EQUITY & TRUSTS

EQUITY & TRUSTS

x Fatema ♡ x

EQUITY & TRUSTS

Sweet & Maxwell's Textbook Series

2nd edition

Professor Michael Haley
School of Law, Keele University

and

Dr Lara McMurtry
School of Law, Keele University

SWEET & MAXWELL

 THOMSON REUTERS

First edition   2006   by Michael Haley and Lara McMurtry
Second edition   2009   by Michael Haley and Lara McMurtry

Published in 2009 by
Thomson Reuters (Legal) Limited
(Registered in England and Wales, Company No 1679046.
Registered office and address for service
100 Avenue Road, Swiss Cottage, London, NW3 3PF)
trading as Sweet & Maxwell

For further information on our products and services, visit
www.sweetandmaxwell.co.uk

Typeset by YHT Ltd, London
Printed in Great Britain by
Ashford Colour Press Ltd, Gosport, Hants

No natural forests were destroyed to make this product;
only farmed timber was used and replanted

A C.I.P. catalogue record for this book
is available from the British Library

ISBN: 9781847037312

DEDICATION

For Fred

PREFACE

The law relating to Equity and Trusts represents notoriously difficult territory for students to navigate. This is not surprising in light of the technical rules, arcane and uncertain principles, ancient wisdoms and contradictory judicial utterances which characterise the subject area. Nevertheless, it is necessary to overcome these obstacles in order to achieve a sound understanding of the law and perhaps for some, more pressingly, to perform successfully in examinations and other forms of assessment. This is (we hope) where this second edition of our textbook assumes relevance.

When writing this book we remain very aware of the strength and depth of other texts on Equity and Trusts that are available for purchase. As a result, we have strived to fashion a book that provides a valuable and interesting alternative to its competitors. We have been selective as to the topics included and, when making this choice, were guided by our own maxim that "the product bought should reflect the product taught". For example, the book offers only a short introduction to history compared to the comprehensive analytical coverage of substantive topics selected in detail. This analysis is designed to blend a rigorous scrutiny of case law authorities (reported and unreported) with an appreciation of the published views of commentators. Our ambition is to offer a product that will well serve students of Equity and Trusts whatever their ability and level. Although the initial assumption is that the reader has no pre-existing knowledge of the subject area (hence a basic glossary and guide to further reading is incorporated), we aim to offer a text that stimulates and educates at all stages of academic development.

The major changes contained in this new edition reflect key developments such as the enactment of the Charities Act 2006 (and the publication in December 2008 of the Charity Commission guidance on the public benefit requirement), the decision of the House of Lords in *Stack v Dowden* affecting co-ownership, the new approach of the Law Commission to the restriction of trustee exemption clauses and the clarification of dishonesty in the context of liability for dishonest assistance. Across all chapters, any recent decisions and statutory amendments of significance and interest are incorporated and analysed.

We would like to thank the editorial team at Sweet & Maxwell (particularly Constance Sutherland) for the assistance and patience they have provided throughout the revision process. We also owe thanks to those behind the scenes who worked on the typesetting, indexing etc.

Lara McMurtry and Michael Haley
February 2009.

TABLE OF CONTENTS

THE THREE CERTAINTIES

CONSTITUTION OF TRUSTS

FORMALITIES AND THE PERPETUITY RULE

POST-MORTEM TRUSTS: MUTUAL WILLS AND SECRET TRUSTS

NON-CHARITABLE PURPOSE TRUSTS

CHARITABLE TRUSTS

CY-PRÈS

RESULTING TRUSTS

CONSTRUCTIVE TRUSTS

TRUSTS OF THE FAMILY HOME

THE APPOINTMENT, RETIREMENT AND REMOVAL OF TRUSTEES

THE DUTIES OF A TRUSTEE

VARIATION OF TRUSTS

SETTING TRUSTS ASIDE

BREACH OF TRUST AND ASSOCIATED REMEDIES

INJUNCTIONS

SPECIFIC PERFORMANCE

A Selected Glossary of Terms

A

AB INITIO: from the beginning.

ACCUMULATION: an increase of principal or capital sum through re-investment of income.

ACQUIESCENCE: an assent to an infringement of rights which can be express or implied from conduct.

ACTUAL NOTICE: actual subjective awareness of another's rights.

AD VALOREM: tax payable on instruments transferring property proportionate to the value of the property.

ADMINISTRATIVE UNWORKABILITY: the size of the beneficiaries must not be so large as to make the administration of the trust unworkable.

ADMINISTRATOR: where a person dies without leaving a will an application must be made to the court for "etters of administration" appointing an administrator. His duties are similar to those of an executor under a will.

ADMINISTRATRIX: a female administrator.

ADMISSIBILITY: the question as to whether evidence is allowable before a court.

ADVANCEMENT, PRESUMPTION OF: a rebuttable presumption whereby a transfer of property is deemed to be by way of advancement, that is under an equitable obligation to provide for another. Applies only to certain special relationships, e.g. from parent to child, from husband to wife.

ADVANCEMENT, POWER OF: a power by which a trustee may apply capital moneys for the advancement or benefit of a beneficiary.

AFTER-ACQUIRED PROPERTY: property acquired after a settlement is created. It was a common feature of marriage settlements to promise to convey to trustees after-acquired property.

AGENCY, AGENT: an arrangement (usually contractual) whereby one person acts on behalf of another (his principal). An act of an agent binds his principal.

ALIENATION: disposition of an interest (e.g. by gift, sale or other transfer).

ANNUITY: provision of an annual payment.

ANTE-NUPTUAL SETTLEMENT: settlement made in contemplation of marriage.

ANTON PILLER ORDER: see search order.

APPOINTMENT, POWER OF: a power, given by deed or will, to appoint a person or persons to take an estate or interest in property, whether real or personal.

ASSIGNMENT: the transfer of property. The transfer of a subsisting equitable interest must be in writing: s53(1)(c) of the Law of Property Act 1925.

ATTESTATION: witness of a signature (e.g. on the execution of a will).

ATTORNEY: a person appointed by another to act in his place or represent him. An attorney can represent his principal for the purpose of executing deeds.

B

BAILMENT: an arrangement (often contractual) whereby an owner (bailor) entrusts possession of his property to another (bailee).

BARE TRUST: a trust where the trustee's duty is simply to convey the property, when required, to the beneficiary.

BENEFICIARY: the party for whose benefit property is held by trustees or executors (sometimes called the cestui que trust).

BENEFICIAL INTEREST: the interest of the beneficiary under the trust.

BEQUEST: a testamentary gift of personal property (i.e. a legacy). A testamentary gift of realty is known as a devise.

BONA FIDE: in good faith.

BONA VACANTIA: property without an owner accrues to the Crown.

BREACH OF TRUST: a trustee is liable for breach of trust if he fails to carry out his duties or commits an unauthorised act.

C

CAPITAL: the fund or property as opposed to income or profits generated from the fund or property.

CAPITAL GAINS TAX: a tax upon gains accruing on the disposal of an asset, other than on death.

CAPITAL MONEY: the proceeds of sale of an asset by a trustee.

CERTAINTIES: the basic requirements of a trust are the certainties of intention, subject matter and objects.

CESTUI QUE USE / CESTUI QUE TRUST: old descriptions for a beneficiary.

CHARGE: a form of security for the payment of a debt or the performance of an obligation where there is a right to receive payment out of a specific fund or out of the proceeds of the realisation of specific property.

CHARITABLE TRUST: a trust of public character such as a trust for the prevention or relief of poverty, the advancement of education, the advancement of religion and a range of other purposes deemed at law to be beneficial to the community.

CHATTEL: an item of personal property such as a car or a watch. This is sometimes termed a chose in possession.

CHOSE IN ACTION: a right of proceeding in a court of law to procure payment of a sum of money or to recover damages for wrongdoing (e.g. debts, bank accounts, shares, copyright, patents or contract rights).

CIVIL PARTNERSHIP: a registered same sex relationship.

CLAIMANT: person bringing a legal action formerly known as the plaintiff.

CLEAN HANDS: reference to an equitable maxim that requires that the claimant in equity must be free from fraud or sharp practice.

COHABITANT: a person who lives with a person in a relationship other than husband and wife or same sex registered partnership.

COMMITTAL: the sending of a person to prison (e.g. for contempt of court).

CONDITIONAL INTEREST: an interest dependent upon the fulfilment of some condition precedent.

CONDITION PRECEDENT: this arises where a gift is to take place on the occurrence of some event (e.g. to X if she marries).

CONDITION SUBSEQUENT: this arises where the gift takes place but is to be forfeited on the occurrence of some event (e.g. to X on condition that she does not marry).

CONSIDERATION: payment under a contract.

CONSTITUTION OF TRUST: this concerns whether the trustee has legal title to the trust property (i.e. where the trust is created by transferring legal title to the trustee, all the necessary formalities to transfer the property must be complied with).

CONSTRUCTIVE NOTICE: knowledge of the rights of a third party that would have been acquired if reasonable care had been taken.

CONSTRUCTIVE TRUST: a trust arising by operation of law imposed as a result of fraudulent or unconscionable conduct or to give effect to the common intentions of the parties.

CONTEMPT OF COURT: conduct which impedes the administration of justice.

CONVERSION, DOCTRINE OF: "equity looks on that as done, that which ought to be done". On entry into a specifically enforceable contract to buy land, the interest of the vendor is treated as an interest in the proceeds of sale and the interest of the buyer is treated as an equitable interest in land.

CONVEYANCE: an instrument (other than a will) transferring property.

CONTINGENT: something which depends on the happening of an event (e.g. reaching the age of 21 years).

COVENANT: traditionally a promise under seal, but in its modern form means a promise contained in a covenant in a formally drafted deed. Covenants are not recognised in equity and are enforceable only in common law.

CUSTODIAN TRUSTEE: a trustee who has care and control of trust property and documents, while leaving the day to day management to a managing trustee. New managing trustees can thus be appointed without vesting trust property in them.

CY-PRÈS: the cy-près doctrine allows gifts for charitable purposes which cannot be carried out to be applied for other purposes as near as possible to those intended by the donor.

D

DEBT: usually a contractual obligation of one party (the debtor) to pay money to another (the creditor).

DECLARATION OF TRUST: one of the two ways of constituting a trust (the other being the transfer of legal title to the trustee). Although declarations of trust usually require no formality, a trust of land must be manifested and proved by some writing signed by the person who is able to declare such a trust (s.53(1)(B) of the Law of Property Act 1925).

DEED: traditionally a document signed, sealed and delivered. The Law of Property (Miscellaneous Provisions) Act 1989 removes the requirement of a seal, but the document must make clear on its face that it is intended to be a deed, is signed in the presence of a witness who attests the signature and is delivered by him or someone authorised by him.

DEHORS THE WILL: outside the will.

DELEGATUS NON POTEST DELEGARE: a delegate cannot delegate. The traditional rule is that a trustee may not, in general, delegate his powers or duties.

DETERMINABLE: an interest which comes to an end upon the happening of some contingency which may never occur.

DEVISE: a testamentary gift of realty.

DISCLAIMER: the refusal by a nominated trustee to act in that capacity.

DISCRETIONARY TRUST: a trust where trustees have a duty to apply the trust property for the benefit of the members of a class of beneficiaries in such proportions as the trustees in their discretion think fit.

DISHONEST ASSISTANCE: where a third party dishonestly participates in a breach of trust without the trust property vesting in him, he is accountable in equity to make good the loss to the trust.

DISPOSITION: a transfer of title by way of sale, assignment, gift etc.

DIVIDEND: payment out of profits to the shareholders of a company.

DONEE: a person receiving a gift.

DONOR: a person making a gift.

DONATIO MORTIS CAUSA: a conditional gift made in contemplation of death.

E

ELECTION: equitable doctrine which prevents a person who accepts a benefit from taking free from an associated burden.

ENDOWMENT: property given in permanent provision (e.g. for educational purposes).

ENTAIL: a settlement whereby property descends exclusively to lineal descendants of the original donee.

EQUITABLE ASSIGNMENT: transfer of property taking effect in equity.

EQUITABLE INTEREST: a right enforceable only in equity.

EQUITABLE MAXIMS: founding and general principles of equity.

EQUITABLE REMEDIES: discretionary remedies created by the Court of Chancery.

EQUITY: the system of principles and rules formulated in the Court of Chancery prior to the Judicature Acts.

ESTATE: a proprietary stake in the land that varies in quality according to whether it is leasehold or freehold. It is also used to describe a deceased person's assets.

ESTATE CONTRACT: a contract for the sale, lease or other disposition of land.

EX PARTE: a "without notice" application to the court—by one party in the absence of the other.

EXECUTOR: a person (personal representative) who carries the provisions of a will into effect. An executor owes fiduciary obligations to the beneficiaries under a will.

EXEMPTION CLAUSE: a clause in an agreement excluding or limiting the liability of one or other of the parties.

EXPRESS TRUST: a trust voluntarily and intentionally granted.

F

FAIR DEALING RULE: sometimes called the rule against insider dealing. It operates where a trustee / fiduciary intends to purchase the interest of a beneficiary.

FALSIFICATION OF ACCOUNTS: the right of a beneficiary to show that an entry in the account is false or erroneous and should be disallowed.

FEE SIMPLE: a freehold estate in land.

FEOFFEE TO USES: forerunner of the trustee who held property subject to a use.

FIDUCIARY: a person who holds a position of trust in relation to another and who must act for their benefit. Typical fiduciary relationships are trustee and beneficiary, principal and agent, director and company, but the categories are not closed.

FIDUCIARY POWER: a power of appointment given to a person in a fiduciary position.

FIXED TRUST: a trust where the beneficial interests are prescribed.

FORMALITIES: the legal requirements to be satisfied before a transaction becomes effective. Formalities usually focus upon the requirement of signed writing.

FREEHOLD: a legal estate of land, unlimited in duration, sometimes called the fee simple.

FREEZING INJUNCTION: formerly known as the "Mareva" injunction. Issued to prevent specified assets from being removed form the jurisdiction of the court.

FULLY SECRET TRUST: a testamentary trust which is not disclosed on the face of the will.

FUTURE PROPERTY: a right or title which has not yet been acquired, but which might be acquired in future (e.g. a covenant to settle after-acquired property on the trusts of a marriage settlement).

G

GENERAL POWER: a power exercisable in favour of anyone, including the donee of the power (e.g. a gift to X for life with remainder to whomsoever he shall appoint).

GIFT: transfer of absolute title to property to another without consideration.

GIFT OVER IN DEFAULT: a provision in a will or settlement providing for a specified gift in the case where a donee of a power fails to exercise that power (e.g. on trust for my wife for life, then to such of our children as she may appoint, but if she fails to do so, to my eldest son absolutely).

GOOD FAITH: acting in a genuine and honest manner. Sometimes referred to as acting bona fide.

GRATUITOUS: a transfer without consideration—a gift.

H

HALF-SECRET TRUST: a trust the existence of which is disclosed in a will where the beneficiary is undisclosed.

HYBRID POWER: sometimes called an intermediate power, this is a power to appoint anyone except a defined group (e.g. to X for life, with remainder to whomsoever X appoints, but X may not appoint himself or his wife).

I

ILLEGALITY: acts forbidden by law.

INALIENABILITY: rights or property that cannot be transferred.

INJUNCTION: an order by the court that the defendant shall do or refrain from doing a particular act.

IN LOCO PARENTIS: a non-parent viewed in the eyes of the law as being in the position of parent.

IN PERSONAM: rights enforceable only as against the person.

IN REM: rights against the world.

IMPLIED TRUST: a trust, which is not express, such as a resulting or constructive trust.

INTANGIBLE ASSET: something which does not have a physical form such as goodwill or shares in a company or intellectual property rights.

INTER PARTES: between the parties.

INTERIM INJUNCTION: a temporary injunction restraining the defendant until trial. Also referred to as an interlocutory injunction.

INTERMEDIATE POWER: a power to appoint anyone except within a certain group. Also known as a hybrid power.

INTER VIVOS: in one's lifetime.

INTESTACY: where a deceased person dies leaving no effective will, he is wholly intestate; if he dies leaving a will which applies only to some of his property he is partly intestate.

J

JOINT TENANCY: a form of co-ownership of property which is characterised by the right of survivorship.

JUDICIAL TRUSTEE: the High Court may appoint a person as judicial trustee under the Judicial Trustees Act 1896.

JUSTIFICATION: a plea in defence of an action which admits the allegations of the claimant, but pleads that they are lawful or justifiable.

K

KNOWING RECEIPT: personal liability imposed on a third party to a breach of trust in circumstances where the third party either knew or ought to have known of the breach of trust.

L

LACHES: a defence to equitable claims whereby the claimant is deemed to have delayed unreasonably in bringing his case.

LANDLORD: a person who allows another exclusive possession of land at a term for a rent (sometimes called a lessor).

LAPSE: the failure of a gift, e.g. where a person to whom property is bequeathed dies before the testator and the property falls into residue.

LEGATEE: a beneficiary under a will.

LETTERS OF ADMINISTRATION: court authorisation to a person to administer the estate of a deceased person who has died intestate.

LIEN: the right to hold property of another as security for performance of an obligation.

LIFE INTEREST: interest in property for the benefit of a person for the duration of his life.

LIVES IN BEING: the common law perpetuity period may be measured by reference to a life or lives in being i.e. of an ascertainable individual or group of individuals living at the time of the disposition plus an additional period of 21 years after the date of the last surviving member.

M

MAINTENANCE: the provision of payments to cover the costs of life's necessities for a person.

MAREVA **INJUNCTION:** see freezing injunction.

MARRIAGE SETTLEMENT: a conveyance of property for the benefit of the parties to, and any prospective issue of, a marriage.

MISREPRESENTATION: a representation which is untrue—where a person is induced to enter into a contract on the basis of a false statement of fact. A misrepresentation may be innocent, negligent or fraudulent.

MONEY HAD AND RECEIVED: a common law action available where money is paid to one person which rightfully belongs to another.

MORTGAGE: a charge by way of legal mortgage providing security for a loan.

N

NOTICE, DOCTRINE OF: the principle that equitable rights do not bind a bona fide purchaser of a legal estate for value without notice. This covers actual notice (knowledge), constructive notice (knowledge that would have been acquired if reasonable enquiries has been made) and imputed notice (the actual or constructive notice of an agent).

O

OBJECTS: beneficiaries under a trust.

OFF-SHORE TRUST: trust situated outside the jurisdiction of the court.

OPTION: a right conferred by agreement to buy property at will according to the terms of the agreement.

OVERREACHING: occurs where the proceeds of sale of land are paid to at least two trustees or a trust corporation. The beneficiaries' interests are shifted to interests in the proceeds of sale and no longer constitute equitable proprietary interest in the land capable of binding a purchaser.

P

PARI PASSU: equally without preference (i.e. an equal percentage of what is owed).

PAROL: oral (e.g. parol/oral evidence).

PERPETUITIES, RULE AGAINST: the rule against remoteness of vesting requires that the gift must vest within prescribed time limits under the common law (lives in being plus 21 years) or under the Perpetuities and Accumulations Act 1964 (maximum of 80 years). The rule against inalienability restricts the duration of private trusts to lives in being plus 21 years and is not affected by the 1964 Act.

PERSONAL PROPERTY: property other than real property (e.g. goods, chattel or choses in action).

PERSONAL REPRESENTATIVES: the executors under a will.

PLAINTIFF: old descriptive label for the claimant.

POSSESSION, INTEREST IN: a person with an immediate right to income produced by settled property has an interest in possession.

POWER OF ADVANCEMENT: the payment or application of capital sums to the beneficiary before he is entitled to demand the fund.

POWER OF APPOINTMENT: a permissive authority to allocate property amongst a class of beneficiaries.

POWER OF ATTORNEY: an instrument empowering one person to represent another.

PRECATORY WORDS: words of hope or confidence which impose merely a moral obligation.

PRIORITY: the right to enforce a claim in preference to others.

PRIVITY: the common law rule by which only those party to a contract can enforce it and have it enforced against them.

PROBATE: a certificate granted by the High Court stating that the will of a person has been proved and registered.

PROPRIETARY ESTOPPEL: equitable doctrine enforcing an informal expectation generated by a representor and relied upon to the detriment of the representee in circumstance where it would be unconscionable to allow the representor to rely on his strict legal rights.

PROTECTIVE TRUST: a trust determinable on the bankruptcy of the beneficiary or other specified event, whereupon a discretionary trust usually in favour of the beneficiary's family arises.

PUBLIC TRUSTEE: a corporation sole under the Public Trustee Act 1906 which acts as custodian or judicial trustee.

PURPOSE TRUST: a trust designed to promote a purpose or object which is prima facie void for want of a beneficiary.

Q

QUIA TIMET **INJUCTIONS:** an injunction to prevent a future or threatened act which would cause the claimant serious damage.

QUISTCLOSE TRUST: arises in a situation in which a lender lends money to a borrower subject to a condition that the money will be used only for the specified purpose. Now classified as a resulting trust.

R

REAL PROPERTY: land.

RECEIVER: a person appointed to receive rents and profits (e.g. for the court or the mortgagee).

RECTIFICATION: an equitable remedy whereby a written contract or other document can, following a mistake, be rewritten by the court to reflect the true agreement of the parties.

REDEMPTION: the discharge of a mortgage debt.

REMAINDER: an interest or estate expectant upon another's estate (e.g. to A for life, remainder to B).

RESCISSION: an equitable remedy used to set aside contracts and to restore the parties to the positions that they had previously occupied.

RESIDUARY ESTATE: the property left by a deceased after discharge of debts and expenses etc and the payment of specific legacies in a will.

RESTITUTION: in its narrow form, a common law process of restoring specific property to its rightful owner or, in its liberal form, the rules concerned with reversing a defendant's unjust enrichment.

RESULTING TRUST: an implied trust where the beneficial interest in property reverts back to the person who transferred the property.

RETENTION OF TITLE: where a supplier of goods stipulates that the property in the goods shall not pass until payment or until the buyer's obligations have been fulfilled.

REVERSION: where land is granted by the owner for an estate less than he himself holds, the undisposed of interest is termed the reversion.

S

SEARCH ORDER: an interim order which requires a person to admit another to premises for the purposes of preserving evidence formerly known as an Anton Piller order.

SECRET TRUST: a testamentary trust which is fully secret (i.e. not disclosed on the face of a will), or half secret (i.e. where the existence of a trust but not its beneficiary is disclosed on the face of the will).

SELF-DEALING RULE: a rule which prevents the trustee dealing with trust property and taking a profit from the transaction.

SEISIN: feudal possession.

SET OFF: a claim by a defendant to a sum of money which is relied on as a defence in whole or in part to an action by the claimant.

SETTLOR, SETTLEMENT: the settlor is the person who creates the trust by conveying property upon trust by way of succession (e.g. to my wife for life, then to my children equally).

SHARE CERTIFICATE: a document certifying that the person named is entitled to a certain number of shares in a company.

SPECIAL POWER: where the field of potential appointees is limited to a class (e.g. to such of the settlor's children as his wife shall appoint).

SPECIFIC PERFORMANCE: equitable remedy enforcing the performance of positive contractual obligations.

SUBROGATION: X taking over the legal rights of Y, so that Y stands in the shoes of X able to assert X's remedies against a third party.

SUB-TRUST: a trust of an existing beneficial interest.

SUI JURIS: of full legal capacity.

SURVIVORSHIP: principle operative in the context of joint tenancies whereby on the death of a joint tenant, the property accrues to the surviving joint tenants.

T

TENANCY IN COMMON: a form of co-ownership in equity whereby each co-owner has a distinct share in the property.

TESTAMENTARY DISPOSITION: a transfer of property on death.

TESTATOR: a male who executes a will.

TESTATRIX: a female who executes a will.

TITLE: a right to ownership of property.

TITLE DEEDS: documents conferring or evidencing the title to land.

TRACING: the process of locating the value of misappropriated assets into substitutions for those assets (e.g. a car purchased with money from trust funds).

TRUSTEE: person who has a duty to administer property for the benefit of others.

TRUSTEE DE SON TORT: one who intermeddles in a trust without authority and, thereby, assumes the duties of a trustee.

TRUST OF LAND: a trust the subject matter of which is land.

U

ULTRA VIRES: beyond powers or in excess of authority.

UNINCORPORATED ASSOCIATION: Two or more persons bound together for one or more common purposes by mutual undertakings, each having mutual duties and obligations, in an organisation which has rules identifying in whom control of the organisation and its funds is vested, and which can be joined or left at will.

USE: the forerunner of the trust.

V

VARIATION OF TRUSTS: the ability of the court to approve an arrangement varying or revoking a trust or the powers of a trustee in the interest of the beneficiaries.

VEST: an estate is said to have vested when it gives present rights.

VOID: of no legal effect.

VOIDABLE: a transaction which is capable of being set aside on the basis of misrepresentation, undue influence or mistake etc.

VOLUNTEER: a person who provides no consideration.

W

WILL: documentary disposition of property on death.

ABBREVIATIONS

Gray and Gray	K. Gray and S.F. Gray, *Elements of Land Law* (5th edn., OUP, 2008)
Hayton	D.J. Hayton, *The Law of Trusts* (4th ed., Sweet & Maxwell, 2003)
Hayton and Marshall	D.J. Hayton and C. Mitchell, *Commentary and Cases on the Law of Trusts and Equitable Remedies* (12th ed., Sweet & Maxwell, 2005)
Hanbury and Martin	J. Martin, *Modern Equity* (18th ed., Sweet & Maxwell, 2009)
Parker and Mellows	A.J. Oakley, *Parker and Mellows, The Modern Law of Trusts* (9th ed., Sweet & Maxwell, 2008)
Pettit	P.H. Pettit, *Equity and the Law of Trusts* (10th ed., OUP 2006)

TABLE OF CASES

Table of Statutes

TABLE OF STATUTORY INSTRUMENTS

TABLE OF NATIONAL LEGISLATION

Chapter 1

AN INTRODUCTION TO EQUITY AND TRUSTS

The term "equity" is, in a general sense, associated with notions of fairness, morality **1.01** and justice. It is an ethical jurisdiction. On a more legalistic level, however, "equity" is the branch of law that was administered in the Court of Chancery prior to the Judicature Acts 1873 and 1875. This was a jurisdiction evolved to achieve justice and to overcome the rigours and deficiencies of the common law.

As Sir Nathan Wright rather grandly explained in *Lord Dudley v Lady Dudley*, "equity is no part of the law, but a moral virtue, which qualifies, moderates, and reforms the rigour, hardness, and edge of the law, and is a universal truth, it does also assist the law where it is defective and weak ... And defends the law from crafty evasions, delusions, and new subtleties intended as contrived to evade and delude the common law, whereby such as, have undoubted right are made remediless, and this is the office of equity, to support and protect the common law from shifts and crafty contrivances against the justice of law. Equity therefore does not destroy the law, nor create it, but assists it."[1]

Although an ethos of conscience pervades this aspect of the law, equity never bestowed an unfettered jurisdiction on the Court of Chancery to do what was fair in the settlement of a dispute. Embodying aspects of ecclesiastical law and Roman law, equity developed and gradually emerged as a distinct body of law. In time, the system became as hidebound by rules and principles as its common law counterpart.

It was not until 1875 that equity was practised in the common law courts. The existence of a dual system entailed that, for example, when a defendant had an equitable defence to a common law action, he would have to go to the Court of Chancery to obtain an injunction to suspend the proceedings in the common law court. He would then begin a fresh action for relief in the Court of Chancery. No court had the ability to offer a complete resolution. This duality persisted until the Judicature Acts which created the Supreme Court of Judicature and allowed all courts to exercise both a

---

[1] (1705) Prec. Ch 241 at 244.

common law and equitable jurisdiction. Although the jurisdictions have been amalgamated for administrative purposes, the two streams of law have not been fused. Both retail their distinctive features and maintain very different rules, remedies and principles.

The history of equity—A shortened version[2]

1.02   In medieval times, the Chancellor (originally a clergyman) was the second most important figure in the country. He was the King's premier minister and presided over the Chancery Court. This court was responsible for the issue of royal writs (i.e. claim forms) which were necessary to commence actions in the common law courts. A defect with the writ system was that a claimant could only bring an action if the complaint corresponded in type to an existing writ. If there was no writ, there was no remedy. At the time of the thirteenth century, the range of writs available was limited and, following the Provisions of Oxford 1258, new writs were rarely innovated. The system was to become fixed and rigid and could no longer adapt to changing needs and changing times. As a consequence hardship and injustice increased.

In cases of injustice, the King had long enjoyed the discretion to interfere for the benefit of his subjects. In order to obtain this discretionary relief, the claimant would need to petition the King or the King's Council. The King dispensed a brand of extraordinary justice in cases where the common law failed the claimant. The Kings of this period were often fighting abroad or too young to deal with petitions. From early times, therefore, the Chancellor was instructed to deal with these petitions. He became the keeper of the King's conscience. The Chancery was the Chancellor's administrative department and operated to process the petitions. By the beginning of the fifteenth century, the petitions were addressed directly to the Chancellor. The petitions were so numerous that it was necessary to establish the Court of Chancery.

The Chancellor heard claims in circumstances where the law was defective because of the inadequacy of damages as a remedy or the slavish insistence upon the satisfaction of formalities. Claims might follow an allegation of bias in favour of Fred, for example, where Fred was a wealthy and powerful individual who might be able to influence proceedings or juries in the common law courts. Understandably, the interference of the Chancellor was not always to be well received by the common law judges.

1.03   During the thirteenth and fourteenth centuries, there was no body of law known as "equity". The Chancellor operated to grant relief on an individual case by case basis. The Chancellor would grant or withhold assistance to a petitioner according to his own sense of what was just. This element of subjectivism and idiosyncrasy explains the criticism levied against Chancery justice that it varied with the size of the Chancellor's foot. Hence, equity operated as a gloss on the common law, offering novel solutions to well-worn problems. It was, therefore, a supplementary jurisdiction which complemented the common law. Indeed, Chancellors tended to consult with the common law judges as to the sorts of case where relief should be granted to a petitioner. This avoided much potential conflict between the competing camps. The Chancery did not

[2] For a full account see W.S. Holdsworth, *A History of English Law*, Vol.1 (London, 1938).

deny the common law and the Chancellor's jurisdiction was framed as being against the person (i.e. in personam). For example, as subsequently became clear as regards the trust, the Chancery has never denied that legal ownership rested with the trustee, but it imposes obligations upon the legal owner to use the trust property for the benefit of a third party. This meant that the Chancellor was making orders to respond to the consciences of the individual parties.

Due to the personal nature of the Chancery's work, it was necessary that the Chancellor could secure the attendance before him of the defendant. The Chancery developed the subpoena as a means of securing such attendance. The subpoena was an order to attend with the sanction that the defendant who failed to comply would forfeit a stipulated amount of money. It also became necessary to devise methods by which the Chancellor's decisions could be enforced. The Chancellor claimed for himself the ability to imprison those who failed to comply on the basis of their contempt of court. In addition, the Chancellor fashioned a novel remedy in the form of injunctive relief. This was an order which either restrained parties to a common law action or prevented a successful claimant in the common law courts from enforcing the judgment. Not surprisingly, the ability of the Chancellor to grant such "common injunctions" was perceived as a direct attack on the common law. The injunction had the potential to render the common law sterile.

Matters came to a head in the sixteenth century when a major conflict developed between Lord Chief Justice Coke and the Lord Ellesmere, the Chancellor. The battle took place as to whether the Chancellor would continue to be able to grant these injunctions. The Lord Chief Justice asserted that they were unlawful and should be prohibited. Lord Ellesmere claimed that he was not intermeddling and that equity acted only in personam. In this contest for supremacy, the King (James I) favoured the Chancellor. Thereafter, the jurisdiction of the Chancellor was rarely challenged.

The key feature in the transformation of equity into a system of set rules, precedents and principles was the appointment of lawyers as Chancellors. Thereafter there was a discernible movement from a conscience based jurisdiction to a precedent driven style of decision making. Lord Nottingham is thought to be the father of the present system of equity. In his nine years (1673–82) as Chancellor, he began the process of moulding a settled system of law. The process of systemisation continued under successive chancellors, particularly Lord Hardwicke (1736–56) and Lord Eldon (1801–27). The reach of equity was, however, wide and extended into the law of mortgages, probate and business law and, of course, trusts law. The impact of equity was also significant in the range of novel remedies that it developed. At common law, the remedy was compensation and this was available as of right. Equity, however, had no power until Lord Cairns' Act 1858 to award damages. Instead, equity had by then long fashioned a number of discretionary remedies which included, most notably, specific performance and injunctions.

It is ironic that, during the seventeenth and eighteenth centuries, the Court of **1.04** Chancery itself became bogged down in procedure, disorganisation, corruption and administrative incompetence. Until 1813 there were only two judges overseeing matters and, when it was abandoned in 1873, this number had only risen to seven judges. Understaffed and over burdened, it became a source of expense and injustice. Although it was subject to piecemeal reform, the Court of Chancery was abolished by the Judicature Acts. Most of its jurisdiction was transferred to the Chancery Division of the

High Court, but all courts subsequently had the ability to exercise both equitable and common law jurisdictions. The Judicature Acts, therefore, fused only the administration of law and equity. According to orthodoxy, they did not fuse law and equity themselves.[3] The legislation achieved an administrative balance which ensured that, if a conflict arose between equity and the common law, equitable rules were to prevail. The Acts did not, however, sweep away the distinctions between equity and the common law. It remains the case that, for example, legal ownership is very different from equitable ownership, legal interests are stronger than their equitable counter-parts, equitable remedies are discretionary, equity has no regard for a covenant and the common law does not recognise a trust. An equitable claim may offer an equitable remedy (e.g. rectification, specific performance, rescission and injunction) and different rules continue to apply to tracing assets whether this process is undertaken at law or in equity. The existing differences, therefore, remain numerous and pronounced. Nevertheless, since the Judicature Acts the ability of equity to devise new rights and remedies has been severely curtailed. The general rule is as stated by Megaw L.J. in *Western Fish Products Ltd v Penwith DC*, "the creation of new rights and remedies is a matter for Parliament, not the judges".[4] The theme was developed further by Bagnall J. in *Cowcher v Cowcher* where he admitted, "This does not mean that equity is past child-bearing; simply that its progeny must be legitimate—by precedent out of principle".[5]

The maxims of equity

1.05   The maxims of equity are the fundamental principles which were worked out by the Court of Chancery and provide general guidelines to judges as to when to exercise their equitable jurisdiction. They reflect equity's general approach to the solution of legal problems. The major maxims are:

- equity will not suffer a wrong to be without a remedy;
- equity follows the law;
- he who seeks equity must do equity;
- he who comes to equity must do so with clean hands;
- equity is equality;
- where the equities are equal the first in time prevails;
- equity imputes an intention to fulfil an obligation;
- equity regards as done that which ought to be done;
- equity looks to substance rather than form;
- delay defeats equity;

[3] See Mummery L.J. in *MCC Proceeds Inc v Lehman Brothers International* [1998] 4 All E.R. 675; cf. Lord Diplock in *United Scientific Holdings Ltd v Burnley BC* [1977] 2 All E.R. 62 at 68.
[4] [1981] 2 All E.R. 204 at 218.
[5] [1972] 1 All E.R. 943 at 948.

- equity acts in personam;
- equity will not allow a statute to be used as an instrument of fraud;
- equity will not assist a volunteer; and
- equity will not perfect an imperfect gift.

Equity will not suffer a wrong to be without a remedy

This maxim is not to be taken too literally as equitable remedies are geared only to strike against unconscionable behaviour and to operate only if that behaviour constitutes a legal (as opposed to merely moral) wrongdoing. As Mann J. commented in *Dubey v HM Revenue & Customs* in relation to the disappointed Farepak customers who received neither their Christmas goods nor a refund of their money, "at the end of the day their claims have to be based in law, not sympathy ... No amount of sympathy can entitle them to be paid moneys to which they are not, or may not be, legally entitled."[6] The underlying rationale of this rule is that equity will strive to interfere in order to remedy a legal wrong when the common law is inadequate to do so. In other words, equity will attempt to ensure that deserving claimants obtain redress. A broad based illustration is the law of trusts under which the beneficiary has no remedy at common law. In the eyes of the common law, it is the trustee who has legal ownership of the trust property and not the beneficiary. The latter could, therefore, only enforce his beneficial interest in equity. A more specific example concerns injunctions which can be employed to prevent an anticipated wrong whereas there is no remedy at common law until the wrongful act has been performed. Modern developments include the evolution of estoppel and the employment of the constructive trust.   **1.06**

Equity follows the law

The general rule is that equity will adhere to the common law unless there is some exceptional justification for not doing so (i.e. where it would be unconscionable). If possible, equity will harmonise its own rules with those of the common law. For example, the common law presumption of a joint tenancy in relation to the co-ownership of land, as discussed in Ch.11, will prevail unless the purchase money was provided unequally or the property was purchased as part of a commercial venture. In the latter circumstances, equity deems the right of survivorship, which arises automatically on the death of a joint tenant, to be unsuited to the transaction and presumes a tenancy in common. A further illustration of this maxim concerns the refusal of equity to contradict the common law rule that a third party cannot be made to perform a contract. Hence, the general rule is that specific performance is available only as against a party to the contract.   **1.07**

---

[6] [2006] EWHC 3272 (Ch).

He who seeks equity must do equity

1.08 A claimant who seeks the relief of equity must himself be willing to act fairly towards the other party. A person seeking equity must be prepared to do equity.[7] For example, a person seeking the grant of an injunction or specific performance must be willing and able to perform his own future obligations.[8] Similarly, if the claimant seeks to rescind (i.e. withdraw from) a contract, the court will ensure that the claimant acts equitably by, say, returning any deposit paid under the contract. The key consideration is that the claimant must be prepared to act fairly towards the defendant. If the claimant cannot or will not perform his obligations, the court will not grant equitable relief. The doctrine of election, which prevents a person who accepts a benefit from taking free from an associated burden, is based on this maxim.[9] Lord Cairns explained, "where a deed or will professes to make a general disposition of property for the benefit of the person named in it, such person cannot accept a benefit under the instrument without at the same time conforming to all its provisions, and renouncing every right inconsistent with them".[10] For example, Adrienne by will leaves a house to her grandson, Jordan, and by a separate legacy leaves her daughter, Fiona, £50,000. Adrienne, however, is mistaken in that the house in fact already belongs to Fiona. Under the doctrine of election, Fiona must elect either to transfer her house to Jordan or to forgo the legacy. She cannot have both.[11]

He who comes to equity must come with clean hands

1.09 While the previous maxim focuses upon future conduct, this maxim concentrates upon the claimant's past actions. As equitable remedies are discretionary in nature, the claimant has to be deserving of equitable intervention.[12] Hence, there will be no specific performance of a contract if the claimant himself is in breach or if the claimant brought about the contract by misrepresentation or fraud.[13] If it were otherwise, equity would be imposing a dual standard. For these purposes, it is the claimant's conduct that is to be examined[14] and not the other party's behaviour. Accordingly, there is no balancing out of fault and bad behaviour between the parties. For example, if a landlord seeks to forfeit the tenant's lease for the latter's breach of covenant, the court has a jurisdiction to grant the tenant relief from forfeiture. Regardless of the landlord's conduct, the tenant will be denied the intervention of equity if the past breach was flagrant. It is to be

---

[7] The court is not bound by any contractual terms which purport to allow the claimant to take free from any equity or cross claim and its discretion is unaffected by such a term: *Quadrant Visual Communications Ltd v Hutchinson Telephone (UK) Ltd* (1991) *The Times*, December 4.

[8] See *Chappell v Times Newspapers* [1975] 2 All E.R. 233.

[9] *Birmingham v Kirwan* [1805] 2 Sch. & Led. 444; see P.H. Pettit, *Equity and the Law of Trusts* (10th edn. Oxford, Oxford University Press, 2006) at pp.764–778.

[10] *Codrington v Codrington* (1875) L.R. 7 HL 854 at 861, 862.

[11] *Douglas v Douglas* (1871) L.R. 12 Eq. 617.

[12] See P.H. Pettit [1990] Conv. 416; M. Halliwell [2004] Conv. 439.

[13] *Cross v Cross* (1983) 4 F.L.R. 235.

[14] In *Boulding Group Plc v Newett* Unreported May 16, 1991 CA, a wife who sought specific performance was not affected by her husband's misconduct.

appreciated, moreover, that the "lack of cleanliness" must relate to the dispute and not to unconnected matters. This means that a general depravity and corruptness does not bar a claim in equity. As Eyre C.B put it in *Dering v Earl of Winchelsea*, "it must be depravity in a legal as well as moral sense."[15] It must concern the equity sought.[16]

For example, in *Fiona Trust & Holding Corporation v Privalov* the defendants pleaded that the claimants should not be granted equitable relief of any kind because of their misconduct in relation to non-disclosure of documents and the improper carrying out of background investigations.[17] In rejecting the defendants' assertions, Andrew Smith J. made several points. First, that the maxim is directed usually to conduct that is in some way immoral and deliberate. Secondly, that not all misconduct deprives a claimant of equitable relief and that the conduct might be too trivial for it to have this effect. Thirdly, the court will assess the gravity and effect of the misconduct cumulatively, "so that, while the elements of misconduct taken individually might be too trivial for the maxim to be applied, they might be sufficient taken together."[18] On the facts before him there was an insufficiently immediate relationship between the misconduct and the relief claimed.

Equity is equality

As regards claims to property under a fixed trust, if the shares are not allocated between the claimants, equity presumes that each was intended to have an equal share.[19] As indicated above (see **1.07**), equity dislikes a joint tenancy and the associated right of survivorship. For example, in *Jones v Maynard* a husband and wife opened a joint bank account together, but made no reference as to how the money was to be shared.[20] The court applied this maxim and determined that each was entitled to an equal share. If no other way forward is outlined by the donor/settlor, this somewhat rough and ready presumption is employed to achieve fairness. It is, however, a default mechanism of last resort. In many cases, equality is most certainly not what was intended.[21]

1.10

Where the equities are equal the first in time prevails

Time assumes importance to equity. In circumstances where two parties have equally strong cases, the party who acquired his equitable rights first will have priority. For example, if two equitable mortgagees are competing for priority in order to determine who will have first claim to the proceeds of sale then, in the eyes of equity, priority will lie with the mortgagee whose interest was created first. This maxim is the founding

1.11

---

[15] (1878) 1 Cox 318 at 320.
[16] See *Grobelaar v News Group Newspapers* [2002] 4 All E.R. 732; *Tinsley v Milligan* (1994) 1 A.C. 340.
[17] [2008] EWHC 1748 (Comm).
[18] [2008] EWHC 1748 (Comm) at [19].
[19] *Burrough v Philcox* (1840) 5 My & Cr 72.
[20] [1951] 1 All E.R. 802.
[21] See Lord Reid in *Gissing v Gissing* [1971] A.C. 886 at 897 (a case decided in the context of the beneficial ownership of the family home).

stone of the doctrine of notice which, prior to any system of registration, regulated the priority between equitable interests in land.

Equity imputes an intention to fulfil an obligation

1.12   This maxim means that where a person is obliged to do something, but instead does something else that could be regarded as a performance of the obligation, equity will regard this as fulfilling the obligation. For example, where a debtor leaves a legacy by will to his creditor, the legacy will be viewed as the satisfaction of the debt. Unless the presumption is rebutted, the creditor will not be able both to sue on the debt and keep the legacy. The debt must, however, be incurred before the will was made, the legacy must be as large as or larger than the debt and the will must not contain a direction to pay debts.[22]

Equity regards as done that which ought to be done

1.13   In the situation where there is a specifically enforceable obligation (e.g. a contract to create a legal lease), equity regards the parties as already being in the position which they would be in following the performance of the obligation (e.g. as if the legal lease had been granted). This maxim is well demonstrated in *Walsh v Lonsdale*[23] where a seven-year lease was granted to the tenant, but no deed was executed. The fixed term lease was, therefore, equitable. In the light that specific performance of the contract to create a legal lease was available, the court admitted that an equitable lease is as good as a legal lease. This was because equity looked on the lease as "legal" as soon as it was informally created. Another example of this maxim is the "doctrine of conversion" that arises on a binding contract, say, for the sale of land. As soon as the contract is entered, the vendor becomes the trustee of the legal estate for the benefit of the purchaser. This ensures that the vendor's interest has been "converted" into the agreed proceeds of sale. Accordingly, if the property is damaged after the contract, the risk potentially falls on the shoulders of the purchaser and the vendor is entitled to the full purchase price.

Equity looks to substance rather than form

1.14   The principle here is that equity will look to substance and not be deceived by the outward appearance of a transaction. This is evident in relation to the intention to create a trust where it is not necessary that the word "trust" be used and it is not conclusive even if the term is employed. The court will look for the true relationship that was created. It will, moreover, unravel any sham or pretence trusts.[24] Similarly, as regards mortgage law and the special protection that is afforded to the mortgagor, the

---

[22] *Sowden v Sowden* (1875) 1 Bro. c.c. 582.
[23] (1882) 21 Ch. D. 9.
[24] *Midland Bank v Wyatt* [1995] 1 F.L.R. 696.

court will look to see the real nature of the bargain entered and whether it is truly a mortgage transaction.[25] By way of a further illustration, a freehold covenant may be construed as being negative even though it is framed in positive language (and, indeed, vice versa).[26]

Delay defeats equity

This is a further illustration of how time is important to equity. It is often said that equity aids the vigilant and not the indolent. The rule is that, if the court concludes that the claimant has allowed too much time to elapse between the wrongdoing and the commencement of legal proceedings, equity will not protect the claimant's rights. The doctrine of "laches" developed in order to prevent stale claims. It is thought that the court's decision will be based upon notions of good conscience in light of the delay. The idea is that the claimant has to act expeditiously. In practice, the role of this maxim has been largely subsumed by the Limitation Acts (which set out time limits within which actions must be commenced), but it still exerts influence when dealing with breach of trust cases and deciding whether equitable remedies should be granted.[27]

1.15

Equity acts in personam

At the heart of equity is the notion that it acts in personam which means that it is designed to prevent a specified individual from acting unconscionably. It strikes at the conduct and conscience of the defendant. This means that equitable remedies are personal in that they are exercised against specific persons. They compel or permit a person to do something or not to do something, for example, search orders and freezing injunctions.[28] In relation to a breach of trust, the beneficiary's redress strikes against the trustees personally. A failure to comply with an order of specific performance or an injunction is viewed as a contempt of court and punishable by a purging visit to the prison cells. It also explains why equity can make an order relating to property situated outside the jurisdiction, provided that the defendant is within the jurisdiction.[29]

1.16

Equity will not allow a statute to be used as an instrument of fraud

This maxim is designed to prevent one party relying on an absence of statutory formalities (e.g. relating to land contracts, the creation of legal leases and express trusts and the registration of land charges), if to do so would be unconscionable and unfair.[30]

1.17

---

[25] *Grangeside Properties Ltd v Collingwoods Securities Ltd* [1964] 1 W.L.R. 139.
[26] *Tulk v Moxhay* (1848) 2 Ph 774.
[27] See *Leaf v International Galleries* [1950] 1 All E.R. 693 (a claim for rescission).
[28] See generally, Ch.18.
[29] *Penn v Lord Baltimore* (1750) 1 Ves. Sen. 444, where specific performance of a contract relating to land in North America was granted.
[30] See *Shah v Shah* [2001] 3 W.L.R. 31 where an improperly attested deed was upheld under this maxim.

For example, in *Bannister v Bannister*[31] an elderly woman conveyed a house on the understanding that she would be able to continue to reside there rent free. Whether viewed as a land contract or an express trust, there was no documentation concerning the transaction. Hence, the bargain was not enforceable by her. Nevertheless, equity stepped in and imposed a constructive trust which gave her a life interest in the property. The consequences of the statutory requirement of writing would otherwise have inflicted injustice upon the woman.

Equity will not assist a volunteer

1.18   The general rule is that the court is prevented from coming to the aid of a volunteer regardless of how undesirable the outcome might appear.[32] Equity will not, therefore, grant specific performance of a gratuitous promise (i.e. an agreement that is unsupported by consideration). Equity will not enforce a covenant ("equity has no regard for a seal"[33]), whereas the common law embodies no such inhibition.[34] In relation to trusts, equity will assist a beneficiary only when there is a perfectly constituted trust (i.e. once legal title to the trust property has vested in the trustee).[35]

Equity will not perfect an imperfect gift

1.19   The underlying notion here is that to make a perfect gift the donor must comply with the requirements necessary to transfer legal title to the property. There are numerous examples where equity has not interfered when, although a transfer was intended, the transferor did not follow the appropriate transfer process. In *Jones v Lock*,[36] a father intended to make a gift of a cheque to his child, but failed to endorse the cheque with the result that legal title did not pass. Equity refused to cure the defect and the gift failed. Similarly, in *Milroy v Lord*[37] an attempt to establish a trust of 50 shares in a bank failed because legal title to the shares never became vested in the trustee. The settlor did not take any steps to transfer the shares before his death. Equity could not perfect the transfer.

As considered in Ch.3, however, this general rule has its exceptions and these include deathbed gifts, fortuitous vesting, proprietary estoppel, unconscionability and the so-called every effort rule.

---

[31] [1948] 2 All E.R. 133.
[32] *Jones v Lock* (1865) L.R. 1 Ch. App. 25.
[33] *Jeffreys v Jeffreys* (1841) Cr. & Ph. 135.
[34] *Cannon v Hartley* [1949] Ch. 213.
[35] *Milroy v Lord* (1862) 4 De. G.F. & J. 264.
[36] (1865) L.R. 1 Ch. App. 25.
[37] (1862) 4 De. G.F. & J. 264.

Key equitable remedies

At common law, the usual remedy is the award of damages and this is available as of   **1.20**
right. One of the most significant contributions of equity is the wide range of remedies
that it has fostered. These remedies are discretionary and, as indicated above, their
availability in any given case may hinge upon the application of the maxims of equity.
They are granted in circumstances where common law damages are inadequate and are
in personam, that is, they are targeted at the defendant personally. The major types of
equitable remedy will now be considered. These are:

- specific performance (discussed in detail in Ch.19);

- injunctions (discussed in detail in Ch.18);

- rectification;

- rescission; and,

- subrogation.

Specific performance

The remedy of specific performance is analysed in detail in Ch.19. For present purposes,   **1.21**
it is to be appreciated that specific performance is an order of the court which directs
the defendant to perform his side of a contract. Specific performance operates in
relation to the entire contract and not merely a part of the agreement. The claimant has
to come with "clean hands"[38] and to apply for relief without unreasonable delay. When
granted, this will be either as an alternative to or in addition to damages for breach of
contract. The remedy will not be granted if damages would adequately compensate the
claimant. An example of where specific performance will be readily granted concerns
contracts for the sale of land. This is because each piece of land is considered to be
unique and damages will not normally be sufficient to compensate a potential purchaser. Although damages may be suitable for the vendor, a need for mutuality allows
the vendor to claim specific performance of a land contract. An action for a specific
performance, moreover, may be commenced even before there has been an actual
breach of contract. This would arise where there is an anticipatory breach, for example,
when one party has stated his intention not to perform his side of the contract.

Specific performance is not, however, available for all types of contract. As regards
contracts for the sale of goods, such as a car or a television, specific performance will
not usually be an appropriate remedy. This rule will give way only when the goods are
rare or unique (e.g. a work of art or shares in a private company) or where special
circumstances make the payment of damages inadequate (e.g. petrol in a time of world
shortage). Obviously, illegal or immoral contracts will not be enforced in this way and
contracts involving personal services (e.g. an agreement under which a singer is to

---

[38] *Coatsworth v Johnson* (1886) 54 L.T. 520 where a breach of covenant disqualified the plaintiff from equitable relief.

appear on a television show) or services which require constant supervision (e.g. an agreement to provide cleaning services in an office block) fall beyond the reach of specific performance.

Injunctions

1.22   An injunction is an order of the court which requires a person either to do something (i.e. a positive or mandatory injunction) or to refrain from doing something (i.e. a negative or prohibitory injunction). Injunctions are considered in detail in Ch.18. Although the remedy is discretionary, any person who suffers from an infringement of an equitable or legal right may apply for injunctive relief. Damages may be awarded in lieu of or in addition to an injunction.

There are various types of injunction, each of which has been designed to achieve a different function. It is perhaps useful at this stage to outline the major categories of injunction:

- the prohibitory injunction is an injunction which forbids the party to do or to continue to do an unlawful act (e.g. not to build upon land in breach of a restrictive covenant);

- the mandatory injunction is an order that an act be undone (e.g. to demolish a building which has been built in breach of a restrictive covenant). Hence, a mandatory injunction when granted is likely to undo a wrongful act rather than to order the defendant to carry out a positive obligation. This type of injunction is uncommon;

- the perpetual or "final" injunction is an order made in final settlement of the dispute between the parties and issued at the completion of the court proceedings;

- the interim injunction (sometimes known as an interlocutory junction) is an injunction made during the course of legal proceedings and which is effective only until the trial of the action takes place. It is designed to restrain the defendant immediately while waiting for a full court hearing;

- the without notice (or ex parte) injunction. This is an injunction granted in an emergency without the other side having been informed or given the opportunity to attend the hearing of the application;

- the *quia timet* injunction is an injunction designed to prevent an anticipatory infringement of the claimant's rights where such an infringement is a realistic threat;

- a search order (formerly known as an *Anton Piller* order) authorises the claimant to enter the defendant's premises to inspect and seize documents relevant to the case. The aim is to protect evidence in relation to impending litigation; and

- a freezing injunction (formerly known as a *Mareva* injunction). This is an injunction that prevents the defendant from removing his assets out of the jurisdiction of the court before the completion of litigation.

As indicated, in certain circumstances the courts may, under s.50 of the Supreme Court **1.23**
Act 1981, award damages instead of injunctive relief. Although the rule of thumb is that
if a right is infringed an injunction may be granted, damages may be substituted where
the claimant's loss is small, the loss can be valued in money terms, money would
provide the claimant with adequate compensation and an injunction would be
oppressive, unduly harsh or disproportionate.[39]

Rectification

The remedy of rectification concerns the rewriting of documents to accord with what **1.24**
the parties agreed in bilateral transactions (such as contracts) or, in the case of a
voluntary deed (such as a trust), with what the settlor truly intended. The remedy is,
therefore, designed to rectify mistakes made. It is crucial that it was intended that the
term appear in the written agreement. If it was deliberately omitted, and the mistake is
as to the legal consequences of the document, rectification is not available.[40] The
purpose of rectification is, therefore, to correct mistakes in the way the translation has
been recorded. It does not allow the parties to change the substance of the agreement
reached. Although it is a discretionary remedy, rectification will usually be awarded
unless damages are a suitable alternative.

As regards bilateral transactions, the remedy operates usually when the mistake is
common to both parties; for example, when both parties intend that a term appear in a
written contract but the term is mistakenly omitted form the final draft. As the contract
fails to record what was agreed, the contract may be rectified by the court. It is less
common for a contract to be rectified because of the mistake of one party only. Indeed,
rectification for a unilateral mistake will be allowed only when there has been some
fraud, sharp practice or other unconscionable conduct on the part of the other contracting party.[41]

Rectification of a voluntary settlement can, however, occur when there is convincing
evidence that, say, a will did not express the clear intention of the testator because of a
drafting error by the testator's solicitor. As regards lifetime settlements, rectification
can be ordered at the behest of the settlor or, indeed, a beneficiary.[42] The mistake here
will usually be of a unilateral nature.

Rescission

Rescission is a remedy employed to set aside a contract and to restore the parties to **1.25**
their pre-contractual positions. The contract is, therefore, voidable and remains, until
rescinded, perfectly valid. Accordingly, rescission reflects the desire of one party no

---

[39] *Shelfer v City of London Electric Lighting Co* [1895] 1 Ch. 287.
[40] *Oun v Ahmad* [2008] EWHC 545 (Ch); *Transview Property Ltd v City Site Properties Ltd* [2008] 2 P. &
C.R. D. 13.
[41] *Commission for New Towns v Cooper (GB) Ltd* [1995] Ch. 259; *Transview Properties Ltd v City Site
Properties Ltd* [2008] 2 P.& C.R. D. 13.
[42] *Thompson v Whitmore* (1860) 1 John & H. 268.

longer to be bound by the contract. As this is a discretionary remedy, the right to rescind may be lost and this will occur when there has been delay, the contract as been affirmed in full knowledge of the facts or it is no longer possible to restore the status quo ante.

Equity claims the ability to set aside a contract where the transaction is tainted by what is known as a vitiating factor. The grounds for rescission include:

- Misrepresentation. A contract may be rescinded if it was induced by misrepresentation. The misrepresentation can be fraudulent, negligent or innocent. Other than with innocent misrepresentation, the victim may also obtain damages.

- Mistake as to fact or law. In *Cooper v Phibbs*,[43] a contract to lease property was entered under the common mistake that the purchaser did not already have an equitable interest in the property. The purchaser later discovered that he had an equitable interest and was entitled to rescind the contract. As regards unilateral mistake, there must be some element of unconscionability arising from the other party's conduct. In both situations the mistake must have induced the contract.[44]

- Undue influence. Where one party exerts undue influence over the other this takes away the free and voluntary will of the victim. Not surprisingly, therefore, the transaction can be rescinded on this basis.[45]

- Breach of fiduciary duty. A fiduciary duty exists, for example, between trustee and beneficiary. In contracts between these parties, the trustee owes a duty of undivided loyalty and utmost good faith and is obliged to make full disclosure. If the fiduciary does not satisfy these duties, a contract may be rescinded.

Subrogation

1.26   The equitable remedy of subrogation allows one person to be subrogated to the existing rights of another. This means that there is a substitution of one claimant by another. It enables the acquisition of the other's rights against a third party. In its simple form, subrogation allows, say, an insurance company who has paid out under a policy to take over the legal rights of the insured and sue any wrongdoer for the loss it has incurred. Subrogation is also a useful remedy where the claimant's money is employed by the defendant to discharge a secured creditor. The idea, which is reliant upon tracing, is that the claimant can stand in the shoes of the secured creditor and the debt, extinguished by the payment, is resurrected for the benefit of the claimant. The claimant will then be able to enforce the security and take priority over the general creditors of the defendant.[46] It is designed to reverse the defendant's unjust enrichment. In *Boscawen v*

---

[43] (1867) L.R. 2 HL 149.
[44] *Oscar Chess v Williams* [1957] 1 W.L.R. 370.
[45] *Allcard v Skinner* (1837) 36 Ch. D. 145.
[46] *Banque Finaciere de la Cite v Parc (Battersea) Ltd* [1999] 1 A.C. 221.

Bajwa,[47] Mr Bajwa intended to sell his house. The purchasers took a £140,000 mortgage from the Abbey National Building Society. From the proceeds of sale, Mr Bajwa intended to redeem a legal charge held by the Halifax Building Society on his property. The purchase money was transferred to Mr Bajwa's solicitors pending completion. Mr Bajwa's solicitors went bankrupt with the purchase money in their client account and the purchase fell through. In breach of trust, the Halifax charge had already been discharged by the solicitors using Abbey National money. Mr Bajwa, therefore, ended up with an unmortgaged property. The Abbey National claimed to be subrogated to the rights of the Halifax in relation to the charge on the property. The Abbey National could trace its money and employed subrogation to deprive Mr Bajwa of the unjust enrichment that he would otherwise have obtained at its expense. The Abbey National was treated as if it had been the mortgagee under the extinguished mortgage. By paying off the legal charge, the Abbey National had in effect "purchased" Halifax's right against the property.

A further example of subrogation is where a trustee brings an unsuccessful legal action against a third party. Costs awarded against the trustee can be charged against the trust property and the third party can stand in the shoes of the trustee and, by way of subrogation, claim the trustee's right to indemnity against the trust property.[48]

Remedies in the context of a breach of trust

In addition to the key equitable remedies, it is necessary to consider the range of   **1.27** personal and proprietary remedies available when there has been a breach of trust.[49] Breaches of trust are many and various, including fraudulent acts, misapplication of trust assets and the failure to act with requisite care and skill. In the case of a breach of trust the beneficiary may require the trustee to account for his stewardship of the trust property. The trustee will be obliged to disclose what trust assets have been in his possession and provide an account of what he has done with such assets. If the beneficiary is not satisfied with the trustee's actions, he has the right to "falsify" or to "surcharge" the account. The account will be "falsified" when the trustee has misapplied trust property, i.e. the trustee has done something that he was not authorised to do. This will entail that the trustee has to account to the trust for the full amount, i.e. the trustee is liable to restore the trust property or its value. As Lord Browne-Wilkinson pointed out in *Target Holdings Ltd v Redferns*, "the basic rule is that a trustee in breach of trust must restore or pay to the trust estate either the assets which have been lost to the estate by reason of the breach or compensation for such loss".[50] Accordingly, if the trustee invests in unauthorised investments and makes a loss, the beneficiaries can elect that the account be falsified and that the money be restored.

The account will be "surcharged" when the trustee has failed to obtain all that should have been obtained for the benefit of the trust. As Peter Millett (writing extra-judicially)

---

[47] [1995] 4 All E.R. 769; see also *Filby v Mortgage Express (No.2) Ltd* [2004] 2 P.& C.R. D. 16 (mortgage fraud).
[48] *Barnett v Semenyuk* Unreported July 10, 2008.
[49] These are considered in detail in Ch.17.
[50] [1996] A.C. 421 at 434.

explains, "The trustee is made to account not only for what he has in fact received, but also for what he might in due diligence have received".[51] Hence, the trustee is accountable for what the value of the trust should have been. The beneficiary will, however, have to prove that the loss would not have happened but for the trustee's failure.

In the case of misapplication of the trust property, the beneficiary may make a proprietary claim to the specific assets or their traceable proceeds.

THE TRUST AND ITS ORIGINS

1.28   The forerunner of the trust was known as the "use" and this had existed, at least in a very basic form, since the eleventh century. By the thirteenth century, however, the "use" had become more sophisticated. At the heart of the "use" was the conveyance of property to a third party (the "feoffee to uses") subject to the proviso that the property was to be held for the benefit of a beneficiary *("cestuis que use")*. In this way, the use fragmented legal and equitable ownership. The feoffee was usually a passive recipient of legal title and held under the duty to account for profits to the beneficiary. In some cases, the feoffee would be under the positive duty to convey the property to another. The popularity of the use in medieval times has been ascribed to the Crusades which encouraged landowners to give control of their property to a feoffee while they fought abroad. The Franciscan monks have also been held responsible for the growth of the use in that it allowed them to retain the benefit of property without contravening their vow of poverty. The use was also employed to facilitate simple frauds whereby property could be put beyond the claims of creditors and feudal lords. Indeed, the avoidance of feudal incidents, such as wardship, marriage and escheat, was a main influence in the growth of the use. As a precautionary measure, it was usual for there to be more than one feoffee appointed and they were directed to hold as joint tenants. As the existing feoffees died new ones could be appointed by the settlor. Hence, there was never an heir and no minor inherited the legal estate.

The use did not suit the common law which did not recognise the divide between legal and beneficial ownership. The beneficiary had no *"seisin"*, i.e. he had no estate in possession, and fell beyond the reach of the common law. Hence, the success of the use rested entirely upon the degree to which the feoffees could be trusted or otherwise enforced to carry out their duties. With the growing popularity of the use in fifteenth century society, the Chancellor was to play a key role. The settlor was reposing trust and confidence in the feoffee which, although not illegal for the feoffee to break, was clearly unconscionable for him to do so. As Simpson puts it, "Thus it was the very impotence of the common law which provided the basis upon which the Chancellor could intervene in the name of good conscience and equity and require the feoffee to hold the land for the benefit of the *cestuis que use* and allow him to take the profits".[52] The Chancellors fashioned rules and principles which were designed to protect the

---

[51] P. Millett (1998) 114 L.Q.R. 214 at p.226.
[52] A.W.B. Simpson, *An Introduction to the History of Land Law* (Oxford: Oxford University Press, 1961) at p.166.

interests of the beneficiary under both an express use and also an implied "resulting use" that arose by operation of law on conveyance for no value or no good reason (e.g. a good reason would be a charitable gift or transfer on marriage). One principle became known as the "doctrine of notice" which was originated to prevent the feoffee transferring use property to a third party and the latter claiming not to be bound by the use. A further rule was that uses could be disposed of by will, whereas common law estates could not. This ability to make testamentary dispositions became an attractive feature of the use.

A number of statutes were passed so as to deal with the evasions of creditors and **1.29** feudal incidents. These provisions were easily sidestepped. The Statute of Uses 1535, however, made a dramatic change in that the legal estate was to be taken away from the feoffees and, instead, vested in the beneficiary. This vesting was termed as "executing the use". It was, in effect, a statutory conveyance of the legal estate and threatened to put to an end to the fragmentation of legal and equitable ownership. The application of feudal incidents was again restored. The power to leave the estate by will was also eroded. In the face of political pressure, however, the latter ability was quickly reinstated and, indeed, extended by the Statute of Wills Act 1540.

Medieval lawyers were keen to identify ways in which the effect of the Statute of Uses could be avoided. First, the statute did not apply to leasehold uses. A settlement to Fred for 1000 years to the use of Jordan entailed that the legal estate would still be vested in Fred. Jordan's beneficial interest would still need to be enforced in equity. Secondly, it quickly became clear that the Statute of Uses did not apply to so-called "active" uses, that is, where the feoffee had to perform some positive duty under the terms of the use. For example, to Fred subject to the obligation that he pays rents and profits from the land to Jordan. Thirdly, a new type of relationship was gradually innovated and this became known as "the use upon a use". A simple example of this new type of relationship would arise where there was a grant to Fred to the use of Jordan to the use of Fiona. In time, the second use was recognised by equity and this entailed that Jordan became the legal owner (by virtue of the first use) for the benefit of Fiona (under the second use). The use upon a use was, therefore, employed to keep alive the distinction between legal ownership and beneficial ownership. With the recognition that the use upon a use was a mere device to outflank the Statute of Uses, a new terminology assumed popularity. By 1700, the relationship had become known as the "trust" and the legal title was held by the "trustee". The terms "use", "feoffee" and *"cestuis que use"* faded into the background. It was then possible to create a "trust" which not being a use, albeit in name only, was not within the Statute of Uses.

During the eighteenth century, the trust became a vehicle by which wealthy land- **1.30** owners could tie up their property for the benefit of future generations of their families. The technique adopted was to settle land successively on the eldest son of each generation for life with the trustees having the flexibility to raise capital for other members of the family. The Settled Land Act 1882 was designed to give the tenant for life powers to dispose of and manage the land and overcome the problem of the land being sterile for substantial periods of time. The Industrial Revolution and the shifting nature of wealth and investment entailed that the trust was to adopt a more dynamic approach in modern times.

Key characteristics of a trust

1.31   Although the trust may be the most important invention of equity, it has proved resistant to precise and exhaustive definition. It is, therefore, safer to describe what a trust is rather than go in pursuit of a definitional chimera. The existence of a trust is dependent upon identifiable property (whether tangible or intangible) being transferred from its legal owner to one or more trustees to hold and manage property for the benefit of ascertainable beneficiaries. The trust may be created inter vivos (i.e. during the lifetime of the settlor) or may be post-mortem (i.e. on the death of the settlor). The trustee labours under the duty to protect the trust assets and to distribute trust income and capital in accordance with the terms of the trust. The trustee, therefore, owes an equitable, fiduciary obligation of good faith and loyalty and must always act to the benefit of the beneficiaries. If the trustee fails to do so, he will be personally liable for his breach of trust. The obligations attach to the trust property and can bind anyone in whom that property becomes vested at a later date.[53] In order that the beneficiaries can police the trust, the trustee is under a duty to maintain financial accounts and to provide other information at their request.

1.32   In general terms, therefore, a trust is either a self-imposed obligation or an obligation imposed on a third party (in whom legal title to the property becomes vested) to act for the benefit of another which is enforceable in equity. The equitable interest in property thereby becoming different and distinct form the nominal legal ownership vested in the trustee. Alternatively, it could be said that a trust is an equitable obligation imposed on the person who has legal title to act for the benefit of others. The Recognition of Trusts Act 1987 promotes the understanding of a trust as the legal relationship created by a settlor who has placed assets under the control of a trustee for the benefit of a person or purpose and which possesses the following characteristics:

- the assets are a separate fund and not part of the trustee's estate;

- legal title to the assets is vested in the name of the trustee or another acting on behalf of the trustee; and

- the trustee has the power and the duty to manage, employ or dispose of the assets in accordance with the terms of the trust.[54]

Types of Trust

1.33   The major reason why the concept of the trust cannot comfortably slot within any promoted definition is that there various types of trust and various ends that they are designed to achieve. As Hayton observes, "Births, marriages, divorces, or intimations of mortality often lead to the creation of trusts. Tax considerations will play a major role in encouraging a settlor to divest himself of his property and in determining the

---

[53] Not, however, a bona fide purchaser of value of the legal estate without notice.
[54] The Act derives this definition from Art.2 of the Hague Convention on the Law Applicable to Trusts.

type of trust to be created to preserve the family wealth from the clutches of the taxman and of improvident spendthrift beneficiaries".[55] Although the major classification is between an express trust and an implied trust, a variety of sub-divisions exist within each class. It is useful to consider these categories at this early stage.

The express trust

Express trusts are created deliberately by the settlor and, as a general rule, may be created by deed, will, writing or orally. The overwhelming majority of trusts are expressly created. The settlor will either declare himself to be a trustee (uncommon) or nominate a third party to act as his trustee. If the latter option is adopted, the settlor must always ensure that the trustee obtains legal title to the trust property by, as appropriate, an inter vivos transfer or by will. The basic ingredients for an express trust are that there is the certainty of intention to create a trust, certainty of subject matter forming the trust and certainty of beneficiary under the trust. By way of an exception to the general rule, some trusts (e.g. those relating to land) must also satisfy additional formalities which usually relate to the need for writing. As will now be demonstrated, there are several brands of express trust.   **1.34**

Bare trusts

A bare or simple trust arises when the trustee holds property for a sole beneficiary who is entitled to the entire beneficial interest without any contingency or encumbrance. The beneficiary can call for a conveyance of the trust property at any time. The trustee has no duties to perform other than holding the property as a nominee for the beneficiary. A bare trust arises where, for example, a solicitor holds client account money in its bank account on trust for its client.[56] Trusts which require the trustee to perform duties are sometimes described as "special trusts".   **1.35**

> chance happening.

Fixed trusts

A fixed trust arises where the trustee holds property on trust for a number of specified beneficiaries and their respective shares under the trust are identified in the trust instrument. For example, "£33,000 on trust for Noel and Adrienne equally". There is no discretion in the trustees as to who is to get what as everything has been pre-determined by the settlor.   **1.36**

---

[55] D.J. Hayton, *The Law of Trusts* at p.49.
[56] *Target Holdings Ltd v Redferns* [1996] A.C. 421.

Executed and executory trusts

1.37   This is a further division of express trusts. An executed trust is one where the settlor has made clear exactly what interests are to be taken by each beneficiary, for example, "£5,000 on trust for each of my two children". The entitlement of the beneficiaries is, therefore, set out in a final form.

An executory trust arises where the settlor has merely expressed a general intention as to how the property is to be applied. Some other document is intended to be executed so as to define more exactly the beneficial interests to be taken. In *Davis v Richards & Wallington Industries Ltd*,[57] a pension scheme was established by an interim (i.e. temporary) trust instrument. This provided for the later execution of a final trust deed. The validity of the later instrument when executed was challenged. Although the court upheld the later deed, it accepted that, had the deed been defective, the interim instrument would have been a valid executory trust. If necessary, the court could have ordered the execution of a new and final instrument corresponding to the terms of the defective one.

Discretionary trusts

1.38   A discretionary trust arises where the trustee is given some power of selecting who is to get what under the trust. For example, "£100,000 to be divided between my children as my trustee sees fit". There the trustee has to divide the money between my children, but is allowed the discretion as to which child will receive what amount. It offers flexibility and can reflect changes in the circumstances and needs of the beneficiaries. Obviously, this makes the job of trustee more difficult and this is particularly so when there is a large class of potential claimants (e.g. a discretionary trust for past and present employees of a particular company). No beneficiary has any property rights until the trustee exercises his discretion. All the beneficiary has is an expectation. There is a further sub-classification of "exhaustive" and "non-exhaustive" discretionary trusts. The former arises where the trustee is under the obligation to distribute all the trust property, and the discretion concerns only who are to be selected as the recipients of the property. The "non-exhaustive" strain of discretionary trust differs in that the trustee is not under an obligation to distribute all the trust property and is given the power to accumulate income.

Sometimes the distinction between a fixed trust and a discretionary trust is not strikingly apparent. For example, "£200,000 to my trustee so that he will divide it in a fair manner between my children". Although this might appear to be a discretionary trust, it is in fact a fixed trust. As the maxim, "equity is equality" can be brought into play, it will be valid. If, however, the trust is instead "£200,000 to be divided in a fair manner between such of my children as my trustee shall select", this will create a discretionary trust because the trustee is given the choice of who gets what.

[57] [1990] 1 W.L.R. 1511.

Public trusts

A private (or non-charitable) trust is one which is to benefit people named or described **1.39** by the settlor (e.g. "my relatives") whereas a public (or charitable) trust is designed promote a purpose which is beneficial in some way to society (e.g. the relief of poverty). Charitable trusts are, not surprisingly, treated differently from private trusts. They enjoy fiscal advantages, are capable of enforcement by the Attorney General (and, hence, do not need to satisfy the rules which require certainty of beneficiary) and need not comply with the rule against inalienability.[58] In order to be a charitable trust, the purpose must be one that the law recognises as charitable, it must have a public benefit and be exclusively charitable.[59]

Secret trusts

A secret trust is one which is created on the death of the settlor with the element of **1.40** secrecy being that the existence of the trust is either not evident at all on the face of the settlor's will (a fully secret trust) or where the trust is disclosed in the will, but the identity of the beneficiary is not (a half-secret trust). The secret trust offers a vehicle by which, say, a married man can provide for his clandestine lover after his death and is discussed in Ch.5.

Statutory trusts

Statutory trusts are imposed in certain circumstances. The major example is where there **1.41** are joint legal owners of land. By virtue of the Trusts of Land and Appointment of Trustees Act 1996, the joint owners must necessarily hold the legal title on statutory trust for themselves and/or others. Statutory trusts arise also on bankruptcy, intestacy and on the conveyance of land to minor.

Employee trusts

Employee trusts have become common in recent years and are often known as **1.42** "Employee Share Ownership Trusts". Such trusts when coupled with approved profit sharing schemes provide an attractive option for companies and their employees. The company establishes the trust fund with tax deductible money and the trustees acquire shares in the company which are then distributed to the employees. The dividends subsequently paid on those shares are taxed in the hands of the employees.

---

[58] See Ch.4.
[59] This is discussed in Ch.7.

Pension trusts

1.43 Pension trusts (otherwise known as superannuation schemes) are central to modern life and an individual's provision for retirement. Private occupational pension schemes have proved popular and attractive. In order to maximise fiscal advantages, the scheme must be approved by the Pensions Regulator and the Inland Revenue. Under such schemes, the employee makes financial contributions through the "pay as you earn" scheme administered by the employer on behalf of the Inland Revenue. The employee receives income tax relief as regards these pay as you go payments. The employer will also make contributions to the pension scheme. The trustees will invest the entire pension fund and, on the retirement of an employee, the idea is that there should be sufficient funds to provide a taxable pension for the retirement years. The payment may be calculated as a percentage of the employee's final salary ("final salary schemes") or may reflect the money earned as a result of the individual's total contributions to the fund ("money purchase schemes"). The use of a trust operates to segregate the pension funds from the employer's funds and to maximise tax advantages.

The choice of scheme to be adopted is up to the employer and it is the employer who will make the initial appointment of the trustees and determine their powers and duties. The danger, of course, lies in the appointment of an employee as trustee because the employer may be able to exert too much influence and prejudice the interests of the employees. The employer, however, owes a fiduciary duty and is obliged to act in good faith towards his employees.[60] The basic aim of the Pensions Acts 1995 and 2004 was to protect beneficiaries from the effects of poor administration, fraud and insolvency. Basic safeguards such as the keeping of proper books and the maintenance of a separate bank account for trust money, and the imposition of criminal liability on an employer who fails to pay over the employee contributions within a set period, were put in place under the 1995 Act. The 2004 legislation introduced the Pensions Regulator who can police pension schemes and can appoint and remove trustees and even bar a person from acting as a trustee. The Pensions Regulator can also impose financial penalties on trustees and, for example, may seek an injunction to restrain a misuse of trust assets and/or apply to court for restitution of assets which have been misused. The Pensions Regulator can even wind-up an occupational pension scheme in order to protect the scheme's members. In addition, the Pensions Ombudsman may investigate complaints and disputes concerning maladministration. The 2004 Act also introduced the Pension Protection Fund which is designed to provide limited compensation for loss suffered by members of a pension scheme when the employer has become insolvent leaving a final salary scheme in deficit.

Outside employee pension trusts, it is possible for an individual (who is, say, self-employed) to maintain a private pension scheme with an insurance company. The individual will pay premiums to the company who will act as trustee, invest the money and, it is to be hoped, provide an adequate pension on the retirement of the individual.

---

[60] *Imperial Group Pension Trust Ltd v Imperial Tobacco Ltd* [1991] 2 All E.R. 597.

Protective trusts

A protective trust is aimed at ensuring that a feckless beneficiary will not lose the trust   **1.44**
property to his creditors or sell his trust interest to someone else. The way in which this
protection is achieved is by giving the beneficiary a life interest in the property which is
made determinable on a given event (e.g. bankruptcy or assignment) and followed by a
discretionary trust in favour of specified beneficiaries.[61] Hence, there are two trusts. The
first is designed to benefit the main beneficiary (e.g. a son) until the happening of the
determining event. The second trust bites once the event has occurred and, thereby,
preserves the trust property and allows the discretionary beneficiaries (which may
include the son) to benefit without bothering about the claims of creditors or the trustee
in bankruptcy. One limitation is that the settlor cannot create a protective trust with
himself having a determinable life interest.[62]

Implied resulting and constructive trusts

There are two types of implied trust: the resulting trust (see Ch.9) and the constructive   **1.45**
trust (see Ch.10). It is helpful if the distinction between the two styles of implied trust is
understood at this early stage.

The resulting trust takes its name from the fact it operates to ensure that beneficial
title "results back" to a transferor. This is more easily understood by considering the
circumstances in which the resulting trust will arise. First, where one party transfers
legal title of property to another in return for no consideration a presumption of a
resulting trust is raised.[63] This is sometimes called a voluntary conveyance resulting
trust. The equitable interest will result back to the transferor.

Secondly, where property is purchased by Fiona with some financial assistance from
Jordan then Jordan may acquire an interest in the property by virtue of a purchase
money resulting trust. Such a trust will be relevant only when there is no common
intention to share the property beneficially and when the payments were made to the
acquisition cost of the property. The examples so far concern what is traditionally
called the "presumed intention resulting trust".

Thirdly, when a settlor who intends to create an express trust fails in some way to
dispose of the entire equitable interest then that which remains results back to the
settlor. This third class is often called an "automatic resulting trust" because it is
traditionally perceived to be an automatic response to the failure to deal with the
property fully and effectively. For example:

---

[61] This is facilitated by s.33 of the Trustee Act 1925 which allows such a trust to be created by merely directing
the trustees to hold on "protective trust". Section 33 of the Act sets out a traditional formula of protective
trust which will then become operative.
[62] See *Re Detmold* (1889) 40 Ch. D. 585.
[63] Unless the presumption is displaced by the counter and outmoded presumption of advancement (i.e. gift).

- Fred transfers legal title to shares to Noel to hold on trust for Adrienne. If Adrienne dies before the transfer, the trust fails and the beneficial interest in those shares results back to Fred;[64]

- as occurred in *Vandervell v IRC*,[65] when Mr Vandervell retained an option to purchase back shares transferred to the Royal College of Surgeons, the entire beneficial interest was not dealt with and, because of this failure to declare in whom the beneficial interest of the option was vested, a resulting trust arose in favour of a very unhappy Mr Vandervell;

- in *Barclays Bank v Quistclose Investments Ltd*,[66] what appeared to be a loan was subject to the condition that the money could only be used to pay dividends to shareholders of a particular company. As the money was never used for these purposes, it was held on resulting trust for the lender; and

- if there is a trust under which specified allocated annuities are to be paid, say, to elderly beneficiaries who die before the fund is exhausted, the surplus will result back to the settlor.[67]

The constructive trust is very different to the resulting trust. It is a trust imposed by the court as a result of conduct and, being designed to ensure good conscience, originally had nothing to do with the intention of the parties. For example, in *Keech v Sandford*[68] a trustee of leasehold property abused his position by negotiating the grant of a new lease of a market in his own favour. Although the landlord had refused to grant a renewal to the trust, his personal interests conflicted with the interests of the trust. Hence, a constructive trust was imposed under which the trustee held the lease for the benefit of the beneficiaries under the express trust. If the property has been disposed of, the constructive trust will attach to the proceeds of sale.[69] These trusts arise by operation of law and are framed so as to prevent unconscionable dealings.[70] Other examples of such dealings include profits from unlawful acts, theft, mutual wills, secret trusts, dishonest assistance in a breach of trust and knowing receipt of trust money.

1.46   Time has, however, marched on and the constructive trust has a new sphere in which to operate, and this is in relation to the joint purchase of the family home. As is demonstrated in Ch.11, the constructive trust has largely subsumed the relevance of the resulting trust in this area of the law. There are two scenarios where this so called "common intention constructive trust" will arise.[71] The first is when there has been some discussion, arrangement or understanding between the parties as to beneficial ownership of the property. If a non-owning party acts to his detriment on the strength of that express bargain, a constructive trust will arise and the court will give effect to the bargain reached. The second instance of a family home constructive trust is when the parties have no discussion at all about the fate of the beneficial ownership of the

---

[64] The objects of the trust failed: see *Bankes v Salisbury Diocesan Council* [1960] Ch. 631.
[65] [1967] 2 A.C. 291.
[66] [1968] 3 All E.R. 651. This case is discussed in detail in both Ch.2 and Ch.9.
[67] See *Re Llanover Settled Estates* [1926] Ch. 626.
[68] (1726) Sel. Cas. Ch. 61.
[69] *Royal Brunei Airlines v Tan* [1995] 2 A.C. 378.
[70] See *Westdeutsche Landesbank Girozentrale v Islington BC* [1996] A.C. 669.
[71] See *Lloyds Bank v Rossett* [1991] 1 A.C. 107.

property, but the non-owner makes a direct financial contribution to the purchase of the property. In such circumstances there will be an implied bargain constructive trust arising from the presumed common intentions of the parties as evidenced by the course of dealings between them.

DISTINGUISHING A TRUST FROM OTHER LEGAL CONCEPTS

Due to the very different legal consequences that attach to a trust relationship than operate in relation to other types of relationship, it is necessary to make some key distinctions at the outset. The alternative concepts that will be considered are debt, bailment, agency, gift as well as the more thorny distinction between a trust and power.   **1.47**

Debt

A debt is usually rooted in a bilateral contractual relationship between the debtor and the creditor. The law of contract is underpinned by the concept of privity of contract which, subject to certain statutory exceptions (e.g. the Contracts (Rights of Third Parties Act) 1999), entails that only a party to a contract can bring an action for breach of contract. Even though no consideration has been provided and no privity of contract exists, a beneficiary can still enforce a trust in equity. The rights afforded under a contract are, moreover, personal whereas a trust interest is a property right. This entails that a trust can be enforced against third parties whereas, due to privity of contract, a contract is not usually enforceable against a non-contracting party. This is important when the recipient of money becomes bankrupt. If the recipient is a debtor and the money is paid under a contract, then the creditor has no special claim and must compete for repayment with other creditors. If the property was trust property, however, the beneficiaries have a prior claim over other creditors. The distinction between a contractual debt and a trust is not, however, always easy to draw.   **1.48**

In *Barclays Bank v Quistclose Investments Ltd*,[72] money was loaned by Quistclose to a company known as Rolls Razor Ltd in order that the latter could pay its shareholders dividends. The money was placed in a separate account at Barclays Bank by Rolls Razor. Before any dividend was paid, Rolls Razor went into liquidation and Barclays Bank laid claim to the money loaned in order to discharge a debt owed to it by the defunct company. If this was merely a contractual loan, Quistclose's position would have been hopeless. The House of Lords, however, discerned the existence of an implied trust (later identified as a resulting trust[73]). The beneficiary of that resulting trust, Quistclose, could thus reclaim its money in priority to the Bank's claims. As examined in Ch.2, numerous cases have been decided in the wake of *Quistclose* and all turn upon there being either a declaration of an express trust or the finding of some condition that has yet to be satisfied.

---

[72] [1968] 3 All E.R. 651.
[73] Per Lord Millett in *Twinsectra Ltd v Yardley* [2002] 2 All E.R. 377.

1.49   Albeit in a different setting, the tension between contract and trust is evident in the cases where there has been no segregation of trust property (also examined in Ch.2). In *Re Goldcorp Exchange Ltd*,[74] customers had paid money for precious metals which were stored for convenience and safekeeping at the dealer's premises. The metals, however, were not separated or segregated in any way. The dealer ceased trading and competing claims arose as to the precious metals. Those that had bought the stored metals claimed the existence of a trust so as to facilitate their claims in advance of the creditors. The court concluded that there could be no trust of tangible objects unless they were clearly identifiable and, as that was not the case here, the owners could not claim priority. It was purely a matter of contract.

Bailment

1.50   If goods are entrusted to another for safe keeping or repair, the relationship at common law is one of bailment. Bailment can be contractual (e.g. as with valet parking of a car) or gratuitous (e.g. when a friend borrows the car). There is, admittedly, some similarity with the trust in that the property is handed over to another and the recipient is under a duty in relation to that property. Nevertheless, they are very different creatures. In the above example, legal title to the car does not pass to the third party and it always remains with the original owner. There is no intention to fragment legal and equitable ownership. The bailee cannot pass title to the property. The duty owed by the bailee is also comparatively slight (i.e. a duty to take reasonable care) when compared to the diverse and onerous equitable duties of a trustee.

Agency

1.51   The key distinction between an agent and a trustee is that an agency is a relationship based upon a contract between principal and agent and, therefore, only offers personal rights in favour of the principal. An agency passes no title to the property and legal and beneficial ownership is unaffected. The extent of the liabilities of an agent will depend upon the terms of the contract. As now should be clear, a trust bestows property rights on the beneficiary which, if necessary, can be enforced against third parties. Like a trustee, an agent owes a fiduciary duty to his principal. This is the most striking similarity as both are prevented from making unauthorised profits and becoming unduly enriched from their position. If an agent makes such a profit, he will hold the money made on constructive trust for his principal.

---

[74] [1994] 2 All E.R. 806.

Gifts

A gift is the complete transfer of property to another. Both legal and equitable title pass   **1.52**
and the donee becomes the absolute owner of the property. A gift is not dependent
upon consideration and is voluntary in nature. To perfect a gift, it is necessary that the
relevant form of transfer relating to the type of property involved is employed. If not,
there is an imperfect gift which equity will not perfect and, as there is no consideration
given, equity will not assist a volunteer. By way of a simple example, Fred approaches
Noel and passes across a £20 note saying something akin to, "I want you to have this as
a birthday present". Absolute ownership has passed to Noel by the parting with possession and the intention to make a gift. If Fred then seeks to claim the money back it is
simply too late. Compare this with Fred giving Noel a £20 note until Noel gets paid at
the end of the week. This is not a gift, but is instead a loan. A contract exists between
Fred and Noel which can be enforced as a debt. In contrast, Fred gives Noel a £20 note
and says, "Will you give this to Jordan when you see him tonight". This is not a gift to
Noel nor is it a loan. There is no contract, but there is a trust. Noel has the legal title to
the money, but holds that £20 on trust for Jordan.

Powers of appointment

A trust will always place mandatory obligations, admittedly of varying degree, on the   **1.53**
shoulders of the trustee. As regards a fixed trust, the duty of the trustee is to distribute
according to the precise allocation made by the settlor. In relation to a discretionary
trust, the duty of the trustee is to exercise his discretion in accordance with the guidance
provided by the settlor and to distribute accordingly. The beneficiary under a fixed trust
has an entitlement to the distribution of his share as laid out in the trust instrument.
The beneficiary under a discretionary trust has no more than a mere expectation that he
will be allocated a beneficial share. He can, however, demand that trustees exercise
discretion in accordance with the trust. A survey of the key duties of trustees is provided
in Ch.13.

A trust will frequently give the trustee powers that are dispositive in nature. These
dispositive powers are those that authorise the trustee to apply trust property (e.g. the
powers of advancement and maintenance) in a different manner than is obligatory
under the terms of the trust.[75] The major dispositive power is the power of appointment.
Usually operating behind a trust, it allows the donee the discretion to divert trust
money from the beneficiaries in favour of another person or purpose, but only to the
extent permitted by the settlor.[76]

---

[75] See Ch.14.
[76] See *Edge v Pensions Ombudsman* [2000] Ch. 602.

Distinguishing a power from a discretionary trust

1.54   It is essential to distinguish a power from a discretionary trust. Although this task is usually a straightforward matter of construction of the words used, a power of appointment and a discretionary trust may share similar characteristics. In both there may be provision for the distribution of assets between members of a class, the selection of who is to benefit and the fixing of the amounts each is to receive. The difference is that under a discretionary trust the trustees are obliged to apply the trust property in the permitted manner (even with a non-exhaustive discretionary trust where the trustees have the power to accumulate income). If the intention is that the discretion must be exercised, then the relationship is a trust. As demonstrated in Ch.16, the beneficiaries together (provided they are of the age of majority and in sound mind) can collectively put an end to the trust, even a discretionary trust, and divide the property between them.

   As regards a power of appointment, appointors are not under such an obligation. Powers are always exercisable at the election of the donee. They are simply permissive in nature. Where a power is not exercised, the property goes to those entitled in default of appointment (e.g. the beneficiaries under the trust). A potential object under a power has no entitlement, whether individual or collective, and must be content to live in hope that the power will be exercised in his favour.[77] As to whether a trust or a power has been created, all turns upon the intention, actual or presumed, of the settlor as divined from the language of the instrument. As stated, the issue is whether the settlor intended a mere power or, instead, a gift to a class subject to the power of selection. As Lord Cottenham observed in *Burrough v Philcox*, "when there appears a general intention in favour of a class, and a particular intention in favour of individuals of a class to be selected by another person, and the particular intention fails, from that selection not being made, the court will carry into effect the general intention in favour of the class".[78] Hence, if there is a gift over in default of appointment then this will demonstrate the lack of intention to create a trust.[79] Similarly, in *Re Weekes*,[80] a testatrix left her husband a life interest in property and gave him the power to dispose of all such property by will amongst their children. He died intestate. The court could not discern a trust and concluded that the intention had been to create a power.

1.55   Powers may be fiduciary or personal. Fiduciary powers are powers vested in an office holder such as the trustee. Where discretion is exercised, the donee must do so responsibly. His duty is to consider periodically, whether or not to exercise discretion to benefit beneficiaries or objects of the power.[81] The power must be exercised in good faith and not in a manner that negates the sensible expectation of the settlor.[82] By contrast, a personal power is vested in an individual in their capacity as an individual. Here the donee is not required to consider periodically whether to exercise the power. In

---

[77] *Re Sayer* [1957] Ch. 423.
[78] (1840) 5 My. & Cr. 72 at 92.
[79] *Re Mills* [1930] 1 Ch. 654. There is no intention to benefit the objects of the power if it is not exercised. The intention is to benefit someone else on default of appointment.
[80] [1897] 1 Ch. 289.
[81] *Re Hay's ST* [1981] 3 All E.R. 788.
[82] *Re Pauling's ST* [1964] Ch. 303.

the absence of a fraud on the power the exercise of discretion cannot be challenged in court. The court is not in a position to take away a personal power from a donee.

A power of appointment may be "general" in that the donee is allowed to exercise it in favour of anyone he chooses (including himself), "special" in that it can only be exercised in favour of specified persons or purposes or "intermediate" or "hybrid" in that it is exercisable in favour of anyone except for specified persons or purposes. For example, a fixed trust of £100,000 in favour of Jordan and Fiona might allow the trustee the special power to pay, at his discretion, income or capital to the settlor's mother, Adrienne. Hence, the donee is permitted to siphon away trust money for the benefit of this person. Similarly, the power might allow the donee the capacity to make charitable donations from trust money. This means that the donee is under no obligation to pay money to Adrienne or to make a charitable donation, but because the donee is a fiduciary he is obliged to consider from time-to-time whether or not to do so.[83] As has been discussed, the donee simply cannot ignore the existence of the power. If it is exercised, it must be exercised reasonably and responsibly. If the power is not exercised, neither Adrienne nor any charity has a claim. The money remains on trust for Jordan and Fiona.

Sometimes, the label "trust power" is employed. This description is, however, apt to confuse and, as it lacks any significance in modern times,[84] should be used sparingly. If the obligation imposed is mandatory, the existence of a discretionary trust must be recognized. If it is, instead, mere permission then it is a power.

OVERSEAS TRUSTS

It is possible that a settlor may wish to create a trust abroad or export an existing trust to foreign shores. This may be desirable for a number of reasons and these may include: **1.56**

- for convenience when the beneficiaries are living abroad or about to live abroad;

- to avoid future tax developments, e.g. the fear of a wealth tax;

- to minimise the risks associated with fluctuations in currency rates;

- to ensure that the trust is subject to an overseas jurisdiction; and

- to reduce tax liabilities.

Tax havens

The popularity of the offshore trusts situated, say, in the Channel Isles is down to the   **1.57**
fiscal advantages that can be enjoyed, both legitimately and otherwise. These trusts are

---

[83] *Re Charteris* [1917] 2 Ch. 379.
[84] Any distinction worthy of note has been erased since the assimilation of the certainty of objects tests which apply to powers and discretionary trusts: *McPhail v Doulton* [1971] A.C. 424.

often used by wealthy individuals who place money overseas in order that the fund is subject to the law of that other country. The site of these trusts is not selected for geographic convenience, and as Lord Walker commented, "they are supposed to offer special advantages in terms of confidentiality and protection from fiscal demands (and, sometimes, from problems under the insolvency laws, or laws restricting freedom of testamentary disposition, in the country of the settlor's domicile) . . . As a further cloak against transparency, the identity of the true settlor may be concealed behind some corporate figurehead".[85] Provided that the purpose of the trust is to avoid tax (and not to evade tax) then there is nothing to stop individuals from placing their money overseas so as to reduce fiscal liability.

GUIDE TO FURTHER READING

A.J. Duggan, "Is Equity Efficient?" (1997) 113 L.Q.R. 601.

S. Gardner, "Two Maxims of equity" (1995) C.L.J. 60.

A. Mason, "The Place of Equity and Equitable Remedies in the Contemporary Common Law World" (1994) 110 L.Q.R. 238.

---

[85] *Schmidt v Rosewood Trust Ltd* [2003] 3 All E.R. 76 at 81.

Chapter 2

THE THREE CERTAINTIES

As shown in Ch.1, the key characteristic of a trust lies in its fragmentation of legal and equitable ownership. Legal (i.e. nominal) title rests with the trustee, whereas equitable (i.e. substantive or real) title vests in the beneficiary. In all cases, the trustee is under a fiduciary duty to use the property according to the terms of the trust and is personally liable to a beneficiary for any breach of trust conditions. Accordingly, it is necessary that the settlor demonstrates that a trust was intended, demarcates the property that is to be the subject of that trust, and identifies who is to benefit under its terms. To cater for this, the law has evolved a test known as the "three certainties" which requires certainty of intention, certainty of subject matter and certainty of objects.[1] The general rule is that the three certainties need to be present so that a trust can be practicable, enforceable and capable of supervision by the court. Different requirements apply to each head of certainty. Accordingly each will be examined in turn.

2.01

INITIAL OBSERVATIONS

It is to be appreciated that all three certainties have to be present as regards express private trusts. In relation to public (i.e. charitable) trusts, however, there is no need to establish certainty of objects (i.e. beneficiaries) because the Attorney General and the Charity Commission have the legal authority to enforce charitable trusts.

2.02

The test as to "certainty of objects" varies between fixed trusts (i.e. where the beneficiaries and their shares are identified) and discretionary trusts (where the trustee selects who exactly is to benefit from a wider class specified by the settlor). Except for charitable trusts, which are the subject of special treatment, the objects must be living individuals. Private purpose trusts (e.g. to care for pets) are thought to have no place in the modern law. This is because of the "beneficiary principle" which requires that there

---

[1] See Lord Langdale M.R. in *Knight v Knight* (1840) 3 Beav. 148 at 173.

is someone with locus standi (i.e. the legal capacity to apply to the court to enforce the trust).[2]

Issues of certainty might arise also in relation to gifts. This is particularly so with conditions that are attached to a gift, for example, a condition precedent[3] or a condition subsequent.[4] Although these eventualities must be conceptually certain,[5] a less strict test applies to these types of gift than applies to trusts.[6] In *Re Allen*,[7] the Court of Appeal was invited to decide whether a devise "to the eldest of the sons of [A] who shall be a member of the Church of England and an adherent to the doctrine of that church" was void for lack of certainty. By a majority, it was held that the personal representative could establish as fact whether the eldest son (the appellant) satisfied the conditions. In *Blathhwayt v Baron Cawley*,[8] a condition for forfeiture if the recipient of a gift should be or become a Roman Catholic was upheld. A further illustration of this liberality emerges from *Re Barlow's Will Trust*[9] (see **2.39**). There a testatrix bequeathed a number of valuable paintings to specified individuals. As to the remainder of her collection, she directed her executor to sell the paintings with the proviso that "any friends of mine who may wish to do so" could buy any of the paintings at less than market value. This direction was upheld because a complete list of friends was not needed. Browne-Wilkinson J. understood the term "friend" to be someone with whom the deceased had a social relationship and had met frequently when circumstances allowed. The friends so defined had options to purchase the artwork. This is a tolerant approach that does not extend to trusts. As will become clear, the term "friend" is insufficiently certain for the creation of a trust.

Consequences of a lack of certainty

2.03   The consequences of an absence of certainty may vary according to which certainty is lacking.[10] First, as regards an absence of the *certainty of intention* to create a trust and depending upon the circumstances, there are alternative options as to what will become of the property. If the property was given or bequeathed to a third party, it will be viewed as an absolute gift to that person.[11] Legal and beneficial title will be transferred to the recipient without the recipient being subject to any legal obligation to do anything with the property. If, however, the settlor has retained legal title to the property,[12]

---

[2] See *Re Astor's ST* [1952] Ch. 534.
[3] For example, an interest vesting only on the donee becoming a solicitor.
[4] For example, an interest ceasing on the donee's bankruptcy. This type of condition is often referred to as a forfeiture clause.
[5] For example, a condition that a person, as appropriate, resides or ceases to reside in a particular area will be void for uncertainty: *Re Gape* [1952] Ch. 743.
[6] See *Re Allen* [1953] Ch. 810, where, as regards certainty of objects, the test is that the gift is valid if it is possible to show that at least one person qualifies even though there may be uncertainty as to others; see generally C.T. Emery (1982) 98 L.Q.R. 551.
[7] Re Allen [1953] Ch. 810.
[8] [1976] A.C. 397.
[9] [1979] 1 W.L.R. 278.
[10] See G. Williams "*The Three Certainties*" (1940) 4 M.L.R. 20, pp.22–16.
[11] *Lassence v Tierney* (1849) 1 Mac. & G. 551; *Hancock v Watson* [1902] A.C. 14.
[12] For example, where the settlor had attempted unsuccessfully to declare himself as a trustee of the property for the benefit of another (see Ch.3).

the property will simply remain in the settlor's estate. This is illustrated in *Re TXU Europe Group Plc*.[13] There the key issue was whether an investment portfolio (valued at more than £8 million) was held by the company on trust to provide top-up benefits to certain senior employees. The High Court held that there was an absence of any positive indication of the intention to hold it on trust. Indeed, such indicators as there were pointed towards the opposite conclusion.[14] Accordingly, the money stayed with the company and was available to its general creditors.

Secondly, if there is a lack of *certainty of subject matter* there are again alternative possibilities. Where there is no certainty of trust property whatsoever, there can be no trust. Applying common sense, and as there is nothing sufficiently identifiable that can leave the legal owner, the property will remain with the settlor (or the settlor's estate). As such, the property will remain susceptible to the claims of the settlor's creditors. In the scenario where there is a lack of certainty of beneficial share, the trust will also fail. If the settlor had intended to act as trustee, the property will obviously remain with him (or his estate). If, however, legal title to the trust property has already left the settlor and become vested in a third party trustee, the trustee will hold the trust property on what is called a "resulting trust". This entails that the property automatically reverts back to the settlor (or his estate).

Thirdly, as regards an absence of *certainty of objects*, if the settlor is the trustee then **2.04** nothing at all happens. No property has left the estate of the settlor. If, however, a third party has been appointed as trustee then, on failure of the trust, the property is again to be held upon automatic resulting trust for the settlor (or his estate).

CERTAINTY OF INTENTION

It is necessary for the settlor to intend to create a trust as opposed to some other type of **2.05** legal relationship (e.g. a gift, a power, bailment or agency). There is, however, no magic formula required to demonstrate the intention to create a trust. It is a well-established principle that equity looks to substance not form. Hence, it is the finding of intention rather than the precise form of expression employed that assumes importance. Trusts can be expressly declared or even inferred from the conduct of the parties and the surrounding circumstances. The test is whether, on a construction of the words used and/or from the behaviour of the parties, there is discernible a clear intention that the property is to be held on trust for the benefit of a third party. The court is advised against taking an unduly technical approach to the interpretation of a homemade document.[15] A mere expression of desire to make a gift or to confer a benefit is insufficient. The unequivocal intention must be to separate legal and equitable own-ership and to impose the obligations of trusteeship on the holder of the legal title.[16] This

---

[13] [2003] EWHC (Ch) 3105.
[14] For example, the company's accounts referred to the investment as an asset. It was also clear that the company's directors (the potential beneficiaries) did not, at the time of the investment, wish for a trust to be created because each would have incurred an immediate liability to tax.
[15] *Wallbank v Price* [2007] EWHC 3001 (Ch); see also *Kynnersley v Wolverhampton City Council* [2008] W.T.L.R. 65.
[16] See *Wright v Atkyns* (1823) Turn & R 143.

raises issues of fact and degree. Although desirable, the use of the word "trust" is not essential.[17] Indeed, even if the term is employed it offers no guarantee that a trust will have been created. It is a word that is capable of various meanings.[18] It is to be noted, moreover, that there is no general requirement that a trust be created[19] or even evidenced[20] in writing.

Precatory words

2.06   Precatory words are words merely of hope and desire (e.g. "in the hope that", "I would like that", "in the expectation that", "I desire that" and "I feel confident that"). Usually, such words appear in non-professionally drafted wills that deal with what is to happen to property on the death of the testator. Since the late nineteenth century, such expressions alone are insufficient to show the necessary intention to create a trust. Older cases are, therefore, no sure guide to modern understanding.[21] The modern approach is to look for imperative words that impose a mandatory legal obligation on the trustee. A moral obligation or mere request is simply not enough.[22] If there is doubt, the burden lies on the claimant to establish the necessary intention on a balance of probabilities.[23] Although sometimes allusion is made to a "precatory trust", care should be taken with this expression. All that this unhelpful descriptive label means is that the intention to create a trust can be discerned from conduct and surrounding circumstances even when the language employed is itself insufficiently imperative. It is, however, to be remembered that there can now be no trust based on precatory words alone. It is, moreover, sometimes argued that there is an interrelationship between the three types of certainty. This is traditionally described as the "reflex action" and emanates from *Mussoorie Bank Ltd v Raynor* where Sir Arthur Hobhouse said, "Uncertainty in the subject of the gift has a reflex action upon the previous words ... and seems to show that he could not possibly have intended his words of confidence, hope or whatever they may be ... to be imperative words".[24] There the House of Lords was cementing the proposition that the

---

[17] As Megarry J. put it in *Re Kayford* [1975] 1 All E.R. 604 at 607, "it is well settled that a trust can be created without using the words 'trust' or 'confidence' or the like: the question is whether in substance a sufficient intention to create a trust has been manifested".

[18] See, for example, *Tito v Waddell (No.2)* [1977] Ch. 106 where government documents referred to a "trust" in the context of mining rights, but no trust was found to have been created; see also *Harrison v Gibson* [2006] 1 W.L.R. 1212.

[19] An exception to this rule concerns sub-trusts which involve the disposition of a subsisting equitable interest (e.g. the transfer of an existing trust interest or the declaration of new beneficiaries) which must be in writing and signed by the settlor: s.53(1)(c) of the Law of Property Act 1925; see Ch.4.

[20] An exception to this rule relates to express trusts of land which need to be evidenced in writing and signed on behalf of the settlor: s.53(1)(b) of the Law of Property Act 1925, see Ch.4.

[21] As Cotton L.J. admitted in *Re Adams and Kensington Vestry* (1884) 27 Ch. D. 394 at 410, "some of the older authorities went a great deal too far in holding that some particular words appearing in a will were sufficient to create a trust ... what we have to look at is the whole of the will which we have to construe ... we must not extend the old cases in any way, or rely upon the mere use of particular words ...".

[22] *Sweeney v Coghill* (1999) 77 P. & C.R. D14. Technically, there is no such thing as a "precatory trust": *Re Williams* [1897] 2 Ch. 12.

[23] *Re Snowden* (1979) Ch. 528; but as Lewison J. accepted in *Wallbank v Price* [2007] EWHC 3001 (Ch), "if there is one interpretation which will produce a valid instrument and another rival interpretation which will make it ineffective, the court should, in my judgment, prefer the former interpretation", (at [44]).

[24] (1882) 7 App. Cas. 321 at 331.

use of "precatory" words cannot alone show the intention to create a trust. As this is now well established law, the "reflex action" appears to lack contemporary significance.[25] It is to be appreciated, however, that a trust can fail for a lack of more than one certainty.

There are two classic examples of the rule that precatory words do not work to create a trust. First, in *Lambe v Eames*[26] the testator left his estate to his widow "to be at her disposal in any way she may think best, for the benefit of herself and her family". It was held that this was a precatory expression and did not connote the necessary intention to create a trust. In relation to the more liberal approach advocated in some earlier cases, James L.J. commented, "I could not help feeling that the officious kindness of the Court of Chancery in interposing trusts where in many cases the father of the family never meant to create trusts must have been a very cruel kindness indeed".[27]

Secondly, in *Re Adams and the Kensington Vestry*[28] the testator's estate was devised by will to the absolute use of his widow, "in full confidence that she will do what is right as to the disposal thereof between my children, either in her lifetime or by will after her decease". These again were merely words of aspiration and did not impose a legal obligation on the widow.

2.07

There are a variety of other case law examples that show the inefficacy of precatory words. These include:

- *Re Hamilton*[29] where the testator left legacies to his two nieces and added the words, "I wish them to bequeath them equally between the families of [X] and [Y] in such mode as they shall consider right". No trust was created in favour of X and Y because the words employed did not impose the obligations of a trustee upon the nieces.[30]

- *Re Diggles*[31] where the testatrix left her property to her daughter with the rider that "it is my desire that she allows to A.G. an annuity of £25 during her life". The added words did not create a trust and the daughter took the property free from this qualification.

- *Margulies v Margulies*[32] where a legacy of the residuary estate was left to one son and expressed to be in confidence that, "if in the interests of family harmony", he would make provision for his brother and sister. The language of the testator did not disclose a sufficient certainty of intention to create a trust. As the words used were precatory in nature, the son could keep the money for himself.

- *Mussoorie Bank v Raynor*[33] where a husband left land to his widow, "feeling confident that she will act justly to our children in dividing the same when no

---

[25] See the views of Rigby L.J. in *Re Williams* [1897] 2 Ch. 12 at 35.
[26] (1871) 6 Ch. App. 597.
[27] (1871) 6 Ch. App. 597 at 599.
[28] (1884) 27 Ch. D. 394.
[29] [1895] 2 Ch. 370.
[30] See also, *Re Johnson* [1939] 2 All E.R. 458 ("I request that…").
[31] (1888) 39 Ch. D. 253. See also *Re Conolly* [1910] 1 Ch. 219 ("I specially desire that.…").
[32] (1999) 77 P. & C.R. D21.
[33] (1882) 7 App. Cas. 321.

longer required by her". The widow mortgaged the land and, eventually, the Bank sought to sell it to recoup the loan. She argued that, as she was a trustee of the land, the mortgage was invalid. The House of Lords held that no trust existed because the husband had used precatory words. She was the legal and beneficial owner of the property and, hence, the mortgagee could sell the property.

2.08   There are a brace of cases that might, at first glance, be viewed as contradicting the accepted wisdom as to the effect of precatory language. The temptation to interpret these cases in this way should, however, be resisted. The first case to be considered is *Comiskey v Bowring-Hanbury*.[34] There a legacy was left to a widow "in full confidence" that she would leave the property on her death to one or more of the testator's nieces. As these were precatory words, they were in themselves ineffective to create a trust.[35] The will, however, went on to declare that, "in default of any disposition by her thereof by her will . . . I hereby direct that all my estate and property acquired by her under this my will shall at her death be equally divided among the surviving said nieces". These added words proved crucial because the House of Lords held that, in looking for certainty of intention, it was necessary to consider the trust document as a whole. The imperative wording of the gift over imposed the mandatory obligation upon the widow.

She held the property on trust for herself for life and then in remainder for the nieces equally. It is to be emphasised that this case is not authority for saying that precatory words can constitute a trust. All that it shows is that the provision made clear the widow could not keep the property for herself.

The second case is that of *Re Steele's Will Trusts*.[36] This involved a solicitor drafting a trust deed for a client, but unfortunately utilising an outmoded precedent that featured precatory words ("I request my said son to do all in his power"). Although this precedent had worked in the past,[37] in the more contemporary setting there should have been no trust because of a lack of certainty of intention. Nevertheless, Wynn-Parry J. concluded that the deliberate use of the precedent (albeit itself defective) demonstrated the necessary intention to declare a trust of a diamond necklace. This is, undoubtedly, a rogue decision and is thoroughly unsafe.[38] It disregards the actual wording of the deed, imputes an artificial intention to the settlor and departs from the general rule that extrinsic evidence is inadmissible in the construction of a trust deed.[39]

---

[34] [1905] A.C. 84; see also *Gibbs v Harding* [2008] Ch. 235 where the words "it is my wish" were followed by the expression "to hold in trust". A trust was upheld.

[35] Indeed, s.22 of the Administration of Justice Act 1982 provides that, unless there is a contrary intention demonstrated, a bequest to a spouse will be regarded as an absolute gift even though it purports to give their children an interest in the same property.

[36] [1948] Ch. 603.

[37] *Shelley v Shelley* (1868) L.R. 6 Eq. 540.

[38] See P. Langan (1968) 32 Conv. 361.

[39] See *Rabin v Gerson Berger Association Ltd* [1986] 1 W.L.R. 526. Extrinsic evidence is allowed to ascertain the testator's intention where there is ambiguity or doubt as to meaning of a provision in a will: s.21 of the Administration of Justice Act 1982. Where there is no will, therefore, s.21 cannot apply.

Fictitious intentions

The working rule is that an express declaration of trust will be conclusive. This rule **2.09** gives way, however, where the intention to create a trust is palpably false (i.e. a "sham" or "pretence" trust has been created). Usually, such a sham trust will be created in order to prevent creditors or an estranged spouse from making a claim against property. If regarded by the court as a sham, however, the trust fails and the title to the property remains with the settlor. Such might occur, for example, when an individual attempts to secrete money in an offshore trust based in the Channel Islands while maintaining control and beneficial ownership of those funds. Hence, in *Rahman v Chase Bank Trust Co Ltd* it was held that the settlor retained total control over the trust funds and, therefore, could never have genuinely intended to set up a trust.[40]

Similarly, in *Midland Bank v Wyatt*,[41] a husband and wife declared a trust in respect of the matrimonial home. The beneficial interest was to be shared equally between the wife and their daughters. The property was mortgaged to the Midland Bank and the husband continued to borrow on the security of the family home. He did not inform the Bank of the trust. The Bank eventually sought to sell the property in order to recover the husband's outstanding debt. In the High Court, the Deputy Judge held that the husband had never had the intention truly to divest himself of his interest in the property. He had declared the trust merely as a means of shielding the family home from the claims of the Bank. Put simply, there was no real intention to create a trust. The declaration was a mere pretence and, therefore, the trust was void. The outcome is not dependent upon there being a finding of fraud and can arise even if the settlor has acted honestly following deficient financial or legal advice.

Inferred intention

Even though there may be no express verbal recognition that a trust is intended, the **2.10** requisite intention might still be inferred. Obviously, much here turns upon the perception of the court and less upon the subjective intentions of the parties. Writing in an extra-judicial capacity, Lord Millett explained that this type of trust, "arises only partly from the language used. In most cases it arises largely, and in some cases wholly, by implication of law ... inferred from the language and conduct of the parties and the circumstances of the case".[42] There is no requirement that the settlor be actually aware that what he is creating is a trust. Instead, the court will investigate whether he intended to make the property subject to an obligation that the law acknowledges as a trust obligation.[43] It is always assumed that the settlor intends the legal consequences of his actions. Although this inference may arise equally in both a family and a commercial context, the different dynamics that are brought into play make it convenient to consider each stream of case law separately. In particular, as regards the commercial sector

---

[40] [1991] J.L.R. 103 (a Jersey case).
[41] [1995] 1 F.L.R. 696.
[42] (1985) 101 L.Q.R. 269 at 284.
[43] See *Duggan v Governor of Full Sutton Prison* [2004] 1 W.L.R. 1010, where the court held that a governor who held prisoner's money was not a trustee, but was instead merely a debtor.

the inferred trust is employed as a guard against the possibility of the recipient of the funds becoming insolvent. For example, a solicitor will pay money received on behalf of clients into a specially designated client account and that account will be shielded from the claims of the solicitor's other creditors.

Inferred intention and the family context

2.11   The primary example of an inferred intention trust is to be found in *Paul v Constance*.[44] Mr Constance repeatedly said to Mrs Paul of a bank account in his sole name, "The money is as much yours as mine". Special arrangements were made so that she could draw on the account and she paid her bingo winnings into it. Mr Constance subsequently died. There was found to be a declaration of an express trust that gave Mrs Paul an equal share in the bank account with the widow of Mr Constance. Scarman L.J. admitted that there was no need for "stilted lawyers' language" and that the court must remember that it is, "dealing with simple people, unaware of the subtleties of equity, but understanding very well indeed their own domestic situation".[45] The words and conduct of Mr Constance had to be viewed against their own background and in their own circumstances. It did not matter that Mr Constance was ignorant of the consequences of his actions.[46] There are, however, two potential difficulties with this case.

First, it was not made clear exactly when the express trust was created. As Scarman L.J. admitted, "It might, however, be thought that this is a borderline case, since it is not easy to pin-point a specific moment of declaration, and one must exclude from one's mind any case built upon the existence of an implied or constructive trust, for this case was put forward at the trial and is now argued by the plaintiff as one of express declaration of trust".[47] Presumably, the trust was created on the first utterance of joint ownership. If so, the relevance of future utterances might be that they serve to embrace the additional payments made into the account by Mr Constance.

2.12   Secondly, it was not made clear what occurred in relation to the bingo winnings paid into the account by Mrs Paul. Imagine a scenario where Mrs Paul won £1 million on the lottery and paid it into the account. There is no way that this additional money would become trust property shared with Mr Constance. The account holder would hold it on resulting trust for the payer. As Mr Constance could not declare a trust in favour of himself over someone else's property, it would seem that the £1 million would fall outside the scope of the trust. Any future payments made by him might, however, fall within the subject matter of the trust if that is deemed to have been his intention. As mentioned, his further utterances of trust may indicate this. This divergence of treatment seems to explain why the widow Constance was able to claim a share of the account (as her deceased husband's next of kin) and why the contents of the bank account were not regarded solely as the property of Mrs Paul. Mr Constance and Mrs Paul could not be regarded as beneficial joint tenants. The unilateral declaration of the

[44] [1977] 1 W.L.R. 527.
[45] [1977] 1 W.L.R. 527 at 530.
[46] See also, *Rowe v Prance* [1999] 2 F.L.R. 787 where frequent reference to a boat (purchased by Mr Prance) as "ours" gave his partner (Ms Rowe) a beneficial interest in the vessel.
[47] [1977] 1 W.L.R. 527 at 532.

trust, coupled with fluctuating nature of the account and the payments in made by her, undermined any intention that they be beneficial joint tenants of the contents of the account.[48] A different outcome would, seemingly, be reached if the couple had opened the bank account together and, although they made unequal contributions, had intended to pool their resources.[49]

The inference of the intention to create a trust was drawn more recently in *Gold v Hill*.[50] In 1993, Mr Gilbert took out a life assurance policy. Mr Gilbert named the beneficiary of the policy as Max Gold and identified Mr Gold as executor under his will. Although a valid will was in existence (it had been executed in 1983), it did not name Mr Gold as executor. It was alleged that Mr Gilbert had said to Mr Gold that he wanted the insurance money to be used to look after his mistress, Carol, and her children. Mr Gilbert was not as charitable towards his wife, Antoinette, "Don't let that bitch get anything". Antoinette was, however, the major beneficiary under his will. Mr Gilbert died in 1995. Mr Gold claimed the money in an individual capacity. The issue was whether he would then be under a duty to pay the money to Carol. Carnwath J. held that the earlier conversation had the effect of nominating Mr Gold as a trustee and that Mr Gilbert had informally explained what he was doing and why.

There must, however, be the intention to declare a trust and not the intention to make an immediate gift. If the latter is intended, there is nothing that the court can do as "equity will not assist a volunteer". This is well illustrated in two cases. First, in *Jones v Lock*[51] a father held out a cheque for £900, which was payable to him, and placed it into the hand of his child. The father said, "I give this to baby and I am going to put it away for him". The father died a few days later and the issue was whether the child was entitled to the cheque. The court held that this was a failed gift (the title to the cheque did not pass because it was not endorsed over to the child) and could not be construed as a declaration of trust because no trust had been intended. As Lord Carnworth L.C. added, "I think it would be a very dangerous example if loose conversations of this sort, in important transactions of this kind, should have the effect of declarations of trust".[52]   **2.13**

Secondly, a similar sentiment was expressed in *Richards v Delbridge*.[53] There a tenant sought to transfer his business premises to his grandson. Unfortunately, he did not execute a conveyance necessary to effect a transfer of legal title to land. The gift, therefore, failed. The grandson argued that the court should instead discern an intention to create a trust. Jessell M.R. rejected this reasoning and made clear that, if it is intended to be a gift, the court cannot regard the failed transfer as amounting to a declaration of trust.[54]

---

[48] See *Standing v Bowring* (1885) 31 Ch. D. 282 where stocks were transferred into the joint name of a widow and her godson. The manifest intention was that they were not to be joint tenants and that the godson was to have sole beneficial entitlement.
[49] See *Re Bishop* [1965] Ch. 450.
[50] [1999] 1 F.L.R. 54.
[51] (1865) L.R. 1 Ch. App. 25.
[52] (1865) L.R. 1 Ch. App. 25 at 29.
[53] (1874) L.R. 18 Eq. 11.
[54] (1874) L.R. 18 Eq. 11 at 15. As Turner L.J. put it in *Milroy v Lord* (1862) 4 De. G.F. & J. 264 at 274, "for then every imperfect instrument would be made effectual by being converted into a perfect trust".

Inferred intention and the commercial context

2.14   This is a more difficult area of trust law and has generated much comment, speculation and analysis. These inferred intention trusts are becoming increasingly prevalent in commercial transactions and are employed as a vehicle through which assets can be protected on the insolvency of their designated holder. For example, a lender may advance money to the recipient on condition that the money be used only for a specified purpose[55] with the result that property rights in those funds do not move from the lender unless and until the money is deployed for that specified purpose. Of course, if the money is advanced unconditionally there is no prospect of an inferred intention trust because there is no retention of a beneficial interest.[56]

The consequence of this ploy is that the obligations in respect of the funds are such that the funds are put beyond the reach of the recipient's creditors. As Deputy Judge Michael Crystal put it in *Freeman v Commissioners for Customs & Excise*, "Company liquidations create many situations where it is claimed that a company's obligations have been transformed from contract into property, or from debt to trust, so that a claimant may claim property as his own rather than it being available for distribution amongst the general body of unsecured creditors".[57]

2.15   The Deputy Judge accepted that the trust arises in circumstances where A advances money to B on the understanding that B is not to have the full use of the money and that it may only be applied for the purpose stated by A. As Lord Millett observed in *Twinsectra v Yardley*, "It is unconscionable for a man to obtain money on terms as to its application and then disregard the terms on which he received it ... This is a classic situation in which a fiduciary relationship arises, and since it arises in respect of a specific fund it gives rise to a trust".[58] The key, therefore, is not that the recipient is bound to apply the money for a specific purpose, but that he is precluded from mis-applying it. The stipulated purpose is normally that B should apply the money for the payment of a creditor, C. In the *Freeman* case, for example, £693,000 was advanced by a purchaser to the seller's solicitors on condition that it be used only for the purposes of paying the VAT (if any was payable) on the sale of commercial premises. The Deputy Judge explained, "The effect of the trust is to reserve in A the beneficial interest in the money, so providing him with proprietary security for his advance ...".[59] He empha-sised that such a trust will only arise when A clearly intends to restrict B's freedom to dispose of the money being advanced to B other than to discharge a stipulated purpose. The Deputy Judge commented, "In the event of B's insolvency the money can be recovered by A. But it cannot be recovered by C whose rights are limited to those of the object of a mere power ...".[60] It appears that an inferred intention to create a trust, in the commercial arena, may arise in the following situations:

[55] For example, to purchase manufactured goods *(Sinclair Investment Holdings v Versailles Trade Finance Ltd* [2004] EWHC 2169 (Ch)) or to acquire brown field sites for building development *(Templeton Insurance Ltd v Penningtons Solicitors* [2006] All E.R. (D) 191 (Feb)).

[56] See *Abou-Rahmah v Abacha* [2005] EWHC 2662 (QB).

[57] [2005] EWHC 582 (Ch) at [10].

[58] [2002] 2 A.C. 164 at 186.

[59] [2005] EWHC 582 (Ch) at [15].

[60] [2005] EWHC 582 (Ch) at [16].

- when funds are transferred and segregated in circumstances where both the payer and the recipient are taken to have intended that the fund be held on trust,

- when, although there is no segregation, both the payer and the recipient have expressly agreed that restrictions are to operate upon the recipient's ability to use of the money, or

- when there has been a unilateral act by the recipient sufficient to demonstrate the intention to create a trust.

Inference from mutual intentions and segregation

This type of inferred intention trust, i.e. where property is transferred and segregated **2.16** from other funds on the shared understanding of both the payer and the recipient that it is to be held on trust, is illustrated most famously in *Barclays Bank v Quistclose Investments Ltd.*[61] Rolls Razor Ltd borrowed £209,000 from Quistclose Investments Ltd under an arrangement whereby the loan was to be paid only for the purposes of providing a dividend for shareholders that the company had already announced. The money was deposited in a specially created bank account at Barclays Bank to whom Rolls Razor was already heavily indebted. Before the payment of the dividend, Rolls Razor went into voluntary liquidation. Quistclose claimed the money in the special account on the ground that the parties had created a trust and that, as its purpose had failed, the funds were to result back to itself. The House of Lords held that the shared intention (of the payer and the recipient) had been that the money was to be held on trust unless it was employed for the purpose specified. If the purpose had been achieved, Quistclose would have been treated like any other unsecured creditor of the company. As the specific purpose had now failed, however, the money was to be held for the benefit of Quistclose and not Barclays Bank.

Two further cases demonstrate the operation of the *Quistclose* approach. First, in *Re* **2.17** *Lewis' of Leicester*,[62] floor space in a department store was rented out of to a number of traders. The traders agreed that their takings would be placed in a separate bank account and, pending payment over, held by the store on trust for them. The store became insolvent and the traders were able to claim their money in priority to the store's creditors. The agreement that the money be kept separate from the store's own funds was sufficient to infer the intention to create a trust.

Secondly, in *Don King Productions Inc v Warren*[63] a partnership was entered under which the benefit of any existing and future sports management agreements acquired by them was to become partnership property. It was argued that certain agreements were non-assignable and could not, therefore, be regarded as partnership property. Lightman J. held that, despite the wording of individual management agreements, the mutual intention was that the benefit of such agreements be held on trust for the partnership.

---

[61] [1970] A.C. 567.
[62] [1995] 1 BCLC 428.
[63] [1998] 2 All E.R. 608.

Although badly drafted, the partnership agreement sufficed to demonstrate this intention.

Inference from restrictions imposed without segregation

2.18   This type of inferred trust arises where both the payer and the recipient have expressly attached restrictions to the recipient's use of the funds.[64] This is illustrated by the decision of the House of Lords in *Twinsectra v Yardley*.[65] In this case, a solicitor received money from a lender (Twinsectra) on behalf of a client (Yardley). The solicitor gave an undertaking that the money would be retained by him and used only for the purposes of purchasing property for the client. The solicitor, however, used the money for other purposes and did not repay the loan. Although there had been no segregation of the funds, Lord Millett held that the limitations placed upon the use of the funds advanced demonstrated the existence of a trust. Under this trust the solicitor held the money for the benefit of Twinsectra, subject to the power of the solicitor to use it for the purposes specified.

A similar stance had previously been adopted by the High Court in *Carreras Rothmans Ltd v Freeman Mathews Treasure Ltd*.[66] Carreras Rothmans are the manufacturers of cigarettes. Carreras employed an advertising firm, Freeman Mathews Treasure Ltd, to place advertisements in the media. The Firm incurred substantial expenses and each month invoiced Carreras Rothmans for the liabilities it had incurred on their behalf. The Firm began to experience financial difficulties and Carreras Rothmans insisted that the Firm open a special bank account into which Carreras Rothmans would make their monthly payments. The Firm agreed that the money should be used only to discharge the debts associated with Carreras Rothmans' advertisement campaign. The Firm became insolvent at a time when there was a substantial amount of money in the special bank account. Under threat that its advertisements would not otherwise run in the media, Carreras Rothmans paid some debts directly and then sought to indemnify themselves from the Firm's bank account. The Firm's liquidator, however, had other ideas. The High Court found in favour of Carreras Rothmans and held that a trust arose as soon as the money was paid into the special account. As Peter Gibson J. put it, "Equity fastens on the conscience of the person who receives from another property transferred for a specific purpose only and not therefore for the recipient's own purposes, so that such person will not be permitted to treat the property as his own or to use it for other than the stated purpose".[67] The key factor was that Carreras Rothmans had intended that the Firm be subject to an enforceable obligation to apply the money for the specified purpose.

2.19   Other authorities concerning this second type of inferred trust include:

---

[64] It is not enough for the payer to have merely a general wish that the money be utilized in a particular way: *Blackburn v H.M. Revenue & Customs* [2008] EWHC 266 (Ch).
[65] [2002] 2 A.C. 164.
[66] [1985] Ch. 207. This was, however, a segregation case.
[67] [1985] Ch. 207 at 222.

- *Re EVTR*[68] in which the appellant, who had won around £250,000 on the premium bonds, loaned £60,000 to his former employer. The loan was on condition that new equipment would be purchased. The company paid over the money to the supplier. Before the equipment arrived, however, the company became insolvent. The supplier then returned £48,000 to the company and the issue was whether this money was available to the company's creditors or was held on trust for the appellant. The Court of Appeal determined that a trust had been created and that, as the purpose of the loan failed, the refunded money was still subject to the trust in favour of the appellant.[69] As to the fact that the £60,000 had already been paid over to the suppliers, Dillon L.J. commented, "... but that was only at half-time, and I do not see why the final whistle should be blown at half-time".[70] Bingham L.J. agreed and spoke of giving effect to, "the common fairness of the situation".[71] Nevertheless, this decision is open to the criticism that any trust should have been extinguished on the payment to the suppliers (i.e. full time had already passed). It is to be appreciated that, if the new machinery had been delivered before the insolvency, the trust would have been discharged and the company's creditors would have had priority over the appellant.

- *Nestle Oy v Lloyds Bank Plc*[72] concerned a ship-owner that paid money to an agent so that the agent could defray expenses incurred on its behalf. The funds were paid into the agent's general bank account. After the agent ceased trading, the ship-owner made a further payment. It was held that an implied trust attached to this final payment and that, regardless of the parties' actual intentions, the beneficial interest remained with the ship-owner. The reasoning was that an honest recipient of the last payment would have returned the money immediately.

- *Cooper v PRG Powerhouse Ltd*[73] involved a director paying £34,239 to the Company in order that it would discharge his debt relating to the purchase of a Mercedes car. The money was placed in the Company's payroll account and a cheque was duly forwarded to the creditor. Unfortunately, the Company went into liquidation before the cheque cleared. The Company's general creditors claimed that the £34,239 was available for them. Mr Cooper argued that a so-called "purpose trust" had been created. Evans-Lombe J. identified the key issue as being whether the money had been at the free disposal of the Company. Although the funds had not been kept in a separate account, the transfer was impressed with a purpose trust. Evans-Lombe J. concluded, "there was clearly to be implied into the arrangement that neither Mr Cooper nor the Company regarded the amount of the payment as part of the assets of the Company at its

---

[68] (1987) BCLC 646.
[69] Dillon L.J. concluded, "... a resulting trust in favour of the provider of the money arises when the money is provided for a particular purpose only, and that purpose fails" ((1987) BCLC 646 at 650).
[70] (1987) BCLC 646 at 651; see also, *R. v Common Professional Examinations Board* (2000) *The Times*, April 19, CA.
[71] (1987) BCLC 646 at 652.
[72] [1983] 2 Lloyds Rep. 658.
[73] [2008] EWHC 498 (Ch).

'free disposal' and available, in particular, as working capital or for the payment of its creditors."[74]

- *Dubey v HM Revenue & Customs*[75] produced a very different outcome. There the High Court rejected an implied trust in favour of the customers of the ill fated Farepak Food & Gifts Ltd. The case dealt with the consequences for customers of Farepak following the Company's insolvency. Although the customers had made advance payments to Farepak's agents for the purpose of acquiring Christmas hampers and vouchers and those specific purposes were not fulfilled by the Company, this was not a *Quistclose*-style trust. Mann J. based this rejection on two grounds. First, that the agents were never obliged to keep the customers' money separate from other money. Secondly, that there was no obligation upon Farepak to put the money on one side pending the dispatch of the customers' orders. Mann J. observed, "If there were a *Quistclose*-style trust then that obligation would have been inherent in it, but the business model would have made no sense. It would have required Farepak to have kept all the customer moneys in a separate account from January until November, untouched until the time when the goods and vouchers were acquired and then sent out. That is completely implausible. It would turn Farepak into a very odd savings organisation. Even banks do not have to do that."[76] The approach of Mann J. appears correct: the money was part of the working capital of the company and at its free disposal. The entitlement of the disappointed customers lay in contract and not trust law.

Inference from a unilateral act: the pre-payment cases

2.20   This next scenario in which an intention to create a trust can be inferred is when the recipient unilaterally acts in a way that evinces the necessary intention to hold the property on trust. The most prominent authority for this proposition is *Re Kayford*.[77] This decision concerned a mail order company that received advance payments from its customers. The company feared insolvency and unilaterally paid these payments into a special Customers' Trust Deposit Account. The company became insolvent and the general creditors laid claim to the money. In the normal course of events, the creditors would be so entitled. On the present facts, however, Megarry J. held that the steps taken by the company overtly demonstrated its intention to create a trust. He viewed this as an express trust for persons with the necessary intention being inferred from the unilateral conduct of the settlor. The trust was not viewed as an implied resulting trust. Megarry J. commented, "The whole purpose of what was done was to ensure that the moneys remained in the beneficial ownership of those who sent them, and a trust is the

---

[74] See also *Azam v Iqbal* [2007] EWHC 2025 (Admin) where there was no mutual intention that the money should not form part of the recipient's ordinary business cash flow.
[75] [2006] EWHC 3272 (Ch).
[76] [2006] EWHC 3272 (Ch) at [34].
[77] [1975] 1 All E.R. 604; see also *Re Nanwa Gold Mines Ltd* [1955] 3 All E.R. 219 where the express understanding was that the money would be kept in a distinct bank account.

obvious means of achieving this".[78] Until the goods were delivered, therefore, the equitable interest in the money remained with the customers.[79] The company had made it clear that it had given up the right to use the money itself.[80] The court viewed this as a proper and honourable act for a company to take. If Megarry J. is correct in his analysis, this case is not properly to be regarded as an example of a *Quistclose*-style trust. There is an absence of any bilateral understanding between the parties and there is instead the express declaration of trust by the settlor company.

A similar approach was adopted in *Re Chelsea Cloisters Ltd*[81] where the dispute concerned deposits paid by tenants as regards potential liabilities for damages and breakage. The landlord experienced financial problems and new deposits were paid into an account ("Tenants' Deposit Account") which was opened for the purposes of keeping the money separate. The Court of Appeal held that the nature of the transaction created a trust in favour of the tenants and that the funds were not to be claimed by the landlord's creditors.[82]

Understanding the *Quistclose*-style trust

The legal nature of the first two types of inferred intention trust has, not surprisingly,   **2.21**
been subject to major doubt and debate both on these shores and in the Commonwealth.[83] In *Barclays Bank v Quistclose*, Lord Wilberforce spoke in terms of there being two trusts: a primary trust to pay the dividend (i.e. one in favour of the shareholders of Rolls Razor) and a secondary trust which would arise if the primary trust could not be carried out (i.e. one in favour of Quistclose).[84] Several difficulties, however, emerge from Lord Wilberforce's approach.

- Lord Wilberforce did not consider whether the primary trust should properly be classified as a private purpose trust and, therefore, potentially void. This has encouraged some to advance the proposition that the primary trust is a non-charitable purpose trust under which the beneficial interest is in suspense until the purpose is satisfied.[85]

---

[78] [1975] 1 All E.R. 604 at 607.

[79] It is generally accepted that a requirement to keep money separately from other funds is indicative of a trust: *R. v Clowes (No.2)* [1994] 2 All E.R. 316. This will not be so, however, where the evidence shows that the customers are to accept the risk of insolvency: *Customs and Excise Commissioners v Richmond Theatre Management Ltd* [1995] S.T.C. 257.

[80] cf. *Re Multi Guarantee Ltd* [1987] BCLC 257 where, although the money (i.e. warranty premiums) was paid into a separate joint account, there was no trust because there was no relinquishing of control of the funds deposited therein. Multi Guarantee Ltd, as Nourse L.J. explained, "never did manifest a sufficient intention to create a trust and the requisite certainty of words was simply not there" (at 268).

[81] (1980) 41 P. & C.R. 98.

[82] See also, *Hill v Phillips* Unreported January 22, 1999 which dealt with a trust of money put into a designated clients' account.

[83] See generally, W. Swadling (ed.). *The Quistclose Trust Critical Essays* (Hart, 2004); see also J.A. Glister, "*The Nature of Quistclose Trusts: Classification and Reconciliation*" [2004] C.L.J. 632.

[84] [1970] A.C. 567 at 580; see also, the analysis of Lord Browne-Wilkinson in *Westdeutsche Landesbank Girozentrale v Islington BC* [1996] A.C. 669 at 708.

[85] See Megarry V.C. in *Re Northern Development Holdings* Unreported October 6, 1978 and Peter Gibson J. in the *Carreras Rothmans* case [1985] Ch. 207.

- Lord Wilberforce did not explain where the beneficial interest was to lie pending the use of the money for the specified purpose.

- Lord Wilberforce did not make clear whether the two trusts were express trusts or implied trusts. Some have viewed them as being express trusts because of the finding of a declared intention that a trust relationship exists.[86] Others, however, have viewed them as implied trusts.[87] Additional difficulty arises as to whether these implied trusts (if they may be so properly categorised) should be classified as resulting or constructive trusts.

Much needed clarification has recently been provided by Lord Millett in a lengthy speech in *Twinsectra v Yardley*, where he concluded that there was only one trust and that the lender of the money was the beneficiary under that trust.[88] Lord Millett claimed that this trust was, "an entirely orthodox example of the kind of default trust known as a resulting trust ...".[89] His reasoning was that the recipient of the funds holds those funds on trust for the person who made the advance subject to a power to use the money only for a specified purpose.[90] It appears, therefore, that these types of inferred intention trust fall properly to be regarded as a single resulting trust that comes into existence as soon as the money is paid over to the recipient. This entails that, first, the donor/lender does not pass over the beneficial interest in the money until the funds are applied for the purposes stipulated. It is only at that point that the trust is discharged. The claim of the donor/lender will then onwards lie only in contract.[91]

2.22   Secondly, if the money is never applied for the specified purposes then, as Lord Millett explained in *Twinsectra*, "the money is returnable to the lender, not under some new trust in his favour which only comes into being on the failure of the purpose, but because the resulting trust in his favour is no longer subject to any power ... to make use of the money".[92] As Lewison J. demonstrated in *Templeton Insurance Ltd v Penningtons Solicitors*,[93] if a firm of solicitors gives an undertaking that client's money can be used only for a specific purpose the firm cannot use any surplus for other purposes, including the payment of its own costs and expenses. The money cannot be applied for unspecified purposes.

Thirdly, this reasoning avoids any need to analyse this style of trust as being a private

---

[86] See, for example, *Re Northern Development Holdings*, Unreported October 6, 1978, where a group of banks paid money into an account (in Northern Development's name) for the sole purpose of discharging the liability of Northern Development's subsidiary company to its general creditors. The money that was unused was held under a *Quistclose*-type trust for the benefit of the banks.

[87] Although largely of academic interest, this classification does assume importance where the subject matter of the trust is land or an existing equitable interest. This is because s.53(1)(b),(c) of the Law of Property Act 1925 imposes added formalities for the creation of such trusts if they are expressly created. By virtue of s.53(2), these formalities do not, however, apply to implied trusts.

[88] [2002] 2 A.C. 164. The earlier view expressed by Peter Gibson J. in the *Carreras Rothmans* case to the effect that the beneficiary was the intended recipient was rejected.

[89] [2002] 2 A.C. 164 at 192; see also *Blackburn v H.M. Revenue & Customs* [2008] EWHC 266 (Ch).

[90] In his article, Lord Millett had previously explained ((1985) 101 L.Q.R. 269 at p.269), "A loan by A to B for a specific purpose, where B is not free to apply the money for any other purpose, gives rise to a fiduciary obligation on the part of B which a court of equity will enforce".

[91] As Lord Millett wrote (1985) 101 L.Q.R. 269, p.270, "This prevents B from obtaining any beneficial interest in the money, at least while the designated purpose is still capable of being carried out. When it is carried out ... A becomes a loan creditor of B and has his normal remedy in debt".

[92] [2002] 2 A.C. 164 at 192.

[93] [2006] All E.R. (D) 191 (Feb).

purpose trust. Due to Lord Millett's view that the beneficial interest remains throughout with the lender, it does not matter whether the trust is regarded as an abstract purpose trust or a trust to benefit an ascertainable class of beneficiary. Lord Millett's analysis explodes the myths that the beneficial interest is somehow maintained in suspense until the purpose either fails or is performed and that the lender merely retains a contractual right (enforceable by injunction) to restrain misapplication.[94] As Deputy Judge Michael Crystal explained in *Freeman v Commissioners for Customs & Excise*:

> "Since it would be illogical to draw a distinction between cases where money is paid for an abstract purpose and those where it can be said that the money is for the benefit of ascertainable individuals, it would appear that, in general, the property is vested in the donor himself on resulting trust, with the trustee having either a power or a duty to apply the money for the stated purpose ... This negates the existence of a 'primary' trust in favour of the intended payee. If the purpose for which the money was given is frustrated, the money returns to the donor, not because there is a new, 'secondary' trust, but because the donor was always its owner and because the resulting trust in his favour is no longer subject to any power or duty on the part of the trustee to make use of the money..."[95]

CERTAINTY OF SUBJECT MATTER

Any existing property may be the subject matter of a trust. It is, for example, permissible to have a trust of land, personal goods, shares, cheques, money, debts and covenants. Existing property must be distinguished from future or after acquired property which cannot be the subject matter of a trust. The concept of existing property, however, includes property that has not yet become vested in the settlor and is awaiting the determination of some other prior interest. This would be the case where, for example, the settlor is entitled absolutely to the property following the death of a life tenant or where the settlor is entitled to the property which is to vest on his reaching a certain age. In both scenarios, the settlor's interest is regarded as being in existing property. After acquired property refers to property that may vest in the future, but as regards which there is no certainty. It is a mere expectation that some property may accrue. Future royalties of a book or an anticipated legacy under a living relative's will cannot, therefore, be the subject matter of a trust. **2.23**

In all cases, the requirement is that the trust property must be identifiable. The settlor must also provide the means by which the interest of the beneficiaries can be ascertained. If either feature is absent, the trust must fail because it cannot be enforced. For example:

---

[94] Potter L.J. sponsored the latter argument at the Court of Appeal stage of the *Twinsectra* litigation ([1999] Lloyds Rep. Bank 438 at 456).
[95] [2005] EWHC 582 (Ch) at [12].

- "£100,000 to be divided equally between my children, Jordan & Fiona". This is a fixed trust that identifies the trust fund (£100,000) and the beneficial entitlement of the children (equal shares).

- "£100,000 to be divided between such of my children as my trustee sees fit". This is a discretionary trust that identifies the trust fund (£100,000) and provides the mechanism by which beneficial entitlement is to be allocated (who gets what is left to the discretion of the trustee).

Trust property

discoverable.

2.24   The entire property that is to be the subject of the trust must be described in such a way that it becomes certain and ascertainable. The straightforward reasoning is that a trustee can perform his duties only if he knows exactly what is trust property and the trust can only be enforced if both the beneficiary and the court are similarly aware. This simply stated rule has, however, caused difficulty both in the family and the commercial context. Three possibilities emerge:

- the fund from which the beneficiary's interest is to be carved out might not itself be identifiable. For example, money paid into an overdrawn account will disappear and cannot be the subject matter of a trust;

- the language used by the settlor might be so vague as to offer no definite meaning whatsoever. This could arise from the use of an uncertain descriptive label (e.g. "most of my money"). This is to be contrasted with a trust of the residue of an estate, which will usually be valid. For example, if a testator leaves a will containing a number of legacies and creates a trust of "whatever is left" then there is certainty of subject matter. The executors can eventually calculate the exact value of the residual estate (see **2.27**); and

- uncertainty might arise from a failure to segregate the trust property from other property owned by the settlor (e.g. "50 stamps from my collection"). This problem most commonly arises following the purchase of goods from a supplier who does not identify specifically the goods bought from general stock. The general rule is that there can be no trust as it is impossible to determine the goods that are to be its subject. A different approach, however, is currently adopted by the courts according to whether the trust property is tangible (e.g. a car, painting or jewels) or intangible (e.g. shares or money in a bank account).[96]

Two cases illustrate the workings of this requirement that there be an identifiable trust fund. First, in *Hemmens v Wilson Browne*[97] a document purported to give X the right to a monetary payment of £110,000 at any time from Y. This did not create a trust because there was no fund identified from which the money was to be paid. Obviously, this is much different from, say, a father who sets up a trust of £110,000 for his daughter.

[96] See R. Goode [2003] LMCLQ 433.
[97] [1995] Ch. 223.

There the trust money will be sourced from his estate and the *Hemmens* problem will not arise.

Secondly, in *MacJordan Construction Ltd v Brookmount Erostin Ltd*[98] a building **2.25** contract provided that the employer would retain three per cent of the price as trustee for the builder. No separate retention fund was set up. On the insolvency of the employer, the builder claimed to have a trust interest and to have priority over a floating charge in favour of a bank. As the source of the money was not identified, there was nothing upon which a trust could be based. The employer had never agreed to set up the retention fund out of its general bank account and, therefore, the builder could make no beneficial claim against the money therein. It follows that, if Fred sets up a trust of a particular bank account, but that account does not exist, the trust must fail.

In search of meaning

The words employed by the settlor must be such that they identify with clarity the **2.26** property to be held on trust or, at least, provide the machinery through which such property can be ascertained (e.g. such furniture as my trustee shall select). The subject mater must be conceptually certain. The following authorities provide useful illustrations of this requirement. In *Palmer v Simmonds*[99] a testatrix by her will left the residue of her estate to her friend, Mr Harrison, subject to the proviso that, if he died childless, "he will ... leave the bulk of my said residuary estate unto" four named persons. The reference to "bulk" was held to be ineffective to create a trust. It has no clear meaning and is thoroughly uncertain. It could mean anything between 51 per cent and 99 per cent. There was nothing designated to which a trust could attach. As Kindersley V.C. explained, she had failed to identify "a definite, clear, certain part of her estate".[1] In *Re Kolb's Will Trusts*[2] the testator (a stockbroker) died and instructed his trustees to sell trust property and from the proceeds to buy "first class" and "blue chip" investments. The reference to "first class" and "blue chip" investments was too subjective in meaning and, therefore, rendered the trust void for uncertainty. As it did not establish an objective standard, the trustees could not know what the testator intended. The trustees, moreover, were not given a power of selection. As Cross J. admitted, "there is no strict definition of the term and the opinions of different stockbrokers and others differ as to what stocks and shares can properly be called 'blue chips' at any given time ... The testator might have made his trustees the judge; but, as he has not done so, that part of the clause is, in my judgment, void for uncertainty".[3] Similarly, in *Peck v Halsey*[4] a gift of "some of my best linen" failed and, in *Jubber v Jubber*,[5] the expression "a handsome gratuity" was held to be conceptually uncertain.

[98] (1991) 56 B.L.R. 1.
[99] (1854) 2 Drew. 221.
[1] (1854) 2 Drew. 221 at 227.
[2] [1961] 3 All E.R. 811.
[3] [1961] 3 All E.R. 811 at 814.
[4] (1720) 2 P.W. 387.
[5] (1839) 9 Sim. 503.

A trust of whatever is left

2.27 There should, normally, be no problem in establishing a trust of "whatever remains" in a deceased's estate after, say, funeral expenses, taxes and legacies have been paid. Indeed, setting up a trust of the residue of an estate is a common practice. Provided the net residue is ascertainable, the trust will be upheld. Despite this straightforward proposition, the area is not entirely liberated from difficulty. Two cases serve to illustrate this tension and demonstrate that much may turn upon the court's construction of the terms of the disposition.

In *Sprange v Barnard*,[6] a testatrix left her husband shares valued at £300, "for his sole use; and at his death, the remaining part of what is left, that he does not want for his own wants and use, to be divided between ..." her brother and sisters. The widower sought to cash in the shares and the dispute arose as to whether he was a trustee of those shares for his deceased wife's siblings. The Court of Appeal held that he was absolutely entitled to the shares. As it would be uncertain as to what would be left on the husband's death, it was a trust that would be impossible to execute. The capital would be wasted away during the lifetime of Mr Sprange.[7] This is an example of where the residue could not be ascertained. Hence, there was no certainty of subject matter.

2.28 This case is, however, to be contrasted with *In the Estate of Last*.[8] There property was left by a testatrix to her brother on terms that "at his death anything that is left, that came from me" was to pass on to specified persons. The court adopted a very different attitude than in the *Sprange* case because it held that the brother was given merely a life interest in the property.[9] It was significant that he could not leave any remaining property under his own will. As the trust (albeit with successive interests) was created on the death of the testatrix, the trust property was sufficiently certain at that date. Consequently, any property not disposed of during his lifetime was to be held on trust. The beneficial interest of the specified beneficiaries was, therefore, suspended during the lifetime of the brother, attaching to the property only on his death.[10] If the brother's interest had not been so limited, the trust would clearly have failed. This decision, therefore, can be understood only in the light that the court was able to find that a life interest, as opposed to an absolute gift, had been created. It will not normally be the case that successive interests can be discerned in this way.[11]

---

[6] (1789) 2 Bro. CC 585.
[7] See also, *Re Jones* [1898] 1 Ch. 438 where a trust of "such parts of my ... estate as she shall not have sold" also failed for uncertainty of subject matter. It was viewed as being an absolute gift to the legatee.
[8] [1958] P 137.
[9] See also, *Re Richards* [1902] 1 Ch. 76 where a widow was held to have a life interest and named legatees under her husband's will were able to claim their entitlement on her death.
[10] See Brightman J. in *Ottaway v Norman* [1972] Ch. 698.
[11] See *Flint v Hughes* (1843) 6 Beav. 342 where a gift expressed to be for life with the proviso that her daughters then take "whatever she can transfer" failed.

A trust of part of property: tangibles

[handwritten annotation: can be touched, seen, weighed, measured or apprehended — something in one's lifetym! that is real & substantial]

Fortunately, the case law relating to an inter vivos trust of part of physical property is **2.29** relatively straightforward. Segregation of the trust property from the remaining bulk is necessary.[12] The judicial approach is encapsulated in *Re London Wine Company*.[13] There a company carried substantial stocks of wine in a number of warehouses. It was common practice that wine would be sold, but remained stored by the company. The customer received a certificate of title, but the customer's wine was not separated from the rest of the stock. Although the company went into receivership, there were sufficient stocks to satisfy all orders. The issue was whether the wine sold was held on trust for the customers or whether the wine was available to the company's creditors. Oliver J. held that, because the property sold was not singled out in any way from the remainder of the company's stock, a customer could not say of any given bottle of wine that he had bought that bottle. Hence, no trust could be created in favour of the customers, "It seems to me that in order to create a trust it must be possible to ascertain with certainty not only what the interest of the beneficiary is to be but also to what property it is to attach".[14]

In *Re Goldcorp Exchange Ltd*,[15] an appeal to the Privy Council concerned a dealership in precious metals that went into receivership. The dealer acted to purchase gold bullion and other metals on behalf of clients and offered a storage service. The usual style of contract entered into with clients required the dealer to hold the whole of an order in its vaults. It transpired that there were woefully insufficient stocks of bullion to meet its obligations. The Bank of New Zealand sought to claim these stocks under a floating charge over the dealer's assets. The customers claimed that the contracts created a series of trusts and that they, as beneficiaries, had first claim to the gold. On the facts, three categories of client emerged.

- Those clients who had claims to identified stocks that had been acquired specifically for them by the dealer. These claimants were successful in establishing a trust because the bullion had been physically and unconditionally segregated from the rest of the stock. This demarcation entailed that the subject matter of these trusts was certain.[16]

- Those customers who had purchased gold for future delivery, but had not been allocated any specific parcel of bullion before the bank's floating charge crystallised. All these claimants could show was a contractual entitlement to an amount of bullion representing a certain value. As they were unable to point to

---

[12] This rule does not apply to testamentary trusts where the selection is made by the executors and no segregation is necessary: *Re Clifford* [1972] 1 Ch. 29.

[13] [1986] PCC 121 HC.

[14] [1986] PCC 121 at 137. The Sale of Goods (Amendment) Act 1995 now offers help to such a purchaser because, in conjunction with the other purchasers, they will be regarded as having proprietary rights against the property as tenants in common. This arises as soon as the contract is entered and allows the purchasers to make a joint claim against the property.

[15] [1995] 1 A.C. 74.

[16] See also, *Re Stapylton Fletcher Ltd* [1995] 1 All E.R. 192, where the trust property (again wine) was separated from the rest of the stock in a distinct part of the warehouse and documentary records identified it as the property of the beneficiary.

any specific bullion as being purchased under their respective contracts, there could be no trust. There was a total absence of certainty of subject matter.

- An individual customer had agreed to purchase a 1,000 gold maple coins. The dealer did not carry such large stocks of coinage. The dealer bought in a larger stock that was required for this particular order. The coins bought for the client were not, however, segregated from the additional coins that the dealer purchased. There was no certainty of subject matter as the customer's property could not be specifically identified from the total stock. Of course, if no extra coins had been bought in there would not then be a problem with ascertainment of trust property.

2.30   In short, *Re Goldcorp Exchange Ltd* emphasises that a commercial contract for the purchase and storage of goods does not, without more, give rise to a relationship of trustee and beneficiary. As Lord Mustill observed, "the essence of a fiduciary relationship is that it creates obligations of a different character from the contract itself".[17] He concluded that no property in the goods could be transferred to the buyers unless the goods themselves were ascertained.

A trust of part of property: intangibles

2.31   The degree of certainty of subject matter required for trusts of so called "choses in action" or intangible assets (such as shares, money in bank accounts and debts) is different to that which is required of trusts of tangible assets. Hayton describes this as an, "old fashioned, but surely specious, distinction".[18] Nevertheless, it is now generally accepted that a trust of, say, shares falls to be treated differently than a trust of chattels.[19] The major case is *Hunter v Moss*,[20] where Mr Hunter was entitled, under his contract of employment with Mr Moss, to claim 50 shares out of 950 shares in a particular company held by his employer. Although this showed the intention to create a trust, Mr Moss did not identify which shares were the subject of this arrangement. Mr Moss later sold the 950 shares and kept the proceeds of sale for himself. Mr Hunter claimed a proportion of those proceeds. The central issue was whether, in these circumstances, Mr Hunter could assert beneficial rights over 50 shares under a trust. A series of points fall to be appreciated.

First, if the orthodox approach (as considered above in relation to tangibles) fell to be applied, the outcome would be against Mr Hunter. It would be impossible to identify precisely which 50 shares were to be the subject matter of the trust. There had been no

---

[17] [1995] 1 A.C. 74 at 98; see also, *Commissioners of Customs & Excise v Richmond Theatre Management Ltd* (1995) *The Times*, February 1, where it was held by Dyson J. that, on paying money over for a theatre ticket, a patron retained no proprietary interest in the payment.
[18] D. Hayton (1994) 110 L.Q.R. 335 at 337. His view is that segregation should always be necessary whatever the nature of property involved. Cf. J. Martin [1996] Conv. 223, who suggests that the tracing rules relating to mixed assets can apply in cases of identifiable mixed funds to negate the need for segregation in every case.
[19] See *Re Harvard Securities Ltd* [1997] 2 BCLC 369 (HC), where it was held that it is possible to create trust of a particular number of shares even though they formed an unidentified part of a bulk of shares.
[20] (1994) 1 W.L.R. 452. In *Re Harvard Securities Ltd*, [1997] 2 BCLC 369 (HC), Neuberger J. followed the *Hunter* approach, but admitted to little enthusiasm in doing so.

segregation whatsoever and, seemingly, no certainty of subject matter. This would, most certainly, be the outcome if, say, Fred (a writer) attempts to create a trust of "50 copies of my latest text book from my personal stock". Although the books are identical, the trust will still fail because they are tangibles and there has been no identification of the exact 50 books to be taken. The only discernible difference between the books and, say, shares being that the books could be physically separated and are, thereby, distinguishable.

Secondly, and nevertheless, the Court of Appeal held that there was a valid trust. The reasoning employed was that, since the shares were essentially identical and indistinguishable, any 50 shares in the company were capable of forming the subject matter of the trust. Dillon L.J. distanced himself from *Re London Wine Company* ("that case is a long way from the present"[21]) and concluded that, "as a person can give by will a specified number of shares in a certain company, so equally, in my judgment, he can declare himself a trustee of 50 of his ordinary shares and that is effective to give a beneficial proprietary interest to the beneficiary under the trust".[22] It is to be appreciated that, if the arrangement had been to give Mr Hunter 50 shares from 950 shares held by Mr Moss in a range of companies, the lack of a homogenous whole would have prevented the existence of an inter vivos trust.

Thirdly, the analogy drawn with what occurs on death has proved controversial **2.32** because, with a testamentary disposition, the shares are to be allocated by the executors of the will. There is no immediate interest vested in the legatee. In contrast, a trust brings with it an immediate interest and, therefore, requires an immediate means of identifying exactly which shares are the subject matter of the trust.[23] In addition, the same justification can equally be invoked in relation to tangibles (e.g. leaving a legacy of "50 copies of my latest textbook"). Not surprisingly, commentators tend to criticise the approach adopted by the Court of Appeal and see no logical distinction to justify the divergent treatment of tangibles and intangibles.[24] Most certainly, *Hunter v Moss* is a curious decision that, seemingly, flies in the face of traditional understanding. Hayton suggests that the court was, "perhaps blinded by the merits of the donee, who had done an awful lot for the subsequently ungrateful donor".[25]

Certainty of beneficial share

Not only must the trust property be certain and ascertainable, but (except as regards **2.33** discretionary trusts[26]) each beneficiary's share under the trust must also be allocated in some way when the trust is established.[27] This is the task of the settlor and the court

---

[21] (1994) 1 W.L.R. 452 at 458.
[22] (1994) 1 W.L.R. 452 at 458, 459.
[23] See D. Hayton (1994) 110 L.Q.R. 335 at 338.
[24] See A. Jones [1994] Conv. 466; M. Ockleton [1994] C.L.J. 448. There are, however, some defenders of the distinction: see J. Martin [1996] Conv. 223; S. Worthington [1999] J.B.L. 1.
[25] D. Hayton, *The Law of Trusts* at p.85.
[26] In relation to discretionary trusts, the very nature of such a trust entails that the beneficial interests are never certain. The essence of a discretionary trust is that the trustees exercise discretion as to who is to get what under its terms.
[27] *Curtis v Rippon* (1820) 5 Madd 434; *Asten v Asten* [1894] 3 Ch. 260.

cannot rewrite the trust instrument in order that the trust can be upheld.[28] As is illustrated by the following cases, this simple proposition as to beneficial share is apt to cause major problems.

- In *Boyce v Boyce*,[29] a fixed trust was set up by will on the death of the testator. The trust property consisted of two houses and there were two named beneficiaries, Maria and Charlotte. Maria was to choose which house she wanted. The other house was to be held on trust for Charlotte. Unfortunately, Maria pre-deceased the testator and died without making any selection. As it was now impossible to say which house Charlotte should have, the entire trust had to fail for uncertainty of beneficial share. As neither the court nor the trustees could decide which house each was to have, both properties stayed in the settlor's estate. The difficulty here was that the testator had prescribed a method of allocation that had subsequently become impossible.

- In *Re Knapton*,[30] the testatrix provided that a number of houses were to be distributed among "my nieces and nephews", a number of named relatives and friends. Unlike in the *Boyce* case, she did not provide any machinery through which the properties were to be divided between them. In these circumstances, the High Court held that the beneficiaries had a right to choose which house they wanted and the order of choice was according to the order that their names appeared in the will. As to those who were described merely as "my nieces and nephews", the order of selection was worked out by the drawing of lots. The court, therefore, felt able to imply a right of selection in order to save the bequests.

- In *Waddington v Waddington*,[31] the testator died leaving to his wife by will, "such articles of furniture not otherwise hereby bequeathed as she shall require". She chose some items and then later sought to choose more. Her stepchildren argued that her initial selection was irrevocable and limiting. In the High Court, Deputy Judge Mackie Q.C. held that she had irrevocably made her choice and was not free to make any further choice.

Equity is equality

2.34   The principle "equity is equality" can be applied where there is a fixed trust that does not declare expressly the beneficial interest to be taken by each beneficiary.[32] The classic example is *Burrough v Philcox*[33] where a trust was set up to benefit the settlor's son and daughter. Their beneficial shares, however, remained unspecified. As such, it might be thought that the trust was irredeemably flawed. The court was, however, able to uphold

---

[28] *Richardson v Watson* (1833) 4 B & AD 787.
[29] (1849) 16 Sim. 476.
[30] [1941] 2 All 573.
[31] Unreported May 26, 1999.
[32] Although usually associated with fixed trusts, the principle that "equity is equality" could arise in relation to a discretionary trust, but only in the unlikely event that the trustees fail to exercise their discretion.
[33] (1840) 5 My & CR 72.

this trust by invoking the equitable maxim "equity is equality". Hence, each child was deemed to have an equal share. This maxim, however, can be invoked only where there is no contrary intention demonstrated. In the unlikely event that the trust had been worded "to benefit my children unequally", the maxim could not then apply and the trust would necessarily fail.[34]

An objective calculus

A difficult case is *Re Golay's Will Trusts*[35] where the testator set up a trust under which   **2.35**
Tossy was, "to enjoy one of my flats during her lifetime and to receive a reasonable income from my other properties". As to the flat, there was no problem as the executors were, on the testator's death, able to choose in which property she could live. The difficulty concerned the calculation of a "reasonable income" and whether that expression rendered that aspect of the trust thoroughly uncertain. Ungoed-Thomas J. held that the word "reasonable" gave it an objective yardstick by which to assess what was an income tailored for any particular person. There are two observations that flow from this decision.

First, if the word "reasonable" had not been employed, the trust of the income would have failed. It was the use of this term which gave the court the ability to undertake the calculation.[36] As Ungoed-Thomas J. acknowledged this offered, "an objective determinant".[37] The court could, thereby, look at Tossy's age, her present income and current outgoings and conjure up a figure that was reasonable for her. He added, "The court is constantly involved in making such objective assessments as to what is reasonable and it is not to be deterred from doing so because subjective influences can never be wholly excluded".[38]

Secondly, if the testator had, for example, wanted to give Tossy a "reasonable   **2.36**
share", "reasonable sum" or "reasonable legacy" then such arrangements would have clearly failed for uncertainty of beneficial share. The difference is that a "reasonable income" (or, it is submitted, "reasonable maintenance" or "reasonable financial provision") is measured solely by taking on board the personal circumstances of the individual concerned. Accordingly, whether the testator's estate was worth £50,000 or £2 million, the income calculated would remain constant (i.e. certain). As regards the alternative and ineffective expressions, the calculation would necessarily reflect the size of the deceased's estate. Put in a slightly different context, say, Jordan agrees with Fred that, if Fred gives Jordan a winning tip on a horse race, Jordan will give Fred a "reasonable share" of the proceeds. At the time the understanding is reached, it is impossible to quantify what would amount to a "reasonable share". All would depend upon how much money Jordan placed on the winning horse and the betting odds

---

[34] See *Margulies v Margulies* (1999) 77 P. & C.R. D21, where the terms of a will contradicted the presumption that the children were to take equally.
[35] [1965] 2 All E.R. 660.
[36] As also occurred in *Jackson v Hamilton* (1846) 3 J & Lat. 702.
[37] [1965] 2 All E.R. 660 at 661. It is to be appreciated that, as this was not a discretionary trust, her entitlement was not at the subjective determination of the trustees. Accordingly, if the court could not ascribe meaning to the subject matter then the trust would fail.
[38] [1965] 2 All E.R. 660 at 662.

prevailing at the time. Unlike "income", therefore, the court has there to look beyond the beneficiary's needs and wants. If, however, Jordan had stated that Fred would have 50 per cent of any winnings then that would offer sufficient certainty of intended entitlement.

CERTAINTY OF OBJECTS

2.37   In order for a trust or, indeed, a power to exist there have to be beneficiaries (i.e. the objects of the trust) who are certain or capable of being rendered certain. As Lord Evershed M.R. put it, "No principle perhaps has greater sanction or authority behind it than the general proposition that a trust by English law, not being a charitable trust, in order to be effective must have ascertained or ascertainable beneficiaries".[39] There must be someone who can enforce the trust or someone in whose favour the court can enforce the trust.[40] If there are no ascertainable beneficiaries there is no trust.[41] As to future interests, the beneficiaries must also be ascertainable within the perpetuity period.[42] The general requirements are that, first, except for charitable trusts, there must be human beneficiaries. A private purpose trust (e.g. the promotion of good relations between nations and the preservation of the independence and integrity of newspapers[43]) cannot be upheld. This is because there would be no-one entitled to enforce such a trust. Secondly, the beneficiaries must be individually identified (e.g. "to hold on trust for Adrienne and Fiona") or must be identified as a member of a clearly defined class (e.g. "to hold on trust for my children"). Such was demonstrated in *Re TXU Europe Group Plc (In Administration)*[44] where it was unclear who were the intended objects of the alleged trust. Some evidence suggested that it was to benefit only existing executives and did not extend to future employees. Other evidence asserted that it was to benefit any employee whether past, present or future. Blackburne J. explained, "There is no reason, of course, why there should not be a trust for a class of persons which may increase in number. The evidence, however, must make this clear".[45]

Conceptual uncertainty?

2.38   The description of the beneficiaries must, as regards both fixed and discretionary trusts, be conceptually certain at the time that the trust is created. This refers to semantic or linguistic expression (i.e. precision of language) as regards the class that is to benefit. The description of beneficiaries must, therefore, be capable of having some ascertainable meaning. There must be provided sufficient definitional criteria so that the trustee

---

[39] *Re Endacott* [1959] 3 All E.R. 562 at 568. It is to be remembered that what follows does not apply to charitable trusts, as the Attorney General and Charity Commission can enforce such public trusts.
[40] See *Morice v Bishop of Durham* (1805) 10 Ves. 522.
[41] *Tackaberry v Hollis* [2007] EWHC 2633 (Ch).
[42] See Ch.4.
[43] *Re Astor's ST* [1952] Ch. 534; see Ch.6.
[44] [2003] EWHC 3105 (Ch).
[45] [2003] EWHC 3105 (Ch) at [29].

can carry out the settlor's instructions. To achieve this end, the court will strain to make sense of the formula that has been used to define the objects. Lord Wilberforce illustrated this in *Blathwayt v Baron Cawley* when he counselled that judges should undertake their task, "without excessive astuteness to discover ambiguities".[46] In *Re Gulbenkians Settlements*, Lord Upjohn added that the court must exercise, "its judicial knowledge and experience in the relevant matter, innate common sense and desire to make sense of the settlor's or party's expressed intentions, however obscure and ambiguous the language that may have been used, to give a reasonable meaning to that language if it can do so without doing violence to it".[47]

If sense cannot be made of the language used, the trustee will be unable to perform his duties and the trust will be entirely void. For example, a fixed trust to distribute money between "my favourite people" or "my relatives who are handsome" would be conceptually uncertain because it would be impossible to ascertain who the settlor truly intended to benefit. The boundaries of meaning are there too imprecise.

Examples of conceptual uncertainty

The most effective way of understanding what will amount to conceptual uncertainty is to consider the authorities. The following cases provide a useful demonstration.

2.39

- In *Re Barlow's Will Trusts*,[48] Browne-Wilkinson J. discussed, albeit by way of obiter, the validity of a trust to benefit "old friends" and concluded that, while such expressions would not invalidate a gift subject to a condition precedent, they would render a trust conceptually uncertain. The terms "old" and "friend" have so many shades of meaning that, whether applying the complete list or the given postulant tests, it was impossible to say who was intended to benefit. If the court was unable to discern any precise meaning then neither would the trustees. As Browne-Wilkinson J. put it, "many people, if asked to draw up a complete list of their friends, would probably have some difficulty in deciding whether certain of the people they knew were really 'friends' as opposed to 'acquaintances' ".[49]

- In *Re Wright's Will Trust*,[50] a trust was designed to benefit "such people and institutions as have helped me or my late husband". Not surprisingly, this was held to be conceptually uncertain. As the High Court concluded, "help" was a term that, "could mean anything from helping the testatrix across the road to saving her from death, dishonour or bankruptcy".

---

[46] [1976] A.C. 397 at 425.
[47] [1970] A.C. 508 at 552.
[48] [1979] 1 W.L.R. 278.
[49] [1979] 1 W.L.R. 278 at 280; see also, Lord Wilberforce in *McPhail v Doulton* [1971] A.C. 424 at 457 where he said, "If there is a trust for 'my old friends', all concerned are faced with uncertainty as to the concept or idea enshrined in these words. It may not be difficult to resolve that 'old' means not 'aged' but 'of long standing'; but then there is the question how long is 'long'. Friendship, too, is a concept with almost infinite shades of meaning".
[50] Unreported July 29, 1982.

- In *Spafax (1965) v Dommett*,[51] a trust established in favour of "customers" was held to be invalid. Although accounts and records could be introduced to show who had dealings with the settlor, it was unclear what was actually meant by the word "customer". For example, it might refer only to those who had made a purchase or it might embrace those who had merely been browsing and had never bought a thing.

- In *Re Astor's ST*,[52] a trust failed on two fronts. First, it was a non-charitable purpose trust that had no living beneficiaries. Secondly, the trust also failed because of conceptual uncertainty. The testator's wishes were to maintain, "good understanding, sympathy and co-operation between nations" as well as, "the independence and integrity of newspapers". The concepts employed here were incapable of any precise meaning.

- *Re Endacott*[53] offers a further example of a failed purpose trust. The testator left money to the local council, "for the purpose of providing some suitable monument to myself". The trust failed also for a lack of conceptual certainty as it was unclear what the term "suitable" encompassed.

Relatives, dependants and children

2.40 It is helpful to consider a couple of cases where the trust was determined to be conceptually certain in circumstances that might be thought of as borderline.

In *Re Baden's Deed Trusts (No.2)*,[54] the issue arose as to whether the definition of the beneficiaries as "relatives" and "dependants" made the trust void for conceptual uncertainty. The Court of Appeal found these expressions to be conceptually certain. The term "dependants" caused the least trouble and, having been employed over many years in trust deeds, lent itself well to conceptualisation. As Sachs L.J. admitted, "I confess that the suggestion that it is uncertain seems no longer arguable".[55] It was, as Megaw L.J. put it, an "ordinary, well understood word".[56] The expression "relatives" was, however, to prove more problematic. Stamp L.J. thought that the term "relatives" was synonymous with next of kin and nearest blood relations. The other members of the Court of Appeal adopted the broader definition of descendants from a common ancestor. Either way, the Court of Appeal was able to uphold the trust. Although such terms might cause evidential difficulties,[57] the trustees can, with discretionary trusts, use their sense and discretion as to who will benefit.

In *Gold v Hill*,[58] the beneficiaries were described as "Carol and the kids". It was

---

[51] (1972) *The Times*, July 14.
[52] [1952] Ch. 534.
[53] [1959] 3 All E.R. 562.
[54] [1973] Ch. 9.
[55] [1973] Ch. 9 at 21.
[56] [1973] Ch. 9 at 22. Stamp L.J. did not doubt that the word, "connotes financial dependence" and agreed that it did not introduce linguistic uncertainty (at 30).
[57] As Lord Evershed M.R. commented of "relations" in *Re Scarisbrick* [1951] Ch. 622 at 632, "That class is, in theory, capable of almost indefinite expansion, but proof of relationship soon becomes extremely difficult in fact".
[58] [1999] 1 F.L.R. 54.

contended that "kids" was uncertain because Mr Gilbert had various children from various relationships. In the context of this trust, Carnwarth J. concluded that there was no serious doubt as to the "kids" referred to, i.e. Carol's children.

Fixed trusts: the complete list rule

It will become clear that a different approach is adopted according to whether the trust **2.41** is a fixed trust or a discretionary trust. A fixed trust is one where both the identity and the interests of the beneficiaries are set out in the trust instrument. The beneficiaries might be named individually or defined by reference to a class (e.g. "my employees" or "my children"). The essence of such a fixed trust is to confer fixed benefits upon fixed beneficiaries. Each and every beneficiary, therefore, is to benefit under a fixed trust. The trustee enjoys no discretion as to the distribution of the trust property.

As the trustee labours under a duty to distribute according to the settlor's expressed wishes, the courts understandably take a strict approach. There can be no division unless all beneficiaries are known. Hence, the rule is that a fixed trust is void unless each and every beneficiary is ascertainable. This is sometimes called the "complete list" test, which demands that the trustee must be able to draw up an exhaustive list of the beneficiaries. If the trustee cannot compile such a comprehensive catalogue, the trust must fail. It was emphasised in *Re Eden*[59] that, although it might be time consuming and expensive, an exhaustive catalogue of beneficiaries must still be compiled. As Wynn-Parry J. accepted, "it may well be that a large part, even the whole of the funds available, would be consumed in the inquiry ... that would be very unfortunate, but that cannot of itself constitute any reason why such an inquiry, whether by the trustees or the court, should not be undertaken".[60]

A useful illustration of the operation of the complete list test is *OT Computers Ltd v* **2.42** *First National Tricity Finance Ltd*.[61] There the claimant (OT Computers) was a retailer of computer products. In 2002, the claimant instructed its bank to open two separate trust accounts for the payment of customer deposits and moneys owed to "urgent suppliers". The claimant compiled two schedules: one containing the names of the customers and the other listing a number of its suppliers. On the claimant going into receivership, the bank sought to discharge a loan due to it from the money in the two accounts. A trust in favour of the customers was upheld because the beneficiaries could be identified in the context of the payments made by them to the company.[62] Pumfrey J. concluded, however, that the trust in favour of the suppliers failed because of a lack of certainty of objects. It was not possible to draw up a complete list of urgent suppliers. The term "urgent" was simply too conceptually vague to identify any class of beneficiary and, therefore, the trustees could draw up no complete list. As Pumfrey J. admitted, "It is not sufficient to be able to say whether or not any identified person is or is not a member of the class entitled to be considered: the purpose of the trust in the

[59] [1957] 2 All E.R. 430.
[60] [1957] 2 All E.R. 430 at 435.
[61] [2003] EWHC 1010 (Ch).
[62] This was a *Re Kayford*-style of trust whereby the company by unilateral conduct made itself a trustee of the funds.

present case is to vest an immediate interest in the suppliers in question ...".[63] The money in the suppliers' account remained in the beneficial ownership of the company.

Untraceable beneficiaries

2.43   It is possible that a fixed trust might be created in circumstances where it is unclear either where a particular beneficiary is or, indeed, whether a particular beneficiary is still alive. In such situations the trustees potentially face a difficult and legally risky choice, i.e. to delay distribution indefinitely until the facts become established or to make an immediate distribution in ignorance of the true facts. The trustee has been helped considerably by a pragmatic solution offered in *Re Benjamin*.[64] There it was demonstrated that, provided the beneficiaries are defined with adequate precision, a fixed trust will not fail simply because a particular beneficiary cannot be found or because there are doubts as to a beneficiary's continued existence. In such cases, the court can authorise the trustees to distribute the trust property amongst the known beneficiaries on the assumption that the beneficiary is dead (i.e. make a "Benjamin order"). This order does not, however, disturb the entitlement of the missing beneficiary.[65] It merely facilitates a speedier distribution. If the beneficiary later reappears, his share can then be recovered from the other beneficiaries. It is common for the court to take an express legal undertaking from the identified beneficiaries to repay the money to any new claimant. If a Benjamin order is not obtained, the trustees run the risk of personal liability to the newly discovered beneficiary. The trustees can, however, take out missing beneficiary insurance to shield themselves against any potential liability.

Fixed trusts: evidential certainty

2.44   Whereas conceptual uncertainty deals with meaning, evidential uncertainty concerns the practical difficulty of proving as a fact whether a person is or is not within the class of beneficiaries. It is, therefore, a totally separate issue from conceptual uncertainty. This requirement of evidential certainty only applies to fixed trusts, which require the trustees to draw up a complete list of the beneficiaries. As demonstrated by the majority in *Re Badens Deed Trusts (No.2)*, because of the employment of the class test (or any given postulant test) a discretionary trust should never fail on this ground.[66] An example of evidential uncertainty would be where the settlor establishes a fixed trust to benefit such students of Larne University who graduated in 1969 with a first class degree in law. If the records of Larne University have been destroyed by fire, it will be impossible to draw up a complete list of beneficiaries and, therefore, the trust will fail for evidential uncertainty. In approaching its task, the court is not to insist upon absolute certainty and, instead, must adopt a pragmatic stance and look to probability

---

[63] [2003] EWHC 1010 (Ch) at [21].
[64] [1902] 1 Ch. 723.
[65] See *Re Greens Trusts* [1985] 3 All E.R. 455.
[66] [1973] Ch. 9. As will become clear below, this is achieved whether through the reversal of the burden of proof (as advocated by Sachs L.J.) or the substantial numbers approach (as canvassed by Megaw L.J.).

rather than theoretic possibility.[67] In *Re Eden*, Wynn-Parry J. explained, "it is only when one reaches, on the evidence, a conclusion that is so vague, or that the difficulty is so great that it must be treated as virtually incapable of resolution, that one is entitled, to my mind, to say that a gift of that nature is void for uncertainty".[68]

Rendering the evidentially uncertain certain?

The trust deed may, however, expressly allow the trustee or a third party to settle any **2.45** evidential dispute as to whether a given individual is a beneficiary. This liberality does not, however, extend to conceptual uncertainty.[69] Three cases offer an insight into the workings of this proposition:

- In *Re Tuck's Settlement Trusts*[70] the beneficiary of a gift was required to be of the Jewish faith. The Chief Rabbi was under the terms of the gift permitted to determine any issues of fact. The expert evidence of the Chief Rabbi was accepted as resolving the issue of whether the donee was of the Jewish faith.[71]

- In *Re Coxen*[72] the settlor made a gift of a house to his widow that was expressed so as to determine if, in the opinion of his trustees, she ceased to reside permanently there. The gift was upheld because any potential evidential uncertainty (as to whether the event occurred) was removed by making the trustees' opinion decisive.[73]

- In *Re Leek*[74] the objects of the trust were expressed to be, "such other persons as the company may consider to have a moral claim". The trust was upheld because, as Harman J. put it, "The trustees are made the arbiters and the objects are such persons as they may consider to have a moral claim; and I do not see why they should not be able on this footing to make up their minds and arrive at a decision".[75]

Discretionary trusts: the class test

Under a discretionary trust, the trustee is given the discretion to select, from amongst a **2.46** specified class of beneficiaries, who will benefit under the trust and often when and to what extent. In modern times, the discretionary trust is used to benefit substantial

---

[67] See Cross J. in *Re Saxone Shoe Co* [1969] 2 All E.R. 904 at 912.
[68] [1957] 2 All E.R. 430 at 433.
[69] *Re Coxen* [1948] 2 All E.R. 492.
[70] [1978] Ch. 49.
[71] See also, *Re Tepper's Will Trust* [1987] 1 All E.R. 970 where evidence of the testator's own beliefs as a Jew were allowed to render certain what he had meant by the word "Jewish".
[72] [1948] 2 All E.R. 492.
[73] See also, *Re Jones* [1953] Ch. 125, where a daughter was to lose her inheritance if, in the opinion of the trustees, she struck up a relationship with a particular man.
[74] [1968] 2 W.L.R. 1385.
[75] [1968] 2 W.L.R. 1385 at 1390.

groups of people, such as employees and their dependants. It is prized as providing a more tax effective means of settling property, maintaining flexibility and offering administrative benefits. The settlor will not usually intend that each person within the designated class will benefit directly under the trust. The settlor will, most certainly, not intend that they each receive an equal share. As Lord Wilberforce explained in *McPhail v Doulton*, "Equal division is surely the last thing the settlor ever intended: equal division among all may, probably would, produce a result beneficial to no one. Why would the court lend itself to a whimsical execution?"[76] Accordingly, it should follow that it is not necessary for each and every potential beneficiary to be identified by the trustee. Indeed, a complete list might often be a practical impossibility. Nevertheless, until the majority decision of the House of Lords in *McPhail v Doulton* the rule for certainty of objects for discretionary trusts was the same as for fixed trusts (i.e. the complete list approach).[77]

In the *McPhail* case, Lord Wilberforce rejected the traditional rule, explaining that the duties of a trustee of a discretionary trust are very different from those under a fixed trust. With a fixed trust, each beneficiary has a specific claim to a specific share of the trust fund and, therefore, the trustee must discover each and every beneficiary. As regards a discretionary trust, however, the trustee is required merely to act as a reasonable trustee and survey the field of potential beneficiaries. As Lord Wilberforce put it:

> "a trustee with a duty to distribute, particularly among a potentially very large class, would surely never require the preparation of a complete list of names, which anyhow would tell him little that he needs to know. He would examine the field, by class and category; might indeed make diligent and careful inquiries, depending upon how much money he had to give away and the means at his disposal, as to the composition and needs of particular categories and of individuals within them; decide on certain priorities or proportions, and then select individuals according to their needs or qualifications. If he acts in this manner, can it really be said that he is not carrying out the trust?"[78]

2.47   The facts before Lord Wilberforce concerned a discretionary trust established to provide benefits for the staff of Matthew Hall & Co Ltd, their relatives and dependants. The objects of the trust, therefore, were so numerous and wide-ranging that it was impossible for the trustee to draw up an exhaustive list of potential beneficiaries. The House of Lords, however, applied a different test that is sometimes referred to as either the "class test", the "any given postulant test", or the "is or is not test".[79] Put simply, the issue is whether it could be said with certainty of any given individual that he is or is not a member of the class.[80] Unfortunately, the House of Lords in *McPhail* felt unable to apply this test on the evidence before it and, instead, referred the case back to the

---

[76] [1971] A.C. 424 at 451.
[77] See *IRC v Broadway Cottages Trust* [1955] Ch. 20.
[78] [1971] A.C. 424 at 449; see also, Megarry V.C. in *Re Hay's Settlement Trusts* (1982) 1 W.L.R. 202 at 209, 210 who spoke of the necessity of the discretionary trustee to address, "the size of the problem".
[79] This test had previously operated only in relation to powers of appointment: see *Re Gulbenkian's ST* [1968] 3 All E.R. 785. Lord Wilberforce saw no difference between the way in which a discretionary trust and a power operate while the selection process is ongoing.
[80] See Lord Wilberforce, [1971] A.C. 424 at 454, 456.

High Court to determine whether the test was satisfied. Eventually, it proceeded to the Court of Appeal under the alternative name of *Re Baden's Deed Trusts (No.2)*.[81]

The class test in operation

The operation of the class test has proved more difficult than, perhaps, might be expected. Although in *Re Baden's Deed Trusts (No.2)* the Court of Appeal tackled the issue directly, each judge gave quite a different interpretation. The major stumbling block concerns the inherent difficulty in proving a negative: how can a trustee prove that a particular person is not, for example, a relative of an employee? Ironically, none of the three approaches is entirely convincing and each is open to criticism. Surprisingly, it remains unclear which approach will be favoured by the courts.

2.48

- Stamp L.J. thought that the class test was to be applied literally, that is, it can only be satisfied when it could be said of any given postulant that he is or is not a member of the class. There is no room for any doubt with this approach. As Stamp L.J. explained, "Validity or invalidity is to depend on whether you can say of any individual—and the accent must be on that word 'any' for it is not simply the individual whose claim you are considering who is spoken of—'is or is not a member of the class', for only thus can you make a survey of the range of objects or possible beneficiaries".[82] The obvious problem with this formulation is that it marks what is, essentially, a retreat to the complete list test previously jettisoned by the House of Lords in *McPhail v Doulton*. It would be remarkable if a discretionary trust, under which only some beneficiaries were intended to benefit, failed because of an inability to say categorically of one person whether he is or is not in a class. Nevertheless, Stamp L.J. believed that the entire class of objects had to be surveyed, "Any survey of the range of objects or possible beneficiaries would certainly be incomplete, and I am able to discern no principle on which such a survey could be conducted or where it should start or finish".[83] Hence, the existence of even a single "don't know" would mean that the trust is doomed.

- Sachs L.J. adopted a more liberal view and stated that it was up to a claimant to prove positively that he is within a class. If he fails to do so, then he is regarded as falling outside the class.[84] Sachs L.J. was promoting the argument that the court should, as regards a discretionary trust, never be defeated by evidential uncertainty. To avoid such outcome, the burden of proving the negative should be reversed. The weakness of this approach is that, when pushed to extremes, it produces some distinctly odd outcomes. It allows for the fact that there might be numerous individuals who cannot prove their entitlement. It also caters for the possibility of a discretionary trust being upheld in circumstances where only

[81] [1973] Ch. 9.
[82] [1973] Ch. 9 at 28.
[83] [1973] Ch. 9 at 28.
[84] [1973] Ch. 9 at 19.

one beneficiary can prove positively that he is in the class. This is clearly not what the settlor would ever have intended.

- Megaw L.J. was also prepared to reject a strict approach. He felt that it sufficed that the trustee could say, as regards a substantial number of beneficiaries, that they fell within the scope of the trust. This would be so even where there were others about whom it could not be said with certainty whether they were in or outside the class.[85] Accordingly, it does not matter that there is a category of "don't knows". This approach overcomes the possibility of there being only one beneficiary under a discretionary trust. Nevertheless, it may mean that the trustee is making a selection from a narrower class than that intended by the settlor.[86]

Administratively unworkable trusts

2.49   This issue is concerned with the width of the class specified (i.e. it is to do with the numerative range of potential beneficiaries). In *McPhail v Doulton*, Lord Wilberforce acknowledged, albeit by way of obiter, that a class of beneficiaries might be, "so hopelessly wide as not to form 'anything like a class' so that the trust is administratively unworkable or ... one that cannot be executed".[87] By way of illustration, he suggested that a trust for "all the residents of Greater London" would necessarily be void.[88] In *Gibbs v Harding*,[89] the objects were defined as "The Black Community of Hackney, Haringey, Islington and Tower Hamlets". Although the trust was upheld as a charitable trust, Lewison J. admitted that the class would be too wide to sustain a private trust. The class would be too extensive for the trustees to perform their duties and for the court to enforce the beneficiaries' claims if the trustee's failed in those duties. Logically, therefore, the case for invalidity appears stronger with a fixed trust than it is with a discretionary trust. For example, a fixed trust to benefit employees of a huge multi-national company and their children might be a ready candidate for classification as an administratively unworkable trust. A discretionary trust, however, in favour of the same beneficiaries would, it is submitted, be less likely to be struck down on this ground. The notion of administrative unworkability appears, therefore, not to be driven solely by numbers, but is concerned with the ability of the trustee to carry out his duty of inquiry and ascertainment.[90]

The only decision directly on this issue is *R. v District Auditor Ex p. West Yorkshire Metropolitan County Council*.[91] An attempt was there made by the soon to be defunct

---

[85] Megaw L.J. concluded, "If it does not mean that, I do not know where the line is supposed to be drawn ..." ([1973] Ch. 9 at 24); see also the approach of Lord Denning in *Re Allen* [1953] Ch. 810.

[86] See the dissenting speech of Lord Hodson in *McPhail v Doulton* [1971] A.C. 424 at 443.

[87] [1971] A.C. 424 at 457.

[88] [1971] A.C. 424 at 457. He added that a trust for "relatives" (even of a living person) did not fall within this category.

[89] [2008] Ch. 235.

[90] L. McKay [1974] 38 Conv. 269 at 283, however, argues that there is no substance to the requirement that a trust must be administratively workable. This author concludes that there are no insurmountable difficulties associated with having a large class of beneficiaries.

[91] (1985) 26 R.V.R. 24.

council to benefit in specified ways "any or all or some of the inhabitants of the County of West Yorkshire". Lloyd L.J. held that the discretionary trust failed because the class (approximately 2.5 million people) was far too large to be workable. He also found it to be a private purpose trust which, as a general rule, will offend the beneficiary principle and fail also on that basis. In *Re Hay's Settlement Trust*,[92] Megarry V.C. accepted (not surprisingly) that a trust to benefit anyone in the world would be ineffective. He did, however, acknowledge that a power of appointment on similar terms might be valid.[93] This distinction was based upon the premise that a trustee's duties are imperative and more stringent than those who are called upon to exercise a power.

Capriciousness

There is no general rule of law that requires a disposition to be sensible and rational. As   **2.50**
Wigram V.C. famously remarked, "No man is bound to make a will in such a manner as to deserve approbation from the prudent, the wise and the good".[94] Although this approach extends to testamentary dispositions and gifts, it does not apply to trusts. Due to the nature of the obligations placed upon a trustee, a trust is void if it is capricious, i.e. it reflects a nonsensical intention on the part of the settlor and precludes any proper consideration by the trustees. For example, a trust to benefit bald men would be struck down in this way.[95] It is submitted that a trust could also be viewed as capricious if the trust fund was woefully inadequate to justify the expense and enquiries of distributing it amongst the specified class of beneficiaries.[96] Although, there has, as yet, been no case decided specifically on the basis of capriciousness, it has been the subject of some judicial consideration.

In *Re Manisty's Settlement*, Templeman J. provided the example of an attempt to benefit the residents of Greater London as being capricious because the terms, "negative any sensible intention on the part of the settlor".[97] While this view may have some merit where the settlor is a private individual, it would surely not apply where the settlor is a local authority. This was the stance adopted by Lloyd L.J. in the *West Yorkshire Metropolitan County Council* case where he concluded that a trust to benefit 2.5 million inhabitants was not capricious. Lloyd L.J. felt that capriciousness would arise where the class was merely, "an accidental conglomeration of persons who had no discernible link with the settlor".[98] On the facts before him, he concluded that, "The council had every reason for wishing to benefit the inhabitants of West Yorkshire".[99]

Two other cases might be invoked as illustrations of when a trust might be classified   **2.51**
as capricious. First, in *M'Caig v University of Glasgow* a private purpose trust to establish various monuments in memory of the settlor was viewed as, "perpetuating at

---

[92] [1981] 3 All E.R. 786.
[93] See also, *Re Manisty's Settlement* [1973] 2 All E.R. 1203.
[94] (1850) Hare 301.
[95] A power will also be rendered void if it is capricious.
[96] See Lord Reid in *Re Gulbenkian's Settlement Trusts* [1970] A.C. 508.
[97] [1973] 2 All E.R. 1203 at 1211.
[98] (1985) 26 R.V.R. 24.
[99] (1985) 26 R.V.R. 24.

great cost, and in an absurd manner, the idiosyncrasies of an eccentric testator".[1] Although the trust failed because of want of beneficiary, it could have failed also on the basis of capriciousness. Secondly, in *Brown v Burdett* the trustees were directed to block up the doors and windows of a house for 20 years.[2] Although the trust was held to fail because it was to advance a private purpose, the direction was undeniably capricious in nature.

GUIDE TO FURTHER READING

C.T. Emery, "Certainty of Beneficiaries of Trusts and Powers of Appointment" (1982) 98 L.Q.R. 551.

Y. Grbich, "*Baden:* Awakening the Conceptually Moribund Trust" (1974) 37 M.L.R. 643.

D. Hayton, "Uncertainty of Subject-Matter of Trusts" (1994) 110 L.Q.R. 335.

L. McKay, "*Re Baden* and the Third Class of Uncertainty" (1974) 38 Conv 269.

P. Millett, "The *Quistclose* Trust: Who Can Enforce It?" (1985) 101 L.Q.R. 269.

T.M. Yeo, H. Tjio, "The *Quistclose* Trust" (2003) 119 L.Q.R. 8.

---

[1] [1907] S.C. 231 at 242 per Lord Kyllachy.
[2] (1882) 21 Ch. D. 667.

Chapter 3

CONSTITUTION OF TRUSTS

This chapter focuses upon the circumstances in which a trust may be properly con- **3.01** stituted or, put more simply, it considers the circumstances where a trustee will have sufficient title to the property in order for the trust to be effective. Constitution can occur by means of an effective self-declaration of trust or an effective transfer of property to the trustees. The classic exposition of this rule of constitution is that of Turner L.J. in *Milroy v Lord*:

> "In order to render a voluntary settlement valid and effectual, the settlor must have done everything which according to the nature of the property comprised in the settlement was necessary to be done in order to render the settlement binding upon him. He may, of course, do this by actually transferring the property to the persons for whom he intends to provide and the provision will then be effectual and it will be equally effectual if he transfers the property to a trustee for the purposes of the settlement, or declares that he himself holds it on trust for those purposes ... but, in order to render the settlement binding one of these modes must, as I understand the law of this court, be resorted to for there is no equity in this court to perfect an imperfect gift".[1]

The requirement of constitution is straightforward and entails that, only if the trust is completely constituted, will the trust bind the settlor and be enforceable by the bene- ficiary. If the trust is not completely constituted then, as a general rule, it will be ineffective. In the latter scenario, the intended beneficiaries have no interest that they can enforce. This is because, unlike a contracting party, the beneficiary usually provides no consideration whatsoever. Equity, moreover, cannot offer assistance because of two interrelated and venerated maxims "equity will not assist a volunteer" and "equity will not perfect an imperfect gift". Hence, the general rule is that the court is prevented from coming to the aid of a volunteer beneficiary regardless of how undesirable the outcome

[1] (1862) 4 De. G.F. & J. 264 at 274.

might appear. In *Jones v Lock*, for example, Lord Carnworth L.C. was unable to uphold a trust of a cheque in favour of a baby and lamented that, "by an act of God, this unfortunate child has been deprived of a provision which his father meant to make for him".[2] Obviously, the courts will, if possible, uphold a trust for as Lord Browne-Wilkinson put it, "Although equity will not aid a volunteer, it will not strive officiously to defeat a gift".[3] In addition, this lack of assistance to a volunteer is not a hard and fast rule and there are, as will become clear, well-established exceptions to it. As Arden L.J. explained in *Pennington v Waine*, "The principle against imperfectly constituted gifts led to harsh and seemingly paradoxical results. Before long, equity had tempered the wind to the shorn lamb (i.e. the donee). It did so on more than one occasion and in more than one way".[4]

3.02   The exceptions to the general rule that equity will not perfect an imperfect gift include:

- when there is a conveyance of land to a minor. Under the Trusts of Land and Appointment of Trustees Act 1996, the conveyance will operate as a declaration that the land is held on trust for that minor. This is the only statutory exception to the rule that equity will not assist a volunteer;

- the so-called every effort rule or the rule in *Re Rose* (see **3.09**);

- as promoted by Arden L.J. in the *Pennington* case, when it would be unconscionable for the donor to change his mind (see **3.13**);

- *donationes mortis causa* or deathbed gifts (see **3.15**);

- the rules as to fortuitous vesting contained in *Strong v Bird* and *Re Rallis WT* (see **3.21**; **3.25**, respectively); and

- proprietary estoppel (see **3.34**).

METHODS OF CONSTITUTION

3.03   As Jessell M.R. explained in *Richards v Delbridge*, there are two methods through which a trust will be perfectly constituted by a settlor, "he may either do such acts as amount in law to a conveyance or assignment of the property, and thus completely divest himself of legal ownership ... or the legal owner of the property may, by one or other of the modes recognised as amounting to a valid declaration of trust, constitute himself a trustee and, without an actual transfer of the legal title, may so deal with the property as to deprive himself of beneficial ownership, and declare that he will hold it from that time forward on trust for the other person".[5]

---

[2] (1865) L.R. 1 Ch. App. 25 CA at 29.
[3] *T. Choithram International SA v Pagarani* [2001] W.L.R. 1 at 11, where the Privy Council construed the words used by the settlor as amounting to a declaration of trust even though they were couched in the language of a gift.
[4] [2002] 4 All E.R. 215 at 226, 227.
[5] (1874) L.R. 18 Eq. 11 at 14.

The first method, therefore, is by transfer of legal title of the property to a third party. This can occur by a valid will[6] or by lifetime (inter vivos) transfer. This applies equally to gifts as it does to the setting up a trust with a third party trustee.

The second method is for the settlor to declare himself as a trustee of his own property. This latter method is obviously more straightforward as the settlor already has legal title and, hence, no transfer is necessary. The declaration will, therefore, operate to strip the settlor of his beneficial interest in the property. He will, of course, retain nominal, legal title to the property.

Transfer of legal title

It is necessary for the settlor to comply with the appropriate formalities in order to transfer legal title to a third party trustee. This, not surprisingly, hinges upon the settlor having legal title in the first place.[7] As will now become clear, the precise mechanism of transfer to be adopted varies according to the nature of the property concerned. As mentioned, the same rules apply also to the making of gifts.   **3.04**

- *Land*. Subject to exceptions relating to short leases,[8] to transfer legal title to *land* a deed of conveyance is needed.[9] In the case of registered land, the transfer only becomes complete on its registration at the Land Registry.[10]

- *Shares*. Legal title to shares is transferred traditionally by executing what is called a share transfer form followed by registration of the new owner in the company's shareholding register.[11] It is upon registration that the transfer is complete. As regards a public company, registration will automatically follow on from the documentary transfer. A private company, however, usually has the discretion to refuse to register a share transfer dealing. If registration is declined, legal title cannot pass and the express trust will be incompletely constituted. There exists, however, a class of shares that are called "bearer" shares and these are treated differently. Legal title of bearer shares passes to whoever has physical possession of the share certificates.

- *Chattels*. Title to chattels is transferred either by deed of gift (uncommon) or by physical delivery of the item to the recipient coupled with the intention to effect a transfer. Delivery includes parting with dominion over an article (e.g. passing over the key to a jewellery box). In *Re Cole*,[12] a husband arranged for furniture to be delivered to the address that he then shared with his wife. She argued that the furniture was a gift to her, but the Court of Appeal held that this delivery

---

[6] That is, one which satisfies the requirements of the Wills Act 1837.
[7] *Re Brook's ST* [1939] 1 Ch. 993.
[8] Section 54(2) of the Law of Property Act 1925 exempts the creation of periodic tenancies and leases not exceeding three years. This exception does not, however, apply to the assignment of such leases.
[9] Section 52 of the Law of Property Act 1925.
[10] Section 7 of the Land Registration Act 2002.
[11] Section 1 of the Stock Transfer Act 1963. Although registration remains key, it is now possible to dispense with a document of transfer. If adopted, the CREST system of share transfer dispenses with paper and allows the transfer to occur electronically.
[12] [1964] Ch. 175.

did not coincide with an intention to transfer title. There was no gift. The appellate court also explained that a transfer does not occur by merely showing the intended donee the goods and uttering words such as "these are now yours".

- *Cheques*. Legal title to a cheque passes on endorsement by the transferor and delivery of the cheque to the third party. This, seemingly, is not possible when the cheque is crossed "account payee only".

- *Copyright*. Writing is necessary for the transfer of copyright.[13]

- *Existing equitable interests*. In order to transfer an existing interest to another, the assignment must be in writing and signed by the assignor or his agent.[14]

Ineffective transfers

3.05 If the correct procedure is not followed, the transfer to the trustees will be ineffective. The maxim "equity cannot perfect an imperfect gift" will apply. This approach reflects a paternalistic stance that ensures that a donor, who acts unwisely and informally, can have a change of mind. It is also important to appreciate that, as *Jones v Lock*[15] demonstrates, a failed gift will not be regarded as a declaration of trust. Examples of ineffective transfers are readily available from decided case law.

In *Richards v Delbridge*,[16] Mr Delbridge purported to assign legal title of a lease to his grandson. He wrote on the back of the original lease, "This deed and all thereto belonging I give to Edward Burnetto Richards from this time forth with all the stock in trade". The gift failed because there was no deed specifically created to convey the transfer (see **3.04**). It could not, moreover, be argued that Mr Delbridge declared himself to be a trustee as there was no intention to create a trust. He intended throughout for there to be an outright gift.

3.06 In *Antrobus v Smith*[17] an attempted transfer of shares by the mere endorsement on the back of a share certificate was clearly ineffective to pass legal title in them to the intended transferee (see **3.04**). Similarly, in *Milroy v Lord*,[18] an attempt to establish a trust of 50 shares in a bank failed because legal title to the shares never became vested in the trustee. The settlor did not take any steps to transfer the shares before his death and, although the intended trustee had previously held an unexercised power of attorney to transfer the shares, this power was revoked by the settlor's death. The shares, therefore, remained in the deceased's estate.[19]

A slightly more difficult case is *Re Fry*.[20] There the intended donor executed a share

---

[13] Section 90(3) of the Copyright Designs and Patents Act 1988; s.5(2) of the Copyright Act 1956.
[14] This is required by s.53(1)(c) of the Law of Property Act 1925. If not it will be ineffectual: see *Re McArdle* [1951] Ch. 669.
[15] (1865) L.R. 1 Ch. App. 25 CA.
[16] (1874) L.R. 18 Eq. 11.
[17] (1806) 12 Ves. 39.
[18] (1862) 4 De. G.F. & J. 264.
[19] See also, *Letts v IRC* [1951] 1 W.L.R. 201 whereby a father merely directed that a company transfer shares to his children. He had not done enough to transfer legal title.
[20] [1946] Ch. 312.

transfer document before his death. As he was resident abroad, the Defence (Finance) Regulations (Amendment No.2) SI 1939/1620 required the consent of the Treasury before the transfer could take place. The donor had completed the necessary forms and returned them. He had also applied for the necessary consent, but this was not given before his untimely demise. With regret, Romer J. held that the transfer was ineffective because the donor had not done everything that he needed to do to pass title. It remained possible that the Treasury would require further information or supplemental answers from the donor or, indeed, refuse its consent altogether. As Romer J. pointed out, if the donor had been asked for further details, he would have been under no compulsion to proceed with the transfer and "he might have refused to concern himself with the matter further".[21] *Re Fry* is often regarded a harsh decision, particularly when contrasted with the two *Re Rose* cases (see **3.09**). Nevertheless, the Defence Finance Regulations ensured that Mr Fry had no power to affect a transfer without Treasury consent. Hence, he attempted to achieve that which was legally impossible and there was no way for the court comfortably to condone a blatant violation of the Regulations.

Self-declaration as trustee

A settlor with a legal interest in property can declare himself a trustee of that property   **3.07** for a beneficiary. This is the less popular method of creating a trust because, somewhat obviously, it can only be created during the lifetime of the settlor (i.e. it only relates to inter vivos trusts). It will also entail that the onerous, and usually unwelcome, duties of a trustee will rest with the person who has just divested himself of beneficial ownership over the property. Several initial points need to be appreciated. First, the general rule is that such declaration can be oral without the need for any additional formality. An exception applies in the case of land when the trust must be evidenced in writing and signed by the settlor or his agent.[22]

Secondly, the settlor can use any form of words to demonstrate the intention to create a trust[23] or this intention might be inferred from conduct. In *Richards v Delbridge*, Jessell M.R. admitted, "the settlor need not use the words 'I declare myself a trustee' but he must do something which is equivalent to it and use expressions which have meaning; for however anxious the court may be to carry out a man's intention, it is not at liberty to construe words other than according to their proper meaning".[24]

Finally, it is crucial to bear in mind that an ineffective gift cannot be construed as a   **3.08** declaration of trust. This is because the settlor has shown the intention to give the property away absolutely and has evinced no intention to retain the legal estate on trust for the intended donee. Accordingly, in *Jones v Lock* the purported gift to a child of a

---

[21] [1946] Ch. 312 at 318.
[22] Section 53(1)(b) of the Law of Property Act 1925; see Ch.4.
[23] See *Paul v Constance* [1977] 1 W.L.R. 527 where it was held that Mr Constance had declared a trust, albeit informally, of a bank account for himself and his mistress. He had used words that indicated the intention to create a trust.
[24] (1874) L.R. 18 Eq. 11 at 14.

cheque failed because the cheque was not endorsed and the court was unable to distil from the facts any declaration of trust.[25] Lord Cranworth L.C. explained, "It all turns upon the facts, which do not lead me to the conclusion that the testator meant to deprive himself of all property in the note, or to declare himself a trustee of the money for the child".[26]

THE EVERY EFFORT RULE

3.09   This rule entails that, if the donor has done everything necessary for him to do to transfer title, the gift or trust will not fail simply because the donor dies before the process of transfer is finalised. This is also known as the rule in *Re Rose*.[27] Put simply, if the only outstanding task is to be carried out by a third party then the settlor has taken all the steps that he personally needs to take. In this way, it is properly to be viewed as an exception to the general rule that a transfer that fails at law will not take effect in equity.

In *Re Rose*, the donor executed a share transfer form in favour of his wife and handed it, together with the share certificate, over to her. He died before the transfer was registered. Although the transfer of the legal title was not concluded at the time of his death, the gift was upheld. In the eyes of equity the transfer was concluded when the signed document was given to the wife for delivery to the company. As there was nothing more for the donor to do to perfect the gift, his death was not fatal to the transfer process. This explains why it is called the "every effort" rule. The same approach has been adopted also in relation to the transfer of registered land. For example, in *Mascall v Mascall*[28] a father delivered an executed land transfer form and land certificate to his son. Following an argument, and before the transfer was registered, the father sought to resile from the transaction. It was held that the every effort rule applied and that it was too late to withdraw from the process.[29]

3.10   *Re Rose* stands in striking contrast to both *Re Fry* and *Milroy v Lord* where, in both cases, it was held that the donor still had something left to do to effect the transfer. Consequently, it could not be said that the transferor had made every effort. The rule, therefore, entails that the settlor need do more than merely sign a document of transfer. The last step in the process will usually be making arrangements for its delivery to, for example, the company or the Land Registry. Accordingly, executing the document and merely placing it in a desk drawer should not, without more, suffice. At that stage, the settlor would surely be free to have a change of heart and tear up the transfer document. There is obviously no question of the transfer being complete in law and it should

---

[25] (1865) L.R. 1 Ch. App. 25 CA. See also *Pappadakis v Pappadakis* Unreported October 25, 1999 (Ch) where the intention to assign a life assurance policy could not be construed as the declaration of a trust.

[26] (1865) L.R. 1 Ch. App. 25 CA at 29.

[27] [1952] Ch. 499; see also the decision of Jenkins J. in the earlier and unrelated case coincidentally bearing the same name: *Re Rose; Midland Bank Executor & Trustee Co Ltd v Rose* [1949] 1 Ch. 78.

[28] (1984) 50 P. & C.R. 119.

[29] See also, *Brown & Root Technology v Sun Alliance & London Assurance Co* [1996] Ch. 51, where Judge Paul Baker Q.C. applied the every effort rule in relation to an assignment of a lease.

also follow that there has been no assignment of the equitable interest to the bene-ficiary/donee.

Although simple to state, the rule has proved at times difficult to apply. The Court of Appeal decision in *Pennington v Waine* has further muddied the waters.[30] This case concerned a purported gift of 400 shares in a private company. The donor signed the appropriate share transfer form and gave it to her adviser to deal with. Prior to the donor's death, the adviser had written to the donee stating that he had been instructed to transfer the shares to him and inviting him to become a director of the company. The donee then signed a form agreeing to become a director and was assured that there was nothing else for him to do. Unfortunately, no further action was taken by the adviser. On the donor's death, the issue arose as to whether the 400 shares formed part of the donor's residual estate or were, instead, held on trust for the donee, pending registra-tion of the transaction.

Arden L.J. admitted that there is no clear answer to the question of when the last step **3.11** necessary is taken by a donor and the equitable assignment of a share takes place. She explained, "The equitable assignment clearly occurs at some stage before the shares are registered. But does it occur when the share transfer is executed, or when the share transfer is delivered to the transferee, or when the transfer is lodged for registration, or when the pre-emption procedure . . . is satisfied or the directors resolve that the transfer should be registered?"[31]

As to whether it was necessary at law for the donor to deliver the form of transfer to the donee, Clarke L.J. felt that this was not a prerequisite of a valid equitable assign-ment. Arden L.J. agreed that delivery could, in some circumstances, be dispensed with. In the interests of legal certainty, she accepted that there has to be an ascertainable point at which it can be said that a gift is completed and that point of no return must be identified on a principled basis. Arden L.J. concluded that this stage is reached when it becomes unconscionable for the donor to renege on the gift. She added, "There can be no comprehensive list of factors which makes it unconscionable for the donor to change his or her mind: it must depend on the court's evaluation of all the relevant considerations".[32]

In the context of the every effort rule, this is an unhelpful and questionable decision **3.12** that flies in the face of well-established authority. It also introduces notions of fairness of outcome into a rule that previously focused exclusively upon the process of transfer. Surely, and unless some arrangement has been made for delivery, the donor truly cannot be said to have taken every step that he has to take.[33] Arden L.J. did, however, accept that, if wrong on the issue of unconscionability, the same end could be reached by finding that the adviser became the agent for the donor for the purpose of submitting the share transfer to the Company. It is, perhaps, unfortunate that the decision was not founded solely upon this more traditional basis.

The every effort rule most certainly conflicts with the traditional stance that equity does not regard an ineffective transfer as a declaration of trust. This tension is not, however, major where the role of the third party is merely a formality, i.e. as with a public company where registration is inevitable. In that situation, there is implied a

---

[30] [2002] 4 All E.R. 215.
[31] [2002] 4 All E.R. 215 at 227.
[32] [2002] 4 All E.R. 215 at 230.
[33] See *Brown & Root Technology v Sun Alliance & London Assurance Co* [1996] Ch. 51 at 67.

constructive trust which assigns the equitable interest to the donee and is timed to span the interim period until the transfer is completed. It is not a trust that is created expressly or permanently. As with a private company, however, it remains possible that the transfer will never be registered because the directors will, in all likelihood, be granted a veto. Although in both *Re Rose* cases the shares were of a private company, registration did eventually occur.[34] The problem to be addressed is what happens if registration is subsequently denied. If the implied trust is to be maintained beyond the refusal of registration, is it not blatantly upholding an ineffective transfer as a declaration of trust? Nevertheless, this is the outcome generated by the every effort rule. Such is confirmed by *Pennington v Waine* where the donee was never registered as the owner of the shares because the directors exercised a right of pre-emption. Although the transfer of legal title was never completed, the donee was entitled to the proceeds of sale of those shares.

THE ROLE OF UNCONSCIONABILITY

3.13   In *Pennington v Waine*, the Court of Appeal concluded that, on the facts, it would have been unconscionable for the donor to recall the gift once the donee had agreed to become a director. It followed, therefore, that it would be equally unconscionable for her personal representative to refuse to hand over the share transfer form to the donee. As Arden L.J. pointed out, "In those circumstances ... delivery of the share transfer before her death was unnecessary so far as perfection of the gift was concerned".[35] Legal title was to remain vested in the donor's estate pending registration of the transaction. Arden L.J. admitted that, during the intervening period, the donor's personal representative became the constructive trustee of the legal title to the shares for the donee.

The prevailing view, however, is that Arden L.J. adopted a mistaken interpretation of previous authority.[36] Halliwell, for example believes that the stance adopted by the Court of Appeal may, "give courts of equity an unfettered discretion as to whether a voluntary gift or trust should take effect".[37] She observes that this is "completely irreconcilable with previous authorities".[38] The key authority relied on by Arden L.J. was the Privy Council decision in *T. Choithram International v Pagarani*.[39] There, on facts considered below (see **3.14**), Lord Browne-Wilkinson admitted that it would be unconscionable for the settlor, who had validly declared a trust, to have a change of heart. The comparison with *Pennington* is, therefore, unconvincing. Parker and Mellows agree, "in contrast, in *Pennington v Waine*, the donor had neither declared a trust nor made a gift nor done everything in her power to make a gift".[40]

---

[34] Albeit in the earlier *Re Rose* it took 18 months for registration of the share transfer to occur.
[35] [2002] 4 All E.R. 215 at 231.
[36] See Parker and Mellows who at p.156 describe Arden L.J.'s judgment as, "a complete misunderstanding"; cf. J. Garton [2003] Conv. 364.
[37] M. Halliwell [2003] Conv. 192 at p.193.
[38] [2003] Conv. 192 at 195.
[39] [2001] 1 W.L.R. 1.
[40] Parker and Mellows at p.156. It is to be noted that the company's regulations required the shares to be offered first to its existing directors and that this was also a step never taken by the donor.

The Settlor as one of several trustees

In *T. Choithram International SA v Pagarani*, the settlor executed a deed of trust in **3.14**
favour of a charitable organisation which he established. He nominated himself and
nine others as trustees. Shortly before his death, the settlor purported orally to settle
money and shares on the organisation. He did not, however, transfer the title of the
assets to the other trustees. On his death, it was argued that the trust was incompletely
constituted and that the assets would pass on intestacy to his next of kin. In the Privy
Council, however, Lord Browne-Wilkinson upheld the trust. It was held that the settlor
had done enough to declare himself a trustee. It did not matter that he intended to be
one of a number of trustees (and not a sole trustee). Lord Browne-Wilkinson explained:

> "There can in principle be no distinction between the case where the donor declares
> himself to be the sole trustee for a donee or a purpose and the case where he
> declares himself to be one of the trustees for that donee or purpose. In both cases
> his conscience is affected and it would be unconscionable and contrary to the
> principle of equity to allow such a donor to resile from his gift".[41]

On these unusual facts, he accepted that it would be unconscionable for the settlor to
renege on the declaration of trust. There was nothing to show that the settlor wanted
the trust to come into effect only when all trustees had legal title. This is a very different
scenario from that which faced the Court of Appeal in *Pennington v Waine*.

DONATIONES MORTIS CAUSA

As shown, the general rule is that equity will not assist a volunteer. One judge-made   **3.15**
exception to this rule is *donationes mortis causa* (DMC) or deathbed gifts. This rule may
have the consequence of constituting what would otherwise be viewed as an incomplete
gift to a donee or an incomplete transfer to a trustee. If a DMC is upheld, the donor's
personal representatives will be obliged formally to complete the gift or transfer. It will,
therefore, take priority over the terms of the will itself. The DMC rule concerns a
conditional, lifetime gift that is made by the donor in contemplation of death. As
Buckley J. put it in *Re Beaumont*, "A *donatio mortis causa* is a singular form of gift. It
may be said to be of an amphibious nature being a gift which is neither entirely *inter
vivos* nor testamentary. It is an act *inter vivos* by which the donee is to have the absolute
title to the subject of the gift not at once but if the donor dies. If the donor dies the title
becomes absolute ... as against his executor. In order to make the gift valid it must be
made so as to take complete effect on the donor's death."[42] Since the defrosting exercise

---

[41] [2001] 1 W.L.R. 1 at 12.
[42] [1902] 1 Ch. 892 at 893.

undertaken by Nourse L.J. in *Sen v Headley*,[43] any type of property can, seemingly, be the subject of a DMC: cheques, promissory notes, chattels, shares (even if in a private company[44]), bonds, insurance policies, land, etc. As Nourse L.J. commented, "Anomalies do not justify anomalous exceptions".[45]

The central notion is that a gift by reason of death may, in certain circumstances, be perfected even though the necessary formalities of transfer have not been followed. It reflects a sentimentality of the court shown towards the dying and the desperate. As such it is an anomaly and, not surprisingly, has been the subject of criticism. For example, as early as 1752 Lord Hardwicke bemoaned the fact that the rule was not abolished in the Statute of Frauds 1677.[46] Lord Eldon later echoed this sentiment and expressed the view that DMC should be, "struck out of our law altogether".[47] Rolfe B. also alluded to the "evils" of this method of side stepping the formalities of transfer.[48] Nevertheless, the rule remains and ironically, with regard to the criticism levied against it, has been enlarged in modern times.

3.16   There are, however, certain conditions that are necessary for an effectual DMC to occur. As Russell C.J. demonstrated in *Cain v Moon*:[49]

- the gift or donation must have been made in contemplation, though not necessarily in expectation, of death;

- the gift must be made under such circumstances as show that the property is to revert to the donor in the case that death does not occur; and

- there must have been delivery to the donee of the subject-matter of the gift.

The burden of proof rests on the donee and, if the claim is unsupported by evidence of any person other than the donee, the court must have before it all material which may be relevant.[50] As acknowledged by the Privy Council in *Cosnahan v Grice*, "Cases of this kind demand the strictest scrutiny. So many opportunities, and such strong temptations, present themselves to unscrupulous persons to pretend these death-bed donations, that there is always the danger of having an entirely fabricated case set up. And without any imputation a fraudulent contrivance, it is so easy to mistake the meaning of a person languishing in a mortal illness, and, by a slight change of words, to convert their expressions of intended benefit into an actual gift of property, that no case of this description ought to prevail, unless it is supported by evidence of the clearest and most unequivocal character."[51]

---

[43] [1991] 2 All E.R. 636; see M. Halliwell [1991] Conv. 307.
[44] Following *Pennington v Waine* [2002] 4 All E.R. 215, if the donee under a DMC is never registered by the company as the shareholder, the donee will still enjoy an equitable interest in the shares and will be entitled to the proceeds of their eventual sale.
[45] [1991] 2 All E.R. 636 at 647.
[46] *Ward v Turner* [1752] 28 E.R. 275.
[47] *Duffield v Elwes* [1827] 4 E.R. 959 at 972.
[48] *Hills v Hills* (1841) 151 E.R. 1095 at 1096.
[49] [1896] 2 QB 283 at 286; see also the similar formulation of Farwell J. in *Re Cravens Estate* [1937] 1 Ch. 423 at 426.
[50] *Calvert v Scholes* [2002] EWHC 2333 (Ch).
[51] (1862) 15 Moo. PC. 215 at 216.

In contemplation of death

The requirement is that the gift be because of or on account of death. In *Duffield v* **3.17**
Elwes, Lord Eldon spoke in terms of "the conceived approach of death".[52] There must
be an impending risk of death occurring and this requires more than mere philosophical
musing or some general contemplation of death. In *Re Cravens Estate*, it was said by
Farwell J. that the contemplation must be of "death within the near future".[53] The
donor does not have to be in *extremis* or at death's door when the gift is made. For
example, a patient admitted to hospital for a routine operation may make a DMC in
contemplation of death even though death might not be the expected outcome. Death
must, however, be contemplated from an identified source. Such a source could be, for
example, illness, the result of an accident, the fear of an air crash or, possibly, suicide.[54]
The gift will still be perfected in the unlikely event of the deceased dying from a different
cause than was anticipated.[55] In *Wilkes v Arlington*, the donor was dying of cancer and
made a valid DMC in contemplation of death, even though he eventually died of
pneumonia.[56]

It is the subjective state of mind of the donor that appears to be relevant. The donor's
actual motivation must surely be the crucial issue and this should not be supplanted by
the fictitious motivations of a reasonable man in the donor's position. Often there will
be an express reference to death (the "if I die I want you to have this" style of case), but
this is not necessary. Such contemplation can be inferred from the circumstances in
which the gift is made.[57] In *Gardner v Parker*, the connection between the gift and the
contemplation of death was inferred from the fact that the donor was terminally ill
when he made the gift and died shortly after the making of it.[58] The circumstances
surrounding the gift demonstrated clearly that this had been the motivation underlying
the gift. A different conclusion, however, was manufactured in *Re Kirkley*.[59] There a gift
made by an aged and bedridden donor was not inferred to be in contemplation of death
because the donor, although worn out, was not ill. The reference to death in this case
would have had to be express for an effectual DMC to be created.

Conditional on death

The gift must be made in circumstances that show that the property is to revert back to **3.18**
the donor if he recovers. As in *Staniland v Willot*,[60] the gift lapses if the donor recovers
from his illness. Over a century later, Nourse L.J. accepted in *Sen v Headley* that the gift

---

[52] [1827] 4 E.R. 959 at 971.
[53] [1937] 1 Ch. 423 at 426.
[54] See *Mills v Shields* [1948] I.R. 367.
[55] This rule might give way when the donor specifies the risk (e.g. "if my plane crashes I want you to have
this"), but then dies of a different cause (e.g. of a heart attack on the way to the airport): see *Re Richards*
[1921] 1 Ch. 513.
[56] [1931] 2 Ch. 104.
[57] *Walter v Hodge* [1818] 36 E.R. 549.
[58] [1818] 56 E.R. 478.
[59] [1909] 25 T.L.R. 522.
[60] [1850] 42 E.R. 416.

becomes absolute only on the donor's death, "being revocable until that event occurs and ineffective if it does not".[61] Accordingly, there can be no DMC if the donor intends to make an absolute and immediate gift.[62] In *Tate v Hilbert*, for example, an elderly donor purported to give money to his two nieces, claiming that he had too much money just for himself.[63] He did not adopt the appropriate method of transfer and died before he could do so. The court held that he had attempted to make an immediate and unconditional gift and, hence, the nieces were denied as there could be no effectual DMC.

This condition can be expressed (e.g. "on my death this is yours") or readily inferred from the circumstances. Indeed, the general rule is that if the gift is made in expectation of death then, absent contrary evidence, it will be regarded as being conditional on the death of the donor.[64] The court will not entertain any argument that, if imminent death is thought to be a certainty, this provides evidence of the intention to create an immediate gift.[65] As Lord Tomlin put it, ". . . when a man is smitten with a mortal disease, he may know, in fact, that there cannot be any recovery; yet I apprehend that a man in that situation . . . is capable of creating a good *donation mortis causa*".[66]

3.19   At any time prior to death, the gift can be revoked. This can occur expressly by words (e.g. "I no longer want you to have my watch")[67] or may be implied from the circumstances (e.g. taking back possession of the watch).[68] In *Hawkins v Blewitt*,[69] however, the donor took back physical possession of a box containing money (the subject matter of the gift) in order to keep it safely hidden under his bed. This did not evince any intention to revoke the DMC. It is important to appreciate that revocation cannot occur by virtue of the deceased donor's will.[70]

Delivery

3.20   The requirement is that, for a valid DMC to exist, dominion (i.e. control and possession) of the subject matter must pass from the donor to the donee before the donor's death.[71] Hence, if delivery occurs after the donor's death, there will be no DMC.[72] There must be something done that demonstrates the intention to transfer the property. Words alone, however, do not suffice for these purposes.[73] Instead, there must be actual and physical delivery of an item[74] or constructive delivery by the passing over the means

[61] [1991] 2 All E.R. 636 at 639.
[62] *Edwards v Jones* [1836] 40 E.R. 361.
[63] (1793) 30 E.R. 548.
[64] *Gardner v Parker* [1818] 56 E.R. 478; *Re Lillingston* [1951] 2 All E.R. 184.
[65] See *Re Mustapha* (1891) 8 T.L.R. 160.
[66] [1931] 2 Ch. 104 at 111.
[67] *Jones v Selby* (1710) Prec. Ch. 303.
[68] *Bunn v Markham* [1816] 129 E.R. 90.
[69] [1798] 170 E.R. 489; see also *Re Hawkins* [1924] 2 Ch. 47 (taking back of bank notes for safe keeping).
[70] *Jones v Selby* (1710) Prec. Ch. 303.
[71] *Ward v Turner* [1752] 28 E.R. 275. Delivery can be made by the donor's agent and accepted by the donee's agent: *Moore v Darton* [1851] 64 E.R. 938.
[72] *Hardy v Baker* [1738] 25 E.R. 1063. Delivery can, however, precede the gift: *Cain v Moon* [1896] 2 Q.B. 283.
[73] *Bunn v Markham* [1816] 129 E.R. 90.
[74] *Birch v Treasury Solicitor* [1950] 2 All E.R. 1198.

of obtaining the property or some indicia of title to the item.[75] Examples of the latter method include handing over the keys to a safety deposit box kept at a bank;[76] passing over of a savings book[77]; handing over the title deeds to house;[78] and giving over the keys to a car.[79] If there is no change of possession, whether real or constructive, there can be no DMC. Accordingly, the mere execution of a deed of transfer without passing the document to the donee will be insufficient.[80] Similarly, if the donee refuses to accept delivery there can be no DMC.[81] In *Reddel v Dobree*,[82] the donor delivered to the donee a locked cash box, but the donor wanted the box back every three months. The donor reserved dominion by retaining the right to deal with the box until his death.

THE RULE IN STRONG V BIRD

A further exception to the rule that equity will not perfect an imperfect gift is the rule regarding fortuitous vesting of which the leading example is the case of *Strong v Bird*.[83] Simply put, in its original and narrow form the rule is that, where there is the forgiveness of a debt and the donee subsequently obtains legal title to the property in the capacity of an executor, the gift (i.e. the release from liability) will then be perfected. This is what is known as "fortuitous vesting" because equity is unconcerned with how the relevant title actually became vested in, say, a trustee. Accordingly, and provided that it can be shown that the intention to make the gift was sustained until the donor's death, the necessary transfer of legal title occurs automatically by operation of law when the donee becomes the executor. It does not matter whether the donee is the sole executor or merely one of a number of executors. As Neville J. acknowledged, "The whole of the property in the personal estate in the eye of the law vesting in each executor, it seems to me immaterial whether the donee is the only executor or one of several ...".[84]

   The facts of *Strong v Bird* concerned a stepson who borrowed £1,100 from his stepmother. She lived in his house and paid £212 every three months for her board. It was agreed that the loan was to be paid off by making a £100 deduction from each of the next eleven payments. The deductions were made on two occasions following which the stepmother orally released the stepson from the remainder of the debt. She paid the £212 each quarter thereafter until her death. The stepson was appointed her executor under her will. Her residuary legatees, however, sought to recover the outstanding debt from the executor. Although there was no formal release made, the intention to forgo the debt was evident and maintained until the stepmother's death. It is to be

3.21

---

[75] *Cain v Moon* [1896] 2 QB 283.
[76] *Re Wasserberg* [1915] 1 Ch. 195.
[77] *Re Weston* [1902] 1 Ch. 680.
[78] *Sen v Headley* [1991] 2 All E.R. 636.
[79] *Woodard v Woodard* [1995] 3 All E.R. 980. A cheque handed to the donee and cashed after the death of the donor can be a valid DMC: *Rolls v Pearce* (1877) L.R. 5 Ch. D. 730.
[80] See *Re Hughes* (1888) 59 L.T. 586.
[81] *Cant v Gregory* (1894) 10 T.L.R. 584.
[82] [1839] 10 Sim. 244.
[83] (1874) 18 Eq. 315.
[84] *Re Stewart* [1908] 2 Ch. 251 at 254, 255.

appreciated that the intention alone would have proved insufficient to effect release of the debt. Without more, her estate would be entitled to claim the remainder of the debt. As Cozens Hardy M.R. said of it in *Re Pink*, "There is no consideration for it. It is not a perfect release; it is not a release at law; and therefore if there is nothing more it would have no operation or effect".[85]

3.22   The stepson being appointed as executor was, however, crucial. It is long established that, at common law, the coincidental appointment of the debtor as an executor (alone or with others) will operate to extinguish the debt.[86] The reasoning is that, as the executors become the owner of the deceased's estate (including the right to bring actions on a debt), it is impossible for the executors to sue themselves. This approach did not, however, originally apply in equity where the deceased's estate would always be allowed to claim against an executor.[87] *Strong v Bird* modified the traditional stance of equity and allowed the common law rule to operate when it was the intention of the deceased to release the debt and that intention continued until death.[88] Accordingly, the oral release of the debt was perfected when the debtor became the executor, i.e. on the death of the testatrix. Jessell M.R. explained, "There being the continuing intention to give and there being a legal act which transferred the ownership ... the transaction is perfected, and he does not want the aid of a Court of Equity to carry it out, or to make it complete, because it is complete already, and there is no equity against him to take the property away from him."[89] Hence, *Strong v Bird* offers an example of a donor inadvertently completing an otherwise imperfect gift. Such was accepted by Astbury J. in *Carter v Hungerford*, "if a donor makes an incomplete gift of real estate and afterwards, though unintentionally, includes it in a conveyance of real estate to the donee, the conveyance perfects the intended gift, and prevents the donor from reclaiming it on the ground of resulting trust or otherwise."[90]

The rule in *Strong v Bird* was widened considerably in *Re Stewart*[91] where it was held that the rule was not limited merely to the release of a debt and, indeed, applied to any imperfect, inter vivos gift. There it was a failed lifetime gift of bonds. As Neville J. explained, "the vesting of the property in the executor at the testator's death completes the imperfect gift made in the lifetime, and ... the intention of the testator to give the beneficial interest to the executor is sufficient to countervail the equity of the beneficiaries under the will, the testator having vested the legal estate in the executor".[92] *Re Stewart*, therefore, extends the equitable rules relating to fortuitous vesting much further than catered for by the common law.

3.23   In *Re James*,[93] it was held that the rule in *Strong v Bird* applied also in the situation where the donor dies intestate (i.e. without leaving a will) and the donee takes out letters of administration (i.e. becomes the administrator of the deceased's estate). There the deceased handed over the deeds of a house to a housekeeper. It will be recalled from *Richards v Delbridge* that this is woefully insufficient to pass legal title to land. On the

---

[85] [1912] 2 Ch. 528 at 535.
[86] *Wankford v Wankford* (1704) 1 Salk 299.
[87] See *Re Bourne* [1906] 1 Ch. 697.
[88] See *Jenkins v Jenkins* [1928] 2 K.B. 501.
[89] (1874) 18 Eq. 315 at 318.
[90] [1917] 1 Ch. 260 at 273.
[91] [1908] 2 Ch. 251.
[92] [1908] 2 Ch. 251 at 254.
[93] [1935] Ch. 449.

death of the donor, the housekeeper was granted letters of administration and legal title to the house then became automatically vested in her capacity as administratrix. As she now had legal title, albeit by this circuitous route, the gift was perfected. This extension to intestacy cases is, however, contentious and was doubted by Walton J. in *Re Gonin*.[94] The debate focuses upon the fact that, unlike executors under a will, the deceased does not nominate an administrator. Instead, probate rules govern who, usually from amongst the deceased's next of kin, can apply to be an administrator. Accordingly, it is unpredictable who eventually will become the administrator(s) of the estate. In addition, at common law (and unlike with an executor) the debt is not extinguished upon becoming an administrator. It is, instead, merely suspended. This is, therefore, fortuitous vesting at its most fortuitous. It is, as Walton J. put it, "to treat what ought to be a simple rule of equity ... as something of a lottery".[95]

The intention of the donor must be to make an immediate gift. In *Re Freeland*,[96] the promise to give a car at a future date fell outside the rule in *Strong v Bird*. There was no intention to make a present and absolute gift of the property. Accordingly, when the donee became the executrix under the donor's will, the gift was not perfected and failed. As Parker J. admitted in *Re Innes*, "it would be extremely dangerous to try to give effect by the appointment of an executor to what is at most an announcement of what a man intends to do in the future, and is not intended by him as a gift in the present ...".[97] The property subject to the gift must, moreover, be in existence at the time of the gift (the rule does not apply to after acquired property) and the property must be specifically identified (e.g. a debt, a bond, shares, land, a specific sum of money or chattels). It is thought that the rule cannot apply to a gift of an unspecified sum of money or unidentified goods (e.g. a gift to X of one of my paintings).

3.24 The intention to make the gift, moreover, has to persist until the death of the donor. If not, the rule in *Strong v Bird* cannot apply.[98] As Kennedy L.J. commented in *Re Pink*, this requires "a continuing intention that the gift should have been given at the time it was given".[99] In *Re Wale*,[1] the testatrix had intended to constitute a trust, but forgot to transfer all of the trust property to the trustees. It was held that the failure to subsequently transfer the trust property showed that she did not have the necessary continuing intention for the rule in *Strong v Bird* to apply. A similar approach might be adopted where, after the gift, the donor leaves the same property by will to another party. It is uncertain whether a temporary change of mind will prevent the rule from operating. Nevertheless, the better view is that there would need to be a fresh attempt to make the gift again in order for it to be brought back within the scope of the rule. Accordingly, a fluctuating intention should prove fatal to a claim under *Strong v Bird*. The issue of whether the intention has continued is an issue of fact and the burden of proof rests with the donee.

Although the rule has been explained in relation to gifts, it will apply equally to the transfer of property to trustees. Accordingly, if the trustee obtains legal title in the

---

[94] [1977] 2 All E.R. 720.
[95] [1977] 2 All E.R. 720 at 734. The extension is defended, however, by G. Kodilinye [1982] Conv. 14.
[96] [1952] Ch. 110.
[97] [1910] 1 Ch. 188 at 193.
[98] *Vavasseur v Vavasseur* (1909) 25 T.L.R. 250.
[99] [1912] 2 Ch. 528 at 538.
[1] [1956] 1 W.L.R. 1346.

capacity of executor or administrator then the trust will be constituted and rendered effective. This possibility was accepted in *Re Wale*.

RE RALLI'S WILL TRUSTS

3.25   In *Re Ralli's WT*,[2] a testator left his estate on trust for his wife for life and then for his daughter. Subsequently, the daughter entered into a covenant to transfer existing and subsequently acquired property to the trustees of her marriage settlement. The subsequent property referred to was the interest that was to come to her, following her mother's death, under her father's will. No transfer was ever made to her trustees. The daughter, however, predeceased the mother. On the mother's death, the trust property reverted back to the father's estate and title vested in the sole executor under the father's will. The executor was, by coincidence, also the remaining trustee under the daughter's marriage settlement. The case was actually decided on the non-contentious ground that the daughter's marriage settlement was a declaration of trust of her existing property and that the reversionary interest under her father's will was existing property at the time of the declaration. Hence, her executor held the property on the same trust when he obtained legal title.

By way of obiter, Buckley J. advanced a broader and more controversial proposition. He believed that, absent an effective declaration of trust of her reversionary interest by the daughter, the trust would still have been perfected. His reasoning was that, as legal title was now (albeit fortuitously) vested in the trustee, the trust of the reversionary interest had become perfectly constituted. The fact that the trustee obtained that title from a different source (i.e. as executor under the father's will) would operate to perfect what might otherwise be an imperfect trust. It should not matter how the trustee acquired title, the key issue was that title had now been acquired, "He is at law the owner of the fund, and the means by which he became so have no effect upon the quality of his legal ownership".[3]

3.26   At first blush, *Re Ralli's WT* might be seen as merely marking an extension to the rule in *Strong v Bird*. It is thought, however, that because of the differences between them, the two rules should be regarded as distinct. First, *Re Ralli's WT* does not require the trustee to be the executor under the settlor's will. There it sufficed that he was the executor under her father's will. *Strong v Bird* would not apply in that instance. Secondly, *Re Ralli's WT* does not require a continuing intention on the part of the settlor and can apply to unspecified and future (i.e. after acquired) property. *Strong v Bird* would be inapplicable in such circumstances. Thirdly, it is to be appreciated, moreover, that *Re Ralli's WT* has never been followed and doubts are raised as to whether it is good law.

Re Ralli's WT appears to contradict the earlier authority of *Re Brook's ST*[4] where, even though the trustees acquired title through a different route, the trust was not perfected. In that case, Lloyds Bank were the trustees of a marriage settlement under

---

[2] [1964] Ch. 288.
[3] [1964] Ch. 288 at 301.
[4] [1939] 1 Ch. 993.

which the wife enjoyed a power of appointment. One of her children made a voluntary settlement of property that he might acquire under his mother's power of appointment. His mother later made the anticipated appointment in his favour. At the time of the appointment Lloyds Bank held legal title to the property on behalf of the mother. The issue was whether the Bank now held the property under the terms of the son's voluntary settlement (the second trust) or whether the son could claim the property absolutely. The court determined that, even though the title to the property was fortuitously vested in the Bank, the second trust was incompletely constituted. The decision of Farwell J. turned on the fact that the case concerned the assignment (by way of voluntary settlement) of a future expected interest. Hence, the son had no more than a mere expectancy under the marriage settlement until the appointment was made. Hence, he purported to assign something to which he may or may not become entitled in the future. This is not a contingent interest and amounted merely to a mere expectancy. As there was no consideration given for the assignment, it could not be enforced in equity.[5] The beneficial interest was, thereby, retained by the son. This decision underscores the maxim that equity will not assist a volunteer. Perhaps significantly, *Re Brook's ST* was not cited before the court in *Re Ralli's WT*.

IMPERFECT CONSTITUTION AND CONTRACTUAL RIGHTS

A completely constituted trust is enforceable by all beneficiaries whether or not they have given consideration. Once created, the trust cannot be revoked by the settlor.[6] If, however, the trust is incompletely constituted all may not entirely be lost for the intended beneficiary. Where the beneficiary has provided consideration, it is open for that beneficiary to rely upon a contractual remedy. In this way an imperfect transfer might be treated as a valid contract to transfer. As will become clear, however, this potential will arise rarely and only in delimited circumstances.   **3.27**

First, there is a need to find consideration underpinning the contract. Unless consideration is provided, equity will not assist the volunteer.[7] Hence, and unless it falls within one of the general exceptions to the rule considered above, an incompletely constituted trust will fail.[8] The concept of consideration includes value as well as money and money's worth. A further type of consideration is "marriage consideration", which arises when a settlement is made before or in consideration of marriage, or is one made in fulfilment of an ante-nuptial agreement. This does not, therefore, include a trust set up by an existing husband and wife. Marriage consideration is recognised by equity,[9] but not by the common law. Accordingly, a marriage settlement can be enforced in equity by those who are within its scope, but not (unless it is contained in a covenant) at law. Those within the ambit of marriage consideration are husband, wife, children and,

---

[5] If there had been consideration found, Lloyds Bank could have enforced the contract to assign future property if and when it was received: *Re Ellenborough* [1903] 1 Ch. 697.
[6] *Paul v Paul* (1882) 20 Ch. D. 742.
[7] *Re Brook's ST* [1939] 1 Ch. 993.
[8] *Ellison v Ellison* (1802) 6 Ves. 656.
[9] *Pullan v Koe* [1913] 1 Ch. 9. It was described by Kay L.J. in *A.G. v Jacobs-Smith* [1895] 2 QB 341 at 354 as, "the most valuable consideration imaginable".

it is thought, grandchildren.[10] Those outside this range remain volunteers and the settlement is not enforceable by them.[11]

3.28   Secondly, when consideration is found, equity is able to specifically perform the contract and, thereby, constitute the trust (i.e. "equity looks on that as done that ought to be done").[12] The contract will also (except where marriage consideration is provided) be recognised at common law and, as an alternative to specific performance, damages made available to the beneficiary. Nevertheless, where the property is in existence and vested in the settlor, any contractual agreement will normally be dispensed with and, instead, the easiest option will be to make an immediate declaration of trust.

In relation to future property (i.e. property which someone merely hopes or expects to receive at a future date), the position is not straightforward. The following propositions emerge:

- as there is nothing yet in existence that can be assigned, there can be *no immediate assignment* of after acquired property. Consequently, the common law will never enforce the purported assignment of a mere expectancy;[13]

- if consideration has been provided, however, equity will deem the failed assignment to be a contract to assign as and when the property is received. The common law will intervene only when there is an express contract to assign;

- a declaration of trust relating to future property is void. When consideration is provided, however, both equity and the common law (unless it is marriage consideration that is given) will enforce *the contract to settle* such after acquired property.[14] This entails that, although a trust of future property is void, a contract to create a trust of future property is enforceable; and

- if the promise to settle future property is contained within a covenant,[15] equity remains powerless to intervene (as there is no consideration), but the common law may award damages for breach of covenant. Hence, no equitable remedies are available to the covenantee.[16] The problems associated with covenants to settle warrant further consideration.

ENFORCEMENT OF COVENANTS TO SETTLE

3.29   Enforcement difficulties can arise in circumstances where a settlor covenants to settle property on trust at a future date, but then changes his mind. There is no transfer at that stage so there is an incompletely constituted trust. All that exists is a mere

---

[10] *MacDonald v Scott* [1893] A.C. 642.
[11] *Re Plumtre's Marriage Settlement* [1910] 1 Ch. 609.
[12] *Pullan v Koe* [1913] 1 Ch. 9.
[13] *Holroyd v Marshall* (1892) 10 H.L.C. 191 (failed assignment of machinery that might in future be substituted for existing machinery).
[14] *Ellison v Ellison* (1802) 6 Ves. Jun. 656.
[15] A covenant is a promise in a deed which itself is a formal document that must be signed, witnessed and delivered: s.1 of the Law of Property (Miscellaneous Provisions) Act 1989.
[16] *Jeffreys v Jeffreys* (1841) Cr. & Ph. 135.

voluntary covenant which, being a gratuitous promise, is unenforceable in equity and outside the scope of equitable remedies such as specific performance. There is no consideration and, therefore, no contract between the parties. Nevertheless, at common law a party to a covenant can sue for breach in the normal way and recover full compensation.[17] This right to sue is classified as a "chose in action". It is a type of property that can be transferred or, as will be considered (see **3.32**), itself become the subject matter of a trust. The problem with covenants to settle is that it will usually be the trustee who is the other party to the covenant and not the intended beneficiary.

In this regard, the effect of the Contracts (Rights of Third Parties) Act 1999 should be noted as this offers third parties, for whose benefit a contract has been entered, to enforce the contract even though they were not a party to the particular contract. Hence, this represents a major incursion upon the common law rules relating to privity of contract. It entails that, if the Act applies, and although not a party to the covenant, a purported beneficiary will be allowed to sue the covenantor directly and to obtain compensation. Several observations should be made about the 1999 Act:

- the covenant /contract must have been entered into after May 11, 2000;

- the rule allowing third party enforceability gives way in the face of a contrary indication in the contract (i.e. it is possible to contract out of the 1999 Act);

- the covenant/contract must expressly cater for third party enforcement or purport to confer a benefit on the third party; and

- the Act covers covenants/contracts to settle both existing and after acquired property.

In cases where the 1999 Act has no application, the enforcement of the covenant is **3.30** not entirely freed from difficulty. As the intended trustee is the only party, it is only the trustee that may sue for breach. The beneficiary cannot sue because he is not a party to the covenant.[18] The trustee's ability to sue is, moreover, subject to major limitations.

First, as demonstrated in *Re Pryce*,[19] the intended trustee cannot be compelled by a beneficiary to sue the covenantor. Eve J. explained, "to do so would be to give the next of kin by indirect means what they cannot obtain by any direct procedure ... the trustees ought not to take any steps to compel the transfer or payment to them ...".[20] The court, therefore, refused to direct the trustee to sue. In *Re Kay's Settlement*, Simonds J. reformulated this proposition and directed the trustees not to sue under the covenant.[21] Accordingly, if the intended trustee applies to the court for directions as to what to do, the court must instruct him not to bring an action for breach of covenant. Elliott, however, contends that this reformulation is unsupported by previous authorities.[22]

[17] *Cannon v Hartley* [1949] Ch. 213.
[18] *Re D'Angibau* (1880) 15 Ch. D. 228.
[19] [1917] 1 Ch. 234; see also, *Re Cook's ST* [1965] Ch. 902.
[20] [1917] 1 Ch. 234 at 241.
[21] [1939] Ch. 329 at 342.
[22] D.W. Elliott (1960) 76 L.Q.R. 100; see also, J.A. Hornby (1962) 78 L.Q.R. 222, who argues that the trustees should not merely be able to sue for damages for breach of covenant, but are bound to do so at the request of the volunteers.

3.31   Secondly, there is some doubt as to whether the trustee, even if he managed to commence an action, could recover full compensation for the breach of covenant. It is to be appreciated that the covenantee cannot, as a general rule, claim damages on behalf of a non-covenanting party (e.g. a beneficiary).[23] It is sometimes thought, therefore, that only nominal compensation can be obtained because the covenantee/trustee has suffered no direct loss.[24] This is, however, a misconceived logic as the common law will not acknowledge the existence of a trust. If the trust limitation is ignored, therefore, the covenantee should surely be able to claim for the loss of the property.[25]

Thirdly, if the intended trustee brings an action for breach of covenant and recovers compensation, the issue that then arises is what is to happen to the money. The obvious question is, does the covenantee/trustee have to apply the damages for the benefit of the otherwise denied beneficiaries or can he keep the compensation for himself? Perhaps surprisingly, the answer to both limbs of the question appears to be in the negative. Equity cannot enforce the intended trust because the beneficiaries remain mere volunteers and the trust is plainly not constituted. Indeed, the trustee has received damages for the very reason that he did not receive the trust property. Similarly, the covenantee cannot keep the damages for himself because the covenantor's intention was to create a trust and not to bestow a benefit on the covenantee. The upshot of this reasoning is that the damages for breach of covenant would be held on resulting trust for the covenantor (i.e. the person who the trustee has just sued!).[26] It is in order to prevent this wasteful and ludicrous outcome that the court strains to prevent the covenantee from embarking on such pointless litigation.

A TRUST OF THE BENEFIT OF THE COVENANT?

3.32   An alternative scenario emerges where the covenantor declares that the covenant (i.e. the promise) is itself the subject matter of the trust. Accordingly, the trust is of the covenant and not, for example, the shares or the land which comprise the subject matter of the promise. In such cases, the beneficiaries will be able to enforce that trust because that trust will be perfectly constituted. They will have immediate equitable rights. This possibility was recognised in the case of *Fletcher v Fletcher*.[27] There Ellis Fletcher covenanted with his trustees to pay them £60,000 to hold for the benefit of his illegitimate son, Jacob. The money was never transferred to the trustees. Jacob succeeded in claiming the money by pleading that there was a completely constituted trust of the promise to pay the £60,000 and that he could enforce the trust of this promise. Accordingly, the subject matter of this trust was the covenant (i.e. the debt or chose in action) and not the money itself. This was a completely constituted trust of the benefit of the covenant and, as with any completed trust, was enforceable by a beneficiary even though he had not given consideration.

---

[23] *Woodar Investments Development Ltd v Wimpey Construction UK Ltd* [1980] 1 All E.R. 571 (HL).
[24] See *West v Houghton* (1879) 4 C.P.D. 197.
[25] *Re Cavendish-Browne's ST* [1916] W.N. 341; see Elliott, above, at p.113.
[26] See D. Hayton, *The Law of Trusts* at p.133.
[27] (1844) 4 Hare 67.

It is perfectly permissible to create a trust of the benefit of a contract or a covenant. As mentioned, a binding promise to transfer property is a form of intangible property. There are, however, two possible limitations on this type of trust. First, the intention to make a trust of the promise (and not a trust of what is promised) must be clearly demonstrated.[28] In modern times, something like the following would, it is suggested, be required: "the benefit of this covenant shall forthwith be held by my trustees upon trust". It is difficult to imagine a situation where the necessary intention could be inferred.

Secondly, it is debatable whether a trust of the covenant could cover after acquired property (e.g. shares acquired in the future). In *Re Cook's ST*,[29] the conclusion drawn was that it could not embrace such future property. Nevertheless, this runs contrary to traditional thinking. As shown above, a covenant to settle after acquired property can be enforced. In *Davenport v Bishopp*,[30] moreover, it was admitted that there could be a perfectly constituted trust of a covenant to settle future property.[31]   **3.33**

PROPRIETARY ESTOPPEL

The doctrine of estoppel can be employed as a mechanism to perfect an otherwise **3.34**   **3.34** imperfect gift or imperfectly constituted trust. In *Yeoman's Row Management Ltd v Cobbe*, Lord Scott acknowledged that, "An 'estoppel' bars the object of it from asserting some facts or facts, or, sometimes, something that is a mixture of fact and law, that stands in the way of some right claimed by the person entitled to the benefit of the estoppel. The estoppel becomes a 'proprietary' estoppel—a sub-species of a 'promissory' estoppel—if the right claimed is a proprietary right, usually a right to or over land but, in principle, equally available in relation to chattels or choses in action."[32] This reflects an expansive jurisdiction of the court to prevent the assertion of a party's strict legal rights in circumstances where it would be unconscionable for that party to rely on such rights.[33] The key characteristics of proprietary estoppel are assurance, reliance, and detriment and satisfaction.[34]

The assurance made by one party to the other might be express (e.g. "the house is yours") or might in more limited circumstances be implied from conduct (e.g. by making payments to the purchase price of the house).[35] In *Greasley v Cooke*,[36] for example, the assurance given to a maid was that she could live in the house as long as

---

[28] *Vandepitte v Preferred Accident Assurance Corp of New York* [1933] A.C. 70.
[29] [1965] Ch. 902.
[30] (1843) 2 Y & CCC 451.
[31] A sentiment echoed in *Lloyds v Harper* (1880) 16 Ch. D. 290.
[32] [2008] 1 W.L.R. 1752 at 1761. While accepting that estoppel is a flexible doctrine that is designed to prevent injustice, Lord Walker added at 1774, "it is not a sort of joker or wild card to be used whenever the Court disapproves of the conduct of a litigant who seems to have the law on his side. Flexible though it is, the doctrine must be formulated and applied in a disciplined and principled way."
[33] See *Taylor Fashions Ltd v Liverpool Victoria Trustees Co Ltd* [1982] Q.B. 133.
[34] As Mummery L.J. explained in *Uglow v Uglow* [2004] W.T.L.R. 1183 at [9], "The overriding concern of the equity to prevent unconscionable conduct permeates all the different elements of the doctrine of proprietary estoppel: assurances, reliance, detriment and satisfaction are all intertwined."
[35] *Thorner v Majors* [2009] UKHL 18.
[36] [1980] 3 All E.R. 710.

she wished, provided that she continued to care for the family without payment. She was able to establish an estoppel which, when satisfied, entitled her to occupy the house rent-free for as long as she wanted. It is also to be appreciated that, although estoppel cases usually feature some express assurance or representation, it is possible that an estoppel by acquiescence can arise. The general idea there is that if A, knowing that B is under a mistaken belief as to the acquisition of a right, allows B to act to his detriment on the basis of his erroneous belief an estoppel might arise as a result of A's acquiescence. The understanding between the parties must, however, be both certain and complete. As Lord Scott pointed out, "Proprietary estoppel requires, in my opinion, clarity as to what it is that the object of the estoppel is to be estopped from denying, or asserting, and clarity as to the interest in the property in question that that denial, or assertion, would otherwise defeat."[37] Although there must be the belief that the representation is binding an irrevocable, this does not mean that there must be an exact specification of what the estoppel claimant is to receive.[38] A general assurance may, therefore, suffice whereas a mere hope will not.[39]

3.35 The reliant conduct of B must, moreover, be referable to A's express or implied assurance. There has to be a causal link between the two.[40] The reliance must necessarily involve a change of position or disadvantage incurred by the claimant on account of the representation that was made.[41] Accordingly, in *Coombes v Smith*[42] the estoppel claimant failed in an attempt to show reliance because she had done nothing more than was to be expected of a woman who was leaving her husband to live with her lover. A more liberal approach was, however, adopted in *Wayling v Jones*.[43] There Mr Jones contributed his unpaid labour in reliance on a promise that he would inherit his cohabitee's business. Although he readily admitted that, had the promise never been made he would have remained in the relationship, an estoppel interest still arose. In these circumstances, an inference of reliance was drawn from the Mr Jones' contribution of 16 years labour. Once the inference is raised, the burden of proof shifts to the representor to show that the claimant's actions were not in reliance on the promise. The cohabitee's estate failed to rebut the presumption of reliance because it became clear that Mr Jones would have quit the relationship had the promise, once made, been subsequently withdrawn.

The reliance must be detrimental to B. Typical acts of reliance will involve expenditure of money or labour, but can also include acts of personal sacrifice.[44] The change of position in *Greasley v Cooke*, for example, was evident from her lengthy services in the family home and sacrificing her career opportunities. Although a change of position can be evidenced from a wide range of circumstances, the claimant's actions must be substantial. In *Brown & Root Technology v Sun Alliance & London Assurance Co*, the

---

[37] *Yeoman's Row Management Ltd v Cobbe* [2008] 1 W.L.R. 1752 at 1768.
[38] *Thorner v Majors* [2009] UKHL 18. Exact specification is, however, common: see *Grundy v Ottey* [2003] W.T.L.R. 1253 (a particular flat in Jamaica).
[39] See *Re Knowles* [2008] UKPC 30 where it was emphasised that the courts should not penalise those who, through kindness, simply allow other family members to live in property rent free. Nothing had been done to encourage any belief that the brother and sister in law could treat the property as their own.
[40] *Thorner v Curtis* [2008] EWCA Civ 732.
[41] *Gillett v Holt* [2001] Ch. 210.
[42] [1986] 1 W.L.R. 808.
[43] (1993) 69 P. & C.R. 170.
[44] In *Jones v Jones* [1977] 1 W.L.R. 438, the detriment comprised of the giving up of a job and home in order to live with the representor.

High Court held that a landlord changing his records and collecting rent from the putative assignee was insufficient for, as Judge Paul Baker Q.C. explained, "The differences were too trivial to satisfy the test of reliance".[45]

Once an estoppel is invoked, it is for the court, in the exercise of a largely unfettered **3.36** discretion, to decide how best it is to be satisfied. The claimant cannot, however, recover more than that which was assured. The court will examine matters in the round (i.e. assess the value of the representation, evaluate the extent of the detriment incurred, factor in any benefits already obtained and consider the conduct of the parties and the interests of others) and then determine what remedy (if any) will be awarded. In some cases, the court may order the donor to complete the gift or transfer (i.e. to perform the representation). This is as occurred in *Pascoe v Turner*[46] where a couple cohabited in a house owned by one partner. He encouraged the other to spend her savings and improve the house in the belief that she would then become the owner. The relationship broke down and he wanted her out of the property. Even though there was no binding contract or express trust declared, the court compelled him to transfer the house to his partner. Similarly, in *Dillwyn v Llewelyn*[47] a father assured his son that certain land now belonged to the son. The father did not, however, transfer the land to his son. The son built a house on the land, but later the validity of the gift was challenged. The son was able to invoke an estoppel and compel the gift to be perfected. The son acquired a right to call on his father's estate to perform the bargain and complete the otherwise imperfect gift. Again, in *Crabb v Arun District Council*[48] the Council led Mr Crabb to believe that he could have a right of way over the Council's land. In reliance, Mr Crabb allowed his land to become land-locked. The Council was estopped from denying the right of way. In the same way as an imperfect donation can be perfected by estoppel, so might an otherwise incomplete transfer of legal title to a trustee.

In other cases the courts will not give effect to the claimant's expectation and will find alternative remedies more appropriate. This represents the modern view which incorporates a notion of proportionality. As Norris J. observed in *Sutcliffe v Lloyd*, "The task is to identify the minimum equity to do justice (the qualification 'minimum' not requiring the court to be constitutionally parsimonious, but simply being an express recognition of the need to do justice not only to the claimant but also to the defendant)."[49] Hence, the court must consider a whole range of events embracing expectations, reliance and unconscionableness. In *Jennings v Rice*,[50] for example, the representation was that the claimant would be left a property worth £420,000 in the representor's will. The property was, however, left to someone else. The claimant invoked an estoppel on the basis that, on the strength of this assurance, he had resided with the deceased and had cared for her during her lifetime. The court held that the extent of his detriment warranted a cash payment of £200,000. It was pointed out by Robert Walker L.J. that a disproportionate remedy did not avoid an unconscionable result. He explained, "if the claimant's expectations are uncertain, or extravagant, or

---

[45] [1996] Ch. 51 at 68.
[46] [1979] 1 W.L.R. 431.
[47] (1862) 4 De. G.F. & J. 517.
[48] [1976] Ch 179. In *Manton Securities Ltd v Nazam* [2008] EWCA Civ 805, Mr Nazam claimed that his landlord had led him to expect that he would be granted a new 21-year lease if he carried out expenditure of money in the repair and improvement of the premises. The landlord was estopped from denying the new lease.
[49] [2008] EWHC 1329 (Ch) at [4].
[50] [2003] 1 P. & C.R. 8.

out of all proportion to the detriment … the court can and should recognize that the claimant's equity should be satisfied in another (and generally more limited) way."[51] In *Sledmore v Dalby*,[52] Mr and Mrs Sledmore encouraged their son-in-law to carry out repair works on a cottage that they owned. In return, he was assured that the property would be left by will to him and his wife (Mr and Mrs Sledmore's daughter). The daughter, however, predeceased her parents. Eventually Mrs Sledmore sought possession of the cottage and the son-in-law advanced an estoppel claim. Although it was clear that there had been an expectation, coupled with detrimental reliance, the son-in-law was awarded nothing. The principal reason was that he had already lived in the property rent-free for over 15 years and that the benefit received satisfied the equity he asserted. In that case, therefore, the remedy fell well below that expected by the claimant. More recently, in *McGuane v Welch*[53] the representation was that Mr Welch would acquire the Mr McGuane's flat. The flat was purchased at a discounted price under the Right to Buy scheme contained in the Housing Act 1985. Mr Welch contributed to the mortgage repayments and expended around £10,000 on the modernization of the property. Although an estoppel was successfully raised by Mr Welch, minimum equity required that he obtain a charge on the lease so that he could be reimbursed for his past expenditure.

GUIDE TO FURTHER READING

D.W. Elliott, "The Power of Trustees to Enforce Covenants in Favour of Volunteers" (1960) 76 L.Q.R. 100.

M. Halliwell, "Perfecting Imperfect Gifts and Trusts: Have We Reached the End of the Chancellor's Foot?" [2003] Conv. 192.

J.A. Hornby, "Covenants in Favour of Volunteers" (1962) 78 L.Q.R. 228.

J. Jaconelli, "Problems in the rule of *Strong v Bird*" [2006] Conv. 432.

G. Kodilinye, "A Fresh Look at the Rule in *Strong v Bird*" [1982] Conv. 14.

---

[51] [2003] 1 P. & C.R. 8 at 22.
[52] (1996) 72 P. & C.R. 196.
[53] [2008] EWCA Civ 785.

Chapter 4

Formalities and the Perpetuity Rules

The general rule is that, once the three certainties are present and legal title to the trust   **4.01**
property is vested in the trustee, there is nothing more demanded of the settlor. By way
of exceptions to this rule, however, Parliament has decreed that certain types of disposition require additional formalities before they can become effective. The most usual
insistence is that the transaction either be in writing or, at the least, be evidenced (i.e.
recorded) in writing and that such writing be signed. All testamentary dispositions (i.e.
dispositions by will) are regulated by s.9 of the Wills Act 1837[1] whereas inter vivos
trusts (i.e. lifetime trusts) are governed by s.53 of the Law of Property Act 1925. These
statutory formalities as they apply to lifetime trusts will be considered in detail. The
latter part of the chapter, however, will serve as an introduction to the arid and complex
perpetuity rules relating to vesting, inalienability and accumulation of income.

The Function of Formalities

There are three broad and interconnected functions which are said to underlie the   **4.02**
requirement for added formalities:[2]

- The evidentiary function. The clearest justification for legal formality is to
  provide documentary evidence of the existence and terms of the transaction. As
  such, it offers some protection against fraud, undue influence and other types of
  wrongdoing. Formalities also provide a provable record of transactions and, in
  particular, lead a paper trail to the individual who currently holds the equitable
  interest under the trust. This is valuable because equitable interests are intangible (i.e. without physical form) and, thereby, difficult to keep track of.

---

[1] Testamentary trusts are considered in Ch.5.
[2] See generally, L.L. Fuller, "Consideration and Form" (1941) 41 *Colom. L. Rev.* 799.

Documentation also helps to establish the obligations of the trustee/executor so that the risk of an inadvertent breach of trust is minimised.

● The cautionary function. This operates to focus the mind of the settlor/testator and to offer a "cooling off" period until the formalities have been attended to. As property rights are often valuable rights, they are not expected to be created or disposed of casually, secretly or informally.

● The channelling function. The presence of authenticated writing relieves the court of the need to enquire whether a legal transaction was intended and, if so, to explore its nature. Fuller explains, "form offers a legal framework into which the party may fit his actions, or, to change the figure, it offers channels for the legally effective expression of intention".[3] This provides administrative relief in that the court has some document to look at in order to divine the settlor/testator's true intentions. In this way, the court does not have to rely solely upon the (often unreliable) testimony and (often incomplete) recollections of witnesses and, thereby, this may avoid costly controversy.

The disadvantage of formalities

4.03   The major problem with formalities is that, if they are not complied with, the genuine intentions of a settlor can be frustrated. For example, the settlor may in the clearest terms declare a trust of land, but fail to adhere to the necessary formalities as to providing written evidence of the terms of the trust. In this situation, the general rule is that the trust will then be unenforceable and the informal disposition rendered of no effect. For example, this may mean that land intended for Fred will remain in the settlor's estate and, on the settlor's death, pass by will or on intestacy to Adrienne as next of kin or residual legatee. Hence, it may generate an unintended outcome that runs contrary both to the wishes of the settlor and, in our example, the expectations of Fred. Gulliver & Tilson describe this as, "enthroning formality over frustrated intent".[4] Nevertheless, it is for the legislature to draw a balance between these conflicting interests and for the judiciary to ensure that the balance is maintained. As Gardner puts it:

> "Deciding whether to require formality involves assessing the advantages and disadvantages either way, and comparing them, to see where the greater benefit lies. So, for example, in having the rule that any attempt to dispose of property on death other than by using the ordained formalities is a nullity, the law takes it that the balance lies in favour of such insistence; that the potential ineffectiveness of attempted informal dispositions is an acceptable price to pay for the advantages of minimising uncertainty".[5]

[3] L.L. Fuller, "Consideration and Form" (1941) 41 *Colom. L. Rev.* 799 at p.801.
[4] A.G. Gulliver & C.J. Tilson, "Classification of Gratuitous Transfers" (1941) 51 Yale L. J. 1 at p.3.
[5] S. Gardner, *An Introduction to the Law of Trusts*, (2nd edn, Oxford, Oxford University Press, 2003) at p.82.

LIFETIME TRUSTS OF LAND

Inter vivos trusts of land are subject to the additional formalities prescribed in   **4.04**
s.53(1)(b) of the Law of Property Act 1925. This provides that, "a declaration of trust
respecting any land or any interest therein must be manifested and proved by some
writing signed by some person who is able to declare such a trust or by his will". These
extra requirements are imposed because of both the value of land and the highly
technical rules that attend its transfer. The settlor is saved, as Hayton puts it, "from the
perils of oral evidence being (mis)used to deprive him of his land".[6] Hence, land is
traditionally treated differently to other types of property. In contrast, no additional
formalities are necessary to create an inter vivos trust of personalty.[7] Gardner argues
that the singling out of trusts of land in this way is justifiable:

> "Trusts of land are particularly likely to be made formally in practice. People
> making dispositions of land are especially likely to perceive that they are doing
> something important, and will almost certainly use professional advisers, who will
> always want to put important matters down on paper. So, as with wills, the danger
> of a requirement of formality frustrating settlors' intentions is slight, allowing the
> balance of advantage to come down in favour of its imposition".[8]

Section 53(1)(b) applies to a declaration of a trust of land regardless of whether the
title is freehold or leasehold and whether the land is registered or unregistered. The
section will catch a trust of land even if the land is situated outside the jurisdiction of
the domestic courts. For these purposes, land is widely defined as embracing mines,
minerals, buildings and incorporeal hereditaments (e.g. easements and profits).[9] It is to
be appreciated, however, that s.53(1)(b) does not require that the trust of land be
created in writing. Instead, it demands that such trusts merely be evidenced in writing.
This requires a documentary memorandum of the existence of the trust, the trust
property and the beneficiaries of the trust.[10]

The consequence of a failure to adhere to s.53(1)(b) is that, although the trust of land   **4.05**
remains valid, the trust is rendered unenforceable by the beneficiary. This distinction
can assume significance where the timing of the creation of the trust is important. For
example, in *Gardner v Rowe*[11] the settlor orally declared certain trusts of land. Subsequently, he became bankrupt and only then did he decide to commit the terms of the
trust to writing. Although the creditors laid claim to the trust property, the court held
that the trusts had been validly created and, due to the presence of writing, were now
enforceable by the beneficiaries. If, of course, the settlor had declined to provide signed

---

[6] D.J. Hayton, *The Law of Trusts* at p.130.
[7] See *Paul v Constance* [1977] 1 All E.R. 195. As Parker and Mellows observe at p.109, "It is indeed rather
surprising that a declaration of trust requires the appropriate writing even if it relates to as little as a square
foot of land while a declaration of trust of millions of pounds worth of cash or investments does not; however,
that is what the statutory provisions provide".
[8] S. Gardner *An Introduction to the Law of Trusts* (2003) at pp.84–85.
[9] Section 205(1)(ix) of the Law of Property Act 1925.
[10] *Smith v Matthews* (1891) 3 De. G.F. & J. 139.
[11] (1828) 5 Russ 258 which was decided in relation to s.7 of the Statute of Frauds 1677 (the precursor of
s.53(1)(b)).

documentary evidence of the trust then the creditors could have claimed the land. As shown in Ch.3, however, this general rule might give way where the beneficiary can establish, for example, an estoppel interest (see **3.34**) or, following the dubious reasoning in *Pennington v Waine*,[12] demonstrate that it would be unconscionable for the settlor to renege on the arrangement (see **3.13**).

There must be writing and this includes typing, printing, lithography, photography and other modes of representing or reproducing words in a visible form.[13] This definition is wide enough to embrace the modern manifestations of writing found in telex, fax and email. The writing may well come into existence contemporaneously with the declaration of the trust. This is not, however, a necessary requirement. The documentary evidence can be created either before or, as demonstrated in *Gardner v Rowe*, after the trust has been declared. Nevertheless, and regardless of when it is brought into being, the writing must recite all the terms of the trust. As there is no prescribed form for this writing to adopt, however, it can be pieced together from more than one document.[14] It may, for example, take the form of correspondence, documents used in court proceedings or a will (valid or otherwise). Indeed, although unlikely, the terms of the trust could even be scrawled on the back of a cigarette packet or beer mat.

4.06   The writing must, moreover, be "signed". Traditionally, the courts have adopted a liberal approach as to what amounts to a signature,[15] but in recent years there has been a tightening up of this requirement. The old cases are, therefore, no sure guide to future decisions.[16] Nevertheless, there remain certain conditions that need to be satisfied:

- there must be some physical manifestation on the document that is intended to identify the declarant. This will entail the presence of the declarant's mark whether represented by a cross, full signature or initials. The mark can be handwritten, typed, made by a rubber stamp or when the law permits, be an electronic signature;

- the declarant's cipher may be placed anywhere on the document provided that it is designed to authenticate and to adopt the document. In *First Post Homes Ltd v Johnson*, for example, the typed insertion of a party's name at the top of a letter as addressee was woefully insufficient to amount to a signature. In *Simpson v Simpson*,[17] the writing relied upon to evidence an oral trust was signed by a person with severe dyslexia. It was argued before the High Court that, because of this disability, he could not be taken to have agreed the contents of the documents. The court was unimpressed and concluded that the dyslexic party would have had the documents explained to him at the time of his signature. In order to escape the effect of signing the document, he would have to show that the content was untrue and that he was improperly persuaded to add his signature. Hence, even though the signatory cannot read or

---

[12] [2002] 4 All E.R. 215.
[13] Interpretation Act 1978, Sch.1.
[14] See *Re Danish Bacon Company Staff Pensions Fund Trusts* [1971] 1 W.L.R. 248.
[15] See further, C.T. Emery, "Statute of Frauds: The Authenticated Signature Fiction—An Illogical Distinction" (1975) 39 Conv. 336.
[16] See *First Post Homes Ltd v Johnson* [1995] 4 All E.R. 355, where Balcombe L.J. admitted (at 363) that, "there was every reason for consigning the old law to the limbo where it clearly belongs".
[17] [2005] EWHC 2098 (Ch).

understand the documents without assistance, they remain sufficient evidence of the oral trust; and

- the signature of the person able to declare the trust is necessary. This person will usually be the settlor, but it has been argued that, if legal title to the property has already been transferred, it is the owner of the equitable interest who must sign and not the original settlor.[18] If the trustee were given the mandate to declare new trusts, in that scenario it would appear that the trustee's signature would be required. There is no express mention made in s.53(1)(b) of the ability of an agent to sign the document. This limitation exists, presumably, because the written evidence of a trust of land can emerge informally and unintentionally and, hence, requires the declarant's direct involvement.

Section 53(2): An exception

As Gray and Gray comment, "However, compelling the policy motivation behind the statutory requirement of written evidence of an express trust of land, there are nevertheless certain circumstances where even this potent rationale is displaced by concerns ranking higher in the scale of values which animate equitable jurisdiction".[19] Such an exception is expressly catered for in s.53(2) which states that the formalities prescribed elsewhere in s.53 as to writing apply only to express trusts and do not extend to resulting, implied[20] or constructive trusts. The latter types of trust are usually informal and may never have been contemplated by the parties. Such implied trusts exist to achieve fairness and to prevent unconscionable outcomes. Hence, to require formalities for the creation of such trusts would undermine the reason for their very existence. Consequently, it is possible for what is originally an unenforceable express trust of land to adopt the guise of an enforceable resulting or constructive trust on the same terms.[21]

4.07

This possibility was demonstrated in *Hodgson v Marks*[22] where a widow was influenced by her lodger to transfer the title to her house into his name on the basis that this would prevent his eviction following her death. The lodger later sold the house to a third party. The Court of Appeal decided that the lodger had held the house on *resulting* trust for the widow and, as this implied trust fell outside s.53(1)(b), it was enforceable against the third party. Sometimes the court will imply a *constructive* trust from the facts in order to take an otherwise unenforceable transaction outside the ambit of the formalities. In *Bannister v Bannister*,[23] two cottages were conveyed to the trustee on the basis that the beneficiary would be allowed to live in one of them for the rest of her life. The court would not allow the trustee to rely upon an absence of writing in these circumstances and invoked a constructive trust.

---

[18] T. Youdan (1984) 43 C.L.J. 306.
[19] *Elements of Land Law* at p.830.
[20] It is, however, unclear whether there is a class of "implied trust" that is totally distinct from either a resulting or a constructive trust.
[21] See *Simpson v Simpson* [2005] EWHC 2098 (Ch).
[22] [1971] Ch. 892.
[23] [1948] 2 All E.R. 133.

4.08   A similar outcome was achieved in *Rouchefoucald v Bousted*[24] which also concerned an oral trust of land that was, at face value, unenforceable. The claimant had, however, relied detrimentally on the strength of this otherwise enforceable bargain. The court concluded that not to enforce the claimant's rights would amount to a fraud. As Lindley L.J. explained, "it is a fraud on the part of the person to whom land is conveyed as trustee, and who knows that it was so conveyed, to deny the trust and claim the land himself".[25] Accordingly, as the maxim of equity is that "statute cannot be used as an instrument of fraud" the need for formality was, thereby, side-stepped.[26] The Court of Appeal, however, spoke in terms of the express trust remaining valid because of the maxim and did not contemplate any new constructive trust arising. Nevertheless, the better view is that the court will, in such cases, be enforcing a constructive trust and not the original express trust.[27] At the least, this disregard of s.53 is expressly condoned in the 1925 Act itself. As whichever route is adopted the outcome remains the same, it appears that nothing much turns upon the correctness of this classification.[28]

A major area for the operation of resulting or constructive trusts concerns informal arrangements relating to the family home. This is discussed in detail in Ch.11. For example, where the title to, say, a house is registered in the name of one partner only, but the other has contributed 20 per cent towards the purchase price, traditionally a resulting trust would arise without any need for formality. The beneficial interest under this resulting trust will be throughout fixed at 20 per cent of the value of the property and that, of course, is itself likely to fluctuate over future years. If the legal owner later allows the other, say, to finance repairs or to give up work to look after their children, a constructive trust may then arise which will subsume the original resulting trust. The attraction of this alternative mechanism is that the assessment of entitlement is not driven solely by monetary contributions and can reflect what the court deems to be fair and reasonable.[29]

DEALING WITH AN EXISTING TRUST INTEREST

4.09   Section 53(1)(c) of the Law of Property Act 1925 provides that "a disposition of an equitable interest or trust subsisting at the time of the disposition, must be in writing signed by the person disposing of the same or by his agent thereunto lawfully authorised in writing or by will". Several initial observations about this provision may be made:

- a failure to comply with s.53(1)(c) makes the transfer entirely void;

---

[24] [1897] 1 Ch. 197.
[25] [1897] 1 Ch. 197 at 206. Note that these cases concern a constructive trust imposed on the transferee in favour of the transferor because of the terms on which the property was acquired.
[26] See also, *Lyus v Prowsa Developments* [1982] 1 W.L.R. 1044, where land was sold on the express, oral understanding that it would be subject to the rights of a third party. The third party acquired enforceable rights under a constructive trust because it would otherwise entail that statute (here the Land Registration Act 1925) was being employed as an engine of fraud.
[27] See Millett L.J. in *Banner Homes Group Plc v Luff Developments Ltd* [2000] 2 W.L.R. 772 at 780.
[28] See *Neale v Willis* (1968) 19 P. & C.R. 836; *Simpson v Simpson* [2005] EWHC 2098 (Ch).
[29] See *Oxley v Hiscock* (2004) 3 All E.R. 703; *Curley v Parkes* [2004] EWCA Civ. 1515.

- section 53(1)(c) applies to all property, that is, personal property as well as land;

- the formalities do not apply to resulting, implied or constructive trusts: s.53(2) (see **4.07**). In *Neville v Wilson*,[30] a dispute arose between the shareholders of a small company as to a series of informal agreements and whether two directors had effectively disposed of their equitable interest in shares of a parent company. Each agreement was oral and the issue, of course, became whether the agreements were rendered ineffectual by virtue of s.53(1)(c). It was contended that the effect of each individual agreement was to constitute the two directors as constructive trustees for the other shareholders so that the writing requirement was dispensed with by virtue of s.53(2) (which exempts such implied trusts from the formal requirements). Nourse L.J. could see no reason why s.53(2) should not extend to these constructive trusts;[31]

- for the purposes of writing, two documents can be read together in order to satisfy s.53(1)(c). By way of illustration, in *Re Danish Bacon Co Ltd Staff Pension Fund Trust*[32] an employee nominated his wife to receive benefits under a pension scheme should he die before he was entitled. He signed the approved form. Later the employee changed the identity of the nominated beneficiary by amending the original form and sending an explanatory letter to the trustee of the pension fund. The issue arose as to whether this was a valid nomination. It was held that the alteration was effective. Although doubtful as to whether the nomination was an assignment of a subsisting equitable interest within s.53(1)(c), Megarry J. held that, even if it was, the two documents (i.e. the form and the letter) were sufficiently interconnected that they could together constitute the necessary writing;

- where an assignee of an equitable interest is to hold in a fiduciary capacity, there is no need for the writing to contain all the terms of the trust. In *Re Tyler*,[33] Miss Tyler appointed King and Green the executors under her will. Shortly afterwards, she gave £1,500 to King. As she did not intend King to have beneficial ownership of the money, and had given no directions as to its application, this gave rise to a resulting trust in her favour. Subsequently, she wrote to King instructing him to use the money for Green as she had previously directed. Although the letter did not contain every detail of the assignment, the letter amounted to a valid disposition of her equitable interest; and

- in contrast with s.53(1)(b), the signature of an agent will suffice for the purposes of s.53(1)(c). This reflects the fact that such written assignments are unlikely to occur inadvertently.

---

[30] [1997] Ch. 144.
[31] See also *Singh v Anand* [2007] EWHC 3346 (Ch).
[32] [1971] 1 All E.R. 486.
[33] [1967] 1 W.L.R. 1269.

Disposition of a subsisting equitable interest?

4.10   It is crucial to understand that s.53(1)(c) applies only after a trust has been created. It has no relevance whatsoever to the original creation of the trust under which the equitable interest arises. This entails that, if both legal and equitable titles are vested in the same person, the law does not regard the equitable title as having an existence distinct from the legal title.[34] Put in other terms, s.53(1)(c) can apply only where the legal and equitable interests in the property are already divorced.[35] Accordingly, the formalities are designed to bite on the transfer of an equitable interest by a beneficiary to someone else or the direction of beneficiary to the trustee to hold the trust property on behalf of another.

It is the disposition (i.e. the transfer itself) of the equitable interest that has to be in documentary form. Hence, it is not enough that the transfer is merely evidenced in writing. Similarly, there can be no scope for any subsequent written ratification of the disposition. Unfortunately, it is not always clear whether a transaction amounts to the declaration of trust (outside s.53(1)(c)) or is, instead, the disposition of an equitable interest (within s.53(1)(c)). The cases, moreover, appear inconsistent and illogical. As Nolan put it, "sadly, common-sense and s.53(1)(c) share only a nodding acquaintance."[36] Indeed, Green criticises the judiciary for confining their attention to adjudicating the facts as appear before them and this entails that judges, "often fail to perceive the wider implications of their particular determinations".[37] Many of the decisions concern tax avoidance cases and involve the Inland Revenue as a major player in the litigation. As dispositions have to be in writing and writing attracts stamp duty, the Inland Revenue tends to argue for a disposition rather than a declaration. This is because stamp duty is charged on an instrument rather than on the transaction itself. In *Bishop Square Ltd v IRC*,[38] for example, the Inland Revenue sought stamp duty of £372,230 whereas the taxpayer claimed that the nominal duty only was payable (a mere 50 pence). The outcome (which favoured the Inland Revenue) turned upon an oral transfer being invalid under s.53(1)(c). Similarly, in the *Vandervell* cases (see below), it was in the interest of the Inland Revenue to establish that an oral disposition had been ineffective due to an absence of writing.

4.11   Section 53(1)(c) does not apply to the disclaimer of an equitable interest by a beneficiary. This is demonstrated in *Re Paradise Motor Co Ltd*[39] where a stepfather gave an equitable interest in certain shares to his stepson. When the stepson discovered this, he made it clear he did not want them. Subsequently, the stepson changed his mind and argued that his disclaimer was ineffective because it was not in writing to comply with s.53(1)(c). The court rejected this reasoning and held that the disclaimer had been effective and stripped him of any rights he might otherwise have had in relation to the shares. It also appears from the views expressed by Megarry J. in *Re Danish Bacon Company Staff Pension Fund* (see **4.09**) that the nomination of a person to receive

---

[34] See *Commissioner of Stamp Duties (Queensland) v Livingstone* [1965] A.C. 694 (PC).
[35] See *Kinane v Mackie-Conteh* [2005] EWCA Civ. 45, where Arden and Neuberger L.JJ. held that s.53(1)(c) did not apply when the legal and equitable estates had not been divided prior to the disposition.
[36] R.C. Nolan, "*Vandervell v IRC*: A Case of Overreaching" [2002] C.L.J. 169 at p.176.
[37] B. Green (1984) 47 M.L.R. 385 at p.385.
[38] (1999) 78 P. & C.R. 169.
[39] [1968] 1 W.L.R. 1125.

payment under a pension scheme is not captured by s.53(1)(c). It is unlikely that the nomination could be regarded as a disposition because it is revocable and transfers nothing at the time it is made. Similarly, in *Gold v Hill*[40] the holder of the life policy orally directed the nominated beneficiary of the policy that, in the event of the pol-icyholder's death, the nominated beneficiary should hold the policy for the benefit of the deceased's family. As nothing was transferred until the death of the policyholder, this was not regarded as an assignment of the existing equitable interest.

In circumstances where an equitable owner declares a sub-trust of his own entire equitable interest, it appears that the application of s.53(1)(c) turns upon whether the equitable owner has active duties to perform (e.g. the exercise of discretion on the creation of a discretionary sub-trust). If there are active duties to perform, or only part of the equitable interest is the subject of the sub-trust, it should be treated as a valid declaration and outside the reach of the formalities.[41] It is to be regarded as a new trust and not merely the transfer of an existing equitable interest. If, however, there are no active duties to perform (i.e. it is a passive or bare sub-trust), the beneficiary will drop from the picture and be regarded as merely having assigned his equitable interest.[42] Hence, the disposition will be invalid unless it satisfies the requirements of s.53(1)(c). Not every one, however, is happy with this line of reasoning. Green describes it has involving a, "somewhat inelegant distinction" and argues that it is a distinction not truly justified on the authorities.[43] Nevertheless, it still reflects the conventional wisdom.

SECTION 53(1)(C): FOUR SEMINAL CASES

Case 1: Grey v IRC

In *Grey v IRC*,[44] the issue was whether a direction by a settlor to his existing trustees to hold shares on trust for a third party fell within s.53(1)(c). In this case, Mr Hunter created six settlements in favour of his grandchildren. Some years later, he transferred legal title in 18,000 shares in Sun Engraving Co Ltd to his trustees (one of whom was Mr Grey) to hold on an express, bare trust for himself. Shortly afterwards, Mr Hunter orally and irrevocably directed his trustees to hold those shares on trust in six parcels for new beneficiaries (his grandchildren). The same trustees were the trustees of the grandchildren's pre-existing settlements. Mr Hunter attempted to do everything orally so as to escape liability to ad valorem stamp duty. Some five weeks later, the trustees executed six documents confirming that they now held the shares on trust for the grandchildren. There was no doubting that the new trusts were valid. The real issue, however, was when the equitable interest in the shares passed: was it on the oral direction or subsequently on the trustees' written confirmation?

The House of Lords had to consider what amounted to a "disposition" for the

4.12

[40] (1998) *The Times*, August 24.
[41] *Grainge v Wilberforce* (1889) 5 T.L.R. 436.
[42] See *Re Lashmar* [1891] 1 Ch. 258.
[43] (1984) 47 M.L.R. 385 at p.397.
[44] [1960] A.C. 1.

purposes of s.53(1)(c). The initial stumbling block concerned the forerunner of this provision as contained in s.9 of the Statute of Frauds 1677. It was argued by the trustees that the Law of Property Act 1925 was merely a consolidating Act and, as such, did not amend the earlier legislation. As s.9 dealt only with "grants and assignments", it was contended that s.53(1)(c) must be similarly limited in scope. It followed that, as the creation of a trust was outside s.9,[45] the present transaction must fall outside s.53(1)(c) because it was neither a grant nor an assignment and was, instead, the declaration of an entirely new trust. This argument was destined to fail.

Although only by way of obiter, Lord Radcliffe was of the opinion that, even if the restricted meaning was adopted, Mr Hunter's direction would still amount to an assignment, "Something had to happen to that equitable interest in order to displace it in favour of the new interests created by the direction: and it would be at any rate logical to treat the direction as being an assignment of the subsisting interest ...".[46]

4.13   Both Viscount Simonds and Lord Radcliffe noted that there were substantial differences in language and subject matter between the two statutory provisions and that there had been interceding legislation in the form of s.3 of the Law of Property (Amendment) Act 1924. Lord Radcliffe emphasised that the 1924 Act had made alterations to the Statute of Frauds and it was these amended provisions that were consolidated in the 1925 Act. These changes were too overt to be ignored and there was no direct link between the two provisions. Lord Radcliffe concluded that the meaning of "disposition" was not to be limited or controlled by the old Act, "It is impossible to regard s.53 ... as a consolidating enactment in this sense ...".[47]

With that argument out of the way, Viscount Simonds felt that the term "disposition" had to be given its ordinary meaning and concluded that, "It cannot, I think, be denied that the direction given by Mr Hunter, whereby the beneficial interest in the shares theretofore vested in him became vested in another or others, is a disposition".[48] Similarly, Lord Radcliffe held no doubts that this was a disposition for the purposes of s.53(1)(c), "Whether we describe what happened in technical or in more general terms the full equitable interest in the 18,000 shares concerned, which at the time was his, was (subject to any statutory invalidity) diverted by his direction from his ownership into the beneficial ownership of the various equitable owners, present and future, entitled under his six existing settlements".[49] Accordingly, the nomination of the new beneficiaries was a disposition of Mr Hunter's equitable interest for the purposes of s.53(1)(c). Mr Hunter had held a subsisting equitable interest at the outset and now claimed to no longer hold such an interest. Commonsense dictated, therefore, that there had been a purported disposition of that interest. As the oral direction could not achieve this transfer, the documents executed by the trustees operated to effect the disposition. Stamp duty was, therefore, payable on those documents.

---

[45] *M'Fadden v Jenkyns* (1842) 1 Hare 458.
[46] [1960] A.C. 1 at 16.
[47] [1960] A.C. 1 at 17.
[48] [1960] A.C. 1 at 12, 13.
[49] [1960] A.C. 1 at 15.

Case 2: Oughtred v IRC

In *Oughtred v IRC*,[50] the House of Lords had to consider whether a formal transfer of   **4.14**
shares following an oral agreement amounted to an assignment for the purposes of
s.53(1)(c). The trustees held 200,000 shares in William Jackson & Son Ltd (a private
company) for the benefit of Mrs Oughtred for life with remainder to her son, Peter.
Between mother and son, they owned the whole equitable interest in those shares. In
return for 72,700 of his mother's own shares in the same company, Peter made an oral
contract to transfer his interest in remainder to her. Her life interest in those shares
would, thereby, become an absolute interest. Following the oral agreement, the mother
transferred her shares to Peter. On the same day two further documents were executed.
First, a deed of release between the trustees, the mother and Peter was executed which
recited that the shares were now to be held on trust absolutely for the mother. Secondly,
and in order to ensure that she was the registered owner of them, the shares were
transferred to the mother by deed made between her and the trustees.

The Inland Revenue claimed ad valorem duty of £663 on the document of transfer,
claiming that it was the document that effectively transferred Peter's reversionary
interest in the 200,000 shares. The mother contended that she fell outside the catchment
of s.53(1)(c) because a contract of this sort was not a disposition of an equitable
interest. It was, she argued, not a complete disposition of Peter's reversionary interest
and was instead the creation of a new equitable interest. In addition, and by virtue of
the doctrine of conversion that operates on a specifically enforceable contract, she
argued that a constructive sub-trust had arisen under which the equitable interest had
already passed to her.[51] This reflects the maxim that "equity looks on that as done that
which ought to be done".[52] Accordingly, the mother claimed that, following the oral
contract, the son was no longer the beneficial owner of the shares. All that the later
transfer conveyed was the legal title to the shares. Her case was, therefore, that the
disposition of the equitable interest fell within the exception in s.53(2) because of the
constructive sub-trust attendant to the contract.

The majority of the House of Lords rejected the mother's appeal. Lord Denning took   **4.15**
the view that, "stripped of all trimmings" the case was simple.[53] He had no doubt that
this was a transfer such as to attract stamp duty. Although it was the trustees and not
Peter who transferred the shares to the mother, "It is clear to me that, by the transfer so
made by his authority, she acquired his reversionary interest as effectively as if he had
conveyed it directly to her. And that is quite enough to attract stamp duty ... the
instrument is the means by which the parties choose to implement the bargain they have
made".[54] The release dealt with the equitable interest and the transfer dealt with the
legal title to the shares. It did not matter that the transaction was designed to wind up
the existence of the trust.

As to the constructive trust argument, Lord Denning said little, but did comment

---

[50] [1960] A.C. 206; see also the similar case of *Bishop Square Ltd v Commissioners of Inland Revenue* (1999) 78
P. & C.R. 169.
[51] See *Lysaght v Edwards* (1876) 2 Ch. D. 499 (the entry into a contract to sell land passing an equitable
interest from vendor to purchaser).
[52] See *Walsh v Lonsdale* (1882) 21 Ch. D. 9.
[53] [1960] A.C. 206 at 232.
[54] [1960] A.C. 206 at 233.

that, "I do not think that the oral agreement was effective to transfer Peter's reversionary interest to his mother ... s.53(1)(c) of the Law of Property Act 1925, clearly made writing necessary to effect a transfer: and s.53(2) does not do away with that necessity".[55] This view was shared also by Lord Cohen. Lord Radcliffe, however, thought that s.53(2) did apply and Lords Keith and Jenkins expressed no view either way. This lack of a majority view enabled Nourse L.J. in *Neville v Wilson*[56] to depart from Lord Denning's view and to apply the statutory exemption to an equitable interest arising under specifically enforceable contract. He felt that to deny the application of s.53(2) would be to restrict the effect of the general words employed therein without justification and to signal problems for the future.[57]

4.16   Lord Jenkins (with whom Lord Keith agreed) took the view that, even if the oral contract did give rise to a constructive trust, the disputed transfer still operated as a transfer of the shares to the mother. He explained, "This interest under the contract is no doubt a proprietary interest of a sort ... But its existence has never (so far as I know) been held to prevent a subsequent transfer, in performance of the contract, of the property contracted to be sold from constituting for stamp duty purposes a transfer on sale of the property in question".[58] Lord Jenkins emphasised that the contract did not pass the full equitable interest in the shares, "In truth, the title secured by the purchaser by means of an actual transfer is different in kind from, and may well be far superior to, the special form of proprietary interest which equity confers on a purchaser in anticipation of such transfer".[59] In this scenario the equitable interest that exists in the purchaser until the contract is performed is of an interim and incomplete nature. This potential vulnerability is what Lord Jenkins was referring to and he was responding to an argument put forward by counsel as to what would happen if the contract was not performed. Lord Jenkins was accepting that, if the contract was rescinded or specific performance for some reason ceased to be available (e.g. the son sold his reversionary interest to a bona fide purchaser), the constructive trust would be discharged. It could not be said that the mother ever had the entire equitable interest until the transfer of the legal title to her.

Battersby, however, argues that this approach is true when the property being purchased (as in *Oughtred*) includes the legal title, "but is not true where the property is a mere equitable interest".[60] This argument enjoys some appeal. It is obvious that a contract to purchase the legal estate in property will, pending completion of the transaction, only pass an equitable interest in that property. Full legal and beneficial title cannot, of course, pass by virtue of the doctrine of conversion. As Millett L.J. explained in *Bishop Square Ltd v Commissioners of Inland Revenue*, "A transfer to a purchaser of the legal estate in property contracted to be sold is nevertheless a 'conveyance on sale', notwithstanding that the beneficial interest in the property has already passed to the transferee under a preceding contract for sale and even though the whole of the purchase consideration has been paid to the transferor before the transfer ...".[61]

[55] [1960] A.C. 206 at 233.
[56] [1997] Ch. 144.
[57] See also, *Chinn v Collins* [1981] A.C. 533.
[58] [1960] A.C. 206 at 240.
[59] [1960] A.C. 206 at 240.
[60] G. Battersby, "Formalities for the Disposition of Equitable Interests under a Trust" [1979] Conv. 17 at p.27.
[61] (1999) 78 P. & C.R. 169 at 173.

Hence, in *Oughtred* the majority of the House of Lords were correct in the conclusion that the full equitable title was transferred only in writing, which was then subject to stamp duty.

If, however, the contract involves the transfer of only the equitable interest (i.e. it is   **4.17** not to be followed by the transfer of the legal estate) different considerations should, surely, apply. There appears no reason why such a contract should not pass a full equitable title in, say, the shares to the purchaser. If so, the equitable interest will transfer under the contract without the need for any written transfer. The vehicle of the constructive trust will, following the approach adopted by the Court of Appeal in *Neville v Wilson*, ensure that s.53(1)(c) is entirely bypassed.

The minority of the House of Lords, namely Lord Radcliffe and Lord Cohen dissented from the majority thinking. Lord Radcliffe accepted that the whole point of the appeal was whether it was open to the court to deduce from the documentation that Mrs Oughtred's title to Peter's reversionary interest rested upon anything more than an oral agreement. He concluded, "my opinion is that such a deduction is not open to a court of law. The materials that would support it are simply not there".[62] On the oral contract, Peter created an equitable interest in his reversion in favour of his mother. He then became a constructive trustee for her of that interest and, having regard to s.53(2), the absence of writing did not prevent that trusteeship arising, "She was the effective owner of all outstanding equitable interests".[63] As to the transfer of legal title in the shares to the mother, this followed on the heels of the release which wound up the trust. Lord Radcliffe reasoned that the release acquitted the trustees from their duties. They were called on to transfer legal title only to the mother, "this transfer cannot be treated as a conveyance of the son's equitable reversion at all. The trustees had not got it: he never transferred or released it to them: how could they convey it?"[64] The other dissentient, Lord Cohen, adopted a similar approach. Although the mother ended up as the absolute owner of the shares, as Lord Radcliffe emphasised, "that is description, not analysis. The question that is relevant ... is how she came to occupy that position; a position which, under English law, could be reached by more than one road".[65]

Case 3: Vandervell v IRC

In *Vandervell v IRC*,[66] the House of Lords had to decide whether a direction by a settlor   **4.18** to his existing trustees to transfer legal and beneficial title to trust property to a third party was within s.53(1)(c). The National Provincial Bank held 100,000 shares in Vandervell Products Ltd on bare trust for Mr Vandervell. In 1958, he directed the Bank to transfer the shares to the Royal College of Surgeons in order to finance (at the expense of £150,000) a chair in pharmacology. The money was to be derived from the dividends paid on these shares. It was decided that the shares should not be given outright to the College and that an option to repurchase them for £5,000 should be

---

[62] [1960] A.C. 206 at 227.
[63] [1960] A.C. 206 at 228.
[64] [1960] A.C. 206 at 228.
[65] [1960] A.C. 206 at 228.
[66] [1967] 2 A.C. 291.

granted to Vandervell Trustees Ltd. It was not, therefore, an unconditional transfer. Lord Reid took an overview, "this case provides yet another illustration of the folly of entering into an important transaction of an unusual character without first obtaining expert advice regarding tax liabilities which it may create".[67] The Inland Revenue mounted two alternative arguments. First, that the transfer of the shares was caught by s.53(1)(c). This argument was destined to fail. Secondly, that the option to repurchase entailed that Mr Vandervell retained some equitable interest in the shares. This argument proved to be more fruitful for the Inland Revenue.

Was the transfer caught by s.53(1)(c)?

4.19   The Inland Revenue argued that there was no written disposition necessary to satisfy s.53(1)(c) and, accordingly, Mr Vandervell had failed to dispose of his equitable interest in the shares and was liable to pay surtax on the dividends paid under those shares. The contention failed because, on the facts, the legal and equitable title to the shares had moved within the same transaction. This was beyond the mischief of the provision which was to prevent hidden oral transactions and fraud which would, in turn, make it difficult for the trustees to ascertain who the true beneficiary is. It is interesting to consider how each of the Law Lords reasoned this outcome. Unfortunately, as Nolan points out, the decision is, "far from easy to understand" and "equally difficult to justify as a matter of legal principle".[68]

Lord Upjohn took the view that, "when the beneficial owner owns the whole beneficial estate and is in the position to give directions to his bare trustee with regard to the legal as well as the equitable estate there can be no possible ground for invoking the section where the beneficial owner wants to deal with the legal estate as well as the equitable estate".[69] Lord Upjohn emphasised that, "the section is, in my opinion, directed to cases where dealings with the equitable estate are divorced from the legal estate ...".[70] Lord Reid agreed that the first argument of the Inland Revenue was unsound, but did not take the matter further.[71]

4.20   Lord Donovan put forward the view that, "If, owning the entire estate, legal and beneficial, in a piece of property, and desiring to transfer that entire interest to another, I do so by means of a disposition which ex facie deals only with the legal estate, it would be ridiculous to argue that s.53(1)(c) has not been complied with, and that therefore the legal estate alone has passed".[72] It did not matter that here the legal and equitable interest in the shares was in separate ownership. Mr Vandervell had the legal competence to direct his trustees to transfer both legal and equitable title to the College and when the trustees did so they disposed of the entire estate in the shares.

Lord Wilberforce acknowledged that s.53(1)(c), "is certainly not easy to apply to the varied transactions in equitable interests that now occur", but concluded, "However, in

---

[67] [1967] 2 A.C. 291 at 305.
[68] R.C. Nolan, "*Vandervell v IRC*: A Case of Overreaching" [2002] C.L.J. 169 at p.169.
[69] [1967] 2 A.C. 291 at 311.
[70] [1967] 2 A.C. 291 at 312.
[71] [1967] 2 A.C. 291 at 307.
[72] [1967] 2 A.C. 291 at 317.

this case no problem arises".[73] Mr Vandervell was the absolute master of the shares and could easily have made himself the sole legal and equitable owner of the shares.[74] Instead, he made a gift of them to the College, "The case should then be regarded as one in which the appellant himself has, with the intention to make a gift, put the College in a position to become the legal owner of the shares, which the college in fact became".[75] No separate transfer of the equitable interest was, therefore, necessary.

Following this unanimous conclusion of the House of Lords in *Vandervell*, it is **4.21** relevant to revisit both *Grey v IRC* and *Oughtred v IRC*. It is seductive to argue that in *Grey*, although the identities of the trustees were unchanged, legal title was subsequently held by them in a different capacity (i.e. as trustees for the grandchildren instead of as trustees for Mr Hunter). If this equation is correct, should this not be treated the same as the directions in *Vandervell*? It would then follow that, because of this perceived movement of equitable and legal title, if *Grey* came before the courts today it would be held that s.53(1)(c) does not apply. This argument is, however, specious. It is clear from the speeches of the Law Lords in *Vandervell* that what was envisaged was the transfer to one entity of the entire estate in the property. In this light, the transfer of the legal estate subsumes and carries in its wake the equitable estate. There is no separate disposition of a subsisting equitable interest. There is not a shred of support therein for the contention that the legal and equitable titles could remain distinct once the transaction is completed. Similarly, it would have been insufficient for Mr Hunter to direct his trustees to transfer legal title to new trustees and transfer equitable title to his grandchildren. Although there is a clear movement of both within the same transaction, the two species of title are treated differently and distinctly. This must amount to a disposition of an equitable interest for the purposes of s.53(1)(c). If it were otherwise, it would drive the proverbial coach and four through the provision. Accordingly, the outcome would, it is submitted, have been very different had Mr Vandervell attempted to move legal title one way and equitable title another.

In *Oughtred v IRC* it would now appear possible (in the post-*Vandervell* era) for the mother and son to have sidestepped s.53(1)(c) altogether by orally directing the trustees to transfer both legal and equitable title to Mrs Oughtred. As legal and equitable title would then move at the same time to the same person, this would surely be a scenario where there would be nothing to which the provision could apply. Of course, the transfer of legal title to the shares will need to be effected by the completion of a share transfer form.

What of the option to purchase?

By virtue of a majority decision, Mr Vandervell lost the appeal on the second ground **4.22** advanced by the Inland Revenue. This alternative argument was that Mr Vandervell had failed to divest himself completely of his equitable interest in the shares because of

---

[73] [1967] 2 A.C. 291 at 329.
[74] Under the rule in *Saunders v Vautier* (1841) 4 Beav. 115 collectively the beneficiaries can call for legal title and put an end to the trust. There is nothing to stop a new trust being declared and this would clearly be outside the scope of s.53(1)(c).
[75] [1967] 2 A.C. 291 at 330.

the option retained to repurchase them.[76] For these purposes, Mr Vandervell and not the College must be regarded as the real grantor of the option. Although the legal title to the option was validly vested in Vandervell Trustees Ltd, no mention whatsoever was made of where the equitable title in the option was to lie. The option deed was too short and too simple. This omission ensured that the title to the option was held on resulting trust for Mr Vandervell. He was, therefore, liable to pay surtax on the dividends. The majority of the Law Lords reasoned as follows.

Lord Upjohn (with whom Lord Pearce agreed) acknowledged that the law relating to resulting trusts was not in doubt, but admitted that, "The difficulty, and it is very great, lies in the application of those well-settled principles to the facts of the case".[77] Lord Upjohn outlined the basic principles to be applied:

> "Where A transfers, or directs a trustee for him to transfer, the legal estate in property to B otherwise than for valuable consideration it is a question of the intention of A in making the transfer whether B was to take beneficially or on trust and, if the latter, on what trusts. If, as a matter of construction of the document transferring the legal estate, it is possible to discern A's intentions, that is an end of the matter ... But, if, as in this case ... the document is silent, then there is said to arise a resulting trust in favour of A".[78]

In Lord Upjohn's eyes, Mr Vandervell had subjectively intended to give away all his beneficial interest in the shares, but had failed to do so because he retained the equitable interest in the option to repurchase them. It followed that, "If the beneficial interest was in A and he fails to give it away effectively to another ... it must remain in him".[79] The trustee company, therefore, held the option on trust for Mr Vandervell until either he or the trustee company (as it was empowered to do so) declared new trusts.

4.23 Lord Wilberforce admitted that whether or not a resulting trust arose in favour of Mr Vandervell hinged upon the interpretation placed on the facts as found. He had no difficulty in concluding as fact that Mr Vandervell had, "failed to bring about the total divestiture"[80] of his interest in the shares. As there had been a failure to securely place the beneficial interest in the option elsewhere, Lord Wilberforce concluded that, "the equitable or beneficial interest cannot remain in the air: the consequence in law must be that it remains with the settlor".[81] The trustee company necessarily held legal title on resulting trust for Mr Vandervell.

Lords Reid and Donovan (the minority voices on this point) both felt that there had been an outright grant of the option to the trustee company and that the company owned the option absolutely. Although Lord Reid agreed that, "the beneficial interest must belong to or be held for somebody: so if it was not to belong to the donee or to be

---

[76] This prompted Megarry J. to observe in *Re Vandervell (No.2)* [1974] 1 All E.R. 47 at 55, "the consequences of granting the option had proved lamentable to all save the Inland Revenue. It was the option which had, I am told, prevented the College from recovering the income tax on the dividends which had constituted the gift, and it was the option which resulted in Mr Vandervell having to pay surtax on dividends that had never been his in any real sense of the word".

[77] [1967] 2 A.C. 291 at 312.

[78] [1967] 2 A.C. 291 at 312.

[79] [1967] 2 A.C. 291 at 313.

[80] [1967] 2 A.C. 291 at 324.

[81] [1967] 2 A.C. 291 at 329.

held by him in trust for somebody it must remain with the donor",[82] on an examination of the transaction he concluded that the trustee company took an absolute right to the option. He could see nothing on which the inference of a resulting trust could be based. Lord Donovan advanced the view that the onus of proof lay with the Inland Revenue to establish a resulting trust of the option and that it had failed to discharge this burden. In any event, there was no hint of any trust evident on the face of the option deed and the language employed was of an absolute grant. There were also compelling fiscal reasons why Mr Vandervell would want the trustee company to hold the option absolutely. In these circumstances, Lord Donovan observed, "it is clear that one must walk a little warily upon the path leading to a resulting trust".[83] Looking at the situation objectively, he concluded that there was no scope for a resulting trust, "There was no reason why the option should be held on trust for the appellant either expressly or by implication. On the contrary there were weighty reasons why it should not".[84]

Case 4: Re Vandervell Trusts (No.2)[85]

To continue the Vandervell saga, Mr Vandervell finally wanted to rid himself entirely of **4.24** any interest that he had in the shares. In 1961, he instructed his trustees to exercise the option given to them and orally directed them to hold the shares so repurchased on trust for his children. The trustees used £5,000 from a trust fund already established to benefit Mr Vandervell's children. Subsequently, the dividends of those shares were transferred to the children's trust fund. In 1965, and to resolve any doubts, Mr Vandervell executed a deed of release by which he transferred to Vandervell Trustees Ltd his equitable interest in the shares, expressly declaring that the shares were to be held on trust for his children. Mr Vandervell died in 1967 and made no further provision for his children in the belief that they were well provided for under the trust. Later that year, the Inland Revenue claimed tax from his executors on the dividends that had been paid between 1962 and 1965 (£769,580 net). The Inland Revenue asserted that Mr Vandervell had not disposed of his equitable interest in the shares until the execution of the deed of release. The executors commenced proceedings against Vandervell Trustees Ltd (the trustees of the children's settlement), claiming that the estate was entitled to the dividends paid (prior to 1965) to the trustee company, less the £5,000 paid on the exercise of the option by the trustee company. The Inland Revenue was not, however, allowed to join in the litigation.[86] The executors succeeded at first instance before Megarry J., but an appeal from this decision was unanimously upheld in the Court of Appeal.

---

[82] [1967] 2 A.C. 291 at 307, 308.
[83] [1967] 2 A.C. 291 at 322.
[84] [1967] 2 A.C. 291 at 323.
[85] [1974] Ch. 269.
[86] As Megarry J. put it in the High Court [1974] 1 All E.R. 47 at 55, "the Inland Revenue is awaiting the outcome of this case in the wings rather than being on the stage".

The reasoning of Megarry J.

4.25   Megarry J. considered the option to purchase the shares and concluded that, "it would be quite unreal to say that in substance it was the college that provided the option; it was Mr Vandervell".[87] The option was, moreover, clearly held on automatic resulting trust for Mr Vandervell, "What a man fails effectively to dispose of remains automatically vested in him . . .".[88] It could not be said that the option was held on trust for the children's settlement. Megarry J. acknowledged that Mr Vandervell had wanted to rid himself of the shares and did not wish to retain any interest under the option, "Yet I cannot see how an intention not to get the shares back can negative a resulting trust . . . I do not see how the donor's intention not to have the beneficial interest can prevail when the resulting trust is automatic".[89] He next considered the effect of the children's £5,000 used to exercise the option and explained:

> "That issue is, in essence, whether trustees who hold an option on trust for X will hold the shares obtained by exercising that option on trust for Y merely because they used Y's money in exercising the option. Authority apart, my answer would be an unhesitating No. The option belongs to X beneficially, and the money merely exercises rights that belong to X. Let the shares be worth £50,000, so that an option to purchase those shares for £5.000 is worth £45,000, and it will at once be seen what a monstrous result would be produced by allowing trustees to divert from their beneficiary X the benefits of what they hold on trust for him merely because they used Y's money instead of X's".[90]

In his opinion, the children had, instead, what is known as a "lien" (a charge) over the shares for the repayment of £5,000 plus interest, "This in effect will restore the status quo ante as regards this payment".[91]

Megarry J. then turned his attention to the issue of estoppel. It was claimed by the trustee company that Mr Vandervell knew that the exercise of the option was to be financed out of the funds of the children's settlement, intending and agreeing that the shares should become part of that settlement. The trustee company did this in reliance on Mr Vandervell's agreement and, therefore, he (and, thereby, his estate) was estopped from asserting any claim to the shares. Megarry J. was unimpressed with this argument. At the time the option was exercised, Mr Vandervell had not known that he was the beneficial owner of it. There could be no estoppel claim made out as, "There is nothing inequitable in a man who has no knowledge that an option is his standing by while the option is exercised for the benefit of a settlement which he has some grounds for believing to be entitled to the option".[92]

4.26   The final aspect of Megarry J.'s judgment concerned the presumption of advancement. The trustee company submitted that the payment of the dividends over to the children's

---

[87] [1974] 1 All E.R. 47 at 61.
[88] [1974] 1 All E.R. 47 at 64.
[89] [1974] 1 All E.R. 47 at 72.
[90] [1974] 1 All E.R. 47 at 72.
[91] [1974] 1 All E.R. 47 at 73.
[92] [1974] 1 All E.R. 47 at 75.

settlement gave rise to the presumption of a gift and prevented Mr Vandervell and his estate from claiming them back. Megarry J. was again unimpressed, "The dividends came from the ... Company and not from Mr Vandervell; there could therefore be no advancement, for the ... Company was neither the father of Mr Vandervell's children nor stood in loco parentis to them".[93]

The divination of a new trust

The reasoning of Megarry J. was not to be followed by the Court of Appeal. Lord Denning M.R. recognised that, when the option was exercised, the trustee company became the legal owner of the shares and held those shares on trust. Seizing upon Lord Upjohn's acceptance that the trust interest remained with Mr Vandervell until new trusts were declared by himself or the trustee company, Lord Denning regarded the children as the beneficiaries under a new trust declared by the trustee. He explained, "This was a different kind of property altogether ... On this occasion a valid trust was created at the time of the transfer. It was manifested in clear and unmistakable fashion. It was precisely defined. The shares were to be held on the trusts of the children's settlement".[94] As the option rights had disappeared when the option was exercised, it was open for Mr Vandervell to direct the trustees to hold the property on new trusts without having to comply with s.53(1)(c).

4.27

The evidence of the intention to create a new trust was, in Lord Denning's view, indisputable. The key indicators of this intention were several-fold. First, that the trustee company had used the children's money to acquire the shares. Lord Denning noted that this would be a breach of trust unless it was intended that the shares were added to the children's settlement. Secondly, the trustees had written to the Inland Revenue declaring that the shares were held by it on trust for the children. Thirdly, all the dividends subsequently received by the trustee company were paid into the children's settlement and treated as part of those funds. This was all done with the full assent of Mr Vandervell. In these circumstances Lord Denning concluded, "Such being the intention, clear and manifest, at the time when the shares were conveyed to the trustee company, it is sufficient to create a trust".[95] It is, however, unclear how the trustee company could have declared a trust when it already believed that it was a trustee of the shares. There was not, as Harris points out, "a conscious dispositive *animus* of any kind".[96] The payment from the children's settlement, moreover, need not be decisive as the general rule (demonstrated by Megarry J. in the High Court) is that he who merely pays will not own. In addition, it could be argued that both the notification to the Inland Revenue and the payment of dividends merely represented what the trustees thought the position was and should not be regarded as declarative of a trust. These actions could have been made under a mistake and, as Megarry J. again demonstrated in the High Court, to yearn is not to transfer.

Stephenson L.J. admitted that he was treading, what was for him, a "dark and

---

[93] [1974] 1 All E.R. 47 at 75.
[94] [1974] Ch. 269 at 319.
[95] [1974] Ch. 269 at 320.
[96] J.W. Harris, "The Case of the Slippery Equity" [1985] 38 M.L.R. 557 at p.559.

unfamiliar path",[97] but was content to uphold the appeal, "as it seems to me to be in accordance with the justice and reality of the case".[98] Lawton L.J. took the view that that the children were the beneficiaries of a new trust which arose from the fact that their money had been used to exercise the option. He concluded, "It follows that once the transfer of the shares had been registered the beneficial interest in them was held by the trustee company on trusts of the children's settlement so that no declaration of trust was necessary".[99]

So what about s.53(1)(c)?

4.28   Not surprisingly, it was submitted that, despite this intention, there could be no trust because Mr Vandervell did not (until the deed of release) comply with s.53(1)(c) and could not, therefore, dispose of his subsisting equitable interest under the resulting trust. Lord Denning could not accept this approach:

> "There is a complete fallacy in that argument. A resulting trust for the settlor is born and dies without any writing at all. It comes into existence whenever there is a gap in the beneficial ownership. It ceases to exist whenever that gap is filled by someone becoming beneficially entitled. As soon as the gap is filled by the creation or declaration of a valid trust, the resulting trust comes to an end. In this case, before the option was exercised, there was a gap in beneficial ownership. So there was a resulting trust for Mr Vandervell. But as soon as the option exercised and the shares registered in the trustees' name, there was created a valid trust of the shares in favour of the children's settlement. Not being a trust of land, it could be created without writing".[1]

The central notion, therefore, was that Mr Vandervell had not disposed of his equitable interest in 1961 (i.e. on the exercise of the option). As Lord Denning made clear, "All that happened was that his resulting trust came to an end—because there was created a new valid trust of the shares for the children's settlement".[2] Lawton L.J. adopted a similar stance and reasoned that, "The exercise of the option and the transfer of the shares to the trustee company necessarily put an end to the resulting trust of the option. There could not be a resulting trust of a chose in action which was no more".[3] Accordingly, neither the extinction of the resulting trust of the option nor the declaration of the new trust fell within the scope of s.53(1)(c). The conclusion that the termination of a resulting trust falls entirely outside the formality provisions is convenient. Although s.53(2) expressly exempts only the "creation" and "operation" of resulting trusts, the gloss applied by the Court of Appeal means that it also encompasses termination. Harris makes the astute observation that the case is authority for the following and novel proposition:

---

[97] [1974] Ch. 269 at 322.
[98] [1974] Ch. 269 at 323.
[99] [1974] Ch. 269 at 325.
[1] [1974] Ch. 269 at 320.
[2] [1974] Ch. 269 at 320.
[3] [1974] Ch. 269 at 320.

"No disposition of an equitable interest needs to be in writing if the interest subsisted only by virtue of a resulting, implied or constructive trust, provided that the disposition brings the trust to an end. This would mean that someone in the position of the settlor in *Grey's* case could avoid the necessity for writing by transferring assets to persons named as trustees, avoiding declaring any trusts and relying on an automatic resulting trust to leave the beneficial interest in him; thereafter, he could make oral declarations shifting the beneficial interest".[4]

The role of estoppel

Lord Denning consolidated his decision by adding that, even if Mr Vandervell had retained a post-option equitable interest in the shares, he would have been estopped from asserting a claim against his children. Lord Denning explained: **4.29**

"Just see what happened. He himself arranged for the option to be exercised. He himself agreed to the shares being transferred to the trustee company. He himself procured his products company to declare dividends on the shares and to pay them to the trustee company for the benefit of the children. Thenceforward the trustee company invested the money and treated it as part of the children's settlement. If he himself had lived, and not died, he could not have claimed it back. He could not be heard to say that he did not intend the children's trust to have it. Even a court of equity would not allow him to do anything so inequitable and unjust. Now that he has died, his executors are in no better position".[5]

Put simply, Lord Denning concluded that Mr Vandervell's conduct was such that it would be inequitable for him to be able to rely upon his strict legal rights under the resulting trust. The children had acted to their detriment by sourcing the purchase money for the shares. Lawton L.J. agreed that Mr Vandevell (and now his executors) would be estopped from denying the existence of a beneficial interest for the children.

There are, however, two problems with this approach. First, when enforcing an estoppel claim the court must afford the "minimum equity" necessary to redress the unconscionable treatment of the claimant.[6] As regards the equity afforded to the children, it is clearly over-generous. The payment of £5,000 as detriment is clearly disproportionate to the eventual benefit of the substantial dividends produced from the shares. By any lights, this is not representative of the "minimum equity" yardstick usually employed in the valuation of the claimant's interest under an estoppel.

Secondly, it is difficult to see what detriment (other than the payment of £5,000 which could easily be refunded) the children had suffered as a result of the representation that they were the beneficial owners of the shares. Indeed, Green argues that the only person who acted to his substantial detriment was Mr Vandervell himself. He had made his will on the basis that his children were otherwise provided for. This mistaken belief, it is contended, could justify an estoppel being raised against Mr Vandervell's executors. As

---

[4] [1985] 38 M.L.R. 557 at p.561.
[5] [1974] Ch. 269 at 321.
[6] See *Crabb v Arun District Council* [1976] Ch. 179.

Green admits, however, this would make Mr Vandervell, "the only person in English law ever to have stood in the shoes of both 'estopped' and 'estopper' at one and the same time".[7]

Is Re Vandervell (No.2) correctly decided?

4.30 The decision of the appellate court in *Re Vandervell (No.2)* has been heavily criticised. For example, Battersby states that the decision of the Court of Appeal is, "unsatisfactory and should be approached with caution by trust lawyers and tax planners".[8] It is, indeed, difficult on the facts to find that there was a genuine declaration of trust by the company who already thought that it was a trustee. It is also difficult to understand why, as there was a resulting trust of the option, there was not also a resulting trust of the shares that resulted from the exercise of such option. The practical consequence was that the beneficial interest passed from Mr Vandervell to his children under their settlements. This, however, appears very much like a disposition. Perhaps a major clue is to be found from the consideration by Lord Denning of what can be called the "hard cases" point. He commented:

> "Every unjust decision is a reproach to the law or to the judge who administers it. If the law should be in danger of doing injustice, then equity should be called in to remedy it. Equity was introduced to mitigate the rigour of the law. But in the present case it has been prayed in aid to do injustice on a large scale—to defeat the intentions of a dead man—to deprive his children of the benefits he provided for them—and to expose his estate to the payment of tax of over £600,000. I am glad that we can overcome this most unjust result".[9]

The Court of Appeal, therefore, felt that it would be unfair to both Mr Vandervell and his children not to uphold the trust. As a result, the Inland Revenue withdrew its tax assessment for the period up to 1965. Any other outcome, as Gardner concludes, "would clearly have been unmeritorious in its disjuncture with the true nature and import of the circumstances. The fact that such distorted reasoning was required to circumvent s.53(1)(c) and to produce a more appropriate result confirms the sense that the law would do better without the section".[10] The problem, of course, is that this form of intuitive justice introduces uncertainty to the law and provides a dubious precedent for future cases. As Clarke comments of the Vandervell saga, "Charles Dickens would perhaps make a second Bleak House from it, but who, apart from the lawyers or the Revenue, really benefits from all this".[11]

[7] B. Green (1984) 47 M.L.R. 385 at p.420.
[8] G. Battersby [1979] Conv. 17 at p.36.
[9] [1974] Ch. 269 at 322.
[10] S. Gardner, *An Introduction to the Law of Trusts*, (2003) at p.99.
[11] P.J. Clarke, "Mr Vandervell Again" [1974] Conv. 405 at p.413.

SECTION 53(1)(C): A SYNOPSIS

The operation of s.53(1)(c) is undeniably complex and defies ready understanding. It is, **4.31**
therefore, convenient to rehearse the key points concerning its application:

- it is the transfer/disposition of an existing equitable interest under a trust that
  has to be in signed writing;

- the transfer of the beneficial interest of one beneficiary to another requires
  writing *(Grey v IRC; Oughtred v IRC)*. This is so whether the transfer takes the
  form of an assignment or a direction to trustees;

- s.53(1)(c) does not apply when the entire legal and equitable interest in the
  property passes to a single entity *(Vandervell v IRC)*. It is a dubious proposition to suggest that the section similarly does not apply where legal title moves
  one way and equitable title another in the same transaction;

- if a sub-trust is created under which the beneficiary retains some function and,
  thereby, does not dispose of the entire beneficial interest, the traditional
  understanding is that this sub-trust is beyond the reach of s.53(1)(c). If the sub-
  trust involves a complete disposal of the beneficial interest, however, it is
  thought that this requires a written transfer;[12]

- it was recognised in *Re Vandervell (No.2)* that the interest under a resulting
  trust can be disposed of without the need for writing;

- it was also recognised in *Re Vandervell (No.2)* that, even though it is not
  specifically identified as an exception in s.53(2), an estoppel can circumvent the
  need for writing; and

- as regards a contract to transfer both legal and equitable title in, say, land or
  shares in a private company, the constructive trust that arises does not pass the
  full beneficial interest to the purchaser *(Oughtred v IRC; Bishop Square Ltd v
  Commissioners of Inland Revenue)*. If it is only the equitable interest that is to
  be transferred, however, the constructive trust will operate outside the parameters of s.53(1)(c) *(Neville v Wilson)*.

THE RULES AGAINST PERPETUITY

An express trust that satisfies the requirements as to certainty, constitution and, when **4.32**
necessary, formality will, as a general rule, be valid. By way of an exception to this rule
there exist the rules against perpetuity. These rules impose temporal limitations on
trusts and operate to restrict the duration that property can be tied up by the settlor.
The rules are based on notions of public policy that property, particularly land, should
not be rendered inalienable for an indefinite period. To allow such sterilisation would

---

[12] *Grainge v Wilberforce* (1889) 5 T.L.R. 436.

prove economically and socially undesirable. As Emery asks, "why should the dead rather than the living prescribe indefinitely who should be entitled to the use and enjoyment of property (the dead hand argument)?"[13] Accordingly, the law has, through the rules against perpetuity, achieved a compromise between the settlor's wishing to restrict the use of property usually with a dead hand (i.e. from the grave) and the ability of future beneficiaries to dispose of the property free from any restraints imposed. This compromise recognises that one person's freedom may well amount to another person's restriction. As Gardner explains, "a settlor cannot legally provide for assets to remain subject to a trust for longer than legal policy will tolerate: there comes a point at which they must return into absolute ownership, and hence full marketability".[14] The law has, therefore, confined such settlements within narrow limits and to invalidate them when they attempt to extend too far into the future.

Perpetuity has, at common law, traditionally been a major cause of trust failure. As will become clear, however, as regards dispositions occurring after the coming into force of the Perpetuities and Accumulations Act 1964, markedly fewer will now fall foul of the perpetuity rules. There are three major rules, each of which will be considered in turn:

- the *rule against remoteness of future vesting* which deals with future gifts and focuses upon how long the property can lie dormant before having to vest in a donee. Put simply, this is to do with the commencement of future interests and relates solely to what may be described as "people trusts";

- the *rule against inalienability* (sometimes referred to also as the rule against perpetual purpose trusts) which deals with how long property can be rendered unmarketable by the donor. As this rule concerns "purpose trusts", the rule against inalienability and the rule against remoteness of vesting operate in mutually exclusive spheres; and

- the *rule against accumulations* which concerns how long the donor can insist that income be added to the capital and, for that period, effectively put income beyond the reach of the donee.

REMOTENESS OF VESTING

4.33 The rule against remoteness of vesting strikes at trust provisions that attempt to sterilise capital (whether real or personal) either indefinitely or for a long period of time. The rule operates by, as Emery explains, "limiting the period of time for which the identity of persons unconditionally entitled to property in trust funds is permitted by law to be unascertainable".[15] All future gifts of property must occur behind a trust whether that trust is testamentary or inter vivos, private or charitable or fixed or discretionary. The rule applies also to powers of appointment. The rule against remoteness of vesting does

---

[13] C. Emery, "Do we need a Rule Against Pepetuities?" (1994) 57 M.L.R. 602 at p.603.
[14] S. Gardner, *An Introduction to the Law of Trusts*, (2003) at p.42.
[15] (1994) 57 M.L.R. 602 at p.602.

not, however, have application to unconditional gifts that vest immediately. The rule is to do with interests that are contingent and not with those that are vested.

The rule against remoteness of vesting demands that the intended recipient acquire his interest in the property (i.e. it must vest in interest) within a finite time frame. It is, therefore, aimed at future gifts that are subject to a condition or contingency that may or may not eventually be satisfied. For example, the donor might make a conditional or contingent gift under which the identity of the beneficiary will be unknown for years to come (e.g. a gift to my first descendant who qualifies as a barrister). Until a descendant actually qualifies as a barrister, the property will be tied up (i.e. it cannot be sold or otherwise disposed of). As it is possible that not one of the descendants ever becomes a barrister, it would be absurd if the property was frozen for hundreds of years awaiting the mere possibility that one of them might one day qualify. The requirement that the gift must vest (i.e. take effect) within the perpetuity period is, therefore, designed to avoid property being tied up longer than a prescribed time. It ensures that the identity of any potential claimant will be ascertained within the permitted perpetuity time frame.

As will become clear, the applicable perpetuity period may differ according to whether the gift is governed by the common law perpetuity rules or, being made after July 15, 1964, is subject to the Perpetuities and Accumulations Act 1964. In either case, if the gift does not vest within the chosen period it is void.   **4.34**

A vested interest?

It is necessary that the property must "vest" within the perpetuity period. Remoteness   **4.35**
of vesting is not concerned with the time that property may be kept once it has vested in the recipient. The example provided by Parker and Mellows is of when, "an outright gift is made to a limited company so that the gift vests in the company immediately, that company may hold the property for more than a thousand years without ever infringing the rule against remoteness".[16] It is, therefore, crucial to understand what is meant by an interest having "vested" for these purposes. The requirement is that the property "vest in interest" within the perpetuity period. The time that it "vests in possession" is irrelevant.

Vesting in interest occurs when a prior interest is all that stands between the interest holder and full enjoyment of the property. For example, consider a trust of property "to Fred for life with remainder to Adrienne". Fred's prior life interest is one vested both in interest and in possession (i.e. he has the right to the present enjoyment and use of the property). While Fred remains in the land of the living, Adrienne's interest is one vested in interest, but not vested in possession (i.e. she does not have a present right to use and enjoyment of the property). Both Fred and Adrienne and their respective interests are ascertained and there are no conditions to be satisfied.

In contrast, if the trust had been "to Fred for life with remainder to Adrienne   **4.36**
provided that she qualifies as a barrister", different considerations then apply to Adrienne. Her interest is now merely a contingent interest and does not become vested

---

[16] At p.257.

in any sense until the condition is fulfilled (i.e. until she qualifies as a barrister). It is with this type of contingent interest the rule against remoteness of vesting is concerned.

The common law perpetuity period

4.37   At common law, every gift of property must vest in its intended recipient within the duration of a finite period of 21 years or specified life or lives in being (i.e. a life or lives existing at the date the gift is made) plus 21 years. Put in a different way, the perpetuity period can extend 21 years beyond the death of the relevant life(s) in being. A life in being may include an embryonic child *(en ventre sa mere)* if this is relevant. For example, if the lives in being are expressed to be "my children" this will include a child who at the time of the gift is merely an embryo. It is not, however, possible to nominate, say, a tortoise or a tree as the life in being. The basic idea was to allow a testator to make provision for his future grandchildren in a way that the property would vest when those grandchildren reached the age of 21. Hayton and Marshall provide a useful example of a testator who leaves his estate on trust for his widow for life, remainder to his only son for life with remainder to such of his grandchildren who attain 21 years of age.[17] As the authors demonstrate, all of these trusts are valid:

- the widow has a life interest that is a present right of present enjoyment (i.e. it is vested in both interest and possession);

- the son also has a vested interest in that it is a present right, but of future enjoyment (i.e. it is not yet vested in possession); and

- the grandchildren under 21 years of age merely have a contingent interest and not a present right (i.e. they have a contingent right to future enjoyment and have no right vested in interest). As the contingent right must necessarily vest in the grandchildren within 21 years of the death of the specified lives in being (the widow and the son) the perpetuity rule is satisfied.[18]

In principle, the donor can expressly select any living person or persons as the chosen yardstick.[19] For example, the trust for grandchildren might nominate the lives in being as the settlor's children (i.e. the parents of the intended beneficiaries). As shown above, this would ensure that all grandchildren who achieve 21 years will do so within the perpetuity period. Nevertheless, it became common practice to adopt what is termed a "royal lives clause". This election entails that the perpetuity period is keyed in to the lifetime of members of the Royal Family.[20] By way of illustration, the perpetuity period could at common law expire 21 years after the death of the last survivor of all the lineal

---

[17] At p.192.

[18] If the testator had, instead, sought to benefit his grandchildren who reached the age of 22 years, this would have been invalid as running contrary to the common law rule against remoteness of vesting.

[19] In *Re Moore* [1901] 1 Ch. 936, however, the settlor selected a perpetuity period as "21 years from the death of the last survivor of all persons who shall be living at my death". This failed for uncertainty because it would be impossible to say when the last person had died.

[20] See *Re Villar* [1928] Ch. 471.

descendants of Queen Elizabeth II alive at the date of the gift. The Royal Family would, thereby, constitute the lives in being.

If no life in being is expressly selected, a life in being might be chosen implicitly. For example, "to the first child of Fred to attain the age of 21 years" would be valid because it is undeniably certain that Fred's first child will attain the required age within 21 years of the death of Fred. Fred would be the measuring life in being.

The wait and see rule

At common law, the vaguest possibility (however ludicrous) that the gift might not vest within the permitted period was enough to invalidate it *ab initio*. For example, in *Re Dawson* the possibility of a 60-year-old woman giving birth was factored in to the equation and rendered the trust void.[21] This was clearly an unsatisfactory state of affairs and entailed that, as Parker and Mellows put it, "common sense has gone straight out of the window and Alice has walked in the front door".[22] As regards the earlier example concerning the first descendant to qualify as a barrister, the gift would be void at common law because it is a possibility that it might not vest within the perpetuity period.   **4.38**

The Perpetuities and Accumulation Act 1964, however, counters the problem of the gift being invalidated at common law by the merest possibility of it failing to vest within the perpetuity period. Section 3 introduces what is styled a "wait and see" approach and this ensures that, if the gift eventually vests within the perpetuity period, it will be upheld. If it transpires that, at the end of the period, the gift has not vested then (and only then) will it become void. The wait and see approach, therefore, focuses upon actual events and not abstract possibilities. For example, a trust to benefit my first grandchild will be rendered void only if and when no grandchild emerges within the relevant perpetuity period.

The wait and see rule, however, only applies to dispositions made after July 15, 1964. The provision, moreover, embodies a major complication. It operates fully only to save gifts that would otherwise be void at common law when the perpetuity period is geared to the "statutory lives in being" listed in s.3(5). If there is no statutory life in being (e.g. a legacy by will to the first person who journeys to the centre of the earth or where a royal lives clause is employed in a will), the perpetuity period for the wait and see provisions is 21 years.[23]   **4.39**

Statutory lives in being for the wait and see provisions

For the purposes of the wait and see rule (and only for this rule), the 1964 Act defines the lives in being. These statutory lives in being are not identical to their common law counterparts. This means that if the interest would be void at common law on the basis   **4.40**

---

[21] (1888) 39 Ch. D. 155. A similar absence of reality was present in *Re Gaite* [1949] 1 All E.R. 459, where the court based its calculation on the basis that a girl below the age of five years could give birth.

[22] At p.256.

[23] Section 3(4)(b).

that it might vest outside the perpetuity period, the interest will not be void until it is established that it will vest outside the perpetuity period as measured by the statutory lives in being. Section 3(5) provides that, for the purposes of the wait and see provision, only the following who are living and ascertainable can be the life or lives in being:

- as regards a lifetime gift, the grantor (s.3(5)(a));

- in the case of a gift to a class, a beneficiary or potential beneficiary (s.3(5)(b)(i));

- the person on whom any power, option or other right is conferred (s.3(5)(b)(v)); and

- any person on the failure or determination of whose prior interest the disposition is to take effect. For example, "to my wife for life with the remainder to be divided between my nephews who marry". The life in being may be the person having that prior interest, i.e. the wife (s.3(5)(d)).[24]

The statutory perpetuity period

4.41 The Perpetuities and Accumulations Act 1964 retains the common law method of stating a perpetuity period with reference to a life or lives in being. It is possible, therefore, that a "royal lives clause" could still be used. Nevertheless, the most attractive feature of the 1964 Act is that it offers an alternative and more practical method of specifying the perpetuity period that is to operate. Section 1 offers the donor the straightforward option of stipulating a fixed period not exceeding 80 years within which the gift must vest in interest. Although the maximum period might be selected, it could manufacture a perpetuity period shorter than that available under common law. The benefit of simplicity outweighs this potential disadvantage. At least, it will be known in advance precisely when the trust will end.

It is hard to escape the conclusion that Parliament should have seized this opportunity to jettison entirely the common law rules. There is no doubt that, in maintaining a dual system, Parliament has created what might be regarded as unnecessary complexity in an already difficult area of the law.

Law reform

4.42 As to future reforms, the Law Commission has considered the law relating to remoteness of vesting on two occasions. In 1993, it published a Consultation Paper[25] within which it was acknowledged that there existed several problems with the post-1964 rules as to vesting. First, the Commission felt that unnecessary conceptual difficulty arises

---

[24] Further provisions apply to powers of appointment and discretionary trusts. In short, ss.3(3), 15(2) ensure that these remain valid to the extent that the trustees exercise their power or discretion within the statutory perpetuity period.

[25] *The Law of Trusts: The Rules against Perpetuities and Excessive Accumulations* (1993) Consultation Paper No.133; see H.W. Wilkinson [1994] Conv. 92.

from the inconsistency between the definitions of the common law lives in being and their statutory counterparts. Secondly, it concluded that that the default position of a 21-year perpetuity period was too short to reflect what the parties would have actually intended, particularly so outside the family context (i.e. in the commercial arena). Thirdly, the Commission took the view that, in certain situations, the present rules can be seen to operate unfairly. It offered the example of a provision in a will that is void if it offends the perpetuity rules as to vesting. This entails that the property will pass instead to the person entitled to the residuary estate. This character is unlikely to be the person who was to have benefited under the invalid disposition. Accordingly, the operation of the rules is capable of producing a result that a testator simply did not intend. Fourthly, the Commission concluded that the rules constituted a trap for an unwary settlor and generated increased legal costs for those sufficiently knowledgeable to ensure compliance with them. Finally, it argued that the rules were out of step with contemporary attitudes to property ownership.

Subsequent to its consultations, in 1998 the Law Commission published a final report.[26] In this Report, the Commission concluded that the rules should be retained, but with modernisation and reform. The aim should be to make the rules more straightforward and easier to operate. The Report recommended that there should be a standard perpetuity period of 125 years and that the notion of a "life in being" should be jettisoned entirely. As a transitional measure, trustees will be able to abandon an existing "life in being" and elect instead for a fixed period of 100 years. The donor could, however, expressly elect for a shorter period. The wait and see rule would also be retained. Although such changes would not be retrospective, it was envisaged that, in certain circumstances, existing trusts would be able to convert to the new scheme. A Perpetuities and Accumulations Bill is currently passing through Parliament to give effect to these proposals. The legislation will not, however, be retrospective.

THE RULE AGAINST INALIENABILITY

This second rule (sometimes described as a rule against excessive duration) is that trust **4.43** property shall not be subject to limitations that effectively render it inalienable. The driving force underlying the rule against inalienability is economic based and reflects the policy that property, particularly land, should not be tied up indefinitely. As Emery comments, "The dead hand argument is another public interest argument based ultimately on the proposition that the deployment of the nation's wealth should not be entirely governed by the wishes and designs of the dead".[27]

The Perpetuities and Accumulations Act 1964 has no effect on the rule against inalienability.[28] Accordingly, the common law period of a specified life or lives in being plus 21 years operates as the relevant perpetuity period. If no life is chosen, the perpetuity period will then be 21 years. No election for an 80-year fixed period is, therefore, possible. Similarly, there is no wait and see rule to be applied. Hence, such purpose

---

[26] *The Rules against Perpetuities and Excessive Accumulations* (1998) Law. Com. No. 251.
[27] C. Emery, "Do we need a Rule Against Perpetuities?" (1994) 57 M.L.R. 602 at p.604.
[28] Section 15(4).

trusts will be void unless it is certain from the outset that persons will become absolutely entitled to the property by the end of the perpetuity period.

4.44   The rule is directed against non-charitable purpose trusts.[29] As discussed in Ch.6, the general rule is that a private purpose trust will be void for want of a beneficiary. There exist, however, anomalous exceptions to this general rule. These exceptions relate to, for example, the maintenance of tombs and monuments and horses and hounds. Hence, the settlor may attempt to set up a fund to maintain his own gravestone by directing his trustee to invest £10,000 and to use the interest obtained solely for this maintenance work. In this example, the settlor is attempting to keep the capital sum (£10,000) locked up permanently and well beyond the perpetuity period. The trust would, therefore, clearly offend the rule against inalienability. The need for a specific rule to cater for these admittedly rare circumstances is provided by Hayton and Marshall, "Such a rule was necessary because purposes unlike individuals can last forever and because a rule against remoteness of vesting is inappropriate when interests cannot vest in purposes as opposed to persons".[30]

THE RULE AGAINST ACCUMULATIONS

4.45   The underlying idea of the rule against accumulations is that it is to sidestep any requirement that income be added to capital (i.e. accumulated) for a period exceeding the perpetuity period. The ambition is to prevent the property (this time income) from being tied up indefinitely and to tackle what may be described as posthumous avarice.[31] This rule is again based upon the broad policy edict that property must not be rendered inalienable. The rule applies both to charitable and private trusts.

At common law, and in the same way as with the rules against remoteness of vesting and against inalienability, this rule was keyed in to the perpetuity period of a life or lives in being plus 21 years. The 80-year term offered by the 1964 Act does not extend to accumulations. As a result of creative drafting of settlements, it became apparent to Parliament that the common law rule alone was insufficient to prevent excessive accumulations.[32]

4.46   Since the Accumulations Act 1800, Parliament has imposed additional restrictions. Their present incarnation is to be found within s.164 of the Law of Property Act 1925 and s.13 of the Perpetuities and Accumulations Act 1964. These provisions add a gloss to the common law and permit accumulation only for the restricted periods allowed therein. The settlor must expressly or impliedly choose one of the following periods for the duration of the accumulation:

- the life of the grantor or settlor;

[29] Note that charities and most pension funds are exempted from the operation of the rule against inalienability.
[30] At p.196.
[31] See *Re Earl of Berkeley* [1968] Ch. 744.
[32] This realisation emerged from the decision in *Thellusson v Woodford* (1798) 4 Ves. Jun. 227, where the income was accumulated for almost 80 years and yet remained valid.

- 21 years from the death of the grantor, settlor or testator;

- the minority of any person(s) alive (or *en ventre sa mere*) at the death of the grantor, settlor or testator;

- the minority of any person(s) who would, if of full age, be entitled to the income to be accumulated;

- 21 years from the making of an inter vivos disposition; and

- the minority of any person(s) in being at the date of making the inter vivos settlement.

Effect of excessive accumulation

In circumstances where an excessive accumulation has been directed, the outcome varies according to whether the direction violates the common law perpetuity period or one of the six statutory periods. A direction that contravenes the common law perpetuity period will be totally void and no income can be accumulated.[33] A direction that satisfies the common law, but exceeds the statutory time frame, will be valid until the lapse of the statutory period. Beyond this cut-off point, the income must be distributed.[34] For example, a direction to accumulate for the life of a member of the Royal Family, while effective at common law, is not one of the listed statutory periods and, therefore, the direction will be valid for 21 years.[35]

4.47

Law reform

There is no doubt that the rule against accumulations is overly complex, uncertain and inconsistent and will, it is expected during 2009/2010, be reformed. In 1998, the Law Commission Report recommended that the common law perpetuity rule in relation to accumulations be abolished. Instead, it would be replaced by a 21 year maximum statutory accumulation period. In 2002, the Lord Chancellor's Department published its own consultation document and this echoed the reforming sentiment of the Law Commission.[36] The Perpetuities and Accumulations Bill 2009 is currently being steered through Parliament and will give effect to these reform proposals. The legislation will not be retrospective.

4.48

---

[33] *Curtis v Lukin* (1842) 5 Beav. 147.
[34] *Re Watts WT* [1936] 2 All E.R. 1555.
[35] *Longden v Simson* (1806) 12 Ves. 295.
[36] *The Rule against Excessive Accumulations*, Consultation Paper C.P. 10/02 (published September 2002).

GUIDE TO FURTHER READING

G. Battersby, "Formalities for the Disposition of Equitable Interests under a Trust" [1979] Conv. 17.

P.J. Clarke, "Mr Vandervell Again" [1974] Conv. 405.

C. Emery, "Do we Need a Rule Against Perpetuities?" (1994) 57 M.L.R. 602.

B. Green, "Grey, Oughtred and Vandervell—A Contextual Reappraisal" (1984) 47 M.L.R. 385.

J.W. Harris, "The Case of the Slippery Equity" (1985) 38 M.L.R. 557.

S.M. Spencer, "Of Concurring Beneficiaries and Transferring Trustees" [1967] Conv. 175.

Chapter 5

POST-MORTEM TRUSTS: MUTUAL WILLS AND SECRET TRUSTS

A testamentary disposition, whether by gift or by trust, must comply with s.9 of the **5.01** Wills Act 1837 (as amended). If it does not, the will fails and the gift or trust cannot take effect. It is to be appreciated, moreover, that the formalities prescribed in s.53 of the Law of Property Act 1925 (as discussed in Ch.4) will not invalidate a trust created by will.[1] Hence the validity of a testamentary trust hinges upon whether the will was validly executed. The policy justification underlying s.9 is to prevent fraudulent claims being made against the deceased's estate when, of course, the testator is no longer able to disprove such claims. As Gulliver and Tilson observe, "The Statute of Wills may therefore reasonably incorporate unusual probative safeguards requiring evidence of testamentary intent to be cast in reliable and permanent form".[2] In the light that most people are aware that there are some formalities attendant upon the making of a will, "the problem of frustrating settlors ignorant of a certainty requirement is negligible, leaving very little to be said against the obvious advantages of imposing such a requirement: as the law does".[3]

A will has no legal significance until the demise of the testator and, hence, it can be modified or, indeed, revoked at any time prior to death.[4] Provided that it is valid, a later version automatically revokes any predecessor. Marriage also has an invalidating effect.[5] The requirements imposed by s.9 are that no will shall be valid unless:

- it is in writing;

---

[1] Section 55 of the 1925 Act.
[2] A.G. Gulliver and C. J. Tilson, "Classification of Gratuitous Transfers" (1941) 51 Yale L.J. 1 at p.6.
[3] S. Gardner, *An Introduction to the Law of Trusts* (2nd edn, Oxford, Oxford University Press, 2003) at p.84.
[4] *Re Heys* [1914] P. 192.
[5] Section 18(1) of the Wills Act 1837.

- it is signed either by the testator or, alternatively, by some other person provided that it is made in the presence of and at the direction of the testator;

- this signature must be made or, alternatively, acknowledged by the testator in the presence of at least two witnesses present at the same time; and

- each witness must sign his name in the presence of the testator, but not necessarily in the presence of the other witness.

5.02   Two key principles underpinning probate law are, first, that the testator enjoys the freedom of testamentary disposition which, as indicated, entails that he is free to revoke a will at his pleasure. A major exception to this rule, however, takes the form of the doctrine of "mutual wills". This operates to curtail the ability of the testator to change his plans. Secondly, the terms of a legacy or a testamentary trust must be disclosed on the face of a validly executed will. If not, the legacy or trust will be invalid. An exception to this rule exists in the doctrine of secret trusts which, at least in appearance, drives the proverbial coach and horses through the provisions of the Wills Act. Each exception will now be considered in turn.

THE DOCTRINE OF MUTUAL WILLS

5.03   Mutual wills arise where two or more parties (usually husband and wife) enter into a binding agreement that they will execute wills in a mutual form on the understanding that those wills are irrevocable and with the intention of benefiting a third party. For example, Adrienne and Fred may enter into an agreement that each executes a will under which the surviving spouse will inherit the property of the deceased spouse. The condition attached is that the surviving spouse must bequeath his or her property to their children. Of course, neither Fred nor Adrienne will know which of them will die first, but on the death of the first the other's estate will be increased. The increased estate will then, on the death of the surviving spouse, devolve to the children as per the arrangement. The parties having entered what might be called a "mutual wills contract".

On the date of death of the first testator, equity regards the mutual wills as being irrevocable.[6] This prevents the survivor from having a change of heart and leaving the property elsewhere (e.g. to a new wife).[7] In order to manufacture this result, equity imposes a constructive trust that binds the survivor and prevents disposal otherwise than under the terms of the mutual agreement.[8] As the agreement between the parties need not be contained in the wills themselves, the imposition of the constructive trust operates by way of an exception to s.9 of the Wills Act and curtails the freedom of testamentary disposition of the survivor. This consequence is justified on the basis that equity will intervene in order to prevent the fraud that would arise if the survivor were

[6] *Birmingham v Renfrew* (1937) 57 C.L.R. 666.
[7] *Dufour v Pereira* (1769) 1 Dick 419; *Olins v Walters* [2008] EWCA Civ 782.
[8] See *Re Cleaver* [1981] 1 W.L.R. 939. This element of trust law was necessary because of the general rule that only a party to a contract can sue on the contract. Hence, without the trust the beneficiaries would, at common law, be unable to enforce the terms of a revoked mutual will; *Olins v Walters* [2008] EWCA Civ 782.

able to take the benefit of the agreement without performing his obligations. For example, in *Re Dale*,[9] a husband and wife entered into mutual wills under which their estates were to be left to their son and daughter equally. The husband died first and his estate devolved according to the agreement. Subsequently, the wife executed a new will under which she left most of her estate to her son. The later will was disputed and the court held that, as the husband and wife had entered into a binding agreement to create mutual wills, the son became the constructive trustee of his mother's estate, holding the property on trust for himself and his sister equally. More recently in *Olins v Walters*, Mummery L.J. emphasized that: "this obligation on the surviving testator is equitable. It is in the nature of a trust of the property affected so the constructive trust label is attached to it. The equitable obligation is imposed for the benefit of third parties, who were intended by the parties to benefit from it. It arises by operation of law on the death of the first testator to die so as to bind the conscience of the surviving testator in relation to the property affected."[10]

A binding agreement

For mutual wills to be recognised by the court, there must be a legally binding **5.04** agreement between the parties that the wills are to be irrevocable.[11] The doctrine is not founded upon some broad-based equitable notion of benefit and burden.[12] The agreement, of course, must be sufficiently certain so that it can be enforced.[13] As Viscount Haldane put it in *Gray v Perpetual Trustee Co Ltd*, "without such a definite agreement there can no more be a trust in equity than a right to damages at law".[14] The agreement must, moreover, be proved and, as Latham L.J. stated, "Those who undertake to establish such an agreement assume a heavy burden of proof. It is easy to allege such an agreement after the parties to it have both died, and any court should be very careful in accepting the evidence of interested persons upon such a question".[15] Dixon J. shared this sentiment, "Such an agreement can be established only by clear and satisfactory evidence. It is obvious that there is a great need for caution in accepting proofs advanced in support of an agreement affecting and possibly defeating testamentary dispositions of valuable property".[16]

It is a matter of construction as to what was agreed that determines the terms of the trust. The terms will, of course, differ on a case by case basis. Leggatt L.J. explained in *Re Goodchild*, "A key feature of the concept of mutual wills is the irrevocability of the mutual intentions. Not only must they be binding when made, but the testators must

---

[9] [1994] Ch. 31.
[10] [2008] EWCA Civ 782 at [37].
[11] *Re Oldham* [1925] Ch. 75.
[12] *Birch v Curtis* [2002] WTLR 965.
[13] As explained at Mummery L.J. in *Olins v Walters* [2008] EWCA Civ 782 at [36], "it is a legally necessary condition of mutual wills that there is clear and satisfactory evidence of a contract between two testators...."
[14] [1928] A.C. 391 (PC) at 400.
[15] *Birmingham v Renfrew* (1937) 57 C.L.R. 666 at 674. Unusually in *Olins v Walters* the agreement was challenged by the surviving testator.
[16] (1937) 57 C.L.R. 666 at 681.

have undertaken, and so must be bound, not to change their intentions after the death of the first testator".[17] If there is no contract, the survivor retains the ability to dispose of the property under a new will at a future date.[18]

5.05   As in *Re Hagger*,[19] it is a much more straightforward matter if the agreement not to revoke is recited in the wills themselves. It is not, however, necessary that the wills make any reference to the agreement. Nevertheless, as Astbury J. demonstrated in *Re Oldham*, a trust is not to be inferred merely because the wills share corresponding terms as this, "does not necessarily connote any agreement beyond that of so making them".[20] He further observed, "Of course it is a strong thing that these two parties came together, agreed to make their wills in identical terms and in fact so made them, but that is not sufficient evidence of an irrevocable interest".[21] The court can, however, scout elsewhere for evidence of the legally binding obligation. The existence of an agreement must be established on a balance of probabilities. In *Re Dale*, Morritt J. commented upon the nature of this agreement:

> "for the doctrine to apply there must be a contract at law ... it is necessary to establish an agreement to make and not to revoke mutual wills, some understanding or arrangement being insufficient ... it is necessary to find consideration sufficient to support a contract at law ... The performance of that promise by the execution of the will by the first testator is in my judgment sufficient consideration by itself".[22]

It is not necessary, as shown in *Re Dale*, that the disposition favours the survivor and it suffices that the mutual agreement is to benefit a third party (e.g. a child or a charitable body). In addition, it appears unnecessary for the wills to be in similar forms. There is no reason why there cannot be mutual wills where the agreement is that Adrienne leaves a will benefiting Fred on condition that Fred leaves a will benefiting Fiona.[23]

Acting on the agreement?

5.06   It is necessary that there must be a disposition in consequence of the agreement to create mutual wills. This gives rise to a number of issues. First, it means that equity will intervene only once one of the parties has died leaving a will as agreed with the other. Until that time, the wills can be revoked by mutual agreement. Unilateral revocation, however, would amount to a breach of contract. The problem with the latter course of

---

[17] [1997] 3 All E.R. 63 at 71. Leggatt L.J. could find no mutual intention that both wills remain unaltered on the facts before him. Although the wife had thought that this would be so, the husband had not.
[18] See *Re Oldham* [1925] Ch. 75.
[19] [1930] 2 Ch. 190.
[20] [1925] Ch. 75 at 88.
[21] [1925] Ch. 75 at 87.
[22] [1994] Ch. 31 at 38. If the property includes land, the normal rule is that the contract must be in writing and signed by both parties: s.2 of the Law of Property (Miscellaneous) Provisions Act 1989. Nevertheless, this formality may also be overidden in order to prevent fraud: *Healey v Brown* [2002] W.T.L.R. 849.
[23] See *Birch v Curtis* [2002] W.T.L.R. 965.

action is that damages recovered are likely to be nominal because the claimant has suffered no real loss.[24]

Secondly, if the first party to die does not leave a will as agreed, it is possible that a survivor can claim (usually only nominal) damages for breach of contract against the deceased's estate. In the normal course of events, the survivor will instead change his own will as he is now released from obligations under the agreement.

Thirdly, as mentioned, if the survivor revokes his will after the death of the other   **5.07**
party, a constructive trust attaches to the property that passes to his executor (under any new will) or his administrator (if the survivor dies intestate).[25] If the agreement identifies specific property, this property can be recovered by the beneficiary from the survivor's estate. Indeed, it would seem that the beneficiary can obtain an injunction restraining any dealing with that specific property. Where, however, the specific property has been disposed of, the beneficiary's entitlement will be for its financial equivalent. If the subject matter of the trust (as is common) is identified as being the survivor's residuary estate, different considerations arise. It is, as Carnwath J. acknowledged in the High Court in *Re Goodchild*, "an unusual form of trust, since it does not prevent the surviving testator using the assets during his lifetime. It is a kind of floating trust which finally attaches to such property as he leaves upon his death".[26] On a practical level, the floating trust approach entails that the value of the residuary estate to which the trust attaches can increase as well as decrease over the intervening years. A trust of such uncertain property would, in the normal course of events, be void.[27] As accepted in *Re Cleaver*,[28] it is only by the special rules of equity that such a suspended, floating obligation can crystallise into a trust on the death of the survivor.

SECRET TRUSTS

As shown above, testamentary dispositions (including trusts) must be executed and   **5.08**
attested in compliance with the formalities prescribed in s.9 of the Wills Act 1837. The key features of that prescription are, it is to be recalled, writing, signature and attestation. The general rule is that any purported legacy or testamentary trust, which is not specified in a valid will is ineffective. An exception to this rule lies with so-called "secret trusts". These are testamentary trusts that usually arise in circumstances where the settlor leaves a legacy in his will on the secret understanding that the legatee (a trusted person such as a solicitor) will hold that property on trust for a third party.[29] Secret trusts can also occur when, on the strength of the recipient's undertaking, a testamentary provision is left unrevoked[30] or no will is made at all.[31] The enforcement of a

---

[24] *Robinson v Ommanney* (1883) 23 Ch. D. 285.
[25] If the deceased's personal representative fails to administer the estate as required by the mutual wills, he can be replaced under s.1 of the Judicial Trustees Act 1896 (but not under s.50 of the Administration of Justice Act 1985): *Thomas & Agnes Carvel Foundation v Carvel* [2007] EWHC 1314 (Ch).
[26] [1996] 1 W.L.R. 694 at 700.
[27] *Re Jones* [1898] 1 Ch. 438.
[28] [1981] 1 W.L.R. 939.
[29] See *Crook v Brooking* (1688) 2 Vern. 50.
[30] See *Tharp v Tharp* [1916] 1 Ch. 142.
[31] See *Re Gardner* [1920] 2 Ch. 523 where the trustee was the deceased's intestate successor.

secret trust appears, therefore, to be a blatant contradiction to the clear requirements of the Wills Act. Nevertheless, the secret trustee cannot deny the trust on the ground of an absence of formality. As Parker and Mellows explain:

> "It is almost inevitable that the existence of secret trusts will only be able to be proved by evidence which does not comply with these requirements; the whole object of the exercise is to exclude the identity of the beneficiary from the formally attested documents admitted to probate. Inevitably, therefore, the evidence of the communication, acceptance and terms of the secret trust in question will be either oral or contained in a document which has not been properly signed and attested. The existence of secret trusts therefore involves a departure from both the letter and the spirit of the Wills Act ...".[32]

The purpose of a secret trust is to keep the identity of the beneficiary undisclosed (e.g. when the secret beneficiary is the testator's illegitimate child or mistress or when it is an organisation that the testator does not wish openly to be associated with). This degree of secrecy might be viewed as necessary because, once probate is granted, a will becomes a document of public record. It can be inspected by anyone who pays the appropriate fee.

5.09 An additional reason for using a secret trust is that it caters for flexibility and allows changes and future dispositions to be made without adherence to the Wills Act 1837. In particular, the so-called "fully secret trust" (where the existence of a trust is not disclosed on the face of the will and the legacy appears to be absolute) caters well for an indecisive testator who cannot make up his mind as to what property to leave to whom. Indeed, the testator's instructions to his trustee might change many times before his death. This prompted Watkin to assert that, "the courts have left the door open for the doctrine to be used, perhaps abused, by the testator who is undecided rather than secretive".[33] Hence, the testator with a fully secret trust can leave a will and thereafter communicate his intentions to his trustee as to how the property is to be held. If those instructions change, the trustee will hold under the revised directions.[34]

As will become clear, however, the same degree of flexibility does not apply to the so-called "half-secret trust" (where the existence of a trust is revealed in the will, but the beneficiary remains undisclosed). It will be shown that, if the terms of the trust are not communicated either before or, at the latest, contemporaneously with the will, there can be no half-secret trust.[35] Watkin suggests that the same rule should be extended to fully secret trusts in order to prevent the will being used as a cloak for the shifting intentions of a testator, "The reformed rule would mean that if the testator wished his plan to be backed by legal sanctions, he would have to make up his mind as to who was to benefit at the latest by the time he made his will".[36] This would ensure that, "Secrecy is indulged, but not indecision".[37] Of course, this revised rule could not apply when the

---

[32] At 123.
[33] T.G. Watkin, "Cloaking a Contravention" [1981] Conv. 335 at p.341.
[34] Such was accepted by Megarry V.C. in *Re Snowden* [1979] 2 All E.R. 172 at 177, 178.
[35] *Re Keen* [1937] Ch. 236.
[36] [1981] Conv. 335 at p.341.
[37] [1981] Conv. 335 at p.341.

fully secret trust arises on intestacy (i.e. when there is no will). It would require this admittedly rare type of fully secret trust to be treated differently from others.

Origins

The equitable principles relating to secret trusts date from at least the seventeenth **5.10** century and their origin is often traced back to *Crook v Brooking*.[38] There a testator bequeathed £1,500 to two brothers (Simon and Joseph) to hold on secret trust, the terms of which had been communicated only to Simon. Subsequent to the death of the testator, Simon revealed the secret trust to Joseph. The beneficiaries of the oral secret trust claimed the £1,500. It was held that, as the testator had declared the terms of the trust to Simon, a secret trust existed and was enforceable. The case demonstrated that, provided that the terms of the trust are communicated to the legatee (or here one of the legatees) during the lifetime of the testator, an equitable obligation becomes attached to the legacy. Accordingly, if an informal secret trust exists, the secret beneficiary can enforce the trust against the actual recipient of the property.

In allowing secret trusts to be binding, equity appears to disregard the statutory requirements relating to testamentary dispositions. The doctrine of secret trusts has always, therefore, been of restricted application and subject to limitations. The enforceability of these post-mortem trusts is historically thought to rest squarely on the equitable maxim that "statute cannot be used as an instrument of fraud".[39] Hence, the doctrine was originally framed to prevent provisions such as s.9 operating to cause injustice. The traditional stance is that it would be a fraud to allow the recipient to keep the property, instead of holding it on trust for the undisclosed beneficiary. The court, as Lord Cairns put it in *Jones v Badley*, "engrafts the trusts on the devise by admitting evidence which the statute would in terms exclude, in order to prevent a devisee from applying property to a purpose foreign to that for which he undertook to hold it".[40] This theme was revisited by Lord Sumner in *Blackwell v Blackwell*:

> "For the prevention of fraud, Equity fastens on the conscience of the legatee a trust, a trust, that is, which would otherwise be inoperative; in other words it makes him do what the will in itself has nothing to do with, it lets him take what the will gives him and then makes him apply it, as the Court of Conscience directs, and it does so in order to give effect to the wishes of the testator, which would not otherwise be effectual".[41]

An alternative theory of more modern vintage is that the secret trust does not run contrary to the Wills Act at all. This is because the trust operates outside the will (i.e. dehors the will) and its existence is not, therefore, dependent upon the finding of fraud or the terms of the will. This approach was advanced by Megarry V.C. in *Re Snowden* who admitted that, "the whole basis of secret trusts . . . is that they operate outside the

---

[38] (1688) 2 Vern. 50.
[39] See *Thynn v Thynn* (1684) 1 Vern. 296; *Devonish v Baines* (1699) Prec. Ch. 3.
[40] (1868) 3 Ch. App. 362 at 364.
[41] [1929] A.C. 318 at 334.

will, changing nothing that is written in it, and allowing it to operate according to its tenor, but then fastening a trust on to the property in the hands of the recipient".[42] The fraud and the *dehors* theories are evaluated below (see **5.34, 5.35**).

Types of secret trust

5.11   There are two types of secret trust: the fully secret trust and the half-secret trust. It is crucial to any understanding of this subject area that the distinction be drawn between these two varieties of secret trust. This is because, in some situations, different rules apply to each. There is also debate as to whether each shares the same theoretic justification for its existence. As to which category of secret trust has been created, it is necessary to look at the wording of the will.

With a fully secret trust it appears from the face of the will that the legatee is entitled to take the legacy absolutely. No indication of a trust or its terms is, therefore, discernible from the will itself. Take, for example, a legacy of "£500,000 for Fred".

5.12   With a half-secret trust, the existence of a trust is not secret (i.e. it is mentioned in the will), but it is the terms of the trust (particularly, the identity of the beneficiary) that will remain private and undisclosed. Take, for example, a provision that reads, "£500,000 for Fred to be held on trust for such purposes as I have communicated to him". The trust (but not its terms) is evident from the will itself.

5.13   Even though the differences between the two categories of secret trust are simple to state, in practice the distinction between them is not always easy to draw. Take, for example, the provision, "£500,000 to Fred knowing that he will carry out my wishes as I have communicated to him". Is this a fully secret or a half-secret trust? As this provision employs precatory words (i.e. words of aspiration and hope, "knowing that he will") no trust obligation is imposed by the will on Fred and, therefore, this is not a half-secret trust.[43] If, however, the previously communicated instructions to Fred imposed a legal obligation on him, the trust will be of the fully secret variety.[44] If Fred is not subject to any fiduciary obligation whatsoever, he can keep the £500,000.

Intestacy

5.14   Although it is usual for a secret trust to be created either behind or within a will, it is possible for a fully secret trust (but not a half-secret trust) to arise when there is no will at all. In *Sellack v Harris*,[45] a father was induced by his son not to make a will. The son assured the father that he would make provision for the mother, wife and child of the intending testator. The court compelled the son to perform the secret trust. As there

---

[42] [1979] 2 All E.R. 172 at 177.
[43] Care should be taken with some of the older cases because, as considered in Ch.2, until the late nineteenth century precatory words could create a trust. This is no longer the case.
[44] *Irvine v Sullivan* (1869) L.R. 8 Eq. 673.
[45] (1708) 2 Eq. Ca. Ab. 46.

was no will, this was necessarily a fully secret trust.[46] A similar line of reasoning would occur when a testator is persuaded to revoke a will because of the inducement by either a legatee under the replacement will or, if none, a beneficiary under the intestacy rules.

Are secret trusts express or constructive trusts?

Sheridan argues that, "The secret trust which arises without mention in the will (or on intestacy) is a constructive trust, not an express trust".[47] He bases his view upon the ground that, where a person has by a representation acquired property which it would be inequitable for him to keep, a constructive trust must arise. He adds that it makes no difference whether there is a transfer by will (as with a fully secret trust) or there is an inter vivos transfer.[48] The same rule must apply in both cases. Sheridan explains, "The fact that the transaction is a secret trust does not make it different in principle. It is but one illustration of the broad principle of constructive trusts, and should be so recognised".[49]

5.15

As regards a half-secret trust, however, Sheridan contends that this must give rise to an express trust created by the will, "That much is clear, for whatever else happens or does not happen, there is a binding trust; the contest is only as to who is the beneficiary. There is certainly no question of the legatee obtaining property which it is inequitable for him to keep".[50] He recognises a lack of clarity emerging from the decided cases as to whether the nomination of the secret beneficiary was testamentary or non-testamentary. He concludes:

> "The decisions are the result of confusing on the one hand a specific type of constructive trust with a specific type of express trust, and on the other hand secret trusts and incorporation by reference. In consequence, a strange third institution has grown up: an express trust, partaking of some of the rules of constructive trusts and some of the rules of incorporation by reference".[51]

Sheridan's distinction between fully secret trusts and half-secret trusts is supported also by Matthews,[52] but represents unpalatable reasoning for Hodge.[53] Hodge believes that both half-secret and fully secret trusts are express trusts. This, he contends, is because in both cases the trust arises from the expressed intentions of the deceased communicated to and accepted by the trustee in the testator's lifetime. The express trust model represents the majority thinking as to the nature of secret trusts.

5.16

The upshot of this distinction is that, if a secret trust of land is classified as an express trust, it should (as discussed in Ch.4) be evidenced in writing by virtue of s.53(1)(b) of

---

[46] The possibility of a secret trust arising on intestacy was accepted also by the House of Lords in *McCormick v Grogan* (1869) L.R. 4 HL 82.
[47] L.A. Sheridan, "English and Irish Secret Trusts" (1951) 67 L.Q.R. 314 at 323.
[48] See *Bannister v Bannister* [1948] 2 All E.R. 133.
[49] (1951) 67 L.Q.R. 314 at p.324.
[50] (1951) 67 L.Q.R. 314 at p.324.
[51] (1951) 67 L.Q.R. 314 at 327.
[52] P. Mathews, "The True Basis of the Half-Secret Trust?" [1979] Conv. 360.
[53] D. Hodge, "Secret Trusts: The Fraud Theory Revisited" [1980] Conv. 341.

the Law of Property Act 1925. Similarly, if it is a secret trust of a subsisting equitable interest, the disposition should be created in writing for the purposes of s.53(1)(c). This would have startling consequences in that the secrecy element would have to be sacrificed. Fortunately, the debate as to whether a secret trust is truly an express trust or a constructive trust is, for practical purposes, rendered somewhat sterile. This is because, even if the secret trust is designated as an express trust, the absence of formality would be overlooked so as to prevent fraud. A constructive trust would then emerge from the ashes of the express trust and, as implied trusts are exempt from formalities by virtue of s.53(2), this remedial trust would ensure that the secret trust is enforceable. Accordingly, the same outcome would be reached regardless of whether the secret trust itself is express or constructive.[54]

Proving a secret trust

5.17   It is usually more difficult to prove the existence of a fully secret trust in circumstances where the intended trustee falsely denies that any communication and acceptance of the trust has occurred. The scope for fraud is obviously great. The testator (and/or where relevant his legal adviser) should take precautionary measures such as keeping copies of letters, maintaining a private record of what was said and when and disclosing the detail of the arrangement to another confidant (e.g. the beneficiary). As Brightman J. put it in *Ottaway v Norman*, "If a will contains a gift which is in terms absolute, clear evidence is needed before the court will assume that the testator did not mean what he said".[55] The ordinary civil standard of proof applies (i.e. on a balance of probabilities) to show the existence of a secret trust.[56]

As regards a half-secret trust, the potential for fraud is reduced because, as the trust is evident on the face of the will, the legatee can never keep the property himself. Nevertheless, there may be future dispute as to the identity of the secret beneficiary. Again the testator should leave some private documentary record of what was agreed and disclose the terms of the trust to someone else. It is to be appreciated, moreover, that as regards half-secret trusts evidence cannot be introduced in order to contradict the will. For example, if the will refers to the terms of the trust having been communicated to the trustee by letter, the court cannot take on board any oral communication that occurred.[57] In *Re Huxtable*,[58] a half-secret trust of property for unspecified charitable purposes was indicated in the will. The trustee sought to convince the court that the trust was only to survive during the trustee's lifetime and that he would be able to dispose of the property under his own will. The court would not admit evidence of this as it conflicted with the statement in the will. In *Re Keen*,[59] the testator bequeathed property on the basis that the terms would be notified to the trustees after the will. The court concluded that evidence of pre-will conversations could not be adduced as it contradicted what was said (in the future tense) in the will. Similarly, a trustee under a

---

[54] See generally, E. Challinor, "Debunking the Myth of the Secret Trust" [2005] Conv. 492.
[55] [1972] 2 W.L.R. 50 at 60.
[56] *Re Snowden* [1979] 2 All E.R. 172.
[57] *Johnson v Ball* (1551) 5 De. G. & Sm. 85.
[58] [1902] 2 Ch. 793.
[59] [1937] Ch. 236.

half-secret trust cannot take as a beneficiary.[60] Evidence can, therefore, be adduced only to complement the terms and not to conflict with those terms.[61] This, of course, does not apply to fully secret trusts.

THE CREATION OF A SECRET TRUST

A leading case concerning a fully secret trust is *Ottaway v Norman*.[62] By his will, Harry **5.18** Ottoway left his bungalow, half of his residuary estate and £1,500 to his housekeeper, Ms Hodges. Before his death, it was orally agreed that she would, in turn, leave by her will the bungalow (and whatever money was left) to Harry's son, William. Ms Hodges later changed her mind and left all her property by will to another. William commenced proceedings against Ms Hodges' executor (Mr Norman) for a declaration that the appropriate parts of her estate were held by him on trust for William. The fully secret trust in relation to the bungalow was upheld, but not the trust in relation to the moneys. The terms of the trust as regards the latter were too unclear, meaningless and unworkable. The arrangement did not require Ms Hodges to keep the Ottaway money separate and distinct form her own funds, "If she had the right to mingle her own money with that derived from Harry, there would be no ascertainable property on which the trust could bite at her death".[63]

In the course of his judgment, Brightman J. described Ms Hodges as the "primary donee" and William as the "secondary donee". He outlined the three vital ingredients of a fully secret trust:

> "The essential elements which must be proved to exist are: (i) the intention of the testator to subject the primary donee to an obligation in favour of the secondary donee; (ii) communication of that intention to the primary donee; and (iii) the acceptance of that obligation by the primary donee either expressly or by acquiescence. It is immaterial whether these elements precede or succeed the will of the donor".[64]

As regards a half-secret trust, the same ingredients must be present: intention, communication and acceptance.[65] As will become clear, however, the rules as to the timing of communication differ markedly between the two types of trust.

[60] *Re Ree's WT* [1950] Ch. 204.
[61] See *Blackwell v Blackwell* [1929] A.C. 318.
[62] [1972] 2 W.L.R. 50.
[63] [1972] 2 W.L.R. 50 at 62.
[64] [1972] 2 W.L.R. 50 at 59.
[65] *Blackwell v Blackwell*, [1929] A.C. 318.

Stage 1: intention

5.19   The Court of Appeal in *Kasperbauer v Griffith*[66] demonstrated that a secret trust (of whatever category) requires the certainty of intention that it is a trust that is to be created. There, at a family gathering, the testator declared that he was to bequeath his house and a lump sum pension benefit to his wife on the understanding that she would use the money to discharge the mortgage on the house. He explained that the house was to be sold within one year of his death and the proceeds of sale divided between his children of a former marriage. The wife remained silent throughout the meeting. The testator eventually made a will in a different form than that predicted which ensured that the wife got everything and the children received no benefit. The children alleged that a fully secret trust had been established because, at the earlier meeting, the testator had said that the wife "knew what she had to do". This argument failed as the testator's words were viewed as being equivocal and sufficient only to impose a moral (i.e. not legal) obligation on the wife. The change of emphasis within the will was deemed to be consistent with the absence of an imperative obligation.

In *Re Snowden*[67] the testatrix bequeathed her estate to her brother with the rider that "he shall know what to do". The brother died shortly afterwards. The testatrix's niece and nephew claimed the benefit of a secret trust. The High Court held that the deceased had shown the intention only to impose a moral obligation on her brother. The words used were insufficient to impose any trust obligations upon him, i.e. there was no certainty of intention to create a secret trust. Similarly, in *McCormick v Grogan*[68] the testator wrote a weakly worded letter which read, "I do not wish you to act strictly to the foregoing instructions, but leave it entirely to your own good judgment to do as you think I would if living, and as the parties are deserving". This again did not reveal the intention to create a secret trust and, therefore, the legatee could keep the money absolutely.

Stage 2: communication

5.20   As regards both a fully secret trust and a half-secret trust, it is crucial that the obligation to hold the property on trust and the terms of the trust (including the subject matter and its beneficiaries) be communicated to the trustee. Exactly what is to be communicated will depend upon the nature of the trust obligation imposed. For example, when there is more than one beneficiary the identity of all the beneficiaries and their entitlements under the secret trust will need to be divulged to the trustee. If, as in *Ottaway v Norman*, the trustee is to be given a life interest in the property then this must be communicated to the secret trustee.

Valid communication can be oral or take the form of, for example, a letter, fax, text message, sign language or email. Communication can also occur via the testator's

---

[66] [2000] W.T.L.R. 333.
[67] [1979] 2 All E.R. 172.
[68] (1869) L.R. 4 HL 82.

agent.[69] It is possible, moreover, that communication of the terms of the trust can be constructive. The classic example is where the trustee is given a letter marked "not to be opened until after my death". Provided the letter is handed to the secret trustee in the testator's lifetime, this will amount to an effective communication of the terms of the trust. In *Re Keen*,[70] the testator made his will and this disclosed the existence of a secret trust relating to the sum of £10,000. The trustee was handed a sealed envelope that contained the name of the secret beneficiary. The letter was not to be opened until after the death of the testator. Lord Wright M.R. drew the parallel that, "a ship which sails under sealed orders, is sailing under orders though the exact terms are not ascertained by the captain till later".[71] The trustee had the means of ascertaining the identity of the beneficiary and this amounted to a sufficient communication. This possibility was also recognised in *Re Batemans WT*.[72]

Communication and the fully secret trust

It is as to the timing of the communication that major differences emerge between the two styles of secret trust. In relation to a fully secret trust, communication must be made during the lifetime of the testator (i.e. it must be made inter vivos).[73] Communication may occur either before or after the will is drafted. As Wood V.C. commented, "it is altogether immaterial whether the promise is made before or after the execution of the will, that being a revocable instrument".[74] The ambulatory nature of a will, therefore, entailed that pre-will communication of the trust is not essential. As without inter vivos communication there cannot be a fully secret trust,[75] it follows that, if the communication is subsequent to death (e.g. by virtue of a letter found amongst the deceased's papers), the legatee can take the property absolutely. There is nothing that affects the conscience of the legatee and equity cannot intervene.[76]

In *Wallgrave v Tebbs*[77] the testator left £12,000 in his will jointly to Mr Tebbs and Mr Martin. After the testator's death, a draft letter was found specifying how the testator wanted them to hold the money. The court held that, because there had been no communication of this to Tebbs and Martin before the testator's death, there could be no binding trust. Tebbs and Martin could, therefore, keep the money. If, however, the trust had been communicated in the testator's lifetime the secret trust would have been effective. As Wood V.C. explained, "Here there has been no promise or undertaking on the part of the legatee. The latter knew nothing of the testator's intention until after his death. Upon the face of the will, the parties take indisputably for their own benefit".[78]

5.21

---

[69] *Moss v Cooper* (1861) 1 J. & H. 352, where one of the secret trustees (acting on behalf of the testator) communicated the trust to the other two secret trustees.
[70] [1937] Ch. 236.
[71] [1937] Ch. 236 at 242.
[72] [1970] 1 W.L.R. 1463.
[73] *Proby v Landor* (1860) 28 Beav. 504.
[74] *Moss v Cooper* (1861) 1 J. & H. 352 at 367.
[75] *Ottaway v Norman* [1972] 2 W.L.R. 50.
[76] *Re Stirling* [1954] 1 W.L.R. 763.
[77] (1855) 25 L.J. Ch. 241.
[78] (1855) 25 L.J. Ch. 241 at 247.

5.22   A less straightforward case is *Re Boyes*.[79] There the testator told the intended trustee (his solicitor) that he was going to leave him property to be applied under a secret trust. The testator said that the terms of the trust would be communicated to the trustee within the testator's lifetime. This did not, however, occur. Following the death of the testator, two documents addressed to the solicitor were discovered and these directed the solicitor to hold the property on trust for the deceased's mistress and illegitimate child. Despite the presence of these documents, the High Court held that this post-mortem communication of the terms of the trust was insufficient. The solicitor could not keep the property for himself and, instead, held it on resulting trust for the deceased's estate. The underlying rationale is that the trustee must be offered the opportunity to refuse to act as the testator would wish. If the trustee refuses, the testator can then make another will and leave the property to some other person willing to act as trustee.[80] As Kay J. commented in *Re Boyes*, "I cannot help regretting that the testator's intention of bounty should fail by reason of an informality of this kind, but in my opinion it would be a serious innovation upon the law relating to testamentary instruments if this were to be established as a trust ...".[81]

Difficulties may also arise, in relation to a fully secret trust, where the testator leaves a legacy to two or more persons jointly and does not communicate with each of them. For example, the settlor communicates with Fred, but fails to communicate with the intended co-trustee, Adrienne. The problem focuses upon whether those that were unaware of the trust will still be compelled to hold the property subject to the secret trust. The court has devised a somewhat elaborate approach to deal with this type of scenario which concentrates upon how the trustees hold the property and the timing of communication to those trustees who were aware of the trust. The mechanics of this approach were set out (albeit briefly) by Farwell J. in *Re Stead*.[82] His approach unfolded as follows:

- if the property is left to the legatees as "tenants in common", i.e. each has a separate share (e.g. "£500,000 to Fred, Adrienne and Fiona equally"), only those with whom the testator has communicated will be bound by the trust. The others will be allowed to keep their shares because as Farwell J. explained, "to hold otherwise would enable one beneficiary to deprive the rest of their benefits by setting up a secret trust".[83] In *Tee v Ferris*,[84] the legacy was to Mr Ferris and three others as tenants in common. The testator intended that they would hold the property on trust for chartable purposes. It was decided that Mr Ferris alone was bound and the others were entitled each to take a quarter share of the property. In short, an innocent tenant in common is never bound by the acceptance of another tenant in common;

- if the property is left to the legatees as "joint tenants", i.e. they own the property together as a single entity and have no distinct shares (e.g. "£500,000

---

[79] (1884) 26 Ch. D. 531.
[80] See *Re Gardner* [1920] 2 Ch. 523.
[81] (1884) 26 Ch. D. 531 at 537.
[82] [1900] 1 Ch. 237 at 241. B. Perrins, "Can You Keep a Half Secret?" (1972) 88 L.Q.R. 225 at p.226 suggests that these rules have been accepted, "generally without enthusiasm".
[83] [1900] 1 Ch. 237 at 241.
[84] (1856) 2 K. & J. 357.

to Fred, Adrienne and Fiona"), and the testator communicated with any of them prior to execution of the will, all three legatees are bound by the trust. This is because, as Farwell J. put it in *Re Stead*, "the will is made on the faith of an antecedent promise ... no person can claim an interest under a fraud committed by another".[85] In *Russell v Jackson*,[86] the testator communicated with some, but not all, of his intended trustees before the making of his will. The court held that the trustees were joint tenants and that all of them were bound by the secret trust. Accordingly, an innocent joint tenant is always bound when the trust was accepted by another joint tenant before the will was made; and

- if the legatees are "joint tenants" and the testator's only communication with them occurred after the execution of the will then only those who were so communicated with are bound. The others are unaffected as, "the will is left unrevoked on the faith of a subsequent promise ... the gift is not tainted with any fraud in procuring the execution of the will".[87] For example, in *Turner v Attorney General*[88] property was bequeathed to four persons as joint tenants. The secret trust was communicated to one of them, but after the will was executed. The living survivor of the joint tenants had known nothing of the arrangement and, hence, he was able to claim the property absolutely.[89] Accordingly, an innocent joint tenant is not bound when the only acceptance of the trust by another joint tenant occurs after the will is executed.

These complicated and admittedly arbitrary rules as to co-trustees under a fully secret trust are not, however, beyond the reach of criticism. Perrins disagrees with the approach adopted in *Re Stead*.[90] He considers the classification promoted by Farwell J. to be contradictory, confusing and based upon a misunderstanding of the authorities. He suggests that the sole matter to be addressed is simply whether the legacy was procured by the co-trustee's promise. Perrins puts forward the alternative view with allusion to A & C who are the co-trustees in this example: **5.23**

> "Returning to A & C, whether they are tenants in common or joint tenants, C is not bound if his gift was not induced by the promise of A because to hold otherwise would be to enable A to deprive C of his benefit by setting up a secret trust; but C is bound if his gift was induced by the promise of A because he cannot profit by the fraud of another; and if the trust was communicated to A after the Will was made, then C takes free if this gift was not induced by the promise of A because if there is no inducement there is no fraud affecting C".[91]

---

85 [1900] 1 Ch. 237 at 241.
86 (1852) 10 Hare 204.
87 Per Farwell J. [1900] 1 Ch. 237 at 241.
88 (1875) 10 Ir. Rep. Eq. 386.
89 See also, *Moss v Cooper* (1861) 1 J. & H. 352.
90 (1972) 88 L.Q.R. 225 at p.226.
91 (1972) 88 L.Q.R. 225 at p.228.

Communication and the half-secret trust

5.24   While communication must still occur before the death of the testator, as regards the half-secret trust a different dimension is added and this is that communication must occur either before the will or, at the very latest, when the will is created. This approach appears entrenched, as demonstrated by Lord Wright in *Re Keen*, "The trust referred to but undefined in the will must be described in the will as established prior to or at least contemporaneously with its execution".[92] The testator, as Lord Sumner admitted, "cannot reserve to himself a power of making future unattested dispositions by merely naming a trustee and leaving the purposes of the trust to be supplied afterwards".[93] If communication takes place after the will is executed, the secret trust must fail. As the intention to create a trust is disclosed on the face of the will, the intended trustee cannot, of course, keep the property for himself. Instead, the legatee will hold the property on resulting trust for the testator's estate.[94]

The adoption of this stricter approach was justified by Lord Sumner in *Blackwell v Blackwell* on the basis that, "to hold otherwise would indeed enable the testator to 'give the go-by' to the requirements of the Wills Act".[95] As to the need for pre-will communication and acceptance, Lord Sumner's reasoning is unconvincing, overlooks the ability of the testator (while alive) to revoke the will and disregards the fact that the same reasoning should equally be applied to fully secret trusts (which have never been subject to the same rule). The requirement of pre-will communication and acceptance has, moreover, been rejected both in Ireland[96] and in Australia.[97]

5.25   It is thought that this requirement emerged due to an erroneous comparison drawn with a doctrine known as "incorporation by reference". This doctrine allows written memoranda, which is referred to in the will, to be allowed in as evidence as to the meaning of a testamentary disposition. The writing must, however, have been in existence before the will was made or, at the latest, the time when the will was executed.[98] While this limitation may have merit in relation to incorporation by reference, it should be distanced form the law relating to half-secret trusts. As Sheridan puts it, "no attempt has yet been made to clear up this branch of the law, which is rich in strange distinctions, and enjoys an uneasy and ill-suited association with the probate rules for incorporation by reference".[99] The communication to trustees under secret trusts, it should not be forgotten, can be oral and there might be no document whatsoever to incorporate into the will. The two doctrines, moreover, have different backgrounds: secret trusts are based upon equitable principle whereas the doctrine of incorporation by reference is rooted in the law of probate.

In relation to the rules relating to the communication to co-trustees under a half-secret trust, the rules have been formulated somewhat haphazardly. As the trust is evident from the will itself, there is no possibility of the trustees keeping the property

---

[92] [1937] Ch. 236 at 246.
[93] *Blackwell v Blackwell* [1929] A.C. 318 at 339.
[94] As occurred in both *Re Keen* [1937] Ch. 236 and *Re Bateman's WT* [1970] 1 W.L.R. 1463.
[95] [1929] A.C. 318 at 339.
[96] *Re Browne* [1944] Ir. R. 90.
[97] *Ledgerwood v Perpetual Trustee* (1997) 41 NSWLR 532.
[98] *Re Jones* [1942] Ch. 328; see further, **5.36**.
[99] (1951) 67 L.Q.R. 314 at p.314.

for themselves. Hence, if a trustee has not been communicated with, his share (co-trustees under a half-secret trust always hold as tenants in common) will either project forward for the benefit of the secret beneficiary or result back to the estate of the testator. All seems to turn upon the wording of the will.

If the will expressly allows communication to "all or any" of the trustees, the **5.26** communication to one trustee (provided that such communication occurs before or at the time of the execution of the will) will bind all the co-trustees and the half-secret trust will be upheld.[1]

If the will states that the terms of the trust have been communicated to "all" the trustees and this has not occurred, the entire trust will fail because the evidence of the informed trustee will contradict the wording of the will and be inadmissible evidence. Hence, a resulting trust will exist in relation to the entire property.[2]

Stage 3: acceptance

The rules concerning the acceptance by the legatee of the obligations of trusteeship are **5.27** the same whether the trust is fully secret or half-secret in nature. Acceptance is crucial because it is this that brings about the "fraud" upon which the doctrine of secret trusts is traditionally based.[3] The intended trustee is also, in this way, presented with the option of declining to act is this capacity. Acceptance can be made at any time before the testator's death. This acceptance of trusteeship can arise in one of two ways, i.e. by express agreement or by implication from silence. Assent can occur, as Lord Westbury put it in *McCormick v Grogan*, "either expressly or by any mode of action which the disponee knows must give to the testator the impression and belief that he fully assents to the request ...".[4]

Silence, in this context, amounts to tacit acceptance.[5] Accordingly, in *Kasperbauer v Griffith* (had there been a sufficiency of intention) the silence of the wife would have signified her acceptance of the trust.[6] In *Wallgrave v Tebbs*, Wood V.C. made clear that the key is whether the trustee's conduct induced the testator to make the legacy and pursue the arrangement of a secret trust. This is because equity will not allow a man to profit by his fraud. In *Wallgrave*, however, the legatees were able to keep the £12,000 because there had been no communication or acceptance that could act as an inducement.[7] By way of contrast, in *Strickland v Aldridge*[8] a son actively induced his father to leave him property on the promise that he would pay £10,000 to his elder brother. The court compelled the younger son to hold £10,000 on trust for his elder brother.

---

[1] *Re Keen* [1937] Ch. 236.
[2] *Re Spence* [1949] W.B.N. 237.
[3] Hence, the secret trustee cannot be the sole beneficiary under the secret trust: *Re Rees* [1950] Ch. 204. As mentioned above, this case made clear also that, with a half-secret trust, such a provision would amount to a contradiction of the terms of the will itself.
[4] (1869) L.R. 4 HL 82 at 82.
[5] *Paine v Hall* (1812) 18 Ves. 475.
[6] [2000] WTLR 333.
[7] See also, *Re Falkiner* [1924] 1 Ch. 88.
[8] (1804) 9 Ves. 517.

Revoking acceptance

5.28 It is open to a person to refuse to act or to continue to act as a trustee.[9] If the disclaimer occurs after the testator's death, it is clear that, with a half-secret trust, the deceased's personal representatives will hold the property on trust for the secret beneficiary. As regards a fully secret trust, the trust will similarly be upheld. Although Cozens-Hardy L.J. doubted the latter conclusion in *Re Maddock*,[10] it is an outcome that received the support of Lords Warrington and Buckmaster in *Blackwell v Blackwell*.[11] If it were otherwise, the legatee would easily be able to frustrate the entire purpose of the secret trust by renouncing the legacy. As Lord Warrington recognised, "a refusal after the death of the testator to give effect to it would be a fraud on the part of the legatee".[12]

If the trustee's disclaimer occurs before the testator's death, different considerations presumably apply. In the normal course of events, the testator can invite another to act as trustee and execute a new will accordingly. The testator is admittedly inconvenienced, but is able to adapt his plans accordingly. If the testator does not do so, it is to be thought that the secret trust will fail.[13] It follows that, in relation to a fully secret trust, the former trustee should be able to keep the property for himself. In the context of a half-secret trust, the property will be held upon resulting trust for the deceased's estate. There is no fraud and nothing to attach to the conscience of the former trustee. Nevertheless, Hayton and Marshall pose the rhetorical question as to what would occur if the testator either dies before he can make a new will or is incurably insane when the disclaimer is communicated to him.[14] The solution to this conundrum is, unfortunately, far from clear. It is arguable that, unless the conscience of the former trustee is affected in some way, equity will not interfere.

5.29 To take a somewhat extreme example, say, the trustee confronted the testator and, having disclaimed the office of trusteeship, proceeded to murder him. In that scenario, and due to the rule of public policy that a wrongdoer cannot profit from his wrongdoing, the homicidal trustee cannot benefit under the will and the legacy to him would be void. Arguably, it should follow that a fully secret trust would fail and the property would remain in the deceased's estate. As regards a half-secret trust, however, the murderous trustee would not, on the face of the will, benefit under the will. No rule of public policy would, therefore, apply. If, by his crime, the trustee stripped the half-secret trust of its validity it would be tantamount to perpetrating a fraud on the secret beneficiary. Hence, the conscience of the trustee would not be freed by having previously informed the testator that he was no longer to be bound by the trust.

---

[9] *Re Sharman's WT* [1942] Ch. 311.
[10] [1902] 2 Ch. 220.
[11] [1929] A.C. 318 at 341, 328 respectively.
[12] [1929] A.C. 318 at 341.
[13] See *Whitton v Russell* (1739) 1 Atk 448, where it was held that there could be no secret trust without fraud. There the testator could have changed his plans, but did not. It was held that the testator's failure to respond did not maintain any obligation on the intended trustees.
[14] At p.118.

Variations on a theme

For a valid secret trust to exist, therefore, it is necessary that there be sufficient intention, communication and acceptance. As regards a fully secret trust, various permutations are possible. Take the example "£500,000 to Fred". **5.30**

- If Fred had previously agreed to the testator's request that he would hold it on trust for Adrienne, Fred will not be able to keep the money. Instead, a fully secret trust will exist and Fred will be compelled to carry out the trust.

- If Fred had assented to act as trustee, but the terms of the trust were never communicated, a resulting trust would arise in favour of the deceased's estate.

- If Fred knew nothing about the trust or had declined to act as trustee, he can keep the £500,000 for himself.

As regards a half-secret trust (e.g. "£500,000 for Fred to be held on trust for such purposes as I have communicated to him"), the following observations are to be made.

- In no circumstances can Fred claim the money for himself.[15]

- If Fred had assented to be the trustee then, provided that the terms were communicated to him before or at the time the will is executed, the trust will be enforceable by the secret beneficiary (Adrienne).

- If Fred had assented to be trustee, but the terms were not communicated at all or were communicated after the execution of the will, the secret trust fails and the property will be held on resulting trust for the testator's estate.

- If Fred had not accepted of the role of trustee, again a resulting trust of the property will arise.

Predeceasing the testator

In circumstances where a fully secret trust is intended, but the sole secret trustee dies before the testator, the legacy lapses and the property will remain in the testator's estate.[16] If, however, other trustees survive the testator, the trust should remain valid in relation to the entire property. As regards half-secret trusts, however, it is thought that the death of the sole trustee will not prevent the trust from taking effect because of the rule that equity will not allow a trust to fail for want of a trustee.[17] **5.31**

In the situation where the secret beneficiary predeceases the testator, the secret trust must fail. It comes into effect via the will, which in turn comes into effect on the death of the testator. If at that time, the beneficiary is no longer living, there can be no trust. The testamentary trust will, therefore, be frustrated in the same way as would occur with an

[15] *Re Ree's* [1950] Ch. 204.
[16] See *Re Maddock* [1902] 2 Ch. 220.
[17] *Re Maddock* [1902] 2 Ch. 220.

inter vivos trust.[18] Hence, with a half-secret trust the property will be held on resulting trust for the testator's estate. As regards a fully secret trust, however, it should follow that the trustee can now keep the property.

Changes to trust property

5.32   In circumstances where the testator wishes to add further property to the intended secret trust, these additional instructions must also be communicated to the trustee. A failure to do so will entail that, as regards the additional property, the secret trust will fail. If it is a fully secret trust, the legatee will be able to keep the excess amount.

If it is a half-secret trust, the additional property will be held on resulting trust for the deceased's estate. This was demonstrated in *Re Colin Cooper*[19] where a testator left £5,000 to trustees on terms that he had already communicated to them. Without the knowledge of the trustees, however, he increased the sum to £10,000 by codicil (i.e. a formal and attested variation of the will). It was held that the trustees held the initial £5,000 on the terms of the trust, but that the remaining £5,000 resulted back to the deceased's estate. As regards the latter sum, there had simply been no communication and acceptance of the revised terms of the trust. As Lord Greene M.R. explained:

"it is impossible to say that the acceptance by the trustees of the onus of trusteeship in relation to the first and earlier legacy is something which must be treated as having been repeated in reference to the second legacy or the increased legacy, which ever way one chooses to describe it ... I cannot myself see that the arrangement between the testator and his trustees can be construed as though it had meant '£5,000 or whatever sum I may hereafter choose to bequeath'. That is not what was said and it was not with regard to any sum other than the £5,000 that the consciences of the trustees (to use a technical phrase) were burdened".[20]

Lord Greene M.R. went on to make two further points. First, he recognised that minor additions would be tolerated under what is known as the de minimis principle. As he put it, "It is not to be thought from what I have been saying that some trifling excess of the sum actually bequeathed over the figure mentioned in the first bequest to the trustees would necessarily be caught".[21] Secondly, he stated that, as regards reductions, a very different approach was to be adopted. He observed:

"Similarly it must not be thought that, if a testator, having declared to his trustees in relation to a specified sum, afterwards in his will inserts a lesser sum, that lesser

[18] *Re Corbishley's Trusts* (1880) 14 Ch. D. 846; but note the opposite conclusion drawn (it is thought incorrectly) in *Re Gardner* [1920] 2 Ch. 523. There Romer J. adopted the unorthodox approach that the secret trust was created when the terms were communicated and accepted.
[19] [1939] Ch. 811.
[20] [1939] Ch. 811 at 817, 818. Although *Re Colin Cooper* concerned a half-secret trust, the same general approach should also apply to a fully secret trust.
[21] [1939] Ch. 811 at 818.

sum would not be caught by the trusts. In such a case the greater would I apprehend be held to include the less".[22]

THE THEORETICAL BASIS OF SECRET TRUSTS

It is apparent that, for whatever reason, secret trusts are treated differently from other forms of testamentary disposition and are properly viewed as forming an exception to the formalities imposed by the Wills Act.[23] The underlying nature of secret trusts has, not surprisingly, been the subject of both academic and judicial speculation. Nevertheless, there is an absence of unanimity as to exactly why secret trusts are treated as operating outside the realms of formality. There are three schools of thought as to what comprises the underlying rationale for the law relating to secret trusts: fraud, the *dehors* theory and incorporation by reference. Unfortunately, none of these suggestions offer an entirely satisfactory explanation. Although it is certain that both fully secret and half-secret trusts will be enforced, it is unclear exactly why this should be so. In this light, the debate is predominantly designed to sate academic interest.

5.33

Fraud

As mentioned, the traditional justification for the enforcement of secret trusts is to prevent fraud.[24] This approach has fallen into some disfavour in recent times. Hodge, however, maintains that, "not only is the principle that equity will not permit a statute to be used as an instrument of fraud capable of being used to support the enforcement of half-secret as well as of fully secret trusts, but also that it is the only principle upon which the enforcement of both kinds of secret trusts can be justified".[25] Unfortunately, there is much divergence of opinion as to the nature of the fraud alleged and this is particularly so with trusts of the half-secret variety.

5.34

As to fully secret trusts, if the legatee/trustee attempts to keep the property for himself this will be a clear fraud. In such a scenario, unless evidence is admitted contrary to the provisions of the Wills Act, the intended trustee will profit from his misconduct. As such, the justification for recognising the fully secret trust is easily made out.[26] In relation to half-secret trusts, however, this reasoning is inapplicable. If the court refused to admit evidence of the terms of the trust, the trustee could not take the property himself, but would instead hold it on resulting trust for the testator's estate. As the trustee will not profit from the failure of the trust,[27] it is thus hard to speak in terms of there being a fraud in connection with a half-secret trust. Nevertheless, it is

---

[22] [1939] Ch. 811 at 818.
[23] See E. Challinor [2005] Conv. 492.
[24] See *McCormick v Grogan* (1869) L.R. 4 HL 82.
[25] D. Hodge, "Secret Trusts: the Fraud Theory Revisited" [1980] Conv. 341 at 341.
[26] See *McCormick v Grogan*, (1869) L.R. 4 HL 82.
[27] Unless, of course, he inherits the testator's residuary estate under the will. In such a case, the notion of fraud by the trustee can be readily invoked.

sometimes argued that the fraud is committed on both the testator and the beneficiary if the trust is not upheld.[28] As Parker and Mellows explain:

> "This view is normally expressed in this way. If evidence of the terms of the trust were not admitted contrary to the provisions of the Wills Act, the testator would be defrauded in that, on the faith of the promise made by the secret trustee, he had either made or revoked a disposition of his property. In the same sort of way, the beneficiaries of the secret trust would be defrauded in that they would be deprived of their beneficial interests".[29]

The problem with this argument is as identified by Sheridan who argues that there is no real fraud on the beneficiary. Instead, the intended beneficiary loses out because the settlor simply did not adhere to the prescribed formalities for creating a testamentary trust.[30] This reasoning, moreover, could apply to any statute that prescribes formalities that if not met will frustrate the settlor's intentions and the beneficiary's expectations. As shown in Ch.4, equity is not prepared to act in this tolerant fashion in relation to a non-compliance with s.53(1)(b),(c) of the Law of Property Act 1925.

Dehors the will

5.35 In the light that the fraud theory is not an entirely satisfactory justification for the recognition of half-secret trusts, both judges and commentators have felt it necessary to look elsewhere. While both types of trust must be similarly enforceable, this has to be justified on a principled basis. Therein lies the problem. A modern view canvassed is that a secret trust (whether fully secret or half-secret) operates *dehors* (i.e. outside) the will. In other words, the trust arises not from the will, but from its lifetime communication to and acceptance by the trustee. This approach was adopted by Viscount Sumner in *Blackwell v Blackwell* where he admitted, "It is communication of the purpose to the legatee, coupled with the acquiescence or promise on his part, that removes the matter from the provisions of the Wills Act and brings it within the law of trusts, as applied in this instance to trustees, who happen to be legatees".[31] It follows that the rules governing wills should not apply to secret trusts. Hence, in *Re Young*[32] the testator made a bequest to his wife with a direction that on her death she should leave £2,000 for their chauffeur. Although the chauffeur had witnessed the will, he was still entitled to the money. The legacy was not void under s.15 of the Wills Act which is designed to prevent a witness to a will being a beneficiary under it. As Danckwerts J. bluntly put it, "The whole theory of the formation of a secret trust is that the Wills Act 1837 has nothing to do with the matter".[33]

The *dehors* school of thought is that secret trusts are enforceable because of the personal obligations placed on the trustee by the inter vivos declaration of trust. This

---

[28] This was accepted by Lord Buckmaster in *Blackwell v Blackwell* [1929] A.C. 318 at 328, 329.
[29] At p.125.
[30] (1951) 67 L.Q.R. 314 at p.324.
[31] [1929] A.C. 318 at 339; see also the approach of Megarry J. in *Re Snowden* [1979] 2 All E.R. 172.
[32] [1951] Ch. 344.
[33] [1951] Ch. 344 at 350.

trust, however, only becomes constituted on the testator's death (i.e. the property vests in the trustee by virtue of the settlor's will). The trust is not, therefore, completely independent of the will as, of course, it is the will that operates to vest title to the property in the secret trustee. Accordingly, if the will is defective (e.g. it is improperly attested or the testator does not have the legal capacity to create it) the secret trust must necessarily fail. This has prompted Penner to conclude that, "The *dehors* the will theory is fundamentally unsound ... the theory should be called the '*dehors* the Wills Act' theory to reflect what it means".[34] He argues that secret trusts are testamentary dispositions and that, simply by revoking the will or by drafting a new will, the testator can prevent the trust being constituted. The *dehors* theory is, therefore, tortuous, "just an attempt to cloak the embarrassing jam equity has got itself into with its willingness to flout the Wills Act".[35] Penner's argument enjoys some force.

Incorporation by reference

A less attractive argument is that the probate doctrine of incorporation by reference offers the true justification underlying the recognition of half-secret trusts. This theoretical basis is put forward by Matthews.[36] He relies on *Johnson v Ball*[37] as providing the "sheet-anchor" of his argument and providing a decision concerning "pure incorporation".[38] There the testator bequeathed the proceeds of a life assurance policy to two trustees, "to hold the same on the uses appointed by letter signed by them and myself". Although no such letter existed at the date of the will, the testator had orally communicated the terms of the trust prior to the execution of the will. The letter was written much later. Following the death of the testator, one of the secret beneficiaries claimed her share. The claim was dismissed because no effectual communication to the trustees had been made. Matthews explains this decision as reflecting the inability to incorporate the document by reference where it is created after the will. By a leap of logic, he concludes that it must necessarily follow that half-secret trusts are based upon the applicability of the rule of incorporation.

5.36

Matthews reasoning is thoroughly unconvincing as it, seemingly, puts the proverbial cart before the equally proverbial horse. The *Johnson* case may well be sound authority on the central notion of incorporation that, as the will must refer to the document to be incorporated, the document must be in existence prior to the will. To view it as propounding the theoretic underpinning of half-secret trusts is a very different matter. First, the *Johnson* case can be (and usually is) viewed as showing that the evidence adduced to establish a half-secret trust cannot contradict the terms of the will. Hence, if the will refers to one mode of communication no other mode will be admissible in evidence. Secondly, the incorporation theory stands in contradiction to key authorities (whether they point in favour of the fraud or the *dehors* theories). Thirdly, it lacks force in that the communication in relation to a half-secret trust may be oral and, hence,

---

[34] J. E. Penner, *The Law of Trusts*, (6th edn, London, Butterworths, 2008) at p.157.
[35] Penner, *The Law of Trusts* (London, 2008) at p.158.
[36] [1979] Conv. 360.
[37] (1851) 5 De. G. & Sm. 85.
[38] [1979] Conv. 360 at p.364.

there may be no document at all that can be incorporated into the will. Finally, the reference in the will to the communication of terms may be general (e.g. "as previously disclosed to you in writing") whereas for the incorporation of a document into the will specificity is required to identify what document is to be read alongside the will.

GUIDE TO FURTHER READING

G. Boughen, "Mutual Wills" (1951) 15 Conv. 28.
D. Hodge, "Secret Trusts: The Fraud Theory Revisited" [1980] Conv. 341.
P. Matthews, "The True Basis of the Half-Secret Trust" [1979] Conv. 360.
P. Meager, "Secret Trusts—Do They Have a Future?" [1995] Conv. 402.
B. Perrins, "Can You Keep Half a Secret?" (1972) 88 L.Q.R. 225.
L.A. Sheridan, "English and Irish Secret Trusts" (1951) 67 L.Q.R. 314.
T.G. Watkin, "Cloaking a Contravention" [1981] Conv. 335.

Chapter 6

Non-Charitable Purpose Trusts

Other chapters focus upon the enforceability of private trusts or public trusts (i.e. **6.01** charitable trusts). The attention of the present chapter, however, falls upon the validity of trusts designed to further non-charitable purposes. The general rule is that non-charitable purpose trusts are void. By their very nature their object is a purpose and they lack a beneficiary to enforce the trust. Accordingly, the aim of this chapter is to consider this primary obstacle to the validity of trusts for non-charitable purposes, the "beneficiary principle". The additional problems that arise in relation to perpetuity and uncertainty will also be considered. First, purpose trusts will be evaluated in the context of the small number of permitted historical exceptions to the general rule. Secondly, the dividing line between trusts for persons and trusts for purposes will be considered and explained. Thirdly, this chapter will focus on property holding by unincorporated associations. Here, the difficulty posed by purpose trusts has been evaded by a movement away from equity and towards a theory based on the contractual relationship that exists between the members. Finally, this chapter will address the alternative means by which non-charitable purposes might be pursued.

The Beneficiary Principle

As indicated, the principal difficulty with private trusts for purposes lies in the absence **6.02** of a beneficiary to enforce the trust. With the exception of charitable trusts, where responsibility for enforcement lies with the Attorney-General and the Charity Commission, it is a historical requirement that a trust has a beneficiary capable of enforcing it. On this basis, the courts have struck down a variety of non-charitable purpose trusts such as for "the preservation of the independence of newspapers"[1] or for "the provision

---

[1] *Re Astor's Settlement Trusts* [1952] Ch. 534.

of some useful monument to myself".[2] The importance of the beneficiary principle was endorsed emphatically by Sir Raymond Evershed M.R. who explained that, "No principle perhaps has greater sanction or authority behind it than the general proposition that a trust by English law, not being a charitable trust, in order to be effective, must have ascertainable beneficiaries".[3] Similarly, in *Leahy v A-G of New South Wales* Viscount Simonds explained that, "A gift can be made to persons (including a corporation) but it cannot be made to a purpose or an object".[4] Put simply, the central concern behind the principle is that, "there must be somebody in whose favour the court can decree performance".[5] A trustee is under no obligation unless there is a correlative right in someone else, a beneficiary, to enforce the trust.

Notwithstanding such forcible expression, the requirement of a beneficiary appears to fall short of absolute. There are two reasons underlying this observation. First, a number of anomalous case law exceptions were admitted historically as valid non-charitable trusts. Sometimes described as trusts of imperfect obligation, they comprise of cases where the court was unable to decree enforcement, but equally did not stand in the way of a person, in the shoes of trustee, prepared to carry out a testator's wishes. As regards such anomalous exceptions, the absence of a cestui que trust has not always proved fatal and, moreover, these decisions have never been overruled. Admittedly, however, their contemporary applicability is highly dubious. Regarded as "concessions to human weakness or sentiment",[6] or "occasions when Homer has nodded",[7] modern courts have emphasised that the scope of the cases should not be extended.

6.03   Secondly, following cases such as *Re Denley's Trust Deed*,[8] the focus of the courts in recent times has been on the practical need for someone with the capacity to enforce the trust, i.e. someone who benefits sufficiently directly. As that person need not be a beneficiary in the strict sense, *Re Denley* suggests that the court's concern lies with the problems of enforcement and not with the absence of a beneficiary per se.

The need for an ascertainable beneficiary to enforce the trust is by no means the only problem associated with purpose trusts. Sometimes the courts offer alternative reasons for holding a non-charitable purpose trust void. The most frequently encountered reasons relate to perpetuity and uncertainty, but excessive delegation of testamentary power and capriciousness are viewed as additional obstacles to validity. In addition, it is not uncommon for trusts to be declared invalid simply on one of these alternative grounds. The award, for example, of an annual cup for a yacht race[9] was held to be void upon the ground of perpetuity without much recourse to argument based on the want of a beneficiary. It is important to recognise that, in this context, questions of uncertainty or perpetuity generally arise only where concerns as to enforceability are satisfied.[10] In other words, the beneficiary principle is viewed as the primary objection to the validity of non-charitable purpose trusts. The other factors are relegated to being of secondary concern. It is only when the court accepts that the lack of a beneficiary will

---

[2] *Re Endacott* [1960] Ch. 232.
[3] [1960] Ch. 232 at 246.
[4] [1959] A.C. 457 at 478.
[5] Per Grant M.R. in *Morice v Bishop of Durham* (1804) 9 Ves. 399 at 405.
[6] Per Roxburgh J. in *Re Astor's Settlement Trusts* [1952] Ch. 534 at 547.
[7] Per Harman L.J. in *Re Endacott* [1960] Ch. 232 at 250.
[8] [1969] 1 Ch. 373.
[9] *Re Nottage* [1895] 2 Ch. 649.
[10] See, for example, *Mussett v Bingle* [1876] W.N. 170 (see **6.11**).

not defeat the trust that the additional obstacles that may stand in the way of purpose trusts are usually considered. It is necessary to look at these further obstacles to validity in more detail.

Perpetuity

There are two major strands to the rule against perpetuities.[11] The first may be described as the rule against remoteness of future vesting, which deals with the maximum length of time for which the vesting of future interests in beneficiaries can be postponed. As Joyce J. explained in *Re Thompson*, "The rule against perpetuities requires that every estate or interest must vest, if at all, not later than 21 years after the determination of some life in being at the time of the creation of some estate or interest, and not only must the person to take be ascertained, but the amount of his interest must be ascertainable within the prescribed period".[12] Although the court now has a statutory discretion to wait and see whether vesting does occur within the perpetuity period,[13] it is clear that the rule against remoteness of future vesting is concerned with commencement of interests.[14]

6.04

The second strand is the so-called rule against inalienability. This rule seeks to ensure that property is not tied up in a trust for longer than an acceptable perpetuity period or, indeed, for an indefinite period. The concern here is as to duration. Accordingly, this second rule plays an important role in the context of trusts for non-charitable purposes, i.e. trusts where there are no beneficiaries in whom property might vest. Where, for example, a testator seeks to cater for the maintenance of a monument or tomb, the maximum duration of the maintenance period may be specified or, in default, the trust will in theory continue indefinitely. It is important, therefore, that a valid perpetuity period is selected. As shown, however, the perpetuity issue only arises as an additional or peripheral obstacle to purpose trusts.[15] The purported purpose trust must first evade the invalidating reach of the beneficiary principle.

At common law, the perpetuity period is measured by a human life or lives in being plus 21 years. As Meredith J. emphasised in *Re Kelly*, "there can be no doubt that 'lives' means lives of human beings, not of animals or trees in California".[16] It is possible to select any number of lives provided that they are identifiable. It used to be common to select royal lives in being because there would be no difficulty identifying the date of death of the last survivor of the group. Accordingly the trust would continue "until the expiry of 21 years from the death of the last survivor of the descendants of Queen Elizabeth II alive at the date of my death". The effect of any uncertainty is aptly

6.05

[11] See Ch.4 for further coverage of this area.
[12] [1906] 2 Ch. 199 at 202. Note that a statutory period is provided by the Perpetuities and Accumulation Act 1964: see below.
[13] Perpetuities and Accumulations Act 1964, s.3(1).
[14] As Romer J. explained in *Re Chardon* [1928] Ch. 464 at 468, the rule is, "not dealing with the duration of interests but with their commencement, and so long as the interests vest within lives in being and 21 years it does not matter how long that interest lasts".
[15] "The rule against inalienability is, in reality, just one of the devices that is employed to keep the development of such trusts in check" (Law. Com. No. 251 (1998) *The Rule against Perpetuities and Excessive Accumulations*, para.1.14).
[16] [1932] I.R. 255 at 261.

illustrated in *Re Moore*, where the testator sought to create a perpetuity period of, "21 years from the death of the last survivor of all persons who shall be living at my death".[17] As it is plainly impossible to ascertain when the last person within that group has died, and thus when the period of 21 years should begin, the gift was held void under the rule against perpetuities. Where no life or lives are selected, the perpetuity period is 21 years from the date when the instrument creating the gift takes effect. In the case of a will, for example, a will takes effect on the date of the death of the testator.

The Perpetuities and Accumulations Act 1964 Act introduced a wholly new perpetuity period, that being a fixed term not exceeding 80 years.[18] Where applicable, it is open to a settlor specifically to select this statutory period, but it will not be implied. It is to be doubted whether the Act is available in cases of trusts for purposes (if indeed it is accepted that such trusts have validity at all).[19] A strong argument has been made that, on the basis of s.15(4) of the 1964 Act, there is no entitlement to use the statute.[20] Section 15(4) provides: "Nothing in this Act shall affect the operation of the rule of law rendering void for remoteness certain dispositions under which property is limited to be applied for purposes other than the benefit of any person or class of persons in cases where the property may be so applied after the end of the perpetuity period". Similarly, the principle of wait and see, whereby a disposition will fail only when it becomes clear that vesting will not occur within the perpetuity period, is logically applicable only to trusts involving people rather than to abstract trusts for purposes.

Certainty

6.06 A further obstacle is uncertainty. Much litigation generated by purpose trusts occurs where there is an intention to create a charitable trust, but the attempt ends in failure. Vagueness of expression within a purported charitable trust may leave it open to the trustee to apply the gift to both charitable and non-charitable purposes. In such cases, the gift will fail because it cannot be construed as exclusively charitable. Often, it is as a last resort that the court is asked to consider the alternative matter of the validity of the trust as a non-charitable purpose trust. It comes as no surprise, therefore, that outside the scope of charity, the issue of uncertainty remains a potential stumbling block for the enforcement of trusts for purposes.

Uncertainty can arise in a range of circumstances. Sometimes the purposes are not prescribed with sufficient precision or conceptual clarity.[21] Alternatively, the means by which the trustee is to achieve or to attain the specified purpose may be ill defined or unacceptably broad.[22] In addition, the class of beneficiaries, or those people intended to benefit, must be sufficiently certain. A classic illustration is provided by *Morice v Bishop*

---

[17] [1901] Ch. 936.
[18] Perpetuities and Accumulations Act 1964, s.1(1).
[19] The Law Commission Report (Law. Com. No. 251) offered no clarification: see para.8.36.
[20] See, for example, Hayton and Marshall where it is argued at p.197 that s.15(4), "prevents the Act having any effect in relation to the rule against inalienability".
[21] See, for example, *Re Endacott* [1960] Ch. 232.
[22] As P.A. Lovell explained of the purported trust in *Re Astor's Settlement Trust* [1952] Ch. 534, it is a case where the trust, "... is a sort of omnibus purpose which expresses really nothing more than an ideal" (Non-Charitable Purpose Trusts—Further Reflections, [1970] Conv. 77 at 82).

of Durham, where a gift was upon trust "to dispose of the ultimate residue to such objects of benevolence and liberality as the Bishop of Durham in his own discretion shall most approve of ...".[23] The especially vague description of the objects left it impossible to determine how the residue was to be applied. From a practical perspective, should the court be called upon to administer or enforce the trust, it will be unable to do so where the purposes are not clear. Accordingly, it is said that, "a court of equity does not recognise as valid a trust which it cannot both enforce and control".[24]

Excessive delegation of testamentary power

The concern as to excessive delegation is that, where a purpose trust is created by will **6.07** and there is no beneficiary to enforce the trust, it is the trustee who must determine how the trust property is to be applied. This is thought to be problematic because in such circumstances, "the testator has imperfectly exercised his testamentary power; he has delegated it, for the disposal of his property lies with them, not with him".[25] Two additional points should be noted. First, this particular objection to purpose trusts does not arise in relation to inter vivos trusts.[26] It is a rule that applies, if at all, to wills that purport to create purpose trusts. Secondly, no case law illustration can be provided of a trust that became void for this reason. Perhaps it is because, as Hoffmann J. explained, "a common law rule against testamentary delegation, in the sense of a restriction on the scope of testamentary powers, is a chimera, a shadow cast by the rule of certainty".[27] Accordingly, it is not apparent whether the commonly cited rule as to excessive delegation carries any contemporary significance.

Capriciousness

This next obstacle to the validity of a purpose trust arises from policy considerations **6.08** concerning purposes that are useless, wasteful, harmful or illegal. Capriciousness is not frequently encountered, but it does provide an additional obstacle to the acceptance of trusts for non-charitable purposes. Consider the extreme request in *Brown v Burdett*[28] that trustees block up all the rooms in a house for a period of 20 years. Needless to say, this purpose failed when Bacon V.C. elected to, "unseal this useless, undisposed of property".[29] Similarly, in relation to gifts for the maintenance of monuments to the testator, the root of the criticism put forward by Lord Salveson appears to lie in capriciousness and the offence to public policy. Memorably, he exclaimed, "The prospect of Scotland being dotted with monuments to obscure persons who happened to

---

[23] (1804) 9 Ves. 339.
[24] Per Roxburgh J. in *Re Astor's Settlement Trust* [1952] Ch. 534 at 549.
[25] Per Viscount Simonds in *Leahy v AG for New South Wales* [1959] A.C. 457 at 484.
[26] As Goff J. explained in *Re Denley's Trust Deed* [1969] 1 Ch. 373 at 387, "If this were a will, a question might arise whether this provision might be open to attack as a delegation of the testamentary power. I do not say that would be so, but in any case it cannot be said of a settlement *inter vivos*".
[27] *Re Beatty's Will Trusts* [1990] 1 W.L.R. 1503 at 1509.
[28] (1882) 21 Ch. D. 667.
[29] (1882) 21 Ch. D. 667 at 673.

have amassed a sufficiency of means, and cumbered with trusts for the purposes of maintaining those monuments in all time coming, appears to me to be little less than appalling".[30]

Administrative workability

6.09   This is the final obstacle to the validity of a purpose trust. It will be recalled from Ch.2 that administrative workability is a necessary ingredient of any trust. The same principle applies in the pursuit of non-charitable purpose trusts. In *R. v District Auditor, Ex p. West Yorkshire Metropolitan County Council*,[31] a local authority in exercise of its statutory powers attempted to create a trust, "for the benefit of any or all or some of the inhabitants of the County of West Yorkshire". The inhabitants, numbering some 2.5 million comprised of a class so large that the trust was deemed to be administratively unworkable.

THE ANOMALOUS EXCEPTIONS

6.10   As referred to above, there are a number of examples of trusts for non-charitable purposes that have been regarded by the courts as valid. These include so called trusts of imperfect obligation, i.e. cases where the "trustee" is not prevented from performing the specified purposes but equally cannot be compelled by the court to do so. Although these cases are viewed in modern times as, "troublesome, anomalous and aberrant",[32] they have yet to be overruled.[33] It is important to consider these exceptions to the general rule.

Monuments and graves

6.11   A notable illustration is *Mussett v Bingle*,[34] where a testator provided £300 to erect a monument in memory of the testator's wife's first husband and a further £200 to provide income for its upkeep. The former was upheld whereas the latter was held void for perpetuity. This category of cases shows that the focus of the court was not on the absence of a beneficiary, but on the danger that such trusts could last for an indefinite period. Nonetheless, in applying the perpetuity rules, the courts have shown flexibility that has allowed the development of this line of authority. First, in cases where the court is concerned only with the construction of the monument (as opposed to upkeep), it has been accepted that the build will take place within the perpetuity period.

---

[30] *M'Caig's Trustees v Kirk Session of United Free Church of Lismore*, 1915 S.C. 426 at 434.
[31] [1986] R.V.R. 24.
[32] *Re Endacott* [1960] Ch. 232 at 251.
[33] For an argument as to the market demand for the creation of such trusts: see J. Brown, "What are we to do with testamentary trusts of imperfect obligation" [2007] Conv 148.
[34] [1876] W.N. 170.

Admittedly, more difficulty surrounds directions as to maintenance because to maintain a grave gives rise to a serious issue in relation to the duration of the future upkeep. A testator who provides for the upkeep of a tomb for the valid common law perpetuity period, i.e. 21 years, could create a valid gift. Where, however, no time limit was specified, the gift would fail. Secondly, somewhat arbitrary equitable intervention has operated to save a variety of gifts in circumstances where testators have stated that their wish is for the gift to last for as long as the law allows. In such circumstances, the courts have been willing to permit the purpose to be pursued for the valid common law period of 21 years.

An unusual approach can be found in *Pirbright v Salway*.[35] There a gift of income to look after a family burial enclosure, "for so long as the law for the time being permitted" was deemed acceptable. Stirling J. was happy to hold the gift as valid for at least a period of 21 years following the testator's death. It has been claimed that *Pirbright v Salwey* is "virtually valueless"[36] as an authority because Stirling J. failed to indicate the maximum duration of the gift. Nevertheless, the case was favourably cited in *Re Hooper*[37] where a bequest to executors and trustees for the upkeep of a vault, the arrangement of which was left to the discretion of the executors, was upheld for a period of 21 years from the testator's death.

In *Re Endacott*,[38] the settlor left his residuary estate to North Tawton Devon Parish **6.12** Council for the purpose of, "providing some useful monument to myself". It was clear to the court that the words imposed a specific obligation on the trustee that the monument was to have the quality of utility and, thereby, serve a public purpose. The trust could not be deemed exclusively charitable, as the use of the money was not confined to strictly charitable purposes. Accordingly, the focus of the court fell upon whether this was a trust of a public character, the type of which the courts had historically accepted as valid. Not surprisingly, the Court of Appeal held the gift to be void. Lord Evershed M.R. accepted the strength of case law authority, but felt that the scope of such cases, "ought not to be extended".[39] Harman L.J. was in full agreement, holding that, "these cases stand by themselves and ought not to be increased in number, nor indeed followed, except where one is exactly like another".[40] *Re Endacott* is an excellent illustration of the contemporary judicial approach to non-charitable purpose trusts because it emphasises that the primary objection to such trusts lies in the beneficiary principle. Perhaps the Court of Appeal was particularly wary that such a large sum of money (£20,000) would be available to the trustee, without anyone to enforce the trust.[41]

Finally it is to be appreciated that the maintenance of private graves is now facilitated **6.13** under s.1 of the Parish Councils and Burial Authorities (Miscellaneous Provisions) Act 1970. A burial authority or local authority may enter into a contract to maintain a monument or other memorial situated within the catchment area of the authority and

---

[35] [1896] W.N. 86.
[36] L.A. Sheridan, "Trusts for Non-Charitable Purposes" [1953] Conv. 46 at p.56.
[37] [1932] 1 Ch. 38.
[38] [1960] Ch. 232.
[39] [1960] Ch. 232 at 246.
[40] [1960] Ch. 232 at 250.
[41] As Roxburgh J. explained in *Re Astor's Settlement Trusts* [1952] Ch. 534 at 542, "it is not possible to contemplate with equanimity the creation of large funds directed to non-charitable purposes which no court and no department of state can control, or in the case of maladministration reform".

in a location to which the authority has a right of access. The obligation as to maintenance runs for a period not exceeding 99 years from the date of the agreement.

Saying of masses

6.14   Trusts for the saying of masses for private individuals are now treated as valid charitable trusts, provided the masses are said in public.[42] Historically, the notion of a mass for a private individual aroused suspicion of superstition and any gift on trust for such purposes was immediately void. In 1919, however, *Bourne v Keane*[43] accepted such a trust as a legitimate private purpose trust. More recently, the Supreme Court of the Straits Settlements has provided an addition to this category holding valid for the perpetuity period a gift for the performance of ceremonies to perpetuate the testator's memory. The gift was not inherently charitable under the head of advancement of religion because there was no worship of a supreme being.[44] Accordingly, the only alternative was to house it within this category of non-charitable purpose trusts.

Care of specific animals

6.15   Gifts for the care or maintenance of particular animals are not charitable. There are, however, a number of cases where gifts for the maintenance of animals have been upheld as valid purpose trusts. In *Pettingall v Pettingall*[45] a testator provided the sum of £50 per annum for the upkeep of his favourite black mare. She was not to be ridden or put in harness and the money was intended to ensure that she was well provided for. Influenced by two separate considerations, Knight Bruce V.C. upheld the gift. First, there was no dispute that a bequest in favour of an animal was valid. Secondly, there were persons interested in the residue that, having regard to decree made, would be able to have the terms of the bequest enforced. The court arrived at a workable solution because the executor under the will provided an assurance that he would use the money to look after the mare. It was accepted that, although he appeared from the will to be entitled to any surplus, he was obliged to provide details of the care whenever required or otherwise face an action by any party interested in the residue should the mare not be properly cared for.

6.16   This approach was followed in *Re Dean*,[46] despite markedly different facts. There the testator provided for a sum of £750 per annum to be paid for a period of 50 years for the maintenance of his horses and hounds if they should live that long. It was clear from the wording that the trustee would have no entitlement to any surplus. North J. upheld the direction even though he was unclear as to who might ask the court to enforce the trust. He explained, "If persons beneficially interested in the estate could do so, then the present plaintiff can do so; but, if such persons could not enforce the trust, still it cannot

[42] *Re Hetherington* [1990] Ch. 1.
[43] [1919] A.C. 815.
[44] See *Re Khoo Cheng Teow* [1932] Straits Settlements L.R. 226.
[45] (1842) 11 L J Ch. 176.
[46] (1889) 41 Ch. D. 552.

be said that the trust must fail because there is no one who can actively enforce it".[47] It is clear, therefore, that North J. did not regard the absence of a beneficiary or person with locus standi to enforce the trust as necessarily being fatal. Nor was he concerned that a period of 50 years did not equate with an acceptable common law perpetuity period. On both points, therefore, *Re Dean* is of questionable authority.

Miscellaneous cases

The most frequently cited case falling into this category is *Re Thompson*.[48] The testator bequeathed a legacy of £1,000 to his friend to be applied by him in such manner as he thought fit towards the promotion and furtherance of foxhunting. His residuary estate was to go to Trinity Hall in the University of Cambridge. Interestingly, all parties concerned were happy to see the testator's wishes carried out. Even the college, as residuary legatee, described itself as "anxious" that the testator's purpose be fulfilled. It was only by virtue of its role as trustee that the college felt duty bound to challenge the validity of the bequest. The judgment of Clauson J. was heavily influenced by the approach previously adopted in *Pettingall v Pettingall*. He allowed the legacy to be applied for the specified purpose subject to an undertaking from the friend that the money only be used towards the expressed object in the testator's will. In the event that the legacy would be applied in any manner other than toward the furtherance of foxhunting, the residuary legatees were at liberty to apply to the court.

6.17

The modern stance

Any movement for the expansion of the categories of anomalous exceptions (described above) was effectively derailed with the decision in *Re Astor's Settlement Trusts*.[49] In 1945, Viscount Astor made a life settlement of most of the shares of the Observer Ltd, the income of which was to be applied to a variety of non-charitable purposes. These included the preservation of the independence of newspapers and the maintenance of good relations between nations. Roxburgh J. held that the trust was void. First and foremost, there was no beneficiary to enforce it. As he explained, "a trustee would not be expected to be subject to an equitable obligation unless there was somebody who could enforce a correlative equitable right ...".[50] Secondly, the trust was void for conceptual uncertainty. Roxburgh J. was unable conjure a certain meaning from such phrases as, "integrity of the press" or "different sections of people in any nation or community". This approach was followed by Harman J. in *Re Shaw*.[51] There the court considered the will of George Bernard Shaw who wished to devote part of his residuary estate to the pursuit of a variety of purposes, such as research into the benefits of a 40-letter alphabet and an inquiry into the number of people speaking or writing English in

6.18

---

[47] (1889) 41 Ch. D. 552 at 557.
[48] [1934] Ch. 342.
[49] [1952] Ch. 534.
[50] [1952] Ch. 534 at 541.
[51] [1957] 1 W.L.R. 729.

the world at the same time. It was held that these purposes, not being charitable in nature, were invalid. In conjunction with *Re Endacott*,[52] these authorities comprise a powerful restatement of the force of the beneficial principle.

TRUSTS FOR PERSONS AND TRUSTS FOR PURPOSES

6.19   The anomalous exceptions considered above are cases involving the pursuit of abstract purposes. A possible area of confusion involves legitimate private trusts for individuals that are expressed in the form of a purpose or limited by a purpose. It is to be remembered that these trusts satisfy the beneficiary principle and adhere to the appropriate test for certainty of objects. The approach of the courts has been to determine, where possible, that the purpose is secondary to the paramount intention of the donor, which is to benefit individuals. Sometimes this has occurred where the court can construe an absolute gift to persons with the purpose merely expressing the motive for the gift (e.g. "£5,000 on trust for the planting of trees on an estate"). Alternatively, a valid fixed trust can be created where a purpose is invoked as the means by which the beneficial share is calculated. These categories of cases are not to be considered as trusts for non-charitable purposes.

In *Re Sanderson's Trust*,[53] the testator's property was left upon trust "to pay or apply the whole or any part of" towards the maintenance, attendance and comfort of his brother. The question arose as to whether the funds remaining at the brother's death devolved to the brother's estate (because he was in receipt of an absolute gift) or to the residuary legatees under the testator's will (because the brother had been entitled only to the amount of income necessary for his maintenance). Wood V.C. decided upon the latter. The brother was a beneficiary under a fixed trust with the right to demand from trustees a distribution to meet the costs of his maintenance expenses. The purpose in this case provided the means to calculate the amount of his beneficial share.

6.20   In the course of his judgment Wood V.C. offered the rule of thumb that has been followed in subsequent cases where there is a trust for persons that appears to be limited by a purpose, "If a gross sum be given, or if the whole income of property be given, and a special purpose be assigned for this gift this court regards the gift as absolute and the purpose merely as the motive of the gift, and therefore holds that the gift takes effect as to the whole sum or the whole income as the case may be".[54]

In *Re Andrew's Trust*,[55] for example, a fund was set aside for the education of the children of Bishop Barclay and it was expressly made clear that the fund was, "by no means intended for the exclusive use of any one of them in particular, nor for equal division, but as deemed as necessary to defray the expenses of all, and that solely in the matter of education". Kekewich J. admitted that the specified object of the trust was solely the education of the children, but he was concerned to adopt a broad view, "Even if it be construed in the narrower sense it is, in Wood V.C.'s language, merely the

---

[52] [1960] Ch. 323.
[53] (1857) 3 K. & J. 497.
[54] (1857) 3 K. & J. 497 at 503.
[55] [1905] 2 Ch. 48.

motive of the gift, and the intention must be taken to provide for the children in the manner (they all then being infants) most useful".[56] Accordingly, the remainder of the fund was available for distribution to the children.

In *Re Osoba*[57] a bequest to the testator's widow upon trust, "for her maintenance and   **6.21** for the training of my daughter Abiola up to university grade and for the maintenance of my aged mother" was held to be a trust for the specified persons absolutely. As at the date of the gift of the residue the testator's mother was deceased, there was an absolute gift to the wife and daughter in equal shares. The expression of the purposes for which the gift was to be used was an indication only of motive. As Buckley L.J. maintained, "The specified purpose is regarded as less significance than the dispositive act of the testator, which sets the measure or the extent to which the testator intends to benefit the beneficiary".[58] Similarly, in *Re Bowes*,[59] £5,000 was left on trust to estate owners for the purpose of planting trees on the estate for shelter. The land would have benefited from £800 worth of trees, any further planting working to the disadvantage of the beneficiaries. Accordingly, it was held that the owners of the estate were absolutely entitled to the £5,000. Again, the purpose merely expressed the motive of the gift.

THE APPROACH IN RE DENLEY

The approach adopted in *Re Denley's Trust Deed*[60] appears to signal some defrosting of   **6.22** the beneficiary principle. The tenor of this decision is that, where a trust is expressed in the form of a purpose, it may still be deemed valid if it can be said to be for the direct or indirect benefit of one or more ascertainable individuals. In other words, the beneficiary principle should invalidate only those trusts that are for abstract non-charitable purposes.

The case concerned an inter vivos trust of land to be maintained and used for the purpose of a recreation or sports ground. It was expressed to be, "primarily for the benefit of the employees of the company and secondarily for the benefit of such other person or persons (if any) as the trustees may allow to use the same". The trustees were afforded the power to raise money for improvements and to adopt such rules and regulations as appropriate to facilitate the specified user of the property. No perpetuity issue arose as the land was to be conveyed to the trustees until the expiration of 21 years from the death of the last survivor of a group of specified persons. The application of the property for the benefit of employees was, therefore, to expire at the end of a valid period of perpetuity giving effect to a gift over. Also contained in the trust deed were three divesting events the occurrence of any one of which would entail that the trustees were to convey the land to the general hospital in Cheltenham.[61]

[56] [1905] 2 Ch. 48 at 53.
[57] [1979] 2 All E.R. 393.
[58] [1979] 2 All E.R. 393 at 402.
[59] [1896] 1 Ch. 507.
[60] [1969] 1 Ch. 373.
[61] For example, where the land was no longer required for the specified purpose.

6.23   As indicated, the stance adopted by Goff J. was to reassess the scope of the beneficiary principle. Importantly, he chose to fashion a distinction between trusts for purely abstract purposes and trusts that are to the benefit of identifiable individuals:

> "in my judgment the beneficiary principle of *Re Astor* . . . is confined to purpose or object trusts which are abstract or impersonal. The objection is not that the trust is for a purpose or object per se, but that there is no beneficiary or cestui que trust . . . Where then, the trust, though expressed as a purpose, is directly for the benefit of an individual or individuals, it seems to me that it is in general outside the mischief of the beneficiary principle".[62]

The essence of the distinction drawn appears to lie in the need for someone who has sufficient capacity to seek enforcement of the trust by applying to the court. Goff J. acknowledged that a line must be drawn to distinguish the *Re Denley*-type enforcer:

> "I think that there may be a purpose or object trust, the carrying out of which would benefit an individual or individuals, where the benefit is so indirect or intangible or which is otherwise so framed as not to give those persons any *locus standi* to apply to the court to enforce the trust, in which case the beneficiary principle would, as it seems to me, apply to invalidate the trust, quite apart from any question of uncertainty or perpetuity . . .".[63]

In the eyes of Goff J., the beneficiary principle should not invalidate cases where persons could be found to have sufficient standing to enforce the trust. This will occur where there is a benefit to that person, provided that the benefit is not too indirect or intangible. In relation to the objects of the trust, Goff J. held that it would be possible to identify easily those employees benefiting at any given time, thus avoiding difficulty relating to certainty of objects.[64] The employees of the company comprised an ascertainable class. The reference to other persons that the trustees may seek to include did not relate to the beneficiaries under the trust but, instead, created a power to permit others to use the land. As Goff J. explained, "the provision as to "other persons" is not a trust but a power operating in partial defeasance of the trust in favour of the employees which it does not therefore make uncertain".[65] The result appears to create a new qualification to the beneficiary principle, a qualification that has been the subject of judicial and academic debate.

6.24   The grounds of immediate challenge to the approach in *Re Denley* centre upon the classification of the trust as either a new type of valid purpose trust or a private trust for individuals. If viewed as a purpose trust, the primary objection remains the want of a beneficiary. As discussed above, it is a general rule that such trusts for purposes are void. By contrast, it can be argued that *Re Denley* is no more than a private trust for the benefit of individuals.[66] Viewed from this perspective, the central role afforded to the

---

[62] [1969] 1 Ch. 373 at 383.
[63] [1969] 1 Ch. 373 at 382.
[64] On the basis of his adoption of *IRC v Broadway Cottages Trust* [1955] Ch. 20, it appears that Goff J. felt that he required a complete list of beneficiaries (see further, **2.41**).
[65] [1969] 1 Ch. 373 at 387.
[66] See P.J. Millett (1985) 101 L.Q.R. 269 at 282.

purpose in *Re Denley* may perhaps present the key obstacle on both a conceptual and a practical level. In particular, two aspects of the *Re Denley*-style trust require clarification. First, if those who benefit are not beneficiaries in the true sense what are their entitlements in terms of enforcement of the trust? Secondly, of what nature and how direct must the benefit be to bring an object of the trust within the approach in *Re Denley?* As McKay argues, the right to enjoy the recreation ground, "gives them a de facto interest in the carrying out of the purpose trust, but Goff J. does not go on to spell out why this factual interest confers standing to enforce...".[67]

Re Denley interpreted: Re Grant's WT

The *Re Denley*-type trust has been the subject of judicial comment on two principal occasions[68] and, although both purport to support the decision, both adopt a markedly different analysis. In *Re Grant's WT*,[69] Vinelott J. appears to argue that the *Re Denley* approach is not about purpose trusts, but that the trust was akin to a discretionary trust for individuals who had sufficient standing to enforce it on their own behalf. On the view as to enforcement postulated by Vinelott J., there is no distinction between, on the one hand, a discretionary trust of income and, on the other hand, the *Re Denley* trust to facilitate the enjoyment of land for a particular purpose amongst a class of individuals. Vinelott J.'s reasoning unfolded as follows:

6.25

> "I can see no distinction in principle between a trust to permit a class defined by reference to employment to use and enjoy land in accordance with rules to be made at the discretion of trustees on the one hand, and, on the other hand, a trust to distribute income at the discretion of trustees among a class, defined by reference to, for example relationship to the settlor. In both cases the benefit to be taken by any member of the class is at the discretion of the trustees, but any member of the class can apply to the court to compel the trustees to administer the trust in accordance with its terms".[70]

The approach of Vinelott J., however, is itself open to criticism. First, his approach overlooks the importance of the purpose in *Re Denley* and deflects attention from the obvious distinctions between the cases. In *Re Denley* the heart of the direction was to achieve a specified goal (i.e. the use of the land as a sports ground). It must not be forgotten that the trustees covenanted that, should the land cease to be required or to be used by the employees as a sports ground, the land would be conveyed to the general hospital, Cheltenham. In such circumstances, the purpose *is* the true object of the trust

[67] L. McKay, "Trusts for Purposes—Another View" [1973] Conv. 420 at p.426.
[68] *Re Grant's WT* [1980] 1 W.L.R. 360; *Re Lipinski's WT* [1976] Ch. 235.
[69] [1980] 1 W.L.R. 360.
[70] [1980] 1 W.L.R. 360 at 370.

and it seems unsatisfactory to hold as a matter of construction that there is a trust for individuals, and not a trust for purposes.

6.26   Secondly, the nature of the entitlement differs as between the *Re Denley*-style trust and the discretionary trust.[71] The employees in *Re Denley* are not entitled to a proprietary interest of any kind. They neither have beneficial ownership of the property, nor have an expectation of receiving it. They could not combine collectively to defeat the specified purpose or to enforce a distribution of the property. Their entitlement extends to the enjoyment of a sports ground, that is, an enjoyment facilitated through the pursuit of the specified purpose. Likewise, the trustees in *Re Denley* did not enjoy discretion as to the distribution of shares of the trust property. Their discretion appertained to administrative decision-making, which involved the adoption of regulations to maximise enjoyment of the land.

Thirdly, the right to benefit from the pursuit of a purpose gives rise to different questions on the issue of enforcement and different regulatory issues for the court. Questions remain unanswered regarding the rights held by the objects of the *Re Denley*-type trust wherein there is a much more limited capacity to demand the performance of trustees' duties. Undeniably, it appears open to members of the specified class to restrain actions for the misuse of the property, for example, the adoption of a regulation that operates to exclude some members, or the perpetration of fraud. It is more difficult to see how the court might positively regulate the relationship between trustees and members of the specified class. When "trustees" refuse to carry out the stated purpose, or a dispute arises as between "trustee" and beneficiaries, there appears to be no effective means of resolution. The terms of the trust appear to dictate that the trustees be divested of the property. This is to be contrasted with the position of beneficiaries under a discretionary trust who hold prospective entitlement to rights in property on the basis that trustees may make a distribution in their favour. *Re Denley* is also very different to those valid trusts which benefit ascertainable individuals where a purpose is construed as merely the motive for the gift.[72] The class to be benefited in *Re Denley* was a large, fluctuating group of persons, the type of beneficiaries traditionally excluded from such construction. As described above, moreover, they held inarguably more limited and non-proprietary entitlements. It is clear, therefore, that the purpose in *Re Denley* is more central than Vinelott J. suggests and that much distinguishes the case from the discretionary trust for individuals.

6.27   Finally, Vinelott J. fails to explain the distinction promoted by *Re Denley* as between abstract purpose trusts to which the beneficiary principle applies and those trusts for purposes where individuals have sufficient capacity to act as enforcers. This distinction was cited with approval by Megarry V.C. in *Re Northern Developments (Holdings) Ltd*[73] and by Oliver J. in *Re Lipinski's WT*.[74] In addition, the distinction drawn by Goff

---

[71] See, for example the arguments put forward by C.E.F. Rickett, "Unincorporated Associations and their Dissolution" (1980) 39 C.L.J. 88 at pp.104–106. Cf. A.R. Everton, "Towards a Concept of 'Quasi-Property'?" [1995] Conv. 118 at p.125 who argues that they, "may exhibit a common feature of a negative kind, in that it is not possible to describe as a strictly proprietary institution either a valid non-charitable non-purpose trust, or a valid discretionary trust in which it is impossible to locate the entire equitable interest".

[72] See, for example, *Re Bowes* [1896] 1 Ch. 507, where £5,000 to the estate owners to be used to plant trees for the purpose of shelter was construed as a gift to the estate owners absolutely, because the specified purpose was no more than an explanation of the motive for the gift.

[73] Unreported October 6, 1978.

[74] [1976] Ch. 235.

J. is at least consistent with previous case law, even though the matter had not been explicitly raised. Consequently, in *Re Drummond*,[75] *Re Taylor*[76] and *Re Turkington*[77] the presence of ascertainable beneficiaries allowed the gift to be upheld whereas, in cases such as *Leahy v AG*[78] or *Re Wood*,[79] the gift failed because there were no such beneficiaries.

Re Denley Interpreted: Re Lipinski's WT

It is necessary now to consider the other count of judicial support (for the *Re Denley* principle) as expounded by Oliver J. in *Re Lipinski's WT*. Although *Re Lipinski's WT* was decided in accordance with the rules governing property holding by unincorporated associations (see below), the *Re Denley* principle was viewed as an alternative justification for upholding the gift. In *Lipinski*, a testator left part of his residuary estate to an unincorporated association solely for the purpose of constructing and effecting improvements to its buildings. As this was a gift to identifiable individuals, albeit framed as a purpose, Oliver J. endorsed the approach in *Re Denley* and hailed it to be, "in accord with authority and common sense".[80]   **6.28**

Upon closer inspection, Oliver J.'s analysis also fails to convince. As will be shown, gifts to unincorporated associations are commonly upheld as gifts to the members of the association, subject to their contractual rights and liabilities. In *Re Lipinski*, therefore, it was open to the members to abandon the specified purpose because there was nothing in the terms or circumstances of the gift, or in the rules of the association, that precluded the members from dividing the subject of the gift between themselves.[81] In *Re Lipinski*, the superadded purpose could simply be ignored. This approach does not sit well with *Re Denley*, where locus standi to enforce the trust can extend logically only to restraint of misapplication. It is clear, moreover, that Goff J. intended the purpose to be carried out, "The court can, as it seems to me, execute the trust both negatively by restraining any improper disposition or use of the land and positively by ordering the trustees to allow the employees and any such other persons (if any) as they may admit to use the land for the purpose of a recreation or sports ground".[82]

Further confusion emerges from the claim of Oliver J. that, "it seems to me that whether one treats the gift as a 'purpose' trust or as an absolute gift with a superadded direction or . . . as a gift where the trustees and the beneficiaries are the same persons, all roads lead to the same conclusions".[83] Both absolute gifts with a superadded direction and gifts where the trustees and beneficiaries are the same persons result in absolute ownership. This is true whether the gift is to private individuals or construed under the special rules that govern property holding by unincorporated associations. More   **6.29**

---

[75] [1914] 2 Ch. 90 (a gift to the old Bradfordians' Club).
[76] [1940] Ch. 481 (a gift to the Midland Bank Staff Association).
[77] [1937] 4 All E.R. 501 (a gift to the Masonic lodge to erect a suitable temple).
[78] [1959] A.C. 457.
[79] [1949] Ch. 498 (a gift towards "The Week's Good Cause" on the BBC).
[80] [1976] Ch. 235 at 248.
[81] [1976] Ch. 235 at 244.
[82] [1969] 1 Ch. 373 at 388.
[83] [1976] Ch. 235 at 250.

difficulty arises where one treats a gift as a purpose trust. As has been discussed, the general rule is that trusts for non-charitable purposes are void. *Re Lipinski's WT*, however, shows only that this conclusion may be avoided in the case of a gift to an unincorporated association if it is construed as a gift in favour of members even where the donor has selected a dedicated purpose for the gift. It is not clear exactly how the principle in *Re Denley* applies in this context.

Notwithstanding, the conceptual and practical difficulties associated with *Re Denley*, it is now an established authority for departure from the rigours of the beneficiary principle in full, to cater for enforcement by those who benefit sufficiently directly, but fall short of being an object of the trust. It is also strongly arguable that the *Re Denley* approach might be employed to validate certain gifts upon trust to unincorporated associations (see below).

GIFTS TO UNINCORPORATED ASSOCIATIONS

6.30   Many groups and societies such as sports and social clubs are committed to the pursuit of non-charitable purposes.[84] Members adhere to the rules of their association and their funds are devoted to the group's activities or purposes. It is, therefore, necessary to consider the role for the beneficiary principle in the context of such societies. Many of these societies can be defined as "unincorporated associations". An unincorporated association is a body or group of individuals that has not been incorporated as a company. Unlike companies, unincorporated bodies or groups do not have legal personality and are, therefore, unable to hold property in their own name.[85] It follows that property belonging to an unincorporated association is held in the name of members on behalf of the association. Much difficulty surrounds the nature of their property holding and the construction of gifts to such societies. It is to be emphasised that the principal objections to purpose trusts as enshrined in the beneficiary principle and in the rules against perpetuities also apply to unincorporated associations. Accordingly the next part of this chapter will focus on these aspects of property holding by unincorporated associations.

Definition

6.31   In *Conservative and Unionist Central Office v Burrell*,[86] Lawton L.J. put forward a definition of an unincorporated association. Albeit submitted for the purpose of interpreting taxation legislation, it is a definition that is of obvious wider applicability. The definition of an unincorporated association offered was, "Two or more persons bound together for one or more common purpose, not being business purposes, by mutual undertakings each having mutual duties and obligations, in an organisation

---

[84] Note that the assets of a society may be held upon charitable trusts which are not subject to the beneficiary principle or the rule against inalienability.
[85] An exception relates to trade unions: Trade Union and Labour Relations (Consolidation) Act 1992, s.10.
[86] [1982] 1 W.L.R. 522.

which has rules which identify in whom control of it and its funds rests and on what terms and which can be joined or left at will".[87]

Inherent difficulties

In *Leahy v A-G for New South Wales*,[88] the testator provided that a large sheep station known as "Elmslea" should be held upon trust, "for such order of nuns as the Catholic Church or the Christian Brothers as my executors and trustees shall select". The gift could not be charitable under the head of advancement of religion because it permitted the selection of purely contemplative orders, which are not considered charitable in law.[89] Although the gift was saved by virtue of a New South Wales statute, which confined the power of selection to exclusively charitable objects, the Privy Council gave detailed consideration to the validity of gifts to unincorporated associations. No intention to create a trust for the benefit of individuals could be discerned where the gift was of a sheep station and the members of the selected orders were so numerous and located worldwide. In addition, the property could have passed to future members of the order for an indefinite period thereby violating the rule against perpetuities. In the alternative, Viscount Simonds explored the possibility that the gift might have been construed as a valid gift to the individual members of the chosen religious orders. Unfortunately, this conclusion was deemed insupportable as the gift was expressed to be for the benefit of religious orders rather than for specified individuals.

Leahy exposed the difficulties inherent in the making of gifts for present and future members. Even in cases where a trust can be discerned, the intention to benefit future members entails that the capital should remain intact and available to future members, thereby offending the rule against remoteness of vesting.[90] If no trust could be said to exist, the only alternative was of an absolute gift to the members. In the view of the Privy Council, this was the case even where the gift purported to be for the general purposes of the society. As Viscount Simonds explained:

> "In law, a gift to an unincorporated association *simpliciter* (i.e., where ... neither the circumstances of the gift nor the directions given nor the object expressed impose on the donee the character of a trustee) is nothing else than a gift to its members at the date of the gift as joint tenants or tenants in common".[91]

6.32

It was inevitable that a new theory of property holding would be developed to deliver the flexibility so patently lacking in the then extant law. In *Neville Estates v Madden*,[92] Cross J. provided the foundations for what has become known as the "contract holding theory" within his outline of possible constructions of gifts to unincorporated associations. The possible constructions were threefold:

6.33

---

[87] [1982] 1 W.L.R. 522 at 525.
[88] [1959] A.C. 457.
[89] See *Gilmour v Coats* [1949] A.C. 426.
[90] Note that *Leahy* was decided prior to the enactment of the Perpetuities and Accumulations Act 1964 and thus before the wait and see rule effected a relaxation of the rules governing remoteness: see further Ch.4.
[91] [1959] A.C. 457 at 477.
[92] [1962] Ch. 832.

- a gift to the members of the association at the date of the gift as joint tenants so that any member could sever his share and claim it whether or not he continues to be a member;

- a gift to the members of the association at the date of the gift not as joint tenants, but subject to their contractual rights and liabilities towards one another as members of the association. In such a case a member cannot sever his share. It will accrue to the other members on his death or resignation, even though such members include persons who become members after the gift took effect. If this is the effect of the gift, it will not be open to objection on the score of perpetuity or uncertainty unless there is something in its terms or circumstances or in the rules of the association which precludes the members at any given time from dividing the subject of the gift between them on the footing that they are solely entitled to it in equity; or

- the terms or circumstances of the gift or the rules of the association may show that the property in question (i.e. the subject of the gift) is not to be at the disposal of the members for the time being, but is to be held in trust for or applied for the purposes of the association as a quasi-corporate entity. In this case the gift will fail unless the association is a charitable body.

The contract holding theory

6.34   The second construction of there being a gift to the members subject to their contractual rights and liabilities towards one another, is the most flexible and convenient approach. Its adoption by the courts has seen the wholesale displacement of the trust as the vehicle to describe property holding by such associations.[93] Its principal attraction lies in the ability to cater for a fluctuating membership without contravening the rules against perpetuity. As the property is held at all times by the existing members in accordance with their rules of association, members who leave or wish to join create no problems. It is not possible for an individual member to claim an individual share. His share will accrue to the remaining members on death or upon leaving the association even though the members may well include persons joining after the date on which the gift took effect. The applicability of this construction will depend upon the rules of the association and the extent to which those rules lend themselves to that construction.[94] If the rules cater for the retention of the gift within the funds of the association, the most natural construction to place upon the gift is that it is held as an accretion to the funds of the association.

[93] Note, however, that technically the treasurer holds funds on trust for the members, to apply the funds in accordance with the rules of the association as laid down in the contract between members.
[94] See generally, P. Matthews, "A Problem in the Construction of Gifts to Unincorporated Associations" [1995] Conv. 302.

Case law developments

In *Re Recher's WT*,[95] the testatrix sought to leave part of her residuary estate to the **6.35**
London and Provincial Anti-Vivisection Society. It transpired that the Society had
ceased to exist by the date of her will, having amalgamated with the National Anti-
Vivisection Society. On these facts, it was not possible to save the gift. Evidently, it
could not be construed as a gift to the members of the Provincial Society subject to their
contractual rights and liabilities. The Society had terminated the contract between its
members and dissolved the association. There was simply no question that the gift
could be construed as a gift to the members of a different association. Had the Society
remained in existence, the gift would have been unproblematic. It would have been
construed as a gift in favour of the members as an accretion to the funds of the society
subject to their contractual rules.[96] This construction was open regardless of whether
the purposes of the society were "inward looking" (to promote the common interest of
the members) or "outward looking" (to promote some outside purpose such as the
abolition of vivisection). Brightman J. appears to have been swayed by the policy
concern that, if every gift was to be construed as a purpose trust or as distributing
shares to members, it would be unnecessarily hard to make a donation to such societies.

In *Re Lipinski's WT*,[97] the testator bequeathed his residuary estate to trustees on trust **6.36**
"as to one half thereof for the Hull Judeans (Maccabi) Association in memory of my
late wife to be used solely in the work of constructing the new buildings for the association and/or improvements to the said buildings". As a gift to a non-charitable
unincorporated association, it fell to Oliver J. to consider the effect of the specification
of the purpose for which the legacy was to be applied. There was no doubt that, had the
gift to the unincorporated association been a gift *simpliciter*, it would have fallen
squarely into the second category drawn up by Cross J. in *Neville Estates v Madden*.
Here, the testator had attached a seemingly specific condition to the use of the subject
matter of the gift. Oliver J. was, however, undaunted and held:

> "If a valid gift may be made to an unincorporated body as a simple accretion to the
> funds which are the subject-matter of the contract which the members have made
> *inter se* ... I do not really see why such a gift, which specifies a purpose which is
> within the powers of the unincorporated body and of which the members of that
> body are the beneficiaries, should fail. Why are not the beneficiaries able to enforce
> the trust or, indeed, in the exercise of their contractual rights, to terminate the trust
> for their own benefit? Where the donee body is itself the beneficiary of the pre-
> scribed purpose, there seems to me to be the strongest argument in common sense
> for saying that the gift should be construed as an absolute one within the second
> category, the more so where, if the purpose is carried out, the members can by

---

[95] [1972] Ch. 526.
[96] As Brightman J. elaborated, "In the absence of words which purport to impose a trust, the legacy is a gift to
the members beneficially, not as joint tenants or as tenants in common so as to entitle each member to an
immediate distributive share, but as an accretion to the funds which are the subject matter of the contract
which the member have made inter se" ([1972] Ch. 526 at 539).
[97] [1976] 1 Ch. 235.

appropriate action vest the resulting property in themselves, for here the trustees and the beneficiaries are the same persons".[98]

Oliver J. felt it to be significant that, under the constitution of the association, the members had the capacity to alter the constitution to provide for the division of the association's assets amongst the members. It was, therefore, open to the members to override the specified purpose even though it had been expressed in strong terms. Accordingly Oliver J. concluded that, "the beneficiaries as members of the association for the time being, are the persons who could enforce the purpose and they must, as it seems to me, be entitled not to enforce it or, indeed to vary it".[99] From the perspective of the testator, moreover, there is merely the hope or expectation that the members will observe the spirit in which the gift was given and apply it to the furtherance of the purpose. As Vinelott J. argued in *Re Grant's WT*:

> "For the validity of a gift within this category rests essentially on the fact that the testator has set out to further a purpose by making a gift to the members of an association formed for the furtherance of that purpose, in the expectation that, although the members at the date when the gift takes effect will be free, by a majority if the rules so provide or acting unanimously if they do not, to dispose of the fund in any way that they might think fit, they and any future members of the association will not in fact do so but will employ the property in the furtherance of the purpose of the association and will honour any special condition attached to the gift".[1]

6.37   In *Re Grant's WT*, the capacity to divide the association's assets amongst the members has been reinforced as a key requirement of the contract holding analysis. Here, the gift ("to the Labour Party property committee for the benefit ... of the Chertsey and Walton Constituency Labour Party") did not take effect as an accretion to the funds of the Constituency Labour Party. The Chertsey and Walton CLP did not control the property sufficiently that they could dispose of it in the way they felt fit or alter the rules and direct that the property be divided amongst themselves beneficially. The rules of the constituency association were clear that its members were controlled by an outside body and simply did not hold those powers. As Vinelott J. confirmed, "It must, as I see it, be a necessary characteristic ... that the members of the association can ... alter the rules so as to provide that the funds, or part of them, shall be applied for some new purpose, or even distributed amongst the members for their own benefit".[2]

6.38   Notwithstanding, the restrictive approach in *Re Grant's WT, Re Horley Town FC*[3] is the latest case to underline judicial preference for the contract holding theory. In 1948 Major Jennings settled land known as "The Defence" on trust, for the purpose of securing a permanent ground for Horley Football Club.[4] It was agreed that at the time the disposition was made, it fell into Cross J's second construction in *Madden*, that is, it

---

[98] [1976] 1 Ch. 235 at 246.
[99] [1976] 1 Ch. 235 at 250.
[1] [1980] 1 W.L.R. 360 at 368.
[2] [1980] 1 W.L.R. 360 at 368.
[3] [2006] EWHC 2386 (Ch).
[4] Despite the reference to "permanent", a perpetuity period was specified by reference to royal lives.

was a gift to the members subject to their contractual rights and liabilities towards one another. The question was whether rule changes, which extended membership and voting rights, precluded the contract holding analysis by limiting the capacity of members to dispose of the property as they saw fit.

Lawrence Collins J. held that such changes made no difference. He reached the common sense view on the facts that extensions to the membership scheme were not designed to confer the benefit of full membership on temporary or associate members. Further, the provision of voting rights to outside bodies in *Re Horley* could not be compared to *Re Grant*, where the level of control over the rules and destination of the association property proved too extensive. Accordingly, Lawrence Collins J. concluded that the beneficial interest was held on bare trust for current full members, each entitled to a share on a per capita basis. Notably, he relied upon the views of Sir Robert Megarry V-C in *Re GKN Bolts & Nuts Ltd etc Works Sports and Social Club*, as to how the court should approach its task:

> "As is common in club cases, there are many obscurities and uncertainties, and some difficulty in the law. In such cases, the court usually has to take a broad sword to the problems, and eschew an unduly meticulous examinations of the rules and regulations ... I think that the courts have to be ready to allow general concepts of reasonableness, fairness and common sense to be given more than their usual weight when confronted by claims to the contrary which appear to be based on any strict interpretation and rigid application of the letter of the rules".[5]

Further possible constructions

Although, the contract holding theory has developed into the preferred construction, a number of alternatives remain arguable bases for property holding by unincorporated associations. These will now be considered in turn.   **6.39**

Charitable purposes

Just as trusts for the furtherance of non-charitable purposes are generally void, a gift to an unincorporated association will fail if construed as creating a non-charitable purpose trust. It is possible, however, for an unincorporated association to pursue charitable objectives such as the alleviation of poverty or the advancement of education. Unincorporated charities hold their assets upon charitable trusts and do not fall subject to the rule against inalienability or the beneficiary principle.   **6.40**

---

[5] [1982] 1 W.L.R. 774 at 776.

Gifts to present individual members

6.41   It remains possible to view a gift to an unincorporated association to be for present members only. Such a gift might be an outright gift to the members,[6] or it may be held on trust for the members as joint tenants or tenants in common. Should the members hold as joint tenants, it is open to each to sever his share and become a tenant in common. On a joint tenant's death, under the right of survivorship, his share will accrue to the remaining members. Should the members hold as tenants in common, however, each has an immediate share and is free to claim it. In contrast to the joint tenancy, on the death of a member his share will devolve by his will or the rules of intestacy. In relation to the vesting of interests in future beneficiaries, no perpetuity problem will arise under this construction. It is somewhat more difficult to avoid other inherent disadvantages. Future members will not automatically acquire any interest in property because it belongs exclusively to those members existing at the date of the gift. If the property is held on trust, the acquisition of an interest in it (being a subsisting equitable interest) appears to require of the vendor/donor a disposition in writing under s.53(1)(c) of the Law of Property Act 1925 (see **4.09**).

Gifts to present and future members

6.42   A gift to an unincorporated association made by way of endowment must necessarily involve a trust. In such cases, the capital sum is held separately upon trust and is used to generate an income to be applied by the members. Unless the gift is framed to be for the benefit of existing members or confined to an appropriate perpetuity period, the principal obstacle will be the rule against perpetuities.[7] The problem relates to the remoteness of future vesting. As Widdows explains, "if it is interpreted as a gift to present and future members, some of the latter presumably being neither alive or ascertainable, it cannot be said by the degree of certainty required by the rule that the gift will vest completely in the period allowed".[8] Presumably, the court will wait and see whether, in appropriate cases, the members wind up the trust and render the capital their own within the statutory timeframe provided for by the 1964 Act.

It will be recalled that such problems were circumvented in *Re Denley's Deed Trust* by the limitation of duration to 21 years from the death of the last survivor of a number of specified persons. It seems, therefore, that a gift may be construed as such for present and future members who benefit sufficiently directly to have *locus standi* to enforce the trust under the approach in *Re Denley*. This construction will be possible where the gift is expressly confined to the perpetuity period or the rules of the unincorporated association are appropriately drafted to avoid problems of perpetuity. More difficulty surrounds the applicability of the Perpetuities and Accumulations Act 1964. Analysis on the basis of the 1964 Act will be dependent upon the way that the trust in *Re Denley*

---

[6] See, for example, *Cocks v Manners* (1871) L.R. 12 Eq. 574.
[7] Where an unincorporated association is at liberty to spend both capital and income a gift will not fail for perpetuity: *Re Price* [1943] Ch. 422.
[8] K. Widdows, "Trusts in Favour of Associations or Societies" [1977] Conv. 179 at p.180.

is classified. If perceived as a straightforward express trust for beneficiaries, it is the rule against remoteness that applies and it is open to the court to apply the statute. If perceived as a valid purpose trust, however, the common law rules must apply because the applicable rule is that which strikes at inalienability.

Mandate or agency

In *Re Grant's WT*,[9] it was the inability to divide the property beneficially amongst the members that precluded the contract holding analysis. The gift failed.[10] Similarly, in *Conservative and Unionist Central Office v Burrell*,[11] the Conservative Party proved ill-suited to the definition of an unincorporated association. The Party was a historical political movement that did not display the necessary mutual rights and obligations between its members. Rules governing control, moreover, lay with the party leader.   **6.43**

It should be pointed out that the courts have at times strained to find the necessary elements in the structure of a given organisation. In *News Group Newspapers v SOGAT 82*,[12] for example, the local branches of a particular union were held to be unincorporated associations with sufficient capacity to take control of their assets, terminate their association and divide their property amongst the members.

In the case of political parties, however, it appears that a different theory is required to explain the structure of their property holding and the construction of gifts to their members. In *Conservative and Unionist Central Office v Burrell*,[13] Brightman L.J. put forward the mandate or agency theory. The theory describes the relationship between the donor and the recipient, usually the party treasurer. In essence, the donor is viewed as the principal and the party treasurer as his agent. The treasurer is required by mandate to apply the money in accordance with the donor's specifications. To the extent that he does so, the recipient discharges his mandate vis-à-vis the contributor. Money applied outside the scope of the mandate exposes the recipient to an action to restrain misapplication or the requirement to replace the money. The contributor can, furthermore, demand a return of the money not expended on the purpose. Once the money is spent the entitlement extends only to an account of expenditure. Alternatively, where the money has been mixed with other party funds, the mandate becomes irrevocable. As Brightman L.J. explained, "The contributor has no legal right to have the mixed fund unscrambled for his benefit".[14] Two areas of potential difficulty arise: **6.44**

- the mandate or agency theory cannot be used to classify testamentary gifts. Agency simply cannot be set up at the moment of death between the testator and his agent. Accordingly, there remains a problem with the construction of testamentary bequests to political parties, and

---

[9] [1980] 1 W.L.R. 360.
[10] *Re Grant's WT* has been criticized as, "a case that has shed more darkness than light, not least because it provided no explanation of how the members of the local Labour Party did in fact hold the local party's assets"; see P. Luxton, "Gifts to Clubs: contract holding is trumps" [2007] Conv 274 at 280.
[11] [1982] 1 W.L.R. 522.
[12] [1986] I.C.R. 716.
[13] [1982] 1 W.L.R. 522.
[14] [1982] 1 W.L.R. 522 at 529.

• more speculatively, it has been suggested that a change of the office-holder to whom the mandate was given may be detrimental to the contractual claim of any complaining contributor. As Brightman L.J. conjectured, "Perhaps only the original recipient can be sued for the malpractices of his successors".[15]

Dissolution of an unincorporated association

6.45 On the dissolution of an unincorporated association, the ultimate destination of any property held by the association requires to be determined. In all cases, the determination is made either by looking at the provisions in the constitution of the association and the nature of the property holding by that association. It will be recalled that the contract holding theory has emerged as the preferred and most convenient construction of property holding by unincorporated associations. Gifts to unincorporated associations will be construed in this way, provided that the contract between the members allows for this construction and the members are able ultimately to divide the assets of the association amongst themselves. Where the contract holding theory is the adopted analysis, there are two possible destinations for the property of the association on dissolution.

Distribution amongst the members

6.46 On the construction that property is held according to the rules of the association as laid out in the contract between members, it would be odd to suggest anything following dissolution other than a distribution of the property amongst the members. The property has always been in the ownership of the members and, accordingly, it is up to them, on the basis of the contract between them, to lay down rules as to distribution. It is to be emphasised that as the matter is one of contract, there is no role for equity and no place, therefore, for the occurrence of the resulting trust. As Walton J. observed in *Re Buckingham Constabulary Widows and Orphans Fund Friendly Society (No.2)*, "It is a matter, so far as the members are concerned, of pure contract, and, being a matter of pure contract, it is, in my judgment, as far as distribution is concerned, completely divorced from all questions of equitable doctrines".[16]

Bona vacantia

6.47 Under the doctrine of bona vacantia, the Crown may claim property that is genuinely ownerless. This can occur where a society is defunct or moribund because all, or all but one, of its members have died and they have, thereby, lost their interest in any remaining assets. As Walton J. commented in *Re Bucks Constabulary (No.2)*:

---

[15] [1982] 1 W.L.R. 522 at 530.
[16] [1979] 1 W.L.R. 936 at 953.

"... although it is difficult to say in any given case precisely when a society becomes moribund, it is quite clear that if a society is reduced to a single member neither he, nor still less his personal representatives on his behalf, can say that he is or was the society and therefore entitled solely to its fund. It may be that it will be sufficient for the society's continued existence if there are two members, but if there is only one the society as such must cease to exist. There is no association, since one can hardly associate with oneself or enjoy one's own society".[17]

The emergence of the contract holding theory is comparatively recent. As such, it is unsurprising that the development of the case law regarding the dissolution of unincorporated associations has traditionally centred on the alternatives of the resulting trust in favour of the contributors[18] or the doctrine of bona vacantia. The conventional equitable approach can be gleaned from *Re West Sussex Constabulary's Widows, Children and Benevolent Fund Trusts*.[19] Money was there raised by a variety of methods to provide for widows and orphans of deceased members of the West Sussex Constabulary, an unincorporated association. The association was subsequently wound up leaving a surplus. It fell to Goff J. to consider the destiny of the surplus property.

- In the case of large donations traceable to identifiable donors, the gifts should be held on trust for those individuals. In cases where it was not possible or practical to trace the donor, the property would pass bona vacantia to the Crown.

- Some of the surplus was comprised of money generated by raffle or via the proceeds of entertainment. In relation to this property, Goff J. felt that subscribers had received the benefit for which they had paid, the contract as between the donor and the unincorporated association excluding the donor's proprietary interest. He believed that the appropriate course for the property was bona vacantia and stated:

  "the relationship is one of contract and not of trust. The purchaser of a ticket may have the motive of aiding the cause or he may not. He may purchase a ticket merely because he wishes to attend the particular entertainment or to try for the prize, but whichever it be he pays his money as the price of what is offered and what he receives".[20]

- In the case of proceeds from collection boxes, again there could be no resulting trust. Those contributors of cash sums must be regarded as intending to part with their money out and out, absolutely.[21]

---

[17] [1979] 1 W.L.R. 936 at 943.
[18] See, for example, *Re Printer's and Transferrers Amalgamated Trades Protection Society* [1899] 2 Ch. 184.
[19] [1971] Ch. 1.
[20] [1971] Ch. 1 at 11. He held, further, that in such cases, "there was no direct contribution to the fund at all. It is only the profit, if any, which is ultimately received, and there may even be none".
[21] See also, *Re Welsh Hospital (Netley) Fund*, [1921] 1 Ch. 655 at 660, where P.O. Lawrence J. felt it to be, "inconceivable that any person paying for a concert ticket or placing a coin in a collecting box presented to him in the street should have intended that any part of the money so contributed should be returned to him when the immediate object for which the concert was given or the collection made had come to an end".

6.48 The conclusions in *West Sussex* are of doubtful authority in light of *Re Buck's Constabulary Fund (No.2)*[22] where, as indicated, the distribution of property on dissolution of an unincorporated association was held to be purely a matter of contract. Walton J. signposted the movement away from equitable principle that had once pervaded judicial thinking. He noted:

> "...judicial opinion has been hardening and is now firmly set upon the lines that the interests and the rights of persons who are members of any type of unincorporated association are governed exclusively by contract, that is to say the rights between themselves and their rights to any surplus assets".[23]

Accordingly, outside the strictly delimited circumstances in which bona vacantia will apply (where all or all but one of the members has resigned or died), the assets of an unincorporated society will usually be divided between the members on dissolution. It is strongly arguable, moreover, that Walton J. would have arrived at a different conclusion than that reached by Goff J. as to the ultimate destination of the property in *Re West Sussex Constabulary's Widows, Children and Benevolent Fund Trusts*.[24]

Walton J. dealt also with the question of the proportions in which members may be entitled on dissolution. Clearly, in many cases the rules will lay down what should happen to property on the termination of a society. Where this is the case, the rules are to be regarded as decisive. Where no such rules are in place, Walton J. rejected any possibility of distribution amongst members according to equitable principles. Faced with the argument that the proportions may vary, he explained, "I completely deny the basic premise. The members are not entitled in equity to the fund; they are entitled at law ... It is a matter of simple entitlement, and that entitlement must be, and can only be, in equal shares".[25]

6.49 Although the contract holding theory is the preferred construction, it is not always possible to analyse gifts to unincorporated associations as falling neatly into this category. It might be clear, for example, that members are individually entitled to property. In that case the rules relating to joint tenancies and tenancies in common will apply on dissolution. In addition, there remains a role for the resulting trust in the case of endowment gifts. In the case of gifts held upon charitable trust, cy-près will operate on the dissolution of an unincorporated association to allow the property to be applied as near as possible to the original purpose for which the gift was intended.[26] Although the approach in *Re Buck's Constabulary Fund (No.2)* has been followed,[27] it is important to remember that both it and *Re West Sussex Constabulary's Widows, Children and Benevolent Fund Trusts* are first instance decisions. No appellate court has yet considered the question of the destination of surplus funds on the dissolution of unincorporated associations.

---

[22] [1979] 1 W.L.R. 937.
[23] [1979] 1 W.L.R. 937 at 952.
[24] See, further, Ch.9.
[25] [1979] 1 W.L.R. 937 at 953.
[26] See Ch.8.
[27] See *Re GKN Bolts & Nuts (Automotive Division) Birmingham Works, Sports and Social Club* [1982] 1 W.L.R. 774.

ALTERNATIVE MEANS OF PURSUING NON-CHARITABLE PURPOSES

Even in the context of unincorporated associations, trusts for purposes are prima facie **6.50** void under the beneficiary principle. The courts have strained to adopt a more flexible approach by developing the contract holding theory or accepting that a trust may be valid if expressed as a purpose, but construed as being directly or indirectly for the benefit of ascertainable individuals. The final matter to consider in this chapter relates to a variety of additional ways to pursue non-charitable purposes.

Using corporations

It is possible to make a gift to a corporate body to advance non-charitable ends. In *Re* **6.51** *Chardon*,[28] a gift of income to a company for as long as it carried out the specified purpose, was deemed valid as it was confined to the perpetuity period. Alternatively, incorporation of a society itself will effect a practical solution to the problem of trusts for purposes as the society becomes a legal entity.

Use of powers

The beneficiary principle only applies to trusts. Hence, it is possible to avoid the pro- **6.52** blem of trusts for purposes by drafting a power. It was, of course, open to George Bernard Shaw to employ a power as the appropriate mechanism to pursue his non-charitable ends. However, once he manifested the intention to create a trust, it was not possible for the court to conclude that there was a power.[29] As was emphasised in *IRC v Broadway Cottages Trust*, "a valid power cannot be spelt out of an invalid trust".[30] Although the express creation of a power would have circumvented the difficulties encountered in *Re Shaw*, it is to be remembered that where a power is employed there is no obligation on the donee necessarily to pursue the purpose.

Employing conveyancing devices

In *Re Tyler*,[31] a gift was made to a charitable body (the London Missionary Society) **6.53** subject to the request that they carry out the maintenance of the family tomb, but with a gift over to another charity (the Bluecoat School) if the request was not complied with. The gift was upheld. The purpose would be pursued as long as the Society felt it to be profitable and would cease when the Society declined to perform the maintenance,

---

[28] [1928] Ch. 464.
[29] Legislation would be required before trusts for non-charitable purposes could be construed as powers, which, if sufficiently certain, would allow trustees to elect to carry out the purposes: see, for example, the Ontario Perpetuities Act 1966.
[30] [1955] Ch. 20 at 36 per Jenkins L.J.
[31] [1891] 3 Ch. 252.

thereby, giving effect to the gift over. The Law Commission has noted the use of this conveyancing device to evade the perpetuity rules and enforce a non-charitable purpose. It makes no recommendation for change to this aspect of the law.[32]

Off-shore trusts

6.54   The use of off-shore trusts has become an increasingly evident means of creating trusts for non-charitable purposes; the motivation of much off-shore legislation is the facilitation of commercial transactions or off-balance sheet transactions that are made difficult in the United Kingdom.[33] In many jurisdictions, legislation has been necessary to remove the obstacles to validity that have hampered the creation of such trusts at home.[34] Accordingly, most provide for extended perpetuity periods[35] and, in some jurisdictions such as Cyprus, purpose trusts are not subject to a perpetuity period at all. In addition, legislation caters for a method of enforcement of such trusts by the use of a protector or an enforcer. The exact means of achieving this may also vary from jurisdiction to jurisdiction. Nevertheless, it has been argued that the approach in jurisdictions such as Bermuda or The Cayman Islands may serve, "as appropriate role models for the introduction of new legislation in England".[36]

- In Bermuda, for example, it was not possible to create a non-charitable purpose trust until the Trusts (Special Provisions) Act 1989. This legislation required the appointment of a person to enforce the trust and provision for the appointment of a successor. Although the original Act has been replaced by the Trusts (Special Provisions) Amendment Act 1998, the Supreme Court can still make an order for the enforcement of a purpose trust. This may be on the application of any person appointed by or under the trust, the settlor, a trustee or any other person whom the court considers has sufficient interest in the enforcement of the trust.[37] If the court is convinced that that there is nobody capable or willing to make an application, the Attorney-General may now himself make such an application.[38]

- In the Cayman Islands there has evolved the STAR trust,[39] which is capable of being perpetual and can only be enforced by dedicated "enforcers". Even in cases where there is a beneficiary, that beneficiary will have no right to enforce the trust as the only persons with standing are those who have been appointed as enforcers. In the case of STAR trusts the defining characteristics of a trust,

---

[32] *The Rules Against Perpetuities and Excessive Accumulations*, Law Com. 251 (1998), paras 7.34, 7.37.
[33] The question of whether a UK court would recognise and assist in the enforcement of a trust of English assets governed by an off-shore jurisdiction may, however, act to discourage the adoption of this method.
[34] No such legislation appears forthcoming in the UK, probably because "there is a feeling that pure purpose trusts may be hijacked for shady dealings involving hiding beneficial ownership" (D. Hayton, *Modern International Developments in Trust Law*, (The Hague, London, Kluwer Law International, 1999) p.305.
[35] See, for example, Belize where a period of 120 years has been adopted.
[36] M. Pawlowski, J. Summers "Private Purpose Trusts—a reform proposal" [2007] Conv 440 at 449.
[37] Trusts (Special Provisions) Amendment Act 1998, s.12B(1).
[38] For detailed analysis of the operation of offshore purpose trusts in specific jurisdictions: see G. Thomas and A. Hudson, *The Law of Trusts*, (Oxford, Oxford University Press, 2004), Ch.39.
[39] Cayman Islands Special Trusts (Alternative Regime) Law 1997.

such as the capacity of beneficiaries to enforce their rights against trustees, are completely missing. Hence, they provide a range of conceptual and practical problems.

By appointment of an enforcer

It has been suggested that a means of sidestepping the problem created by an absence of **6.55** beneficiaries might be to appoint an enforcer of the trust.[40] This argument is based on the view that the beneficiary principle ought to be regarded as the enforcer principle. In effect, this would as Hayton and Marshall argue:

> "clearly supply a mechanism for the positive enforcement of the trusts so that the trustees are under an obligation to account to someone in whose favour the court can positively decree performance unlike the cases of void non-charitable purpose trusts so far considered by the English courts where there was no-one who had been given locus standi positively to sue to enforce the trust".[41]

To adopt this approach would allow non-charitable purpose trusts to be valid where the settlor has appointed an enforcer provided the circumstances are such that the trust is administratively workable and restricted to a valid perpetuity period. Perhaps unfortunately, this is the least likely alternative method of successfully pursuing non-charitable purposes. The traditional approach of the courts has been to regard the need for a beneficiary with rights enforceable against trustees as fundamental to notion of a trust.

GUIDE TO FURTHER READING

D.J. Hayton, "Developing the Obligation Characteristic of the Trust" (2001) 117 L.Q.R. 96.

P. Matthews, "A Problem in the Construction of Gifts to Unincorporated Associations" [1995] Conv. 302.

L. McKay, "Trusts for Purposes—Another View" (1973) 37 Conv. (NS) 420.

M. Pawlowski, J. Summers "Private Purpose Trusts—a reform proposal" [2007] Conv. 440.

L.A. Sheridan, "Trusts for Non-charitable Purposes" (1953) 17 Conv. (NS) 46.

---

[40] See D. Hayton, "Developing the Obligation Characteristic of the Trust" (2001) 117 L.Q.R. 96.
[41] At p.204.

Chapter 7

CHARITABLE TRUSTS

In order to be charitable a trust must satisfy three requirements. It must be for a purpose that the law deems to be charitable; it must be for the public benefit[1] and it must be exclusively charitable in nature.[2] Until recently, charitable trusts were required to fall within a well established four-fold classification, that is, of trusts for the relief of poverty, advancement of education, advancement of religion or other purposes beneficial to the community.[3] As this classification was itself based on almost three hundred years of case law developments,[4] the need for a modern and flexible statutory definition became essential.[5] Accordingly, the Charities Act 2006, which lists 13 descriptions of purposes deemed charitable at law, now provides an encompassing test of inherent charity and more accurately reflects contemporary societal values and understandings of what charity entails. In order to be charitable, therefore, a purpose is required to fall within at least one of these statutory descriptions[6] and it must be for the public benefit.[7] It is these core characteristics of charitable trusts that this Chapter is primarily concerned.[8]

In addition, and, notwithstanding recent legislative change, a large body of pre-existing case law continues to be relevant to the definition of charity. For this reason, a solid understanding of the empirical evolution of the law of charities remains   **7.01**

---

[1] It must be of benefit to the public at large or a sufficient section thereof: see *Verge v Somerville* [1924] A.C. 497.

[2] That is property must be capable of dedication to charitable purposes only.

[3] *Commissioners for Special Purposes of Income Tax v Pemsel* [1891] A.C. 531 at 583 per Lord MacNaughten.

[4] Stemming from the Preamble to the Charitable Uses Act 1601: see further **7.09**.

[5] As stated in the Government's Strategy Unit Report, *Public Action, Private Benefit* (2002) at [4.9], "The law is confusing and unclear. The four 'heads' do not accurately represent the full range of different types of organisations with charitable status today, nor the range of organisations that should have charitable status".

[6] Charities Act 2006 s.2(1)(a).

[7] Section 2(1)(b).

[8] Accordingly, this chapter is not concerned with the administration of charities or reforms thereto.

challenging and essential.[9] In particular, an appreciation of historical developments explains the technical meaning ascribed to the concept of charity, to public benefit and to the approach of the courts to the key requirements of charitable trusts. Further, it elucidates the process of recognising new charitable purposes by analogy to existing charitable purposes, the essence of which has been retained within the final statutory description within the 2006 Act.[10]

7.02   This Chapter aims to provide an overview of the law of charitable trusts, and includes discussion of the advantages of charitable status, the problem with political purposes, the pursuit of charity overseas and the need for exclusively charitable objectives. Due regard will be had, of course, to the role of the Charity Commission in developing the law within the new statutory framework. This is because the 2006 Act appears to carve out a prominent role for the Commission in clarifying the public benefit requirement and producing guidance as to compliance for organisations seeking charitable status. It must not be forgotten nonetheless, that, "The Commission will be subject to the existing law of charities ... just as it was before enactment".[11]

THE ADVANTAGES OF CHARITABLE STATUS

7.03   Charitable trusts benefit from a range of advantages or privileges that do not attach to other trusts. Special treatment is afforded on the grounds that trusts for the promotion of charitable ends are valuable in the community as providing a benefit to the public and not merely to private individuals. Much of the litigation as regards charitable trusts is spurred by the need to filter out those trusts which do not benefit a sufficient section of the community and, therefore, do not deserve the advantages bestowed on charities. These advantages range from relaxed legal rules vis-à-vis other trusts to a variety of tax exemptions that accompany charitable status. Not surprisingly, tax advantages are of particular prominence. Indeed, some have gone as far as to point to an inextricable tie between the question as to whether a purpose should be deemed charitable at law and the consequent fiscal privileges which attach to charitable status.[12] Although this view is by no means universally shared,[13] it is difficult to ignore the colossal value of tax exemptions generated per annum and the motivation for manipulation of the system by individuals. As is clear from the brief categories listed below, moreover, charitable trusts benefit from relaxed rules as to certainty and perpetuity.

---

[9] The difficulty is that, as Lord Simonds noted, "A great body of law has ... grown up. Often it may appear illogical and even capricious. It could hardly be otherwise when its guiding principle is so vaguely stated and is liable to be differently interpreted in different ages" (*Gilmour v Coats* [1949] A.C. 426 at 443).

[10] Section 2(2)(m) includes, "other purposes currently recognised as charitable and any new charitable purposes which are similar to another charitable purpose".

[11] J. Hackney, "Charities and Public Benefit" (2008) 124 L.Q.R. 347 at p.350.

[12] As Lord Cross stated in *Dingle v Turner* [1972] A.C. 601 at 624, "In answering the question whether any given trust is a charitable trust the courts—as I see it—cannot avoid having regard to the fiscal privileges accorded to charities ... It is of course unfortunate that the recognition of any trust as a valid charitable trust should automatically attract fiscal privileges, for the question whether a trust to further some purpose is so little likely to benefit the public that it ought to be declared invalid and the question whether it is likely to confer such benefits on the public that it should enjoy fiscal immunity are really two quite different questions".

[13] See, principally, the views of Lord MacDermott [1972] A.C. 601 at 614.

Purpose trusts

As is clear from the Ch.6, a trust for non-charitable purposes is prima facie void for want of a beneficiary to enforce it. This rule is redundant in the case of charitable trusts where, as will become apparent, the so-called beneficiary principle does not apply.[14] Charitable purpose trusts are, therefore, valid and responsibility for enforcement of lies with the Attorney-General. Hence, these trusts do not require ascertainable beneficiaries to enforce them. In addition to their wide powers of administration, the Charity Commission can exercise powers of enforcement as are exercisable by the Attorney General.[15]   **7.04**

Certainty of objects

Charitable trusts differ from private trusts in that the objects of a charitable trust need not be certain. Provided the objects are wholly and exclusively charitable, the courts or the Charity Commission can remedy any vagueness by preparing a scheme for the application of funds. The cy-près doctrine, which allows for the dedication of trust property to purposes as near as possible to those originally selected, is considered in Ch.8.   **7.05**

Perpetuity

A charity is not subject to the rule against alienability that applies to pure purpose trusts.[16] Accordingly, property can be dedicated indefinitely to, for example, the relief of poverty or the advancement of religion. In addition, although a gift to charity must vest within the perpetuity period, a gift over from one charity to another can occur outside the perpetuity period.[17] In this regard, the Perpetuities and Accumulations Act 1964 does not apply a rule against remoteness. Where, however, the gift is from a non-charitable source to a charity, or from a charity to a non-charitable recipient, the rule against remoteness will apply. In this case, it is a major innovation of the 1964 Act that it is possible to wait and see whether a gift takes effect within the perpetuity period.[18]   **7.06**

---

[14] Note that charity can be carried out in a variety of legal forms which range from the charitable trust with individual or corporate trustees to unincorporated associations or registered companies.
[15] Charities Act 1993 s.32.
[16] See **6.04**.
[17] *Christ's Hospital v Grainger* (1849) 1 Mac. & G. 460.
[18] See Ch.4 for a detailed discussion of the perpetuity rules.

Tax advantages

7.07   Last but most certainly not least, charitable status attracts a range of significant tax advantages.[19] These include:

- relief from income tax on investment income applicable to exclusively charitable purposes;[20]

- exemption from tax on trading income where either the trade is exercised in the course of carrying out a primary purpose of the charitable trust or the work in connection with the trade is mainly carried out by beneficiaries of the charitable trust[21];

- exemptions from capital gains tax;[22]

- a claim to at least 80 per cent relief from the payment of non-domestic rates for premises wholly or mainly used for charitable purposes; and

- exemptions from payment of stamp duty on conveyances.

THE DEFINITION OF CHARITY

Legal meaning

7.08   The legal meaning of charity has always been somewhat elusive and stands distinct from any understanding of charity in a general or popular sense. As Lord Wright observed, the word "charitable" in its legal sense is, "a word of art, of precise and technical meaning".[23] It is curious, therefore, that prior to the enactment of the Charities Act 2006 a prominent characteristic of the development of charity was the reluctance both of the courts and of the Legislature to provide an authoritative definition.[24] Rather, in the course of past centuries, it has been necessary to have regard to any prevailing or accepted descriptions of charitable purposes in order to determine whether a trust or an institution was of an inherently charitable nature.[25] The Charities Act 2006, however, provides a modern statutory definition of charity by listing 13 descriptions of purposes deemed to be charitable at law. These descriptions are

---

[19] Note that there were over 190,000 charities registered with the Charity Commission at the end of March 2008, with a total annual income of £45 billion generated: Charity Commission, *Annual Report 2007/8*.
[20] The income must, in fact, be applied to charitable purposes: *IRC v Educational Grants Association Ltd* [1967] Ch. 993.
[21] Income Tax Act 2007 s.525.
[22] See Taxation of Chargeable Gains Act 1992.
[23] *National Anti-Vivisection Society v IRC* [1948] A.C. 31 at 41.
[24] In *Baddeley v IRC* [1955] A.C. 572 at 583, Viscount Simonds remarked that, "no comprehensive definition of legal charity has been given either by the legislature or in judicial utterance, there is no limit to the number and diversity of ways in which man will seek to benefit his fellow men".
[25] In the view of Lord Normand in *Oppenheim v Tobacco Securities Trust Co Ltd* [1951] A.C. 297 at 309, it is this, "empirical development which has so often baffled efforts to reduce the law to systematized definitions".

considered in detail below, but it is first necessary to consider the evolution of the general law.

The historical development of charitable purposes

A natural and necessary starting point is the Preamble to the Charitable Uses Act **7.09** 1601.[26] The Preamble, containing a detailed list of purposes then regarded as charitable, was to assume a central role for the courts as a reference point, or catalogue of accepted instances of charity. The list was as follows:

> "The relief of aged, impotent and poor people; the maintenance of sick and maimed soldiers and mariners, schools of learning, free schools and scholars in universities; the repair of bridges, ports, havens, causeways, churches, sea banks and highways; the education and preferment of orphans; the relief, stock or maintenance for houses of correction; the marriage of poor maids, the supportation, aid and help of young tradesmen, handicraftsmen and persons decayed; the relief or redemption of prisoners or captives; the aid or ease of any poor inhabitants concerning payment of fifteens, setting out of soldiers and other taxes".

The Preamble became pivotal to the development of the law. As Picarda notes, "the practice of the courts was to refer to the preamble as a guide and gradually this practice became an accepted rule of law".[27] The interpretation of charitable objects, furthermore, was not confined to only those purposes enumerated. Any purpose listed or analogous thereto was deemed to be charitable at law. As Sir William Grant spelled out in *Morice v Bishop of Durham*, "Those purposes are considered charitable, which that Statute enumerates, or which by analogies are deemed within its spirit and intendment".[28] Accordingly, by reference to the Preamble and analogous purposes thereto, the categories of charitable purposes had the capacity to grow. In the equity of the statute (or its spirit and intendment), the courts found the necessary flexibility to develop the law to meet the needs of changing times. A responsive approach was necessary. In the view of Lord Greene M.R., "The Preamble set out what were then regarded as purposes which should be regarded as charitable in law. It is obvious that as time passed and conditions changed common opinion as to what was properly covered by the word charitable also changed".[29]

Two hundred years were to pass before any further re-classification of charitable **7.10** objects was put forward[30] and almost a further hundred years before Lord MacNaughten in *Pemsel's Case*, famously classified charitable objects in the form to be

---

[26] Otherwise referred to as the Statute of Elizabeth I, the Act was repealed by the Mortmain and Charitable Uses Act 1888. Although s.13(2) of the 1888 Act expressly preserved the Preamble, both were repealed by the Charities Act 1960, s.38(4).

[27] H. Picarda, *The Law and Practice Relating to Charities* (3rd edn, London, Butterworths, 1999) at p.10.

[28] (1804) 9 Ves. 399 at 405. In order to be within the spirit and intendment of the Preamble, Lord Greene M.R. identified that the court, "must find something charitable in the same sense as the recited purposes are charitable" (*Re Strakosch* [1949] Ch. 529 at 537).

[29] [1949] Ch. 529 at 537.

[30] By Sir Samuel Romilly, in argument, in *Morice v Bishop of Durham* (1805) 10 Ves. 522.

adopted from then until the 2006 Act.[31] He claimed that charity in its legal sense was comprised of four principal divisions:

- trusts for the relief of poverty;

- trusts for the advancement of education;

- trusts for the advancement of religion; and

- trusts for other purposes beneficial to the community not falling under any of the preceding heads.

The alleviation of poverty and the advancement of education or religion were evidently clear in terms of the types of purposes contained therein. The fourth division or head was to prove the most cumbersome as not every purpose of possible benefit was deemed to be a purpose "beneficial to the community". Accordingly, the spirit and intendment of the Preamble continued to have a pervasive influence, in that it remained necessary to look at the Preamble and the decided cases under the Preamble to determine whether a given purpose was sufficiently analogous.[32]

In *Re Strakosch*, for example, a gift for the purpose of strengthening bonds between South Africa and the United Kingdom was perceived by Lord Greene M.R. to be, "undoubtedly for the benefit of the community [but] . . . not charitable in the sense in which the benefits to the community instanced in the preamble are charitable".[33] Similarly in *Williams's Trustees v IRC*[34] a trust to promote the interests of Welsh people living in London was of clear benefit to the public in a general sense. As the purpose could not be said to be sufficiently distinguishable from the mere social or recreational purposes, however, it was not within the spirit and intendment of the Preamble. It was not beneficial in a way the law regarded as charitable.

Proceeding by analogy

7.11 A valuable illustration of the process of drawing analogies from the Preamble is to be found in *Scottish Burial Reform and Cremation Society v Glasgow City Corporation*.[35] There the House of Lords was required to consider whether the provision of a crematorium was caught by the fourth head as being within the spirit and intendment of the Preamble. Lord Upjohn objected that the spirit and intendment of the Preamble had been, "stretched almost to breaking point",[36] but he highlighted the series of cases that drove him to conclude that the provision of a crematorium was charitable.[37] As a starting point the Preamble makes specific reference to the repair of churches. By

---

[31] *Commissioners for Special Purposes of Income Tax v Pemsel* [1891] A.C. 531 at 583.
[32] A less restrictive approach to the Preamble is promoted by Russell L.J. in *Incorporated Council of Law Reporting for England and Wales* [1972] 1 Ch. 73 at 88 where he argues as regards a given purpose, ". . . the proper question to ask is whether there are any grounds for holding it to be outside the equity of the Statute".
[33] [1949] 1 Ch. 529 at 538.
[34] [1947] A.C. 447.
[35] [1968] A.C. 138.
[36] [1968] A.C. 138 at 153.
[37] [1968] A.C. 138 at 152.

analogy, a trust for the repair of a parish churchyard was held charitable in *Re Vaughan*.[38] By way of analogy to *Re Vaughan*, the provision of burial ground for members of the Society of Friends was held charitable, there being no distinction to be drawn between a gift to repair God's house and God's acre.[39] Building further, a link could be drawn to validate a public burial ground in *Re Eighmie*[40] and, accepting that, the provision of a crematorium on the instant facts.

By far the most enterprising approach is to be found in the Canadian authority of **7.12** *Vancouver Regional Freenet Association v Minister of National Revenue*,[41] where the provision of internet access was held charitable by analogy to the repair of bridges or highways referred to in the Preamble. Although doubtless creative in adapting long-standing principles to meet the needs of contemporary society, it is difficult to imagine a more compelling case for statutory reform. On the evidence of such cases, the spirit and intendment of the Preamble had long ceased to function as a sensible measure of the appropriateness of adopting new charitable purposes.

The Charities Act 2006

The question of the inherent charitable nature of any given purpose or institution is no **7.13** longer answered by reference to the four heads of charity as laid down in *Pemsel*. Regard must be had to the new statutory descriptions of purposes contained in paragraphs (a)–(m) of s.2(2) of the 2006 Act:

(a) the prevention or relief of poverty;

(b) the advancement of education;

(c) the advancement of religion;

(d) the advancement of health or the saving of lives;

(e) the advancement of citizenship or community development;

(f) the advancement of the arts, culture, heritage or science;

(g) the advancement of amateur sport;

(h) the advancement of human rights, conflict resolution or reconciliation or the promotion of religious or racial harmony or equality and diversity;

(i) the advancement of environmental protection or improvement;

(j) the relief of those in need, by reason of youth, age, ill-health, disability, financial hardship or other disadvantage;

(k) the advancement of animal welfare;

---

[38] (1886) 33 Ch. D. 187.
[39] *Re Manser* [1905] 1 Ch. 68.
[40] [1935] Ch. 524.
[41] (1996) 137 D.L.R. 406; see A. Iwobi, "Rolling Down the Information Highway in Search of Charitable Status" (1998) 5 Web JCLI.

(l)   the promotion of the efficiency of the armed forces of the Crown, or of the efficiency of the police, fire and rescue services or ambulence services;

(m) other purposes currently recognised as charitable and any new charitable purposes which are similar to another charitable purpose.

The idea is that in order for a trust or institution to exist for the furtherance of charitable purposes, it must fall within at least one of the statutory purposes listed above. In addition, a charitable purpose must be for the public benefit and exclusively charitable in nature. The approach adopted in this chapter is briefly to introduce the general concepts of public benefit and exclusivity of charitable nature before examining in detail each of the statutory purposes in the Charities Act 2006. Thereafter, it remains only to consider charitable trusts in two important and specific contexts: first, where political objects are promoted and, secondly, where charitable purposes are pursued overseas.

PUBLIC BENEFIT

Statutory requirements

7.14   Section 2(1)(b) of the Charities Act 2006 makes clear that a charitable purpose is a purpose that is for the public benefit, i.e., "as that term is understood for the purposes of the law relating to England and Wales".[42] No new statutory definition of public benefit is, therefore, provided. It follows that regard must be had as to how the concept of public benefit evolved under the general law. Under s.3(2), however, it can no longer be presumed that a purpose of a particular description is for the public benefit.[43] The public benefit must now, in all cases, be demonstrated.

The approach of the courts

7.15   Traditionally, the public benefit requirement for charitable trusts could be stated succinctly, that is, the benefit must be available to the public at large, or to a sufficient section of the community.[44] In the words of Lord Wrenbury in *Verge v Somerville*, "To ascertain whether a gift constitutes a valid charitable trust ... a first inquiry must be whether it is public—whether it is for the benefit of the community or of an appreciably important class of the community".[45] Thus, the need for public benefit in this technical or legal sense has always been paramount and for hundreds of years the courts have been at the forefront in developing and enforcing the requirement. In practice, different

---

[42] Section 3(3).
[43] Previously, (in the absence of evidence to the contrary) trusts falling under the first three *Pemsel* heads were presumed to be for the public benefit.
[44] The question as to whether a trust is exclusively charitable may then be considered separately (**7.20–7.25**).
[45] [1924] A.C. 497 at 499.

"tests" of public benefit evolved to meet the specific concerns of the courts arising under the four *Pemsel* heads of charity. Invariably, therefore, the answer as to what amounted to a "sufficient section of the community" reflected the mix of pragmatic, economic and social concerns arising under each of these separate heads.

A prominent example of the specificity of public benefit is to be found under advancement of education where the presence of a personal link (of blood or contract) between potential beneficiaries will indicate a private trust.[46] In contrast, as regards a trust for the alleviation of poverty, no such constraints are operative. The relief of poverty is considered so altruistic that trusts under this head are exempt from the rule that there can be no personal nexus. Indeed, the legitimacy of longstanding authorities to this end has been confirmed by the courts[47] and the Charity Commission.[48] In a trust for the relief of poverty, therefore, it is perfectly permissible to define objects by reference to a class of poor employees or poor relatives. As will be demonstrated, however, the distinction between a trust to benefit a class of poor persons (public trust) and a trust to benefit particular poor persons (private trust) is sometimes difficult to draw. This difficulty is addressed in detail below.[49]

7.16

As regards trusts for the advancement of religion, again, there must be a benefit to the public or a sufficient section thereof. Unlike education, a less rigorous approach applies which reflects the absence of specific concerns regarding exploitation of charitable benefits under this head. It is difficult to see what possible objection might be raised to a trust for the advancement of religion amongst one's employees, for example.

The final *Pemsel* head was comprised of "other purposes beneficial to the community", i.e. it housed all those charitable purposes other than those for the advancement of religion, education and for the alleviation of poverty.[50] The development of this public benefit test has been influenced by the nature of purposes collectively charitable under the fourth head. As Viscount Simonds emphasised, "It is, ... in my opinion, particularly important ... to keep firmly in mind the necessity of the element of general public utility and I would not relax this rule".[51] By the very nature of trusts that fell under this head, the benefits provided required to be available to the public at large.

7.17

Accordingly, the courts have enforced a particular public benefit requirement, that the possible beneficiaries must not be "a class within a class". In *IRC v Baddeley*, benefits were confined to inhabitants of a particular area who were members of a particular church.[52] In *Williams v IRC* the class of potential objects was confined to "Welsh people living in London".[53] In both cases, a class had been highlighted and then restricted further by the imposition of an additional qualification. In *IRC v Baddeley*, the difference was explained to be "between a form of relief extended to the whole community yet, by its very nature, advantageous only to the few, and a form of relief

---

[46] *Oppenheim v Tobacco Securities Trust Co Ltd* [1951] A.C. 297 (**7.45**).

[47] See *Dingle v Turner* [1972] A.C. 601.

[48] The Charity Commission acknowledged that the law must be followed until it is overruled, but urged caution and flexibility in its application: see Charity Commission: *Public Benefit—The Legal Principles* (January 2005) at [A11]–[A15].

[49] See **7.32**.

[50] A trust in this category was required to be, in the words of Viscount Simonds in *IRC v Baddeley* [1955] A.C. 572 at 585, "a trust of general public utility and must be within the spirit and intendment of the preamble".

[51] *IRC v Baddeley* [1955] A.C. 572 at 591.

[52] [1955] A.C. 572.

[53] [1947] A.C. 447.

accorded to a selected few out of a larger number equally willing and able to take advantage of it".[54] The former is charitable; the latter is not. Viscount Simonds' oft quoted illustration is that,

> "a bridge which is available for all the public may undoubtedly be a charity and it is indifferent how many people use it. But confine its use to a selected number of persons, however numerous and important: it is then clearly not a charity. It is not of general public utility, for it does not serve the public purpose which its nature qualifies it to serve".[55]

It was permissible, therefore, to provide relief to the whole community in a form that only a few take advantage, for example, by the provision of a rest home. It was not, however, beneficial to a sufficient section of the community to confine that benefit arbitrarily to a section of the community to the exclusion of others who may otherwise take advantage. Accordingly, as the cases cited above suggest, it was not possible to create a trust of general public utility for those people living in London, if its benefits are confined to those of a particular nationality or a particular church.

Admittedly, the purposes charitable under the old fourth *Pemsel* head have now been divided up into a range of statutory descriptions, but there is nothing to suggest that the courts will not continue to apply the "class within a class" test to future cases, as appropriate. Thus, a trust for the relief of unemployment, for example, may not be for the public benefit if confined, say, to a particular group within a particular area.

The Charity Commission guidance

7.18 The Charity Commission now has a statutory obligation (following appropriate consultation) to issue (and from time to time revise) guidance as to the operation of the public benefit requirement[56] in order "to promote awareness and understanding" as to its operation.[57] The Commission's guidance does not create a new definition of public benefit or alter the general law. Nonetheless, the Charity Commission plays a key role in assessing public benefit and in determining whether an organisation should acquire, or continue to hold, charitable status. This, in turn, is of influence when the courts are called upon to distinguish charitable from non-charitable purposes.

Accordingly, in its recent publication, "Charities and Public Benefit", the Commission has produced general interpretative guidance on public benefit[58] and what charity trustees should consider in order to show that their charity's aims are for the public benefit.[59] The Commission acknowledges the need to determine broad questions, such as whether a purpose has an identifiable benefit, but also more specific issues, such as

---

[54] [1955] A.C. 572 at 592.
[55] [1955] A.C. 572.
[56] Charities Act 2006 s.4(1).
[57] Section 4(2).
[58] (January 2005). This publication replaces previous guidance on public benefit contained in RR8: *The Public Character of Charity*.
[59] Charity trustees are now required to report on their charity's public benefit in their Trustees' Annual Report.

the provision of any benefit to private individuals, or the effective exclusion from benefit of a particular section of the community. This encompassing approach is reflected in the promotion of two main principles. The first applies when deciding whether a purpose is beneficial in a way that the law regards as charitable. The second is concerned with whether a purpose benefits the public or a sufficient section thereof.

By way of a general introduction, these principles, as introduced by the Charity Commission, are outlined directly below.[60] More detailed analysis of the public benefit requirement is found within the substantive discussion of each head of charity.

7.19

Principle 1: there must be an identifiable benefit or benefits

- It must be clear what the benefits are.[61]
- The benefits must be related to the aims.[62]
- Benefits must be balanced against any detriment or harm.[63]

Principle 2: benefit must be to the public or a sufficient section of the public[64]

- The beneficiaries must be appropriate to the aims.
- Where benefit is to a section of the public, the opportunity to benefit must not be unreasonably restricted:

    - by geographical or other restrictions,
    - by ability to pay any fees charged.[65]

- People in poverty should not be excluded from the opportunity to benefit.[66]
- Any private benefits must be incidental.

[60] Charity Commission, "Charities and Public Benefit" (January 2008).
[61] Although it will usually be for trustees to provide evidence that aims are for the public benefit, "evidence of independent, expert opinion" from someone suitably qualified may be required (Charity Commission, "Charities and Public Benefit" (January 2008), p.14).
[62] Where a charity has more than one aim, each of those aims should have a demonstrated public benefit requirement.
[63] For example, "something that is damaging to the environment" or, "to mental or physical health", or that, "encourages hatred towards others" (Charity Commission, "Charities and Public Benefit" (January 2008), p.16).
[64] As is clear from the general law, the benefit must be to the public at large, or to a sufficient section of the public. The question as to what is deemed "sufficient" in terms of "a sufficient section of the community" is dependent on the charitable purpose in issue. See **7.14–7.19**.
[65] This factor affects a wide range of charitable purposes such as those pursued by educational organisations, private hospitals, recreational charities and charities that charge for membership, publications, or entry into performances or exhibits.
[66] Trustees will be required to consider ways in which people who cannot afford fees can benefit in some material way related to their charity's aims, for example, "the educational benefits to state school pupils arising from collaboration and partnerships between state schools and independent schools" (Charity Commission, "Charities and Public Benefit" (January 2008), p.25).

EXCLUSIVITY OF CHARITABLE PURPOSE

7.20 The final principle of a general nature is that the objects of a trust (or the purposes of a charitable institution) must be exclusively charitable. It follows that in determining the charitable nature of a trust the courts are called upon to look closely at the terms of a trust to work out whether trust property can be dedicated to non-charitable purposes. Sometimes the distinction between cases is very fine and almost imperceptible. The awkwardness in drawing firm principles derives from the sheer volume of case law decided over hundreds of years in which the courts have engaged with the subtleties of construction.[67] Nowhere is this better illustrated than in the similarly worded provisions of *Farley v Westminster Bank*[68] and *Re Simson*.[69] In the former, a gift to a vicar "for parish work" was deemed invalid. Lord Atkin considered that parish work,

> "seems to me to be of such vague import as to go far beyond the ordinary meaning of charity, in this case in the sense of being a religious purpose. The expression covers the whole of the ordinary activities of the parish, some of which no doubt fall within the definition of religious purposes, and all of which no doubt are religious from the point of view of the person who is responsible for the spiritual care of the parish in the sense that they are conducive, perhaps, to the moral and spiritual good of his congregation. But that, I think, quite plainly is not enough".[70]

In *Re Simson*, however, a gift to a vicar "for his work in the parish" was upheld as a gift to that person limited to purposes defined by his office. Hence, there was a sufficient nexus between the vicar and his charitable work for Romer J. to distinguish from previous authority. He concluded:

> "A gift to a vicar and churchwardens 'for parish work' is a general phrase covering a multitude of activities, and, as such, was held to be too wide, but a gift to a vicar 'for his work in the parish' involves a totally different conception. It merely means that the gift is to be used for the purposes of such part of his work, i.e. his functions connected with the care of souls in the particular district—as lie within the particular parish. In my judgment, such work is both sufficiently definite and is charitable".[71]

Difficulties in determining the ambit of a trust extend also to cases where the precise description of objects is not stated such as in a gift on trust for "charitable purposes" or "deserving purposes". A gift on trust for "charitable purposes" is unproblematic. It may be, for example, that the trustee is given a discretion or a power to allocate property to charitable purposes of his own choosing. Whatever objects are selected, the trustee must ensure they are charitable. Where, however, a gift is on trust for

---

[67] As J. Martin reflects in *Modern Equity* at p.464, "The many pages in the reports dealing with these refinements bring no credit to our jurisprudence".
[68] [1939] A.C. 430.
[69] [1946] Ch. 299.
[70] [1939] A.C. 430 at 435.
[71] [1946] Ch. 299 at 305.

"benevolent" purposes[72] or "public" purposes[73] or "deserving" purposes,[74] the gift will fail because its use is not confined to exclusively charitable purposes. Although purposes benevolent, public or deserving may incorporate much that falls within the definition of charity, there is a chance that some part of the gift may be applied outside the confines of charity and, for this reason, the gift will fail. Despite such a seemingly strict approach, there are a variety of means to construe as exclusively charitable, trusts which appear, at first glance, to provide for both charitable and non-charitable ends. It is open to the court to:

- adopt a conjunctive construction;

- sever charitable and non-charitable ends;

- deem non-charitable ends to be merely incidental; or

- apply the Charitable Trusts Validation Act 1954.

Each will now be considered in turn.

Conjunctive/disjunctive construction

Sometimes a charitable purpose is linked with another purpose and it is necessary to look at matters of construction to determine whether the trust property must necessarily be devoted to exclusively charitable purposes. Generally speaking, it is clear that the courts have been minded to accept that purposes linked by the word "and", such as "charitable *and* deserving" or "charitable *and* educational" should be viewed conjunctively and not disjunctively. This entails that such gifts are exclusively charitable as there is no possibility that property can be applied to deserving objects or educational objects that are not also charitable. By way of illustration, in *Re Best* property was left upon trust, "for such charitable and benevolent institutions" in the city of Birmingham as the Lord Mayor should choose.[75] Farwell J. had no difficulty declaring this to be a good charitable gift and claimed, "I think the testator here intended that the institution should be both charitable and benevolent; and I see no reason for reading the conjunction 'and' as 'or'".[76]

By contrast, purposes linked by the word "or" such as "charitable or deserving" should be viewed disjunctively. When construed in this way, such purposes are not exclusively charitable as they permit the dedication of property to purposes which are

7.21

---

[72] See, for example, *Re Barnett* (1908) 24 T.L.R. 788 (benevolent objects or purposes of a company).
[73] *Blair v Duncan* [1902] A.C. 37.
[74] See *Harris v Du Pasquier* (1872) 26 L.T. 689.
[75] [1904] 2 Ch. 354.
[76] [1904] 2 Ch. 354 at 356. See also, *Re Sutton* (1885) 28 Ch. D. 464 at 465, where Pearson J. considered the Will of a testatrix to leave property to "charitable and deserving purposes" that, "To my mind the words 'charitable and deserving objects' mean only one class of objects, and the word 'charitable' governs the whole sentence. It means objects which are at once charitable and deserving".

either charitable or non-charitable. Accordingly, in *Houston v Burns*,[77] a gift made for "public, benevolent or charitable" purposes in a Scottish parish failed because the words were wide enough to justify the trustees in disposing of the fund to benevolent or public purposes which were not charitable. Similarly in *A-G v National Provincial & Union Bank of England*, a gift "for such patriotic purposes or objects and such charitable institution or institutions or charitable object or objects in the British Empire" as my trustees may select was construed disjunctively and failed.[78] There were several categories of objects, each of which could not be said to be charitable.

7.22   Although it is possible to find a large number of authorities that adhere to the general rule as to conjunctive/disjunctive construction, it is necessary to adopt a cautious approach to the case law. For example, it is not difficult to unearth authorities with markedly different standpoints. In *A-G Bahamas v Royal Trust Co*,[79] a gift for the "education and welfare" of young people was interpreted disjunctively on the ground that welfare could not be said to be restricted to educational welfare. Lord Oliver remarked, "it is not easy to imagine a purpose connected with the education of a child which is not also a purpose for the child's welfare. Thus if 'welfare' is to be given any separate meaning at all it must be something different from and wider than mere education, for otherwise the word becomes otiose".[80] Perhaps, therefore, this is a legitimate point of distinction from, say, the conjunctive reading of "charitable and benevolent" in *Re Best*. There, Farwell J. found it easy to conceive of charitable purposes which were not also benevolent[81] and found it of no surprise that the testator should seek to ensure that the objects of the trust were both charitable and benevolent. Furthermore, as proffered by Sargant J. in *Re Eades*, "The more qualifications or characteristics enumerated, the more probable it is that there was an intention to multiply rather than restrict the scope of the disposition".[82] As to his approach to construction of the specified class of "such religious, charitable and philanthropic objects", Sargant J. objected that, "the ordinary careful student of English language and literature would, I think, almost certainly come to the conclusion that the three epithets here are epithets creating conjunctive or cumulative classes of objects, not epithets creating conjunctive or cumulative qualifications for each object".[83] As one or more of the selected objects might be merely philanthropic and not necessarily charitable, the gift in favour of charity failed.

Severing charitable and non-charitable parts

7.23   A charitable trust will fail for uncertainty where the property to be applied for the charitable purpose is not stated and no guidance is provided as to how that property

---

[77] [1918] A.C. 337; see also, *Chichester Diocesan Fund and Board of Finance v Simpson* [1944] A.C. 341, where the words "charitable or benevolent" were construed as sufficiently wide to allow property to be applied to benevolent objects which were not also charitable.
[78] [1924] A.C. 262.
[79] [1986] 1 W.L.R. 1001.
[80] [1986] 1 W.L.R. 1001 at 1005.
[81] Such as in advancing the writings of Joanna Southcote: see *Thornton v Howe* (1862) 31 Beav. 14 (see **7.51**).
[82] [1920] 2 Ch. 353 at 357.
[83] [1920] 2 Ch. 353 at 357.

might be ascertained. Commonly, moreover, difficulties are created where a variety of beneficiaries are specified, but there is uncertainty as to the beneficial share. In *Salusbury v Denton*,[84] however, the court was able to employ a severance of purposes where the trust was comprised of charitable and non-charitable objects. There, a testator left property by will to his widow to apply in part to the foundation of a charity school and, as to the rest, for the testator's relatives. On the facts, the courts ordered an equal division between the charitable and the non-charitable parts in line with the maxim "equity is equality". Two points require consideration. First, severance is possible only where it is not open to the trustee to apply the property solely towards the non-charitable ends. As Page-Wood V.C. claimed, "It is one thing to direct a trustee to give *a part* of a fund to one set of objects, and the *remainder* to another, and it is a distinct thing to direct him to give 'either' to one set of objects 'or' to another ... This is a case of the former description. Here the trustee was bound to give a part to each".[85] Secondly, equal division will be patently inappropriate in some cases. If so, the court may endeavour to calculate the percentage to be held on invalid trusts in order to hold the remaining part charitable.[86]

Incidental non-charitable purposes

Provided it is truly ancillary to the achievement of the main charitable purpose, an incidental non-charitable purpose will be accommodated. In *Re Coxen*,[87] therefore, a sum of money set aside for an annual dinner for trustees did not taint the whole trust as the amount was an insignificant fraction of the total and provided for the better administration of the trust. Jenkins J. considered of the testator that, "his motive and object in providing for the annual dinner ... was I think clearly to benefit the charity and not the members for the time being ... It cannot be said that these particular modes of furthering his charitable purpose are in fact incapable of furthering it. On the contrary I think there is every reason to suppose that it will be furthered thereby".[88]

7.24

It is important not to confuse the stated charitable purposes of a trust with the incidental consequences of carrying out those purposes. In *London Hospital Medical College v IRC*,[89] Brightman J. held that a students' union would be charitable if it existed to further the educational and therefore charitable purposes of the college to which it was attached. He claimed that, "If, put shortly, the union existed for the benefit of the college, it would be immaterial that the union also provided a personal benefit for the individual students who were elected members of the union and chose to make use of its facilities".[90] This is much in line with the thinking of Atkin L.J. in *IRC v Yorkshire*

---

[84] (1857) 3 K. & J. 529.
[85] (1857) 3 K. & J. 529 at 539.
[86] See *Re Coxen* [1948] Ch. 747 at 753 where Jenkins J. admitted that, had the provisions under consideration been invalid, the court, "would find means to quantify the income applicable to the invalid trusts rather than divert from purposes admittedly charitable (say) eleven twelfths of the income of a fund because a part of such income incapable of exact quantification but incapable on any reasonable estimate of exceeding (say) one twelfth is directed to be held on invalid trusts".
[87] [1948] Ch. 747 (a trust for orthopaedic hospitals).
[88] [1948] Ch. 747 at 755.
[89] [1976] 1 W.L.R. 613.
[90] [1976] 1 W.L.R. 613 at 620.

Agricultural Society that, "if the benefit given to its members is only given to them with a view of giving encouragement and carrying out the main purpose which is a charitable purpose, then I think the mere fact that the members are benefited in the course of promoting the charitable purpose would not prevent the society being established for charitable purposes only".[91] A problem arises where non-charitable activities are not incidental or subsidiary, but form part of the trust purposes. Clearly, the determination of whether a benefit is an incidental benefit falls to be addressed in the circumstances of the case. The more substantial the non-charitable activity or the weaker the connection between the activity and the main charitable purpose the greater the assumption that the activity is an object in its own right.

Charitable Trusts (Validation) Act 1954

7.25   The Charitable Trusts (Validation) Act 1954 applies to trusts taking effect before December 16, 1952. The confinement of its ambit in this manner has ensured that the Act is of increasingly less relevance with the passage of time.[92] It was enacted to render charitable the so called "imperfect trust provisions" invalid under the common law in that the property thereof could be applied either for exclusively charitable purposes or, indeed, non charitable purposes. The effect of the Act was to allow for the terms of such trusts to be treated as though they were capable of application for charitable purposes only. By way of example, in *Chichester Diocesan Fund and Board of Finance v Simpson*, trusts for "charitable or benevolent purposes" were not deemed to be trusts for exclusively charitable purposes.[93] The Charitable Trusts (Validation) Act 1954 would have allowed this wording to permit the disposal of property towards charitable ends alone. More difficulty is involved in cases where there is no express mention of charitable purposes. Harman J. preferred a restrictive view in the case of a trust for "worthy causes",[94] but in *Re Wykes*[95] the use of the phrase "welfare purposes" had a "sufficient flavour of charity"[96] that Buckley J. was prepared to deem this to fall within the meaning of the Act. In essence, the court is required to make an assessment as to whether anyone would have a legitimate complaint if the whole were applied for charity. Thus in *Ulrich v Treasury Solicitor*, where Hart J. was called upon to construe the very vague language used there by a testator, he was happy to follow *Re Wykes* and hold that the entirety of a fund was one to be devoted to the relief of poverty amongst the specified class.[97] On the facts, the class was in practice limited to those exposed to financial hardship and the size of the fund was not calculated to be of much obvious use except as a fund to be resorted to in the case of genuine hardship. Accordingly, it is now

---

[91] [1928] 1 K.B. 611 at 631.
[92] As Cross J. professed in *Re Harpur's Will Trusts* [1961] Ch. 38 at 48, "The Act leaves the law untouched for the future but, for some reason which I do not pretend to understand, validates retrospectively a limited number of dispositions which had already failed. I do not know on what principle these particular dispositions were selected for favourable treatment and I see no reason for construing this Act liberally".
[93] [1944] A.C. 341.
[94] *Re Gillingham Bus Disaster Fund* [1958] Ch. 300.
[95] [1961] Ch. 229.
[96] To adopt the phrase used by Cross J. in *Re Saxone Shoe Co Ltd's Trust Deed* [1962] 1 W.L.R. 943 at 957.
[97] [2006] 1 W.L.R. 33.

clear that the Act is not confined to cases where a specific charitable purpose has been expressed.

THE STATUTORY DESCRIPTIONS OF CHARITABLE PURPOSES

Bearing in mind that for a purpose to be charitable it must be for the public benefit and **7.26** exclusively charitable in nature, it is appropriate now to consider the 13 heads of charity as described in the Charities Act 2006. In order to be charitable within the law's definition, a purpose must fall within at least one of the statutory descriptions of purposes contained in s.2(2). As indicated above, the first three of Lord McNaughten's *Pemsel* heads are ostensibly retained. Thereafter, other purposes beneficial to the community (the fourth head) are sub-divided and added to in order that the new heads reflect closely the contemporary understanding of the types of purposes charitable at law. Accordingly, each description will be considered in turn and any particular requirement as to public benefit will be highlighted and analysed.

(a) THE PREVENTION OR RELIEF OF POVERTY

The "prevention or relief of poverty" is the first purpose listed in s.2(2)(a) of the 2006 **7.27** Act. This description is amended from that adopted by Lord McNaughten in *Pemsel's Case*, in that it refers both to the "prevention" and "relief" of poverty. "Prevention" and "relief" are to be read disjunctively, examples of the former ranging, perhaps, from "providing debt or money management advice" to "providing emergency aid in the wake of a natural disaster to people who are at imminent risk of becoming poor because of the loss of their home, possessions, crops or business".[98] As to the latter, much can be gleaned from the case law preceding the Act as to purposes inherently charitable and the public benefit requirement.[99]

The meaning of poverty

Although relieving poverty, of course, includes helping the destitute, it is a central **7.28** feature of the law that poverty, as a condition, is viewed broadly. As Eve J. put it in *Re Gardom*, "there are degrees of poverty less acute than abject poverty or destitution, but poverty nevertheless".[1] Similarly, in *Re Coulthurst* it was held that "Poverty does not mean destitution. It is a word of wide and somewhat indefinite import, and, perhaps, it

---

[98] See Charity Commission's latest guidance, *The Prevention or Relief of Poverty for the Public Benefit*, (December 2008), p.20.
[99] It will be recalled that the Preamble to the Charitable Uses Act 1601, listed as a charitable, trusts for the "relief of the aged, impotent and poor persons" (**7.09**). The relief of the impotent and aged will now fall within a different description, i.e. s.2(2)(j): "the relief of those in need by reason of youth, age, ill-health, disability, financial hardship or other disadvantage".
[1] [1914] 1 Ch. 662 at 668.

is not unfairly paraphrased for present purposes as meaning persons who have to 'go short' in the ordinary acceptation of that term, due regard being had to their status in life and so forth".[2] Nowadays, the Charity Commission is of the view that anyone unable to afford things taken for granted in modern society can qualify for assistance.[3] Accordingly, in its dealings with the Garfield Poverty Trust,[4] the provision of interest free loans was accepted as charitable for the relief of those unable to take out a mortgage under usual commercial terms. There are further means by which trustees of charities may relieve poverty[5] and these include grants of money,[6] the provision of domestic items whether outright or on loan,[7] payment for services,[8] or the provision of facilities such as tools, books or vocational training.

Poverty inferred from the nature of the gift

7.29   Poverty may most clearly be inferred where a gift is on trust to an organisation or body whose aim is the relief of poverty. It may also be inferred from the nature of the gift itself. Sometimes the description of the objects of the trust is illustrative. In *Re Gosling*, the provision of a superannuation fund for, "pensioning off old worn out clerks" was held to be charitable, being implicitly for the relief of poverty.[9] Similarly, the disposition for the relief of distressed gentlefolk in *Re Young* was held charitable, as "distressed" suggested to the court an implicit poverty requirement.[10] The courts have accepted, moreover, that descriptors such as "in needy circumstances"[11] or "of limited means"[12] are apt to indicate poverty, whereas the more general label of "deserving"[13] is insufficiently referable to the poverty requirement. In other cases, the provision of particular services may connote poverty. In *Biscoe v Jackson*,[14] the provision of a soup kitchen in Shoreditch was implicitly for the alleviation of poverty. A less clear-cut example is provided by *Re Niyazi*.[15] There, Megarry V.C. upheld a trust to build a working mens' hostel in Cyprus. The reference to working men in conjunction with hostel accommodation was sufficient to point to poverty although he acknowledged the case was, indeed, borderline. This decision may be usefully compared to *Re Sanders' WT* where a trust to provide dwellings for the working classes around Pembroke Dock in Wales was held not charitable.[16] It appears, therefore, that the mere limitation of the scope of a gift to the "working classes" is not, of itself, sufficient to indicate poor persons. Neither is

---

[2] [1951] Ch. 661 at 666 per Lord Evershed M.R.
[3] Charity Commission, *Commentary on the Descriptions of Charitable Purposes in the Charities Bill*, (December 2005) at [6].
[4] (1995) 3 Decisions 7–10.
[5] Charity Commission CC4: *Charities for the Relief of Financial Hardship* (August 2004).
[6] For example, to relieve sudden distress or to meet expenses associated with visiting people.
[7] Such as furniture, fridges or even radio and television.
[8] Such as child-minding or meals on wheels.
[9] (1900) 16 T.L.R. 152.
[10] [1951] Ch. 344.
[11] *Re Scarisbrick* [1951] Ch. 662.
[12] *Re Gardom* [1914] 1 Ch. 662.
[13] *Re Cohen* [1973] 1 W.L.R. 415.
[14] (1887) 35 Ch. D. 460.
[15] [1978] 3 All E.R. 785.
[16] [1954] Ch. 265.

extrinsic evidence of poverty admissible in court to evidence need. The requirement of poverty must be imposed by the terms of the trust.[17]

Public benefit

It will be recalled that in order to be charitable at law, a trust must be for the benefit of **7.30** a sufficient section of the community. Thus, where the community to benefit is restricted to a particular class of persons the question arises as to whether a sufficient section of the community is benefited. The idea was introduced that different "tests" are applicable depending on the head of charity in question. With regard to advancement of education, a gift which defines its objects by reference to a blood relationship or a contractual relationship cannot be regarded as being of public benefit, regardless of the number of people to benefit.[18] This so-called "personal nexus test" or "blood and contract rule"[19] does not apply to trusts for the relief of poverty.

A trust for a testator's poor relations has long been accepted as charitable,[20] illustrating clearly that evidence of a blood relationship between settlor and beneficiaries was no bar to public benefit. Such trusts were seemingly always deemed to be of benefit to a sufficient section of the community. It followed that no objection was raised to trusts the object of which was the relief of poverty of poor members of an association. In *Spiller v Maude*,[21] a fund for the relief of orphans of deceased members of a theatrical society to provide medical advice and annuities to members incapacitated by age accident or infirmity was held charitable. A number of cases demonstrate, furthermore, that objects can be limited to one's poor employees. In *Re Coulthurst*,[22] for example, a gift for the benefit of widows and orphans of deceased officers and deceased ex-officers of a bank was held by the Court of Appeal to be a charitable trust for the relief of poverty.

This generous treatment of public benefit in the context of the relief of poverty has **7.31** been the subject of considerable comment. In *IRC v Educational Grants Association*, Harman J. objected that, not being permitted under other heads, such cases "stick out like a sore thumb".[23] Lord Evershed M.R. commented in *Re Scarisbrick* that, "The 'poor relations' cases may be justified on the basis that the relief of poverty is of so altruistic a character that the public element may necessarily be inferred thereby; or they may be accepted as a hallowed, if illogical, exception".[24] The matter of the appropriate public benefit test fell to be considered by the House of Lords in *Dingle v Turner*.[25] There the testator directed his trustees to invest a specified sum on trust, "to

---

[17] *Re Sanders' WT* [1954] Ch. 265.
[18] As Jenkins L.J. emphasised in *Re Scarisbrick* [1951] Ch. 622 at 649, "An aggregate of individuals ascertained by reference to some personal tie (e.g. of blood or contract), such as the relations of a particular individual, the members of a particular family, the employees of a particular firm, the members of a particular association, does not amount to the public or a section thereof for the purposes of the general rule".
[19] See **7.45**.
[20] *Isaac v Defriez* (1754) Amb. 595.
[21] (1881) 32 Ch. D. 158.
[22] [1951] Ch. 661; see also, *Gibson v South American Stores (Gath & Chaves) Ltd* [1949] 2 All E.R. 985.
[23] [1967] Ch. 993 at 1011.
[24] [1951] Ch. 622 at 639.
[25] [1972] A.C. 601. See further, T. Watkin, "Charity: The Purport of Purpose" (1978) 42 Conv. (NS) 277.

apply the income thereof in paying pensions to poor employees" of his company. Lord Cross, (giving the leading speech) decided that, even though the poor relations cases were anomalous, they were too well established to overrule. He claimed that:

> "the 'poor members' and the 'poor employees' decisions were a natural develop-
> ment of the 'poor relations' decisions and to draw a distinction between certain
> sorts of poverty trusts would be quite illogical and could certainly not be said to be
> introducing 'greater harmony' into the law of charity ... and assuming, as one
> must, that they are properly administered in the sense that benefits under them are
> only given to people who can be fairly said to be, according to current standards,
> 'poor persons', to treat such trusts as charities is not open to any practical
> objection".[26]

Although all their Lordships were in agreement with this conclusion, Lord Cross put forward his own opinion on the unsatisfactory application of the personal nexus test.[27] Regarding the determination of charitable status, he argued that, "validity and fiscal immunity march hand in hand"[28] and, that the cases under the head of education were, "pretty obviously influenced by the consideration that if such trusts as were there in question were held valid they would enjoy an undeserved fiscal immunity".[29] He explained:

> "To establish a trust for the education of the children of employees in a company
> in which you are interested is no doubt a meritorious act; but however numerous
> the employees may be the purpose which you are seeking to achieve is not a public
> purpose. It is a company purpose and there is no reason why your fellow taxpayers
> should contribute to a scheme which by providing 'fringe benefits' for your
> employees will benefit the company by making their conditions of employment
> more attractive. The temptation to enlist the assistance of the law of charity in
> private endeavours of this sort is considerable ... and the courts must do what they
> can to discourage such attempts".[30]

The distinction between education and poverty was, thereby, that, "In the field of poverty the danger is not so great as in the field of education—for while people are keenly alive to the need to give their children a good education and to the expense of doing so, they are generally optimistic enough not to entertain serious fears of falling on evil days much before they fall on them".[31] In the view of Lord Cross, the taking on board of this fiscal advantages point adequately explained why trusts for the relief of poverty fall legitimately outside the blood and contract rule. They are simply not the trusts at which the blood and contract rule was developed to prevent. With the exception of Lord Simon, however, each other Law Lord expressly asked to be

---

[26] [1972] A.C. 601 at 623.
[27] See also, the views of Lord MacDermott (dissenting) in *Oppenheim v Tobacco Securities Ltd* [1951] A.C. 297.
[28] [1972] A.C. 601 at 624.
[29] [1972] A.C. 601 at 625.
[30] [1972] A.C. 601 at 625.
[31] [1972] A.C. 601 at 625.

dissociated from these further remarks. Even Lord MacDermott stressed, "I would prefer not to extend my concurrence to what [Lord Cross] ... goes on to say respecting the fiscal privileges of a legal charity. This subject may be material on the question whether what is alleged to be a charity is sufficiently altruistic in nature to qualify as such, but beyond that, and without wishing to express any final views on the matter, I doubt if these consequential privileges have much relevance to the primary question whether a given trust or purpose should be held charitable in Law".[32]

Distinguishing a class of objects

It remains necessary, nonetheless, under the head of the prevention or relief of poverty, to distinguish between trusts of a private and, therefore, non-charitable nature and those of sufficient public character to be charitable at law.   **7.32**

It should be noted that case law has focused on a sufficient section of the community for the purpose of "relieving" poverty rather than "preventing" it. The Commission has warned, however, that, "what is a section of the public for the prevention of poverty is not necessarily the same as what is a section of the public for the relief of poverty".[33] Accordingly, it might follow that a, "more restricted beneficial class, which can be sufficient in certain circumstances for the relief of poverty, is unlikely to be sufficient for the prevention of poverty".[34]

Historically, as regards trusts for the relief of poverty, a distinction was once made on the basis of whether the capital sum was retained, with the income applied for the benefit of the objects (charitable) or whether there was an immediate distribution of capital amongst objects (private).[35] This unhelpful distinction was emphatically rejected initially, by the Court of Appeal in *Re Scarisbrick* and latterly (unanimously) by the House of Lords in *Dingle v Turner*. The difference depends only, as Lord Cross put it in *Dingle v Turner* on, "whether as a matter of construction the gift was for the relief of poverty amongst a particular description of poor people or was merely a gift to particular poor persons, the relief of poverty among them being the motive of the gift".[36] Only if construed as the former would the gift be upheld as charitable.   **7.33**

This test was met with the most liberal of interpretations in *Re Segelman*.[37] There, a testator established a trust fund for the poor and needy of six named members of the testator's family and their issue alive at the expiry of 21 years after the testator's death. At the date of the testator's death there were 26 persons in the class. Chadwick J. acknowledged that the gift could not be charitable if it was in essence a gift to the individual members of the class. In his view, the gift was not of that character. The selection of named beneficiaries focused on need and not mere closeness of relationship. In addition, Chadwick J. drew upon a similarity between the instant case and *Re Scarisbrick* in that, as regards both, the class of those eligible to benefit was not closed

[32] [1972] A.C. 601 at 614.
[33] See Charity Commission's guidance, *The Prevention or Relief of Poverty for the Public Benefit*, (December 2008), p.16.
[34] Charity Commission, *The Prevention or Relief of Poverty for the Public Benefit*, (December 2008), p.16.
[35] *A-G v Price* (1810) 17 Ves. 371.
[36] [1972] A.C. 601 at 617.
[37] [1996] Ch. 171.

upon the testator's death, but remained open for a further period of 21 years. Chadwick J. explained:

> "During that period issue of the named individuals born after the death of the testator will become members of the class. It is, in my view, impossible to attribute to the testator an intention to make a gift to those after-born issue as such. His intention must be taken to have been the relief of poverty amongst the class of which they would become members. It follows that I am satisfied that the gift to the poor and needy of the class of persons set out in the second schedule to the will falls on the charitable side of the line...".[38]

It has been argued, perhaps harshly, that the outcome of *Re Segelman* extends, in an unwarranted way, the anomaly that is presented by the charitable trust for the relief of poor relations.[39] It is more accurate to say that the case is borderline.[40] The Court of Appeal in *Re Scarisbrick* made clear that a trust for the relief of poverty would not be charitable if the poor persons to benefit are either named, or comprise a narrow class of close family.[41] Arguably, *Re Segelman* falls just outside the narrow class of the type excluded by Jenkins L.J. Although it is perhaps problematic that the objects comprised named individuals as well as their after born issue, the members of the class in *Re Segelman* were potentially numerous, of a number unforeseen by the testator and selected originally on the basis of need. For these reasons, it is arguable that *Re Segelman* was correctly decided, albeit positioned uncomfortably close to the dividing line between the public and the private.

Exclusivity

7.34   However weak the public benefit test is in relation to trusts to relieve poverty, any such trust must aim exclusively at the relief of poverty. In *Re Gwyon*[42] a testator left his residuary estate on trust to establish a clothing foundation to provide trousers for boys in the Farnham district aged between five and 15 years old. The further conditions imposed were: first "that he shall not belong to or be supported by any charitable institution"; secondly, "that neither he nor his parents shall be in receipt of parochial relief"; thirdly "that he shall not be black";[43] and, finally, "that on a second or subsequent application he shall not have disposed of any garment received within the then preceding year from the Foundation and that when he comes for a new pair of knickers

---

[38] [1996] Ch. 171 at 192.

[39] See P. Luxton, *The Law of Charities* (Oxford, Oxford University Press, 2001), p.175. "the decision in *Re Segelman* on this point ... must be considered to have been reached *per incuriam*".

[40] See H. Picarda, *The Law and Practice Relating to Charities*, (3rd edn, London, Butterworths, 1999) p.43.

[41] As Jenkins L.J. argued in *Re Scarisbrick* [1951] Ch. 622 at 651, "One can conceive of a testator making a limited provision ... for a child or children whose conduct in his view had reduced their claims on his bounty to a minimum. A disposition of that sort would obviously not be for the relief of poverty in the charitable sense. The same must be said of gifts to named persons if in needy circumstances, or to a narrow class of near relatives, as for example to such of a testator's statutory next of kin as at his death shall be in needy circumstances".

[42] [1930] 1 Ch. 255.

[43] See generally, T. Watkin, "Discrimination and Charity" [1981] Conv. 131.

or trousers the legend 'Gwyon's Present' shall still be decipherable on the waist band of his old ones".

Eve J. was adamant that the trust was not limited to the relief of poverty in that there were no grounds for exclusion of the well off. He claimed:

> "None of these conditions necessarily import poverty nor could the recipients be accurately described as a class of aged, impotent or poor persons ... I think that according to the true construction of these testamentary documents the bene- volence of the testator was intended for all eligible boys other than paupers, and I cannot spell out of them any indication which would justify the Foundation Trustees refusing an applicant otherwise eligible on the ground that his material circumstances were of too affluent a character".[44]

(b) Advancement of Education

The meaning of education

The head of advancement of education is derived from the Preamble to the Statute of Elizabeth wherein there is reference to "the maintenance of schools ... and scholars in universities" as well as to the "education and preferment of orphans". The Charities Act 2006 retains this head and, consequently, much of the case law preceding the Act remains of relevance in determining what is charitable under the statutory description. The Charity Commission maintain that education covers both formal education, which may arise through schools and universities and other educational institutions, and less formal education which may arise in the community, "It therefore covers education, training and research in specific areas of study and expertise, and broader education in the development of individual capabilities, competencies, skills and understanding".[45] Accordingly, the copious case law detailing all things inherently charitable under this head is here categorised as follows:

7.35

- knowledge and research,
- formal teaching and study,
- public services and facilities,
- art and aesthetics, and
- sport and education.

---

[44] [1930] 1 Ch. 255 at 260.
[45] Charity Commission, *Commentary on the Descriptions of Charitable Purposes in the Charities Bill* (December 2005) at [8].

Knowledge and research

7.36   The conventional understanding of the head of advancement of education is that there must be more than simply an accumulation of knowledge. Learning needs to be imparted.[46] In *Re Shaw*, for example, George Bernard Shaw directed his trustees to use his residuary estate for a number of designated purposes.[47] In particular, trustees were to make inquiries into the number of persons speaking or writing the English language by the official alphabet of 26 letters and to determine how much time could be saved by the use of an alphabet containing at least 40 letters. In addition, a phonetics expert was to be employed to transliterate his play entitled, "Androcles and the Lion" into the proposed new alphabet and to advertise and publish the transliteration. Harman J. perceived the object to be an increase of knowledge. Unless combined with an element of teaching or education, this was not, of itself, a charitable object. As Harman J. explained:

> "The research and propaganda enjoined by the testator seem to me merely to tend to the increase of public knowledge in a certain respect, namely, the saving of time and money by the use of the proposed alphabet. There is no element of teaching or education combined with this, nor does the propaganda element in the trusts tend to more than to persuade the public that the adoption of the new script would be 'a good thing', and that, in my view, is not education. Therefore I reject this element".[48]

Logically, different considerations must apply to the work of academic researchers who are not engaged in the teaching process. The ambit of education in this respect was examined in *Re Hopkin's WT*.[49] There a testatrix gave part of her residuary estate to the Francis Bacon Society to be applied towards the discovery of the Bacon-Shakespeare manuscripts. A central aim was to "encourage the general study of the evidence of Francis Bacon's authorship of plays commonly ascribed to Shakespeare". Wilberforce J. held that the object was within the law's conception of a charitable purpose. He claimed, "it would seem to me that a bequest for the purpose of search, or research, for the original manuscripts of England's greatest dramatist (whoever he was) would be well within the law's conception of charitable purposes. The discovery of such manuscripts, or of one such manuscript, would be of the highest value to history and to literature".[50]

7.37   As to the absence of an element of active teaching or education, Wilberforce J. took a wider view than that of Harman J. in *Re Shaw*. The decision in *Re Shaw* appears to

---

[46] As Eve J. recognised in *Re De Noailles* (1916) 114 L.T. 1089 at 1094, "The mere stuffing of information into a boy or girl may make them very priggish, but it does not make them of much use in life, unless they know how to apply that information for the purpose of becoming useful citizens".

[47] [1957] 1 W.L.R. 729.

[48] [1957] 1 W.L.R. 729 at 738.

[49] [1965] Ch. 669; see also, *McGovern v A-G* [1982] Ch. 321, for discussion of research into human rights abuses.

[50] [1965] Ch. 669 at 679.

suggest that a mere increase in knowledge could not be a charitable purpose unless combined with an element of active teaching or educating. Wilberforce J. felt that this could not apply to researchers engaged in work of educational value. He claimed that the words "combined with teaching or education", were, "not easy to interpret in relation to other facts", and concluded that he would be, "unwilling to treat them as meaning that the promotion of academic research is not a charitable purpose".[51] Accordingly, he put forward the requirements to be met before research could be regarded as charitable. The research must:

> "either be of educational value to the researcher or must be so directed as to lead to something which will pass into the store of educational material, or so as to improve the sum of communicable knowledge in an area which education may cover—education in this context extending to the formation of literary taste and appreciation".[52]

Formal teaching or study

The head of advancement of education clearly embraces formal teaching including the study or promotion of individual subjects. The many illustrations are varied and uncontroversial. *Re British School of Egyptian Archaeology*,[53] for example, concerned a school whose objects were the discovery of knowledge connected with ancient Egypt, the publication of related works and the training of students in the craft or art of excavation. Harman J. concluded, "I cannot doubt that this was a school for the diffusion of a certain branch of knowledge, namely, knowledge of the ancient past of Egypt, and that the school has a direct educational purpose, namely, to train students in that very complicated branch of knowledge known as Egyptology. On that view, the school is clearly a charity".[54] Further examples include objects such as general advancement of mechanical science,[55] typing and book-keeping,[56] the study of economics[57] or the provision of postgraduate scholarships.[58]

7.38

More difficulty surrounds objects that might be considered too trivial or frivolous to fulfil a truly educational purpose. Care must be taken not to confuse the development of skill or understanding by learning, with a mere hobby or pastime to which there is an educational element. Whilst the former is charitable, the latter is not. As will become clear, this line is, on occasion, difficult to draw.

---

[51] [1965] Ch. 669 at 680.
[52] [1965] Ch. 669 at 680.
[53] [1954] 1 All E.R. 887.
[54] [1954] 1 All E.R. 887 at 890.
[55] *Institute of Civil Engineers v IRC* [1932] 1 K.B. 149.
[56] *Re Koettgen's WT* [1954] Ch. 252.
[57] *Re Berridge* (1890) 63 L.T. 470.
[58] *Re Gott* [1943] Ch. 193.

Public services or facilities

7.39 Advancement of education extends to the provision of educational public services and facilities such as museums,[59] botanical gardens,[60] zoos,[61] training opportunities for the unemployed[62] or public libraries.[63] Even the preparation of law reports by the Incorporated Council of Law Reporting was held by a majority in the Court of Appeal to fall under the head of advancement of education.[64] In *IRC v White*, Fox J. highlighted a substantial range of activity which would foster, promote and increase the interest of the public in craftsmanship, such as the holding of public exhibitions of works of modern craftsmanship,[65] the preservation and exhibition to the public of works of good craftsmanship of earlier centuries[66] and, as was directly in issue, the maintenance for the public use of a collection of books relating to craftsmanship whether old or modern. In doing so he was influenced by the approach of Farwell J. in *Re Cranstoun*, who had explained why a devise of ancient cottages to the Royal Society of Arts was inherently charitable. Farwell J. claimed:

> "It must be for the advantage of the whole of the people of this country that they should have an opportunity of seeing beautiful and picturesque buildings and cottages of this kind, which have in addition the historical interest which such buildings necessarily bear; and it must also be for the benefit of the community that any devices of good craftsmanship in the building of these cottages should be preserved".[67]

Such an explanation is readily illustrative of the importance attached by the courts to the advancement of culture and heritage. It comes as no surprise, therefore, that such a worthy purpose is explicitly recognised under s.2(2)(f) the advancement of the arts, culture, heritage or science (see **7.64**).

Artistic and aesthetic education

7.40 Advancement of education embraces the promotion of artistic and aesthetic objects. In *Associated Artists Ltd v Commissioners of Inland Revenue*, Upjohn J. claimed it to be a charitable object, "to foster, promote and increase the interest of the public in the dramatic art and in the co-related arts as well by the presentation of dramatic works as

---

[59] *Re Holburne* (1885) 53 L.T. 212.
[60] *Townley v Bedwell* (1801) 6 Ves. 194.
[61] *Re Lopes* [1931] 2 Ch. 130.
[62] See further, Charity Commission RR3: *Charities for the Relief of Unemployment* (March 1999).
[63] *IRC v White* (1980) 55 TC 651 (maintenance of a collection of books on craftsmanship).
[64] *Incorporated Council of Law Reporting v A-G* [1972] Ch. 73 (Russell L.J. dissenting). The court was unanimous in finding this purpose charitable under the then fourth head containing other purposes beneficial to the community.
[65] As Fox J. illustrated, "it seems to me that an exhibition of modern works of, say, good quality stained glass, or fine book binding or engraving, or of the silversmith's craft, would be educative of the public taste in a field in which it is to the general public benefit that such instruction should be available".
[66] As occurred in *Re Cranstoun* [1932] 1 Ch. 537.
[67] [1932] 1 Ch. 537 at 545.

by other means".[68] An illustration is provided by *Royal Choral Society v IRC* wherein the object was the promotion, practice and performance of choral works.[69] Lord Greene M.R. argued strongly in favour of a broad inclusive approach. In his opinion, "a body of persons established for the purpose of raising the artistic taste of the country and established by an appropriate document which confines them to that purpose, is established for educational purposes, because the education of artistic taste is one of the most important things in the development of a civilised human being".[70] Further, he argued that it does not matter that the persons involved derive pleasure from the given activity, provided that it is incidental and not the primary purpose of the trust, "Curiously enough", he observed, "some people find pleasure in providing education. Still more curiously, some people find pleasure in being educated: but the element of pleasure in those processes is not the purpose of them, but what may be called a by-product which is necessarily there".[71]

In *Re Delius*,[72] the wife of the composer Delius bequeathed her residuary estate for the advancement of her late husband's work. This object was to be achieved by the production of gramophone recordings, the publication of his works and the financing of public performances. Roxburgh J. perceived the purpose of the trust to be, "the spreading and establishment of knowledge and appreciation of Delius's works amongst the public of the world".[73] Following *Royal Choral Society v IRC*, he was clear that a charitable trust was created.[74]

Whereas there is little doubt surrounding the inherent educational value of advancing the works of great writers and composers such as Shakespeare or Beethoven, the same cannot be assumed of less meritorious artists or, indeed, more mundane gifts for the furtherance of appreciation of the arts. As Russell L.J. reminds in *Re Pinion*, "The mere fact that a person makes a gift of chattels to form a public museum cannot establish that its formation will have a tendency to advance education in aesthetic appreciation or in anything else. Inquiry must first be made ...".[75] The danger of subjective evaluation is undeniably present where the court is called upon to adjudicate the quality of lesser-known artists' work. As will become clear, the court must draw on expert evidence in order that, in the end, it is satisfied as to the artistic merit of the object in question. Where no benefit or utility to the public can be discerned, there cannot be a sufficient educational and, thereby, charitable element.[76]

7.41

Such difficulties came to the fore in *Re Pinion*. There an art enthusiast bequeathed his studio and its contents to trustees to enable it to be used as a museum to display his collection of works. Harman L.J. pointed to "a strong body of evidence" that as a means of education the collection was "worthless".[77] The testator's own paintings (of which there were around 50), were described as being "atrociously bad".[78] The

---

[68] [1956] 1 W.L.R. 752 at 759.
[69] [1943] 2 All E.R. 101.
[70] [1943] 2 All E.R. 101 at 105.
[71] [1943] 2 All E.R. 101 at 104.
[72] [1957] Ch. 299.
[73] [1957] Ch. 299 at 305.
[74] See also, *Re Shakespeare Memorial Trust* [1923] 2 Ch. 389.
[75] [1965] Ch. 85 at 108.
[76] See, for example, *Re Hummeltenberg* [1923] 1 Ch. 237 (a college for the training of spiritualist mediums).
[77] [1965] Ch. 85 at 106.
[78] [1965] Ch. 85 at 106.

assembly was so haphazard and without purpose or style that it could not properly be called a collection. Particularly telling was the surprise expressed by one expert that "so voracious a collector should not by hazard have picked up even one meritorious object".[79] Although there were some items that were not altogether worthless, these were "stifled by a large number of absolutely worthless pictures and objects".[80] Memorably, Harman L.J. concluded, "I can conceive of no useful object to be served in foisting on the public this mass of junk. It has neither public utility nor educative value".[81]

7.42   Understandably, more success was occasioned by the wife of George Bernard Shaw, who gave the residue of her estate to be held on trust for, "the teaching promotion and encouragement in Ireland of self-control, elocution, oratory deportment, the arts of personal contact, of social intercourse and the other arts of public private professional and business life".[82] Vaisey J. likened this to a finishing school and was satisfied as to the inherent educational benefit in, "the promotion or encouragement of those arts and graces of life which are, after all, perhaps the finest and best part of the human character".[83] A sharp contrast might be drawn between qualities deemed admirable and those less fine parts of the human character. Needless to say, as Harman L.J. did in *Re Pinion*, that a public library devoted entirely to works of pornography or of a corrupting nature would, by contrast, not be permitted.[84]

Sports, activities and educational institutions

7.43   The promotion of amateur sport is a head of charity in its own right, but the traditional approach of the courts has been to deny that sport per se is of charitable or, indeed, educational benefit.[85] This reservation has never been pertinent where sport is ancillary to another charitable purpose, for example, the formal education of the young.[86] In *Re Mariette*, therefore, a gift for the provision of five squash courts to Aldenham school was held charitable on the ground that learning to play games at a boarding school was just as important as learning from books.[87] As Eve J, put it, "No one of sense could be found to suggest that between those ages (10 to 19) any boy can be properly educated unless at least as much attention is given to the development of his body as is given to the development of his mind. It is necessary, therefore, in any satisfactory system of education to provide for both mental and bodily occupation".[88] Similarly, in *IRC v*

---

[79] [1965] Ch. 85 at 107.
[80] [1965] Ch. 85 at 107.
[81] [1965] Ch. 85 at 107.
[82] *Re Shaw's WT* [1952] Ch. 163.
[83] [1952] Ch. 163 at 172.
[84] [1965] Ch. 85 at 106.
[85] As Lopes L.J. affirmed in *Re Nottage* [1895] 2 Ch. 649 at 656, "I am of the opinion that a gift, the object of which is the encouragement of a mere sport or game ... cannot upon the authorities be held to be charitable, though such sport or game is to some extent beneficial to the public" (the instant case concerned the provision of a cup to "encourage the sport of yacht racing").
[86] The advancement of the physical education of young people not undergoing formal education is now a recognised charitable purpose: see Charity Commission RR11: *Charitable Status and Sport* (April 2003).
[87] [1915] 2 Ch. 284.
[88] [1915] 2 Ch. 284 at 288.

McMullen,[89] the House of Lords upheld a trust to provide facilities in schools and universities to play football and other sports. Lord Hailsham embraced the idea that education of the young should not be limited to formal education and he painted a picture of, "a balanced and systematic process of instruction, training and practice containing . . . spiritual, moral, mental and physical elements".[90] He continued, "I reject any idea which would cramp the education of the young within the school or university syllabus, confine it within the school or university campus, limit it to formal instruction, or render it devoid of pleasure in the exercise of skill".[91]

Besides activities that might generally be classified as sport, the courts have considered the educational benefit of a wide range of pursuits. To adopt the approach of Lord Hailsham, it is probably the case that that where an activity contains something of the process of instruction, training and practice, perhaps involving some spiritual, moral, mental and physical elements, an argument can be made as to its inherent charitable nature. Thus, in *Re Lopes*, Farwell J. claimed that, "A ride on an elephant may be educational. At any rate it brings the reality of the elephant and its uses to a child's mind, in lieu of leaving him to mere book learning. It widens his mind, and in that broad sense is educational".[92]

Re Dupree's Deed Trusts[93] involved a trust to promote chess playing through the organisation of an annual tournament for boys under the age of 21 in the Portsmouth area. Vaisey J. made apparent his discomfort in admitting, "One feels perhaps that one is on a rather slippery slope. If chess, why not draughts? If draughts, why not bezique? And so on, through to bridge, whist, and by another route stamp-collecting and the acquisition of birds' eggs".[94] Notwithstanding this practical concern, there is nothing in the remainder of his judgment to cast doubt as to his view of the educational worth in learning and playing the game. Such is evident from his admission in the opening paragraph of his judgment that, "the nature of the game is such as to encourage the qualities of foresight, concentration, memory and ingenuity. Even unguided by actual evidence, I should not have been surprised if the conclusion could have been reached that the game is essentially one which does possess an educational value".[95] Essentially, it is possible to argue that those qualities are present in a very much wider range of activities undertaken by children. Picarda, for example, is happy to make the argument that, "stamp-collecting may bring the reality of geography and history to a child's mind" or that the acquisition of birds' eggs may stimulate "his or her enthusiasm for natural history".[96] Perhaps more problematic are the activities where educational value is not so readily apparent or where chance plays a greater role, as in many card or board games.

7.44

[89] [1981] A.C. 1.
[90] [1981] A.C. 1 at 18.
[91] [1981] A.C. 1 at 18.
[92] *Re Lopes* [1931] 2 Ch. 130 at 136.
[93] [1945] Ch. 16.
[94] [1945] Ch. 16 at 20.
[95] [1945] Ch. 16 at 19.
[96] Picarda, M., *The Law and Practice Relating to Charities* (3rd edn, London, Butterworths, 1999), p.53.

Public benefit

7.45 It is clear that a trust is incapable of being charitable unless it is for the benefit of the public or a sufficient section of the public. Unlike trusts for the relief of poverty, a more stringent rule applies to trusts for the advancement of education to deny the benefits of charitable status to those who seek to benefit their relatives or employees at the expense of the taxpayer. In *Re Compton*,[97] for example, a trust providing for the education of the descendants of three named persons was not a valid charitable trust because the objects were defined by reference to a personal nexus. The trust lacked a sufficiently public quality.

Guidance as to the operation of the personal nexus test was supplied by the House of Lords in *Oppenheim v Tobacco Securities Trust Co*.[98] The case concerned a settlement to provide for the education of children of employees and ex-employees of British American Tobacco or any allied company, of which there were over 110,000. Despite the large number to benefit, the nexus between them was employment by a particular employer. Accordingly, there could not be said to be a benefit to a sufficient section of the community. As Lord Normand identified, "there is no public element to be found in the bare nexus of common employment".[99] Lord Simonds explained the approach of the courts to the issue of public benefit under the second head as follows:

> "the question is whether that class of persons can be regarded as such a 'section of the community' as to satisfy the test of public benefit. These words 'section of the community' have no special sanctity, but they conveniently indicate first, that the possible (I emphasise the word 'possible') beneficiaries must not be numerically negligible, and secondly, that the quality which distinguishes them from other members of the community, so that they form by themselves a section of it, must be a quality which does not depend on their relationship to a particular individual. It is for this reason that a trust for the education of members of a family ... cannot be regarded as charitable. A group of persons may be numerous, but, if the nexus between them is their personal relationship to a single propositus or to several propositi, they are neither the community nor a section of the community for charitable purposes".[1]

In essence, therefore, if beneficiaries are ascertained by reference to some personal tie (whether of blood or contract), this cannot amount to the public or a sufficient section thereof. This test has been accepted despite the legitimate criticisms of its utility voiced by Lord MacDermott in his dissenting speech. He highlighted that whilst there was no problem with a trust to advance the education of railwaymen, there could be no charitable trust for the advancement of education of the workers of a particular railway even where there would be little difference in the make-up of the group to benefit. He explained:

---

[97] [1945] 1 Ch. 123.
[98] [1951] A.C. 297, noted at (1951) 67 L.Q.R. 162 (A.L. Goodhart).
[99] [1951] A.C. 297 at 310.
[1] [1951] A.C. 297 at 306.

"if the bond between those employed by a particular railway is purely personal, how should the bond between those who are employed as railwaymen be so essentially different? Is a distinction to be drawn in this respect between those who are employed in a particular industry before it is nationalised and those who are employed therein after that process has been completed and one employer has taken the place of many?"[2]

The arbitrariness of the test was such that, "had the present trust been framed so as to provide for the education of the children of those engaged in the tobacco industry in a named county or town, it would have been a good charitable disposition, and that even though the class to be benefited would have been appreciably smaller and no more important than is the class here".[3] Accordingly, Lord MacDermott (alone) was of the view that public benefit should be a matter of evidence in each case without out the need to resort to a hard and fast rule.

The Charity Commission has consistently acknowledged that it must apply the law as   **7.46** set out in *Oppenheim* unless and until it is overruled.[4] Nonetheless, it is pointed out that that a class whose distinguishing feature is an impersonal quality may be a sufficient section of the public even if its constituent members happen to share a personal characteristic. Accordingly, even in a case where all the potential beneficiaries are connected by blood or contract there may still be a sufficient section of the public if, in view of all relevant considerations, it is clear that a public class is intended and that the class can be (and, as a rule, is in fact) described otherwise than by reference to a blood or contract relationship.[5] Where a class cannot be defined by objective and impersonal terms, however, this will be sufficient to indicate the intention to establish a private rather than public benefit. In adopting this approach, the Charity Commission hopes to deal with the potentially anomalous application of *Oppenheim*, in that there may be different treatment of bodies serving the same section of the community according to the description of the group by reference to, for example, common employment, or by some other public quality.[6]

A preference to a private class

It is permissible to create a charitable trust for a primary class wherefrom the trustees   **7.47** have a power to prefer a smaller private class.[7] Controversially, in *Re Koettgen's WT*[8] Upjohn J. held charitable a trust containing an imperative duty upon trustees to prefer, as to up to 75 per cent of the income, the employees of a selected company or any of their family members. The trust in issue was established to further the education of

---

[2] [1951] A.C. 297 at 317.
[3] [1951] A.C. 297 at 318.
[4] Charity Commission: *Public Benefit—The Legal Principles* (January 2005) at [A11].
[5] The Charity Commission cite *Springhill Housing Action Committee v Commissioner of Valuation* [1983] NI 184 as authority for this proposition. Unfortunately, no further practical illustration is provided.
[6] Charity Commission: *Public Benefit—The Legal Principles* (January 2005) at [A15].
[7] Note that as the public benefit requirement must now be demonstrated, the Charity Commission view that the requirement will be met, "only if the class that is preferred is, in itself, a section of the public" (Charity Commission, *The Advancement of Education for the Public Benefit* (December 2008)).
[8] [1954] Ch. 252.

"persons of either sex who are British born subjects and who are desirous of educating themselves or obtaining tuition for a higher commercial career but whose means are insufficient or will not allow of their obtaining such education or tuition at their own expense". Upjohn J. was, evidently, influenced by the argument that it could not be certain in any future year how much (if any) of the 75 per cent would be used by the preferred class. By looking at the primary class, he was satisfied that the trust was of a sufficiently public character, and he maintained that it is, "when the primary class of eligible persons is ascertained that the question of the public nature of the trust arises and falls to be decided".[9] This conclusion is essentially problematic and cannot safely be followed. Upjohn J. looks to have accepted as charitable a trust whereby trustees have a discretion as to the distribution of income between charitable and non-charitable ends. It is difficulty to see, therefore, how such a trust can be regarded as exclusively charitable.

A different approach prevailed in *IRC v Educational Grants Association Ltd*[10] in relation to a charitable corporation the object of which was, "to advance education in such ways as shall from time-to-time be thought fit and in particular by making grants to or for the benefit of and for the education of all such persons as shall be considered likely to benefit from education at a preparatory, public or other independent school, including boarding schools, and at technical colleges". The Association was supported by payments under a deed of covenant by the Metal Box Company. The question arose as to whether the payments were made for charitable purposes only when it emerged that 80 per cent of the income of one year was paid towards the education of children connected to the company. *Re Koettgen's WT*, was considered but Pennycuick J. was clearly minded not to follow the thinking previously employed by Upjohn J.[11] Instead he felt compelled to follow *Oppenheim* and held that a charitable corporation was not entitled to recover income tax on income applied for the non-charitable purposes of advancing the education of a preferred group with a wider class of charitable objects. This sensible and practical approach is much to be preferred.

Public benefit and fee-charging

7.48   As all organisations seeking or holding charitable status are now required to demonstrate public benefit, a greater level of Charity Commission scrutiny will fall on educational providers which charge fees and, thereby, restrict benefit to those who can afford to pay. The Charity Commission position is that, where charities do charge fees, those who are unable to pay must not be entirely excluded from benefit. As the Commission points out, "This does not mean that charities have to offer services for free. Nor does it mean that people who are unable to pay the fees must actually benefit, in the sense that they choose to take up the benefit. They must not be excluded from the opportunity to benefit, whether or not they actually do so".[12] In addition, the sense of

---

[9] [1954] Ch. 252 at 258.
[10] [1967] Ch. 123.
[11] He cited the criticism levied at Upjohn J.'s judgment by Lord Radcliffe in *Caffoor v Comr. Of Income Tax, Colombo* [1961] A.C. 584 at 604, that the *Re Koettgen* decision, "edges very near to being inconsistent with *Oppenheim's* case".
[12] Charity Commission: *Charities and Public Benefit* (January 2008), p.23.

"not excluding" people from benefit requires more than providing, "minimal or nominal benefit".[13] Opportunity to benefit should be "genuine and meaningful".[14] Examples of ways in which education providers might satisfy the public benefit requirement include a demonstration of, "the educational benefits to pupils in state schools arising from collaboration and partnerships between state schools and independent schools", or "the educational benefits to state school pupils who are able to attend certain lessons or other educational events at independent schools".[15]

Political objects

A final reference needs to be made regarding the potential for a variety of non-charitable purposes to be dressed up as educational. As the Charity Commission warned in its Annual Report for 1966, "Ingenious draftsmen have found it possible to embrace within this word a vast variety of activities, mainly propagandist, which do not come within the meaning of the 'advancement of education' as it is used in charity law. A purpose which is not charitable cannot be made charitable merely by representing it to be a form of education".[16] Accordingly, a trust to educate the public that peace is best secured through pacifism and disarmament was held not charitable on the ground that the object was political albeit advanced by educational means.[17]

7.49

(c) ADVANCEMENT OF RELIGION

Section 2(2)(c) of the 2006 Act lists the "advancement of religion" as falling within the new statutory descriptions of charitable purposes. No definition of religion is provided although further clarification can be found in s.3(a), which states that "religion" includes, "a religion which involves belief in more than one God", and "a religion which does not involve belief in a God". The clarification was deemed necessary to take account of the growing diversity of faiths practised in England and Wales and the consequent concern that the law should be flexible and inclusive. Accordingly, the large body of case law as to charitable trusts which advance religion will remain relevant although in the view of the Charity Commission, decisions as to what is charitable must now be considered, "in the context of current social and economic circumstances".[18]

7.50

---

[13] Charity Commission: *Charities and Public Benefit* (January 2008), p.23.
[14] Charity Commission: *Public Benefit and Fee Charging* (December 2008), p.12.
[15] Charity Commission: *Charities and Public Benefit* (January 2008), p.25.
[16] At [38].
[17] *Southwood v A-G* [2000] W.T.L.R. 1199 (see **7.84**).
[18] Charity Commission, *The Advancement of Religion for the Public Benefit* (December 2008), p.24.

Meaning of religion

7.51 It is a central feature of the head of "advancement of religion" that the courts adopt a stance of neutrality and decline to distinguish between different religions. The case law is littered with examples of trusts for the advancement of religions ranging from the well established such as Islam or Catholicism to the more peripheral or new age such as the Unification Church or small spiritualist groups.[19] Both polytheistic and monotheistic religions are embraced alike.[20] The presumption is held, furthermore, that any religion is better than none.[21] Naturally, the existence of a wide variety of fringe religious groupings or sects has tested the boundaries of what is generally an inclusive approach. As Romilly M.R. accepted in *Thornton v Howe*, "It may be that the tenets of a particular sect inculcate doctrines adverse to the very foundations of all religion, and that they are subversive of all morality. In such a case, if it should arise, the Court will not assist the execution of the bequest, but will declare it to be void . . .".[22] This test has been adopted as the appropriate point at which the pursuit of one's "religion" ceases to be regarded as charitable. Whilst some groups readily fall to be excluded,[23] an interesting variety of trusts for the advancement of religion have been held to be charitable.

Thornton v Howe, for example, concerned the publication of the obscure works of Joanna Southcote who alleged that she had been impregnated by the Holy Ghost and would give birth to the second Messiah. Romilly M.R. described her as an, "ignorant woman, of an enthusiastic turn of mind, who had long wished to become an instrument in the hands of God to promote some great good on earth".[24] Although he deemed her writings to be foolish, he could find nothing that was, "likely to make persons who read them immoral or irreligious".[25] Accordingly, the publication of her work was held charitable for the advancement of religion. Similarly, in *Re Watson* property was left on trust "for the continuance of the work of God as it has been maintained by Mr HG Hobbs and Myself".[26] Expert evidence showed that Mr Hobbs numerous fundamentalist writings were of no intrinsic worth. Following *Thornton v Howe*, Plowman J. acknowledged that the court did not prefer one religion to another or one sect to another. There being nothing properly subversive in the teachings, a valid charitable trust was created. By way of a final illustration, in *Holmes v A-G*[27] Walton J. was called upon to determine whether the purposes of a particular trust deed were charitable, i.e. whether enabling a meeting-house to be built and used for the benefit of an ultra-puritan sect known as the "Exclusive Brethren" or the "Plymouth Brethren" was charitable. Despite the well-documented opposition of the Charity Commissioners to

[19] In practice, however, it has appeared more difficult for newly established religions to persuade the Charity Commission of the genuineness of belief. See, for example, the problems encountered by the Church of Scientology discussed below (see **7.53**).
[20] This development might be regarded as relatively recent. In *Bowman v Secular Society* [1917] A.C. 406 at 449, the House of Lords embraced the more restrictive view that, "a trust for the purpose of any kind of monotheistic theism would be a good charitable trust".
[21] *Gilmour v Coates* [1949] A.C. 426.
[22] (1862) 31 Beav. 14 at 20.
[23] For example, Satanists and devil-worshippers.
[24] (1862) 31 Beav. 14 at 18.
[25] (1862) 31 Beav. 14 at 19.
[26] [1973] 1 W.L.R. 1472.
[27] (1981) *The Times*, February 11.

some of the group practices, Walton J. was bound to consider only evidence that had been put in front of him. He could find nothing in their doctrines, "to which exception could properly be taken".[28] Accordingly, he declared the "Kingston Meeting Rooms Trust, Feltham", a valid charitable trust, with the reminder that, "it has long been settled that the law presumes that it is better for a man to have a religion—a set of beliefs which take him outside his own petty cares and lead him to think of others— rather than to have no religion at all".[29]

Belief in a supreme being

Traditionally, a trust for the advancement of atheist or agnostic purposes could not be charitable because belief in, and worship of, a god were deemed essential features of religion.[30] Nowhere was this principle more emphatically demonstrated than in *Re South Place Ethical Society*.[31] There Dillon J. observed that   **7.52**

> "It seems to me that two of the essential attributes of religion are faith and worship; faith in a god and worship of that god. This is supported by the definitions of religion given in the Oxford English Dictionary ... The Oxford English Dictionary gives as one of the definitions of religion: 'a particular system of faith and worship ... recognition on the part of man of some higher, unseen power as having control of his destiny and as being entitled to obedience, reverence and worship.' "[32]

The society before him existed to "study and disseminate ethical principles" and to cultivate "rational religious sentiment". It was an agnostic society interested in the values of love, truth and excellence, the members of which neither believed in nor denied the existence of God. Accordingly, Dillon J. had the opportunity to put forward the fundamental principle that, "Religion is concerned with man's relations with God and ethics are concerned with man's relations with man".[33] As there was no belief in a supreme being, the society could not be a charity for the advancement of religion.

The requirement of belief in a Supreme Being posed problems for a number of groups, religions and religious practices. A prominent example was that of Buddhism, with regard to which there has been much debate as to whether a supreme being is recognised. In *R. v Registrar General Ex p. Segerdal*, for example, Lord Denning M.R. treated it as something of an exception to the rule requiring belief in a god.[34] In *Re South Place Ethical Society*, however, Dillon J. (accepting without issue that Buddhism was a religion), countered the argument that Buddhism was not theist, but admitted to possessing insufficient knowledge to determine whether there was belief in a god.[35]

[28] (1981) *The Times*, February 11.
[29] (1981) *The Times*, February 11.
[30] As discussed, the Charities Act 2006 now includes, "a religion which does not involve belief in a god" (s.2(3)(a)(ii)).
[31] [1980] 1 W.L.R. 1565.
[32] [1980] 1 W.L.R. 1565 at 1572.
[33] [1980] 1 W.L.R. 1565 at 1571.
[34] [1970] 2 QB 697 at 707.
[35] [1980] 1 W.L.R. 1565 at 1573.

Nowadays, a number of Buddhist groups have been granted charitable status[36] and, within the Charities Act 2006, any persisting doubt has been eradicated by the statutory description of religion. As explained above, the new head includes, "religion which does not involve belief in a God".[37] Obvious conceptual difficulty will arise, nonetheless, from the adoption of a definition that is at odds with the conventional understanding of religion as being comprised of the elements of belief in, and, as necessarily follows, the worship of a God. The Charity Commission recognition, that adherents must have "belief in a god (or gods) or goddess (or goddesses), or supreme being, or divine or transcendental being or entity or spiritual principle, which is the object or focus of the religion" is a common sense approach to the current legal position.[38] It remains to be seen how the courts will respond when the boundaries of this new description are tested.

The act of worship

7.53   Traditionally, there has been much judicial focus on the act of worship as an inherent facet of religious practice. This has seen the courts and the Charity Commission spell out the types of activities that constitute worship. In *R. v Registrar General Ex p. Segerdal*, Buckley L.J. argued that worship must have some of the characteristics of, "submission to the object worshipped, veneration of that object, praise, thanksgiving, prayer, or intercession".[39] The absence of such qualities in the practice of the Church of Scientology led directly to the conclusion that a building used for instruction in Scientology was not a "place of meeting for religious worship" under the Places of Worship Registration Act 1855.

Similar difficulties beset the Church of Scientology in its application to the Charity Commissioners in 1999. Like the Court of Appeal, the Charity Commissioners decided that at least some elements of worship were required. The Commissioners accepted that there was a belief in a supreme being, but they could find no evidence of worship. Rather the dominant practices were "auditing" and "training". The former, which could be described as the one to one exploration of an individual's past life, was more akin to counselling than worship. The latter was no more than intensive scripture study and, therefore, more of an educational activity than an act of worship.

In light of the 2006 Act, the requirement of worship must now be construed liberally so as not to exclude legitimate religious groups where there is no worship of a supreme being or entity.[40]

---

[36] For example the Ambedkar International Mission, registered as a charity since 1978, is a charity to advance the teachings of Buddhism as revived by the late Dr Ambedkar.
[37] Section 2(3)(a)(ii).
[38] See Charity Commission, *The Advancement of Religion for the Public Benefit* (December 2008), at p.8.
[39] [1970] 2 Q.B. 697 at 709.
[40] The Commission cite the example of Jainism where adherents do not "connect" with a supreme being or entity, but adopt a belief system based on attainment of a state of purity or oneness after death by living good lives: see Charity Commission, *The Advancement of Religion for the Public Benefit* (December 2008), at p.23.

Churches and the clergy

Trusts for the repair, maintenance or enhancement of churches are charitable trusts. **7.54**
Accordingly, there have been valid trusts to provide for stained-glass windows in a
church,[41] to maintain the church organ[42] and to assist in the training of the clergy.[43] A
gift for the advancement of religion that fails to specify a particular faith to be benefited
will be presumed to be for the established church.

Advancement of religion

Valid charitable trusts under this head are required positively to advance religion. In **7.55**
United Grand Lodge of Ancient, Free and Accepted Masons of England v Holborn BC,
Donovan J. explained that, "to advance religion means to promote it, to spread the
message ever wider among mankind; to take some positive steps to sustain and increase
religious belief; and these things are done in a variety of ways which may be comprehensively described as pastoral or missionary".[44] For Lord Denning, the question of
advancement inevitably brought to mind the concept of public benefit. In *National
Deposit Friendly Society Trustees v Skegness UDC*, he provided the simple and effective
illustration that, "When a man says his prayers in the privacy of his own bedroom, he
may be truly concerned with religion but not with the advancement of religion".[45]
Naturally, therefore, the question as to what comprises a sufficient section of the
community must be answered by reference to the decided case law falling under this
head.

Public benefit

Under the head of advancement of religion, the distinction between practice in public **7.56**
and practice in private is uppermost. As the Charity Commission reflected in the
application for registration as a charity by the Church of Scientology, "the decided
cases indicated that the public or private nature of the 'religious practice' of the
organisation in question was central to determining the presence or absence of public
benefit".[46] As will become clear, nowhere is a public benefit more lacking than in the
case of enclosed orders where religious practice is carried out in private. Although the
practices that occur behind closed doors are no doubt devoutly religious, they will
seldom provide a tangible public benefit. There must, therefore, be a benefit beyond
that experienced by adherents to the religion itself. By way of illustration, the public
benefit test will be analysed by reference to the following:

---

[41] *Re King* [1923] 1 Ch. 243.
[42] *Adnam v Cole* (1843) 6 Beav. 353.
[43] *Re Williams* [1927] 2 Ch. 283.
[44] [1957] 1 W.L.R. 1080 at 1090.
[45] [1959] A.C. 293 at 322.
[46] Decisions of the Charity Commissioners (November 17, 1999) p.47.

- enclosed orders;

- retreat houses, and

- the saying of masses.

Enclosed orders

7.57 The line of authority as regards enclosed orders dates back to the nineteenth century. In *Cocks v Manners*,[47] Wickens V.C. held that a gift to the Dominican convent was not a gift on charitable trust. He reasoned that, "It is said, in some of the cases, that religious purposes are charitable, but that can only be true as to religious services tending directly or indirectly towards the instruction or the edification of the public".[48] As the gift was for the purposes of an enclosed order of nuns, there was no benefit to the public, direct or otherwise. *Cocks v Manners* was cited by Lindley J. in *Re White*, who argued, similarly, that, "A society for the promotion of private prayer and devotion by its own members, and which has no wider scope, no public element, no purposes of general utility, would be a 'religious' society, but not a 'charitable' one".[49] More recently, the House of Lords has emphasised that no public benefit accrues from the religious activities of enclosed orders. In *Gilmour v Coats*, property was left on trust for the purposes of a Carmelite convent.[50] Although, the Carmelites are a purely contemplative order that remain strictly cloistered, the Roman Catholic Church maintained that there was, nonetheless, a public benefit. First, through intercessory prayer the nuns prayed to God to help members of the public. Secondly, it was argued, their cloistered lives brought spiritual edification to the community. Lord Simonds disregarded this view. Those benefits have to be proven as a matter of law not simply faith. Intercessory prayer and spiritual belief were not capable of judicial proof and the benefit to the public was, therefore, intangible and vague.[51] Any benefit was felt not by the public at large or even a sufficient section of it, but by individuals within the walls of the convent.

The order of Carmelite nuns in *Gilmour v Coats* may be usefully compared with the closed community of Anglican nuns in the Society of the Precious Blood.[52] In the 1990's, the Society of the Precious Blood applied for charitable status.[53] Its constitution disclosed purposes similar to those of the Carmelite nuns in that they concerned themselves with contemplation and intercessory prayer. In distinction to *Gilmour v Coats*, however, they were not entirely cut off from the outside world. The Society had associate members who lived outside in the community. It ran a counselling and support program that involved the community. In addition, community members,

[47] (1871) L.R. 12 Eq. 575.
[48] (1871) L.R. 12 Eq. 575 at 585.
[49] [1893] 2 Ch. 41 at 51.
[50] [1949] A.C. 426.
[51] Lord Simonds regarded the benefit derived by others from the example of pious lives, as too "indirect, remote, imponderable and ... controversial" to be admitted into the category of public benefit ([1949] A.C. 426 at 447).
[52] See also, *Caldey Abbey* [1969] Ch. Com. Rep. 9, which too provides ready comparison.
[53] *Society of Precious Blood* (1995) 3 Decisions 11 (an Anglican contemplative community at Burnham Abbey).

particularly school children, were permitted to visit the Abbey, to take classes on the history and archaeology of Burnham Abbey and to hear talks on religious issues. The Abbey also offered retreat facilities to needy outsiders.[54] In light of these substantially charitable activities, the Charity Commissioners felt that the constitution did not reflect the truly charitable purposes carried out by the nuns. Crucially, much of its real work was carried out in public. Accordingly, the Society was asked for amendments to be made to its constitution to reflect its inherently charitable work. The Society was duly registered as a charity.

Retreat houses

At first glance, the arguments about the absence of public benefit in relation to closed orders are also applicable to retreat houses. In *Re Warre's WT*, Harman J. explained that a retreat house is, "a form of religious experience well understood in the Church of England. It is a retirement from the activities of the world for a space of time for religious contemplation and the cleansing of the soul".[55] He did not hesitate to hold, therefore, that the provision of a retreat house for the Church of England was not charitable. Harman J. continued, "No doubt that is a highly beneficial activity for the person who undertakes it, but it is not an activity, which for the reasons so often set out in English law is a charitable activity".[56] No public benefit attached to a trust where only the few who stayed there derived benefit. Unfortunately, this perspective ignores the indirect, but nonetheless discernible benefit, to the public at large when individuals return to society. As Cross J. acknowledged in *Neville Estates v Madden*, "the court is entitled to assume that some benefit accrues to the public from the attendance at places of worship of persons who live in this world and mix with their fellow citizens".[57] The authority of *Re Warre's WT* is now legitimately questionable.

Retreat houses were again considered in *Re Banfield*.[58] The court was required to consider a residuary bequest in favour of "Pilsdon Community House," a religious community that received and tended to members of the public who needed help for reasons such as drug or alcohol abuse. Goff J. easily distinguished the *Gilmour v Coats* line of cases as dealing with, "cloistered nuns whose community was essentially introspective and existed for the purpose of sanctifying the souls of the members ...".[59] There was no impact on the public, "save the benefit of the example of the pious life and the benefit of intercessory prayer, which were too intangible to be recognised and evaluated by a court of law".[60] In his view, the very purpose of the Pilsdon Community House in *Re Banfield* was to do good works in the community. Goff J. also faced the more formidable argument that the community house was a retreat house, which for Harman J. in *Re Warre's WT* lacked the necessary element of public benefit. Of the

7.58

---

[54] The provision of a retreat house has been held, of itself, to carry no public benefit: *Re Warre's WT* [1953] 1 W.L.R. 725.
[55] [1953] 1 W.L.R. 725 at 728.
[56] [1953] 1 W.L.R. 725 at 728.
[57] [1962] Ch. 832 at 853.
[58] [1968] 1 W.L.R. 846.
[59] [1968] 1 W.L.R. 846 at 850.
[60] [1968] 1 W.L.R. 846 at 850.

retreat house in *Re Warre's WT*, Goff J. explained that, "Such a house exists for private meditation and improvement only, and is therefore lacking in the necessary public element. Pilsdon Community House is quite different, as it opens out to reach the public. No doubt the retreat is practised on particular occasions as part of the religious discipline of the community ... but that is not the be all and end all of the establishment".[61] Accordingly, and for the future, it may be that evidence of reaching out to the community will be sufficient to display the public benefit patently lacking in the cases of enclosed orders.

Religious masses

7.59   Not surprisingly, the question of public benefit arises where there is a trust for the saying of masses or the performance of religious ceremonies. The position is straightforward. Where the masses or ceremonies are held in public, the trust will be charitable. If held in private, however, no public benefit attaches. In *Re Hetherington's WT*, the testatrix made a bequest of £2,000 to the Bishop of Westminster for the saying of masses for the souls of herself, her husband, her parents and her sister.[62] The bequest was deemed charitable for the advancement of religion. Although in this case the will did not specify how the masses were to be said, Browne-Wilkinson V.C. placed a benign construction on the words so they were construed as capable of being carried out by charitable means only. He explained, "Where there is a gift for a religious purpose which could be carried out in a way which is beneficial to the public (i.e. by public masses) but could also be carried out in a way which would not have sufficient element of public benefit (i.e. by private masses) the gift is to be construed as a gift to be carried out only by the methods that are charitable, all non-charitable methods being excluded ...".[63]

(d) THE ADVANCEMENT OF HEALTH OR THE SAVING OF LIVES

7.60   The advancement of health or the saving of lives is now a distinct head of charity under s.2(2)(d) of the 2006 Act.[64] Dating back to the Statute of Elizabeth I, the promotion of health has long been accepted as a charitable purpose. The Preamble makes reference to relief of the aged or impotent and to trusts for the maintenance of sick or maimed soldiers and mariners. As will be discussed, relief of the aged will be charitable under its own separate description.[65] Trusts for the advancement of health generally will fall to be considered as a separate category.

---

[61] [1968] 1 W.L.R. 846 at 852.
[62] [1990] Ch. 1.
[63] [1990] Ch. 1 at 12.
[64] Section 3(b) defines, "the advancement of health" as "including the prevention or relief of sickness, disease or human suffering".
[65] *The Relief of those in Need by Reason of Youth, Age, Ill-health, Disability, Financial Hardship, or other Disadvantage* (see **7.71**).

Traditionally, the advancement of public health has been served in a variety of ways, for example, in the provision of hospitals,[66] the supply of contraceptives,[67] the provision of healthcare advice[68] or recreational activities deemed to be for the betterment of public health.[69] This new head of charity also incorporates the prevention or relief of sickness, disease or human suffering.[70] This object is underlined by the Charity Commission, for which the advancement of health includes:

> "the prevention or relief of sickness, disease or human suffering, as well as the promotion of health. It includes conventional methods as well as complementary, alternative or holistic methods which are concerned with healing mind, body and spirit in the alleviation of symptoms and the cure of illness".[71]

As to the relief of sickness, charitable purposes extend, "beyond the treatment or provision of care, such as a hospital, to the provision of items, services and facilities to ease the suffering or assist the recovery of people who are sick, convalescent, disabled or infirm or to provide comforts for patients".[72] The "saving of lives" incorporates those bodies whose work involves the provision of rescue services such as fire brigades,[73] lifeboat associations[74] and search and rescue organisations such as mountain[75] or cave rescue.[76] It also includes charities that ensure the proper standards of medical practice,[77] charities set up to assist the victims of natural disasters or war[78] the provision of life saving or self defence classes and the provision of blood transfusion services.[79]   **7.61**

Public benefit

A legitimate and sometimes difficult question arises as to whether charities which charge fees (for example, in this context private hospitals or care homes) are of benefit to a sufficient section of the community. As has been discussed, the Charity Commission promotes the view that those who are less well off must not be entirely excluded from benefit.[80] Accordingly, it is acceptable that fees are charged, even if at a higher   **7.62**

---

[66] Note that hospitals may charge fees but cannot be charitable where the poor are excluded: see *Re Resch's Will Trust* [1969] 1 A.C. 514.
[67] The *Family Planning Association* [1969] Ch. Com. Rep. 11.
[68] For example, the *British Pregnancy Advisory Service* [1978] Ch. Com. Rep. 26.
[69] Such as the provision of an ice-rink in *Oxford Ice Skating Association* [1984] Ch. Com. Rep. 11
[70] Charities Act 2006, s.2(3)(b).
[71] Charity Commission, *Commentary on the Descriptions of Charitable Purposes in the Charities Bill* (December 2005) at [12]; note that sufficient evidence of the efficacy of the method is required.
[72] Charity Commission, *Commentary on the Descriptions of Charitable Purposes in the Charities Bill* (December 2005) at [12]. Further guidance as to the ways in which charities can relieve sickness is provided by Charity Commission CC6: *The Relief of Sickness* (March 2000).
[73] *Re Wokingham Fire Brigade Trusts* [1951] Ch. 373 (provision for a local fire brigade).
[74] Such as the Royal National Lifeboat Institution.
[75] For example, Buxton Mountain Rescue Team.
[76] For example, Cave Rescue Organisation.
[77] Such as the General Medical Council.
[78] For example, OXFAM.
[79] For example, The British Blood Transfusion Society.
[80] See generally, "*Charities and Public Benefit*" (January 2008).

level than required for the provision of the service, as long as they are not so high as to effectively exclude the less well off.[81] Where high fees are charged, the question arises as to whether the level of fees has the effect of deterring or preventing the less well off from accessing the services. If so, there must be evidence to show that the less well off are not wholly excluded from possible benefits, whether direct or indirect. For example, the existence or otherwise of accessible medical insurance schemes may provide evidence of whether, and how, the less well off can access private hospital services. Similarly, by looking at the nature and extent of the benefit provided, it might be possible to conclude that the type of service provided is one for which there is a public need and, that the service provided goes some way to meeting that need. For example, a private hospital may have, and make available, specialised equipment not available in the local NHS hospital.

(e) THE ADVANCEMENT OF CITIZENSHIP OR COMMUNITY DEVELOPMENT

7.63   This purpose is found in s.2(2)(e) and includes rural or urban regeneration as well as the promotion of civic responsibility, the voluntary sector or the effectiveness or efficiency of charities.[82] As to urban or rural regeneration, permissible charitable purposes are required to relate to an area of social and economic deprivation. The Commission cite as key means to achieve regeneration the, "maintenance or improvement of the physical, social and economic infrastructure and by assisting people who are at a disadvantage because of their social and economic circumstances".[83] An organisation might provide, therefore, public facilities, advice and assistance to businesses where it would lead to training and employment opportunities for the unemployed[84] or for the maintenance and improvement of roads and accessibility to main transport routes. It is important, however, that the benefit to the public outweighs any private benefit to individuals or companies.

As to the promotion of civic responsibility, a broad collection of associated purposes will be housed here. Charities concerned with promotion of the voluntary sector are a recent and prominent example.[85] The Charity Commission deemed this purpose to be charitable, "by analogy to purposes which promote a whole category of the social and economic life of a community such as the promotion of commerce and industry for the public benefit and the promotion of individual industries for the public benefit[86] . . . or

---

[81] *Re Resch's WT* [1969] 1 A.C. 514.
[82] Charities Act 2006, s.3(c).
[83] Charity Commission RR2: *Promotion of Urban and Rural Regeneration* (March 1999) at [2].
[84] See further Charity Commission RR3: *Charities for the Relief of Unemployment* (March 1999).
[85] Charity Commission RR13: *Promotion of the Voluntary Sector for the Benefit of the Public* (September 2004), Annex A at [4]; see also Charity Commission RR14: *Promoting the Efficiency and Effectiveness of Charities and the Effective Use of Charitable Resources for the Benefit of the Public* (September 2004).
[86] Such as agriculture (*IRC v Yorkshire Agricultural Society* [1928] 1 K.B. 611), or horticulture (*Re Pleasants* [1923] 39 T.L.R. 675).

as furthering the mental and moral welfare of the community[87] and promoting good citizenship".[88] It is also now accepted that the provision of tangible as well as intangible benefits to organisations and bodies that receive help directly is evidence of a public benefit to society at large.

(f) THE ADVANCEMENT OF THE ARTS, CULTURE, HERITAGE OR SCIENCE

As has been discussed in the context of advancement of education, the provision of a **7.64** museum or an art gallery is a charitable purpose, provided that the works therein are of sufficient merit. Such purposes are charitable also under the head of advancement of the Arts.[89] As indicated, this head embraces the wider purposes of advancement of culture, heritage and science and there are, of course, many prominent organisations whose contribution to charity lies chiefly in this context. The purposes of the National Trust, for example, are accepted as charitable in that they promote "the permanent pre-servation for the benefit of the nation of lands and tenements (including buildings) of beauty or historic interest and as regards lands for the preservation (so far as prac-ticable) of their natural aspect features and animal and plant life".[90] The overlap with education is also present in relation to research carried out for the advancement of science and in the work of societies such as the Royal College of Surgeons,[91] which would be considered charitable under either head.

The Charity Commission has published guidance on the scope of organisations set up for the charitable purposes of preservation and or conservation.[92] Naturally, this has an impact on those bodies that seek to claim involvement in the advancement of heritage. As regards preservation, expert evidence is required that the site or building is of sufficient historical interest[93] and that there is sufficient public benefit.[94] Where a building is preserved because of its connection to a particular person, for example, to commemorate a birth or death, expert evidence is required to satisfy that the person is of sufficient educational, historical or scientific interest. In addition, the building should have a real connection with the person and a significant part of the surviving fabric of the building should relate to the period during which the person occupied it. None-theless, considerable flexibility is maintained in that the Commission regards this as a starting point from which it is prepared to take on board other factors in assessing the merits of a particular case.[95]

---

[87] In *Re Scowcroft* [1862] 2 Ch. 638, for example, the furtherance of principles of religious and moral improvement was accepted as a charitable purpose.
[88] Charity Commission, *Commentary on the Descriptions of Charitable Purposes in the Charities Bill* (December 2005) at [15].
[89] See Charity Commission RR10: *Museums and Art Galleries* (August 2002).
[90] *Re Verrall* [1916] 1 Ch. 100.
[91] *Royal College of Surgeons of England v National Provincial Bank Ltd* [1952] A.C. 631.
[92] Charity Commission RR9: *Preservation and Conservation* (February 2001).
[93] This can be assumed in the case of a famous historic building where the existence of merit is considered obvious, or evidenced in the case of listed buildings.
[94] For example, that there is sufficient public access provided.
[95] Charities Commission RR9: *Preservation and Conversation* (February 2001), Annex at [7].

7.65 Outside preservation, it remains necessary to consider whether it is charitable to erect (as opposed to maintain) a building or memorial for the advancement of purposes under this head. In *Re Endacott*, there was no charitable quality to the provision by a testator of "some useful monument to myself".[96] It is, perhaps, safer to suggest that some useful monument in furtherance of an accepted charitable purpose will be more readily acceptable, although there is surprisingly little authority to this effect. If the monument is itself a work of art, for example, there could conceivably be little objection to its inclusion under this head or others. The provision of memorials to police officers who lost their lives in the course of their duties was deemed a charitable purpose on the ground that it promoted good citizenship and public awareness.[97] Of more long standing authority, it was held in *Murray v Thomas* that to promote for the benefit of the two villages some useful memorial preferably of the type of a village hall was in law a charitable purpose.[98] Although Clauson J. was minded to think that a fund collected to erect a memorial of something in the nature of a cross would also be charitable, he was not compelled to come to any firm view. He held, "I can feel no doubt that the object for which these funds were collected and the object of the association was to benefit the people of these two areas by having some commemorative institution which would be of public service to those two areas".[99]

(g) THE ADVANCEMENT OF AMATEUR SPORT

7.66 Traditionally the advancement of sport per se has never been charitable.[1] If ancillary to a charitable purpose,[2] however, the promotion of sport has been held to be charitable under the applicable head. The old fourth head of "other purposes beneficial to the community" housed a number of such examples. In *Re Gray*, Romer J. was happy to accept that sport in the form of shooting, fishing, cricket, football and polo would increase the efficiency of the armed forces, holding for that reason that a gift was charitable.[3] He claimed of the testator that, "it was his intention to benefit the officers and men of the Carabiniers by giving them an opportunity of indulging in healthy sport. It is to be observed that the particular sports specified were all healthy outdoor sports, indulgence in which might reasonably be supposed to encourage physical efficiency".[4]

More recently, the Charity Commission has recognised as charitable, first, "the promotion of community participation in healthy recreation by providing facilities for

---

[96] [1960] Ch. 232.
[97] *The Police Memorial Trust* [1984] Ch. Com. Rep. 10.
[98] [1937] 4 All E.R. 545.
[99] [1937] 4 All E.R. 545 at 550.
[1] *Re Nottage* [1885] 2 Ch. 649 (yacht racing).
[2] Such as the advancement of education: see *IRC v McMullen* [1981] A.C. 1 (see **7.43**).
[3] [1925] Ch. 362.
[4] [1925] Ch. 362 at 365. Similar arguments were accepted in relation to the police force in *IRC v City of Glasgow Police Athletic Association* [1953] A.C. 380, but the association was deemed to be non-charitable on the ground that the provision of recreation was a primary purpose. As Lord Normand explained at 396, "The private advantage of members is a purpose for which the association is established and it therefore cannot be said that this is an association established for a public charitable purpose only".

particular sports" and, secondly, "the advancement of the physical education of young people not undergoing formal education".[5] Whilst the latter is merely an extension of the principles of decided cases (see **7.43**), the former was a new departure recognising as charitable the work done by many Community Amateur Sports Clubs (CASC's).[6] It has since been possible for a CASC to be a charity where the sport in question is capable of improving health and fitness. Open membership is required, in that access to the club's facilities must be genuinely available to anyone who wishes to take advantage of them. A failure to adhere to this requirement will result in private as opposed to public benefit.

The Charities Act 2006 embraces the advancement of amateur sport as a head of charity in its own right, but with the explicit restriction that sport is understood to be an activity which, "involves physical or mental skill or exertion".[7] This reflects the Charity Commission view that it is the, "close and obvious connection between physical exercise and physical health that makes the provision of facilities for health recreation charitable".[8] Accordingly, it is no surprise that "sports" such as snooker, pool or ballooning do not in the eyes of the Charity Commission constitute healthy recreation in the sense that the activities will not improve physical health and fitness.   **7.67**

It remains possible that other charitable purposes may be furthered by sport. In the relief of disability, sport can be charitable where it improves the conditions of people with a mental or physical disability. The Charity Commission provide a range of examples of charities engaging in sports[9] such as bowls,[10] shooting,[11] gliding[12] and sailing.[13] In addition, physical training towards the alleviation of stiffness and immobility was cited as charitable as being for the relief of old age.[14]

(h) THE ADVANCEMENT OF HUMAN RIGHTS, CONFLICT RESOLUTION, OR RECONCILIATION, OR THE PROMOTION OF RELIGIOUS OR RACIAL HARMONY OR EQUALITY AND DIVERSITY

By analogy with existing charitable purposes,[15] it is clear that the advancement of human rights had become a recognised charitable purpose under the fourth *Pemsel* head. The Charities Act 2006 provides a statutory basis for treating the promotion of human rights as charitable. Human rights can be promoted, whether at home or abroad, in a wide variety of ways. Examples range from obtaining redress for, or   **7.68**

---

[5] Charity Commission RR11: *Charitable Status and Sport* (April 2003).
[6] "Facilities" extends beyond the provision of lands, buildings and equipment to include the organisation of sport.
[7] Charities Act 2006, s.2(3)(d).
[8] Charity Commission RR11: *Charitable Status and Sport* (April 2003) at [8].
[9] Charity Commission RR11: *Charitable Status and Sport* (April 2003) at [5].
[10] British Wheelchair Bowls Association.
[11] Great Britain Paraplegics Shooting Association.
[12] Flyability.
[13] Sailability.
[14] Charity Commission RR11: *Charitable Status and Sport* (April 2003), Annex at [8].
[15] For example, those purposes beneficial to the community by virtue of their moral or spiritual welfare and improvement: Charity Commission RR12: *The Promotion of Human Rights* (January 2005).

alleviating the need of, victims of human rights abuses, to educating the public and promoting public support for human rights.[16] It is not problematic that trustees of a charity may engage in political activity provided that that activity is not the continuing and sole means by which a charity carries out its adopted objects.[17] The provision of technical advice to government and participation in governmental consultations on changes to the law are perfectly legitimate aims consistent with charitable status.

As to public benefit, the Charity Commission concluded that there is an obvious and clear public benefit in promoting human rights:

> "For individuals whose human rights are thereby secured, the benefit is immediate and tangible. There is also a less tangible, but nonetheless significant, benefit to the whole community that arises from our perception that the fundamental rights of all members of the community are being protected. That provides sufficient benefit to the community to justify treating the promotion of human rights as a charitable purpose in its own right".[18]

7.69 This head of charity is not confined to the advancement of human rights, but extends to "conflict resolution or reconciliation". The Charity Commission has explained that the advancement of conflict resolution or reconciliation involves:

> "the resolution of international conflicts and relieving the suffering, poverty and distress arising through conflict on a national or international scale by identifying the causes of the conflict and seeking to resolve such conflict. It includes the promotion of restorative justice, where all the parties with a stake in a particular conflict or offence come together to resolve collectively how to deal with its aftermath and its implications for the future. It also includes purposes directed towards mediation, conciliation or reconciliation as between persons, organisations, authorities or groups involved or likely to become involved in dispute or inter-personal conflict".[19]

Accordingly, the Charity Commission has registered a wide range of organisations whose purposes are charitable in this context, such as Mediation UK, The Restorative Justice Consortium and The Foundation for Reconciliation in the Middle East.

The statutory description, the "promotion of religious or racial harmony or equality and diversity" will include a broad range of charitable activities such as the promotion of good race relations, the tackling of discrimination whether on the basis of age, gender or sexual orientation or the enabling of people to understand the religious beliefs of others. The Community Security Trust, for example, exists to promote good race relations between the Jewish community and other members of society, to promote the efficiency of the police within society at large, to relieve the hardship of victims of racial or religious harassment and to promote public education about racism and anti-

---

[16] See generally: RS16: *Charities Working in the Field of Human Rights* (Dec 2007).
[17] See **7.82**.
[18] Charity Commission RR12: *The Promotion of Human Rights* (January 2005) at [12].
[19] Charity Commission, *Commentary on the Descriptions of Charitable Purposes in the Charities Bill* (December 2005) at [26].

semitism.[20] A further and frequently cited illustration is the Womens Service Trust which sought to promote equal rights and responsibilities between men and women as citizens.[21]

(i) THE ADVANCEMENT OF ENVIRONMENTAL PROTECTION OR IMPROVEMENT

The Charity Commission consider that the advancement of environmental protection   **7.70**
and improvement "includes preservation and conservation of the natural environment and the promotion of sustainable development".[22] As to the scope of the head, it is said that, "Conservation of the environment includes the conservation of a particular animal, bird, or other species or 'wildlife' in general; a specific plant species, habitat or area of land, including areas of natural beauty and scientific interest; flora, fauna and the environment generally".[23] Typical examples of charitable purposes falling within this description include the conservation of the environment generally, of a particular geographical area or of a particular species. In relation to the promotion of sustainable development, charitable purposes include research or practical efforts to promote biodiversity, recycling, sustainable waste management and the use of renewable energy resources. It was previously thought that no public benefit accrued from keeping the public away from the protected object or area, i.e. that public access was a key determinant of public benefit.[24] There is little evidence that such a rule will, in future, be applied rigidly. A broader view is adopted in line with developing understanding and appreciation of the need for environmental protection and improvement generally.

(j) THE RELIEF OF THOSE IN NEED BY REASON OF YOUTH, AGE, ILL-HEALTH, DISABILITY, FINANCIAL HARDSHIP, OR OTHER DISADVANTAGE

The Preamble to the Statute of Charitable Uses 1601 contained a range of charitable   **7.71**
purposes that now fall under this new statutory head, such as "the relief of aged, impotent and poor people". It was rapidly acknowledged that the wording thereof was to be construed disjunctively so that distinct categories evolved which concerned the relief of those in need because of age, disability and financial hardship. In *Joseph Rowntree Memorial Trust Housing Association Ltd v A-G*, Peter Gibson J. upheld as

---

[20] See *Community Security Trust* (1995) 4 Ch. Com. Dec. 8.
[21] [1977] Ch. Com. Rep. at [34–36].
[22] Charity Commission, *Commentary on the Descriptions of Charitable Purposes in the Charities Bill* (December 2005) at [29].
[23] Charity Commission, *Commentary on the Descriptions of Charitable Purposes in the Charities Bill* (December 2005) at [29]. Expert evidence may be required to demonstrate the worthiness of an object for conservation: see Charity Commission RR9: *Preservation and Conservation* (February 2001).
[24] See *Re Grove-Grady* [1929] 1 Ch. 557, discussed below (see **7.73**).

charitable the provision of housing for the elderly without regard to any poverty requirement.[25] He claimed that the word "relief" requires that the persons in question have a need attributable to their condition as aged, impotent or poor persons which requires alleviating.[26] Accordingly, relief of the aged can be achieved in a number of ways, such as, the provision of advice, medical care, rest homes or day centres and is not confined to the poor and aged. Similarly the provision of children's care homes and orphanages is charitable[27] along with the provision of apprenticeships, which are charitable in terms of the establishment in life of children or young people. Again the development of this category of charitable trusts stems from the specific inclusion in the Preamble of, "the education and preferment of orphans".

Ill health and disability can take many forms and, understandably, the relief of those who are suffering is achieved through a very wide variety of charitable purposes such as the training of guide dogs[28] and the provision of personal transportation.[29] The Charities Act 2006 s.2(3)(e) expressly includes under this head relief given by the provision of accommodation or care to the persons outlined and in need. The reference to "other disadvantage" leaves open a variety of possibilities, such as that a trust for the relief of alcoholics or drug users may well be charitable under this head. Whilst the prevention of such social evils through the promotion of temperance will be categorised as the advancement of health, the relief of those who are suffering seems best placed under this statutory description.

(k) THE ADVANCEMENT OF ANIMAL WELFARE

7.72   The charitable nature of trusts for the protection of animals has long been accepted and its inclusion as a head in its own right has not been regarded as a significant change in the law.[30] Nonetheless, it is not entirely clear how this category developed. There is no mention of such a purpose in the Preamble and the approach of the courts has been markedly shaped by prevailing notions as to the benefit to the community of activities such as the destruction of animals, vivisection or the importance of environmental protection. Historically, charitable purposes associated with animal welfare have grown by the ready acceptance of new purposes analogous to those appearing in the decided case law. In *London University v Yarrow*, a hospital for the treatment of animals useful to mankind was held charitable.[31] This paved the way for the acceptance of, for example, the Home for Lost Dogs[32] and, further, the protection of animals.[33] Although

---

[25] [1983] Ch. 159.

[26] [1983] Ch. 159 at 171.

[27] As Lord Hailsham claimed in *D v NSPCC* [1978] A.C. 171 at 228, "the welfare of children, particularly of young children at risk of maltreatment by adults, has been, from the earliest days, a concern for the Crown, as *parens patriae*, an object of legal charities and in latter years the subject of a whole series of Acts of Parliament".

[28] Guide Dogs for the Blind Association.

[29] Motability.

[30] *Hanchett-Stamford v AG* [2009] 2 W.L.R. 405 at 411 per Lewison J.

[31] (1857) 1 De F. & G. 72.

[32] *Re Douglas* (1887) 35 Ch. D. 472.

[33] *Armstrong v Reeves* (1890) 25 L.R. Ir. 325.

now overruled, in *Re Foveaux*[34] Chitty J. developed the category further when he declared that particular societies for the abolition of vivisection were charities within the legal definition of charity.[35]

There has never been a presumption that trusts for the advancement of animal welfare are for the public benefit. The most prominent issue for the courts has been in establishing the sense in which such trusts are beneficial to the community. The pervading obstacle is that in the course of advancing welfare, a benefit must accrue to mankind. The nature of this benefit came to the fore in *Re Foveaux*, where Chitty J. claimed that:

> "Cruelty is degrading to man, and a society for the suppression of cruelty to the lower animals, whether domestic or not, has for its object, not merely the protection of the animals themselves, but the advancement of morale and education among men. The purpose of these societies, whether they are right or wrong in the opinions they hold, is charitable in the legal sense of the term. The intention is to benefit the community".[36]

Similarly in *Re Wedgwood*[37] the Court of Appeal was called upon to consider the charitable nature of a trust for "the protection and benefit of animals". The trust was upheld with emphasis again placed on the benefit to humanity. As Swinfen Eady L.J. commented:

> "It is a gift for a general public purpose, beneficial to the community. A gift for the benefit and protection of animals tends to promote and encourage kindness towards them, to discourage cruelty, and to ameliorate the condition of the brute creation, and thus to stimulate humane and generous sentiments in man towards the lower animals; and by these means promote feelings of humanity and morality generally, repress brutality, and thus elevate the human race. That such purposes are eminently charitable, in the accepted legal sense of that term, is amply established ...".[38]

Re Grove-Grady provided further elucidation.[39] There the Court of Appeal held that a **7.73** sanctuary for the preservation of all animals or birds to keep them safe from molestation by man was not a charitable purpose. The court could discern no public benefit. Lord Hanworth M.R. identified that the sanctuary in question was not a straightforward case of a sanctuary for endangered species. He claimed that, "no such purpose is indicated—nor indeed possible".[40] Crucially, on the facts of *Grove-Grady* the gift was neither to the advantage of the animals nor the betterment of humankind. He observed, therefore that, "The one characteristic of the refuge is that it is free from the molestation of man, while all the fauna within it are to be free to molest and harry each other.

---

[34] [1895] 2 Ch. 501.
[35] *Re Foevaux* was overruled by *National Anti-Vivisection Society v IRC* [1948] A.C. 31 where it was held by the House of Lords that anti-vivisection is not a charitable purpose.
[36] [1895] 2 Ch. 501 at 507.
[37] [1915] 1 Ch. 113.
[38] [1915] 1 Ch. 113 at 122.
[39] [1929] 1 Ch. 557.
[40] [1929] 1 Ch. 557 at 573.

Such a purpose does not, in my opinion, afford any advantage to animals that are useful to mankind in particular, or any protection from cruelty to animals generally. It does not denote any elevating lesson to mankind".[41]

The advancement of animal welfare will continue to be accepted as an inherently charitable purpose under the new Act. As to whether the traditional approach to public benefit will continue to pervade the modern law, it may be that future courts adopt a lenient approach to long-standing authority.

(l) The Promotion of the Efficiency of the Armed Forces of the Crown, or of the Efficiency of the Police, Fire and Rescue Services or Ambulance Services

7.74 Trusts for national or local defence, such as those that promote the efficiency of the armed and emergency services[42] were accepted charitable purposes under the fourth *Pemsel* head. For example, a trust for training boys as officers in the Royal Navy was upheld in *Re Corbyn*.[43] Indeed, the endorsement of trusts for certain patriotic purposes had extended even to a gift to the National Revenue, as in *Nightingale v Goulbourn*, where a testator made a charitable bequest to the Chancellor of the Exchequer, "to be by him appropriated to the benefit and advantage of my beloved country Great Britain".[44]

The new statutory description specifically covers the need to ensure that the armed forces are trained and equipped in times of conflict. It extends to the provision of facilities and benefits for the armed forces. Many examples of such charitable purposes provided by the Charity Commission would be charitable under other statutory descriptions, such as increasing technical knowledge of members of the armed forces through the provision of educational resources or maintaining a museum or other collection for the preservation of artefacts connected with a military unit.[45] Other examples of charitable purposes are more particularly relevant such as promoting and strengthening bonds between allied units or encouraging recruitment to the armed services.

Any Other Purposes

7.75 Section 2(2)(m) lists as charitable any other purposes within subsection (4). These purposes are:

---

[41] [1929] 1 Ch. 557 at 573.
[42] As to the reference to "fire and rescue services", these are defined by the Fire and Rescue Services Act 2004 Pt 2.
[43] [1941] Ch. 400.
[44] (1848) 2 Ph. 594.
[45] See Charity Commission, *Commentary on the Descriptions of Charitable Purposes in the Charities Bill* (December 2005) at [36].

(a) Any purposes not listed within paras (a)–(l) (above) but which are recognised as charitable purposes under the existing law or by virtue of the Recreational Charities Act 1958 s.1.

(b) Any purposes which "may reasonably be regarded as analogous to, or within the spirit of", purposes listed in paras (a)–(l), or, indeed s.2(4)(a).

(c) Any purposes which "may reasonably be regarded as analogous to, or within the spirit of", any purposes which have been recognised under charity law as falling within s.2(4)(b) or (c).

It is important to emphasise that purposes recognised as charitable under existing law or by virtue of the Recreational Charities Act 1958 (considered below) continue to be charitable purposes. The Act, furthermore, permits the inclusion of any purpose that may reasonably be regarded as analogous to, or within the spirit of the accepted charitable purposes whether new or pre-existing. The Charity Commission has identified a range of charitable purposes that will continue to be charitable, notwithstanding the absence of direct reference in the new descriptions of purposes discussed above. The most noteworthy charitable purposes listed by the Charity Commission are as follows:[46]

- purposes charitable under the Recreational Charities Act 1958 (as amended);[47]

- the provision of public works and services such as the repair of bridges, ports, havens, causeways and highways or the provision of water and lighting;[48]

- the relief of unemployment;[49]

- the promotion of mental or moral improvement;

- the preservation of public order;[50]

- the promoting of the sound administration and development of the law;[51]

- the promotion of ethical standards of conduct and compliance with the law in the public and private sectors; and

- the rehabilitation of ex-offenders and the prevention of crime.

---

[46] Charity Commission, *Commentary on the Descriptions of Charitable Purposes in the Charities Bill* (December 2005) at [38].
[47] See **7.77**.
[48] Such purposes were contained in the Preamble and developed by analogy to include a broad range of public works and amenities (e.g. the provision of sewers, public gardens or museums).
[49] See Charity Commission RR3: *Charities for the Relief of Unemployment* (March 1999).
[50] See *IRC v City of Glasgow Police Athletic Association* [1953] A.C. 380.
[51] Examples of charitable purposes include the provision of a court house (*A-G v Heelis* (1824) 2 Sim. & St. 67), mediation services or free legal advice to those in need (such as that provided by JUSTICE to prisoners who believe they have suffered a miscarriage of justice).

Public benefit

7.76   It will be recalled that charitable purposes falling within the old fourth *Pemsel* head, "other purposes beneficial to the community" developed and modernised through the process of drawing analogies with accepted charitable purposes.[52] As regards trusts classified as beneficial to the community, the courts have been vigilant to ensure a sufficient section of the community benefited, more specifically, that benefit was not restricted to a "class within a class".[53] It may be that the courts continue to adopt this test where to do so would be to draw a sensible inference from a statutory description that a purpose should benefit the public at large. There seems to be a legitimate role for the continued application of the test under para. (m), which catches purposes not expressly listed, but nevertheless charitable, or charitable by analogy thereto.

THE RECREATIONAL CHARITIES ACT 1958

7.77   As indicated above, purposes rendered charitable under the Recreational Charities Act continue to be charitable. The scope of the 1958 Act requires to be considered.[54] It is useful to note that by contrast to the promotion of mere sport, a trust for the provision of public recreational facilities such as a park[55] or a recreation ground[56] is a legitimate charitable trust. Accordingly, a considerable number of charities have existed for many years to pursue such purposes.[57] The Recreational Charities Act 1958 was enacted to allay fears that many charities, such as women's institutes and miners' welfare trusts, would cease to be charitable as a result of the House of Lords decision in *IRC v Baddeley*.[58] There, a trust to promote the moral, social and physical well-being of persons resident in West Ham and Leyton who were or were likely to become members of the Methodist Church was deemed not charitable. It was considered that the concept of well-being was too vague to be recognised as a charitable purpose under the fourth head. In addition, and most importantly, the objects were deemed to comprise a class within a class i.e. a class restricted by reference to one criterion (e.g. geographical area) from which a further class were selected to benefit (e.g. those of a particular creed). The development of this general test of public benefit under the fourth *Pemsel* head called into question the status of many existing charities whose beneficiaries were not only confined to a particular area, but narrowed further to a particular class within that class. The object of the 1958 Act was not to enlarge the definition of charity or to acknowledge new institutions as charitable, but to recognise by statute that the provision of recreational facilities in the interests of social welfare is a valid charitable purpose.

---

[52] See **7.11–7.12**.
[53] *IRC v Baddeley* [1955] A.C. 572; see **7.17**.
[54] See S. Maurice, "Recreational Charities" (1959) 23 Conv. (NS) 15. For a summary of the Charity Commission's views, see Charity Commission RR4: see *The Recreational Charities Act* (August 2000).
[55] *Re Hadden* [1932] 1 Ch. 133.
[56] *Re Morgan* [1955] 1 W.L.R. 738.
[57] For example, the Oxford Ice Skating Association.
[58] [1955] A.C. 572.

Section 1(1) of the Act provides that, "it shall be and be deemed always to have been   **7.78**
charitable to provide, or assist in the provision of, facilities for recreation or other
leisure-time occupation, if the facilities are provided in the interests of social welfare".[59]
The requirement that the facilities[60] are provided in the interests of social welfare[61] is
not treated as satisfied unless, the facilities are provided with the object of, "improving
the conditions of life for the persons for whom the facilities are primarily intended".[62]
In addition those persons must, "have need of the facilities by reason of their youth,
age, infirmity or disablement, poverty or social and economic circumstances" or "the
facilities are to be available to male, or to female, members of the public at large"[63]

The intended application of s.1 is confirmed in s.1(3) where it is emphasised that
s.1(1) applies in particular to:

> "the provision of facilities at village halls, community centres and women's insti-
> tutes, and to the provision and maintenance of grounds and buildings to be used
> for purposes of recreation or leisure-time occupation, and extends to the provision
> of facilities for those purposes by the organising of any activity".[64]

POLITICAL PURPOSES

A trust for political purposes can never be a charitable trust.[65] The basis of the court's   **7.79**
objection was explained by Lord Parker in *Bowman v Secular Society:* "A trust for the
attainment of political objects has always been held invalid, not because it is illegal, for
everyone is at liberty to advocate or promote by any lawful means a change in the law,
but because the court has no means of judging whether a proposed change in the law
will or will not be for the public benefit".[66] Further, as Lewison J. explained in *Hanchett-Stamford v AG*, "the law cannot stultify itself by holding that it is for the public
benefit that the law should be changed ... each court must decide on the principle that
the law is right as it stands".[67] No charitable trust or organisation can exist, therefore,
primarily to further the interests of a political party,[68] to change the law (or oppose

---

[59] The principle still applies that for a trust or institution to be charitable it must be for the public benefit.
[60] Facilities provided need not be educative.
[61] The "social welfare" element has been sufficient to exclude groups or societies that exist exclusively for the enjoyment of members, for example, the Birchfield Harriers Athletics Club: Decisions, Vol. 1 (1993), p.4. Many Community Amateur Sports Clubs are now recognised as charitable as advancing amateur sport (**7.66**).
[62] No specific social disadvantage is necessary as long as facilities are provided with the object of improving the conditions of life for members of the community generally: see *Guild v IRC* [1992] 2 A.C. 310 (North Berwick Sports Centre); cf. *IRC v McMullen* [1979] 1 W.L.R. 130, where the majority of the Court of Appeal held that deprivation was necessary.
[63] Section 1(2A) as amended by the Charities Act 2006 s.5(2). Note the scope for overlap with the description in para.(j) "the relief of those in need by reason of youth, age, ill health, disability, financial hardship or other disadvantage".
[64] The specific provision to cater for Miners' Welfare Trusts, has been repealed by the Charities Act 2006.
[65] See generally, C. Forder, "Too Political to be Charitable" [1984] Conv. 263.
[66] [1917] A.C. 406 at 442.
[67] *Hanchett v Stamford v AG* [2009] 2 W.L.R. 405 at 411.
[68] As Finlay J. held in *Bonar Law Memorial Trust v IRC* (1933) 17 TC 508 at 517, "it would not be right to say—that a trust for the promotion of Conservative principles, or the principles, I need hardly say, of any other political party, would be a good charitable trust".

proposed changes)[69] or to seek to influence government to those ends, whether central or local, here or abroad.[70] It is the job of Parliament to legislate and of the courts to apply the law.

Changing the law

7.80   In *National Anti-Vivisection Society v IRC* a trust to abolish vivisection was not charitable, as it required the repeal of the Cruelty to Animals Act 1876 in order to achieve its purpose.[71] The court acknowledged the difficulties in determining whether the purpose was charitable by analogy to existing charitable purposes. Crucially, the aims could not be achieved except by the alteration of legislation. As stated above, the courts have no sufficient standing to determine whether such a change is in the public benefit. If the court felt able to conclude that a change in the law was for the public benefit, this would be to confuse its role with that of the legislature.

In *McGovern v A-G* Amnesty International (a non-charitable organisation) sought charitable status for the Amnesty International Trust under which charitable aspects of the organisations work were carried into operation.[72] At this time, its objects included:

(i) the relief of needy persons who are, were or are likely to become prisoners of conscience and their relatives;

(ii) the attempt to secure the release of such prisoners;

(iii) the abolition of torture or inhumane or degrading treatment or punishment; and

(iv) the promotion and commission of human rights research and dissemination of results.

7.81   Although no objection was raised as to the part that comprised research, Slade J. could not ignore other overtly political objects. He interpreted securing the release of prisoners of conscience as involving the, "direction of moral pressure or persuasion against governmental authorities".[73] As to the "abolition of torture or inhumane or degrading treatment or punishment", Slade J. concluded that:

> "reference to the word 'punishment' really puts the matter beyond doubt. In its context, this word to my mind primarily connotes punishment by process of law and, as I have indicated, is wide enough to include capital and corporal punishment by such process. Correspondingly, the phrase 'procuring the abolition of' necessarily includes the procurement of appropriate reforming legislation, which is the first and most obvious way to put an end to such forms of punishment".[74]

[69] *National Anti-Vivisection Society v IRC* [1948] A.C. 31.
[70] See *McGovern v A-G* [1982] Ch. 321.
[71] [1948] A.C. 31.
[72] [1982] Ch. 321; see R. Nobles, (1982) 45 M.L.R. 704.
[73] [1982] Ch. 321 at 347.
[74] [1982] Ch. 321 at 351.

Accordingly, the trust was deemed to be non-charitable on the ground that it required pressure on foreign governments to change their policies. Although it is possible to create a valid charitable trust for the relief of human suffering, it cannot be charitable if its aims can only be secured by a change in government policy here or abroad.

Campaigning

Although a trust for political purposes cannot be a charitable trust, there is considerable debate as to the extent to which political and campaigning activities can (and should) be carried out by charitable bodies. In other words, the stated aims of a charitable body cannot be political, but a question arises as to what extent activities carried out in furtherance of charitable aims may, indeed, be political. Much campaigning work carried out by charities does not involve "political" campaigning, such as fundraising and promoting awareness. The Government recognises the particular strengths of charities in carrying out a legitimate role in campaigning and advocacy.[75] For example, strong links between charities and local communities entail that charities are well placed to monitor, evaluate and comment upon implemented policies. Government acknowledges a benefit, moreover, from the diversity of causes represented by charities and the scope therein to give voice to a wider range of perspectives and interests than otherwise possible.

    The approach of the Charity Commission has been positive in terms of emphasising the campaigning activities that are indeed compatible with charitable purposes. Previously, it took the view that any political activity must be in furtherance of, and ancillary to, a charity's stated objects i.e. it must serve and be subordinate to the charity's purpose.[76] Its current guidance serves to emphasise that political campaigning must not be the continuing and sole activity, but acknowledges that, "a charity may choose to focus most, or all, of its resources on political activity for a period".[77] The balance to be achieved by trustees is to ensure that the activity in question does not become the reason for the charity's existence.

7.82

Education and politics

Where it is clear that a trust or an organisation carries some educational benefit, it is necessary to be careful that that benefit does not mask truly political objects. In *Re Hopkinson*[78] Vaisey J. made clear that political propaganda masquerading as education is not for the public benefit. Here, a trust to educate the public in the values of a particular political party had some educational character, but it was clear that it could not be charitable. As Vaisey J. claimed, "In my judgment, there can be no doubt that the testator's object was, not education in the proper sense of that word, but the

7.83

---

[75] *Private Action, Public Benefit* (September 2002).
[76] See Charity Commission CC9: *Campaigning and Political Activities by Charities* (September 2004).
[77] Charity Commission CC9: *Speaking out—Guidance on Campaigning and Political Activity by Charities* (March 2008).
[78] [1949] 1 All E.R. 346.

furtherance of his political views and the better equipping of those who make it their business to further them".[79]

A similar conclusion befell a gift for, "the advancement and propagation of the teaching of socialised medicine".[80] The testator had died in 1944. Even though the NHS was introduced after his death, at the point of his death a legislative change would have been required to bring about this purpose. There, Goulding J. concluded, "I am quite unable to avoid the conclusion that the main or dominant or essential object is a political one. The testator never for a moment, as I read his language, desired to educate the public so that they could choose for themselves, starting with neutral information, to support or oppose what he called 'socialised medicine'. I think he was trying to promote his own theory of education, if you will by propaganda ...".[81]

7.84   By way of a more recent example, in *Southwood v A-G* a trust for the advancement of the education of the public in the subject of militarism and disarmament was denied charitable status because the aim of the promoters was to challenge the policies of Western governments.[82] On close examination the object was not to educate the public in the differing means of achieving peace and avoiding war, but to educate the public to an acceptance that peace is best secured by "demilitarisation". Accordingly, Chadwick L.J. concluded:

> "The court is in no position to determine that promotion of the one view rather than the other is for the public benefit. Not only does the court have no material on which to make that choice; to attempt to do so would be to usurp the role of government. So the court cannot recognise as charitable a trust to educate the public to an acceptance that peace is best secured by 'demilitarisation' ".[83]

A distinction must be drawn between political propaganda which is a political, non-charitable object and education with a political flavour. As the latter does not seek to change the law or government policy, it is capable of being charitable. *Re Koepplers' WT*, for example, concerned the purposes of the Wilton Park Project, more specifically the provision of conferences to promote greater co-operation in Europe and the West in general, involving an exchange of views on political, economic and social questions of common interest.[84] Slade L.J. identified that:

> "(i) the conferences sought to improve the minds of the participants, not necessarily by adding to their factual knowledge but by expanding their wisdom and capacity to understand;
>
> (ii) the subjects discussed at conferences were recognised academic subjects in higher education;
>
> (iii) the conferences operated by a process of discussion designed to elicit an exchange of views in a manner familiar in places of higher education;

[79] [1949] 1 All E.R. 346 at 352.
[80] *Re Bushnell* [1975] 1 W.L.R. 1596; noted at (1975) 38 M.L.R. 471 (R. Cotterrell).
[81] [1975] 1 W.L.R. 1596 at 1605.
[82] (2000) *The Times*, July 18.
[83] (2000) *The Times*, July 18.
[84] [1986] Ch. 423.

(iv) the conferences were designed to capitalise on the expertise of participants who were there both to learn and to instruct".[85]

He acknowledged, therefore, that although the topics touched on the political, the activities of Wilton Park were not of a party political nature. They were not designed to procure changes in the laws or policies of the government. "Even when they touch on political matters, they constitute, so far as I can see, no more than genuine attempts in an objective manner to ascertain and disseminate the truth".[86]

CHARITABLE PURPOSES OVERSEAS

Provided a purpose or activity would be charitable at home, it is no objection that a   **7.85**
charitable purpose is carried out abroad. Many well-known organisations such as OXFAM carry out valuable charitable work outside this country. The principal difficulty occasioned by such trusts lies in the question as to the community to be benefited, i.e. whether the benefit relates to a sufficient section of the community in the United Kingdom or the community abroad.[87] Early cases appear either to ignore, or fail to recognise as important, the issue of public benefit. In *Whicker v Hulme*, for example, the House of Lords upheld a trust, "for the benefit and advancement, and propagation, of education and learning in every part of the world as far as circumstances will permit".[88] Lord Evershed M.R. in the Court of Appeal in *Camille and Henry Dreyfus Foundation Inc v IRC*[89] adopted a more cautious approach. Recognising the existence of many charities where the benefit accrued to populations outside the United Kingdom, he claimed:

> "It may be that, on very broad and general grounds, relief of poverty or distress in any part of the world, or the advancement of the Christian religion in any part of the world, would be regarded as being for the benefit of the community in the United Kingdom. I see formidable difficulties, however, where the objects of the trust were, say, the setting out of soldiers or the repair of bridges or causeways in a foreign country".[90]

The Charity Commission appears to endorse the tenor of this approach in the sense that outside relief of poverty and distress (where precedent is plentiful), a more cautious tack is to be adopted. Accordingly, other purposes deemed charitable if carried out at home

---

[85] [1986] Ch. 423 at 436
[86] [1986] Ch. 423 at 437.
[87] For example, in *Keren Kayemeth Le Jisroel Ltd v IRC* [1932] A.C. 650 (a trust for the purchase of land in Israel for the settlement of Jews) it was not possible to identify the community to be benefited, leaving open the question of whether a benefit to a sufficient section of an overseas community will suffice.
[88] (1858) 7 HL 124.
[89] [1954] Ch. 672.
[90] [1954] Ch. 672 at 684.

can be charitable when carried out overseas provided that there is no offence to public policy.[91] In addition, there must be some benefit to the UK community,[92] however indirect[93] or an accepted, identifiable benefit to the community abroad. On this view, a trust to reduce the national debt of a foreign state may be contrary to public policy[94] whereas a trust to promote the protection of the environment in another part of the world will be (and has been) accepted as charitable.[95]

A GUIDE TO FURTHER READING

M. Chesterman, "Foundations of Charity Law in the New Welfare State" (1999) 62 M.L.R. 333.

H. Cohen, "Charities—A Utilitarian Perspective" (1983) 36 C.L.P. 241.

N. Gravells, "Public Purpose Trusts" (1977) 40 M.L.R. 397.

M. Harding, "Trusts for Religious Purposes and the Question of Public Benefit" (2008) 71 M.L.R. 159.

F. Newark, "Public Benefit and Religious Trusts" (1946) 62 L.Q.R. 244.

G. Plowright, "Public Benefit in Charitable Trusts" (1975) 39 Conv. (NS) 183.

---

[91] See "Charities Operating Overseas: Charities for Fourth Head Purposes" (1993) 1 Dec. Ch. Com. 16.
[92] As assumed in *McGovern v A-G* [1982] Ch. 321 at 338; see generally, H. Cohen, (1983) 36 C.L.P. 241 at pp.253–254.
[93] Such as a moral benefit.
[94] To adopt the example provided by Jenkins L.J. in *Camille and Henry Dreyfus Foundation Inc v IRC* [1954] Ch. 672 at 704. Note also the difficulties posed by trusts for the advancement of political purposes.
[95] See Annual Report (1989) at para.29.

Chapter 8

CY-PRÈS

The term cy-près loosely translated means "as near as possible". The doctrine to which **8.01** it lends its name fulfils an important role in the law of charities because it determines what happens when trust property devoted to charitable purposes cannot be applied in the manner intended by the donor. Prior to the Charities Act 1960, cy-près was available only where it was "impossible" or "impracticable" to give effect to the donor's intentions.[1] Such would occur, for example, where the donor elected to benefit a specified institution that had ceased to exist or, in fact, had never have existed at all. Alternatively, it might transpire at some point during the running of the trust that the charitable purpose can no longer be carried out. The effect of s.13(1) of the Charities Act 1993 (which replaced s.13(1) of the Charities Act 1960) was to extend the range of circumstances in which cy-près is available. Where cy-près is, indeed, applicable, it is open to either the court or the Charity Commission to draw up a scheme for the application of the property to purposes "as near as possible" to those originally selected by the donor.[2] In other words, a cy-près scheme is a scheme that involves the alteration of the original charitable purposes.

---

[1] *Re Weir Hospital* [1910] 2 Ch. 124.
[2] There is no compulsion to apply the property to the very nearest possible alternative purpose: see *A-G v Ironmongers' Company* (1834) 2 My. & K. 576, where the redemption of Christian slaves captured by Barbary pirates was no longer capable of being carried out and the property was applied cy-près for the benefit of schools.

The Court's Inherent Jurisdiction

Impossibility and impracticability

8.02   Impossibility or impracticability may be apparent from the outset or it may become clear at some later date that the charitable purpose cannot be carried into effect. "Initial impossibility" occurs where it has never been possible for the specific charitable end to be pursued. Failure must occur, therefore, before the date when the trust comes into existence. In the case of testamentary gifts, this initial failure covers cases where it has always been impossible for a charitable end to be achieved or where it becomes impossible at some point between the making of a will and the death of the testator. Hence, initial impossibility encompasses situations such as the selection of a charity that has never existed,[3] the selection of a charity that has ceased to exist prior to the testator's death[4] or where there is an absence of certainty as to the property to be dedicated to charitable purposes.[5]

Failure or impossibility will be termed "subsequent" or "supervening" if it occurs after property has been effectively dedicated to charity (i.e. after the trust comes into effect). It is at this moment that the claims of the donor and those claiming through him are excluded permanently. In relation to cases of initial impossibility, it is necessary to infer a general or paramount charitable intention on the part of the donor before the property can be applied cy-près. In contrast, cy-près is nearly always available in instances of subsequent impossibility regardless of the generality of charitable intention exhibited by the donor.

General charitable intention

8.03   As indicated above, the availability of cy-près to cases of initial failure will depend upon there being a general charitable intention on the part of the donor. In some cases, the generality of intention is readily apparent.[6] In many other cases, however, the discernment of this general charitable intention is by no means as straightforward. The court will construe the relevant trust instrument as a whole to work out whether the primary intention was to benefit a particular object (in which case the intention is specific) or to give effect to a general mode of charity despite the indication as to a specific object. Where the reference to the specific can be said to be secondary to the donor's general charitable intention, it will be possible to apply the property cy-près. As Kay J. explained in *Re Taylor:*

---

[3] *Re Harwood* [1936] Ch. 285 (gift to the "Peace Society of Belfast").
[4] See, for example, *Re Rymer* [1895] 1 Ch. 19 (St. Thomas' Seminary).
[5] See *Harwood v Harwood* [2005] EWHC 3019 (Ch.) where a testator bequeathed the "Harwood Collection" to trustees for the purpose of establishing a museum but there was no certainty as to what comprised the collection.
[6] One obvious example of general charitable intention concerns cases where a donor has expressed that the gift is to be dedicated to a charitable purpose, but has omitted to identify a mode of application, e.g. "for the relief of poverty".

"If upon the whole scope and intent of the will you discover the paramount object of the testator was to benefit not a particular institution but to effect a particular form of charity independently of any special institution or mode, then, although he may have indicated the mode in which he desires that to be carried out, you are to regard the primary paramount intention chiefly, and if the particular mode for any reason fails, the court, if it sees a sufficient expression of a general charitable intention of charity, will, to use the phrase familiar to us, execute that *cy-près*, that is, carry out the general paramount intention indicated without which his intention itself cannot be effected".[7]

Where, on the other hand, the particularisation is paramount there can be no execution cy-près. As Megarry V.C. put in *Re Spence*, "Where the difficulty or impossibility not only afflicts the method but also invades the concept of the alleged general charitable intention, then I think that the difficulty of establishing that the will displays any general charitable intention becomes almost insuperable".[8] Undeniably, the dividing line is difficult to draw. This has led Vinelott J. to claim that, "To search for such a paramount or dominant charitable purpose or intention is in many cases to follow a will-o-the-wisp".[9] The process is best illustrated through a consideration of case law examples where a general charitable intention was necessary.

INITIAL FAILURE

Although, as will become apparent, there is a marked inconsistency in approach, it is possible to categorise those cases to which the issue of general charitable intention has been central.   **8.04**

Gifts for charitable purposes

In *Biscoe v Jackson*[10] a testator made provision for a soup kitchen and cottage hospital for the parish of Shoreditch. It was impossible to carry out the testator's wishes and initially the gift failed. Despite the degree of particularity in the description of the charitable purpose, the court was able to discern a general charitable intention to benefit the sick and poor of the parish. It was simple to determine those who were intended to benefit and the difficultly lay in the method of carrying out the testator's intention. As Lindley L.J. explained, "The object here is to establish a charity for the benefit of the poor with a particular mode of doing it; and if you cannot accomplish the   **8.05**

---

[7] (1888) 58 L.T. 538 at 542.
[8] [1979] Ch. 483 at 496.
[9] *Re Woodhams* [1981] 1 W.L.R. 493 at 502.
[10] (1887) 35 Ch. D. 460.

object in that mode, then in some other mode in which you can".[11] Accordingly, *Biscoe v Jackson* illustrates the court's readiness to execute a general charitable purpose cy-près where the impossibility extends only to the form of the gift. As explained in *Re Wilson*, "the gift is given to a particular charitable purpose, but it is possible, taking the will as a whole, to say that, notwithstanding the form of the gift, the paramount intention, according to the true construction of the will, is to give the property in the first instance for a general charitable purpose rather than a particular charitable purpose".[12]

By way of contrast, other cases suggest that the more detailed the description of the charitable purpose, the narrower the generality of charitable intention. *Re Good's WT*,[13] for example, concerned a trust to provide rest homes in Hull. The testator had drawn up extremely detailed provisions for the erection of six or more rest homes, including plans for the management and day-to-day running of the project. Insufficient funds entailed that it was impracticable to proceed with the development. Wynn-Parry J. noted the specificity with which the testator's plans were drawn up and the technical and particular language used. He felt that both were inconsistent with the finding of a general charitable intention. The testator in *Re Good's WT* had formulated a very specific intention and, accordingly, there could be no cy-près application.

8.06   Similarly in *Re Spence*,[14] a gift to the defunct, "Old Folks Home at Hillworth Lodge, Keighley" was held to be a gift for a specific charitable purpose. Megarry V.C. was unable to construe a general charitable intention to benefit old people within the general area. The existence of the home at the time of the making of the will militated against a general intention as to charity even though that particular home had closed.

Institutions that cease to exist

8.07   As is clear from *Re Spence*, it is difficult to construe a general intention as to charity where the institution selected is specific and in existence at the time of the testator's will. *Re Rymer*,[15] for example, concerned a bequest of £5,000, "to the rector for the time being of St. Thomas Seminary for the education of priests in the diocese of Westminster for the purposes of such seminary". Before the testator's death, the seminary ceased to exist and the students moved to an alternative seminary outside Birmingham. Lindley L.J. could not avoid the very specific intention evidenced in the nature of this gift. Refusing to apply it cy-près, he commented, "It is a gift of £5,000 to a particular seminary for the purposes thereof, and I do not think it is possible to get out of that".[16] His conclusion sprang from the premise that the court must, "consider whether the

---

[11] (1887) 35 Ch. D. 460 at 470; see also, *Moggridge v Thackwell* (1802) 7 Ves. 36 at 69, where Lord Eldon laid down the principle that, "if a testator has manifested a general intention to give to charity, the failure of that particular mode in which the charity is to be effectuated shall not destroy the charity, the law will substitute another mode of devoting the property to charitable purposes".

[12] [1913] 1 Ch. 314 at 320 per Parker J.

[13] [1950] 2 All E.R. 653.

[14] [1979] Ch. 483.

[15] [1895] 1 Ch. 19.

[16] [1895] 1 Ch. 19 at 35; see also, *Re Wilson* [1913] 1 Ch. 314, where no general intention attached to the very specific provisions drawn up by the testator relating to the erection of a school and the provision of a salaried schoolmaster.

mode of attaining the object is only machinery or whether the mode is not the substance of the gift".[17] In *Re Rymer*, impossibility afflicted both the mode and the substance of the gift.

Continuation in another form

Sometimes a testator will seek to benefit a charity that has not ceased to exist as such, but has amalgamated with other organisations and, thereby, is continued in another form. Continuation in another form can occur where the name or the objects of the charity have changed, perhaps via the making of a scheme[18] or by trustees in accordance with the trust deed.[19] It is important to distinguish those institutions that genuinely cease to exist from those that continue to exist albeit in another guise. In the latter case, there is no issue of initial failure. Where a charity has funds held on trust for its purposes, the charitable purposes will continue despite the alteration to its constitution or its objects.[20] *Re Faraker*[21] is an oft-cited example. In 1911, a legacy was left to "Mrs Bailey's Charity, Rotherhithe". The only similar charity that had operated was Hannah Bayly's Charity founded in 1756. In 1905, it had been consolidated with 13 other charities and new trusts were declared for the benefit of the poor in Rotherhithe. It was held that the testatrix had sought to benefit Hannah Bayly's Charity. Accordingly this was not a case of initial failure. The objects of the charity had developed over the years. Rather than being destroyed by the consolidation, this charity continued in another form.[22] Accordingly, the consolidated charities were entitled to the legacy.

Gifts to incorporated and unincorporated associations

In *Re Vernon's WT*[23] Buckley J. laid down the principles governing gifts to unincorporated charities and gifts to charities with corporate status. In relation to the former he stated that:

> "Every bequest to an unincorporated charity by name without more must take effect as a gift for a charitable purpose ... a bequest which is in terms made for a charitable purpose will not fail for lack of a trustee but will be carried into effect ... by means of a scheme. A bequest to a named unincorporated charity, however, may ... show that the testator's intention to make the gift at all was dependent on

8.08

8.09

---

[17] [1895] 1 Ch. 19 at 35.
[18] See *Re Lucas* [1948] Ch. 424.
[19] See *Re Bagshaw* [1954] 1 W.L.R. 238.
[20] As Kennedy L.J. tentatively put it, "It seems to be the law, that an endowed charity, to whatever purpose its funds are devoted, if and so long as they are devoted to some charitable purpose under some duly authorised scheme, remains still existent so as to draw to it a sum of money given by a will for, presumably, the same purpose as the original charity" (*Re Faraker* [1912] 2 Ch. 488 at 495).
[21] [1912] 2 Ch. 488.
[22] As Farwell L.J. concluded, "Neither the Charity Commissioners nor the Court can take an existing charity and destroy it: they are obliged to administer it" ([1912] 2 Ch. 488 at 495).
[23] [1972] Ch. 300.

the named charitable organisation being available at the time when the gift takes effect. If so and the named charity ceases to exist in the lifetime of the testator, the gift fails...".[24]

On this basis, a gift to an unincorporated charity will be construed as a gift for the purposes of that charity, even though the charity itself may cease to exist in the lifetime of the testator. Unless there is something to demonstrate the need for the continued existence of the donee, the gift will not fail for want of a trustee and effect will be given to it. As to the gifts to charities with corporate status, Buckley J. continued:

"A bequest to a corporate body, on the other hand, takes effect simply as a gift to that body beneficially ... There is no need in such a case to infer a trust for any particular purpose ... the natural construction is that the bequest is made to the corporate body as part of its general funds, that is to say, beneficially and without the imposition of any trust. That the testator's motive in making the bequest may have undoubtedly been to assist the work of the incorporated body would be insufficient to create a trust".[25]

Accordingly, strong evidence is required to demonstrate that a corporate body is to hold property on trust for charitable purposes. In the absence of such evidence, a gift to a corporate charity will fail should the body cease to exist before the death of the testator.

Re Finger's WT[26] concerned two testamentary gifts of residue, first, to the National Radium Commission (an unincorporated association) and, secondly, to the National Council for Maternity and Child Welfare (a corporate charity). Both had ceased to exist before the death of the testator. As to the gift to the Commission, it was interpreted as being a purpose trust that did not depend on the continued existence of the Commission. As the purposes continued, the gift would not fail for initial impossibility. By contrast, the gift to the Council was a gift to a corporate charity. As this type of gift takes effect as a gift to that body beneficially, it could not be construed as a gift on trust for its purposes. The result was a case of initial failure. Somewhat fortunately, Goff J. was able to construe a general charitable intention from looking at the will as a whole and the portion of property intended for the Council was capable of application cy-près.

8.10   Although a different approach has been adopted to the construction of gifts to unincorporated charities and corporate charities, it is a distinction which has been criticised[27] and one capable of producing unfortunate results. This was recognised by Harman J. in *Re Meyers*[28] where he dealt with a number of legacies to both corporate and unincorporated hospitals all of which had been taken over by the Ministry of Health under the National Health Service Act 1946. As to the legacies to

---

[24] [1972] Ch. 300 at 303.
[25] [1972] Ch. 300 at 303.
[26] [1972] Ch. 286.
[27] In *Re Roberts* [1963] 1 W.L.R. 406, for example, Wilberforce J. admitted that, "The mere fact that there is a gift to an unincorporated charity does not seem to me to be enough to enable me to come to the conclusion that a gift is for charitable purposes".
[28] [1951] 1 All E.R. 538.

unincorporated hospitals, there was no difficulty posed by the construction of those gifts as being for the purposes of the hospitals. By contrast and, in line with the distinction promoted in *Re Vernon's WT*, the gifts to the corporate hospitals could not be so construed. If viewed as gifts to those hospitals beneficially, the prima facie conclusion is that those gifts should fail. Harman J. held it to be, "contrary to common sense"[29] not to give a like construction to each gift. He explained, "In my judgment I am doing no violence to the language that the testator has used in the context in which he has used it in saying that in every case when he gives money to a hospital he does not regard the fact whether it was corporate, but he gives for the purposes of the work that that hospital is carrying on".[30]

The distinction has been recently reapplied in *Re ARMS (Multiple Sclerosis Research) Ltd.*[31] There in the context of legacies made to an incorporated charity, the testator died after the charity had run into financial difficulties and a winding-up order had been made. As the legacies were construed as a beneficial gift to that institution, the liquidator successfully claimed entitlement for the benefit of the charity's creditors.

Gifts subject to a condition

A further category of cases concerns gifts that are limited by a condition. In this context, the courts have proved eager to dismiss unacceptable and specific qualifications or conditions as inessential to the testator's paramount intention.[32] For example, in *Re Lysaght*[33] there was a gift of £5,000 to the Royal College of Surgeons to create medical studentships, subject to the qualification that students must be British born and not of Jewish or Roman Catholic faith. The restriction was unacceptable to the Royal College and regarded by it as, "so invidious and so alien to the spirit of the college's work as to make the gift inoperable in its present form".[34]   **8.11**

The gift was saved and the offensive provision deleted because the court was able to rely on the general charitable intention of the testatrix to establish the studentships. First, (and somewhat questionably), it was held that the detail within the bulk of the provisions did not form an essential part of her true intention. Buckley J. gave an assured statement of principle when he concluded that, "the fact that a testator has condescended to details cannot be conclusive that those details, or all of them, are essential parts of his true intention".[35] Less convincing, was the conclusion as a matter of construction that the details did not form part of that intention. Secondly, he determined that it did form part of her paramount intention that the College should act as trustee.[36] This enabled Buckley J. to conclude that the fact that the College would not accept the gift subject to the condition should not be allowed to deflect from her

[29] [1951] 1 All E.R. 538 at 542.
[30] [1951] 1 All E.R. 538 at 542.
[31] [1997] 2 All E.R. 679.
[32] See further **8.19–8.20**.
[33] [1966] Ch. 191.
[34] [1966] Ch. 191 at 200 per Buckley J.
[35] [1966] Ch. 191 at 204.
[36] As Buckley J explained, "It is of the essence of the trust that the trustees selected by the settlor and no one else shall act as the trustees of it and if those trustees cannot or will not undertake the office, the trust must fail" ([1966] Ch. 191 at 207).

paramount intention to create the studentships. In doing so, he invoked the general principle that, "A general charitable intention ... may be said to be a paramount intention on the part of the donor to effect some charitable purpose which the court can find a method of putting into operation, notwithstanding that it is impracticable to give effect to some direction by the donor which is not an essential part of his true intention—not, that is to say, of his paramount intention".[37]

8.12   A further, less troublesome, example is that of *Re Woodhams*.[38] There, a gift to the London College of Music to fund annual scholarships was expressed to be subject to the restriction that the scholarships be available only to boys coming from two specific and high profile orphanages. Vinelott J. held that the selection of orphans from those particular homes merely identified those orphans in greatest need of assistance. It was not, he claimed, "an essential part of the scheme that the scholarships be so restricted, whatever needs might present themselves in changed circumstances".[39] Accordingly, the restriction was deleted.

Non-existent institutions

8.13   In *Re Harwood*,[40] the court was called upon to consider the availability of cy-près in relation to two testamentary gifts. The first, to the "Wisbech Peace Society, Cambridge", suffered initial failure because the society had ceased to exist prior to the death of the testatrix. The second, to the, "Peace Society of Belfast", had failed because there was no evidence that any such society had existed at all. As regards the first gift, Farwell J. felt that the testatrix had gone out of her way to specify that particular charity. This specific identification made it difficult to discern a general intention. As Farwell J. acknowledged:

"where the testator selects as the object of his bounty a particular charity and shows in the will itself some care to identify the particular society which he desires to benefit, the difficulty of finding any general charitable intent in such a case where the named society once existed, but ceased to exist before the death of the testator, is very great".[41]

As regards the second gift, cy-près was available. The testatrix had elected to benefit a non-existent institution and, accordingly, Farwell J. readily found a general charitable intention to, "benefit societies whose object was the promotion of peace".[42] Notwithstanding the doubt that such an intention was political rather than charitable, this case is an excellent illustration of the relative ease with which the court may find a general intention. The idea is that only a general charitable intention can be attributed to a

[37] [1966] Ch. 191 at 202.
[38] [1981] 1 W.L.R. 493.
[39] [1981] 1 W.L.R. 493 at 505.
[40] [1936] Ch. 285.
[41] [1936] Ch. 285 at 287.
[42] [1936] Ch. 285 at 288.

donor who fails correctly to specify an existing charity. At the very least, the court, "is more ready to infer a general charitable intention than to infer the contrary".[43]

Groups of objects

In *Re Satterthwaite's WT*[44] an eccentric testatrix, who declared that she hated all human **8.14** beings, left the residue of her estate to nine separate bodies concerned with the welfare of animals. There was evidence that most of the list had been compiled from the London classified telephone directory. The Court of Appeal was asked to consider whether there could be a cy-près application of the share left to the London Animal Hospital. No such charity ever existed and the share was being claimed by a vet who worked under that trade name prior to the death of the testatrix. Here, a number of factors point to a general charitable intention: the random selection of charities; the mode of selection (by phonebook); her public hatred of people and the nature of the charities selected, all of which were concerned with the welfare of animals.

Russell L.J. was happy to construe the residuary gift as a whole. As each share was intended to go to some object connected with the care of animals, he did not question that there was a general intention to benefit that sort of charity, "Here I have no doubt from the nature of the other dispositions ... that a general charitable intention can be discerned in favour of charity through the medium of kindness to animals".[45] Harman L.J., however, expressed, "the gravest doubts" as to whether a general charitable intention had, indeed, been shown. It was for another reason that he felt compelled to arrive at the same conclusion as Russell L.J. namely that the judge at first instance had discerned, in respect of a similar gift, the general charitable intention necessary to apply cy-près. As no appeal had been made as to the judge's findings in respect of that gift, Harman L.J. was forced to arrive at the same conclusion as to the gift to the London Animal Hospital.[46]

Re Satterthwaite's WT suggests, therefore, that a general charitable intention is easier **8.15** to discern in cases where a group of objects has been selected. The approach adopted by Russell L.J. appears to rely on the detection of a range of similar objects as a means of construing a general, rather than a specific, intention. It is an approach that is not without support. In *Re Knox*,[47] for example, there was a residuary gift to be apportioned in quarters to two named infirmaries, a particular nursing home and Dr Barnardo's Homes. Although the named nursing home had never existed, Luxmoore J. was still able to see a general charitable intention. He explained of the name of the nursing home that, "the object of each of the other charities is a kindred object to that which might be inferred from the name".[48]

---

[43] *Re Davis* [1902] 1 Ch. 876 at 881 per Buckley J.
[44] [1966] 1 W.L.R. 277.
[45] [1966] 1 W.L.R. 277 at 286.
[46] Diplock L.J. offered no opinion, blithely stating that, "With that humility that is becoming in a common law lawyer when confronted with an arcane branch of the Chancery law, I agree with the judgments that have been delivered" ([1966] 1 W.L.R. 277 at 287).
[47] [1937] Ch. 109.
[48] [1937] Ch. 109 at 113. This approach was followed in *Re Hartley* Unreported March 15, (1978), where a general charitable intention sufficed for a cy-près application of one part of a residuary gift in quarters to service charities where one charity no longer existed at the date of the will.

In *Re Spence*,[49] however, Megarry V.C. was unimpressed both with the reasoning in *Re Knox* and with the argument that the principle could apply where as few as two objects had been selected. He distinguished between the case of initial failure where the object had never existed and one where the gift was to a body that had existed at the date of the will, but had ceased to exist before the death of the testator.[50] In the case of the latter, "the court is far less ready to find such an intention".[51] As Megarry V.C. observed, "It is difficult to envisage a testator as being suffused with a general glow of broad charity, when he is labouring and labouring successfully, to identify some particular specified institution or purpose as the object of his bounty".[52] A similar reluctance was evident in the approach of Buckley J. in *Re Jenkin's WT*.[53] There, a gift to the British Union for the Abolition of Vivisection, a non-charitable association, was one non-charitable bequest amongst a group of nine gifts to charitable associations. Buckley J. refused to accept that a general charitable intention motivated the gift, claiming that, "if you meet seven men with black hair and one with red hair you are not entitled to say that there are eight men with black hair".[54] On the basis that a non-charitable object was selected in *Re Jenkin's WT*, it appears that the case is readily distinguishable from *Re Satterthwaite's WT* where the testatrix had selected an animal hospital that had never existed.

SUBSEQUENT FAILURE

8.16   The application of cy-près is broader in relation to instances of subsequent or supervening failure. Unlike initial failure, no general charitable intention need be discerned on the part of the settlor. In the event that property becomes dedicated to charity, it remains dedicated to charity and it is not possible for a previous owner to assert a claim over it. In the case of a will, the relevant date at which this exclusion occurs is that of the testator's death. More generally, this principle is as Jenkins L.J. put it, "once the charity for which the fund was raised had been effectively brought into action the fund was to be regarded as permanently devoted to the charity to the exclusion of any resulting trust".[55]

Timing

8.17   In *Re Slevin*[56] the testator left a variety of legacies one of which was a legacy to a Tyneside orphanage. Shortly after the testator died, but before the legacy was paid, the

[49] [1979] Ch. 483.
[50] Logically, the distinction must also apply to the object that had ceased to exist before the date of the will as the intention is specific, albeit, impossible.
[51] [1979] Ch. 483 at 495.
[52] [1979] Ch. 483 at 493.
[53] [1966] Ch. 249.
[54] [1966] Ch. 249 at 256.
[55] *Re Ulverston and District New Hospital Building Trusts* [1956] Ch. 622 at 636.
[56] [1891] 2 Ch. 236.

orphanage ceased to exist. It was held that the date of the testator's death was crucial. At that point the legacy became dedicated to charity and applicable by the Crown for charitable purposes. It did not matter that the orphanage did not obtain receipt of the legacy. As Kay L.J. commented, "Obviously it can make no difference that the legatee ceased to exist immediately after the death of the testator. The same law must be applicable whether it was a day, or month, or year, or, as might well happen, 10 years after".[57] Similarly, in *Re Wright*,[58] a testatrix died in 1933 providing for the foundation, on the death of her tenant for life, of a convalescent home. Although the failure occurred during the existence of a life interest before the charity became entitled in possession to the property, it was held that the property had been dedicated to charity to the exclusion of the claims of next of kin and residuary legatees.

Surplus

A different problem was posed in *Re King*[59] wherein the question arose as to what to do **8.18** with surplus remaining after the purpose had been carried out. There, a sum of money had been put aside for the setting of a stained-glass window in a parish church to the memory of the testatrix and her family. Having established that such a gift was, indeed, charitable Romer J. readily applied the surplus cy-près. As the whole fund had been dedicated to charity, the surplus was to be applied as near as possible to the original purpose and a second stained-glass window was ordered. Romer J. considered this to be an application of a basic principle that, "Where a gift is made for a particular charitable purpose which is sufficiently provided for without the gift, the gift will be applied *cy-près*".[60]

Somewhat confusingly, there is authority to suggest that the issue of general charitable intention has relevance in this particular context. In *Re Welsh Hospital (Netley) Fund*,[61] for example, a fund was collected for the charitable purpose of building a hospital to benefit sick and wounded soldiers. When the hospital was wound up, the question arose as to whether the surplus was available for application cy-près or whether it was, instead, to be held on resulting trust for subscribers. Unfortunately P.O. Lawrence J. sought to look for a general charitable intention as a basis for deciding upon the former, even though intention is viewed as irrelevant in cases of subsequent failure. He felt it to be clear that subscribers, "did not intend that the surplus, if any, of their contributions should be returned to them".[62] Although in ordering a cy-près application the correct outcome was reached, the appropriate analysis of such cases was provided in the later case of *Re Wokingham Fire Brigade Trusts*.[63] This case concerned a voluntary fire brigade funded by donations, subscriptions and fees for attending fires.

[57] [1891] 2 Ch. 236 at 241; see also, *Re Wright* [1954] Ch. 347 at 363, where Romer L.J. observed that, "no question of subsequent lapse, or of anything analogous to lapse, between the date of the testator's death and the time when the money actually becomes available for actual application to the testator's purpose can affect the matter so far as they are concerned".
[58] [1954] Ch. 347.
[59] [1923] 1 Ch. 243.
[60] [1923] 1 Ch. 243 at 246.
[61] [1921] 1 Ch. 655; see also, *Re North Devon and West Somerset Relief Fund Trust* [1953] 1 W.L.R. 1260.
[62] [1921] 1 Ch. 655 at 661.
[63] [1951] Ch. 373.

After operating a service for many years, it became no longer practicable to continue with the brigade. This was by reason of the sale of the assets to a different body charged with similar duties. Accordingly, Dankwerts J. held that, "Though that purpose is no longer practicable ... the charitable trusts do not fail. It is not necessary to consider whether there was any general charitable intention, and the trusts should be modified by means of a cy-près application".[64]

ALTERING CHARITABLE PURPOSES

8.19   Prior to the statutory reforms introduced by the Charities Act 1960, the court enjoyed a limited discretion to apply funds cy-près only where it was "impossible" or "impracticable" to carry out the terms of the trust. The narrow ambit of the discretion reflected the policy concern that the original wishes of the settlor should be respected. In other words, the court felt constrained to give effect to the expressed wishes of the settlor and was not free to divine a more beneficial use for the property. As Kennedy L.J. noted of the court's inherent jurisdiction, "neither the Court of Chancery, nor the Board of Charity Commissioners ... is entitled to substitute a different scheme for the scheme which the donor has prescribed in the instruments which creates the charity, merely because a coldly wise intelligence, impervious to the special predilections which inspired his liberality, and untrammelled by his directions, would have dictated a different use of his money".[65]

Notwithstanding the limited application of the cy-près doctrine, it is clear that that "impossibility" has long been given a broad meaning.[66] Hence in *Re Dominion Students' Hall Trust*[67] a colour bar (i.e. a condition limiting the class of beneficiaries by reference to their colour) was removed so as to include all students of the overseas dominions of the British Empire. The rationale for so doing was that, "times have changed ... and it is said that to retain the condition, so far from furthering the charity's main object, might defeat it and would be liable to antagonise those students, both white and coloured, whose support and goodwill it is the purpose of the charity to sustain".[68]

8.20   Similarly, in looking to the question of "practicality", it is not necessary, as Evershed J. points out, "to go to the length of saying that the original scheme is absolutely impracticable".[69] In *Re Robinson*,[70] for example, a condition in an endowment gift to an evangelical church requiring the preacher to wear a black gown in the pulpit was dispensed with as impracticable under the court's inherent jurisdiction. P. O. Lawrence J. noted that the use of such a gown had become unusual in more modern times. In addition, he concluded that the wearing of the gown would be detrimental to the teaching and practice of evangelical doctrines and services and would, moreover, be

---

64 [1951] Ch. 373 at 377.
65 *Re Weir Hospital* [1910] 2 Ch. 124 at 140.
66 See, for example, *Re Campden Charities* (1881) 18 Ch. D. 310.
67 [1947] Ch. 183.
68 [1947] Ch. 183 at 186 per Evershed J.
69 [1947] Ch. 183 at 186.
70 [1923] 2 Ch. 332.

interpreted as an act of eccentricity. He found the evidence corroborated by the fact that, "no incumbent has attempted to comply with the condition during the long period which has elapsed since the fund was paid into court".[71] To negate the unwanted practical consequence that the fund would remain in court, P.O. Lawrence J. felt justified in deeming the condition to be impracticable and, hence, deleting it from the terms of the bequest.

Different considerations apply where the court is asked to make an alteration to the administration of a charity.[72] In *Re J. W. Laing Trust*,[73] Peter Gibson J. viewed the job of the court, under its inherent jurisdiction, to consider, "whether it is expedient" to regulate the administration of a charity by removing a requirement as to distribution of a capital sum. There, a trust fund worth £15,000 set up in 1922 had, by 1982, appreciated in value to an astonishing £24 million. The settlor had anticipated that trustees would distribute the fund within 10 years of his death and, in the intervening period, the income would benefit a variety of Christian evangelical causes. In recognition that the settlor had come to view the requirement as inexpedient, and that various charitable causes had come to depend on that continued support, the court approved a scheme under which the trustees were discharged from the obligation as to distribution. It is clear, therefore, that a distinction may be drawn between an alteration in the administration of a charity to cater for the continued support of selected causes, and those cases where there is required an alteration in the charitable purposes or objects themselves. As Peter Gibson J. rationalised, "it cannot be right that any provision, even if only administrative, made applicable by a donor to his gifts should be treated as a condition and hence part of its purpose".[74]

The statutory widening of cy-près

The statutory basis for the cy-près doctrine is to be found within the Charities Act 1993 (as amended). The modernisation of the law governing charitable trusts originally occurred with the Charities Act 1960,[75] but the reforms were re-enacted as s.13(1) of the 1993 Act and have been subject to further amendment by the Charities Act 2006. Accordingly, cy-près is no longer confined to cases where it is "impossible" or "impracticable" to implement the terms of the trust. The statutory grounds, listed in paras (a)-(e) (outlined below), embrace circumstances such as where the original purposes have been fulfilled as far as possible, or have become harmful to the community, or where the purposes have been catered for by another means. It is, moreover, possible to invoke cy-près where the original purposes relate to an area or a class of persons that has since ceased to be suitable for pursuit of the original charitable ends.

8.21

---

[71] [1923] 2 Ch. 332 at 337.
[72] The court has a well established inherent jurisdiction as to alteration in the administration of charities: *AG v Dedham School* (1857) 23 Beav. 350.
[73] [1984] Ch. 143.
[74] [1984] Ch. 143 at 153. See also, *Oldham Borough Council v A-G* [1993] Ch. 210, where Dillon L.J. interpreted a requirement that the actual land given be used as a playing field as being administrative in nature and outside the concept of the charitable purpose.
[75] See the recommendations of the Nathan Committee on the Law and Practice Relating to Charitable Trusts (1952) Cmd. 8710.

8.22   The effect of s.15 of the Charities Act 2006 is to alter the occasions for applying property cy-près to take full account of current social and economic circumstances. Formerly, a particular focus of s.13 fell on "the spirit of the gift" or, in the words of Pennycuick V-C, "the basic intention underlying the gift".[76] Indeed, the expression "spirit of the gift" appeared in four separate paragraphs within s.13(1).[77] On all but one occasion, (that is, para.(a)), s.13 has now been amended to substitute the words, "the spirit of the gift" and replace them with a new expression, "the appropriate considerations". The expression "appropriate considerations" is defined to cover, "(on the one hand) the spirit of the gift concerned", and "(on the other) the social and economic circumstances prevailing at the time of the proposed alteration of the original purposes".[78] The effect is to require the Charity Commission, when making a scheme to alter the purposes for which property is to be applied, to take into account not only the intention underlying the gift of property, but the social and economic circumstances prevailing at the time of the proposed alteration in the purpose.[79]

Overall, therefore, s.13 (as amended) expands and clarifies the jurisdiction and aims to meet the need for greater efficiency and modernisation of the cy-près doctrine. It would be wrong, however, to assume that the intentions of the donor have been largely relegated as a factor in determining the ultimate destination of property. The Charity Commissioners acknowledged almost 40 years ago, "The paramount principle that the donor's intent must be followed as closely as possible has been preserved but his intention is now interpreted in light of modern conditions and having regard to the spirit of the gift".[80] As will become apparent, these sentiments continue to have at least some resonance.

Paragraph (a): fulfilment or failure

8.23   Section 13(1)(a) allows for cy-près where the original purposes, in whole or in part (i) "have been as far as may be fulfilled" or (ii) "cannot be carried out or not according to the directions given and to the spirit of the gift". In interpreting para.(a), it is clear that the case law generated by the Charities Act 1960 remains of primary relevance. In *Re Lepton's Charity*[81] a testator provided that the income from a trust would be applied in the annual payment of £3 to the minister of Pudsey with the balance being applied to poor and aged residents of Pudsey. As between the date of the testator's death in 1715 and the date at which the case was heard in 1972, the annual income had risen from £5 to almost £800. It was contended that the annual amount paid to the minister should be increased to reflect modern conditions.

8.24   Pennycuick V.C. was required to consider whether the expression, "the original purposes" of a charitable gift in s.13(1) should be construed as referring to the trusts as

---

[76] *Re Lepton's Charity* [1972] Ch. 276 at 285.
[77] Paras (a), (c), (d) and (e)(iii): see below.
[78] Section 13(1)(1A).
[79] Note that it is now the duty of trustees, where property may be applied cy-près, to take steps to have the property so applied (s.13(5)).
[80] Annual Report 1970, para.41.
[81] [1972] Ch. 276.

a whole or must be determined individually in relation to the trust for the fixed annual income and the trust for the payment of the residuary. He accepted that, "in a trust of the present character there is an obvious interrelation between the two trusts in that changes in the amount of the income and the value of the money may completely distort the relative benefits taken under the respective trusts".[82] Accordingly, Pennycuick V.C. concluded that the trusts comprised a single charitable gift.[83] On this basis he proceeded to hold that the original purposes could not be carried out in adherence to the spirit of the gift. Paragraphs a(ii) or e(iii)[84] provided alternative routes to the same conclusion,[85] "The intention underlying the gift was to divide a sum which, according to the values of 1715, was modest but not negligible, in such a manner that the minister took what was then a clear three fifths of it. This intention is clearly defeated when in the conditions of today the minister takes a derisory £3 out of a total of £791".[86] Thus, Pennycuick V.C. approved an application to increase the minister's income to £100 per annum.

Paragraph (b): A use provided for part only

Section 13(1)(b) permits cy-près where the original purposes provide a use for part only   **8.25** of the property available by virtue of the gift. This paragraph is straightforward in application and does not appear to alter the common law position. Hence, para.(b) will apply to facts such as those arising in *Re North Devon and West Somerset Relief Fund*.[87] There, surplus funds raised for those who suffered in the floods in 1952 were applicable cy-près. The contributors had parted with their money out and out and did not intend that the surplus, if any, would be returned to them should the immediate object of charity come to an end. In the language of para.(b), cy-près would be available because the original purposes provided a use for part only of the property.

Paragraph (c): More effective use in conjunction with other property

Section 13(1)(c) is applicable, "where the property available by virtue of the gift and   **8.26** other property applicable for similar purposes can be more effectively used in conjunction, and to that end can suitably, regard being had to the appropriate considerations, be made applicable to common purposes".

Paragraph (c), therefore, admits schemes such that embarked upon by the Charity Commissioners in *Re Faraker*.[88] There, it will be recalled, Hannah Bayly's Charity

---

[82] [1972] Ch. 276 at 285.
[83] Note that the same conclusion would not be reached where, for example, a trust caters for the distribution of income between charities in aliquot shares, or in cases of trusts for charities in succession because, "the possibility of carrying out the trusts of one share according to the spirit of the gift could hardly react upon the possibility of carrying out the trusts of the other share according to the spirit of the gift" ([1972] Ch. 276 at 285).
[84] That the original purposes had, "ceased in any other way to provide a suitable and effective method of using the property available by virtue of the gift, regard being had to the spirit of the gift".
[85] Pennycuick V.C. was of the view that, "Subsection (1)(e)(iii) appears to be no more than a final writing out large of paragraph (a)(ii)" ([1972] Ch. 276 at 285).
[86] [1972] Ch. 276 at 285.
[87] [1953] 2 All E.R. 1032.
[88] [1912] 2 Ch. 488.

(established to provide for poor widows of Rotherhithe) was amalgamated with 13 other charities each of which benefited the poor. As Luxton points out, however, the Charity Commissioners acted without jurisdiction to make this alteration to the purposes of Hannah Bayly's Charity as there continued to be poor widows in Rotherhithe.[89] There is no doubt that that such an alteration would now be permitted under s.13(1)(c).

Paragraph (d): The area or class has ceased to be suitable

8.27   Section 13(1)(d) applies where the original purposes:

> "were laid down by reference to an area which then was but has since ceased to be a unit for some other purpose, or by reference to a class of persons or to an area which has for any reason since ceased to be suitable, regard being had to the appropriate considerations, or to be practical in administering the gift".

In *Peggs v Lamb*,[90] for example, an application was made to the court for a cy-près scheme in relation to a longstanding trust for the benefit of the freemen of Huntingdon. The basis of the application was the decline in numbers of the particular group to be benefited. Morritt J. identified the original purpose as being general in nature and for the benefit of the freemen of Huntingdon and their widows. Although hindered somewhat by the absence of a founding instrument, Morritt J. divined that, "the original basic intention or spirit of the gift was the benefit of the borough of Huntingdon".[91] Accordingly, he was able to apply para.(d) to hold that the original purposes had been laid down by reference to a class of persons who had since ceased to be suitable regard being had to the spirit of the gift.[92] The effect of the scheme was to enlarge the class of persons to benefit to include all of the inhabitants of Huntingdon.

Paragraph (e): Where purposes have been adequately provided for, ceased to be charitable or ceased to be suitable or effective

8.28   Section 13(1)(e) makes cy-près applicable to purposes which, in whole or in part, have, since they were laid down:

> "(i) been adequately provided for by other means; or
>
> (ii) ceased, as being useless or harmful to the community or for other reasons, to be in law charitable; or

---

[89] P. Luxton, *The Law of Charities* (Oxford, Oxford University Press, 2001), p.567.
[90] [1994] Ch. 172.
[91] [1994] Ch. 172 at 197.
[92] Note that s.13(1A) permits consideration of the social and economic circumstances prevailing at the time of the proposed alteration in addition to the "spirit of the gift": see **8.22**.

(iii) ceased in any other way to provide a suitable and effective method of using the property available by virtue of the gift, regard being had to the appropriate considerations".

Of the occasions on which s.13(1)(e) has been considered judicially, it is para.(e)(iii) that is viewed as the most encompassing.[93] Presumably, para.(e)(ii) ("ceased, as being useless or harmful to the community or for other reasons, to be in law charitable") will assume relevance only in circumstances where statute declares a purpose to be no longer charitable or illegal. It has been suggested, for example, that this subsection could apply to the endowments of independent schools should charitable status be withdrawn.[94]

As indicated above in *Re Lepton's Charity*,[95] Pennycuick V.C. regarded para.(e)(iii) as a viable alternative to (a)(ii). On the facts before him, the original purposes could not be carried out "according to the directions given and to the spirit of the gift" (as required by para.(a)(ii)). Equally, the original purposes had, "ceased to provide a suitable and effective method of using the property ... regard being had to the spirit of the gift" (as required by para.(e)(iii)).[96] *Varsani v Jesani*[97] provides further, and more recent, guidance as to the breadth of para.(e)(iii). Under the court's inherent jurisdiction cy-près would not have been available on the ground that it was still possible to carry out the original purposes of the charity.[98] The case concerned a charitable trust to promote the faith of a particular Hindu sect. The sect split into rival factions following a disagreement as to the divine status of the successor to their founder, with one group refusing to continue to worship in the communal temple. Chadwick L.J. was of the view that the spirit of the gift was to provide facilities for a small community of followers of a particular sect in the worship of a particular faith. The division of the community entailed that the original purposes were no longer a suitable and effective method of using the property because the fragmented community were no longer able to worship together. Regard being had to the spirit of the gift, he elected sub-para.(e)(iii) as the basis upon which a cy-près scheme could be directed, the aim being to facilitate a division of the charity property amongst the feuding groups.

Charities Act 1993 s.13(2)

Section 13(2) provides that s.13(1), "shall not affect the conditions which must be **8.29** satisfied in order that property given for charitable purposes may be applied cy-près, except in so far as those conditions require a failure of the original purposes".

In *Re J. W. Laing Trust*, Peter Gibson J. was clearly of the view that the consequence of this section would be to preserve the requirement existing prior to statutory

---

[93] Paragraph e(i) has proved useful in relation to charitable purposes which are the duty of government authorities (e.g. repair or maintenance of the roads). In such cases the Charity Commission can use its statutory powers to apply the property cy-près towards the improvement of other local amenities.
[94] See J. Jaconelli [1996] Conv. 24.
[95] [1972] 1 Ch. 276.
[96] Note that the expression "spirit of the gift" employed in both paragraphs under s.13(1) has been replaced by "the appropriate considerations" to permit consideration not only of the spirit of the gift but also the prevailing social and economic circumstances at the time of the proposed alteration: see **8.22**.
[97] [1999] Ch. 219.
[98] [1999] Ch. 219 at 237 per Chadwick L.J.

intervention that the donor must show a general charitable intention.[99] If inclusive of cases of subsequent failure, this conclusion is open to question.[1] The majority of s.13(1) cases concern subsequent failure where no finding of general charitable intention is, under the general law, deemed necessary.[2]

CHARITY COLLECTIONS AND APPEALS

8.30   It remains to consider the statutory provisions enacted to deal with the problems of failure in the context of charity collections and public appeals. Here, difficulties have arisen where charitable funds are raised by public appeal and it proves impossible or impracticable to apply the property to that purpose or it transpires that the funds are not required to pursue the original purposes at all. In such cases, it is often difficult or impossible to locate the donors to such charitable funds in order to effect a return of their property. It is important to appreciate that problems arise in cases of initial failure alone. If the case is one of subsequent failure, no possibility of a return of the property arises, and cy-près is available as of course.[3]

Conventionally, in the case of initial failure, a general charitable intention was required before a cy-près application of property was possible. Where the intention of the donor was deemed to be specific, cy-près was not available. Instead, the courts were forced to grapple with the less attractive alternatives of a return of property to the original donors under a resulting trust or payment of the funds to the Crown as bona vacantia. Accordingly, s.14 of the Charities Act 1993, (re-enacting s.14 of the Charities Act 1960), was designed to ensure that property, donated for specific charitable purposes which fail, could be applied cy-près as though the donation was for general charitable purposes.

Unknown or disclaiming donors

8.31   Section 14(1) deals with the application cy-près of the gifts of donors "unknown or disclaiming". Here, property may be applied cy-près as if given for charitable purposes generally, in either of two specified cases. The first is where the donor cannot be identified or found but the prescribed advertisements and inquiries have been published and made, and the prescribed period beginning with the publication of those

---

[99] [1984] Ch. 143 at 149.
[1] As J. Warburton argues [1984] Conv. 319 at p.320, "Peter Gibson J. has, by a back door, purported to introduce a restriction into the application of trust property cy-près which did not exist prior to 1960".
[2] *Re Wright* [1954] Ch. 347.
[3] See, further, *Re Ulverston and District New Hospital Building Trusts* [1956] Ch. 622, where Jenkins L.J. promotes the understanding that, where any of the property has been applied towards the charitable purpose, the failure is a subsequent failure, automatically allowing a cy-près application irrespective of the s.14 jurisdiction.

advertisements has expired.[4] The second covers the case of a donor who has executed a disclaimer, in the prescribed form, of his right to have the property returned.[5]

Where, however, property consists of, "the proceeds of cash collections made by means of collecting boxes or by any other means not adapted for distinguishing one gift from another" or, "the proceeds of any lottery, competition, entertainment, sale or similar money-raising activity, after allowing for property given to provide prizes or articles for sale or otherwise to enable the activity to be undertaken," it is conclusively presumed (without any advertisement or inquiry) to belong to donors who cannot be identified.[6] Thus, where the method of donation makes it difficult to tell one contribution from another, there is a presumption of donation to general charitable purposes. The idea is to avoid the need to impute a fictitious general charitable intention on the part of the donor, or to seek (often in vain), to return the property.

As to property not falling within s.14(3), the court or the Charity Commission[7] may direct that property be treated, without advertisement or enquiry, as belonging to donors who cannot be identified.[8] Such an order may be made if it appears that, "it would be unreasonable, having regard to the amounts likely to be returned to the donors, to incur expense with a view to returning the property" or that "it would be unreasonable, having regard to the nature, circumstances and amounts of the gifts, and to the lapse of time since the gifts were made, for the donors to expect the property to be returned".

The impact and usefulness of s.14 has been much criticised. Indeed, s.14(7) appears to be limiting in scope as it provides that "charitable purposes will be deemed to 'fail' where any difficulty in applying the property to those purposes makes that property, or the part not applicable cy-près, available for return to the donors". On this basis of this wording, it might be argued that the section only covers cases where, under the general law, the property is held on resulting trust for the donors. The unfortunate conclusion may be that s.14(7) excludes many of the cases it was intended to encompass, i.e. where property will pass to the Crown as bona vacantia.   **8.32**

In the case of cash collections, for example, the judgment of Goff J. in *Re West Sussex Constabulary's Fund* provides an obvious starting point.[9] Goff J. held that those who make anonymous cash contributions to collection boxes do not intend to, and therefore do not, retain any interest in the donations. This is both sensible and correct.[10] In consequence, s.14 is not engaged in relation to the donations listed in s.14(3)(a) (proceeds of cash collections), precisely because the common law deems this type of contributor to have divested himself of all interest in the donation. If viewed from this perspective, the property would not be available for return to its original donors as is required under s.14(7).

Similarly, in relation to the class of contribution cited in s.14(3)(b), (proceeds from

[4] Section 14(1)(a).
[5] Section 14(1)(b).
[6] Section 14(3).
[7] Prior to the Charities Act 2006, only the court had the power to make such a direction.
[8] Charities Act 1993, s.14(4) as amended by Charities Act 2006 s.16.
[9] [1971] Ch. 1. Although the case concerned non-charitable donations where a surplus remained after the fund was wound up, there is no distinction here to be drawn between donations for charitable and non-charitable purposes.
[10] A different (and less plausible) view was taken by Harman J. in *Re Gillingham Bus Disaster Fund* [1958] Ch. 300, that such donations should be held on resulting trust.

entertainment), again, this contributor retains no interest in the property. As Goff J. explains, "The purchaser of a ticket may have the motive of aiding the cause or he may not. He may purchase a ticket merely because he wishes to attend the particular entertainment or to try for the prize, but whichever it be he pays his money as the price of what is offered and what he receives".[11] As such, therefore, he attains the advantage for which he has contracted and thereby loses his entitlement to any interest in the property.

In consequence, s.14 has been argued to be redundant. Wilson, for example, takes the view that, "the general law itself would seem to be perfectly capable of performing the task which, it appears, section 14 was intended to perform but which, due to the way in which it was drafted . . . it is unable to perform".[12] For others, it is less than clear that the courts would adopt this interpretation and "rob the section of most of its significance".[13] As to the correct interpretation of s.14, it probably matters little. This is because the conventional stance of the Attorney General is to waive the claim for bona vacantia and allow the cy-près application of the property derived from anonymous donors.[14]

Solicitations, statements and relevant declarations

8.33 As regards the cy-près application of gifts made in response to certain solicitations, the Charities Act 2006 amends the 1993 Act to include the new s.14(A).[15] The section applies to property given for a specific charitable purpose in response to a solicitation or appeal. A solicitation will be within the subsection where it is made for a specific purpose and it is accompanied by a statement to the effect that property given in response to it will, in the event of those purposes failing, be applicable cy-près as if given for charitable purposes generally. The statement will apply unless the donor makes a relevant declaration in writing at the time of making the gift that, in the event of the specific charitable purpose failing, he wishes the trustees holding the property to give him the opportunity to request the return of the property in question (or a sum equal to its value at the time of the making of the gift).[16]

Where the specific charitable purposes fail and the donor has made the relevant declaration, trustees are charged with informing the donor of the failure of the purposes, enquiring whether he wishes to request a return of the property (or a sum equal to its value), and if such a request is made within the prescribed period, to return the property (or such a sum) to him.[17] Where trustees have taken all appropriate prescribed steps but they have failed to find the donor, or the donor fails to request a return of the property (or a sum equal to its value) within the prescribed period, the property will be

---

[11] [1971] Ch. 1 at 11. He held, further at [11], that in such cases, "there was no direct contribution to the fund at all. It is only the profit, if any, which is ultimately received, and there may even be none".
[12] D. Wilson [1983] Conv 40 at 49.
[13] P. Luxton, *The Law of Charities*, (Oxford University Press, Oxford, 2001), p.587.
[14] *Re Ulverston and District New Hospital Building Trusts* [1956] Ch. 622.
[15] Charities Act 2006 s.17.
[16] Section 14A(2), (3).
[17] Section 14A(5). "Prescribed" means prescribed by regulations made by the Commission: s.14A(9).

applied as though the donor had disclaimed any right to its return.[18] If, however, the purposes have failed and the donor has not made a relevant declaration, the property is to be applied cy-près as though the donor had disclaimed the right to have the property returned to him.[19]

Further s.14A(8)(c) now caters for appeals that consist of both solicitations which contain the statement described in s.14A(2) and solicitations that are not so accompanied. It is made clear that a person giving property as a result of such an appeal will be taken to have responded to a solicitation containing the statement, unless he can prove otherwise.

Cy-près schemes

In addition, s.18 of the Charities Act 2006 has effected a further alteration of the cy-près rules by inserting into the 1993 Act a new s.14B to be considered by the court or the Charity Commission when making a scheme to change charitable purposes. Section 14B applies either when the scheme is transferring property from one charity to another or, where there is no transfer and the scheme simply changes the purposes of the charity that holds the property.[20] There are three matters to which the court or the Charity Commission must have regard,[21] each of which carries equal weight. The matters are: **8.34**

- "the spirit of the original gift",

- "the desirability of securing that the property is applied for charitable purposes which are close to the original purposes", and

- "the need for the relevant charity to be able to make a significant social or economic impact".

Under s.14B(4), the court or the Commission, when making a scheme to transfer a charity's property to another charity, can require trustees of the recipient charity to use the property for purposes as similar as practicable to the original purposes for which the property was held. The aim of the section is to cover cases where the original purposes are considered to be useful but the court or the Commission believe that the property can be more effectively used in conjunction with other property.

---

[18] Section 14A(6).
[19] Section 14A(7).
[20] References to "property given" include the property in the form in which it was originally given and any property derived from it (s.14(B)(5)).
[21] Section 14(B)(3).

Guide to Further Reading

J. Garton, "Justifying the Cy-Près Doctrine" (2007) 21 Trust Law International 134.

P. Luxton, "In 'Pursuit of Purpose' through Section 13 of the Charities Act 1960" [1985] Conv. 313.

J. Warburton, "*Re J. W. Laing Trust*" [1984] Conv. 319.

D. Wilson, "Section 40 of the Charities Act 1960: A Dead Letter" [1983] Conv. 40.

Chapter 9

RESULTING TRUSTS

The focus of the book so far has been on express trusts wherein the settlor must comply **9.01** with the three certainties[1] and adhere to requirements as to proper constitution.[2] Trusts, however, need not be express. This chapter is concerned with a form of implied trust called the resulting trust.[3] The resulting trust (as with the constructive trust[4]) arises by operation of law and without the concerted actions of a settlor to constitute an express trust. As such, the resulting trust does not come into being by design, but arises only where equity stipulates that a trust should be imposed on account of the particular circumstances. Consequently, there are no formal requirements for its creation. Hence, the resulting trust is exempt from the requirement of writing laid down in s.53(1) of the Law of Property Act 1925.[5] Even a minor can act as a resulting trustee.[6] The essential characteristic of the resulting trust is that the settlor is also its beneficiary. Its fundamental function is to "re-direct" the beneficial ownership of trust property back to the former title owner.

The resulting trust arises in two principal contexts.[7] The first is that of failed trusts, where there has been an attempt to create a trust and some part of the beneficial interest remains undisposed of.[8] The function of the resulting trust here is restorative. As equity is said to abhor a vacuum, someone must be entitled to that property.[9] The resulting trust is, thus, the mechanism whereby property jumps back to the settlor or it is the tool to establish that the settlor retains an equitable interest in the property.

---

[1] *Knight v Knight* (1840) 3 Beav. 148; see Ch.2.
[2] See generally, Ch.3.
[3] The term "resulting trust" is derived from the Latin *"resalire"* meaning to jump back.
[4] This is a concept analysed in Ch.10.
[5] This is of particular importance for unmarried cohabitants who may, through a contribution to the purchase or upkeep of the home, acquire a property interest without compliance with formality: see Ch.11.
[6] *Re Vinogradoff* [1936] W.N. 68.
[7] Per Lord Browne-Wilkinson in *Westdeutsche Landesbank v Islington LBC* [1996] A.C. 669 at 708.
[8] See further, **9.09**.
[9] As Lord Reid put it in *Vandervell v IRC* [1967] 2 A.C. 291 at 308, "the beneficial interest must belong to or be held for somebody: so if it was not to belong to the donee or to be held by him in trust for somebody it must remain with the donor".

9.02   The second context is that of apparent gifts. This includes cases where there is a voluntary transfer of property or a contribution to the purchase price of property without an express indication as to how equitable title is to be held.[10] In such cases, there is a rebuttable presumption of resulting trust. In other words, there is a presumption (capable of displacement by evidence to the contrary) that the intention of each transferor or contributor was not to make a gift, but that they should hold a proprietary right proportionate to their contribution.

Typically broad definitions have been put forward to explain or describe a doctrine that has grown to operate in such specific, but varied circumstances. Martin, for example, continues to regard the resulting trust as arising in, "a situation in which the transferee is required by equity to hold property on trust for the transferor; or for the person who provided the purchase money for the transfer".[11] Such explanations are helpful only to the extent that they offer a descriptive setting in which the resulting trust has traditionally operated. Other commentators have pondered the adaptability of the resulting trust mechanism and promoted an extended role for the resulting trust. It has been suggested, for example, that such trusts might work to effect restitution where X has been unjustly enriched at the expense of Y.[12] In *Westdeutsche Landesbank v Islington LBC*,[13] however, the House of Lords rejected this liberal reasoning and effectively confined the resulting trust to its more traditional role. As regards that role, Chambers looks to the issue of why such trusts are imposed and argues that, "all resulting trusts come into being because the provider of property did not intend to benefit the recipient".[14] As regards the conventional contexts in which the resulting trust operates this is, perhaps, the unifying link between the category of failed trusts and the category of apparent gifts or informal contributions to the purchase price of property. Where it cannot be established that the transferee of property was intended to take property beneficially, a resulting trust is imposed by law to effect a return of the property to the transferor.

9.03   The subject area of resulting trusts is notoriously difficult. Recent academic discourse has exposed its theoretical complexity and highlighted the classificatory problems.[15] The principal issues of contention concern the conceptual basis of the resulting trust, the extent to which such trusts give effect to the common intentions of the parties and the nature of the obligations of the resulting trustee. The primary aim of this chapter, however, is to evaluate the circumstances in which resulting trusts arise. As a corollary, the situations in which a resulting trust will be excluded are also highlighted. This chapter will draw together a range of case law illustrations to paint a comprehensive picture of the modern judicial approach to resulting trusts. In addition, the manner in which resulting trusts are classified will be evaluated and some of the principal conceptual difficulties confronted.

---

[10] See further, **9.33**.
[11] J. Martin, *Modern Equity*, at p.251.
[12] P. Birks, "Restitution and Resulting Trusts" in S. Goldstein (ed.) *Equity: Contemporary Legal Developments* (Hebrew University of Jerusalem, 1992) at p.335.
[13] [1996] A.C. 669.
[14] R. Chambers, *Resulting Trusts* (Oxford, Clarendon Press, 1997) at p.2.
[15] Most recently, see W. Swadling "Explaining Resulting Trusts" (2008) 124 L.Q.R. 72, for a discussion of the operation of presumptions.

CLASSIFICATION OF RESULTING TRUSTS

As described above, the resulting trust is encountered in a variety of circumstances. In **9.04** search of an analytical overview, the classification of resulting trusts has assumed a high priority for judges and commentators alike. Prior to the decision in *Westdeutsche Landesbank v Islington LBC*, the accepted categorisation of resulting trusts was that put forward by Megarry J. in *Re Vandervell's Trusts (No.2)*.[16] Megarry J. divided resulting trusts into two main categories: resulting trusts that arise automatically and those based on the presumed intention of the transferor of property. The former, he felt, did not depend on the intention of the parties, but arose as an automatic consequence of the transferor's failure to dispose of the entirety of the beneficial interest. For Megarry J. the "automatic resulting trust" was deemed to arise:

> "where the transfer to B is made on trusts which leave some or all of the beneficial interest undisposed of. Here B automatically holds on a resulting trust for A to the extent that the beneficial interest has not been carried to him or others. The resulting trust here does not depend on any intentions or presumptions but is the automatic consequence of A's failure to dispose of what is vested in him. Since ex hypothesi the transfer is on trust, the resulting trust does not establish the trust but merely carries back to A the beneficial interest that has not been disposed of. Such resulting trusts may be called 'automatic resulting trusts' ".[17]

By contrast, as regards a trust based on presumed intention:

> "the question is not one of the automatic consequences of a dispositive failure by A, but one of presumption: the property has been carried to B, and from the absence of consideration and any presumption of advancement B is presumed not only to hold the entire interest on trust but also to hold the beneficial interest for A absolutely. The presumption thus establishes both that B is to take on trust and also what that trust is. Such resulting trusts may be called 'presumed resulting trusts' ".[18]

The distinction posited by Megarry J. provides a useful starting point in that he **9.05** identifies two essential categories of trust that were adopted by judges in much of the case law decided subsequently. However, the dividing line between his categories is not without difficulty. In particular, as regards the automatic resulting trust, there appears to be no focus at all upon the intention of the parties. Megarry J. sees the so-called "automatic resulting trust" as a self-activating or mechanical response to the dispositive failure of the settlor, whereas his "presumed intention resulting trust" arises because there is a rebuttable presumption of trust based on inferred intention. In the latter case, the settlor makes no express indication as to how the beneficial interest lies. Equity presumes, however, that the property belongs to the person who advances the purchase

---

[16] [1974] Ch. 269.
[17] [1974] Ch. 269 at 294.
[18] [1974] Ch. 269 at 294.

money, that is, in the absence of evidence to rebut the presumption. It might, nonetheless, be argued of the former that where an express trust fails to dispose of some part of the beneficial interest, an intention can be implied on the part of the settlor that, in so far as there is any, the unexhausted beneficial interest should revert to him. Somewhat artificially, however, this process involves deciding what the settlor would have intended had the thought occurred to him that some part of the beneficial interest may remain undisposed of. It was inevitable that the distinction promoted by Megarry J. would attract further scrutiny.

In his speech in *Westdeutsche Landesbank v Islington*,[19] Lord Browne-Wilkinson clarified the circumstances in which the resulting trust arises. First, category A:

> "Where A makes a voluntary transfer to B or pays (wholly or in part) for the purchase of property, which is vested either in B alone or in the joint names of A and B, there is a presumption that A did not intend to make a gift to B: the property is held on trust for A (if he is the sole provider of the money) or in the case of a joint purchase by A and B in shares proportionate to their contribution. It is important to stress that this is only a presumption, which presumption is easily rebutted either by the counter presumption of advancement or by direct evidence of A's intention to make an outright transfer...".[20]

Secondly, category B:

> "Where A transfers property to B on express trusts, but the trusts declared do not exhaust the whole beneficial interest ... and *Barclays Bank v Quistclose Investments Ltd*...".[21]

9.06   He warned, moreover, that the distinction drawn by Megarry J. between the "automatic resulting trust" and the "presumed intention resulting trust" was untenable.[22] In particular, he illustrated that the so-called "automatic resulting trust" was not irrebuttable in the manner that Megarry J. appeared to suggest. Lord Browne-Wilkinson argued that:

> "Megarry J. ... suggests that a resulting trust does not depend on intention but operates automatically. I am not convinced that this is right. If the settlor has expressly, or by necessary implication, abandoned any beneficial interest in the trust property, there is in my view no resulting trust: the undisposed-of equitable interest vests in the Crown as bona vacantia".[23]

In addition, he hailed as a general feature of the resulting trust that it gave effect to the common intentions of the parties.

[19] [1996] A.C. 669.
[20] [1996] A.C. 669 at 708. Note that in the context of the family home, regard must be had to the new approach by the House of Lords in *Stack v Dowden* [2007] 2 A.C. 432: see Chapter 11 for detailed discussion of trusts of the family home.
[21] [1996] A.C. 669 at 708.
[22] It is to be noted that Megarry J. viewed his propositions as, "the broadest generalizations" which did, "not purport to cover the exceptions and qualifications which doubtless exist" ([1974] Ch. 269 at 294).
[23] [1996] A.C. 669 at 708.

Despite the obvious authority underpinning Lord Browne-Wilkinson's views, his principles of resulting trusts have themselves encountered criticism. First, it is not immediately apparent that resulting trusts must give effect to the common intention of the parties. A common intention may be discerned in the case of the purchase money resulting trust where two or more people evince the intention to share the beneficial interest in property.[24] It is much less clear how, if at all, a resulting trust can give effect to common intention where it comes into being because the settlor has failed to divest himself effectively of his beneficial interest. In such cases, the only intention of any relevance to the destination of the equitable interest can be that of the settlor. In addition, this explanation also fails to consider the imposition of the resulting trust where the settlor never intends that a transferee act as trustee[25] or, moreover, ever desires that the remainder of trust property result back.[26] In such cases, the imposition of a resulting trust is antithetical to the intentions of the settlor and casts doubt on Lord Browne-Wilkinson's view that all resulting trusts give effect to presumed intention.

Secondly, the circumstances in which one can be said to have simply abandoned property are, indeed, very rare. The courts have proved willing to uphold the resulting trust even when faced with evidence that the transferor did not intend to retain any interest. In *Air Jamaica v Charlton*,[27] for example, the Privy Council held that a resulting trust arose in favour of a company over the surplus funds of a pension trust determined to be void under the perpetuity rules. In doing so, Lord Millett overcame a formidable obstacle presented by cl.4 of the trust deed, which stated that, "No moneys which any time have been contributed by the Company under the terms hereof shall in any circumstances be repayable to the Company". Nonetheless, and, in elucidating further the principles of resulting trusts, he held that:

9.07

> "Like a constructive trust, a resulting trust arises by operation of law, though unlike a constructive trust it gives effect to intention. But it arises whether or not the transferor intended to retain a beneficial interest—he almost always does not—since it responds to any absence of intention on his part to pass a beneficial interest to the recipient. It may arise even where the transferor positively wished to part with the beneficial interest, as in *Vandervell* ... In that case the retention of a beneficial interest by the transferor destroyed the effectiveness of a tax avoidance scheme which the transferor was seeking to implement. The House of Lords affirmed the principle that a resulting trust is not defeated by evidence that the transferor intended to part with the beneficial interest if he has not in fact succeeded in doing so".[28]

It is, therefore, a perceived limitation of both Megarry J.'s distinction and the views as to intention postulated by Lord Browne-Wilkinson that they fail to examine accurately the role of intention in all cases of resulting trusts. Within his adopted category of

---

[24] The bilateral intention of the parties is, however, the distinguishing feature of the constructive trust, which arises to give effect to a bargain between the parties as to beneficial ownership.

[25] In *Re Vinogradoff* [1935] W.N. 68 the transferee was a child of seven years of age.

[26] In *Vandervell v IRC* [1967] 2 A.C. 291, for example, Mr Vandervell sought to dispose of his interest completely in order to avoid liability to taxation.

[27] [1999] 1 W.L.R. 1399.

[28] [1999] 1 W.L.R. 1399 at 1412.

"automatic resulting trusts", Megarry J. identifies the response of equity as being detached from the question of intention altogether. For Lord Browne-Wilkinson, all resulting trusts give effect to the presumed intentions of the parties. More convincingly, as shown above, both types of trust must now properly be viewed as a response to the absence of intention that the recipient of property should have the benefit of it.[29]

9.08   The remainder of this chapter is concerned to explore the operation of resulting trusts as they apply in the context, first, of failed trusts and secondly, the voluntary transfer or the purchase in the name of another. It is important to note that Lord Browne-Wilkinson positioned the *Quistclose* trust as falling within his category of trusts which fail. The *Quistclose* trust is, as Lord Millett reminds, "an entirely orthodox example of the kind of default trust known as the a resulting trust. The lender parts with the money to the borrower by way of loan, but he does not part with the entire beneficial interest in the money, and so far as he does not it is held on a resulting trust for the lender from the outset".[30] *Quistclose* trusts have been detailed in Chapter 2, but discussion of this type of resulting trust will be incorporated here as is necessary.[31]

FAILURE OF TRUST CASES

9.09   As indicated above, where an express trust fails to dispose of the entirety of the beneficial interest, the remainder is held by implication on resulting trust for the settlor. The purpose of the resulting trust in this context is to restore equitable title in property to its previous owner or to establish that that person continues to hold an equitable interest in the property. Many examples of the operation of resulting trusts feature in other parts of the book. Accordingly, some of the illustrations offered below will be familiar to the reader. Although there is no attempt to produce an exhaustive list, examples of resulting trusts will be considered under the following four broad headings:

- failure to declare a trust;
- failure of a trust;
- the failure of a specific purpose, and
- unexhausted beneficial interests.

Failure to declare a trust

9.10   Where property is conveyed to persons with the intention that they act as trustees, the failure to declare the manner in which all of the beneficial interest is to be held on trust will entail that any property unaccounted for is held on resulting trust for the grantor.

---

[29] See R. Chambers, *Resulting Trusts* (Oxford, Clarendon Press, 1997) for a forceful argument that the resulting trust arises because the provider of the property did not intend to benefit the recipient.
[30] *Twinsectra v Yardley* [2002] 2 All E.R. 377 at 403.
[31] See further, **9.15**.

The classic illustration is provided by *Vandervell v IRC*[32] (considered in detail in Ch.4). It will be recalled that in 1958 Vandervell wished to found a Chair of Phamacology at the Royal College of Surgeons. He planned to transfer shares in Vandervell Productions Ltd to the College, in whose favour dividends on the shares would subsequently be declared. As a charity, the College enjoyed fiscal privileges, the attraction of the transaction being that the dividends, (amounting to some £250,000), would not give rise to tax liability. The shares were to be transferred subject to the option to repurchase in favour of Vandervell Trustees Ltd, a company administering trusts connected to Vandervell's family and business enterprises. Once the dividends were paid, the shares could be retrieved by Vandervell Trustees Ltd. Vandervell was sure that if the option was not vested in him he could avoid any liability for tax.

Until 1961, the College was in receipt of dividend payments on the shares. The Inland Revenue sought to claim surtax on the dividends, arguing that Vandervell had failed to divest himself absolutely of the beneficial interest in the shares. The basis of this view was that, on the failure to declare a trust of the option, its benefit must be held on resulting trust for Vandervell. By a majority of three to two in the House of Lords the Inland Revenue was successful. As no trust of the option had been declared, the option was held on resulting trust. In the view of the court, retention of the option involved retention of part of the beneficial interest in the shares. As Lord Wilberforce commented, there was:

> "no need or room to invoke a presumption. The conclusion, on the facts found, is simply that the option is vested in the trustee company as a trustee on trusts, not defined at the time, possibly to be defined later. But the equitable, or beneficial interest, cannot remain in the air: the consequence in law must be that it remains in the settlor".[33]

9.11 In *Re Vandervell's Trusts (No.2)*[34] the Court of Appeal concluded that the resulting trust terminated when the option was exercised. In 1961, Vandervell had sanctioned the use of money from his children's settlement to exercise the option. Legal title vested in Vandervell's trust company accordingly. It was not until 1965, however, that Vandervell expressly declared that the company was to hold the shares on trust for the children's settlement. The Inland Revenue sought to argue that he had not divested himself of his equitable interest in the shares until that point and, hence, incurred liability for surtax on dividends paid during that period. At first instance, Megarry J. observed that the trust company acquired the shares on trust. He held that there had been no valid declaration of trust in favour of the children's settlement. Accordingly, the shares, like the option to purchase them, were held on resulting trust for Vandervell. Ultimately successful in the Court of Appeal, Vandervell's executors fended off the Inland Revenue. The much-maligned reasoning of the decision is considered in Ch.4. Although, the judgment given by Megarry J. at first instance was reversed, there was nothing said in the appellate court to cast doubt on his propositions on resulting trusts. It remains a fundamental principle that, where a transfer is made on trusts which leave

---

[32] [1967] 2 A.C. 291.
[33] [1967] 2 A.C. 291 at 329.
[34] [1974] Ch. 269.

some or all of the beneficial interest undisposed of, the transferee holds on resulting trust for the transferor to the extent that the beneficial interest has not been carried to him or others. Here, the resulting trust functions, "to fill in evidential lacunae as to the location of the beneficial interest".[35]

Failure of the trust

9.12   A trust can fail for a variety of reasons, whether it is by lapse,[36] illegality[37] or a failure to comply with the rules against perpetuity and accumulations.[38] Where such failure occurs, the resulting trust effects a transfer of property back to the settlor. It will be recalled from Ch.2, that a resulting trust can arise where a trust fails for a lack of certainty of beneficial interest or uncertain objects. Provided that a trust was intended (i.e. there is certainty of intention) there is no question that a trustee can take the property as an absolute gift. Thus, in *Boyce v Boyce*[39] a testator left two houses on trust to convey to Maria, "whichever house she may think proper to choose or select" and to convey the other to Charlotte. On Maria's death, it proved impossible for the court to determine which of the houses was held on trust for Charlotte. Maria had died before making her selection. Consequently, the houses were held on resulting trust for the testator's residuary estate. Similarly, in *Re Atkinson's Will Trusts*,[40] the uncertainty prevalent in a residuary gift from a testatrix to be divided between, "such worthy causes as have been communicated by me to my trustees in my lifetime" could lead only to the finding of a resulting trust when no such causes had been communicated.

Other prominent case law examples of failed trusts are consequent to the failure of a condition precedent[41] or condition subsequent.[42] As will become clear from the following illustrations, when a transfer of property is made subject to a condition which is not achieved the resulting trust effects a return of the property to the transferor. First, in *Essery v Cowlard*,[43] a settlement was executed in 1877 in consideration of a then intended marriage. The intended wife transferred property to trustees to be held on trust for the benefit of herself, her intended husband and any children resulting from their marriage. Although the couple cohabited and had children, no marriage took place. In 1883, therefore, they brought an action against the trustees to recover the property. Pearson J. was confident that the contract to marry had been, "definitely and absolutely put an end to"[44] and ordered that the property be transferred back to the woman. As the property was held on the terms of a marriage that never took place, the condition precedent had not been achieved and, accordingly, the property moved back under a resulting trust.

---

[35] C.E.F. Rickett, R. Grantham, "Resulting Trusts—The Nature of the Failing Trust Cases" (2000) 116 L.Q.R. 15 at p.20.
[36] See, for example, *Ackroyd v Smithson* (1780) 1 Bro. C.C. 503.
[37] See **16.12–16.14**.
[38] *Re Drummond's Settlement* [1986] 3 All E.R. 45.
[39] (1849) 6 Sim. 476.
[40] [1978] 1 All E.R. 1275.
[41] For example, that X must marry, but X fails to marry.
[42] For example, where the beneficiaries must remain married but they fail to do so.
[43] (1884) 26 Ch. D. 191.
[44] (1884) 26 Ch. D. 191 at 193.

Failure also occurred in *Re Ames' Settlement*, which was, in the words of Vaisey J., **9.13**
"a simple case of money paid on a consideration which failed".[45] In a marriage settlement of 1908, the bridegroom's father covenanted to pay to trustees, within one year
of the solemnisation of marriage, the sum of £10,000. This was to be held on trust, the
income payable to the husband for life and after his death to the wife for life or until her
remarriage, with the remainder to any issue of the intended marriage. The parties lived
together until 1926 when a decree of nullity was made on the wife's petition on the
grounds of non-consummation of marriage. The effect of the decree was to render the
marriage void ab initio (i.e. as if it had never occurred). The husband received the
income until his death some 20 years later. The question for the court was whether the
capital sum was held on trust for the husband's next of kin or was, instead payable
under resulting trust for the settlor's estate. Vaisey J. decided on the latter. As the
money was vested on trusts which failed, the money was held on resulting trust. In
Westdeutsche Landesbank Girozentrale v Islington LBC[46] Lord Browne-Wilkinson
described the judgment as confused and preferred the view that the ultimate trust failed
because it was only expressed to take effect in the event of the failure of the issue of a
non-existent marriage, which he described as an impossible condition precedent. Ultimately, as Lord Browne-Wilkinson accepted, it makes no difference because on either
view the funds were vested in trusts which failed.

Finally, *Re Cochrane*[47] concerned a post-nuptial settlement into which both husband
and wife brought property. In essence, the income generated was to be paid to the wife
on the condition that she continued to reside with her husband. Should either die, the
other would be entitled to the entirety beneficially. A problem arose when the wife left
her husband and he died shortly thereafter. This was a scenario that had not been
envisaged at the outset. The draftsman had failed to provide for this event. Harman J.
felt that the gap in the trusts declared could not be filled by construction because it was
difficult to see clearly what it was that would have been inserted to cover that particular
eventuality. His hesitancy was evident from his reluctance to fall back on to the
resulting trust in such situations. He warned, "A resulting trust is the last resort to
which the law has recourse when the draftsman has made a blunder or failed to dispose
of that which he has set out to dispose of".[48] Nonetheless, Harman J. could arrive at no
other conclusion than that there must be a resulting trust of the income of the fund in
favour of the settlors in proportion to their several interests. As to the property contributed by the husband, it passed to his estate.

Excluding the resulting trust

Obviously, no resulting trust can arise where property is deemed to be the subject of an **9.14**
absolute gift. In *Adams and Kensington Vestry*,[49] the testator left his estate to his wife,
"in full confidence that she would do what was right as to the disposal thereof between

---

[45] [1946] 1 Ch. 217 at 223.
[46] [1996] A.C. 669.
[47] [1955] 1 Ch. 309.
[48] [1955] 1 Ch. 309 at 316.
[49] (1884) 27 Ch. D. 394.

my children, either in her lifetime, or by will after her decease". No trust arose to which the widow was subject and it was held that she was entitled to retain the property as an absolute gift to herself. In other cases there is an absolute gift of property onto which failed trusts are subsequently engrafted. In such a case the rule in *Hancock v Watson*[50] might apply. As Lord Davey explained, "if you find an absolute gift to a legatee in the first instance, and trusts are engrafted or imposed on that absolute interest which fail, either from lapse or invalidity or any other reason, then the absolute gift takes effect so far as the trusts have failed to the exclusion of the residuary legatee or next-of-kin as the case may be".[51] The court will construe the language of the instrument as a whole, therefore, to determine whether there has been an initial absolute beneficial gift onto which inconsistent trusts have been engrafted. In *Palmer v Simmonds*,[52] for example, a testatrix left her estate to her husband, "for his own use and benefit" subject to a trust on his death to leave, "the bulk of my residuary estate" to specific named relatives. As the engrafted trust failed for a lack of certainty of subject matter, the husband took the property absolutely. This was not the case in *Boyce v Boyce*, however, where mandatory words evidenced an intention to create a trust and not to provide an absolute gift to trustees in the first instance. It is only in those cases where the rule in *Hancock v Watson* will not apply that the property will be held on resulting trust.

Outside the context of private trusts, the resulting trust has also assumed a prominent role in dealing with failed charitable gifts. A purported charitable trust will fail, for example, where the purposes described are not exclusively charitable. In *Morice v Bishop of Durham*,[53] property was provided for "charitable and benevolent" purposes, but the trust failed with the consequence of a resulting trust in favour of the settlor. In this context, however, the resulting trust is by no means an automatic consequence of the failure of the trust. As discussed in Ch.8, the cy-près doctrine can, in delimited circumstances, allow the application of the trust property to purposes "as near as possible" to the original purposes specified by the settlor. In cases where failure occurs before the property has been effectively dedicated to charity, a general charitable intention is required on the part of the donor in order to exclude the resulting trust.[54]

The failure of a specific purpose

9.15 This category involves a class of case where the transferor intends that the property revert back to him unless it is used for the particular purpose specified. The principal example is that of *Barclays Bank v Quistclose Investments Ltd*.[55] It is to be recalled that Quistclose Investments advanced money to Rolls Razor (a company in financial difficulties) for the purpose of paying a dividend on its shares.[56] The transfer was in the form of a loan. Money was advanced on the basis that it would be used solely for the specified purpose and that it would be paid into a separate account. Unfortunately,

---

[50] [1902] A.C. 14.
[51] [1902] A.C. 14 at 22.
[52] (1854) 2 Drew. 221.
[53] (1805) 10 Ves. 522.
[54] See **8.03**.
[55] [1970] A.C. 567; see W. Goodhart, G. Jones (1980) 43 M.L.R. 489.
[56] See Ch.2 for detailed coverage of *Quistclose* trusts.

Rolls Razor became insolvent before the dividend was paid. The Bank contended that the money held in the share dividend account should be set off against Rolls Razor's overdraft with the Bank on the basis that Quistclose Investments was simply an unsecured creditor of Rolls Razor with no priority over other creditors. The House of Lords held unanimously that the money advanced was held on trust for Quistclose Investments on the basis that the purpose for which it had been advanced had not been carried into effect.

Lord Wilberforce analysed the position in *Quistclose* as giving rise to two trusts. In his view, a primary trust arose to use the money for the specified purpose. Failing that, a secondary trust obliged the recipient to return the money to Quistclose Investments. As Lord Wilberforce carefully stated, "In the present case the intention to create a secondary trust for the benefit of the lender, to arise if the primary trust, to pay the dividend, could not be carried out, is clear and I can find no reason why the law should not give effect to it".[57] The problems associated with Lord Wilberforce's analysis are substantial. First, there is an obvious obstacle in that the primary trust appears to be a purpose trust for the payment of a dividend, i.e. a trust that offends the rule against pure purpose trusts. Such trusts are prima facie void. Secondly, if the primary trust is an express trust, there is difficulty surrounding the location of the beneficial interest. Indeed, a variety of arguments and counter-arguments have tested the claims that it lies in the lender, in the borrower, in the beneficiaries or, somehow, in suspense.

Accordingly, the precise nature of the trusts identified has invited much judicial scrutiny and considerable academic debate over the last 35 years or so.[58] As a consequence, it is possible to see *Quistclose* trusts classified variously, using the language of express trusts, constructive trusts and resulting trusts.[59] Fortunately, the uncertainty as to categorisation has been convincingly dispelled by the analysis put forward in *Twinsectra v Yardley*.[60] There, Lord Millett clarified that, "if the borrower is treated as holding the money on a resulting trust for the lender but with power (or in some cases a duty) to carry out the lender's revocable mandate, and the lender's object in giving the mandate is frustrated, he is entitled to revoke the mandate and demand the return of money which never ceased to be his beneficially".[61]

9.16

Lord Millett, therefore, discounts the existence of primary and secondary trusts that had characterised Lord Wilberforce's original analysis. He identified one single trust in evidence throughout, that is, a trust in favour of the person advancing the money. His construction stems from the policy perspective that the *Quistclose* trust is:

"a simple, commercial arrangement ... which enables the borrower to have recourse to the lender's money for a particular purpose without entrenching on the lender's property rights more than necessary to enable the purpose to be achieved. The money remains the property of the lender unless and until it is applied in accordance with his directions, and in so far as it is not so applied it must be returned to him. I am disposed, perhaps predisposed, to think that this is the only

---

[57] [1970] A.C. 567 at 582.
[58] See generally, W. Swadling (ed.). *The Quistclose Trust—Critical Essays* (Oxford, Hart Publishing, 2004).
[59] For a discussion of alternative analyses see C. Rickett, "Different Views on the Scope of the Quistclose Analysis" (1991) 107 L.Q.R. 608.
[60] [2002] A.C. 164.
[61] [2002] A.C. 164 at 192.

analysis which is consistent both with orthodox trust law and with commercial reality".[62]

9.17   Accordingly, the *Quistclose*-style trust is now accepted as a species of resulting trust. Such trusts will be upheld where by express agreement both the payer and recipient intend that the money be held for a specific purpose,[63] but also in cases where there has been an agreed restriction on the use of the money such that it is not at the ready disposal of the recipient.[64] Even in circumstances where part of the money has been expended on the specific purpose, there is nothing to prevent the *Quistclose* trust arising in respect of whatever is left.[65] In addition, the scope of the *Quistclose* has extended beyond the confines of money advanced by way of loan. In *Carreras Rothmans v Freeman Matthews Treasure*,[66] for example, money was advanced in satisfaction of a contractual debt, in respect of which Peter Gibson J. claimed that, "the principle in all these cases is that equity fastens on the conscience of the person who receives from another property transferred for a specific purpose only and not therefore for the recipient's own purposes, so that such person will not be able to treat the property as his own or to use it for other than the stated purpose".[67] Characterising each of these examples is a common intention or mutual agreement consistent with Lord Millett's view that the *Quistclose* trust will arise only where the parties intended the restriction, i.e. that the money would not be at the free disposal of the recipient.

Unexhausted beneficial interest

9.18   The final failure of trust example involves the destination of property in the event that a trust has been performed and a surplus remains. Here, the desirability of the resulting trust can depend on the context in which the trust is created. Different policy concerns arise, for example, according to whether the trust is private or charitable. In addition, different obstacles are encountered where the surplus arises from a desire to maintain individuals, public appeals, the dissolution of unincorporated associations or the complex commercial arena of over-funded pension trusts. Each will be considered in turn.

Maintenance cases

9.19   A resulting trust arises in respect of any surplus remaining once the purposes of the trust have been carried out. However, no resulting trust will arise where the trust instrument explicitly excludes this possibility[68] or where an inference can be drawn that

---

[62] [2002] A.C. 164 at 187.
[63] *Re Lewis's of Leicester* [1995] 1 BCLC 428.
[64] See *Twinsectra v Yardley* [2002] 2 A.C. 164.
[65] See *Re EVTR* (1987) BCLC 647 which concerned a loan for the purchase of equipment, part of which was not delivered leading to a money refund to the debtor.
[66] [1985] Ch. 207.
[67] [1985] Ch. 207 at 222.
[68] *King v Denison* (1813) 1 Ves. & B. 260.

some other person was intended to take the property beneficially.[69] It is merely a general principle that where money is held on trust, and the trusts declared do not exhaust the fund, the surplus will revert back to the settlor under a resulting trust. *Re Trusts of the Abbott Fund*[70] provides a classic illustration where Dr Fawcett collected a sum of money, raising subscriptions from the public, and set up a fund to be applied for the relief of two ladies who were deaf and dumb. No provision was made as to the disposal of the ultimate surplus. It was argued that the balance of the fund belonged to the survivor of the two ladies, because the subscriptions were in the form of absolute gifts and the donors could never have intended a return of any unused funds. Stirling J. in a brief judgment, could not believe that the subscriptions were, "ever intended to be an absolute gift to the ladies".[71] He denied that they would have been in a position to demand a transfer of the property to themselves or that in the case of bankruptcy, for example, such sums could be claimed by their trustee in bankruptcy. Accordingly, he upheld a resulting trust of the remaining sums to the subscribers of the Abbott Fund.

A different outcome was reached, however, in *Re Andrew's Trust*[72] wherein a fund was subscribed for the education of the children of a deceased clergyman. Once the formal education of the children was complete, the court was asked to consider the destination of the surplus funds. Unlike *Re Trusts of the Abbott Fund*, where the beneficiaries had died, the children in this case were still alive. Consequently, Kekewich J. would not consider the purpose exhausted merely because the children had attained ages where, "education in the vulgar sense" was no longer necessary.[73] Instead, he ascribed the broadest possible meaning to "education" and held that the children were entitled to what remained in equal shares. Unlike *Re Trusts of the Abbott Fund*, it appears, therefore, that the overriding goal of benefiting the children could still be achieved.[74]

The Court of Appeal in *Re Osoba*[75] drew a similar conclusion. This case concerned a testamentary trust for the maintenance of the testator's widow, his mother, and, "for the training of my daughter Abiola up to university grade". By the time the case was heard, both the widow and mother had died. Abiola, moreover, had been fully trained up to university grade. It was held that the women took the fund as joint tenants and, on the death of two of the joint tenants, the daughter would succeed to the entire fund. Clearly anxious to avoid the contrary conclusion, Buckley L.J. felt that the testator had parted beneficially with the whole fund. As the subject matter was the testator's residue, any failure of the gift would result in intestacy which was most certainly not what the testator had intended.

For Megarry V.C. in the High Court in *Re Osoba*,[76] the presence or absence of living beneficiaries was a key distinction to be drawn between cases. He claimed:

9.20

---

[69] *Westdeutsche Landesbank Girozentrale v Islington LBC* [1996] A.C. 669 at 708.
[70] [1900] 2 Ch. 326.
[71] [1900] 2 Ch. 326 at 330.
[72] [1905] 2 Ch. 48.
[73] [1905] 2 Ch. 48 at 53.
[74] In the alternative, he was content to construe education as being merely the motive for the gift and that the intention was to provide for the children in the manner most useful.
[75] [1979] 1 W.L.R. 247.
[76] [1978] 1 W.L.R. 791.

"If a trust is constituted for the assistance of certain persons by certain stated means there is a sharp distinction between cases where the beneficiaries have died and cases where they are still living. If they are dead, the court is willing to hold that there is a resulting trust for the donors; for the major purpose of the trust, that of providing help and benefit for the beneficiaries, comes to an end when the beneficiaries are all dead and so are beyond earthly help whether by the stated means or otherwise. But if the beneficiaries are still living, the major purpose of providing help and benefit for the beneficiaries can still be carried out even after the stated means have all been accomplished, and so the court will be ready to treat the standard means as being indicative and not restrictive".[77]

9.21   Where beneficiaries are alive, it appears, therefore, that the courts are reluctant to conclude other than that the expression of a purpose is merely an indicator of motive. A similar principle is at play in the context of gifts to persons on trust for purposes,[78] where the preferred approach of the courts is to construe the gift, where possible, as an absolute gift and prevent the resulting trust. This is evident in the rule of construction laid down in *Re Sanderson's Trust* where Page Wood V.C. claimed, "If a gross sum be given, or if the whole income of the property be given, and a special purpose be assigned for that gift, the court always regards the gift as absolute, and the purpose merely as the motive for that gift, and therefore holds that the gift takes effect as to the whole sum or the whole income as the case may be".[79] Thus, in *Re Bowes*[80] a gift of £5,000 on trust for the purpose of planting trees on an estate was construed as an absolute gift to the estate owners, the purpose being no more than an expression of motive. In all cases, it will be a matter of construction as to whether the donor parted with his property out and out. As Lord Browne-Wilkinson clarified in the *Westdeutsche* case, if the donor has expressly or by necessary implication, abandoned any beneficial interest in the trust property, there is no resulting trust and the undisposed of equitable interest vests in the Crown as bona vacantia.

Disaster appeals

9.22   In the context of public appeals for good causes, a similar approach to *Re Trusts of the Abbott Fund* was adopted in *Re Gillingham Bus Disaster Fund* where the court upheld a resulting trust.[81] There an appeal was raised in 1951 in response to a road traffic accident in which 24 Royal Marine Cadets were killed, with a number of others suffering serious injuries. Publishing the appeal in a newspaper, the mayors of the surrounding towns avowed that the memorial fund would be devoted, "to defraying the funeral expenses, caring for the boys who may be disabled, and then to such worthy causes in memory of the boys who lost their lives, as the Mayors may determine". A sum of nearly £9,000 was collected via methods such as large donations from known

[77] [1978] 1 W.L.R. 791 at 796.
[78] See **6.19**.
[79] (1857) 3 K. & J. 497 at 503.
[80] [1896] 1 Ch. 507.
[81] [1958] Ch. 300.

donors, street collections, football matches and whist drives. The trustees spent £2,368 on the stated purposes and then sought guidance from the court as to how the surplus was applicable. The alternatives were as follows:

- cy-près, that is, the surplus may be available to apply to a charitable purpose as near as possible to the original charitable purpose;

- resulting trust, that is, the surplus is returnable to the donors because they are deemed to hold an interest in the undisposed of property, and

- bona vacantia, that is where the surplus is deemed to be genuinely ownerless it becomes available to the Crown.

Harman J. was forced to discount the possibility of cy-près. The trust fund had not been devoted to purposes deemed exclusively charitable at law and the doctrine was, thereby, unavailable to the court. Of the two remaining alternatives, he opted for the resulting trust. He applied the general principle that where money is held upon trust and the trust does not exhaust the fund it will revert to the donor under a resulting trust. He explained that the reasoning is that, "the settlor or the donor did not intend to part with his money out and out ...",[82] but only to the extent that his wishes could be carried into effect. Harman J. emphasised that the doctrine did not rest upon evidence as to the state of mind of the donor, "The resulting trust arises where the expectation is for some unforeseen reason cheated of fruition, and is an inference of law based on after-knowledge of the event".[83] Three aspects of Harman J's judgment are worthy of note.

First, he deemed there to be no intention on the part of donors to contribute their **9.23** money out and out. This, it is submitted, has the unfortunate practical consequence that bona vacantia is excluded and that all sums from anonymous donors are paid into court awaiting unlikely claims under a resulting trust. The strong inference of his judgment is that in a case where it can be said that a donor intends to part out and out with his donation, the destination of any surplus would be as bona vacantia.

Secondly, Harman J. drew no distinction between the differing categories of donation. He saw no difference between the person who makes a small anonymous cash donation in a collecting tin and the person who makes a large personal contribution under his own name. As Harman J. concluded, "I see no reason myself to suppose that the small giver who is anonymous has any wider intention than the large giver who can be named. They all give for the one object. If they can be found by inquiry the resulting trust can be executed in their favour. If they cannot, I do not see how the money could then ... change its destination and become bona vacantia".[84] Despite the intuitive appeal to his argument, it was considered and rejected by Goff J. in *Re West Sussex Constabulary Fund*.[85] In that case, Goff J., adopting the approach of Upjohn J. in *Re Hillier's Trusts*,[86] held that people who contribute to collection boxes make their contributions out and out. This excluded the possibility of a resulting trust and entitled the Crown to the money as bona vacantia on a failure of the trusts.

---

[82] [1958] Ch. 300 at 310.
[83] [1958] Ch. 300 at 310.
[84] [1958] Ch. 300 at 314.
[85] [1971] Ch. 1.
[86] [1954] 1 W.L.R. 9 at 22.

9.24   Although both *Re West Sussex Constabulary Fund* and *Re Gillingham Bus Disaster Fund* are first instance decisions, (and, thus, an argument can be made as to which is to be preferred in this context), Goff J. did embark on a careful review of authority where he encountered strong support for his view,[87] often forcefully expressed.[88] Admittedly, it is appropriate to acknowledge the different context from which such support is derived. Goff J.'s supporting authorities may be distinguishable on the ground that they deal with cases of charitable funds and the question of whether surplus is available cy-près. As explained above, there was no possibility that the surplus could be applied cy-près in *Re Gillingham Bus Disaster Fund* because the purposes were not exclusively charitable.

Thirdly, Harman J. failed to make explicit whether there is a distinction between the proceeds of entertainment and donations by collection tin or otherwise. There is specific mention of events such as whist drives, concerts and football matches, and it is unclear whether Harman J. simply lumps the proceeds from these together with other donations as forming the subject matter of a resulting trust. In any event, the view postulated by Goff J. in *Re West Sussex Constabulary Fund* is, on this point, almost certainly correct. There, he claimed it to be "impossible" to apply the doctrine of resulting trust to the proceeds of entertainment and sweepstakes.[89] Goff J.'s reasoning unfolds on two levels. His primary objection is that the relationship is one of contract and not of trust, "the purchaser of a ticket may have the motive of aiding the cause or he may not; he may purchase the ticket merely because he wishes to attend the particular entertainment or to try for the prize, but whichever it be, he pays his money as the price of what is offered and what he receives".[90] Quite apart from this, Goff J. could see no direct contribution to the fund at all. He observed, "It is only the profit, if any, which is ultimately received and there may even be none".[91]

9.25   The facts of *Re West Sussex Constabulary Fund* raise a separate issue as to the destination of surplus funds on the winding up of an unincorporated association. Whereas *Re Gillingham Bus Disaster Fund* concerned an appeal in respect of a specific tragic event, *Re West Sussex Constabulary Fund* concerned a fund set up to benefit the widows and dependants of deceased members of the West Sussex Constabulary, an unincorporated association. Although given in this very different context, Goff J.'s conclusions are of obvious applicability to cases such as *Re Gillingham Bus Disaster Fund*, where a surplus remains on completion of a specific appeal. Outside the cases involving unincorporated associations, therefore, the exact role of the resulting trust remains arguable. To follow *Re Gillingham Bus Disaster Fund* would see the proceeds from entertainments and the contributions from donors held on resulting trust. In the view of Goff J. in *Re West Sussex Constabulary Fund*, any surplus would go to the Crown as bona vacantia.

---

[87] *Re Hillier's Trusts* [1954] 1 W.L.R. 700 at 715 per Denning L.J. approving the approach of Upjohn J. at first instance; *Re Welsh Hospital (Netley) Fund* [1921] 1 Ch. 655 at 659 per P. O. Lawrence J.
[88] See, for example, the views of P.O. Lawrence J. who describes it to be "inconceivable" and "absurd" that a donor to a street collection did not part with money out and out ([1921] 1 Ch. 655 at 659).
[89] [1971] 1 Ch. 1 at 11.
[90] [1971] 1 Ch. 1 at 11.
[91] [1971] 1 Ch. 1 at 11.

Unincorporated associations

The construction of gifts to unincorporated associations is dealt with in detail elsewhere **9.26**
in the book.[92] It is to be recalled, however, that unlike companies these associations lack
legal personality and cannot hold property in their own name. Consequently, the courts
have struggled with the question of how such societies hold their property and, perti-
nently, what happens to it on dissolution. In this context, three differing approaches
have enjoyed prominence: the resulting trust, bona vacantia and distribution in
accordance with the contract between members.

As to the resulting trust approach, historically, it was thought that the destiny of
property on dissolution would be determined by the resulting trust. In *Re Printers and
Transferrers Amalgamated Trades Protection Society*,[93] for example, it fell to Byrne J. to
decide how the unexpended funds of a society, which contained the unequal contributions of two classes of member (printers and transferrers), were to be distributed.
He found the true principle to be that, "there is a resulting trust in favour of those who
have contributed to these funds, and I think that the proper and legitimate way of
dividing, therefore, will be in accordance with the amounts contributed by the existing
members at the time of the passing of the resolution".[94] This principle was followed in
Re Lead Company's Workmen's Fund Society[95] and is also evident in *Re Hobourn Aero
Components Limited's Air Raid Disaster Fund*.[96] In the latter case, it was held that any
contributor to the disaster fund was entitled to an interest in the surplus under a
resulting trust in proportion to the amount contributed, but subject to any adjustment
made on the basis of a benefit derived from the fund.

As to the bona vacantia approach, this was approved by the Court of Appeal in **9.27**
Cunnack v Edwards,[97] (and commended itself to Goff J. in *Re West Sussex Constabulary
Fund*). There, a society was established in 1801 to raise a fund by the subscriptions, fines
and forfeitures of its members, to provide annuities for the widows of its deceased
members. By 1879 all the members had died. On the passing of the last widow-
annuitant in 1892, there was a large surplus fund. At first instance, Chitty J. followed
the established approach based on the resulting trust doctrine.[98] He claimed:

> "Where a man provides a fund by way of trust for payment of a specified annuity
> to his widow during her life and makes no further declaration of trust affecting the
> fund, the beneficial interest in the fund, or as much of it as is not required ...
> results to himself. The same doctrine would apply in the case of several persons ...
> providing such annuities for their widows; there would be an ultimate trust in their
> favour when the purposes of the fund had come to an end ... Insomuch, then, as
> all the purposes for which the funds of the society were raised by contributions of
> the members have been exhausted, and there is no indication to be found in the

---

[92] See Ch.6.
[93] [1899] 2 Ch. 184.
[94] [1899] 2 Ch. 184 at 189.
[95] [1904] 2 Ch. 196.
[96] [1946] Ch. 86 per Cohen J. (affirmed by the Court of Appeal [1946] Ch. 194).
[97] [1896] 2 Ch. 679.
[98] The Society was not a charity to which the doctrine of cy-près applied. The stark choice was that the surplus
was held either on resulting trust for the personal representatives or as bona vacantia for the Crown.

rules as to what was to be done with the funds ... I am constrained to hold, according to the principles of equity, that the doctrine of resulting trust applies".[99]

The Court of Appeal reversed his judgment. A. L. Smith L.J. contended that as each member paid money to the society, "he divested himself of all interest in his money for ever, with this one reservation, that if the member left a widow she was to be provided for during her widowhood".[1] Accordingly, he was unimpressed with the analogy drawn by Chitty J. in the court below. Rigby L.J. also denied that the doctrine of resulting trust could aid the personal representatives of deceased members to claim entitlement. The members, he felt, were, "persons who, under contracts or quasi-contracts with the society, secured for valuable consideration certain contingent benefits for their widows which could be enforced by the widows in the manner provided".[2] Consequently, they had received everything to which they were entitled. The surplus in *Cunnack v Edwards* was, therefore, available to the Crown as bona vacantia.

9.28   Similarly, in 1968, when the West Sussex Constabulary was amalgamated with other forces, it fell to Goff J. to determine how its outstanding funds were to be dealt with. Goff J. identified that the fund was comprised of four different types of contribution:

   (i) the contributions of past and present members;

   (ii) entertainments, raffles and sweepstakes;

   (iii) collecting boxes, and

   (iv) donations and legacies.

Only in relation to (iv) donations and legacies, did Goff J. identify the resulting trust as the appropriate mechanism to account for surplus. All other contributions went as bona vacantia to the Crown. The past and present members had no claim under a resulting trust because as widows and dependants they had received that to which they were entitled. This entailed for Goff J. that there is no question of trust. In addition, as indicated above, the proceeds of entertainments, etc. raised an issue of contract, this time between the seller and the buyer. An additional obstacle was evident, moreover, in the fact that the money accrued would be in the nature of profit and not a direct contribution to the fund. In relation to the proceeds of collecting boxes, again, as is already clear, contributors are taken to have parted with their money out and out.

As regards the approach to dissolution based on the contract between members, *Re Bucks Constabulary Fund (No.2)*[3] is the principal authority. Although based on markedly similar facts to *Re West Sussex Constabulary Fund*, Walton J. arrived at a strikingly different conclusion when he held that the members were entitled to the remaining property in equal shares. Walton J. criticised Goff J.'s approach, determining that the remaining assets on the instant facts were held, "to the total exclusion of any claim on behalf of the Crown".[4] According to the developed rules regarding property

[99] [1895] 1 Ch. 489 at 497.
[1] [1896] 2 Ch. 679 at 683.
[2] [1896] 2 Ch. 679 at 689.
[3] [1979] 1 W.L.R. 936.
[4] [1979] 1 W.L.R. 936 at 951.

holding by unincorporated associations (the contract-holding theory), the distribution of property on dissolution was to be governed by the contract between the members. The funds are held subject to the contractual rights and liabilities between the members in accordance with the rules of their association. Only in the case of a moribund society (i.e. where all or all but one of the members had died) would bona vacantia be viable. Similarly, Walton J. saw no residuary role for the resulting trust. Where the rules of the association are silent as to what should happen on dissolution, there is a presumption of equal division amongst the existing members.

In relation to each of the types of contribution identified by Goff J. in *Re West Sussex* **9.29** *Constabulary Fund*, it is readily apparent that Walton J. would have reached a contrary conclusion. Even in the case of donations and legacies, it is strongly arguable that such contributions would be held subject to the contractual rights and liabilities of the members. In *Re Recher's WT*, for example, Brightman J. explicitly considered the status of a donation from an outside source and also that of a legacy:

> "In the case of a donation which is not accompanied by any words which purport to impose a trust, it seems to me that the gift takes effect in favour of the existing members of the association as an accretion to the funds which are the subject-matter of the contract which such members have made *inter se*, and falls to be dealt with in exactly the same way as the funds which the members themselves have subscribed. So, in the case of a legacy. In the absence of words which purport to impose a trust, the legacy is a gift to the members beneficially".[5]

The approach of Walton J. in *Re Bucks Constabulary Fund (No.2)* is consistent with the approach adopted in the general law towards property-holding by unincorporated associations and has been followed subsequently. In *Re GKN Bolts & Nuts Sports and Social Club*, for example, Megarry V.C. held that proceeds from the sale of a social club should be divided equally amongst those persons who were members of the club on the date of dissolution.[6] More recently, Peter Smith J. hailed as a statement of the general law that, "the principles of trust and resulting trust do not generally govern the principles of distribution and dissolution ... The rules are a contract whereby persons who become members of the association are entitled to benefit and their rights and their entitlements in the funds on dissolution are governed by that contract".[7] Although the area has yet to be considered by the appellate courts, it is hardly contentious to argue that, as regards unincorporated associations, *Re West Sussex Constabulary Fund* follows the wrong course.

Outside this context, say where a surplus remains from a specific appeal, it may be **9.30** that *Re West Sussex Constabulary Fund* is correctly decided. If so, and for the reasons explored above, contributions in the form of legacies and donations from identifiable donors would be held on resulting trust, whereas, those from anonymous contributors, and any proceeds from entertainments would go as bona vacantia. It must not be forgotten, however, that in *Re Gillingham Bus Disaster Fund*, Harman J. makes a convincing case for treating as the same the contributions from identifiable donors and

[5] [1972] Ch. 526 at 539.
[6] [1982] 1 W.L.R. 774.
[7] *Elvidge v Coulson* [2003] EWHC 2089 (Ch).

those (smaller) contributions from anonymous sources. It seems right that there is no compelling reason to distinguish the two on the grounds of intention. The only difference, he argues, is the ease with which their contribution can be returned. For Harman J. the principled approach is payment into court awaiting claim under resulting trust. In practical terms, nonetheless, the resulting trust is highly problematic. Bona vacantia is much to be preferred in view of the futility of awaiting the claims of anonymous contributors for miniscule sums. In this light, for many, a review of key case law by the appellate courts would bring a welcome clarification to the law.[8]

Resulting trusts and pension funds

9.31 Much has been made of dicta in the context of pension trusts where a similar problem has arisen over what to do with over funded pensions. In *Davis v Richards and Wallington Industries Ltd*,[9] Scott J. considered the winding up of a pension fund that contained contributions from three specific sources: those of employers, those of employees and money transferred from other funds. His conclusions appear to cast doubt on the approach taken by Walton J. in *Re Bucks Constabulary Fund (No.2)*.[10] As regards the employers' overpayments, he observed that these would be returnable under a resulting trust. By contrast, the employees' contributions would go as bona vacantia to the Crown. Scott J. acknowledged that the fact that a party had received everything he had bargained for was not necessarily a decisive argument against a resulting trust. On the facts before him, however, there could be no resulting trust in favour of the employees. First, he could see no workable scheme to apportion the surplus contributions amongst different classes of employee. Scott J. would not, "impute to them an intention that would lead to an unworkable result".[11] Secondly, no intention could be imputed to the employees that they should receive a surplus in excess of the maximum permitted by the rules governing administration of the scheme.

In *Air Jamaica v Charlton*[12] the Privy Council criticised the approach adopted as to imputation of intention as "erroneous". In Lord Millet's view, it was not obvious, in the case of employees promised certain benefits under a scheme to which they had contributed, that they should be regarded as having no expectation of a return of any surplus. Lord Millett pointed out that a resulting trust cannot be avoided simply because there is no intention to retain the beneficial interest:

> "Like a constructive trust, a resulting trust arises by operation of law, though unlike a constructive trust it gives effect to intention. But it arises whether or not the transferor intended to retain a beneficial interest—he almost always does not—since it responds to the absence of any intention on his part to pass the beneficial interest to the recipient. It may even where arise the transferor positively wished to part with the beneficial interest as in *Vandervell v IRC*".[13]

---

[8] See, for example, Parker and Mellows at p.330.
[9] [1990] 1 W.L.R. 1511.
[10] [1979] 1 W.L.R. 936.
[11] [1990] 1 W.L.R. 1511 at 1544.
[12] [1999] 1 W.L.R. 1399.
[13] [1999] 1 W.L.R. 1399 at 1412.

Air Jamaica v Charlton, however, concerned the failure of certain trusts of a pension **9.32** scheme which were void for perpetuity. On these facts, it was impossible to say that the members had received all that they had bargained for; the surplus arose through the invalidity of the trusts. A resulting trust for employers and employees was, therefore, upheld in proportion to their respective contributions. It arose by operation of law outside the pension scheme and outside the Jamaican tax legislation. In *Davis v Richards and Wallington Industries Ltd*, Scott J. could find no workable scheme to apportion the surplus funds because he had felt it necessary to value the benefits that each member had received in order to ascertain his share. In *Air Jamaica v Charlton*, it was emphasised that no such process is required. Instead there should be a pro rata division between the members and the estates of deceased members in proportion to contributions made, without regard to benefits received and irrespective of the dates on which contributions were made.

It is unlikely that this approach as to the role for the resulting trust will impact outside the limited confines of surplus pension funds. Most schemes are statutorily regulated. Some are exceedingly complex and almost all will provide expressly for what should happen in the case of any surplus. Accordingly, it is advisable to hold as distinct to its particular subject matter the judicial pronouncements as to the role of resulting trusts in this context.

THE "APPARENT GIFT" CASES

It remains to consider the second category of cases in which the resulting trust tradi- **9.33** tionally makes an appearance, that of apparent gifts. This category contains those resulting trusts that arise where there has been a contribution to the purchase price of property but the property is held in the name of another or in joint names.[14] or a voluntary transfer of property into the name of another.[15] Although both transactions have the outward appearance of a gift, equity adopts a realistic interpretation of the parties' motivations and assumes, in the absence of contrary evidence, that they intended bargains not gifts. In this manner, the imposition of the resulting trust is based on the unrebutted presumption that the transferor did not intend to benefit the transferee. Lord Diplock described the role of the court in making presumptions in *Pettitt v Pettitt*.[16] He explained how the courts engage in a process of:

> "imputing an intention to a person whenever the intention with which an act is done affects its legal consequences and the evidence does not disclose what was the actual intention with which he did it ... When the act is of a kind to which this technique has frequently to be applied by the courts the imputed intention may acquire the description of a 'presumption'—but presumptions of this type are not

[14] No presumption of resulting trust now arises in the context of the family home where legal title is held in joint names: see *Stack v Dowden* [2007] 2 A.C. 432.
[15] As Bagnall J. aptly outlined in *Cowcher v Cowcher* [1972] 1 W.L.R. 425 at 431, a resulting trust arises, "where a person acquires a legal estate but has not provided the consideration for its acquisition, unless a contrary intention is proved".
[16] [1970] A.C. 777.

immutable. A presumption of fact is no more than a consensus of judicial opinion disclosed by reported cases as to the most likely inference of fact to be drawn in the absence of evidence to the contrary".[17]

Accordingly, and as the presumption of resulting trust is made only in cases where there is an absence of evidence as to the intentions of the parties, it can be, "readily rebutted by comparatively slight evidence",[18] ousted by the more flexible constructive trust[19] or (in the context of specific relationships where a gift is deemed to have been intended), displaced by a counter-presumption of equity such as the presumption of advancement (see below, **9.40**).

Purchase in the name of another

9.34   The presumption of resulting trust applies where property is purchased in the name of X, but X has provided only part (or perhaps no part at all) of the purchase price. The resulting trust arises by operation of law in favour of Y to reflect the contribution provided by Y. Thus, if Fred was to provide the entire purchase price for property held solely by Trevor and, there is no evidence of contrary intention,[20] Trevor will hold legal title on resulting trust for Fred. This is because a proprietary interest, to adopt the frequently cited words of Eyre C.B., "results to the man who advances the purchase money".[21] As to cases of shared legal ownership, until recently, the consistent approach of the courts has been that, "where the purchase money for property acquired by two or more persons in their joint names has been provided by those persons in unequal amounts, they will be beneficially entitled as between themselves in the proportions in which they provided the purchase money".[22] In the context of the family home, this approach no longer applies. Following the recent House of Lords' decision in *Stack v Dowden*,[23] there is a strong presumption that equity follows the law and that equitable ownership, like legal ownership, is jointly held. As Baroness Hale explained, "cases in which the joint legal owners are to be taken to have intended that their beneficial interests should be different from their legal interests will be very unusual".[24] In the commercial context, however, and in the absence of evidence to the contrary, it is still assumed that neither party wished to make a gift of their contribution to the purchase price. Here the resulting trust is presumed to arise.[25]

---

[17] [1970] A.C. 777 at 823.
[18] *Pettitt v Pettitt* [1970] A.C. 777 at 814 per Lord Upjohn.
[19] Which arises to give effect to the parties' bargain as to their beneficial entitlements and prevent an unconscionable assertion of sole beneficial ownership by the holder of legal title.
[20] As Robert Walker J. observed in *Stockholm Finance Ltd v Garden Holdings Inc* [1995] N.P.C. 162, "the equitable presumptions … are presumptions of fact only, which will rarely be decisive today except where there is a complete lack of evidence as to the parties' intentions".
[21] *Dyer v Dyer* (1788) 2 Cox Eq. Cas 92 at 93.
[22] *Walker v Hall* [1984] F.L.R. 126 at 133 per Dillon J.
[23] [2007] 2 A.C. 432.
[24] [2007] 2 A.C. 432 at 459.
[25] See further *Laskar v Laskar* [2008] 1 W.L.R. 2695.

Voluntary conveyance or transfer

In the case of a gratuitous transfer of property into the name of the transferee or into   **9.35**
the joint names of the transferor and transferee, it is necessary to take on board the
effect of s.60(3) of the Law of Property Act 1925. As such, a distinction is drawn
commonly between a voluntary transfer of land and of personalty.

Land

The subsection provides that, "In a voluntary conveyance a resulting trust for the   **9.36**
grantor shall not be implied merely by reason that the property is not expressed to be
conveyed for the use or benefit of the grantee." The provision is, in essence, a word
saving mechanism to ensure that, as had been required in the past, it is no longer
necessary to employ a particular formulation of words in order to render a voluntary
conveyance for X effective.[26]

The subsection acts, therefore, to prevent a resulting trust arising simply because   **9.37**
certain words of benefit have been omitted. There is, however, nothing to prevent the
resulting trust where there is other evidence indicative of the transferor's intention. It is
merely the presumption that, absent words of benefit, the resulting trust arises is ousted
by s.60(3). Thus in *Ali v Khan*, Morritt V.C. emphasised that there is nothing to inhibit
reliance on extrinsic evidence from which a resulting trust may be inferred.[27]

Personalty

It has long been established that a gratuitous transfer of personal property into the   **9.38**
hands of a transferee gives rise to a resulting trust in the transferor's favour.[28] Some
debate has centred on the question of the scope of s.60(3), in particular, whether it is
applicable both to real and personal property.[29] Quite legitimately, the references to
"conveyance" within the section have led most commentators to the conclusion that
s.60(3) operates solely in relation to transfers of land. This view is supported by the
absence of decided case law on the applicability of the section to transfers of personal
property. In the post-1926 case law, there is nothing to suggest that s.60(3) has altered
this position. Thus, in *Re Vinogradoff*,[30] a grandmother transferred a bond into the joint

---

[26] This may have been rendered necessary after 1926 by the repeal of the Statute of Uses under which it was
the practice to include the words, "unto and to the use of" where a gift was intended.
[27] [2002] EWCA Civ. 974.
[28] *Fowkes v Pascoe* (1875) 10 Ch. App. 343.
[29] Section 205 of the Law of Property Act 1925 provides an inclusive definition of property that, unless the
context otherwise requires, property means "any interest in real or personal property".
[30] [1935] W.N. 68.

names of herself and her granddaughter. Although the evidence was unclear as to her intentions, she continued to receive dividends until her death. Farwell J. found that the property was held on resulting trust for the grandmother's estate. The presumption of resulting trust, arising on the voluntary transfer of personalty, was not rebutted by the evidence or displaced by the counter presumption of advancement (considered below).[31]

Displacing the presumption of resulting trust

9.39 The presumption of resulting trust is occasionally displaced by evidence of intention or a counter-presumption of equity. Where there is evidence that money was provided by way of loan, for example, there can be no room for the presumption of resulting trust. The debtor/creditor relationship is regulated by contract and should not entitle the lender to a beneficial interest under a resulting trust. Similarly, the presumption of a resulting trust will be displaced by evidence that the transferor or contributor intended to confer a gift. The ease with which donative intent can be assessed will obviously depend upon the strength of the evidence adduced. Not surprisingly, most of the cases arise in the context of the family. In *Walker v Walker*,[32] the public declaration by a father that he intended to give his newly wedded son the money to set up a home was sufficient to show an intention to benefit the son by way of gift. Consequently Browne-Wilkinson L.J. accepted that, "Once ... the father had said that he was making a gift to the son, any claim based on the resulting trust must fail".

The presumption of advancement

9.40 The counter-presumption of advancement arises in the context of specific relationships wherein equity recognises that there is an obligation of conscience owed by the transferor "to advance" or to support the welfare of the transferee.[33] This will occur, for example, in the case of a voluntary conveyance from the transferor to his wife, child or someone to whom he stands in loco parentis. In such cases, there is no presumption of resulting trust because the transferor is presumed to transfer the property freely to the transferee on account of the relationship of obligation. The transferor is deemed to intend, as Spence J. explains, "to make a gift of the subject matter of the transfer to the transferee".[34] The effect of the presumption is to shift the burden of proving equitable ownership in the absence of declared intention. Hence, if X transfers shares for no

---

[31] The grandparent was not deemed to stand in loco parentis to her grandchild. The contrary conclusion would have brought her within the category of relationships wherein the transfer would have been seen to be by way of gift "to advance" the child (see **9.43**).

[32] Unreported April 12, 1984.

[33] In *Murless v Franklin* (1818) 1 Swans 13 at 17, Lord Eldon described the duty to advance as being a, "species of natural obligation to provide ...".

[34] *Goodfriend v Goodfriend* [1972] 22 D.L.R. (3rd) 699 at 703.

consideration into the name of Y, and the presumption of advancement applies, the shares are deemed to be owned by Y and the onus lies with X to rebut the presumption that he intended to "advance" Y.

The operation and rationale of the presumption of advancement has been legitimately and extensively criticised. As will be clear from the discussion below, the presumption has the propensity to produce diverse outcomes and, furthermore, it reflects the prevailing moral and socio-economic values of by-gone days. In the words of McHugh J., the presumption arises, "where the relationship between the parties falls into a class where dependency, past, present or future, commonly exists or, at all events, commonly existed in the nineteenth century".[35] In 1970, moreover, Lord Diplock famously and viciously attacked its contemporary relevance. In *Pettitt v Pettitt*[36] he exclaimed:

> "It would in my view, be an abuse of the legal technique for ascertaining or imputing intention to apply to transactions between the post-war generation of married couples 'presumptions' which are based upon inferences of fact which an earlier generation of judges drew as the most likely intentions of earlier generations of spouses belonging to the propertied classes of a different social era".[37]

Despite such stern criticism, modern courts have felt constrained to work within its parameters. In *Harwood v Harwood*, Slade L.J. held that the presumption of advancement, "must be applied with caution in modern social conditions" but he could find, nonetheless, "nothing sufficient to displace" it on the facts of the case before him.[38] Accordingly, it remains necessary to consider the relationships which give rise to the presumption of advancement.

Husband and wife

The presumption as it operates on transfers from husband to wife is long established **9.41** and historically prominent.[39] As Malins V.C. declared in the latter part of the nineteenth century, "The law of this court is perfectly settled that where a husband transfers money or other property into the name of his wife only, then the presumption is, that it is intended as a gift or advancement to the wife absolutely at once . . .".[40] In this context, the reach of the presumption is somewhat limited given that it will not apply where the

---

[35] *Nelson v Nelson* (1995) 184 C.L.R. 538 at 600.
[36] [1970] A.C. 777.
[37] [1970] A.C. 777 at 824.
[38] [1991] 2 F.L.R. 274 at 294.
[39] It also operates in the case of a transfer made in contemplation of marriage: *Moate v Moate* [1948] 2 All E.R. 486.
[40] *Re Eykyn's Trusts* (1877) 6 Ch. D. 115 at 118.

transfer is from wife to husband[41] as between co-habiting spouses or, furthermore, from a man to his mistress.[42]

Parent and child

9.42   The presumption of advancement is also strong where a transfer is from a father to his child. As Sir George Jessel M.R. observed, "The father is under that obligation from the mere fact of his being the father, and therefore no evidence is necessary to shew the obligation to provide for his child. In the case of a father, you only have to prove that he is the father, and when you have done that the obligation at once arises".[43] Much less certainty surrounds the operation of the presumption in the context of other relationships. As between mother and child, for example, equity has rarely construed that relationship as bestowing on the mother an obligation to advance her child either financially[44] or morally.[45] This is apparent even in cases where the father has died[46] or where the mother is the primary earner. Not surprisingly, therefore, this aspect of the operation of the presumptions has been the subject of much criticism. The application of presumed advancement has, as the Grays comment:

> "become hopelessly out of touch with the egalitarian nature of contemporary society and fails, moreover, to reflect the fact that both parents, if married to each other, are nowadays statutorily burdened with 'parental responsibility' for their minor children ... Today it seems scarcely conceivable that the presumption can survive, in the parental context, in its offensively differential form".[47]

Kodilinye agrees, "It is based on the absurd notion that a mother, unlike a father, has no moral obligation to advance her child. Even in the context of Victorian custom and morality such a distinction between a mother and a father seems curious, but it is completely inappropriate in the conditions of the modern family".[48]

Although in such cases it is the presumption of resulting trust which technically arises, the presumption may, of course, be rebutted with evidence of any intention to the contrary. The strength of the evidence required will vary according to the given circumstances. As Jessel M.R. points out, "in the case of a mother very little evidence beyond the relationship is wanted, there being very little additional motive required to induce a mother to make a gift to her child".[49] Accordingly, the apparent harshness in the operation of the presumption is, to a degree, mitigated by the relative ease with which the courts will deem an intention to make a gift.[50] Arguably, the presumption should be abandoned altogether as it carries little legitimacy in modern times. At the

---

[41] *Heseltine v Heseltine* [1971] 1 W.L.R. 342.
[42] *Diwell v Farnes* [1959] 1 W.L.R. 624.
[43] *Bennet v Bennet* (1879) 10 Ch. D. 474 at 477.
[44] See *Re De Visme* (1863) 2 De. G.J. & S 17.
[45] *Bennet v Bennet* (1879) 10 Ch. D. 474.
[46] See, for example, *Bennet v Bennet* (1879) 10 Ch. D. 474.
[47] *Elements of Land Law*, at 856–857.
[48] G. Kodilinye, "Resulting Trusts, Advancement and Fraudulent Transfers" [1990] Conv. 213 at p.214.
[49] *Bennet v Bennet* (1979) 10 Ch. D. 474 at 480.
[50] cf. *Sekhon v Alissa* [1989] 2 F.L.R. 94.

very least, it would be reasonable to expect the courts to adopt a more pro-active approach and eliminate its indefensible gender bias. Such was the approach of the High Court in Australia where in *Nelson v Nelson*[51] the presumption was deemed equally applicable to fathers and mothers.[52]

In Loco Parentis

Outside the relationship of parent and child, the courts will look for evidence that the **9.43** donor stands in loco parentis to the transferee. This means simply that a person stands in the shoes of a parent and assumes parental obligations of support or provision. Such may occur in relation to an illegitimate child,[53] or an adopted child.[54] It is also common for relatives such as uncles, aunts or grandparents to act in loco parentis where circumstances demand. In *Ebrand v Dancer*,[55] for example, a grandfather acted in loco parentis to his grandchild on the death of the child's father.

REBUTTING THE PRESUMPTION OF ADVANCEMENT

The effect of a presumption of equity is to shift the burden of evidential proof to the **9.44** party against whom the presumption operates. Rebutting the presumption simply comes down to issues of evidence. As James L.J. declared in *Fowkes v Pascoe*, "Where the Court of Chancery is asked, as an equitable assumption or presumption, to take away from a man that which by the common law of the land he is entitled to, he surely has a right to say: 'Listen to my story as to how I came to have it, and judge that story with reference to all the surrounding facts and circumstances'".[56] Showing some distaste for the presumption of advancement, modern courts have endorsed a flexible approach to the admissibility of evidence. Recently Lord Phillips M.R. emphasised that:

> "Equity searches for the subjective intention of the transferor. It ... is not satisfactory to apply rigid rules of law to the evidence that is admissible to rebut the presumption of advancement. Plainly, self-serving statements or conduct of a transferor, who may long after the transaction be regretting earlier generosity, carry little or no weight. But words or conduct more proximate to the transaction itself should be given the significance that they naturally bear as part of the overall picture. Where the transferee is an adult, the words or conduct of the transferor

---

[51] (1995) 184 C.L.R. 538.
[52] For a recent Court of Appeal of Singapore decision endorsing this approach: see: *Lau Siew Kim v Terence Yeo Guan Chye* [2007] SGCA 54, noted by K. Low, (2008) 124 L.Q.R. 369.
[53] See, for example, *Beckford v Beckford* (1774) Lofft 490.
[54] *Standing v Bowring* (1886) 31 Ch. D. 282.
[55] (1680) 2 Ch. Cas 26.
[56] (1875) 10 Ch. App. 343 at 349.

will carry more weight if the transferee is aware of them and makes no protest or challenge to them".[57]

In light of this liberal approach, older authorities that seek to impose restrictions on the admissibility of evidence[58] must now be viewed with some scepticism.[59]

Reliance upon evidence of illegality

9.45 "He who comes to equity must come with clean hands" is a historic equitable principle which continues to resonate in the context of illegality and resulting trusts. It is encountered in the case of a gratuitous transfer of property into the hands of another as part of an illegal or fraudulent scheme where, in accordance with this maxim, the presumption of advancement cannot be rebutted by adducing evidence of illegality or fraudulent activity.[60] Thus, a transferor is prevented from arguing illegality to show that he intended to retain a beneficial interest in the property. In *Gascoigne v Gascoigne*,[61] for example, property was transferred from husband to wife in order to put that property beyond the reach of the husband's creditors. In the light that, as between husband and wife, the presumption of advancement arose, it was necessary for the husband to adduce evidence of his fraudulent activities to show that a gift was not intended and establish his entitlement in equity under a resulting trust. The clear adjudication of the court was that he was not entitled to rely upon his own illegality to assert his claim and to rebut the presumption of advancement. As Lush J. commented, he had, "concocted the scheme of putting his property in her name, while retaining the beneficial interest, for the purpose of misleading, defeating and delaying present or future creditors".[62]

Similarly, in *Chettiar v Chettiar (No.2)*[63] the presumption of advancement proved decisive. The case concerned the evasion of regulations governing the holding of rubber plantations in Malaya. Once the father had reached the threshold of 100 acres, (to hold more would subject him to further regulations) he transferred additional plantations into the name of his son. The Privy Council was unimpressed with the adducement of evidence of a fraudulent purpose to show that he did not plan to divest himself of his equitable interest in the additional plantations. Lord Denning could only conclude that the legal and equitable estate should lay where it had fallen, "The father has used the transfer to achieve his deceitful end and cannot go back on it".[64]

9.46   In *Tinker v Tinker*[65] a husband purchased a house and a garage business in Cornwall.

---

[57] *Lavelle v Lavelle* [2004] 2 F.C.R. 418 at [19].
[58] See *Shephard v Cartwright* [1955] A.C. 431 at 445 per Viscount Simonds.
[59] As E. Fung argues in (2006) 122 L.Q.R. 651 at p.688, "The rule in *Shephard v Cartwright* is an anomalous relic of the common law from former times and should be recognised as such".
[60] This rule is a principle of policy and not a principle of justice: *Holman v Johnson* (1775) 1 Coup 341.
[61] [1918] 1 K.B. 223.
[62] [1918] 1 K.B. 223 at 226, see also *SMQ v RFQ* [2008] EWHC 1874 (Fam) where a father transferred assets to his children with the illegal purpose of defrauding the Inland Revenue.
[63] [1962] A.C. 294.
[64] [1962] A.C. 294 at 302, see also *Barrett v Barrett* [2008] 2 P. & C.R. 17 where reliance on the agreement between the parties necessitated reliance on an underlying illegal purpose.
[65] [1970] P. 136.

To safeguard himself from the claims of creditors in the event that his business should fail, he purchased the house in the sole name of his wife. On the breakdown of their relationship, the husband sought to recover the property from his wife. The outcome of the case illustrates the effect of the presumption of advancement. As Lord Denning M.R. explained, the husband had, "simply found himself on the horns of a dilemma in that, as between himself and his wife, he wished to say that the property belonged to him whereas, as between himself and his creditors, he wished to say that it belonged to her".[66] It was clear to Salmon L.J. that, "The burden of displacing the presumption of advancement is therefore on the husband. This burden can in many cases be displaced without much effort. It seems to me, however, that in this case the husband's evidence, far from displacing the presumption has done much to reinforce it".[67]

Where evidence of illegality is unnecessary

Where a proprietary interest can be established under a resulting trust without recourse to reliance on evidence of illegality, the "clean hands" principle has no role to play.[68] Such was demonstrated by the House of Lords in *Tinsley v Milligan*.[69] The case concerned the joint purchase of a home for two women as co-habiting lovers. By mutual agreement, the property was registered in Ms Tinsley's name as the sole proprietor so as to enable Ms Milligan to make false social security claims, thereby benefiting both parties. On the breakdown of their relationship, Ms Tinsley moved out and claimed possession of the house as its legal owner. Ms Milligan counterclaimed for an order for sale claiming that the house was held on trust for the both of them equally. As between the ending of their relationship and Ms Tinsley's claim to possession, Ms Milligan had discontinued her fraudulent activity and had settled the matter with the relevant authorities. It is instructive to consider the approach both of the Court of Appeal and the House of Lords.

9.47

The Court of Appeal[70] attempted to fashion a flexible approach broadly based on a test of public conscience. The majority agreed that, "The court should keep in mind that the underlying principle is the so-called public conscience test. The court must weigh, or balance, the adverse consequences of granting relief against the adverse consequences of refusing relief. The ultimate decision calls for a value judgment".[71] Nicholls L.J. highlighted a range of relevant factual considerations[72] and concluded, "I have no doubt that, far from it being an affront to the public conscience to grant relief in this case, it would be an affront to the public conscience not to do so. Right-thinking people would not consider that condemnation of the parties' fraudulent activities ought

---

[66] [1970] P. 136 at 141.
[67] [1970] P. 136 at 142.
[68] See *Slater v Simm* [2007] EWHC 951 (Ch) where lies contained in a financial statement did not prevent the assertion of a beneficial interest.
[69] [1994] 1 A.C. 340, see also *Gibson v Revenue & Customs Prosecution Office* [2008] EWCA Civ 645 where a drug trafficker's wife was able to assert her interest in property subject to a confiscation order.
[70] [1992] 2 All E.R. 391.
[71] [1992] 2 All E.R. 391 at 398 per Nicholls L.J. (with whom Lloyd L.J. agreed).
[72] Such as the relatively small sums of money involved, the limited contribution of those sums to the acquisition of the house, the act of repentance, and that the illegality had ceased.

to have the consequence of permitting the plaintiff to retain the defendant's half share of this house".[73]

9.48   The approach of the majority appears to run contrary to a long standing line of authority that the court will not give effect to a trust established for a fraudulent purpose, but will instead, "let the estate lie where it falls". Nicholls L.J. sought to argue that cases such as *Gascoigne v Gascoigne*,[74] *Chettiar v Chettiar*[75] and *Tinker v Tinker*[76] were merely illustrations or examples of cases where the court considered it to be an affront to public policy to grant relief. In his view, they laid down no immutable principle. Ralph Gibson L.J. dissented and felt that, although the fairer result would be to uphold the resulting trust, previous case law authority precluded such an outcome. For him, there was no balancing exercise to be performed by the courts. The present facts fell within the rule, as in cases such as *Tinker v Tinker*, that the court should not give effect to an equitable right based upon a transaction which is unlawful.

In the House of Lords there was unanimous agreement that to apply a test of public conscience was outside the proper jurisdiction of the court. Lord Browne-Wilkinson dismissed out of hand that the consequences of being a party to an illegal transaction could depend, "on such an imponderable factor as the extent to which the public conscience would be affronted by recognising rights created by illegal transactions".[77] By a majority, the House of Lords determined that a resulting trust could be upheld where it was not necessary to rely on illegality as the basis of the claim. Lord Browne-Wilkinson enlisted support from a category of cases dealing with the informal acquisition of an interest in the family home. In accordance with principles set out in well-known cases such as *Lloyds Bank v Rosset*,[78] he held that the source of Ms Milligan's rights in equity was her contribution to the purchase price. Although illegality had been raised by Ms Tinsley in an effort to rebut the presumption of resulting trust in Ms Milligan's favour, it was by the latter's direct contribution to the purchase price that she acquired an equitable proprietary interest. Consequently, it was unnecessary to adduce evidence of the illegal purpose that had driven her to consent to the conveyance of legal title into the sole name of her lover. Neither, moreover, was she subject to the clean hands principle. As Lord Browne-Wilkinson clarified, "A party to an illegality can recover by virtue of a legal or equitable property interest if, but only if, he can establish his title without relying on his own illegality".[79]

9.49   As to the dissenting views expressed by Lords Goff and Keith, both were content to embrace the traditional principles of decided case law. Their view was that the capacity of the court to intervene in cases of illegality did not depend upon whether evidence of illegality of fraudulent activity was necessary to support the participant's claim. This view is rooted in the approach of the court laid down by Lord Eldon in *Mucklestone v Brown*, to the effect that where a plaintiff seeks to rely on illegality to establish a claim to equitable relief, the appropriate response is to, "let the estate lie, where it falls".[80] Indeed, regardless of whether the claim to a resulting trust depended upon the evidence

[73] [1992] 2 All E.R. 391 at 399.
[74] [1918] 1 K.B. 223.
[75] [1962] 1 All E.R. 494.
[76] [1970] 1 All E.R. 540.
[77] [1994] 1 A.C. 340 at 369.
[78] [1991] 1 A.C. 107.
[79] [1994] 1 A.C. 340 at 375.
[80] (1801) 6 Ves. 52 at 68.

of illegality or stood independently without the need to adduce such evidence, it was a matter of equitable principle that a court of equity would not intervene. There is no shortage of authority to support the strict approach to the clean hands doctrine endorsed by Lord Goff.[81] His was the view that equity should not assist someone who transfers property into the hands of another in furtherance of an illegal purpose to establish an equitable claim to that property. Policy and practicality pervaded his judgment and he was of the firm opinion that should the stance of Lord Browne-Wilkinson be adopted, it would, "open the door to far more unmeritorious cases".[82]

Despite such strong dissenting protestation, the effect of *Tinsley v Milligan* may be viewed as carving out an exception to the general principle of clean hands and, thereby, effecting a relaxation in the approach of equity. Where it is unnecessary to adduce evidence of illegality in order to establish a proprietary interest, the presence of illegality will not preclude the availability of equitable relief. Accordingly, where the relationship between the parties is one in which the presumption of advancement does not apply, the transferor is at liberty to recover the property on the basis that there is no need to rely on illegality. The transferor need rely merely on the resulting trust that arose when the transfer occurred. Nonetheless, as Lord Browne-Wilkinson admitted, in cases where the presumption of advancement does apply, the transferor is faced with the presumption that property was transferred freely. The transferor cannot claim under a resulting trust unless and until he has rebutted that presumption of gift for those purposes. As he must rely on the underlying illegality, his claim will fail.

Although expedient on the facts, *Tinsley v Milligan* shows that the outcome of future **9.50** cases will pivot, perhaps unfairly, on the nature of the relationship of the parties involved and the presumption of equity raised to cater for their inferred intentions. Understandably, therefore, *Tinsley v Milligan* has been the subject of robust criticism from commentators and ill-disguised regret in the Court of Appeal that, for at least the present time, the House of Lords authority requires to be followed.[83] Stowe, for example, makes the convincing argument that, "availability of relief depends entirely on a fact which is completely irrelevant from a policy perspective (viz whether there is a presumption of advancement in relation to the person to whom the property is transferred); and ... is in no way related to the seriousness of the underlying illegality".[84] Other commentators have focused upon the impact of the obvious gender bias that pervades the historic presumptions of equity and which are implicitly retained by the House of Lords. As Halliwell argues, "The opportunity for authoritative review of the gender discrimination contained within this presumption rarely arises and it is regrettable that the House of Lords failed to seize the opportunity to advance equality in the law".[85]

The potential for hardship was illustrated in *Silverwood v Silverwood*.[86] Here, the testatrix placed her assets in the names of her grandchildren in order to facilitate a claim for income support from the Department of Social Security. Albeit with some

---

[81] Lord Goff spoke of a "long line of unbroken authority stretching back over 200 years" ([1994] 1 A.C. 340 at 363).
[82] [1994] 1 A.C. 340 at 362.
[83] See, for example, *Silverwood v Silverwood* (1997) 74 P. & C.R. 453.
[84] H. Stowe "The 'Unruly Horse' Has Bolted" (1994) 57 M.L.R. 441 at p.446.
[85] M. Halliwell [1994] Conv. 62 at p.67.
[86] (1997) 74 P. & C.R. 453.

reluctance, Nourse L.J. held that her executor was entitled to recover the assets on the basis of a resulting trust that arose in her favour. In line with *Tinsley v Milligan*, no adducement of the evidence of an illegal purpose was necessary, as the presumption of advancement did not operate in the context of a grandparent/grandchild relationship. Of particular note, was the forceful support voiced by Nourse L.J. in favour of the Court of Appeal test of public conscience in *Tinsley v Milligan*. The adoption of such a test would, in his view, bring the flexibility lacking in the extant law.

9.51   Similarly, in *Lowson v Coombes*[87] the operation of the presumptions led to an unfortunate, but inevitable outcome. There a man and his mistress contributed to the purchase price of a number of properties, each of which was held in the sole name of the mistress to prevent any claim from the man's estranged wife.[88] In reliance on the presumption of resulting trust and, without the need to adduce evidence of illegality, the man was entitled to recover. Robert Walker L.J. lamented the continuing operation of the presumption of advancement under the *Tinsley v Milligan* approach. He emphasised that it does, "create difficulties because the presumption has been cogently criticised both as being out of date in modern social and economic conditions ... and as being uncertain in its scope".[89]

It is noteworthy also that the High Court of Australia has rejected the *Tinsley v Milligan* approach in favour of a flexible test based on public policy considerations. In *Nelson v Nelson*,[90] a woman who purchased property in the name of her children in order to take advantage of particular housing subsidies was permitted to rebut the presumption of advancement by leading evidence of her illegal purpose. As a condition of equitable relief, she was obliged to repay the sums accrued improperly via the illegal scheme. Similar flexibility would be provided in England and Wales by implementation of the Law Commission proposal that there be a statutory discretion when illegality is raised.[91] Amongst the range of factors to influence this discretion of the court would be the seriousness of the illegality; the knowledge and intention of the party seeking enforcement of the transaction; the extent to which refusal to assist would deter illegality or would further the purpose of the rule which renders the trust illegal and the extent to which refusal to assist would be a proportionate response to involvement in illegality. Unfortunately, and as with many of the Law Commission consultation exercises, no further progress has been made to enact these proposals.

Abandonment of fraudulent activity

9.52   A notable relaxation of the "clean hands" requirement is discernible from *Tribe v Tribe*.[92] In this case, the question arose as to whether the transferor could rebut the presumption of advancement by adducing evidence of an illegal purpose that had not subsequently been carried into effect.[93] The plaintiff held 459 out of 500 shares in a

---

[87] [1999] Ch. 373.
[88] An illegal purpose under the Matrimonial Causes Act 1973 s.37.
[89] [1999] Ch. 373 at 385.
[90] (1995) 132 A.L.R. 133.
[91] *Illegal Transactions: The Effect of Illegality on Contracts and Trusts* ((1999) Law. Com. No. 154).
[92] [1996] Ch. 107.
[93] See also *Painter v Hutchison* [2007] EWHC 758 (Ch).

family company and was tenant under two leases. When a notice of dilapidations was served on him, he feared that the demands of extensive repairs would lead to losses to the family companies. In order to avoid liability by deceiving the landlord, Mr Tribe purported to sell the shares to his son for the sum of £78,000, which was never paid. It transpired that the deception was not necessary because the landlord later agreed to a surrender of one of the leases. The son, however, claimed that he was now absolutely entitled to the shares under the presumption of advancement. The Court of Appeal held that as the father had not carried out his illegal purpose he was able to adduce evidence of it to rebut the presumption of advancement.

The principle in *Tribe v Tribe* can be simply stated. When the planned illegal activity is never carried out, the transferor is not precluded from relying on evidence of his proposed activities to support his claim or rebut the presumption of advancement. This principle is not novel. In the nineteenth century, for example, it was held that, "Where the purpose for which the assignment was given is not carried into execution, and nothing is done under it, the mere intention to effect an illegal object when the assignment was executed does not deprive the assignor of his right to recover the property from the assignee who has given no consideration for it".[94] Many older authorities appear to require some kind of repentance from the illegal purpose. This is not an approach that has found favour in modern courts. The withdrawal from fraud before it was implemented was, in the view of the Court of Appeal in *Tribe v Tribe*, a no less desirable end than the discouragement of fraud from the outset.[95] In *SMQ v RFQ*, moreover, Black J. explained, "... genuine repentance is not required. Justice is not a reward for merit".[96]

The present state of the law on illegality and resulting trusts is helpfully set out in the judgment of Millett L.J. in *Tribe v Tribe*.[97] By way of summary, seven propositions may be identified from the judgment of Millett L.J.:   **9.53**

- title to property passes both in law and in equity even if the transfer is made for an illegal purpose. The fact that title has passed to the transferee does not prevent the transferor from bringing an action for restitution;

- the transferor's action will prove unsuccessful if it would be illegal for him to retain any interest in the property;

- the transferor can otherwise recover the property if this can be done without relying on the illegal purpose. This will usually be possible when the property was transferred without consideration in circumstances where the transferor can rely on an express declaration of trust or a resulting trust in his favour;

- the transferor can usually recover property where the illegal purpose has not been carried out. A contrary conclusion may be drawn where the illegal purpose has been carried out and the transferee can rely on the transferor's conduct as inconsistent with his retention of a beneficial interest;

[94] *Symes v Hughes* (1870) L.R. 9 Eq. 475 per Lord Romilly M.R.
[95] As Millett L.J. reasoned [1996] Ch. 107 at 134, "if the policy which underlies the primary rule is to discourage fraud, the policy which underlies the exception must be taken to be to encourage withdrawal from a proposed fraud before it is implemented, an end which is no less desirable".
[96] [2008] EWHC 1874 (Fam) at [125].
[97] [1996] Ch. 107.

- the transferor can lead evidence of the illegal purpose whenever it is necessary for him to do so provided that he has withdrawn from the transaction before the illegal purpose has been wholly or partly put into effect. This will be necessary where the transferor initiates legal proceedings and needs to rebut the presumption of advancement;

- the only way in which a man can protect his property from his creditors is by divesting himself of all beneficial interest in it. Evidence that he transferred the property in order to protect it from his creditors, therefore, does nothing by itself to rebut the presumption of advancement. Indeed, it reinforces the presumption. To rebut the presumption it is necessary to show that he intended to retain a beneficial interest and conceal it from his creditors; and

- the court should not conclude that his intention was to protect property from his creditors without compelling evidence to this effect. The identity of the transferee and the circumstances in which the transfer was made may assume major relevance. It is unlikely that the court would reach such a conclusion where the transfer was made in the absence of an imminent and perceived threat from known creditors.

Although the broad principles emanating from *Tinsley v Milligan* and *Tribe v Tribe* are compatible, the law remains in a patently unsatisfactory state. In *Tribe v Tribe*, Millett L.J. felt compelled to deal with the prospect that injustice might result from continued recourse to equitable presumption. He argued, therefore, that a transferor would not automatically succeed in every case where the presumption of resulting trust applied. For example, where a transferee led evidence of a transferor's subsequent conduct, the presumption of resulting trust may be rebutted by evidence inconsistent with the transferor's intention to retain a beneficial interest. Unfortunately, in the illustration provided by Millett L.J. (transfer between uncle and nephew to conceal property from creditors with whom the uncle subsequently deals as though he has no interest in the property), there seems little to distinguish the *Tinsley v Milligan* style case where the opposite conclusion was reached—that the transferor can rely on the resulting trust. It seems both certain and sensible, therefore, that the higher courts will re-visit these principles in future.

A GUIDE TO FURTHER READING

R. Ellison, "Pension Fund Surpluses" (1991) Trust Law International 60.

M. Halliwell, "Equitable Proprietary Claims and Dishonest Claimants: A Resolution?" [2004] Conv. 439.

C.E.F. Rickett, "Different Views on the Scope of the Quistclose Analysis" (1991) 107 L.Q.R. 608.

C.E.F. Rickett & R. Grantham, "Resulting Trusts—The True Nature of the Failing Trust Cases" (2000) 116 L.Q.R. 15.

H. Stowe, "The 'Unruly Horse' Has Bolted" (1994) 57 M.L.R. 441.

W. Swadling, "A New Role for Resulting Trusts" (1996) 16 Legal Studies 110.
W. Swadling, "Explaining Resulting Trusts" (2008) 124 LQR 72.

Chapter 10

Constructive Trusts

Like the resulting trust (considered in Ch.9), the constructive trust is a form of implied **10.01** trust that arises by operation of law and not by the deliberate act of the parties.[1] No formalities are required for its creation.[2] It is a trust implied in a variety of circumstances where the defendant has knowledge of some factor that affects his conscience in respect of specific property.[3] In the words of Costello J., "The principle is that where a person who holds property in circumstances which in equity and good conscience should be held or enjoyed by another he will be compelled to hold the property in trust for another".[4] The circumstances in which the constructive trust will be encountered are many and varied.[5] It follows that the constructive trust is notoriously difficult to define. As Edmund Davies L.J. admitted in *Carl Zeiss Stiftung v Herbert Smith & Co*, "English law provides no clear and all-embracing definition of a constructive trust. Its boundaries have been left perhaps deliberately vague, so as not to restrict the court by technicalities in deciding what the justice of a particular case may demand".[6] It is clear, nonetheless, that the general trigger activating the constructive trust is unconscionability. Equity acts in personam to "construe" the defendant to be a trustee of property when he has knowledge of some factor that affects his conscience. Typically, equity is seen to intervene to remedy wrongful actions[7] or to give effect to an agreement between the parties upon which the claimant has relied.[8]

The most notable recent analysis of the basis of the constructive trust is that of Lord

---

[1] See further, A. Oakley, *Constructive Trusts* (3rd edn, London, Sweet & Maxwell, 1997).
[2] The constructive trust is exempt from the requirement of writing laid down in s.53(1) of the Law Property Act 1925.
[3] *Westdeutsche Landesbank Girozentrale v Islington LBC* [1996] A.C. 669.
[4] *HKN Invest OY v Incotrade PVT Ltd* [1993] 3 I.R. 152 at 162.
[5] As Lord Scott acknowledges in *Cobbe v Yeoman's Row Management Ltd* [2008] 1 W.L.R. 1752 at 1769, "It is impossible to prescribe exhaustively the circumstances sufficient to create a constructive trust but it is possible to recognise particular factual circumstances that will do so and also to recognise other factual circumstances that will not."
[6] [1969] 2 Ch. 276 at 300.
[7] For example, in the case of property obtained by unlawful killing.
[8] For example, the common intention constructive trust: see Ch.11.

Browne-Wilkinson in *Westdeutsche Landesbank Girozentrale v Islington LBC*.[9] The case concerned payments made under an interest rate swap agreement between a bank and a local authority.[10] The agreement entered into in 1987 was intended to run over a period of 10 years. In 1992, however, the House of Lords ruled that such agreements were ultra vires and void ab initio.[11] The Bank sought to recover the money paid to the local authority on the basis that the local authority was a constructive trustee. Lord Browne-Wilkinson held that from the point of entry into the transaction until the point at which the property ceased to be traceable, both parties believed they had entered into a valid contract. There was nothing to affect the conscience of the local authority and, accordingly, no basis upon which to impose a constructive trust. Lord Browne-Wilkinson laid down the following general principles:

> "(i)   Equity operates on the conscience of the owner of the legal interest. In the case of a trust, the conscience of the legal owner requires him to carry out the purposes for which the property was vested in him (express or implied trust) or which the law imposes on him by reason of his unconscionable conduct (constructive trust).
>
> (ii)   Since the equitable jurisdiction to enforce trusts depends upon the conscience of the holder of the legal interest being affected, he cannot be a trustee of the property if and so long as he is ignorant of the facts alleged to affect his conscience, i.e. until he is aware that he is intended to hold the property for the benefit of others in the case of an express or implied trust, or, in the case of a constructive trust, of the factors which are alleged to affect his conscience.
>
> (iii)   In order to establish a trust there must be identifiable trust property. The only apparent exception to this rule is a constructive trust imposed on a person who dishonestly assists in a breach of trust who may come under fiduciary duties even if he does not receive identifiable trust property.
>
> (iv)   Once a trust is established, as from the date of its establishment the beneficiary has, in equity, a proprietary interest in the trust property, which proprietary interest will be enforceable in equity against any subsequent holder of the property (whether the original property or substituted property into which it can be traced) other than a purchaser for value of the legal interest without notice".[12]

10.02   At its core, therefore, the constructive trust requires the defendant to have knowledge of factors which affect his conscience such that he is prevented from asserting his own sole beneficial entitlement to the property in question. At this level of generality, there appears much scope for the invocation of a constructive trust whether in a remedial capacity or where the justice of the case demands. Nonetheless, the English constructive trust may not be viewed as a remedial device imposed at the discretion of the court. Developed rules determine its invocation, as is evident from a close evaluation of its nature and incidents.

---

[9] [1996] A.C. 669.
[10] An agreement whereby each party agrees to pay the other an amount calculated by reference to the interest that would have accrued over a given period on a notional principal sum.
[11] *Hazell v Hammersmith and Fulham BC* [1992] 2 A.C. 1.
[12] *Westdeutsche Landesbank Girozentrale v Islington LBC* [1996] A.C. 669 at 705.

Institutional or remedial?

Generally speaking, constructive trusts may be institutional or remedial in nature (these terms are explained below). Unlike other jurisdictions, however, English law recognises only the former, i.e. what is sometimes termed the "institutional constructive trust". As Lord Browne-Wilkinson observed:

10.03

> "Under an institutional constructive trust, the trust arises by operation of law as from the date of the circumstances which give rise to it: the function of the court is merely to declare that such trust has arisen in the past. The consequences that flow from such trust having arisen (including the possibly unfair consequences to third parties who in the interim have received the trust property) are also determined by rules of law, not under a discretion".[13]

Rather than the court imposing or creating a remedy by way of a response to the defendant's wrong, the institutional constructive trust is a substantive constructive trust where the court deems the acts of the parties already to have brought the trust into being. We will see that the obligation of trustees under express trusts is determined through the express terms of the trust instrument and also under the general law.[14] The obligations of constructive trustees will, by contrast, reflect the circumstances in which the trust has arisen.[15] Necessarily, the court is acutely aware that a constructive trustee in a pre-existing fiduciary relationship to the claimant will already have assumed onerous obligations as part of an ongoing professional relationship to the claimant. The imposition of similar levels of liability is patently unsuitable, say, where the defendant is an individual who is credited with an overpayment of the claimant's money or the payment of money by mistake. In each case, the court will determine the specific obligations of the constructive trustee when it acts to recognise the claimant's pre-existing rights.

For Lord Browne-Wilkinson in *Westdeutsche*, the distinction between institutional and remedial trusts was simple to state. He claimed, "A remedial constructive trust, as I understand it, is different. It is a judicial remedy giving rise to an enforceable equitable obligation: the extent to which it operates retrospectively to the prejudice of third parties lies in the discretion of the court".[16] A principal practical distinction between these forms of constructive trust lies in the date at which the claimant may assert proprietary rights. Under the institutional version, the court merely confirms the pre-existing proprietary interest in effect before the order of the court. Under the remedial constructive trust, the court creates a remedy by order of the court and exercises discretion to determine any retrospective effect. This matter of timing is of obvious relevance to third parties who acquire an interest in the property before the order of the court.

---

[13] [1996] A.C. 669 at 714.
[14] See Ch.13.
[15] As Millett L.J. warned in *Lonhro Plc v Al-Fayed (No.2)* [1992] 1 W.L.R. 1 at 12, "it is a mistake to suppose that in every situation in which a constructive trust arises the legal owner is necessarily subject to all the fiduciary obligations and disabilities of an express trustee".
[16] *Westdeutsche Landesbank Girozentrale v Islington LBC* [1996] A.C. 669 at 714.

10.04   Outside England and Wales, the approach adopted in countries such as the United States, is to regard the constructive trust as a remedial instrument imposed, broadly speaking, when the constructive trustee has been unjustly enriched in some way. As Cardozo J. once put it, the constructive trust is thereby a, "formula through which the conscience of equity finds expression".[17] It is difficult to ignore the refusal of the English courts to develop the law in line with the approach of other jurisdictions. On many occasions the remedial constructive trust has been rejected outright[18] or it has been clearly emphasised that, "English law has not followed other jurisdictions where the constructive trust has become a remedy for unjust enrichment".[19] Such reluctance is, perhaps, underpinned by the fear that future equitable intervention must be principled as well as flexible. For Nourse L.J., it is simply unpalatable to grant a proprietary right by way of remedy to someone who, beforehand, had no such right. His objection is based on the established principle that property rights can only be varied by statute. As he emphasised in *Re Polly Peck International Plc (in administration) (No.2)*, "you cannot grant a proprietary right to A who has not had it beforehand, without taking some proprietary right away from B. No English court has ever had the power to do that, except with the authority of Parliament".[20]

Notwithstanding, this general intransigence, it remains open to future courts to develop the law. In *Westdeutsche*, for example, Lord Browne-Wilkinson adopted a more positive stance in charting the likelihood of future reform. He argued:

> "Although the resulting trust is an unsuitable basis for developing proprietary restitutionary remedies, the remedial constructive trust, if introduced into English law, may provide a more satisfactory road forward. The court by way of remedy might impose a constructive trust on a defendant who knowingly retains property of which the plaintiff has been unjustly deprived. Since the remedy can be tailored to the circumstances of the particular case, innocent third parties would not be prejudiced and restitutionary defences, such as change of position, are capable of being given effect. However, whether English law should follow the United States and Canada by adopting the remedial constructive trust will have to be decided in some future case when the point is directly in issue".[21]

10.05   It remains only to note the efforts, (principally) of Lord Denning, during the 1970s to introduce a remedial constructive trust to this jurisdiction. It took the form of a constructive trust "of a new model".[22] In *Hussey v Palmer*, Lord Denning described it as a, "trust imposed by law whenever justice and good conscience require it … It is an

---

[17] *Beatty v Guggenheim Exploration Co* (1919) 225 NY 380 at 385; see also Restatement of Restitution, "Where a person holding title to property is subject to an equitable duty to convey it to another on the ground that he would be unjustly enriched if he were permitted to retain it, a constructive trust arises" ((American Law Institute, 1937) at [160]).

[18] See *Re Polly Peck International Plc (In Administration) (No.5)* [1998] 3 All E.R. 812, where to impose a constructive trust on the assets of an insolvent company would confer on the claimant a priority not accorded by the relevant legislation.

[19] *Halifax Building Society v Thomas* [1996] Ch. 217 at 229.

[20] [1996] Ch. 217 at 831.

[21] *Westdeutsche Landesbank Girozentrale v Islington LBC* [1996] A.C. 669 at 716.

[22] *Eves v Eves* [1975] 1 W.L.R. 1338.

equitable remedy by which the court can enable an aggrieved party to obtain restitution".[23] The "new model" constructive trust failed to become established on the basis that Lord Denning's broad concepts of justice and good conscience lacked the necessary circumscription to cater for a principled and certain law. Criticism of the new model was forthcoming both here[24] and abroad.[25] As Dillon L.J. put it, "The court does not yet sit, as under a palm tree, to exercise a general discretion to do what the man in the street, on a general overview of the case, might regard as fair".[26]

Personal or proprietary?

Constructive trusts may give rise to personal or proprietary claims. The proprietary **10.06** constructive trust occurs where the defendant stood in a fiduciary relationship to the claimant or in cases where the defendant received property and acted unconscionably. Where the property remains in the defendant's hands, reliance on his proprietary rights will enable the claimant to recover his interest in the property (and any increase in value) in priority to the constructive trustee's general creditors. If the property has passed into the hands of a third party, the imposition of the constructive trust may be the basis of an equitable proprietary claim against the third party.[27] In addition, it is open to the claimant to rely on the personal liability of the constructive trustee. This avenue will be preferable, say, where no proprietary claim is possible because the property can no longer be recovered.[28] A personal claim may supplement a proprietary claim where damages are sought for any depreciation in value in the property.

Personal liability to account as a constructive trustee[29] is encountered in two principal situations. The first is where the defendant receives property in the knowledge that receipt is further to a breach of trust (knowing receipt)[30] and, secondly, where the defendant dishonestly assists in a breach of trust (dishonest assistance).[31] In the latter example, the language of constructive trusteeship is apt to confuse. No trust property vests in the defendant. He is merely an accessory to a trustee's breach of trust, but he is liable to account in equity as though he were a trustee.[32] As explained above, Lord Browne-Wilkinson treated, as an "apparent exception" to the rule regarding identifiable trust property, the imposition of the constructive trust on the dishonest assistant.[33] Nonetheless, the fictional nature of the constructive trust has led to convincing calls for replacement terminology. Notably, Lord Millett claimed:

---

[23] [1972] 3 All E.R. 744 at 747.
[24] See, for example, the approach of Fox L.J. in *Ashburn Arnold v Anstalt v Arnold* [1989] Ch. 1.
[25] See *Allen v Snyder* [1977] 2 NSWLR 685 at 701, where it was claimed that, "the legitimacy of the new model is at least suspect; at best it is a mutant from which further breeding should be discouraged".
[26] *Springette v Defoe* [1992] 2 F.L.R. 388 at 393.
[27] See Ch.17.
[28] It may have passed into the hands of a bona fide purchaser or have been somehow dissipated.
[29] That is, personal liability to make good any loss to the trust: see Ch.17.
[30] *Twinsectra v Yardley* [2002] 2 All E.R. 377.
[31] *Royal Brunei Airlines v Tan* [1995] 2 A.C. 378.
[32] As Ungoed-Thomas J. put it in *Selangor v Cradock (No.3)* [1968] 1 W.L.R. 1555 at 1579, the imposition of a constructive trust is, "nothing more than a formula for equitable relief. The court of equity says that the defendant shall be liable in equity, as though he were a trustee"; see also, *Coulthard v Disco Mix Club Ltd* [2000] 1 W.L.R. 707 at 731.
[33] *Westdeutsche Landesbank Girozentrale v Islington LBC* [1996] A.C. 669 at 705.

"Equity gives relief against fraud by making any person sufficiently implicated in the fraud accountable in equity. In such a case he is traditionally (and I have suggested unfortunately) described as a 'constructive trustee' and is said to be 'liable to account as a constructive trustee'. But he is not in fact a trustee at all, even though he may be liable to account as if he were. He never claims to assume the position of trustee on behalf of others, and he may be liable without ever receiving or handling the trust property ... In this second class of case the expressions 'constructive trust' and 'constructive trustee' create a trap ... I think that we should now discard the words 'accountable as constructive trustee' in this context and substitute the words 'accountable in equity' ".[34]

Irrespective of the debate as to the correctness of applying constructive trusts in the context of assistance in a breach of trust, it remains convenient and logical to examine together third party liability in cases of dishonest assistance and knowing receipt. Detailed analysis is provided in this chapter. A broad discussion of the range of further personal and proprietary remedies for breach of trust is provided in Ch.17.

Constructive trusts proper

10.07   The remaining distinction of relevance to the forthcoming illustrations of constructive trusts is that put forward by Millett L.J. in *Paragon Finance Plc v Thakerar & Co.*[35] There he drew a distinction between two classes of constructive trust that is, arguably, indicative of the problems of classification and definition that pervade the current law.

He explained that the first type concerns cases where the defendant, although not expressly appointed as trustee, assumes the duties of a trustee by an earlier, independent lawful transaction which is not impeached by the plaintiff. As he put it,

"the constructive trustee really is a trustee. He does not receive the trust property in his own right but by a transaction by which both parties intend to create a trust from the outset and which is not impugned by the plaintiff. His possession of the property is coloured from the first by the trust and confidence by means of which he obtained it, and his subsequent appropriation of the property to his own use is a breach of that trust. In these cases the plaintiff does not impugn the transaction by which the defendant obtained control of the property. He alleges that the circumstances in which the defendant obtained control make it unconscionable for him thereafter to assert a beneficial interest in the property".[36]

10.08   The second type concerns cases where the trust obligation arises because of an unlawful transaction which is subsequently impeached by the plaintiff. It was never envisaged that the recipient would hold property as a trustee. Millett L.J. observed:

---

[34] *Dubai Aluminium Co v Salaam* [2002] 3 W.L.R. 1913 at 1946.
[35] [1999] 1 All E.R. 400.
[36] [1999] 1 All E.R. 400 at 408.

"The second class of case is different. It arises when the defendant is implicated in a fraud. Equity has always given relief against fraud by making any person sufficiently implicated in the fraud accountable in equity. In such a case he is traditionally though I think unfortunately described as a constructive trustee and said to be 'liable to account as constructive trustee'. Such a person is not in fact a trustee at all, even though he may be liable to account as if he were. He never assumes the position of a trustee, and if he receives the trust property at all it is adversely to the plaintiff by an unlawful transaction which is impugned by the plaintiff. In such a case the expressions 'constructive trust' and 'constructive trustee' are misleading, for there is no trust and usually no possibility of a proprietary remedy".[37]

As to Millett L.J.'s adopted classification, the purpose served in distinguishing between his two types of trust lies in the application of statutory limitation periods in cases of breach of trust. The first class of trusts were, indeed, trusts capable of breach and, therefore, subject to the statutory limitation period. As to the second category, he was able to conclude, "there is in truth no breach of trust, but merely a breach of some other duty in response to which equity imposes a form of 'constructive trusteeship' ".[38]

Categories of constructive trusts

It is clear that the constructive trust is imposed in a variety of circumstances and there is little agreement as to how best to categorise the many examples that are found in the case law. The approach undertaken in this chapter is to provide a selective overview of the established cases of "constructive trusts" (rightly or wrongly described), to bring into focus the more abstract discussions highlighted above. Accordingly, a variety of applications of the constructive trust will be illustrated and explained. In many cases, the illustrations will be familiar from discussions in other chapters. Where this is so, the reader will be referred to the more substantive coverage of relevant material in other chapters. The categories of cases will be considered as follows:

10.09

- unauthorised fiduciary gains;

- liability imposed on strangers to the trust who knowingly receive trust property or dishonestly assist in cases of breach of trust;

- equitable response to wrongdoing or unconscionability; and

- enforcing the agreement between the parties.

---

[37] [1999] 1 All E.R. 400 at 408.
[38] [1999] 1 All E.R. 400 at 415. For a discussion of limitation periods in the context of breach of trust: see **17.27**.

Unauthorised Fiduciary Gains

10.10 One of the clearest situations in which a constructive trust will operate is that of unauthorised fiduciary gains. In essence, a fiduciary is liable to his principal in respect of unauthorised gains obtained by reason of his fiduciary office. Unauthorised gains may take a variety of forms, such as a secret profit,[39] a bribe[40] or the use of confidential information to make an unauthorised profit.[41] This principle is long-standing and well understood. As Lord Hershell observed in *Bray v Ford*, "It is an inflexible rule of the court of equity that a person in a fiduciary position, such as the plaintiff's, is not, unless otherwise expressly provided, entitled to make a profit; he is not allowed to put himself in a position where his interest and duty conflict".[42] The nature of fiduciary duties is examined in detail in Ch.13.[43] For present purposes, it is sufficient to note that fiduciaries include not only trustees, but also others who owe similar duties of loyalty and good faith to their principal, such as solicitors and company directors, partners and agents. The imposition of a constructive trust is an important remedy to the claimant, providing him with a claim to the property in priority to general creditors. As is discussed in Ch.17, fiduciaries are under a personal obligation to account for any unauthorised gain.[44]

Supporting authority for the invocation of the constructive trust is long-standing and oft cited. In *Keech v Sandford*[45] a landlord's trustee renewed a lease for his own purposes when it became apparent to him that the landlord was not prepared to offer a renewal to the current tenant, an infant beneficiary of the trust. Upholding the claim made on behalf of the infant beneficiary, Lord King L.C. explained:

> "I must consider this as a trust for the infant, for I very well see that if a trustee, on the refusal to renew, might have a lease to himself, few trust estates would be renewed to *cestui que use*. Although I do not say there is a fraud in this case, yet the trustee should rather have let the lease run out, than to have had it to himself. It may seem hard that the trustee is the only person of all mankind who might not have the lease, but it is very proper that rules should be strictly pursued, and not in

---

[39] For example, an unauthorised commission: see *Williams v Barton* [1927] 2 Ch. 9 at 11, where Russell J. explained that, "A person who has the management of property as a trustee is not permitted to gain any profit by availing himself of his position, and will be a constructive trustee of any such profit for the benefit of the persons equitably entitled to the property".

[40] See Sir P. Millett, "Bribes and Secret Commissions" (1993) 1 R.L.R. 7.

[41] See *Boardman v Phipps* [1967] 2 A.C. 46 (see **10.11**).

[42] [1896] A.C. 44 at 51. See also, the strict formulation of principle by Lord Cranworth L.C. in *Aberdeen Railway Co v Blaikie Brothers* [1843–60] All E.R. Rep. 249 at 252, that, "it is a rule of universal application that no one having such duties to discharge shall be allowed to enter into engagements in which he has or can have a personal interest conflicting or which possibly may conflict with the interests of those whom he is bound to protect".

[43] For a discussion of the defining characteristics of the fiduciary, see *Bristol & West Building Society v Mothew* [1998] Ch. 1 at 18 per Millett L.J.

[44] *Target Holdings v Redferns* [1996] 1 A.C. 421.

[45] (1726) Sel. Cas. Ch. 61.

the least relaxed; for it is very obvious what would be the consequence of letting trustees have the lease on refusal to renew to *cestui que use*".[46]

The strict application of equity's general principles has been a marked feature of   **10.11**
more recent case law. In *Boardman v Phipps*,[47] trustees had a minor shareholding in a poorly managed company. Boardman, as solicitor to the trust took the view that in acquiring more shares the trust could take control and, thereby, improve the fortunes of the company. As the trust was not in the financial position to purchase further shares, Boardman and a beneficiary purchased shares on their own behalf. Following the re-structure of the company, both Boardman's personal investment and that of the trust increased in value. Notwithstanding that Boardman's actions were in good faith, the House of Lords held that he was a constructive trustee of the profit made on his personal shareholding. The opportunity to make a profit had arisen from his fiduciary office and he had used confidential information in the process.[48] Although compensa-tion was payable to Boardman in return for the work he had completed, the funda-mental principle was upheld that, unless otherwise expressly provided, a person in a fiduciary position is not entitled to make a profit because he is not allowed to put himself in a position where his interest and duty conflict.

Bribes

By way of a final illustration, where a bribe is accepted by a fiduciary as an inducement   **10.12**
for his breach of duty, the fiduciary becomes, in equity, a debtor to his principal for the amount of the bribe. He holds the bribe and any property acquired therewith on constructive trust for that person. In the case of a depreciation of value in the property representing the bribe, the fiduciary is liable for that difference in value. Likewise, the fiduciary may not retain any increase in value, in line with the principle that a fiduciary must not profit from his breach. Until *A.G. for Hong Kong v Reid*,[49] the prevailing understanding (derived for the Court of Appeal in *Lister & Co v Stubbs*[50]) was that the bribed fiduciary does not become a constructive trustee.[51] In *A.G. for Hong Kong v Reid*, however, the Privy Council rejected the reasoning of the Court of Appeal and laid out policy reasons for the invocation of a constructive trust. As Lord Templeman explained:

"The decision in *Lister & Co v Stubbs* is not consistent with the principles that a fiduciary must not be allowed to benefit from his own breach of duty, that the fiduciary should account for the bribe as soon as he receives it and that equity

---

[46] (1726) Sel. Cas. Ch. 61 at 62.
[47] [1967] 2 A.C. 46.
[48] As Lord Hodson commented, [1967] 2 A.C. 46 at 106, "Mr. Boardman used the strong minority share-holding which the trustees held, that is to say eight thousand shares in the company, wielding this holding as a weapon to enable him to obtain the information of which he subsequently made use".
[49] [1994] 1 All E.R. 1.
[50] (1890) 45 Ch. D. 1; see further, Sir P. Millett, "Remedies: The Error in *Lister v Stubbs*", in P. Birks (ed.), *The Frontiers of Liability* (Oxford, Oxford University Press, 1994) Vol.1 at 56.
[51] He will, nonetheless, be liable to account for the sum received.

regards as done that which ought to be done. From these principles it would appear to follow that the bribe and the property from time to time representing the bribe are held on a constructive trust for the person injured. A fiduciary remains personally liable for the amount of the bribe if, in the event, the value of the property then recovered by the injured person proved to be less than that amount".[52]

It is instructive to consider, in outline, the facts of *A. G. for Hong Kong v Reid*. Mr Reid, a public prosecutor in Hong Kong accepted bribes to obstruct the prosecution of criminals in Hong Kong, the proceeds of which he invested profitably in three freehold properties in New Zealand. The Crown sought to argue his constructive trusteeship of the investments in order to assert its beneficial entitlement. Lord Templeman seemed minded to reach the politically correct outcome and did not hold back his view of the repugnant nature of the crime committed. As he put it:

> "Bribery is an evil practice which threatens the foundations of any civilised society. In particular bribery of policemen and prosecutors brings the administration of justice into disrepute. Where bribes are accepted by a trustee, servant, agent or other fiduciary, loss and damage are caused to the beneficiaries, master or principal whose interests have been betrayed. The amount of loss or damage resulting from the acceptance of a bribe may or may not be quantifiable. In the present case the amount of harm caused to the administration of justice in Hong Kong by the first respondent in return for bribes cannot be quantified".[53]

10.13   Although it seems likely that the House of Lords will, on any future consideration of such matters, endorse the Privy Council approach there remain arguable difficulties in imposing constructive trusteeship on the fiduciary that accepts a bribe. Not least, the trust is imposed despite the absence of any pre-existing proprietary interest of the principal or any intention in the principal to obtain such an interest. On this ground alone, it is hard to justify the argument that the bribe belonged to the principal from the moment the fiduciary received it. Lord Templeman's response, that is, to apply the maxim, "equity sees as done that which ought to be done" fails altogether to convince.

LIABILITY IMPOSED ON STRANGERS TO THE TRUST

10.14   The second incidence of constructive trusteeship concerns the personal liability imposed on third parties or strangers to the trust. Speaking of the obligations of the trustee generally, Lord Selborne L.C. observed in *Barnes v Addy*[54] that such responsibilities, "may no doubt be extended in equity to others who are not properly trustees, if they are

---

[52] [1994] 1 All E.R. 1 at 9.
[53] [1994] 1 All E.R. 1 at 4.
[54] (1874) 9 Ch. App. 244.

found either making themselves trustees *de son tort*, or actually participating in any fraudulent conduct of the trustee to the injury of the *cestui que trust*".[55]

Lord Selborne L.C. made reference, therefore, to the constructive trust imposed on a person who intermeddles or interferes with the trust so that he assumes the responsibilities of a trustee and faces consequent liability on that basis. He also spoke of the extension of liability to those who participate in the fraudulent conduct of the trustee. Although future courts have many times developed and re-formulated the basis of liability, the personal liability of strangers to the trust now advances on two fronts. Liability will be imposed as against third parties who, first, dishonestly assist in a breach of trust or, secondly, receive trust property in breach of trust.

In the development of case law, the courts have guarded against the incautious extension of these categories. As Lord Selborne L.C. warned:

> "strangers are not to be made constructive trustees merely because they act as the agents of trustees in transactions within their legal powers, transactions, perhaps of which a Court of Equity may disapprove, unless those agents receive and become chargeable with some part of the trust property, or unless they assist with knowledge in a dishonest and fraudulent design on the part of the trustees".[56]

This cautious approach as to the imposition of third party liability found favour with James L.J. who added:

> "I have long thought, and more than once expressed my opinion from this seat, that this Court has in some cases gone to the very verge of justice in making good to *cestuis que trust* the consequences of the breaches of trust of their trustees at the expense of persons perfectly honest, but who have been, in some more or less degree, injudicious. I do not think it is for the good of *cestuis que trust*, or the good of the world, that those cases should be extended".[57]

Trusteeship de son tort

As described, where a third party intermeddles with the business or management of the   **10.15**
trust so as to assume the responsibility for the trust or appear to act as trustee, he may be described as a trustee *de son tort* (meaning by his own wrong). As A.L. Smith L.J. reflected in *Mara v Browne*:

> "Now, what constitutes a trustee *de son tort*? It appears to me if one, not being a trustee and not having authority from a trustee, takes upon himself to intermeddle with trust matters or to do acts characteristic of the office of trustee, he may thereby make himself what is called in law a trustee of his own wrong—*i.e.*, a trustee *de son tort*, or, as it is also termed, a constructive trustee".[58]

---

[55] (1874) 9 Ch. App. 244 at 251.
[56] (1874) 9 Ch. App. 244 at 251.
[57] (1874) 9 Ch. App. 244 at 255.
[58] [1896] 1 Ch. 199 at 209.

The responsibilities of the trustee *de son tort* are the same as those of the express trustee. As Viscount Cave explained in *Taylor v Davies*[59] such persons, "though not originally trustees had taken upon themselves the custody and administration of property on behalf of others; and though sometimes referred to as constructive trustees, they were, in fact, actual trustees, though not so named".[60] More recently, in *Dubai Aluminium Company v Salaam*,[61] Lord Millett sounded his distaste for the terminology employed in the case law. He claimed:

> "we would do better today to describe such persons as de facto trustees. In their relations with the beneficiaries they are treated in every respect as if they had been duly appointed. They are true trustees and are fully subject to fiduciary obligations. Their liability is strict; it does not depend on dishonesty. Like express trustees they could not plead the Limitation Acts as a defence to a claim for breach of trust".[62]

The dishonest assistant in a breach of trust

10.16   A stranger to a trust can be liable in equity for assisting in a breach of trust, even though he has never received trust property. Where the third party assists,[63] in a dishonest manner, in the misapplication of trust property, he may be held personally liable in equity to restore the trust fund or to compensate the beneficiary for the loss occasioned to the trust fund. Originally, termed liability for "knowing assistance" the elements of this personal action were laid down by Lord Selborne L.C. in *Barnes v Addy*.[64] There the husband of a life tenant under a trust was appointed as a sole trustee. He proceeded to misappropriate trust property. The court was called upon to consider whether his solicitors, acting as trustees, were liable to make good the misappropriations. The court decided in the negative. In the course of his speech Lord Selborne L.C. effectively imposed the requirement that a defendant must assist in a dishonest breach of duty. This marked a shift in the development of the law as no such requirement that the breach be dishonest had hitherto been imposed.[65]

In *Royal Brunei Airlines v Tan*,[66] however, the opportunity was taken to re-evaluate the requirements for the imposition of liability on strangers to the trust.[67] Here Royal Brunei Airlines entered into an agency agreement with Borneo Leisure Travel ("BLT") under which BLT were required to sell tickets for the airline and hold the money

---

[59] [1920] A.C. 636.
[60] [1920] A.C. 636 at 651.
[61] [2002] 3 W.L.R. 1913.
[62] [2002] 3 W.L.R. 1913 at 1946.
[63] Note that the third party must assist. Mere presence does not constitute assistance: see *Brinks Ltd v Abu-Saleh (No.3)* (1995) *The Times*, October 23, 1995, where a wife who made a number of trips to Switzerland with her husband in order to keep him company was not deemed to assist in his disposal of the proceeds of a robbery.
[64] (1874) 9 Ch. App. 244.
[65] See *Fyler v Fyler* (1841) 3 Beav. 550.
[66] [1995] 2 A.C. 378.
[67] Lord Nicholls bemoaned the tendency of judges to construe Lord Selborne's formulation, "as though it were a statute" ([1995] 2 A.C. 378 at 386).

received on express trust. With the assistance of Tan, its managing director and principal shareholder, the company paid the money into its current account and, in breach of trust, used the money to cover a range of expenses incurred by BLT. The airline sought to recover the money owed. In light of BLT's insolvency, it moved against Tan on the ground of "knowing assistance" in a breach of trust. Tan was held liable for assisting in a breach of trust.

In a departure from the approach in *Barnes v Addy*, Lord Nicholls acknowledged that, in a case of an honest trustee and a dishonest third party who assists in a breach of trust, dishonesty on the part of the third party was a sufficient basis for third party liability. His dishonesty was sufficient, "notwithstanding that the trustee, although mistaken and in breach of trust, was honest".[68] Lord Nicholls explained:

10.17

"If the liability of the third party is fault-based, what matters is the nature of his fault, not that of the trustee. In this regard dishonesty on the part of the third party would seem to be a sufficient basis for his liability, irrespective of the state of mind of the trustee who is in breach of trust. It is difficult to see why, if the third party dishonestly assisted in a breach, there should be a further prerequisite to his liability, namely that the trustee also must have been acting dishonestly. The alternative view would mean that a dishonest third party is liable if the trustee is dishonest, but if the trustee did not act dishonestly that of itself would excuse a dishonest third party from liability. That would make no sense".[69]

In the course of his analysis, Lord Nicholls rejected outright the possibility that a third party should never be liable. He also dismissed the possibility that liability should be strict so that a third party would be liable even if he did not know or had no reason to suspect that he was dealing with a trustee. In his preferred fault-based approach, Lord Nicholls hailed the criteria of dishonesty as the corner stone of liability for the assistant in a breach of trust. Formulating what is now regarded to be the "accessory liability principle," Lord Nicholls concluded:

"Drawing the threads together, their Lordships' overall conclusion is that dishonesty is a necessary ingredient of accessory liability. It is also a sufficient ingredient. A liability in equity to make good resulting loss attaches to a person who dishonestly procures or assists in a breach of trust or fiduciary obligation. It is not necessary that, in addition, the trustee or fiduciary was acting dishonestly, although this will usually be so where the third party who is assisting him is acting dishonestly. 'Knowingly' is better avoided as a defining ingredient of the principle, and in the context of this principle the *Baden* ... scale of knowledge is best forgotten".[70]

[68] [1995] 2 A.C. 378 at 384.
[69] [1995] 2 A.C. 378 at 385.
[70] [1995] 2 A.C. 378 at 392; see, however, *Jyske Bank (Gibraltar) Ltd v Spjeldnaes* (1999) *The Times*, September 28, where Nourse L.J. considered that the Baden classification, "will sometimes continue to be helpful in identifying different states of knowledge which may or may not result in a finding of dishonesty". Note that the *Baden* scale (discussed below, **10.26**) was influential in the development of the now jettisoned liability for "knowing assistance".

It is, therefore, beyond doubt that a claimant does not need to show that the breach in which the defendant assisted was itself a dishonest breach by the trustee.[71]

The test for dishonesty

10.18   It remains to consider the question of when a defendant will be deemed to be dishonest. In *Royal Brunei Airlines v Tan*, Lord Nicholls put forward his interpretation of the standards of behaviour that will suffice for dishonesty to be found. He claimed:

> "Honesty has a connotation of subjectivity, as distinct from the objectivity of negligence. Honesty, indeed, does have a strong subjective element in that it is a description of a type of conduct assessed in the light of what a person actually knew at the time, as distinct from what a reasonable person would have known or appreciated. Further, honesty and its counterpart dishonesty are mostly concerned with advertent conduct, not inadvertent conduct. Carelessness is not dishonesty. Thus for the most part dishonesty is to be equated with conscious impropriety. However, these subjective characteristics of honesty do not mean that individuals are free to set their own standards of honesty in particular circumstances. The standard of what constitutes honest conduct is not subjective. Honesty is not an optional scale, with higher or lower values according to the moral standards of each individual. If a person knowingly appropriates another's property, he will not escape a finding of dishonesty simply because he sees nothing wrong in such behaviour".[72]

This substantially objective test was reviewed in *Twinsectra Ltd v Yardley*:[73] There, the House of Lords acknowledged that the courts had frequently drawn a distinction between subjective and objective dishonesty. Lord Hutton proceeded to consider three different tests of dishonesty:[74]

- a wholly subjective standard, whereby a person is deemed to be dishonest if he transgresses his own standard of honesty, even if that standard is contrary to that of the reasonable and honest person. Otherwise referred to as the "Robin Hood test," this approach has not found favour with the courts. By way of example, Sir Christopher Slade stated in *Walker v Stones*, "A person may in some cases act dishonestly, according to the ordinary use of language, even though he genuinely believes that his action is morally justified. The penniless thief, for example, who picks the pocket of the multi-millionaire is dishonest even though he genuinely considers the theft is morally justified as a fair redistribution of wealth and that he is not therefore being dishonest"[75];

[71] *Twinsectra Ltd v Yardley* [2002] 2 All E.R. 377.
[72] [1995] 2 A.C. 378 at 389.
[73] [2002] 2 All E.R. 377.
[74] [2002] 2 All E.R. 377 at 384.
[75] [2000] 4 All E.R. 412 at 444.

- a purely objective standard whereby a person acts dishonestly if his conduct is dishonest by the ordinary standards of the reasonable and honest person, even if he does not realise this; or

- a combined test of objective and subjective elements which requires that the defendant's conduct is dishonest by the ordinary standards of the reasonable and honest person and that the defendant himself realises that by those standards his conduct is dishonest.

The majority of the House of Lords agreed that the combined test applied. To be **10.19** liable as an accessory to a breach of trust, an individual must act dishonestly by the ordinary standards of reasonable and honest people and also be aware that by those standards he was acting dishonestly. This test requires knowledge by the defendant that honest people would regard his conduct as dishonest. He should not escape a finding of dishonesty if he adopts his own threshold and does not regard as dishonest that which he knows would offend the standards of honest and reasonable people. Lord Hutton identified a pragmatic consideration in support of the view that for liability as an accessory to arise the defendant must himself appreciate that his actions were dishonest by the standards of honest and reasonable people. He claimed:

"A finding by a judge that a defendant has been dishonest is a grave finding, and it is particularly grave against a professional man, such as a solicitor. Notwithstanding that the issue arises in equity law and not in a criminal context, I think that it would be less than just for the law to permit a finding that a defendant had been 'dishonest' in assisting in a breach of trust where he knew of the facts which created the trust and its breach but had not been aware that what he was doing would be regarded by honest men as being dishonest".[76]

Despite the logical appeal of Lord Hutton's argument, it is the alternative vision of Lord Millett (dissenting) which is to be preferred. Lord Millett considered that the key question was not whether Lord Nicholls used the word "dishonesty" in a subjective or objective sense in *Royal Brunei Airlines v Tan*. Instead the issue was whether a claimant should be required to establish that an accessory to a breach of trust had a dishonest state of mind or whether it should be sufficient to establish that he acted with the requisite knowledge, i.e. so that his conduct was objectively dishonest. Although Lord Millett acknowledged that the House was free to resolve the question either way, he opted for a substantially objective approach. He explained:

"In my opinion Lord Nicholls was adopting an objective standard of dishonesty by which the defendant is expected to attain the standard which would be observed by an honest person placed in similar circumstances. Account must be taken of subjective considerations such as the defendant's experience and intelligence and his actual state of knowledge at the relevant time. But it is not necessary that he should actually have appreciated that he was acting dishonestly; it is sufficient that he was".[77]

---

[76] [2002] 2 All E.R. 377 at 387.
[77] [2002] 2 All E.R. 377 at 408.

Accordingly, Lord Millett took the view that Lord Nicholls employed an essentially objective test wherein there was scope to look at very limited subjective factors. In his view, it was not necessary that the defendant realise that he acted dishonestly. The defendant did not need to know the details of the trust. It was sufficient that the defendant recognise that the money was not at the free disposal of the person to whom he lent assistance. Three reasons were put forward by Lord Millett in support of this conclusion.

10.20   First, he observed that consciousness of wrongdoing is an aspect of mens rea and, therefore, an appropriate condition of criminal liability.[78] Lord Millett did not view mens rea as an appropriate condition of civil liability, which generally results from negligent or intentional conduct. He claimed, "For the purpose of civil liability, it should not be necessary that the defendant realised that his conduct was dishonest; it should be sufficient that it constituted intentional wrongdoing".[79]

Secondly, "The objective test is in accordance with Lord Selborne's statement in *Barnes v Addy* ... and traditional doctrine. This taught that a person who knowingly participates in the misdirection of money is liable to compensate the injured party. While negligence is not a sufficient condition of liability, intentional wrongdoing is. Such conduct is culpable and falls below the objective standards of honesty adopted by ordinary people".[80]

10.21   Finally, Lord Millett discussed the claim for "knowing assistance" as the equitable counterpart of the economic torts. He explained, "These are intentional torts; negligence is not sufficient and dishonesty is not necessary. Liability depends on knowledge. A requirement of subjective dishonesty introduces an unnecessary and unjustified distinction between the elements of the equitable claim and those of the tort of wrongful interference with the performance of a contract".[81]

Twinsectra considered

10.22   In *Barlow Clowes International Ltd (in liquidation) v Eurotrust International Ltd*[82] the Privy Council took the opportunity to reflect on developments in *Twinsectra*, particular as regards the approach of Lord Hutton therein to the dishonesty of the assistant. Barlow Clowes International Ltd had, in the mid-1980s, operated a fraudulent off-shore investment scheme in which high returns were offered for the skilled investment of funds in UK gilt-edged securities. The scheme collapsed in 1998 and Mr Clowes was duly imprisoned. Some of the money received from investors had been diverted through off-shore bank accounts held by a company providing off-shore services. The principal director of the company (Eurotrust International Ltd) faced an action by Barlow Clowes (in liquidation) for dishonest assistance in the misappropriation of the investment monies.

---

[78] In *R. v Ghosh* [1982] Q.B. 1053, Lord Lane C.J. held in the context of theft that dishonesty requires that the defendant himself must realise that what he is doing is dishonest by the ordinary standards of reasonable and honest people.

[79] [2002] 2 All E.R. 377 at 410.

[80] [2002] 2 All E.R. 377 at 410.

[81] [2002] 2 All E.R. 377 at 410.

[82] [2006] 1 W.L.R. 1476.

At first instance, the defendants were found liable for dishonest assistance in the misappropriation of the investment funds. The judge had proceeded on the basis that liability for dishonest assistance required a dishonest state of mind on the part of the assistant to a breach of trust. The judge found that although a dishonest state of mind was a subjective mental state, the standard by which the law assessed whether it was dishonest was objective and was to be determined by ordinary standards. In relation to one director, Mr Henwood, the judge pointed to this director's strong suspicion that the funds passing through his hands were moneys that Barlow Clowes had received from members of the public who thought that they were investing in gilt-edged securities. If those suspicions were accurate, it followed that no honest person could have assisted in the disposal of the moneys. In addition, he had consciously decided not to make inquiries so as to avoid the risk of discovering the truth of his suspicions. Accordingly, he was deemed to have had a dishonest state of mind. In the Court of Appeal, Mr Henwood succeeded on the basis that there was no evidence to show that he had acted as a dishonest assistant. Although he was deemed to be dishonest by objective standards, there was no evidence at trial as to his subjective state of mind.[83] Barlow Clowes appealed.

In the Privy Council, Lord Hoffmann focused on the views of Lord Hutton in *Twinsectra* upon which Mr Henwood had relied. There, Lord Hutton had spoken of the injustice in finding dishonesty where the defendant: **10.23**

> "had not been aware that what he was doing would be regarded by honest men as being dishonest ... although he should not escape a finding of dishonesty because he sets his own standards of honesty and does not regard as dishonest what he knows would offend the normally accepted standards of honest conduct".[84]

Mr Henwood submitted that he could not be said to be consciously dishonest unless he had been aware that his actions would be dishonest by ordinary standards. The matter to be determined was, therefore, the extent to which an examination of the defendant's views about standards of honesty was required. Lord Hoffmann accepted that there was an element of ambiguity in Lord Hutton's remarks, "which may have encouraged a belief, expressed in some academic writing, that the *Twinsectra* case had departed from the law as previously understood and invited inquiry not merely into the defendant's mental state about the nature of the transaction in which he was participating but also into his views about generally acceptable standards of honesty".[85] Nonetheless, the Privy Council declined to accept that this is what Lord Hutton meant. As Lord Hoffmann explained, "the reference to 'what he knows would offend normally accepted

[83] The judge found that Mr Henwood may well have lived by different standards and seen nothing wrong in what he was doing, in that he had an, "exaggerated notion of dutiful service to clients, which produced a warped moral approach that it was not improper to treat carrying out clients' instructions as being all important".
[84] *Twinsectra Ltd v Yardley* [2002] 2 All E.R. 377 at 387.
[85] [2006] 1 W.L.R. 1476 at 1481.

standards of honest conduct' meant only that his knowledge of the transaction had to be such as to render his participation contrary to normally acceptable standards of honest conduct. It did not require that he should have had reflections about what those normally acceptable standards were".[86] Ruling that the judge's findings of fact should not have been set aside, Lord Hoffmann considered that the appellate court had erred in two respects. First, Mr Henwood's clear suspicions that the moneys were misappropriated in breach of trust were sufficient. It was not necessary that he conclude that the disposals were of money in breach of trust. Secondly, it was "quite unreal"[87] to suppose that Mr Henwood needed to know all the details to which the court referred before he had grounds to suspect that the moneys were misappropriated. The money, "was either held on trust for the investors or else belonged to the company and was subject to fiduciary duties on the part of the directors. In either case, Mr Clowes ..., could not have been entitled to make free with it".[88]

Although it had been suggested in previous case law that a person cannot be liable for dishonest assistance in a breach of trust unless he knows of the existence of the trust or at least the facts giving rise to the trust,[89] the Privy Council did not agree. Citing *Twinsectra Ltd v Yardley*, Lord Hoffmann observed, "Someone can know, and can certainly suspect, that he is assisting in a misappropriation of money without knowing that the money is held on trust or what a trust means".[90]

Barlow Clowes considered

10.24   Although *Twinsectra* clearly established an approach based on both objective and subjective tests, the *Barlow Clowes* approach appears to be essentially objective. In other words, it was more than a mere refinement of an ambiguity in the reasoning of the House of Lords. Unfortunately, however, recent case law has ostensibly failed to clarify the relationship between these approaches.[91] Most notably, *Barlow Clowes International Ltd (in liquidation) v Eurotrust International Ltd* was applied in *Abou-Rahmah v Abacha* where the Court of Appeal had its first opportunity to consider this increasingly complex body of case law.[92] It involved an action by the claimants against a Nigerian registered bank for dishonest assistance in a fraudulent scheme.

At first instance,[93] Treacy J. could find no evidence that the defendant was aware of a situation giving rise to a fiduciary duty or that any such duty had been breached. There was nothing to indicate that the funds passing through the third party's account were

---

[86] [2006] 1 W.L.R. 1476 at 1481; As T.M. Yeo argues in (2006) 122 L.Q.R. 171 at p.172, this clarification is unconvincing: "It is difficult to understand the role of a combined test if the two limbs are testing for the same thing and one limb does not make sense without the other. It is also difficult to see how the question whether a person has realised that he has breached ordinary standards of honest behaviour can be answered without considering his view on what those standards are".
[87] [2006] 1 W.L.R. 1476 at 1483.
[88] [2006] 1 W.L.R. 1476 at 1483.
[89] *Brinks Ltd v Abu-Saleh (No.3)* [1996] C.L.C. 133 at 151 per Rimer J.
[90] [2006] 1 W.L.R. 1476 at 1484.
[91] See, for example, *Statek Corp v Alford* [2008] EWHC 32 (Ch) where an objective approach to dishonesty was applied without question.
[92] [2007] 1 Lloyd's Rep 115.
[93] [2006] 1 Lloyd's Rep 484.

the misappropriated funds or that they had been obtained by fraud. Accordingly, it was felt that no claim for dishonest assistance was sustainable. Treacy J. appeared, nonetheless, to endorse the *Barlow Clowes* "refinement" that no subjective appreciation that conduct is dishonest by normally acceptable standards is required.

In the Court of Appeal, Arden L.J. upheld the findings of the trial judge. She met **10.25** head on the widely held view that, *Twinsectra* required both an objective and subjective test of dishonesty and, that in applying the subjective element of the test, this, "would mean that the defendant would not be guilty of dishonesty unless he was conscious that the transaction fell below normally acceptable standards of conduct".[94] She advanced the view that the Privy Council, in the *Barlow Clowes* case, regarded this an incorrect reading of the *Twinsectra* decision: "It is not a requirement of the standard of dishonesty that the defendant should be conscious of his wrongdoing".[95] As to the extent that *Barlow Clowes* departs from *Twinsectra*, she emphasised that the approach in *Twinsectra* had not been jettisoned. As Arden L.J. explained, the Privy Council merely, "gave guidance as to the proper interpretation to be placed on it as a matter of English law".[96]

For those who disliked the combined test in *Twinsectra*, this readiness to promote the Privy Council interpretation will be a welcome development. Unfortunately, however, there is much more caution in the approach of both Rix and Pill L.JJ. in the *Abou-Rahaman* decision. As to Rix L.J., his uncertainty and reticence is palpable:

"I would merely hazard this analysis. It would seem that a claimant in this area needs to show three things: first, that a defendant has the requisite knowledge; secondly, that, given that knowledge, the defendant acts in a way which is contrary to normally acceptable standards of honest conduct (the objective test of honesty or dishonesty); and thirdly, possibly, that the defendant must in some sense be dishonest himself (a subjective test of dishonesty which might, on analysis, add little or nothing to knowledge of the facts which, objectively, would make his conduct dishonest)".[97]

Pill L.J., moreover, was content to, "fully and respectfully acknowledge the value of *Barlow Clowes* in its explanation of *Twinsectra*", but he did not want to enter the debate.[98]

In short, there is still much uncertainty. It should not be long before the courts look again at what Arden L.J. (somewhat optimistically) described as, "a consistent corpus of law"[99] which stems from *Royal Brunei* to the present day.

---

[94] [2006] 1 Lloyd's Rep 115 at [65].
[95] [2006] 1 Lloyd's Rep 115 at [65].
[96] [2006] 1 Lloyd's Rep 115 at [68].
[97] [2007] 1 Lloyd's Rep 115 at [16].
[98] "...the implications are in my view best considered in a case in which a real issue arises on its impact", [2007] 1 Lloyd's Rep 115 at [16]; see also the view of Rix L.J. at [23] that he did not "need to enter into that controversy for the purposes of this appeal".
[99] [2006] 1 Lloyd's Rep 115 at [68].

Knowing receipt of trust property

10.26 Personal liability to account on the basis of knowing receipt of trust property applies to strangers to the trust who receive trust property or its traceable proceeds[1] in the knowledge that the property has been misapplied or transferred in breach of trust. It is a pre-condition of liability that there has been a breach of trust. Accordingly, where property is transferred to a stranger in an authorised manner or within the terms of the trust there can be no liability for knowing receipt. In addition, the success of the claim does not depend on the recipient's continued possession of the property. As Lawrence Collins J. explained, "The main purpose of seeking to establish constructive trust liability on the basis of knowing receipt is when the alleged constructive trustee has disposed of the property so that a personal remedy for its value is sought against him".[3] The accepted formulation of the requirements for liability to be imposed in the context of knowing receipt are those identified by Hoffmann L.J. in *El Ajou v Dollar Land Holdings*.[4] Namely, there must be:

- a disposal of assets in breach of trust or fiduciary duty;

- the receipt by the defendant of assets which are traceable as representing the assets of the claimant; and

- knowledge on the part of the defendant that the assets he received are traceable to a breach of fiduciary duty.

It is for the claimant to demonstrate, therefore, that the defendant received trust property[5] and that he knew of some breach of trust or fiduciary duty. Whereas the concept of receipt is well understood, the requisite knowledge of the defendant is a markedly more complex question. Unlike liability for dishonest assistance, dishonesty is not a pre-requisite. As Vinelott J. emphasised in *Eagle Trust Plc v SBC Securities Ltd*, "it is not necessary, and never has been necessary, to show that the defendant was in any sense a participator in a fraud".[6]

As to what constitutes knowledge, in *Baden v Societe Generale pour Favoriser le Developpement du Commerce et de l'Industrie en France SA*[7] Peter Gibson J. identified five categories:

---

[1] In accordance with the tracing rules discussed in detail in Ch.17. Note that as Megarry V.C. highlighted in *Re Montagu's Settlement* [1987] Ch. 264 at 277, "The equitable doctrine of tracing and the imposition of a constructive trust by reason of the knowing receipt of trust property are governed by different rules and must be kept distinct. Tracing is primarily a means of determining the rights of property, whereas the imposition of a constructive trust creates personal obligations that go beyond mere property rights".

[2] A proprietary remedy may be available where the recipient retains trust property or its proceeds requiring the return of the specific property or its proceeds: see further, Ch.17.

[3] *Re Loftus* [2005] EWHC 406 (Ch) at [172].

[4] [1994] 2 All E.R. 685 at 700; see also, *Sinclair Investment Holdings SA v Cushnie* [2004] EWHC 3055 (Ch).

[5] Receipt means, "receipt by one person from another of assets". For example, mere entry into a binding contract cannot constitute a "receipt" of assets: see *Criterion Properties Plc v Stratford UK Properties LLC* [2004] UKHL 28 at [27] per Lord Nicholls.

[6] [1992] 4 All E.R. 488 at 501.

[7] [1983] BCLC 325 at 407.

(i)   actual knowledge;

(ii) wilfully shutting one's eyes to the obvious;[8]

(iii) wilfully and recklessly failing to make such inquiries as an honest and reasonable man would make;

(iv) knowledge of circumstances which would indicate the facts to an honest and
reasonable man; and

(v)   knowledge of circumstances which would put an honest and reasonable man
on inquiry.

Categories (ii) and (iii) are generally considered to be types of actual knowledge or
similar, where the defendant's behaviour exhibits a level of wilfulness or recklessness.
Categories (iv) and (v) are not governed by similar words and appear to be aligned
more clearly with mere carelessness or negligence. Unfortunately, as will become clear,
there is little consensus in the case law as to the role and utility of the *Baden* categories.
The utter lack of coherence evident in much of the case law has fuelled debate as to the
appropriateness of a strict liability claim to which the recipient could raise a defence of
change of position.[9]

In *Re Montagu's Settlement Trusts*,[10] Megarry V.C. qualified the scope of the *Baden*   **10.27**
categories of knowledge to deny a claim of knowing receipt on difficult facts. Particular
chattels had been transferred to a beneficiary, the 10th Duke of Manchester, in breach
of trust. During his lifetime the 10th Duke did as he pleased with the property and some
of the property was disposed of. After his death, the 11th Duke argued that the trustees
had been in breach of trust in failing to make an appropriate inventory of the chattels
and in transferring the property to the 10th Duke. He further alleged that in taking
possession of, and in dealing with the items delivered to him in the knowledge that the
items were subject the trusts of the settlement, the 10th Duke held the property as a
constructive trustee. Megarry V.C. made explicit reference to the inherent difficulties of
grappling with judicial precedent. He claimed that he would:

> "make no attempt to reconcile all the authorities and *dicta*, for such a task is
> beyond me; and in this I suspect I am not alone. Some of the difficulty seems to
> arise from judgments that have been given without all the relevant authorities
> having been put before the judges. All I need do is to find a path through the wood
> that will suffice for the determination of the case before me, and to assist those who
> have to read this judgment".[11]

By way of a starting point, Megarry V.C. deemed the crucial question to be whether the
conscience of the recipient is sufficiently affected to justify the imposition of a

---

[8] Otherwise termed "Nelsonian knowledge".
[9] See further, **10.31**.
[10] [1987] Ch. 264.
[11] [1987] Ch. 264 at 285.

constructive trust.[12] He emphasised the distinction between knowledge and notice in this context:

> "It should also be remembered that the doctrines of purchaser without notice and constructive trusts are concerned with matters which differ in important respects. The former is concerned with the question whether a person takes property subject to or free from some equity. The latter is concerned with whether or not a person is to have imposed upon him the personal burdens and obligations of trusteeship. I do not see why one of the touchstones for determining the burdens on property should be the same as that for deciding whether to impose a personal obligation on a man. The cold calculus of constructive and imputed notice does not seem to me to be an appropriate instrument for deciding whether a man's conscience is sufficiently affected for it to be right to bind him by the obligations of a constructive trustee".[13]

Cautioning against "a fertile source of confusion",[14] he proffered that the knowledge of the recipient was paramount and, accordingly, the word "notice" should be avoided in such cases. Megarry V.C. qualified "knowledge" as including not only actual knowledge, but knowledge of types (ii) and (iii) in the *Baden* case. This includes actual knowledge that would have been acquired but for shutting one's eyes to the obvious, or the wilful and reckless failure to make such inquiries as a reasonable and honest man would make. In both types, he identified a want of probity that would justify the imposition of the constructive trust. As to whether knowledge of the *Baden* types (iv) and (v) would suffice, Megarry V.C. felt it to be at best doubtful. In his view, he could not see that the carelessness involved would normally amount to a want of probity.

Imputed knowledge

10.28 On the question of a general doctrine of "imputed knowledge" that corresponds to "imputed notice", Megarry V.C. felt that any doctrine would not apply so as to fix the beneficiary with the knowledge of his solicitor if the beneficiary has not employed the solicitor to investigate his right to receive the property and has done nothing else that can be treated as accepting that the solicitor's knowledge should be treated as his own.[15] It followed that any such doctrine, "should be distinguished from the process whereby,

---

[12] As Lawrence Collins J. put it in *NABB Brothers Limited v Lloyds Bank International (Guernsey) Limited* [2005] EWHC 405 (Ch) at [71], "the recipient's state of knowledge must be such as to make it unconscionable for the recipient to retain the benefit of the receipt"; see also, *Bank of Credit and Commerce International (Overseas) Ltd v Akindele* [2001] Ch. 437 at 455.

[13] [1987] Ch. 264 at 272.

[14] [1987] Ch. 264 at 277.

[15] As Megarry V.C. illustrated, "I cannot see why equity should say to that donee or beneficiary, 'True, your solicitor, who had not been employed to investigate title, told you that the property was yours, and you believed him; but he was wrong, and as he had actual knowledge that the property was subject to a trust, you too had actual knowledge of that trust. This bound your conscience, and therefore you took the property as a constructive trustee'. This would in no way be equity as I know it" ([1987] Ch. 264 at 284).

under the name 'imputed knowledge', a company is treated as having the knowledge that its directors and secretary have".[16]

Forgotten knowledge

Megarry V.C. also considered the issue of forgotten knowledge to hold that a person is not to be taken to have knowledge of a fact that he once knew but has genuinely forgotten. He claimed, "I suppose that there may be some remarkable beings for whom once known is never forgotten; but apart from them, the generality of mankind probably forgets far more than is remembered".[17] On this basis the test to be applied is whether the knowledge continues to operate on that person's mind at the time in question. The clear implication of the decision in *Re Montagu's Settlement Trusts* is that, in order to establish liability in knowing receipt, the recipient must have actual knowledge (or its equivalent) that the assets received are traceable to a breach of trust or fiduciary duty. For these purposes actual knowledge is extended to include *Baden* types (ii) and (iii), namely, actual knowledge that would have been acquired but for shutting one's eyes to the obvious or wilfully and recklessly failing to make such enquiries as a reasonable and honest man would make. As Megarry V.C. admitted, "in such cases there is a want of probity which justifies imposing a constructive trust".[18]

10.29

Towards a single test of knowledge?

In *Bank of Credit and Commerce International (Overseas) Limited v Akindele*,[19] Nourse L.J. embarked on a thorough review of the relevant authorities. He noted the divergence of opinion on the degree of knowledge necessary to found recipient liability and acknowledged that, of the many authorities which suggested that mere constructive knowledge would suffice,[20] the question had not been considered in any great depth. He acknowledged the judgment of Megarry V.C., as a, "seminal judgment, characteristically penetrative in its treatment of authority and, in the best sense, argumentative".[21] Nevertheless, as to the *Baden* scale of knowledge, Nourse L.J. concluded that there was no need for such a categorisation at all.[22] In the view of Nourse L.J., "All that is necessary is that the recipient's state of knowledge should be such as to make it unconscionable for him to retain the benefit of the receipt".[23] He continued:

10.30

[16] [1987] Ch. 264 at 285.
[17] [1987] Ch. 264 at 284.
[18] [1987] Ch. 264 at 285.
[19] [2001] Ch. 437 at 455.
[20] For example, *Belmont Finance Corp v Williams Furniture Ltd (No.2)* [1980] 1 All E.R. 393; *Polly Peck International Plc v Nadir (No.2)* [1992] 4 All E.R. 769.
[21] [2001] Ch. 437 at 455.
[22] As Nourse L.J. explained [2001] Ch. 437 at 455, "although my own view is that the categorisation is often helpful in identifying different states of knowledge which may or may not result in a finding of dishonesty for the purposes of knowing assistance, I have grave doubts about its utility in cases of knowing receipt."
[23] [2001] Ch. 437.

"I have come to the view that, just as there is now a single test of dishonesty for knowing assistance, so ought there to be a single test of knowledge for knowing receipt. The recipient's state of knowledge must be such as to make it unconscionable for him to retain the benefit of the receipt. A test in that form, though it cannot, any more than any other, avoid difficulties of application, ought to avoid those of definition and allocation to which the previous categorisations have led. Moreover, it should better enable the courts to give commonsense decisions in the commercial context in which claims in knowing receipt are now frequently made".[24]

It is unfortunate that Nourse L.J. did not subject his new test of unconscionability to more rigorous examination. It is not clear, for example, exactly when the recipient's knowledge will be such that he cannot in conscience retain the benefit of his receipt. Although it cannot be denied that such a test caters for maximum flexibility against diverse factual circumstances, recourse to a test of unconscionability lacks the relative certainty provided by the particular test of dishonesty as advanced in *Twinsectra* for cases of dishonest assistance.[25] Although its modern day utility is much in dispute, the *Baden* categorisation of knowledge provides, at least, a scale against which receipt can be measured and an important reference point in evaluating past cases. In addition, it is as yet unclear how the relative concepts of dishonesty and unconscionability are to be distinguished in this important context. It is to be acknowledged that in *Royal Brunei*, Lord Nicholls explicitly discounted the usefulness of a test based on unconscionability. There he concluded:

"Unconscionable is a word of immediate appeal to an equity lawyer. Equity is rooted historically in the concept of the Lord Chancellor, as the keeper of the Royal Conscience, concerning himself with conduct which was contrary to good conscience. It must be recognised, however, that unconscionable is not a word in everyday use by non-lawyers. If it is to be used in this context, and if it is to be the touchstone for liability as an accessory, it is essential to be clear on what, in this context, unconscionable means. If unconscionable means no more than dishonesty, then dishonesty is the preferable label. If unconscionable means something different, it must be said that it is not clear what that something different is. Either way, therefore, the term is better avoided in this context".[26]

10.31   By way of a footnote to his judgment, Nourse L.J. contributed to the argument that the recipient of misapplied trust property should be strictly liable to a claim in unjust enrichment subject to the change of position defence. As will be discussed, such arguments accord with recent developments in the law of remedies for breach of trust.[27] Not least, the House of Lords has recognised the legitimacy of the defence of change of

---

[24] [2001] Ch. 437 at 455.
[25] [2002] 2 All E.R. 377.
[26] [1995] 2 A.C. 378 at 392.
[27] See Ch.17.

position to the personal action at common law for money had and received.[28] Nourse L.J. cited the extra-judicial view of Lord Nicholls[29] that:

"In this respect equity should now follow the law. Restitutionary liability, applicable regardless of fault but subject to a defence of change of position, would be a better-tailored response to the underlying mischief of misapplied property than personal liability which is exclusively fault-based. Personal liability would flow from having received the property of another, from having been unjustly enriched at the expense of another. It would be triggered by the mere fact of receipt, thus recognising the endurance of property rights. But fairness would be ensured by the need to identify a gain, and by making change of position available as a defence in suitable cases when, for instance, the recipient had changed his position in reliance on the receipt".[30]

It is noteworthy that Nourse L.J. provided a committed response which doubted the wisdom and workability of restitutionary liability.[31] In doing so, he both accepted and underlined the lack of coherence in the law as it currently stands, but he emphasised that the law has yet to develop in the fashion outlined. He observed:

"We must continue to do our best with the accepted formulation of the liability in knowing receipt, seeking to simplify and improve it where we may. While in general it may be possible to sympathise with a tendency to subsume a further part of our law of restitution under the principles of unjust enrichment, I beg leave to doubt whether strict liability coupled with a change of position defence would be preferable to fault-based liability in many commercial transactions, for example where, as here, the receipt is of a company's funds which have been misapplied by its directors. Without having heard argument it is unwise to be dogmatic, but in such a case it would appear to be commercially unworkable ... that, simply on proof of an internal misapplication of the company's funds, the burden should shift to the recipient to defend the receipt either by a change of position or perhaps in some other way. Moreover, if the circumstances of the receipt are such as to make it unconscionable for the recipient to retain the benefit of it, there is an obvious difficulty in saying that it is equitable for a change of position to afford him a defence".[32]

10.32 It is currently accepted that the approach in *Akindele* represents the current law. Accordingly, "liability for 'knowing receipt' depends on the defendant having sufficient knowledge of the circumstances of the payment to make it 'unconscionable' for him to

---

[28] *Lipkin Gorman v Karpnale Ltd* [1991] 2 A.C. 548.
[29] See "Knowing Receipt: The Need for a New Landmark" in Cornish, Nolan, O'Sullivan and Virgo (eds) *Restitution Past, Present and Future* (Oxford, Hart Publishing, 1998) at p.238.
[30] Cited at [2001] Ch. 437 at 456. See further *Criterion Properties Plc v Stratford UK Properties LLC* [2004] 1 W.L.R. 1846.
[31] For a rejection of the restitutionary analysis by the High Court of Australia: see *Farah Constructions Pty Ltd v Say-Dee Ltd* [2007] HCA 22.
[32] [2001] Ch. 437 at 456.

retain the benefit or pay it away for his own purposes".[33] This test, of course, is extremely flexible but it provides no clarity as to the approach of future courts. Again, in this context, it is inevitable that the House of Lords will review the ambit of recipient liability and, perhaps, that moment will arrive soon.[34] Until then, as noted by Parker and Mellows, "the test is going to require virtually every claim to impose liability for knowing receipt to be litigated, something which is far from an ideal state of affairs for potential litigants".[35]

UNCONSCIONABILITY GENERALLY

10.33   The preceding sections have considered the constructive trust in the context of, first, unauthorised fiduciary gains and, secondly, third party liability in cases of breach of trust. A further context in which constructive trusts arise concerns general unconscionable behaviour. This interventionist jurisdiction is one, "by which a court of Equity, proceeding on the ground of fraud, converts the party who has committed it into a trustee for the party who is injured by that fraud".[36] As will be demonstrated, the courts have proved willing to apply constructive trust principles to a range of cases where the defendant acquires property belonging to another by unconscionable means. Further, the principle that a criminal should not benefit from his crime not only underpins the law as to unlawful killing (discussed below), but also as to property obtained as a result of fraud.[37]

Acquisition of property by killing

10.34   It is a statement of general principle that a person should not benefit from the commission of a criminal act. A specific manifestation of this general principle is to be found in the forfeiture rule, i.e. a rule of public policy that precludes a person who has unlawfully killed another from acquiring a benefit as a consequence of the killing. As Sir Samuel Evans P. stated *In the Estate of Crippen*, "It is clear that the law is, that no person can obtain, or enforce, any rights resulting to him from his own crime; neither can his representative, claiming under him, obtain or enforce any such rights. The human mind revolts at the very idea that any other doctrine could be possible in our system of jurisprudence".[38] Accordingly, when Mr Crippen murdered his wife and inherited her property, he could not leave that property by will to a legatee. As Mr

---

[33] *Charter Plc v City Index Ltd* [2008] 2 W.L.R. 950 at [8]. See also *Hollis v Rolfe* [2008] EWHC 1747 (Ch) at [172].
[34] See S. Gardner, "Moment of Truth for Knowing Receipt?" (2009) 125 L.Q.R. 20, noting that leave to appeal has been granted in *Charter Plc v City Index Ltd* litigation.
[35] Parker & Mellows, p.436.
[36] *McCormick v Grogan* (1869) L.R. 4 HL 82 at 97 per Lord Westbury.
[37] As Lord Browne-Wilkinson states obiter in *Westdeutsche Landesbank Girozentrale v Islington LBC* [1996] A.C. 669 at 716, "when property is obtained by fraud equity imposes a constructive trust on the recipient: the property is recoverable and traceable in equity".
[38] [1911] P. 108 at 112.

Crippen was not allowed to benefit by his crime, his legatee was also unable to benefit. In the memorable words of Hamilton L.J., "A man shall not slay his benefactor and thereby take his bounty".[39]

In the cases where legal title has passed to the killer, forfeiture is enforced through the mechanism of the constructive trust. The application of the forfeiture rule may arise, for example, in the context of co-ownership. It is the essence of a joint tenancy that each co-owner individually owns nothing, but that together they are wholly entitled to the entirety of the property. The right of survivorship entails that on the death of a joint tenant the co-owned estate is said to "survive" to the remaining joint tenants. The last surviving joint tenant becomes the sole owner of the once co-owned property. The operation of the survivorship principle exposes the possibility that the death of a joint tenant will bestow a practical financial benefit upon the remaining co-owner(s) in whom, in consequence, entitlement to the whole of the property remains.[40] The killing of one co-owner by the other is, thus, sufficient to invite an equitable response. The prevailing understanding is that, through the imposition of a constructive trust, the killer holds legal title in the co-owned property on trust for himself and the victim's estate in equal shares.

Some limited statutory relief is provided by the Forfeiture Act 1982. The Act applies **10.35** to cases of unlawful killing other than murder and permits the court to grant relief from forfeiture where the justice of the case requires. As Mummery L.J. explained in *Dunbar v Plant*, "The provision requires that the judge should look at the case in the round, pay regard to all the material circumstances, including the conduct of the offender and the deceased, and then ask whether 'the justice of the case requires' a modification of the effect of the forfeiture rule".[41] The court may grant relief in respect of all or merely part of the property.

Absence of statutory formalities

Equity will not permit a statute to be used as an instrument of fraud.[42] *Bannister v* **10.36** *Bannister*[43] provides a simple illustration. X conveyed legal title to two cottages to her brother-in-law for less than the market price. She did so on the basis of his oral promise that she could reside in one of the cottages rent free for the remainder of her life. No mention of the promise was contained in the conveyance. When the brother-in-law sought to evict X from her home, the Court of Appeal held that legal title was held on constructive trust to give effect to X's life interest. Scott L.J. identified that the constructive trust, "is raised against a person who insists on the absolute character of a conveyance to himself for the purpose of defeating a beneficial interest, which, according to the true bargain, was to belong to another".[44] It is not open to the defendant in such cases to argue the absence of written evidence of the bargain between the parties. As Scott L.J. added, "The fraud which brings the principle into play arises

---

[39] *In the Estate of Hall* [1914] P. 1 at 7 per Hamilton L.J.
[40] See further, T. Youdan "Acquisition of Property by Killing" (1973) 89 L.Q.R. 235.
[41] [1998] Ch. 412 at 427.
[42] *Rochefoucauld v Boustead* [1897] 1 Ch. 196.
[43] [1948] 2 All E.R. 133.
[44] [1948] 2 All E.R. 133 at 136.

as soon as the absolute character of the conveyance is set up for the purpose of defeating the beneficial interest, which, according to the true bargain, was to belong to another".[45]

Property acquired expressly subject to personal rights

10.37   In delimited circumstances, and provided his conscience is affected, a constructive trust can arise to bind the purchaser of property who agrees to take subject to a pre-existing interest. In *Binions v Evans*,[46] Mr Evans was employed by Tredegar Estate and was permitted to live rent free in a cottage owned by his employer. On his death, he left a wife aged 73. Three years later the trustees of the estate entered into an agreement with Mrs Evans that she could continue to live in the cottage for the remainder of her life as a tenant at will rent free. In return, she agreed to keep the cottage in good repair. Subsequently, the Estate sold the cottage to Mr and Mrs Binions expressly subject to the interest held by Mrs Evans. As a consequence, a reduced price was paid for the cottage. The Binions sought to evict Mrs Evans but this attempt failed. In the Court of Appeal, Lord Denning M.R. argued that the Binions took the property subject to a constructive trust in favour of Mrs Evans.[47] In the course of his judgment, he put forward the broad proposition that, "Whenever the owner sells the land to a purchaser, and at the same time stipulates that he shall take it 'subject to' a contractual licence, I think it plain that a court of equity will impose on the purchaser a constructive trust in favour of the beneficiary ... It would be utterly inequitable that the purchaser should be able to turn out the beneficiary".[48] In *Ashburn Anstalt v Arnold*,[49] Fox L.J. admitted the legitimacy of this application of the doctrine of constructive trusts, but clarified the narrow principles on which it is operative. The Estate had sold the cottage to the Binions expressly subject to the pre-existing agreement with Mrs Evans and for which a lower purchase price was accepted. It was, therefore, "a proper inference that on the sale to the plaintiffs, the intention of the estate and the plaintiffs was that the plaintiffs should give effect to the tenancy agreement".[50] The payment of the lower price was significant. The fact that land is expressed to be conveyed subject to a contract is not, of itself, sufficient to give rise to a constructive trust.[51] As Fox L.J. emphasised, "The court will not impose a constructive trust unless it is satisfied that the conscience of the estate owner is affected".[52]

---

[45] [1948] 2 All E.R. 133 at 136.
[46] [1972] Ch. 359.
[47] Lord Denning M.R. sought also to argue that the contractual licence to occupy was an equitable interest in land; Megaw and Stephenson L.J. decided the case on the ground that the defendant was a tenant for life under the Settled Land Act 1925.
[48] [1972] Ch. 359 at 366.
[49] [1989] Ch. 1.
[50] [1989] Ch. 1 at 23.
[51] This is "at least consistent with an intention to protect the grantor against claims by the grantee as an intention to impose an obligation on the grantee" ([1989] Ch. 1 at 26 per Fox L.J.).
[52] [1989] Ch. 1 at 25.

Property acquired by joint venture

Equity will impose a constructive trust on property acquired by X in furtherance of an **10.38**
understanding with Y that, if Y refrains from entering the market, Y will be granted an
interest in the property. The equity arises notwithstanding that their understanding falls
short of creating contractual obligations that are enforceable at law. The defendant will
hold property acquired in this manner on constructive trust for the claimant. By way of
example, in *Banner Homes Group Plc v Luff Developments Ltd (No.1)*[53] Luff wished to
acquire a development site. It entered into negotiations with Banner to form a joint
venture for the purpose of acquiring the site. The parties agreed to acquire the site
through a new company owned equally between them, which would be the vehicle for
the joint venture. Subsequently, Luff decided against the proposed joint venture, but
omitted to inform Banner for fear that Banner would proceed itself to bid for the site.
Throughout, Banner conducted itself on the basis that the joint venture was proceeding
and that the parties would enter into a formal agreement reflecting their pre-agreed
terms. It was not until after the site had been acquired that Luff informed Banner of its
withdrawal from the proposed joint venture. Banner contended that Luff's actions gave
rise to a constructive trust in its favour over half the shares in the new company.

The Court of Appeal agreed and outlined the necessary ingredients of liability. For
an equity to arise,[54] there must be a pre-acquisition understanding that the acquiring
party will take steps to acquire the relevant property and that the non-acquiring party
will obtain an interest in that property.[55] In reliance on the understanding, the non-
acquiring party should do something which confers an advantage on the acquiring
party or refrain from doing something detrimental to the ability of the non-acquiring
party to acquire the property on equal terms. In other words there must be an
advantage to one gained, or a detriment to the other suffered as a consequence of the
understanding.[56] It then becomes unconscionable to allow the acquiring party to retain
the property for himself, in a manner inconsistent with the parties' agreement or
understanding.[57]

This is a specific illustration of the broad principle to which Millett J. made reference **10.39**
in *Lonrho Plc v Al-Fayed (No.2)*.[58] There he argued that equity will intervene by way of
constructive trust, not only to compel the defendant to restore the claimant's property
to him, but also, "to require the defendant to disgorge property"[59] which he should
have acquired for the claimant. In this latter case, the defendant's wrong arises from his
subsequent failure to acknowledge the claimant's beneficial interest. For Millet J., "the
defendant must either have acquired property which but for his wrongdoing would

---

[53] [2000] Ch. 372.
[54] The so-called "*Pallant v Morgan* equity" deriving its name from *Pallant v Morgan* [1952] 2 All E.R. 951; see
N. Hopkins "The *Pallant v Morgan* Equity?" (2002) 66 Conv. 35.
[55] No such understanding arose in *Button v Phelps* [2006] EWHC 53 (Ch) (defendant's participation in rival
bids to that entered into by the claimant and defendant for the acquisition of bars and nightclubs), where
"open competition" and an absence of reliance precluded the finding of a constructive trust.
[56] It is clearly necessary, that the non-acquiring party is not informed before the acquisition that the acquiring
party no longer intends to honour the understanding.
[57] Note that where negotiations are subject to contract, withdrawal does not involve the requisite unconscionability to give rise to a constructive trust: see *London Investments Ltd v TBI Plc* [2002] EWCA Civ 855.
[58] [1991] 4 All E.R. 961.
[59] [1991] 4 All E.R. 961 at 969.

have belonged to the plaintiff, or he must have acquired property in circumstances in which he cannot conscientiously retain it as against the plaintiff".[60]

ENFORCEMENT OF AGREEMENTS

10.40   The following illustrations mark out the role of the constructive trust in preventing a defendant from unconscionably resiling from an agreement entered into with the claimant. As will be demonstrated, equity operates in diverse contexts ranging from binding contracts (such as to enforce contracts for the sale of land) to informal arrangements (such as bargains to share beneficial interests in the family home). The selection of examples considered includes specifically enforceable contracts, mutual wills and secret trusts.

Specically enforceable contract

10.41   Under a specifically enforceable contract for sale, the vendor becomes a trustee of the property for the purchaser.[61] Equity treats that as done which ought to be done and deems the purchaser already to be the real owner of the property. In the case of a contract for the sale of land, for example, a constructive trust is imposed and the vendor of the estate is considered to assume his trusteeship from the time at which he enters into the contract. Consequently, and subject to variation by agreement, it is for the purchaser to insure against damage to the property by fire or flood in the intervening time between contract and completion.[62] If the vendor proceeds to sell to a third party, he is deemed to hold the purchase money on trust for the purchaser.[63]

    Although the proposition that the vendor becomes a trustee for the purchaser dates back several centuries, the nature of his trusteeship is markedly less certain. No doubt when the purchase money is paid and the purchaser has no remaining obligations to perform under the contract, the vendor is but a bare trustee who must convey legal title to the purchaser forthwith.[64] Prior to this stage, many judges point in diverse terms to a qualified trusteeship with the vendor described variously as a "constructive trustee or a trustee *sub modo*"[65] a "quasi-trustee",[66] or a trustee "in a modified sense".[67] It is important to recognise that the vendor-trustee occupies an unusual position. He is at liberty to safeguard his own interest in the property until conveyance. In other words, he can act in a capacity which seems at odds with the office of trustee.

---

[60] [1991] 4 All E.R. 961 at 969.
[61] For the availability of specific performance: see Ch.19. As a general rule specific performance will be available where damages are an inadequate remedy for breach of contract.
[62] See, however, M.P. Thompson [1984] Conv. 43.
[63] *Lake v Bayliss* [1974] 2 All E.R. 1114.
[64] *Lloyds Bank Plc v Carrick* [1996] 4 All E.R. 630.
[65] Per Stamp L.J. in *Berkley v Poulett* (1977) 242 E.G. 39 at 42.
[66] Per Lord Greene M.R. in *Cumberland Consolidated Holdings Ltd v Ireland* [1946] K.B. 264 at 269.
[67] Per Kekewich J. in *Royal Bristol Permanent Building Society v Bomash* (1887) 35 Ch. D. 390 at 397.

Informal trusts of the family home

As regards the informal acquisition of an interest in the family home, the so-called **10.42** common intention constructive trust arises on the basis of the bargain between the parties (evidenced by their express discussions or conduct) as to their shared equitable interests.[68] A full analysis of the operation of constructive trusts in this context is provided in Ch.11.

Mutual wills

It will be recalled from Ch.5 that mutual wills arise where two or more parties enter into **10.43** a binding agreement that they will execute wills in a mutual form on the understanding that the wills will be irrevocable. Typically, a husband and wife may enter into an agreement that each will execute a will whereby the survivor will inherit the property of the deceased spouse. On the death of the survivor, their pooled property will pass to nominated beneficiaries, usually, the children of the marriage. On the date of death of the first testator, a constructive trust comes into effect and it is no longer open to the surviving party to leave that property to an alternative beneficiary (e.g. to a new wife).[69] As Lord Camden explained in *Dufour v Pereira*: "It might have been revoked by both jointly ... but I cannot be of opinion ... that after the death of either, it could be done by the survivor by another will ... The first that dies, carries his part of the contract into execution".[70]

Accordingly, it can be seen that a constructive trust binds the survivor and prevents disposal otherwise than under the terms of the mutual agreement. By this means, equity intervenes in order to prevent the fraud that would arise if the survivor were able to take the benefit of the agreement without performing his obligations. The imposition of a constructive trust is widely viewed as a clumsy mechanism to give effect to the parties' intentions. As Jill Martin comments, "It is a kind of salvage operation; a salvage of a wreck which competent legal advice would have avoided in the first place".[71]

Secret trusts

A final illustration of the capacity of equity to enforce the agreement of the parties by **10.44** means of constructive trust lies in the context of secret trusts. It will be recalled that a secret trust is a trust where the testator makes a gift of property in a will to a recipient who agrees to hold that property on trust for a third party.[72] Such trusts may be fully secret (i.e. where the existence of the trust and its terms are concealed) or half secret (i.e.

---

[68] *Lloyds Bank Plc v Rosset* [1991] 1 A.C. 107.
[69] "The obligation on the surviving testator is equitable. It is in the nature of a trust of the property affected, so the constructive trust label is attached to it": *Re Walters (Deceased)* [2008] EWCA Civ 782.
[70] (1769) I Dick 419 at 420.
[71] *Modern Equity*, at p.354.
[72] See Ch.5.

where only the terms are concealed). The classification of secret trusts as express or constructive remains a controversial question and one on which the commentators disagree. Hodge, for example, views both half-secret and fully secret trusts as express trusts, where the trust arises from the expressed intentions of the deceased communicated to and accepted by the trustee in the testator's lifetime.[73] Although this view appears to be widely held, not all commentators accept the express trust model. Sheridan argues that the secret trust which arises without mention in the will or on intestacy is constructive and not express[74] He bases his view upon the ground that, where a person has by a representation acquired property which it would be inequitable for him to keep, a constructive trust must arise. He adds that it makes no difference whether there is a transfer by will (as with a fully secret trust) or there is an inter vivos transfer. The same rule must apply in both cases. As Sheridan explains, "The fact that the transaction is a secret trust does not make it different in principle. It is but one illustration of the broad principle of constructive trusts, and should be so recognised".[75] Sheridan accepts, nonetheless, that as regards a half-secret trust, this must give rise to an express trust created by the will. He holds this view on the basis that there is a binding trust with the contest concerning only the question as to the identity of the beneficiary. There is no issue of the legatee obtaining property which it is inequitable for him to keep. The relevance of the debate as to the classification of secret trusts rests in the application of formalities. If a secret trust of land is classified as an express trust, it should be evidenced in writing by virtue of s.53(1)(b) of the Law of Property Act 1925 with the attendant consequence that the desired secrecy would be lost.[76]

GUIDE TO FURTHER READING

P. Birks, "Persisted Problems in Misdirected Money" [1993] LMCLQ 218.

H. Delaney, D. Ryan "Unconscionability: A Unifying Theme in Equity" [2008] Conv 401.

S. Gardner, "Knowing Assistance and Knowing Receipt: Taking Stock" (1996) 112 L.Q.R. 85.

C. Harpum, "Accessory Liability for Procuring or Assisting a Breach of Trust" (1995) 111 L.Q.R. 545.

B. McFarlane, "Constructive Trusts arising on a receipt of Property Sub Conditione" (2004) 120 L.Q.R. 667.

L. Smith, "Constructive Trusts and Constructive Trustees" [1999] C.L.J. 294.

---

[73] D. Hodge, "Secret Trusts: The Fraud Theory Revisited" [1980] Conv. 341.
[74] L. A. Sheridan, "English and Irish Secret Trusts" (1951) 67 L.Q.R. 314; see also P. Mathews, "The True Basis of the Half-Secret Trust?" [1979] Conv. 360.
[75] (1951) 67 L.Q.R. 314 at p.324.
[76] A similar principle applies if it is a secret trust of a subsisting equitable interest, the disposition should be created in writing for the purposes of s.53(1)(c): see Ch.4.

Chapter 11

TRUSTS OF THE FAMILY HOME

This chapter is concerned with the property rights of those who jointly own a home. **11.01** These persons are usually, but not necessarily, married or unmarried couples. Other persons who may share a home, of course, include friends and relatives. This type of shared ownership is becoming prevalent and the Law Commission noted that, by 2000, seven out of 10 homes were co-owned.[1] The social importance of co-ownership should not, therefore, be under-estimated.[2] The family home is not only the major asset that most families will possess, but also the stage upon which family life is enacted. It is, moreover, utilised as a means of raising substantial amounts of cash whether to finance lifestyle improvements or to guarantee business debts. Hence, there are a number of circumstances where it will be crucial to determine what rights, if any, each party has in the property. The issue could arise, for example:

- on the breakdown of the relationship between the co-owners. Attention then will focus upon whether the sharers are entitled to a payment of a capital sum representing their share of the home. It is at this point that the law traditionally draws a distinction between married couples and other types of relationship. The Matrimonial Causes Act 1973 gives the court the general power to redistribute property rights on divorce. An identical stance is now adopted in relation to same-sex registered partnerships under the Civil Partnership Act 2004. As will become clear, there is (as yet) no special treatment of family assets of unmarried and non-registered partnerships;

- on the death of one of the co-owners. The issue here will concern whether the deceased had an interest in the property and, if so, what is now to happen to it;

---

[1] "Sharing Homes: A Discussion Paper" (2002) Law Com. 278 at para.1.7. According to the Government Actuaries Department "Marital Status Protection for England and Wales" (2005)), by 2031 one in four of couples living together will be unmarried.

[2] Nor, indeed, should the financial costs to the parties: see "Cohabitation: The Financial Consequences of Relationship Breakdown" (2006) Law Com (Consultation Paper) No.179.

- when the property has been purchased with the aid of a mortgage and the borrower has subsequently defaulted. The lender will seek to exercise its power of sale, wish to obtain vacant possession and hope to discharge the debt from the proceeds of sale. It is, therefore, imperative for the lender to ascertain whether there is anyone living in the property who can claim priority and, thereby, defend possession proceedings or make a superior claim against the sale proceeds;

- when an unsecured creditor seeks to sell the property so that the debt can be satisfied. The question then arises as to whether any co-owner can resist the creditor's claim against the home; and

- in relation to liability to tax or, as in *Heron v Sandwell MBC*,[3] the additional payment of owner-occupier's supplement following compulsory purchase of land.

Not surprisingly, the key purpose of this chapter is to examine when co-ownership arises and how, once it has arisen, the shares of the co-owners are quantified. Unlike with divorce or the dissolution of a registered same-sex partnership, on the breakdown of non-marital and non-registered relationships there is no overarching principle under which the parties' assets can be redistributed, nor is there the ability for a judge always to produce a result that is fair and reasonable in the circumstances. There is no doctrine of "family assets".[4] The entitlement of a party turns purely upon the application, as between strangers, of cold and inflexible principles of law and equity. As admitted by Waite J. in *Hammond v Mitchell*:

> "Had they been married, the issue of ownership would scarcely have been relevant, because the law these days when dealing with the financial consequences of divorce, adopts a forward-looking perspective in which questions of ownership yield to the higher demands of relating the means of both to the needs of each ... Since this couple did not marry, none of that flexibility is available to them ... their financial rights have to be worked out according to their strict entitlements in equity, a process which is anything but forward-looking and involves, on the contrary, a painfully detailed retrospect".[5]

The relevance of legal title: *Stack v Dowden*

11.02   In *Stack v Dowden*,[6] the House of Lords considered the effect of a conveyance into the joint names of a cohabiting couple in circumstances when there was no explicit declaration of their respective beneficial interests. Lord Hope observed that the legal title cases may be broken down into those where there is simple legal ownership and those where there is joint legal ownership. In the former, sole beneficial ownership is the

---

[3] (1980) 255 E.G. 65.
[4] *Pettitt v Pettitt* [1970] A.C. 777.
[5] [1991] 1 W.L.R. 1127 at 1129.
[6] [2007] 2 A.C. 432.

starting point.[7] Lord Hope explained, "So in a case of sole legal ownership the onus is on the party who wishes to show that he has any beneficial interest at all, and if so what that interest is."[8] This may only be done by establishing the existence of a trust.[9] If established, the trust will establish both beneficial ownership and its extent.[10]

In contrast, in domestic relationships joint legal ownership carries with it the presumption that beneficial ownership is to be divided between the beneficial owners equally. As Baroness Hale put it, "It should only be expected that joint transferees would have spelt out their beneficial interests when they intended them to be different from their legal interests ... the starting point where there is joint legal ownership is joint beneficial ownership".[11] The onus lies heavily with a party who wishes to show that the beneficial interests are otherwise divided.[12] It will, therefore, only be in unusual circumstances that the beneficial interests be found to be different from the legal interests. It appears that the party must establish some form of unjust enrichment of the other in order to rebut this evidential presumption.[13] This majority view of the House, however, departs from the traditional approach[14] and was rejected by Lord Neuberger. In his dissenting speech, he accepted that equal beneficial ownership in joint names cases was a starting point, but felt that, when the parties had contributed unequally to the purchase price, it should be displaced by the presumption of a resulting trust. He explained:

> "Where the only additional relevant evidence to the fact that the property has been acquired in joint names is the extent of each party's contributions to the purchase price, the beneficial ownership at the time of acquisition will be held, in my view, in the same proportions as the contributions to the purchase price. That is the resulting trust solution."[15]

Subsequently, in *Laskar v Laskar*[16] Neuberger L.J. (now sitting in the Court of Appeal) made clear that the joint names presumption, as advocated in *Stack v Dowden*, does not apply to commercial cases (e.g. where property is bought for development or letting). In *Laskar*, the property was purchased primarily as an investment for rental income and capital appreciation. It was not purchased as a home. Hence, and even though the parties were mother and daughter, the resulting trust presumption still applied.

The way of rebutting the evidential presumption of equal ownership is to demonstrate that the shared, common intention of the parties was that there should be **11.03**

---

[7] *Roy v Roy* [1996] 1 F.L.R. 541.

[8] [2007] 2 A.C. 432 at 439; see also *Crisp v Mullings* (1976) 239 E.G. 119.

[9] *Gissing v Gissing* [1971] A.C. 886.

[10] *Mountney v Treharne* [2003] Ch. 135.

[11] [2007] 2 A.C. 432 at 453.

[12] See *Gibson v Revenue & Customs Prosecution Office* [2008] EWCA Civ 645 where, unusually, it was a third party (the Revenue & Customs) who attempted to challenge the presumption of equal division (there between husband and wife).

[13] See T. Etherton, "Constructive trusts: a new model for equity and unjust enrichment" (2008) C.L.J. 265.

[14] Which was that this presumption could easily be displaced: see *McKenzie v McKenzie* [2003] EWHC 601 (Ch).

[15] [2007] 2 A.C. 432 at 468. He also counselled against imputing a fictional agreement between the parties so as to justify the imposition of a common intention constructive trust.

[16] [2008] 1 W.L.R. 2695.

ownership in different proportions.[17] In determining this common intention, the court may consider a wide range of issues. These could include, for example, financial and indirect contributions, advice received, discussions between the parties, reasons why the property was bought in joint names, the purposes for which the home was acquired, whether it was a home for the parties' children, how the parties arranged their finances and the nature of the parties' relationship.[18] The court may also take into account how the circumstances have changed since the purchase.[19] Unsurprisingly, Mrs Dowden raised a variety of factors which indicated a common intention that the beneficial interests were to be unequal and justified her successful claim to a 65 per cent share. Primarily, she contributed far more to the acquisition of the property than did Mr Stack. Similarly, she contributed more to the repayment of the mortgage than did her partner. Although the couple had lived together for 18 years, this was not a case where the parties pooled their resources for the common good. As Baroness Hale observed, "There cannot be many unmarried couples who have lived together for as long as this, who have had four children together, and whose affairs have been kept as rigidly separate as this couple's affairs were kept. This is all strongly indicative that they did not intend their shares, even in the property which was put into both their names, to be equal...".[20]

In *Adekunle v Ritchie*, it was argued that the *Stack* approach applied only when there was some sexual relationship between the parties. This was rejected by Judge John Behrens, but he did accept that "It may well be, however, that where one is not dealing with the situation of a couple living together it will be easier to find that the facts are unusual in the sense that they are not to be taken to have intended a beneficial joint tenancy".[21] The judge noted that on the facts before him the context of the acquisition of the property was very different from that of the normal cohabiting couple. This was a very unusual case in that it concerned the purchase of a council house by a tenant under the right to buy scheme with the benefit of a generous discount in a situation where the tenant could not alone fund the mortgage. The primary purpose was to provide a home for the mother and the parties' finances were separate. The facts that the property was purchased in joint names, that both were jointly and severally liable under the mortgage and that her son contributed to the mortgage repayments, pointed to the conclusion that he was to have a beneficial interest in the property. Adopting a holistic approach, the judge awarded the son a one-third beneficial interest in the property.

Similarly, in *Laskar v Laskar*[22] the presumption of equality fell to be rebutted on the grounds that the parties' financial affairs were kept separate; the property was not purchased as a home; there was no reason why the mother would favour one child over her other children; the contributions were significantly different and the reason why the daughter became a co-owner was simply because the mother could not afford the property on her own.

---

[17] *Fowler v Barron* [2008] EWCA Civ 377. Any unilateral or secret intentions do not constitute a shared intention.
[18] See *Adekunle v Ritchie* [2007] 2 P. & C.R. D20.
[19] In *Kali v Chawla* [2007] EWHC 2357 (Ch), the High Court felt it necessary to look at the parties' interests as at the time of their divorce and not at the time of purchase (some 19 years earlier). It was important here that for the last nine years the parties had been leading separate physical and financial lives.
[20] [2007] 2 A.C. 432 at 465.
[21] [2007] 2 P. & C.R. D20 at D21.
[22] [2008] 1 W.L.R. 2695.

AN EXPRESS DECLARATION OF TRUST

The displacement of the working rule that legal title carries with it the equitable title **11.04** will, of course, arise when it can be shown that the legal owner holds the property subject to an express trust in favour of an ascertainable beneficiary. Retreating to basics, an express trust will arise where the legal owner expressly declares himself to be a trustee or conveys the property to a third party expressly subject to a trust. Either way, this will ensure the separation of legal and equitable title. Nominal ownership vests in the legal owner whereas true entitlement rests with the beneficiary. It will, however, be recalled that express trusts of land are subject to additional formalities as prescribed in s.53(1)(b) of the Law of Property Act 1925. The statutory prescription is that, in order for an express trust of land to be enforceable, the declaration of trust must be evidenced in writing, which is signed by the settlor. As shown in Ch.4, the use of formal means of rights creation reflects the need for certainty and clarity in dealings with land.

Accordingly, if Fred is the sole legal owner of a house and seeks to declare an express trust of the land in favour of his grandson, Jordan, he is expected to comply with s.53(1)(b). Fred should, therefore, set out his intention to create a trust and its terms in writing and attach his signature to the relevant document. Only then will the express trust become enforceable by Jordan.

In *Simpson v Simpson*,[23] a daughter (Phyllis) claimed that, in 1966 when her father **11.05** (James) transferred his home to a family company in return for £15,000, there was an express trust created in her favour. The property was now worth somewhere in the region of £1 million. Her difficulty was that there was no written contemporaneous evidence of what was agreed in 1966. It was clear that the ostensible sale to the Company was either not the real transaction or, at least, not the whole of the transaction that took place. The father had entered the transaction in order to ensure that the family home was beyond the reach of potential creditors. There was sufficient evidence to show the intention to create an express oral trust in favour of Phyllis. In order to satisfy s.53(1)(b), the judge found documentation that prima facie qualified as evidence of the trust. In 1981, a director of the Company (Harry) had executed a statutory declaration stating that the property was held on trust for Phyllis. In 1983, Harry signed a statement that also recognised that the directors had agreed that the property was to be held on trust for Phyllis.

Harry, however, was profoundly dyslexic and the Company argued that he could not be taken to have agreed the contents of the documents. The judge was unimpressed and concluded that Harry would have had the documents explained to him at the time of his signature. Accordingly, for Harry to escape the effect of signing the documents he would have to show that they were untrue and that he was improperly persuaded to sign them. He could show neither of these events. Even though Harry could not read or understand the documents without assistance, they offered signed, written evidence of the oral trust in favour of Phyllis. The High Court added that, for the trust to be

---

[23] [2005] EWHC 2098 (Ch).

enforced, Phyllis would be required to repay the £15,000 or other sum due to the Company. It is to be borne in mind that, "He who seeks equity must do equity".

11.06   Of course, an implied trust might arise from the ashes of a failed trust[24] and, indeed, it might be that any written, but unsigned, documentation will shape the terms of that implied trust.[25] It will become clear that equity attaches major significance to the underlying intent of dealings and the prevention of fraud and unconscionable conduct. For example, Adrienne is the sole legal owner a house in which she lives with her partner, Fred. She encourages Fred to spend money on the family home based upon the informal assurance that he will have a beneficial interest in the property. These factors should give rise to a constructive trust under which Fred will be able to claim a share even though there is no signed, written evidence in support. Such informal trusts are considered later in this chapter.

Joint legal owners

11.07   By way of a further gloss, a statutory trust of land arises automatically under s.1(2) of the Trusts of Land (Appointment of Trustees) Act 1996 when two or more persons become the holders of the legal title to the land. In such joint enterprises, the existence of a trust does not have to be spelled out on the face of the conveyance. The statutory trust instead arises by operation of law. Nevertheless, the best way forward has always been to acknowledge the trust expressly and, more importantly, to specify the beneficial interests thereunder in the conveyance itself. Not surprisingly, the courts have long urged conveyancers to insert an express declaration as the invariable standard practice.[26] Although a failure to do so might expose the conveyancer to an action in negligence,[27] this best practice is still not always adopted.[28] As Ward L.J. lamented, "Perhaps conveyancers do not read the law reports. I will try one more time: always try to agree on and then record how the beneficial interest is to be held. It is not very difficult to do".[29]

11.08   Indeed since 1998, it has been possible (but it is not mandatory) under the Land Registration Rules that the joint registered proprietors make a declaration as to the beneficial interests under the trust of land. The transfer will, however, be valid whether or not this part of the form is completed. As Baroness Hale pointed out in *Stack v Dowden*, "so there may still be transfers of registered land into joint names in which there is no express declaration of the beneficial interests."[30] Although this facility does not assist those involved with pre-1998 purchases, the attraction of such a compulsory declaration is that it promotes certainty and is usually determinative of whether the

---

[24] Section 53(2) states that implied, resulting and constructive trusts are not subject to the formality of signed writing.
[25] *Sleebush v Gordon* [2004] EWHC 2287 (Ch).
[26] See Bagnall J. in *Cowcher v Cowcher* [1972] 1 W.L.R. 425 at 442, "The just resolution of future disputes would be facilitated; the additional costs would be insignificant; and I cannot think that connubial harmony would be unduly jeopardised".
[27] See *Walker v Hall* [1984] 5 F.L.R. 126.
[28] See *McKenzie v McKenzie* [2003] EWHC 601 (Ch).
[29] *Carlton v Goodman* [2002] EWCA Civ. 545 at [44].
[30] [2007] 2 A.C. 432 at 453.

parties are to hold as joint tenants or as tenants in common with individual shares. The Law Commission explained:

> "Where two people buy a home together, there is rarely a problem. They are likely to seek legal advice. If they are married, or, although not married, are in a long-term relationship, it is very likely that they will decide to have title to the home registered in their joint names. They will also execute a declaration of trust stipulating what their respective shares in the property are to be—this will then govern the proportions into which the proceeds of sale of the house would be divided in the event of sale".[31]

An interesting, but unusual, issue arose in *Sleebush v Gordon*.[32] There a declaration of **11.09** a tenancy in common was duly inserted in a conveyance into the joint names of a son and his mother. Inexplicably, both had failed to sign the conveyance. Mrs Sleebush later claimed that the absence of the signatures invalidated the declaration of a tenancy in common. She asserted that, as the original purchasers had contributed to the purchase price in equal proportions, a beneficial joint tenancy should, instead, be presumed. On this understanding, and by virtue of the right of survivorship, Mrs Sleebush would become the sole legal and beneficial owner of the property. The High Court felt that the absence of the signatures did not connote a rejection of the declaration of a tenancy in common and that any presumption of a joint tenancy was effectively rebutted by the declaration in the conveyance. Accordingly, the unexecuted declaration offered conclusive proof of the parties' intentions as to beneficial ownership. Even though the declaration did not satisfy the formalities set out in s.53(1)(b), the transfer took effect according to its terms.[33]

The involvement of conveyancers offers to the parties the ready opportunity to make an express declaration of trust. Obviously, the same opportunity is denied when the co-ownership arises after the purchase of the property. For example, where Fred buys a house in 1990 and Adrienne moves in with him in 2000 it is highly improbable that either will seek professional advice. Accordingly, as the Law Commission acknowledged:

> "In this latter situation, it is relatively rare for the parties to make an express declaration of their respective beneficial entitlements. It is unusual for such persons to seek legal advice at such a time, and there is no occasion equivalent to registration of title to the property following a purchase which would afford an opportunity to advise those sharing the home of the advantages of making formal provision".[34]

---

[31] "Sharing Homes: A Discussion Paper" (2002) Law Com. 278 at p.vi, para.3.
[32] [2004] EWHC 2287 (Ch).
[33] See also, *Roy v Roy* [1996] 1 F.L.R. 541; *Pink v Lawrence* (1978) 36 P. & C.R. 98.
[34] "Sharing Homes: A Discussion Paper" (2002) Law Com. 278 at para.2.45.

In search of a declaration of trust

11.10   The first step, therefore, is to scour the conveyance for an indication of how the parties are to hold beneficially. Absent a direct incantation, this is not always a straightforward task. In *Stack v Dowden*,[35] for example, the conveyance to the parties contained no words of trust. The parties, however, necessarily held the property on statutory trust for themselves. The issue concerned the extent of their respective beneficial interests under that trust. As a conveyance into joint names does not always lead to the conclusion that the parties were entitled beneficially in equal shares, the court has to look for indication from the wording of the conveyance. The conveyance contained a declaration that the survivor of them was entitled to give a valid receipt for capital money. The insertion of this type of clause is indicative of a joint tenancy as it is consistent with the right of survivorship.[36] Indeed, the appropriate declaration when a tenancy in common has been created is that a valid receipt for capital monies cannot be obtained from one survivor alone. The case considered the evidential weight to be given to the receipt clause.

It was held that there was no express declaration of trust arising from the mere insertion of the receipt clause.[37] The House did, however, accept that, if the parties had understood the significance of the receipt clause (i.e. it was consistent only with the right of survivorship), the inference that they intended a beneficial joint tenancy would be drawn.

Departing from the declared terms of an express trust

11.11   On the finding of an express declaration of trust, only in exceptional circumstances will its terms not be definitive of the parties' true beneficial entitlement.[38] As Sir Peter Gibson put it, "Where the parties have reached a consensus on the beneficial interests in the property, the court will give effect to it, unless there is very good reason for not doing so, such as a subsequent renegotiation ...".[39] This reluctance was evidenced in *Goodman v Gallant*.[40] There a couple bought a house in 1978 and the conveyance defined their respective beneficial interests by stating that they held "upon trust for themselves as joint tenants". In 1983, the couple separated and Mrs Goodman served a written notice of severance on Mr Gallant. The effect of this notice was to convert the pre-existing beneficial joint tenancy into a tenancy in common. Mrs Goodman claimed that, as she had paid three-quarters of the purchase price, she was entitled to a three-quarter share of the proceeds of sale. The Court of Appeal rejected this claim on the basis that the parties could not go behind the express declaration of trust and that the declaration was conclusive. On a subsequent sale, each party was, thereby, entitled to a

---

[35] [2007] 2 A.C. 432.
[36] *Re Gorman* [1990] 1 W.L.R. 616.
[37] See also, *Huntingford v Hobbs* [1993] 1 F.L.R. 736.
[38] *Pettitt v Pettitt* [1970] A.C. 777.
[39] *Crossley v Crossley* [2005] EWCA Civ. 1581 at [32]; see *Mortgage Corporation v Shaire* [2001] Ch. 743 (evidence of one co-owner's subsequent interpretation of intention did not establish a common intention).
[40] [1986] Fam. 106.

half share of the proceeds. As Slade L.J. observed, "there is no room for the application of the doctrine of resulting implied or constructive trusts unless and until the conveyance is set aside or rectified; until that event the declaration contained in the document speaks for itself".[41] Accordingly, there is no need usually for the court to look beyond the four-corners of the declaration. As the Law Commission concluded, "It is essential, in order to reward those who make proper provision, that courts continue rigorously to enforce express declarations of trust".[42]

The declaration of trust is not, however, entirely sacrosanct. It is possible that the transaction may be set aside on the basis of fraud or mistake, misrepresentation or other equitable wrongdoing (e.g. undue influence or duress).[43] This explains the (albeit unsuccessful) attempt in *Simpson v Simpson* to avoid a written declaration on the basis of severe dyslexia on the part of the signatory.[44] An express declaration of trust cannot, moreover, bind those who are not a party to the purchase. This was demonstrated in *City of London Building Society v Flegg*[45] where a house was purchased by X and Y for themselves as joint tenants in law and in equity. Over half of the purchase price was provided by Y's parents and, as such, the parents were able to claim an interest in the property by virtue of a resulting trust. The arrangement between X and Y governed their entitlement only as regards their interest in the property, but as the parents had not executed the declaration it could not affect their interests.

The Privy Council was invited to look beyond the terms of a declaration in *Potter v Potter*.[46] This litigation arose out of the breakdown of the relationship between two cousins, the appellant (Mr Potter) and the respondent (Ms Potter). In 1998, they bought a home in New Zealand for the sum of $875,000. Before the purchase was completed, they took the precaution of sorting out the financial arrangements between them. Following the receipt of independent legal advice, the parties entered into a "Property Sharing Agreement". The agreement covered issues such as the declaration of beneficial ownership to the intention to create a formal family trust. The property was registered in their joint names. Six months after moving into the property the parties' relationship ended, but no family trust had yet been executed. Mr Potter commenced litigation, seeking an order of sale and orders that would exclude Ms Potter from any share in the proceeds. She argued that she was entitled to a share in the net proceeds of sale.

11.12

The resolution of the dispute turned upon the content and construction of the written agreement. Lord Scott read the agreement as giving the respondent a half-share. This was so even though Mr Potter had provided the purchase monies and defrayed the acquisition costs of the purchase. Mr Potter, however, attempted to vary the agreement by contending that Ms Potter's beneficial half share was impliedly subject to defeasance on the breakdown of the relationship. This argument was rejected. There was no express term to this effect and, in order for such a defeasance condition to be implied, it would be necessary to show that this was Ms Potter's intention at the time of the agreement. This was clearly not possible on the present facts. Once purchased, the

---

[41] [1986] Fam. 106 at 111.
[42] "Sharing Homes: A Discussion Paper" (2002) Law Com. 278 at para.2.52.
[43] *Pink v Lawrence* (1978) 36 P. & C.R. 98. For example, in *Re Colebrook's Conveyances* [1972] 1 W.L.R. 1397 rectification was available where the parties intended to be tenants in common, but the conveyance stated that they were joint tenants.
[44] [2005] EWHC 2098 (Ch).
[45] [1988] A.C. 54.
[46] [2004] UKPC 41.

property was to be held by the couple in equal shares both at law and beneficially. Although the breakdown of the relationship led to a frustration of their intentions to create a family trust, it did not justify reversing the parts of the agreement that had been implemented.

11.13   In *Wade v Grimwood*,[47] property was purchased in joint names and an ancillary trust deed was drafted. This contained a declaration that the purchasers were to hold as beneficial tenants in common and that after all expenses and debts were discharged, the proceeds of sale were to be divided between the couple with an 80 per cent entitlement in favour of Mr Wade. Clause 4 of the trust deed stated that the parties were to bear equally the costs, expenses and outgoings payable in respect of the property. The property was sold for £510,000 and Mr Wade then commenced proceedings seeking a declaration that he was entitled to the whole of the proceeds of sale or, in the alternative, an account for the payments made solely by him of Clause 4 costs. Sir Martin Nourse felt that this argument was untenable. First, Clause 4 did not disturb the allocation of beneficial shares, which remained at 80 per cent in favour of Mr Wade. Secondly, and although agreed beneficial entitlements can be varied under the equitable principle of accounting, this was not an accounting situation. The accounting principle caters for an account to be taken only when it is necessary to discover the ultimate balance between the parties on a sale of the property. The present facts gave rise to a set-off situation, with each obligation being enforceable immediately. Clause 4 imposed mutual, but independent, obligations on the parties to contribute to costs, expenses and outgoings as they became payable. Hence, if one party made an entire payment, that party acquired an immediate cause of action against the other for reimbursement. Mr Wade had, however, impliedly waived any rights to a contribution from his partner. He had led his former partner to believe that he was not going to enforce any right to reimbursement against her and she had ordered her affairs accordingly. As Sir Martin Nourse concluded, "this was not a commercial agreement between strangers ... As between parties living happily together, that is surely enough to establish waiver. It is not appropriate to insist on the formalities of waiver in its application to an informal relationship".[48]

A change of entitlement

11.14   The principle of equitable accounting is rooted in concepts of fairness and justice. For present purposes, it assumes relevance where one party makes substantially greater post-purchase payments relating to the property than the other. The question is whether such additional expenditure obliges one party to account to the other when the property is sold.[49] Sir Martin Nourse commented in *Wright v Johnson* that the question whether there should be equitable accounting, "depends on the intention of the parties to be inferred from all the facts of the case".[50] In *Re Pavlou*, Millett J. explained, "The guiding principle for the court of equity is that the proportions in which the entirety

---

[47] [2004] EWCA Civ. 999.
[48] [2004] EWCA Civ. 999 at [18].
[49] See generally, E. Cooke, "Equitable Accounting" [1995] Conv. 391.
[50] [2002] 2 P. & C.R. 210 at 215.

should be divided between former co-owners must have regard to any increase in its value which has been brought about by means of expenditure by one of them".[51] There the court ordered equitable accounting as regards the post-separation payment of mortgage instalments and the carrying out of improvements by the wife. On similar facts, in *Bernard v Josephs*[52] credit was given to the partner remaining in occupation for five years after the relationship ended in respect of mortgage payments, but this was counterbalanced by an occupation rent that he was expected to pay to the non-occupying partner.

In *Re Pavlou*, Millett J. emphasised that there was no difference here between a joint tenancy and a tenancy in common, "neither party could take the benefit of an increase in the value of the property without making an allowance for what had been expended by the other in order to obtain it".[53] Millett J., however, made no reference as to whether the expenditure must occur only after the separation of the parties. This issue of timing was addressed by the High Court in *Clarke v Harlowe*.[54]

In 2001, Mr Harlowe and Ms Clarke purchased Bank House. The purchase price was £396,500 and the acquisition was assisted by a mortgage of £124,970. The property was conveyed to them as legal and beneficial joint tenants. Following the purchase, Mr Harlowe made the mortgage repayments. In addition, he paid for substantial works of renovation on the property, totalling more than £90,000. The relationship broke down in 2003 and Bank House was eventually sold at a sale price of £700,000 which, after the mortgage was redeemed and expenses paid, produced net proceeds of £611,495. Ms Clarke contended that she was entitled to one half the net proceeds of sale, i.e. she relied upon the declaration of the beneficial joint tenancy. Mr Harlowe, however, invoked the principle of equitable accounting. His argument was that, in making the distribution, he should be given credit for the £90,000 spent on improvements to the property. Ms Clarke made the fundamental point that the moneys were spent at a time when the relationship was continuing and that there was no scope for the rules of equitable accounting to come into play. She asserted that the principles come into play only in relation to post-separation expenditure.

11.15

Mr Harlowe countered that, while most cases had indeed been concerned with post-separation equitable accounting, there was no reason why it could not take place in respect of the period prior to separation. He offered the example of where a joint owner spent £10,000 on the day before separation and another joint owner spent £10,000 on the day after separation. He submitted that it would be unfair and inequitable if only one of these joint owners should be entitled to benefit from equitable accounting.

Judge Behrens considered the express declaration of trust and accepted that, in the absence of fraud or mistake, the declaration of trust was conclusive and the parties were not permitted to go behind it. He did, however, recognise that it is possible for the parties to vary their beneficial interest after the acquisition of the property. This could be achieved by the making of a new express declaration of trust. The mere fact that one party has spent time and money in carrying out improvements will not be sufficient and, indeed, a variation will be inferred only in exceptional circumstances. Judge Behrens provided the example of an agreement between the parties in a business setting where

11.16

---

[51] [1993] 3 All E.R. 955 at 959.
[52] (1982) 1 Ch. 391.
[53] [1993] 3 All E.R. 955 at 958.
[54] [2005] EWHC 3062 (Ch).

one of the parties is unable to honour the agreement to pay towards the outgoings. If the other party has to pay more than a fair share, the judge concluded that this must be taken into account, "I equally do not see that such equitable accounting is prohibited simply because the relationship is not at an end"[55]. He continued, "Before there can be a duty to account by one party to the other there must be a breach of or failure to comply with some obligation owed by that party to the other. There may be a debate in individual cases as to the nature of the obligation necessary to give rise to a duty to account but there must still be an obligation"[56]. The judge felt that this applied in an ordinary cohabitation case as in any other. In the cohabitation case, the common purpose of the trust subsists while the relationship continues. While ordinary arrangements for the discharge of outgoings exist, there is no breach or failure.

Although Mr Harlowe had met all of the mortgage payments, there was no suggestion that Ms Clarke was under an obligation to reimburse him. After the relationship ends, the common purpose of the trust has generally come to an end, "At that stage there are no common arrangements between the parties with the result that each ought to discharge his or her proportionate share of the outgoings. There is thus at that time an obligation on each of the parties. If one party fails to honour its obligation an appropriate account can be taken on the sale of the property"[57]. Accordingly, there were sound reasons for concluding that, in an ordinary case, equitable accounting commences at the date of separation. Prior payments of outgoings are referable to the common purpose underlying the trust. Unless exceptional circumstances prevail, there is no room for equitable accounting. As the improvements were carried out in the period prior to separation, and absent an agreement that Ms Clarke would make financial contribution, she was not in breach of any obligation. Hence, there was no reason why a court of equity should now compel her to contribute to the cost of the improvements.

Unexpressed beneficial ownership

11.17 In circumstances where there is no valid express declaration of trust, the courts have devised analytical tools through which the existence of a trust may be implied and its terms divined. In the absence of a declaration of trust the solution must be found in the principles of law relating to resulting, implied or constructive trusts. It becomes necessary for the court to consider the intentions of the parties as discerned from the evidence or from presumptions to be drawn from their conduct. Unlike on divorce or the dissolution of registered same-sex partnerships, Parliament has not afforded to the court a general discretion to direct a division fair and equitable to both parties.

Unfortunately, the area of implied co-ownership is marked with some uncertainty concerning, for example, the current role of the resulting trust, the co-existence between estoppel and the constructive trust and whether the timing of intention dictates which remedial vehicle is to be adopted. The quantification of a party's beneficial share may also vary greatly according to which mechanism is employed. Be warned, however,

---

[55] [2005] EWHC 3062 (Ch) at [33].
[56] [2005] EWHC 3062 (Ch) at [35].
[57] [2005] EWHC 3062 (Ch) at [38].

judges and commentators alike do not always speak with one voice on such matters. As the Law Commission put it, " 'Who owns what?' may be very simple to ask, but in a short time the enquirer will find themselves immersed in the off-putting, and sometimes obscure, terminology of the law of trusts and estoppel".[58]

THE PURCHASE MONEY RESULTING TRUST

The purchase money resulting trust arises where property is conveyed into the name of one party, but another has made a contribution to the purchase price. In that scenario, it is presumed that a beneficial interest in the property passes to the contributing party. As Eyre C.B. acknowledged over 200 years ago, "the trust of the legal estate . . . whether taken in the name of the purchasers and others jointly, or in the name of others without that of the purchaser; whether in one name or several; whether jointly or successive, results to the man who advances the purchase money".[59] This view still enjoys contemporary resonance.[60] By affording a beneficial interest to the provider of the purchase money, equity assumes bargains and not gifts. Such was demonstrated in *Karis v Lewis*[61] where the legal title was transferred into the name of an associate, allegedly on the payment by him of £1,150,000. The issue was who really provided the purchase money. If it was the transferor himself, a resulting trust would arise in his favour. The presumption that the legal title owner was also the beneficial owner was displaced by evidence which showed that the transferee could not have afforded the purchase price and that the transferor continued to treat the property as his own. The transfer was a mere cloak so that the transferor could hide real ownership of the property.

The resulting trust operates in circumstances where no common or express intention is apparent.[62] If, however, the evidence displays a common or express intention that each should have a beneficial share in the property, the case falls outside resulting trust territory.[63] As Sir Peter Gibson put it in *Crossley v Crossley*, "The presumption [of a resulting trust] yields to the intentions of the parties, upon which the judge made findings of fact".[64] Such facts will instead promote a claim in constructive trust or proprietary estoppel.[65] The delights of exploring these other legal concepts will be experienced later in this chapter.

Take the example where Fred and Adrienne each contribute to the purchase price, but the property is conveyed into Fred's sole name. Although Fred is the legal owner, he holds the property on trust for himself and Adrienne. Adrienne has acquired her beneficial interest by virtue of her payments to the purchase price that have triggered a resulting trust. If they each contribute equally to the purchase price, the traditional

11.18

11.19

---

[58] "Sharing Homes: A Discussion Paper" (2002) Law Com. 278 at para.1.12.
[59] *Dyer v Dyer* (1788) 2 Cox Eq. 92 at 93.
[60] *Pettitt v Pettitt* [1970] A.C. 777. Cf. the situation where this conveyance is into joint names and there is no declaration of trust: *Stack v Dowden* [2004] 2 A.C. 432 (see **11.02**).
[61] [2005] EWCA Civ. 1627.
[62] *Themistokli v Spyrou* [2005] EWHC 1822 (Ch).
[63] *Ahmad v Gould* Unreported December 6, 2005.
[64] [2005] EWCA Civ. 1581 at [21].
[65] *Oxley v Hiscock* [2004] 3 W.L.R. 715.

presumption is that they have a beneficial joint tenancy. If the contributions are unequal the presumption is of a beneficial tenancy in common.[66]

Quantification

11.20 The issue of quantum is, once the facts are established, a straightforward matter. In *Arogundade v Arogundade*,[67] a flat was purchased for £207,000. The claimant contributed £62,000 to the purchase price and, by virtue of resulting trust principles, in the High Court obtained a 30 per cent share in the property. Similarly, in the earlier example, the quantification of Adrienne's interest will be proportionate to her contribution to the purchase price. If she contributed 50 per cent of the purchase price, therefore, a 50 per cent share of the proceeds of any sale will result back to her. If she contributed 10 per cent, her interest will be pegged at 10 per cent.

At the outset, it is important to note that this is very unlike the assessment process under a constructive trust where the court attempts to produce an outcome that is fair and just. This divergence of treatment was made apparent in *Drake v Whipp*.[68] There the total expenditure on the purchase was £195,790 and Mrs Drake's total contribution was assessed at £38,000. Applying resulting trust principles, her entitlement would be 19.4 per cent of the current value of the property. Based upon her financial contributions, Mrs Drake's share was £43,650. The case was, however, decided on the basis that a constructive trust arose. This entitled Mrs Drake to a share now quantified at £75,000.

Rebutting the presumption

11.21 The presumption of a resulting trust may always be rebutted, in whole or in part, by contrary evidence.[69] For example, an oral or unsigned written declaration of express trust might operate to displace the presumption of a resulting trust. Similarly, evidence of a common intention may take the bargain outside the realm of the resulting trust and into the more flexible world of the constructive trust.[70] The presumption of a resulting trust might also be defeated in circumstances where the financial contribution was by way of a loan[71] or a gift.[72]

The counter, but now anachronistic, presumption of advancement (operative, say,

---

[66] *Lake v Gibson* (1729) 1 Eq. Ca. Abr. 290.
[67] [2005] EWHC 1766 (Ch).
[68] [1996] 1 F.L.R. 826, noted by A. Dunn [1997] Conv. 467.
[69] In *Stack v Dowden* [2007] 2 A.C. 432, the transfer of legal title into joint names rebutted the presumption of a resulting trust.
[70] See *Midland Bank v Cooke* [1995] 4 All E.R. 562; *Oxley v Hiscock*, [2004] 3 W.L.R. 715.
[71] *Vajpeyi v Yusaf* [2003] EWHC 623 (Ch).
[72] *Levin v Beatt* [2005] EWHC 828 (Ch).

when a husband/father supplies the purchase money and the conveyance is taken in the wife's/child's name alone) may support the conclusion that a gift was intended.[73] Nevertheless, the presumption of advancement is nowadays easily dislodged[74] and, because of its gender bias, arguably contravenes the European Convention on Human Rights. In *Kyriakides v Pippas*,[75] a father purportedly made a gift of a house to his daughter upon her marriage. Although the evidence was vague and unsatisfactory, the High Court concluded that there was no intention to make an immediate gift to the daughter. The father had made statements as to the house having been a dowry merely to maintain appearances in front of fellow Greek Cypriots rather than sacrificing the interests of his wife and other children. Put simply, the donative intention was lacking and a resulting trust arose in the father's favour. Deputy Judge G. Moss Q.C. commented, "I suspect the position we have now reached is that the courts will always strive to work out the real intention of the purchaser and will only give effect to the presumptions of resulting trust and advancement where the intention cannot be fathomed and a 'long-stop' or 'default' solution is needed".[76]

Much turns, therefore, upon the strength of the presumption in favour of a resulting **11.22** trust for as Mellish L.J. observed in *Fowkes v Pascoe*, "the presumption must, beyond all question, be of very different weight in different cases".[77] In some cases it will be very strong indeed, as in *Abrahams v Abrahams*[78] where a wife continued to pay her own and her estranged husband's share in a lottery syndicate. It was held that the presumption of a resulting trust in her favour was not rebutted on the evidence. She was, therefore, successful in her claim. In other cases it will be a weak presumption and easily displaced.

In *Fowkes v Pascoe*, a woman of considerable fortune (Mrs Pascoe) purchased £250 of shares and registered them in the name of the son of her former daughter-in-law. The son lived with Mrs Pascoe and she provided for him. She also purchased a further £250 of shares in the name of her female companion. Mellish L.J. concluded, "applying one's common sense to that transaction, what inference is it possible to draw, except that the purchases were intended for the purpose of gifts?"[79] The appellate court was influenced by two factors. First, that had a trust been intended there would be no reason for the two sums not to be invested in the same name. Secondly, Mrs Pascoe already had a large sum of stock in her own name. Mellish L.J. thought that it would be absurd for a woman with so much stock to seek to invest a comparatively meagre £500 in the names of the others and yet intend for it to be held on trust for herself. As there was no plausible reason why she should transfer the shares to either the son or the companion as her nominee, the appellate court concluded from the surrounding circumstances that

---

[73] *Silver v Silver* [1958] 1 W.L.R. 259. There the matrimonial home was bought in the name of the wife and was presumed to be a gift to her by the husband.
[74] It is, in the words of Nourse L.J. in *McGrath v Wallis* [1995] 2 F.L.R. 114 at 115, "reclassified as a judicial instrument of last resort". As Arden L.J. added in *Gibson v Revenue & Customs Prosecution Office* [2008] EWCA Civ 645 at [26], "... this presumption is no longer in keeping with modern conditions or at least is much diminished, or more easily rebutted, nowadays...".
[75] [2004] EWHC 646 (Ch).
[76] [2004] EWHC 646 (Ch) at [76].
[77] (1875) 10 Ch. App. 343 at 352
[78] (1999) *The Times*, July 26.
[79] (1875) 10 Ch. App. 343 at 353.

she intended to make a gift of the shares. This promotes a pragmatic approach that requires sensible inferences to be drawn from the available evidence.

11.23   In *Vajpeyi v Yusaf*,[80] the High Court accepted that the rebuttal of the presumption of a resulting trust might appear to be a straightforward process. Nevertheless, difficulties may arise when the transaction occurred a long time ago and the parties do not accurately remember its details or, indeed, may have died. As Deputy Judge Peter Prescott Q.C. puzzled, "After such a lapse of time, how is the court to arrive at the truth?"[81] In the case before him, the defendant accepted that the presumption of a resulting trust arose and the onus was upon him to rebut that presumption. As to the evidence necessary to achieve this rebuttal, the Deputy Judge commented, "This depends on the strength of the presumption. And the strength of the presumption depends upon the facts and circumstances which give rise to it. This is because the doctrine of resulting trusts is supposed to be based on common sense. In each case the court is trying to find the answer to the question: what would the parties have intended if they had given thought to the position?"[82]

The Deputy Judge in the *Vajpeyi* case acknowledged that, depending upon the circumstances, it is possible for the presumption of a resulting trust to be rebutted by comparatively slight evidence. The evidence admissible for this purpose will focus upon the acts and declarations of the parties. He provided two examples. First, when an unmarried couple intend to live together in property and both contribute to the purchase price there is a presumption that they intend to hold it in proportionate shares even though the property is conveyed into the name of one of them alone. The fact that both came up with the money calls for a common sense explanation of which the most obvious is that they intended the property to be acquired for their joint benefit.

11.24   The second example provided concerned a young woman in her first job who raised as much as she could on mortgage to buy a flat and turned to her uncle to pay a minor part of the purchase price. The common sense explanation in this scenario might well be that the uncle did not want an interest in the property. The Deputy Judge added, "It is more credible that it was meant to be a loan or, perhaps, a gift".[83] On a general level, this example bore some passing resemblance to the facts of *Vajpeyi* where £10,000 was advanced to the defendant (a young man with limited resources) by the claimant (an older woman who was very fond of him) in order that he could purchase a house in his sole name. In concluding that the plausible explanation was that this was a loan and not an investment in the venture, the Deputy Judge added, "And we must not have our judgment clouded because of their respective sexes. Imagining they were reversed: what might we expect the position of the older and wealthier man to be?"[84]

While there is no limitation period in respect of a resulting trust, the amount of time that has elapsed before the resulting trust is asserted is also capable of helping to rebut the presumption. The Deputy Judge in *Vajpeyi* observed, "The fact that no complaint is made for a long time calls for an explanation. If no sufficiently credible explanation is forthcoming when one might have expected this may, in my judgment, serve to rebut

---

80   [2003] EWHC 2339 (Ch).
81   [2003] EWHC 2339 (Ch) at [66].
82   [2003] EWHC 2339 (Ch) at [71].
83   [2003] EWHC 2339 (Ch) at [77].
84   [2003] EWHC 2339 (Ch) at [83].

the presumption, or help to do so".[85] On the facts before him, the defendant was allowed to collect and keep rents from the property for nearly 21 years. This made no sense if the transaction was a shared venture. Similarly, Dr Vaipeyi's failure to seek interest for almost 21 years told against her claim. On the facts, therefore, the presumption of a resulting trust was not a strong one and was easily rebutted by Mr Yusaf.

What payments suffice?

The presumption of a purchase money resulting trust is based upon the making of a **11.25** direct contribution in money or money's worth to the purchase price. The relevant principle is that the resulting trust of a property purchased arises once and for all at the date on which the property is acquired. It is at the date of purchase that the intention is presumed to exist and the entitlement under the trust fixed.[86] The working rule, therefore, is that payments made subsequent to the purchase do not generate the presumption.[87] As will become clear, such post-acquisition expenditure may well, instead, fuel a constructive trust.[88] The shift towards the latter device has diminished the currency of the resulting trust analysis and reduced it to a "judicial instrument of last resort".[89]

The clearest example of a purchase money resulting trust arises where, say, Fred and Adrienne purchase a house together and Adrienne contributes 30 per cent of the purchase price. Adrienne will acquire her beneficial interest as a result of that contribution. Nevertheless, this is not the only type of payment that may be made and it has been left to the courts to determine which types of payment qualify and which do not.

A direct contribution to the deposit or the cash price of the property will, without **11.26** more, activate the presumption of a resulting trust.[90] Nevertheless, it is not every contribution of value that will be regarded as "purchase money" for these purposes. It is useful to consider some common examples of payments that may be made and to see whether or not they will generate the presumption of a resulting trust.

The right to buy discount under the Housing Act 1985

In *Springette v Defoe*,[91] the sitting tenant of a local authority house was entitled to a 41 **11.27** per cent discount on purchasing the property with her partner. The financial advantage achieved by her discount was regarded as her contribution to the purchase price and factored in the calculation of her equitable interest in the property. This method of contribution to the purchase price was recognised also in *McKenzie v McKenzie* where it was again held that the benefit from the discount could give rise to a resulting trust of

[85] [2003] EWHC 2339 (Ch) at [78].
[86] *Pettitt v Pettitt* [1970] A.C. 777; *Gissing v Gissing* [1971] A.C. 88.
[87] *Bernard v Josephs* [1982] Ch. 391.
[88] *Curley v Parkes* [2004] EWCA Civ. 1515.
[89] Per Blackburne J. in *Nightingale Mayfair Ltd v Mehta* [2000] W.T.L.R. 901.
[90] *Samad v Thompson* [2008] EWHC 2809 (Ch).
[91] [1992] 2 F.L.R. 388.

a beneficial interest proportionate to the value of the discount in relation to the purchase price.[92] The discount obtained can be substantial. For example, in *Day v Day*[93] the discount was 60 per cent. In *Crossley v* Crossley,[94] the market value of the property was £56,500 but the price paid, reflecting a 38 per cent discount, amounted in total to £35,051.

A similar approach should be adopted in circumstances where, in the private sector, a sitting tenant and another buy the freehold reversion at a discount from the landlord.[95]

Mortgage repayments

11.28 There is no doubt that the discharge of mortgage repayments can give rise to a resulting trust, but this is not always so. The distinctions that are drawn as regards purchase by instalments reflect the difficulty of adapting the traditional resulting trust theory to such elongated transactions. In *Stack v Dowden*, Lord Neuberger acknowledged that a simple and clear treatment of a mortgage liability is questionable both in terms of principle and authority.[96] Instead, as Peter Gibson L.J. acknowledged in *Curley v Parkes*, reliance is generally placed on a constructive trust where an agreement or common intention can be found or inferred from the circumstances.[97] Nevertheless, in the context of the resulting trust:

- the assumption of legal liability under a mortgage to purchase the property will normally suffice.[98] Peter Gibson L.J. explained in *Curley v Parkes*, "Because of the liability assumed by the mortgagor in a case where monies are borrowed by the mortgagor to be used on the purchase, the mortgagor is treated as having provided the proportion of the purchase price attributable to the monies so borrowed".[99] Hence, if Fiona and Jordan buy property together with the aid of a mortgage taken out in both names, the legal liability to which each is exposed under this acquisition mortgage will be usually regarded as a contribution to the purchase price. This occurred in *Laskar v Laskar* where the parties purchased the property with the aid of a mortgage and as an investment;[1]

- a mere exposure to risk as a result of becoming party to a mortgage will not be a qualifying condition when the evidence shows that it was not intended at the time of the initial acquisition and mortgage that the claimant should actually pay instalments.[2] This is regardless of any potential liability under the mortgage or, indeed, any payment made upon subsequent enforcement. The important

---

[92] [2003] EWHC 601 (Ch); see also, *Laskar v Laskar* [2008] 1 W.L.R. 2695.

[93] [2005] EWHC 1455 (Ch).

[94] [2005] EWCA Civ. 1581.

[95] *Carlton v Goodman* [2002] 2 F.L.R. 259.

[96] [2007] 2 A.C. 432 at 471.

[97] [2004] EWCA Civ. 1515; see also, *Driver v Yorke* [2003] EWHC 746 (Ch).

[98] In *Samad v Thompson* [2008] EWHC 2809 (Ch), the fact that Mr Samad promised the Thompsons that he would make payments under the mortgage did not give him an interest under a resulting trust. He had no liability to the lender.

[99] [2004] EWCA Civ. 1515 at [14].

[1] [2008] 1 W.L.R. 2695.

[2] *McKenzie v McKenzie* [2003] EWHC 601 (Ch).

factor is, instead, that it was intended that the party should be responsible for paying, and actually pay, part of the mortgage instalments;

- a voluntary and subsequent making of mortgage repayments will not be enough for resulting trust purposes. As Peter Gibson L.J. noted in *Curley v Parkes*, such payments, "are not part of the purchase price already paid to the vendor, but are sums paid for discharging the mortgagor's obligations under the mortgage".[3] Accordingly, if Fiona is the sole borrower under the acquisition mortgage, any repayments made by Jordan will not count for resulting trust purposes. At the time the property was purchased, Jordan was under no legal compulsion to discharge the mortgage debt; and

- any payments made towards mortgage instalments on an occasional basis, or commenced some time after the original acquisition, do not enjoy, as the Deputy Judge in *McKenzie v McKenzie* put it, "the requisite direct nexus with the purchase to be treated as a contribution to the purchase price...".[4]

Payment of conveyancing and other expenses

The effect of a payment of conveyancing expenses is, somewhat surprisingly, unclear.   **11.29**
Traditionally, such payments were thought sufficient to give rise to a resulting trust as comprising part of the composite cost of purchasing the property.[5] Nevertheless, recently in *Curley v Parkes* the Court of Appeal adopted the view that such expenditure is not to be regarded as a contribution to the purchase price. Peter Gibson L.J. concluded, "The payment was no part of the purchase price, though I accept that for the purposes of a constructive trust (as distinct from a resulting trust) any ancillary payment, such as the payment of expenses, may be relevant".[6] The appellate court concluded that the payment of legal fees and stamp duty could not be treated as part of the purchase cost for the purposes of a resulting trust. It also demonstrated that the payment of removal costs plainly did not form part of the purchase price and, therefore, fell to be disregarded for these purposes. These payments are either non-acquisition costs or are made only after the purchase has taken place. For example, the payment of general household expenses will be insufficient.[7] Such payments are referable to the running of a home and not the acquisition of property.[8]

---

[3] [2004] EWCA Civ. 1515 at [14].
[4] [2003] EWHC 601 (Ch) at [82].
[5] See generally, *Davis v Vale* [1971] 1 W.L.R. 1022.
[6] [2004] EWCA Civ. 1515 at [21].
[7] *Gross v French* (1976) 238 E.G. 39.
[8] *Gissing v Gissing* [1971] A.C. 886.

Domestic labour and payment of rent

11.30   Activities such as work in or on the house or child rearing do not amount to "purchase money" for the purposes of giving rise to a resulting trust.[9] Such services are geared to the running of a household rather than to the purchase of a house. As Lord Denning M.R. observed in relation to painting and decorating and gardening work carried out by one partner, "Those are the sorts of things that a wife does for the benefit of the family without altering the title to, or interests in, the property".[10]

The periodic payment of rent will also prove insufficient. Rent equates with a payment for the use of the property and is not to do with its purchase. Plowman J. explained in *Savage v Dunningham*, "Rent, unlike purchase-money, is not paid for the acquisition of a capital asset, but for the use of a property during the term ... the fact that the plaintiffs and the defendant shared the rent does not establish a resulting trust in favour of the plaintiffs".[11] This, of course, stands in marked contrast with a capital contribution towards the purchase price of a lease (i.e. premium), which is clearly a contribution towards the purchase of the property.

Employer relocation packages and informal agreements

11.31   In *Curley v Parkes*, Mr Curley was asked by his employer to move to Luton and was offered a relocation package. The employer was prepared to pay removal costs, solicitor's fees and a contribution to any increased mortgage costs if the move entailed buying in a more costly housing area. Although the title to the new property and the attendant mortgage would be in the name of Ms Parkes, the employer agreed to let Mr Curley take advantage of the relocation scheme. No part of the purchase price was paid by Mr Curley. Mr Curley eventually paid the £9,213 to Ms Parkes. As it was not established that Mr Curley had incurred a liability to pay the £9,213, what arose between the parties was, as Peter Gibson L.J. put it "an agreement such as is reached between members of a family and others living together which is not intended to have legal consequences".[12] Any obligation that existed was owed by Mr Curley's employer and was owed to Mr Curley.

Doctrinal divergence

11.32   The traditional view is that the recognition and enforcement of resulting trusts ensures the realisation of the unexpressed, but presumed positive intention of the party making the financial contribution to create a trust.[13] Hence, such trusts are often referred to as "presumed intention resulting trusts". The purchase money resulting trust is one

[9] *Burns v Burns* [1984] Ch. 317.
[10] *Button v Button* [1968] 1 W.L.R. 457 at 462.
[11] [1974] Ch. 181 at 185.
[12] [2004] EWCA Civ. 1515 at [20].
[13] See the views expressed by Megarry J. in *Re Vandervell's Trusts (No.2)* [1974] 2 Ch. 269.

example of a presumed intention resulting trust. The other example is the gratuitous transfer resulting trust which arises when an owner of property transfers it to a third party for no consideration.

There is, however, an alternative underlying principle for the existence of resulting trusts that has assumed a popular currency. The alternate assertion is that it is the absence of any positive intention to pass by way of gift the beneficial interest to the transferee that is crucial. This absence of intention to benefit theory was, most famously, expounded by Lord Millett in *Air Jamaica Ltd v Charlton*.[14] The theory is, therefore, posited upon what the transferor did not intend as opposed to what was intended. In other words, the resulting trust is responsive to the absence of intention to pass the beneficial interest and not to the positive intention to retain it. This emphasis upon the negative entails that the resulting trust arises by operation of law and has nothing to do with any presumption as to the positive intentions of the settlor. As explained by Potter L.J. at the Court of Appeal stage in *Twinsectra Ltd v Yardley*:

"the role of intention in resulting trusts is a negative one, the essential question being whether or not the provider intended to benefit the recipient and not whether he or she intended to create a trust. The latter question is relevant to whether the provider succeeded in creating an express trust, but its relevance to the resulting trust is only as an indication of lack of intention to benefit the recipient...".[15]

Although the differences between the two theories appear to carry little practical importance (i.e. in most cases both routes lead to the same destination),[16] the conundrum has stirred much intellectual argument. Rickett and Grantham[17] offer an interesting perspective that attempts to unify these seemingly opposing theories. The writers accept that all resulting trusts are a response to the presumed intention of the transferor or settlor. Nevertheless, they identify the key issue as being, "whether the transfer of property to B is intended by A to be beneficial to B. It is presumed that A did not intend B to acquire a beneficial interest in the property".[18] They continue, "intention is established not by the actual evidence but by appeal to presumptions supplied by the law. Resulting trusts comprise a group of trusts that are founded upon intention, although neither express nor implied ... All resulting trusts are more accurately termed 'presumed trusts'".[19] Hence, these commentators see the resulting trust and its associated presumptions operating as a series of default rules locating the beneficial interest in property in circumstances where there is uncertainty as to the placement of that interest.

11.33

This overarching approach has received some judicial support. In *McKenzie v McKenzie*,[20] the High Court accepted that the true doctrinal basis of a resulting trust

---

[14] [1999] 1 W.L.R. 1399 at 1412. This is, however, a decision of the Privy Council and, thereby, is only of persuasive authority.
[15] [1999] Lloyd's Rep. Bank 438 at 457. In the House of Lords [2002] 2 A.C. 164, only Lord Millett made reference to this absence of intention theory. It does not, therefore, form part of the ratio of that decision.
[16] This was recognised by Mummery L.J. in *Carlton v Goodman* [2002] 2 F.L.R. 259 at 267.
[17] C.E.F. Rickett and R. Grantham, "Resulting Trusts—The True Nature of the Failing Trust Cases" (2000) 116 L.Q.R. 15.
[18] Rickett and Grantham, (2000), at p.18.
[19] Rickett and Grantham, (2000), at p.19.
[20] [2003] EWHC 601 (Ch).

was disputed (that is, whether it is based upon an inferred intention or, instead, the absence of intention). Nevertheless, Deputy Judge Robert Hildyard Q.C commented:

> "there does seem to me to be much in the view that in the case of a resulting trust the basis for equity's intervention is not proof of a common intention; but a presumption ... that a person is unlikely to have paid for property altruistically without some expectation of return by way of a beneficial interest in it ... a resulting trust is equity's response to the failure of a gift or proof of lack of intention to make one. In any event, as it seems to me, conduct on the part of the contributor that it is explicable on a basis other than the expectation of return by way of beneficial interest will not suffice to give rise to the presumption that is the basis of such a resulting trust".[21]

Distinguishing a constructive trust

11.34   It is crucial that the fundamental differences between the resulting trust and the more far-reaching constructive trust are appreciated at the outset. As Lord Browne-Wilkinson writing extra-judicially observed, these types of trust "are two different animals" and as to which a failure to tell them apart has led to "great confusion".[22] As shown, the resulting trust is based upon financial contributions to the purchase of land and the intention that is presumed to underlie the making of those payments. In contrast, a constructive trust is underpinned by the twin tenets of common intention and change of position. As indicated above, the reliance upon mortgage finance, and the difficulty of classifying mortgage repayments for resulting trust purposes, has reduced the importance of the resulting trust. Indeed, the Law Commission has endorsed the view that the resulting trust has become limited to those relatively rare instances where there is no evidence of the parties' actual intentions, but some contribution has been made to the purchase price.[23]

There are two distinguishing features of a constructive trust. First, it is concerned with the enforcement of the bilateral intentions of the parties arising from some antecedent arrangement, whether express or implied, relating to equitable ownership.[24] As acknowledged by Chadwick L.J. in *Oxley v Hiscock*, it is the element of consensus that each should have a beneficial share which, "provides the foundation for Mrs Oxley's claim in constructive trust or proprietary estoppel; and which distinguishes that claim from one founded on resulting trust alone".[25] Similarly, in *McKenzie v McKenzie* Deputy Judge Robert Hildyard Q.C. took the view that, "a constructive trust arises out of, and is equity's way of giving effect to, the common intentions of the parties. Where a common intention can be proven or imputed to the parties by reference to some express agreement or arrangement between them the technique of equity is to impose a constructive trust to fulfil it".[26] The finding of this agreement or arrangement will normally

---

[21] [2003] EWHC 601 (Ch) at [76].
[22] "Constructive Trusts and Unjust Enrichment" (1996) 10 Trust Law International 98, p.99.
[23] "Sharing Homes A Discussion Paper" (2002) Law Com. 278 at para.2.61.
[24] *Crossley v Crossley* [2005] EWCA Civ. 1581.
[25] [2004] 3 W.L.R. 715 at 722.
[26] [2003] EWHC 601 (Ch) at [70].

be based upon evidence of express discussions between the parties, however imprecise and imperfectly remembered. In the absence of any communicated intention, a common intention may be inferred from the conduct of the parties.

Secondly, and following *Gissing v Gissing*,[27] this common intention trust is imposed only when the claimant has acted in reliance on the bilateral intention in circumstances where it would be inequitable to allow the other party to refuse to give it effect. As the Deputy Judge in *McKenzie v McKenzie* explained, "Consensus (whether express or inferred) will not suffice to give rise to a constructive trust without proof of detrimental reliance".[28] Conscience and the prevention of equitable fraud, therefore, underpin the constructive trust.   **11.35**

Under both a constructive trust and a proprietary estoppel, the fundamental ingredient is that the legal owner of the property has acted unconscionably. As Browne-Wilkinson L.J. admitted in *Grant v Edwards*, "In both, the claimant must to the knowledge of the legal owner have acted in the belief that the claimant has or will obtain an interest in the property. In both, the claimant must have acted to his or her detriment in reliance on such belief. In both, equity acts on the conscience of the legal owner to prevent him from acting in an unconscionable manner by defeating the common intention".[29] The shared need for detrimental reliance gives rise to further difficulties in that it becomes difficult to draw a clear demarcation between the constructive trust and proprietary estoppel in this context.[30]

As regards quantification of the beneficial interest, different rules apply according to whether the implied trust is resulting or constructive. In relation to the former, it will be remembered that the claimant should obtain a share commensurate with the value of the contribution. In the case of a constructive trust, quantification should, when possible, be according to what the parties intended. Under a constructive trust, therefore, the court can adopt a more creative approach to the calculation of the parties' respective shares. As demonstrated in *Grant v Edwards*, this involves looking beyond direct financial contributions (which, obviously, still assume relevance) and considering the parties' entire course of conduct together.   **11.36**

If the intention is not clear the court traditionally favours a contribution-based assessment. As will become clear, these contributions need not be to the purchase price. As Peter Gibson L.J. put it in *Curley v Parkes*, "In a constructive trust case one looks at the entire conduct of the parties and a broader approach as to what constitutes contributions is appropriate".[31]

CONSTRUCTIVE TRUSTS AND THE FAMILY HOME

A constructive trust arises in order to prevent one party resiling from an understanding as to beneficial entitlement in circumstances where it would be unconscionable to do so.   **11.37**

---

[27] [1971] A.C. 886.
[28] [2003] EWHC 601 (Ch) at [73]; see also *Midland Bank v Dobson* [1986] 1 F.L.R. 171.
[29] [1986] Ch. 638 at 656.
[30] See *Banner Homes Ltd v Luff Developments Ltd* [2000] Ch. 372 at 397 where Chadwick L.J. admitted, "the concepts of constructive trust and proprietary estoppel have much in common in this area".
[31] [2004] EWCA Civ. 1515 at [16].

This will occur primarily where the estate owner has by words or conduct induced the claimant to act to his detriment in the reasonable belief that, in so acting, he will obtain a beneficial interest in the property.[32] The concepts of bargain, change of position and conscience, therefore, lie at the heart of the constructive trust. This was demonstrated by the House of Lords in *Lloyds Bank Plc v Rosset* where Lord Bridge took the opportunity to restate the law as it related to the acquisition of an interest in the family home.[33] Lord Bridge identified two rules under which a beneficial interest could arise, one following on from an express, but informal, arrangement between the parties, the other arising from their unexpressed, but inferred, common intentions. It is helpful to consider these settings separately.

Rule 1: express bargain constructive trusts

11.38   The traditional context for the creation of a constructive trust is where the legal owner of land has informally agreed that another is to acquire some beneficial interest in the property.[34] As Lord Bridge explained:

> "The first and fundamental question which must always be resolved is whether ... there has at any time prior to acquisition, or exceptionally at some later date, been any agreement, arrangement of understanding reached between them that the property is to be shared beneficially. The finding of an agreement or arrangement to share in this sense can only, I think, be based on evidence of express discussions between the partners, however imperfectly remembered and however imprecise their terms may have been. Once a finding to this effect is made it will only be necessary for the partner asserting a claim to a beneficial interest against the partner entitled to the legal estate to show that he or she has acted to his or her detriment or significantly altered his or her position in reliance on the agreement in order to give rise to a constructive trust or a proprietary estoppel".[35]

Discussion and shared intention

11.39   Accordingly, there must be some discussion as to property rights between the parties and, consequently, some arrangement, agreement or understanding reached between them as to ownership. This discussion will usually, but need not necessarily, occur prior to the acquisition of legal title.[36] Following *Hammond v Mitchell*,[37] and in order to avoid the case failing due to vagueness, it is necessary that the express discussions alleged should be pleaded in detail. Provided that the claimant has acted to his

---

[32] *Gissing v Gissing* [1971] A.C. 886.
[33] [1991] 1 A.C. 107.
[34] For example, in *Williamson v Sheikh* [2008] EWCA Civ 990 a draft declaration of trust (never executed) constituted the necessary agreement.
[35] [1991] 1 A.C. 107 at 132; see also *Morris v Morris* [2008] EWCA Civ 257 where there was no discussion and, therefore, no "Rule 1" common intention constructive trust.
[36] *Clough v Killey* (1996) 72 P. & C.R. D22.
[37] [1991] 1 W.L.R. 1127.

detriment (or significantly altered his position) in reliance upon that arrangement, either a constructive trust or a proprietary estoppel will be invoked in favour of the claimant. The trust or estoppel will be employed to give effect to the express and shared intention. This approach is well illustrated by two case law examples.

First, in *Eves v Eves*[38] Stuart told his partner, Janet, that their joint home was to be acquired in his sole name because, at the time of purchase, she was under 21 years of age. Hence, it was explicitly made clear that, had she been older, the property would have been transferred into joint names. Subsequently, the relationship ended and she then claimed an interest in the quasi-connubial home. Stuart ran the defence that he had used Janet's age as an excuse for not having to put the house in both names. Although it had never been Stuart's real intention that Janet should acquire any beneficial interest, his excuse was viewed as evidence of some intention to share. He had led her to believe that she was to have an interest in the house. As Janet acted on that belief, a constructive trust was invoked under which she was entitled to a one quarter share in the property. As Lord Denning M.R. explained, "he should be judged by what he told her—by what he led her to believe—and not by his own intent which he kept to himself".[39] Brightman J. added, "It seems to me that this ... raises the clear inference that there was an understanding between them that she was intended to have some sort of proprietary interest in the house: otherwise no excuse would be needed".[40]

Secondly, in *Grant v Edwards*[41] George informed his partner, Linda, that the only **11.40** reason why the property was conveyed into his sole name was that her on-going divorce might be prejudiced if she was to be a joint legal owner. Again it was not the genuine desire of George that Linda become a beneficial owner. Nevertheless, by this trick she was led to believe that the property was to be theirs jointly. Hence, a constructive trust was imposed to ensure that she received the half-share in the house that George had led her to believe she would have. As Nourse L.J. explained, "Just as in *Eves v Eves*, these facts appear to me to raise a clear inference that there was an understanding between plaintiff and defendant, or a common intention, that the plaintiff was to have some sort of proprietary interest in the house; otherwise no excuse for not putting her name onto the title would have been needed".[42] Mustill L.J. added, "Whatever the defendant's actual intention, the nature of the excuse which he gave must have led the plaintiff to believe that she would in future have her name on the title, and this in turn would justify her in concluding that she had from the outset some kind of right to the house".[43] Browne-Wilkinson V.C. also agreed that the representation made to the Linda, albeit untrue, was clear direct evidence of a common intention that she was to have an interest in the house.[44]

The shared intention for these purposes, however, needs to be express. If no discussion occurs, as demonstrated in *Burns v Burns*,[45] there is no scope for a constructive trust under the first rule in *Rosset*. It is also to be recalled that, where there is an intention expressed, there is no scope for a resulting trust.

[38] [1975] 1 W.L.R. 1338.
[39] [1975] 1 W.L.R. 1338 at 1342.
[40] [1975] 1 W.L.R. 1338 at 1344.
[41] [1986] Ch. 638.
[42] [1986] Ch. 638 at 649.
[43] [1986] Ch. 638 at 653.
[44] [1986] Ch. 638 at 655.
[45] [1984] Ch. 317; see also *Driver v Yorke* [2003] EWHC 746 (Ch).

The thoughts of the parties necessarily have to be communicated as, in the words of Steyn L.J., "Our trust law does not allow property rights to be affected by telepathy".[46] Nevertheless, as Arden L.J. admitted in *Lightfoot v Lightfoot-Brown*, "The fact that an agreement or arrangement is reached as a result of express discussions which are imprecise in their terms does not prevent the court from finding that there was an express agreement that a party should have a beneficial interest even though he or she is not the legal owner".[47] This entails that there has to be evidence (whether direct or circumstantial) that proves the existence of a specific statement about ownership. The court will, therefore, look for some signs of a consensual understanding. This forensic exercise was described by Waite J. in *Hammond v Mitchell* as involving a, "painfully detailed retrospect".[48] He added that the emphasis upon express discussions between the parties:

> "means that the tenderest exchanges of a common law courtship may assume an unforeseen significance many years later when they are brought under equity's microscope and subjected to an analysis under which many thousands of pounds of value may be liable to turn on fine questions as to whether the relevant words were spoken in earnest or in dalliance and with or without representational intent".[49]

11.41 In both *Eves v Eves* and *Grant v Edwards* the court was able to discern the necessary element of "agreement" in order to activate the constructive trust. This was despite the deceit and trickery underlying the statements made. Some commentators, however, dispute whether this finding should have been made and regard the agreement as a fiction. Clarke looks at these excuse cases and concludes, "Surely this is not agreement: it is disagreement ... it is surely converting the intention of one party—albeit on these facts the innocent one—into an agreement".[50] Gardner shares the incredulity and notes that, "in both, the partner had explicitly told the woman that she was not to have a share. So on the face of it, there was most decidedly no agreement that she should".[51] He continues, "It is hard to think that the judges concerned really believed in it. One can only conclude that they ... were engaged in the business of inventing agreements on women's behalf ... the judges are prepared to take an inventive approach to the facts, so as to discover a common intention when in truth none exists ...".[52] Nevertheless, both cases survived scrutiny by the House of Lords in *Lloyds Bank v Rosset* and represent the current state of the law. Subsequently, in *Hammond v Mitchell*[53] the Court of Appeal upheld a constructive trust based upon the statement of the male partner (a second hand car dealer) that "I'll have to put the house in my name because I have tax problems" which explained why the house was conveyed into his sole name. He added that she was not to worry as when they married (this happy event, however, never occurred) the property would be half hers. As a result, she allowed her rights in the

---

[46] *Springette v Defoe* [1992] 2 F.L.R. 388 at 394.
[47] [2005] EWCA Civ. 201 at [23].
[48] [1991] 1 W.L.R. 1127 at 1129.
[49] [1991] 1 W.L.R. 1127 at 1139.
[50] P. Clarke, "The Family Home: Intention and Agreement" [1992] 22 Fam. Law 72 at p.74.
[51] S. Gardner, "Rethinking Family Property" (1993) 109 L.Q.R. 263 at p.265.
[52] (1993) 109 L.Q.R. 263 at p.265.
[53] [1991] 1 W.L.R. 1127.

property to be subordinated to those of a subsequent mortgagee and worked for her partner on an unpaid basis. Again the court construed this excuse as amounting to an assurance that the house was to be shared with his partner. Such declaration of intent operated as the basis of the understanding upon which she acted to her detriment. It appears, therefore, that the common intention is to be tested objectively and not subjectively.

More recently, in *Oxley v Hiscock*[54] the shared intention was that the couple were to live **11.42** together and to pool their financial and other resources as would a married couple. The fact that the title was registered in the sole name of Mr Hiscock was expressly stated to be in order to defeat any claim that her former husband may have against the property. Again a Rule 1 constructive trust arose.

Other examples of informal arrangements

The informal arrangements that might be entered between the parties are various and **11.43** include the following examples:

- an agreement that X should retain an interest in land purchased from X by Y. In *Bannister v Bannister*,[55] a woman conveyed land at an undervalue to her brother-in-law on the oral understanding that she would be allowed to occupy rent free for the remaining years of her life. It was held that, when he tried to evict her, there was a constructive trust that enabled the enjoyment of the beneficial life interest as promised. In short, there was a bargain, detrimental reliance and equitable fraud;

- an agreement that X should retain an interest in land purchased from Z by Y. In *Lyus v Prowsa Developments Ltd*,[56] a building plot was sold by a mortgagee to a development company subject to the subsisting rights of a named party who had paid a deposit on one of the still to be constructed houses. The contract to buy the house had not, however, been protected by an appropriate entry on the Land Register. The development company subsequently threatened not to honour its commitment. The High Court held that the development company had taken the legal title subject to a constructive trust in favour of the third party. There had been an express arrangement that formed, in part, the basis of the sale transaction which gave the house buyer new rights. For the development company to renege on that stipulation would amount to an unconscionable act;

- an agreement that X should acquire an interest in land to be purchased from Z by Y. In *Pallant v Morgan*,[57] there was a joint venture involving an antecedent and unenforceable bargain that one party could buy the land without competition from the other in return for a promise of shared rights in the land. In

---

[54] [2004] 3 W.L.R. 715.
[55] [1948] 2 All E.R. 133.
[56] [1982] 1 W.L.R. 1044.
[57] [1953] Ch. 43.

these circumstances, equity will not permit Y to acquire the property and keep it for his own benefit to the exclusion of X. The key ingredients of the *Pallant*-style equity are, as Sir Martin Nourse put it in *Kilcarne Holdings Ltd v Targetfollow (Birmingham) Ltd*, "first, that there be an arrangement or understanding between the parties that A will acquire the property and that if he does so B will obtain some interest in it; and secondly, that B must act in reliance on that arrangement or understanding".[58] The claim failed in the *Kilcarne Holdings* case because there was no understanding between the parties that the property should be acquired for their joint benefit or that Kilcarne would obtain some interest in it;

- an agreement that X should acquire an interest in land already owned by Y. In *Gissing v Gissing*,[59] there was an unenforceable post-acquisition under-standing that a cohabitant was to acquire an interest in the family home. Absent signed writing, this was not an effective declaration of an express trust. Nevertheless, the oral agreement, coupled with detrimental reliance, made it unconscionable for the cohabitant's interest to be denied. The House of Lords gave effect to it by utilising a constructive trust. Similarly, in *Hussey v Palmer*,[60] Mrs Hussey was invited to live with her son-in-law, Mr Palmer. In return, she financed an extension to the house in which she was to be accommodated. The pair fell out and the majority of the Court of Appeal held that a constructive trust arose under which she was entitled to a share in the property as a result of her financial contributions. The problem with this decision is that the existence of an agreement between the parties is not readily apparent on the evidence. Indeed, in his dissenting judgment Cairns L.J. felt that this was a loan and that the elderly woman was not entitled to invoke a trust; and

- an agreement that X should acquire a greater interest in land owned by Y. In *Re Densham*,[61] there was originally a purchase money resulting trust which fixed the beneficial interest of X according to the financial contributions made towards the acquisition of the property. Subsequently, it was agreed orally that X would acquire a larger share in the property. In light of X's reliance upon the agreement, a constructive trust arose in order to give effect to the understanding between the parties. In *Gissing v Gissing*, Lord Diplock alluded to there being, "some subsequent fresh agreement, acted upon by the parties, to vary the original beneficial interests created when the . . . home was acquired".[62]

Rule 1: change of position

11.44 Once the court has divined an express agreement, arrangement or understanding relating to the equitable ownership of the property, it remains for the detection of

---

[58] [2005] EWCA Civ. 1355 at [21]; see also, *Banner Homes Plc v Luff Developments Ltd* [2000] Ch. 372.
[59] [1971] A.C. 866.
[60] [1972] 1 W.L.R. 1286.
[61] [1975] 1 W.L.R. 1519.
[62] [1971] A.C. 886 at 906.

conduct by the claimant acting upon that intention. This is usually called "detrimental reliance" or "change of position". It is necessary, as Lord Diplock observed in *Gissing v Gissing*, "to show that he or she has acted to his or her detriment or significantly altered his or her position in reliance on the agreement".[63] In *Layton v Martin*, Scott J. described this as some "*quid pro quo* moving from the claimant".[64] There has, however, to be a causal linkage between the informal understanding and the detrimental conduct. The conduct must be referable in some way to the informal arrangement reached between the parties. This required nexus was the subject of analysis, albeit somewhat divergent, by the Court of Appeal in *Grant v Edwards*.[65] There the claimant had made significant contributions to household expenses so that the other could pay the mortgage instalments.

First, Nourse L.J. favoured a restrictive approach which was to consider whether the claimant would have performed the acts, but for the understanding with the defendant. He spoke in terms of, "conduct on which the woman could not reasonably have been expected to embark unless she was to have an interest in the house".[66] Accordingly, no interest will accrue if the claimant would, without the understanding, have performed the acts anyway.[67] Conduct that results merely from the mutual love and affection of the parties, therefore, will not be sufficient to activate a constructive trust. Accordingly, merely moving in to live with another will not suffice.[68] In contrast, Nourse L.J. felt that a woman would not be expected to wield a 14lb sledge hammer in the front garden. It remains unclear whether he would have adopted the same reasoning if it had been a male claimant who had wielded the sledge hammer.

Secondly, Mustill L.J. adopted a different stance and contended that, if the bargain is express (e.g. "give up your existing Rent Act tenancy, move in with me and you will have a share in my house"), there is usually no difficulty. The surrender of the tenancy and the moving in completes the bargain (it may be added without recourse to a sledge hammer) and should not now be defeated by the fact that you might have moved in with me anyway. The difficulty, of course, is when the bargain is not as clear-cut. In such a case, the court has to fill in the blanks. As Mustill L.J. explained, "the proprietor promises the claimant an interest in the property on the basis that the claimant will do something in return. The parties do not themselves make explicit what the claimant is to do. The court, therefore, has to complete the bargain for them by means of implication".[69] As regards whether the conduct will satisfy the test, all will turn upon the nature of both the conduct and the bargain. In this default position, however, the court will again speculate as to what the claimant would have been prepared to do anyway in the absence of any informal understanding.

Thirdly, Browne-Wilkinson V.C. suggested what has become known as the "joint

11.45

---

[63] [1971] A.C. 886 at 905. The form of the reliance does not have to be specified in the agreement: *Parris v Williams* [2008] EWCA Civ 1147.

[64] [1986] 2 F.L.R. 227 at 236. The court felt that she would have moved in with her partner regardless of his vague assurances as to her future financial security. Her conduct was not induced by financial considerations.

[65] [1986] Ch. 638.

[66] [1986] Ch. 638 at 648.

[67] *Midland Bank Plc v Dobson* [1986] 1 F.L.R. 171 (periodic decorating and household chores).

[68] *Layton v Martin*, [1986] 2 F.L.R. 227; see also, *Coombes v Smith* [1986] 1 W.L.R. 808 where living with her lover for 10 years and bearing him a child was an insufficient change of position for the purposes of an estoppel.

[69] [1986] Ch. 638 at 652.

lives" approach to the linking of the intention and the acts relied upon to show detriment. Promoting a very liberal and popular approach, he explained:

> "it is impossible to say whether or not the claimant would have done the acts relied on as a detriment even if she thought she had no interest in the house. Setting up house together, having a baby, making payments to general house-keeping expenses (not strictly necessary to enable the mortgage to be repaid) may all be referable to the mutual love and affection of the parties and not specifically referable to the claimant's belief that she has an interest in the house ... once it has been shown that there was a common intention that the claimant should have an interest in the house, any act done by her to her detriment relating to the joint lives of the parties is, in my judgment, sufficient detriment to qualify".[70]

Browne-Wilkinson V.C. felt that in these "joint lives" cases, the inference is that the claimant acted in reliance on the understanding that a beneficial interest will be acquired and the burden lies on the legal owner to displace that inference. Of the three competing views, the approach of Browne-Wilkinson V.C. has much to commend it not least because it affords flexibility and is better suited to cope with the tangled web of modern living arrangements and diverse relationships.

11.46   For the purposes of Rule 1 of *Rosset*, the conduct relied upon can adopt a variety of guises. As will become clear, this is a more liberal test than is employed in relation to Rule 2 implied bargain constructive trusts. In *Grant v Edwards*,[71] the claimant contributed to household expenses so that the defendant could meet the mortgage repayments. In *Eves v Eves*,[72] the claimant did not make any financial contribution, but did carry out substantial physical labour (including wielding a 14lb sledgehammer) relating to internal and external decorating, gardening and general maintenance. She also performed the role of mother and housewife. The detriment must, however, be material and not merely emotional or psychological in nature. As Lord Templeman put it, "Equity operates on conscience but is not influenced by sentimentality".[73] In *Christian v Christian*,[74] the claimant asserted as "detriment" the fact that she had to live with her partner in a house which was located near her partner's wife's property. This "social embarrassment" was not regarded as a relevant detriment and the Court of Appeal emphasised that equity was not concerned with shielding people's feelings.

The court sometimes assesses the degree of detriment by adopting a balance sheet approach. In other words, the court looks for a net disadvantage to the claimant. There must be a substantial and not trivial detriment incurred. For example, gardening work put in by a claimant in his son-in-law's garden has been regarded as merely the carrying out of a hobby and, hence, did not suffice.[75] A similar approach was adopted where housekeeping services were relied upon, but the claimant had already been compensated by the payment of a regular housekeeping allowance and free accommodation.[76]

---

[70] [1986] Ch. 638 at 657.
[71] [1986] Ch. 638.
[72] [1975] 1 W.L.R. 1338.
[73] *Winkworth v Edward Baron Development Co Ltd* [1986] 1 W.L.R. 1512 at 1516.
[74] (1981) 131 N.L.J. 43.
[75] *Hannaford v Selby* (1976) 239 E.G. 811.
[76] *Layton v Martin* [1986] 2 F.L.R. 227. A similar approach is adopted in relation to satisfying an estoppel claim: see *Jennings v Rice* [2003] 1 P. & C.R. 100.

Rule 1: quantification

If the express bargain prescribes the shares that the parties are to take, the quantifi-   **11.47**
cation of the beneficial interest is straightforward. In *Clough v Killey*,[77] there was an
express bargain that the beneficial interest be shared on a 50/50 basis. Mrs Killey
argued that, under the first rule in *Rosset*, a constructive trust arose which, due to the
express agreement, gave her a 50 per cent interest. Subsequent to this arrangement, Mrs
Killey had undeniably acted to her detriment by making the proceeds of her divorce
settlement available to Mr Clough and undertaking work on the cottage. As to the
extent of her share, Peter Gibson L.J. admitted, "it is only common sense that where the
parties form a common intention as to specific shares they are to take, those shares
prima facie are the shares to which the court will give effect".[78] The correct starting
point, therefore, was to take the shares as established by the parties' express common
intention and to depart from this only when there was good cause. Although Peter
Gibson L.J. failed to indicate what would constitute such a cause, he here did conclude
that, on the present evidence, there was no justification for such departure, "It seems to
me only just that Mr Clough should be held to, and not allowed to renege on, his
promise on which Mrs Killey relied to her detriment".[79] Accordingly, *Clough v Killey*
demonstrates the fundamental point that when the parties expressly agree on beneficial
shares, provided there is some detrimental reliance, that understanding will almost
certainly be enforced by the courts.

Difficulties arise, however, when the express bargain is silent as to the beneficial share
to be taken. The court is then forced to do its best to allocate on the basis of fairness
and justice. The maxim "equity is equality" has little role to play in these circumstances.[80] As Lord Reid put it in *Gissing v Gissing*, "I think that the high-sounding
brocard 'equity is equality' has been misused. There will of course be cases where a half-
share is a reasonable estimation, but there will be many others where a fair estimate
might be a tenth or a quarter or sometimes more than half".[81]

In *Drake v Whipp*,[82] there was an express agreement to share beneficial ownership,   **11.48**
but the respective shares were left unstated. The issue was whether the calculation
should be based upon constructive trust principles (i.e. a broad brush approach) or
resulting trust principles (i.e. an arithmetical approach). The argument promoted was
that there was no scope for a constructive trust because of the lack of a common
understanding or intention as to the respective shares to be taken. The Court of Appeal
rejected this line of reasoning. Although it was necessary for there to be a common
intention that Mrs Drake should have some beneficial interest, it was not necessary for
constructive trust purposes that the exact shares be specified between them. Instead, the
court could assess her share by evaluating her change of position, including direct
financial contributions made, as a result of the informal agreement. Peter Gibson L.J.

---

[77] (1996) 72 P. & C.R. D22.
[78] (1996) 72 P. & C.R. D22 at D24. In *Parris v Williams* [2008] EWCA Civ 1147, the Court of Appeal
emphasized that, although the contributions of the parties differ significantly, the agreement will still be
enforced.
[79] (1996) 72 P. & C.R. D22 at D24.
[80] See Waite J. in *Hammond v Mitchell* [1991] 1 W.L.R. 1127 at 1137.
[81] [1971] A.C. 886 at 897.
[82] [1996] 1 F.L.R. 826.

acknowledged that the court would also take into account, "the fact that Mr Whipp and Mrs Drake together purchased the property with the intention that it should be their home, that they both contributed their labour in 70 per cent/30 per cent proportions, that they had a joint bank account out of which the costs of conversion were met, but that that account was largely fed by his earnings, and that she paid for the food and some other household expenses and took care of the housekeeping for them both".[83]

Somewhat surprisingly, the same issues were once more canvassed in *Oxley v Hiscock* where again there was an agreement to share, but in unspecified proportions.[84] The first question on appeal was whether the court was to follow the constructive trust approach or whether the shares were to be calculated simply according to the respective financial contributions to the acquisition cost. Chadwick L.J. reiterated that, for the purposes of an express bargain constructive trust, the agreement need not recite the extent of the parties' beneficial interests. The primary issue was to establish an express discussion to share and, once that was demonstrated, there was no practicable alternative to the determination of a fair share. "It must now be accepted that ... the answer is that each is entitled to that share which the court considers fair having regard to the whole course of dealing between them in relation to the property".[85] This includes arrangements which they make from time to time in order to meet the outgoings (e.g. housekeeping, mortgage contributions, council tax and utilities) which have to be met if they are to occupy the property as a home. Accordingly, the court is simply imputing a common intention as to the parties' respective shares on the basis of that which, in the light of all the material circumstances (including the acts and conduct of the parties after the acquisition) is shown to be fair and reasonable. Chadwick L.J. acknowledged that, "the courts have not found it easy to reconcile that final step with a traditional, property-based approach".[86]

11.49 Chadwick L.J. noted that this "fair share" approach had been criticised by Dillon L.J. in *Springette v Defoe*[87] as offering palm tree justice, but he felt that the court must make such an order as the circumstances require to give effect to the beneficial interest of the one party, "the existence of which the other party (having the legal title) is estopped from denying".[88] Chadwick L.J. preferred his reasoning to that adopted in *Midland Bank v Cooke*[89] which attributed to the parties a fictitious common intention that their respective beneficial interests should be fixed as from the time of the acquisition when, in reality, they had given no thought to the matter. Chadwick L.J. also believed his approach to be better than that promoted by Lord Diplock in *Gissing v Gissing*[90] which was that, at the time of acquisition, the common intention was that their respective shares should be left for later determination.

[83] [1996] 1 F.L.R. 826 at 831.
[84] [2004] 3 W.L.R. 715.
[85] [2004] 3 W.L.R. 715 at 750. This approach was approved by Baroness Hale in *Stack v Dowden* [2007] 2 A.C. 432 (cf. Lord Neuberger's view at 476).
[86] [2004] 3 W.L.R. 715 at 750.
[87] [1992] 2 F.L.R. 388.
[88] [2004] 3 W.L.R. 715 at 750. Chadwick L.J. expressed the view that the *Springette* case did not accurately reflect the state of the law even when it was decided. The primary issue was to establish an express discussion to share and, once you get to that stage, there is no practicable alternative to the determination of a fair share.
[89] [1995] 4 All E.R. 562.
[90] [1971] A.C. 886.

The "fair share" approach is based upon three strands of reasoning:

- the court must operate on the basis that the parties have agreed that their shares are to be determined in such a way at the end of their relationship or upon sale;

- following a review of the whole of the parties' course of dealing, the court must assume that this was the parties' assumed common intention at the time of purchase; and

- the fairness approach must operate because it invoked principles that were almost indistinguishable from those applied under the doctrine of proprietary estoppel.

In the Court of Appeal in *Stack v Dowden*,[91] Chadwick L.J. was offered the opportunity   **11.50** to revisit his earlier decision in *Oxley v Hiscock*. He emphasised that the same approach was to be adopted regardless of whether the property is registered in the joint names of the cohabitants or is, instead, registered in the sole name of one of them. He also took the opportunity to consider the relevance of financial contributions. He again rejected the proposition that, absent agreement as to shares, the property is necessarily to be held in beneficial shares proportionate to their respective contributions to the purchase price. He admitted that quantification might reflect the parties' contributions when it was fair and just that this should follow. This may be, for example, where the majority of the purchase price has been provided by one party and the other has made a comparatively slight financial input. Although the parties may have agreed that each should have an undefined beneficial interest, it would not be fair, having regard to the whole course of dealing between the parties in relation to the property, to treat their beneficial shares as equal. An alternative conclusion would, of course, fail to give proper weight to the financial contributions made to the acquisition of the property.

A role for proprietary estoppel?

Lord Bridge in *Lloyds Bank Plc v Rosset* envisaged that a beneficial interest could be   **11.51** acquired by proprietary estoppel as well as by constructive trust.[92] The traditional distinction between a constructive trust and an estoppel lies in the emphasis of the former upon "bargains" and the emphasis of the latter upon "representations".[93] There are three characteristics of proprietary estoppel: there must be a representation or assurance; there must be reliance or change of position; and there must be detriment or unconscionable disadvantage.[94] Hence, under the first rule in *Rosset*, a constructive trust and a "common expectation" proprietary estoppel can arise on the same facts. They both share common characteristics in that there is the need for some form of shared understanding, detrimental reliance and equitable fraud. The conventional

---

[91] (2006) 1 F.L.R. 254; affirmed at [2007] 2 A.C. 432.
[92] [1991] 1 A.C. 107 at 132.
[93] See generally, P. Ferguson, "Constructive Trusts—A Note of Caution" [1993] 109 L.Q.R. 114.
[94] *Morris v Morris* [2008] EWCA Civ 257. Sir Peter Gibson noted that the representation or assurance, "must be specific, such as would entitle the person to whom it is made reasonably to rely on it or change his or her position" (at [28]).

response is that both are, "concerned with equity's intervention to provide relief against unconscionable conduct".[95] As Browne-Wilkinson V.C. put it in *Grant v Edwards*, "The two principles have been developed separately without cross-fertilisation between them, but they rest on the same foundation ...".[96] It is, therefore, common for alternative arguments based upon the constructive trust and estoppel to be pleaded.[97] Nevertheless, the scope for semantic and conceptual confusion is so profound that, in *Simpson v Simpson*, the High Court unhelpfully spoke in terms of a constructive trust based on equitable estoppel.[98]

The role for estoppel in the co-ownership arena appears to concentrate on Rule 1 cases where there has been an informal agreement and even then only when the informal agreement is inconclusive as to the parties' beneficial shares. This is a sensible restriction as the usual outcome will be that a complete informal agreement will be enforced as it stands. This is regardless of the degree of the change of position undertaken by the claimant. Under an estoppel, however, what is represented (i.e. the expectation generated) is far from determinative of the outcome of the case. Such was demonstrated in *Jennings v Rice*,[99] where the Court of Appeal admitted that the court had to look at matters in the round and have regard to the nature and quality of the representation and the expectation engendered, the detriment incurred and the proportionality of any award having regard to the detriment. If the claimant's expectations are uncertain, extravagant or out of proportion to the detriment suffered, the court should recognise that the claimant's equity should be satisfied in another and generally more limited way than that which was expected.[1] To honour the representations in the *Jennings* case (i.e. to award the claimant a house worth £435,000) would have been entirely disproportionate to satisfy the equity.[2] Instead, the claimant was awarded a sum of £200,000. The touchstone of unconscionability, therefore, comes into play when satisfying the equity. A disproportionate remedy is not the correct way of doing what is right to avoid an unconscionable result. It is also an adage of estoppel that the court will confer only the minimum equity to do justice on the facts of each case. Such concerns do not bother the court when there is an express bargain to share in specified proportions.

11.52 Estoppel may assume relevance in the scenario where there has been an express agreement as to sharing, but the agreement is totally silent as to the parties' shares. It was in this context that Chadwick L.J. in *Oxley v Hiscock* surveyed the relationship between the two legal concepts and concluded, "the time has come to accept that there is no difference in outcome ... whether the true analysis lies in constructive trust or in proprietary estoppel".[3] This assimilation was, however, doubted by Lord Walker in *Stack v Dowden*, "proprietary estoppel typically consists of asserting an equitable claim against the conscience of the 'true' owner. The claim is to a 'mere equity'. It is to be

[95] Per Robert Walker L.J. in *Yaxley v Gotts* [2000] Ch. 162 at 176. Note, however, his later reluctance to accept that the two concepts can be assimilated: *Stack v Dowden* [2007] 2 A.C. 432 at 448; *Cobbe v Yeoman's Row Management Ltd* [2008] 1 W.L.R. 1752 at 1776.

[96] [1986] Ch. 638 at 656.

[97] See *Pineld v Eagles* [2005] EWHC 477 (Ch).

[98] [2005] EWHC 2098 (Ch).

[99] (2003) 1 P. & C.R. 100.

[1] *Powell v Benney* [2007] EWCA Civ 1283.

[2] See also, *Murphy v Burrows* [2004] EWHC 1900 (Ch).

[3] [2004] 3 W.L.R. 715 at 751.

satisfied by the minimum award necessary to do justice ... which may sometimes lead to no more than a monetary award. A 'common intention' constructive trust, by contrast, is identifying the true beneficial owner or owners, and the size of their beneficial interests."[4]

As shown, in cases where there is an agreement to share and the agreement expressly allocates the parties' respective interests, a constructive trust analysis will prevail. Accordingly, where the parties have informally agreed that each is to have an equal share this will usually be definitive. It is, however, possible that subsequent to the agreement X acts further to his detriment without there being a positive representation made by Y. If Y stands back and allows X to change his position in the mistaken belief that he (X) has rights and although there is no bargain between them, X's additional detriment could be recognised by an added value estoppel interest built upon the finding of a constructive trust.[5] This theme was pursued in *Sleebush v Gordon*[6] where the High Court felt that an express declaration of trust contained in the conveyance could be departed from by the invocation of proprietary estoppel. There the co-owner made clear and unequivocal representations and, as a result, the claimant took over total financial responsibility for the property over many years. This reliance warranted an increased entitlement to the property which was awarded on an estoppel basis.

Rule 2: the implied bargain constructive trust

The second rule in *Rosset* applies where there is no evidence of an express discussion **11.53** having occurred between the parties. In this situation, the court looks in detail at the conduct of the parties with the prospect of presuming a common intention to share beneficial ownership. There are two key ingredients. First, the claimant must convince the court that there was a common intention to share the property beneficially. As Arden L.J. noted in *Lightfoot v Lightfoot-Brown*, "In the absence of a common intention, no common intention constructive trust will arise".[7] Secondly, the claimant must demonstrate that he changed his position on the basis of the unexpressed common intention. The court may look at conduct both prior and subsequent to the acquisition of the property.

It will quickly become clear that, under this second rule, the role of direct financial contributions made by a non-owner is multifaceted. This was discussed by Arden L.J. in *Lightfoot v Lightfoot-Brown* where she concluded that such contributions serve:

- as evidence from which a common intention can be inferred;
- as corroboration of direct evidence of intention;
- as evidence that the claimant has acted in reliance on the intention; and

---

[4] [2007] 2 A.C. 432 at 448; see also Black J. in *SMQ v RFQ* [2008] EWHC 1874 (Fam).
[5] *Preston & Henderson v St Helens MBC* (1989) 58 P. & C.R. 500. This case concerned who was entitled to the owner occupier's supplement on compulsory purchase of an unfit dwelling house.
[6] [2004] EWHC 2287 (Ch).
[7] [2005] EWCA Civ. 201 at [24].

- as an aid to the quantification of the size of the beneficial interest.[8]

Common intention

11.54 The process of finding a common intention has been eased somewhat by the stance of the Court of Appeal in *Oxley v Hiscock*.[9] This appeal concerned a female claimant who had made a 20 per cent contribution towards the purchase of the family home. Under constructive trust principles, however, she was awarded a 40 per cent share. As regards the threshold issue relating to the intention to share beneficially, Chadwick L.J. emphasised that, "direct contributions to the purchase price will be conduct from which such common intention can readily be inferred".[10] The appellate court, therefore, acknowledged that proof of the common intention will normally take the form of financial contributions made by the claimant to the acquisition cost of the property. This was an approach shared also by the High Court in *McKenzie v McKenzie* where it was admitted that, "the Court is unlikely to consider the inference justified unless there is proof that the claimant made direct contributions to the purchase price which are not explicable except on the basis that the parties must have intended that the property would be beneficially shared ...".[11] In *Morris v Morris*, Sir Peter Gibson acknowledged that, "a common intention constructive trust based only on conduct will only be found in exceptional circumstances."[12]

It follows that even a small contribution can afford evidence of the common intention and, as it is an inference drawn by the court from conduct, the fact that the parties never gave any thought to the matter is irrelevant.[13] The common intention is not, therefore, undermined by the lack of any consensus as to beneficial shares. Intention should not be difficult to establish.

Change of position

11.55 In contrast with the first rule in *Rosset*, there is a more demanding test employed here as regards what amounts to a change of position. It is not enough for the purposes of Rule 2 that the claimant's conduct is merely attributable to the inferred agreement between the parties. It should not be overlooked that, as Lord Bridge observed, the claimant is relying upon his own conduct, "both as the basis from which to infer a common intention to share the property beneficially and as the conduct relied on to give rise to a constructive trust".[14] Consequently, the change of position is localised only to direct financial contributions made to the initial and/or ongoing purchase of the property.[15]

---

[8] [2005] EWCA Civ. 201 at [24].
[9] [2004] 3 W.L.R. 715.
[10] [2004] 3 W.L.R. 715 at 734.
[11] [2003] EWHC 601 (Ch) at [72].
[12] [2008] EWCA Civ 257 at [23].
[13] *Midland Bank v Cooke* [1995] 4 All E.R. 562.
[14] *Lloyds Bank Plc v Rosset* [1991] 1 A.C. 107 at 133.
[15] *Gissing v Gissing* [1971] A.C. 886. Hence, it would cover mortgage repayments. It is thought that improvements to the property will not suffice.

Arden L.J. explained in *Lightfoot v Lightfoot-Brown*, "In this respect the expenditure has to be referable to the acquisition of the house".[16] Indeed, as Lord Bridge acknowledged, "it is at least extremely doubtful whether anything else will do".[17] Accordingly, if direct contributions are found the courts will readily imply a constructive trust,[18] whereas, if no such contributions are made then co-ownership under the second rule simply does not arise.

The insistence upon there being monetary contribution to the purchase of the property ignores other valuable contributions that a claimant may have made. This was patently demonstrated in *Burns v Burns*[19] where years of domestic labour and child rearing were disregarded. There had been no express agreement (so Rule 1 could not apply) and no direct financial contribution whatsoever (so she could not invoke a Rule 2 constructive trust or, indeed, a purchase money resulting trust). Hence, Ms Burns acquired no interest at all in the family home. As Fox L.J. put it, "the mere fact that the parties live together and do the ordinary domestic tasks is . . . no indication at all that they thereby intended to alter the existing property rights of either of them".[20] In a similar vein, a daughter's unpaid work managing a public house did not trigger a constructive trust in relation to the family home that was purchased out of the profits of the pub business.[21] The contribution was indirect and showed no intention that she was to acquire an interest in the house.

Quantification

Although the making of direct financial contributions is necessary to buy entry into the   **11.56**
co-ownership arena, it is important to appreciate that, once the constructive trust is invoked, the court can look beyond the direct contributions.[22] In doing so it is able to divine a beneficial share which, on the facts of each case, accords with justice and good conscience.[23] As Chadwick L.J. pointed out in *Oxley v Hiscock*, "the relevant common intention is that each party should have some beneficial interest. Direct contributions to the purchase price may lead to an inference that each party should have some beneficial interest without necessarily leading to the further inference that their respective shares should be proportionate to the amount of the direct contributions".[24] This is apparent also from *Midland Bank Plc v Cooke* where Waite L.J. refused to accept that the shares were to be fixed solely by reference to the wife's direct contributions which, in turn, would make all other conduct irrelevant.[25] Instead, he believed that the court was to undertake a survey of the whole course of dealing between the parties relevant to their

---

[16] [2005] EWCA Civ. 201 at [24].
[17] *Lloyds Bank Plc v Rosset*, [1991] 1 A.C. 107 at 133.
[18] See *Pineld v Eagles* [2005] EWHC 477 (Ch).
[19] [1984] Ch. 317; see also, *Button v Button* [1968] 1 W.L.R. 457.
[20] *Burns v Burns*, (1984) Ch. 317 at 331; see also *James v Thomas* [2007] EWCA Civ 1212.
[21] *Ivin v Blake* (1994) 67 P. & C.R. 263.
[22] See the Privy Council decision in *Abbot v Abbot* Unreported July 26, 2007. There Baroness Hale observed at [19], "The parties' whole course of conduct in relation to the property must be taken into account in determining their shared intentions as to its ownership."
[23] *Drake v Whipp* [1996] 1 F.L.R. 826.
[24] [2004] 3 W.L.R. 715 at 734.
[25] [1995] 4 All E.R. 562.

ownership and occupation of the property and their sharing of its burdens and advantages. The contemporary tendency is, therefore, for the court to adopt a broad brush approach to the calculation of shares under the implied bargain. Without the sanction of Parliament, the courts have in the post-*Rosset* world employed the flexibility of an implied bargain constructive trust to effect a back-door redistribution of family assets according to perceptions of what is a fair outcome.

A fair share, however, does not necessarily equate with an equal share in the property.[26] This is a further area which is usually unsuited to an application of the equitable maxim, "equity is equality".[27] This maxim will only be invoked as a measure of last resort.[28] Accordingly, it is common for the determination to be of unequal shares.

11.57 The financial contributions made by the claimant may be a persuasive, but not necessarily decisive, factor in the calculation of beneficial interests. As demonstrated in *Midland Bank Plc v Cooke*, the court must look at the entire course of dealings between the parties. This flexible approach entails that factors which are totally irrelevant in discerning the existence of co-ownership can assume major relevance when calculating the parties' shares once co-ownership has been established. Accordingly, and as the Court of Appeal in the *Cooke* case made clear, when deciding the issue of quantum the court can survey the parties' shared endeavours, past family life, pooling of resources and mutual commitment.

Non-financial and indirect financial contributions assume much relevance in the evaluation process. The court can have regard to payments towards the financing of substantial improvements to the property[29] and to the discharge of utilities such as council tax, electricity and household insurance.[30] Account may be taken of indirect assistance such as the payment of other household expenses, contributions by way of labour and other unquantifiable actions of the claimant.

Scope for proprietary estoppel

11.58 In contrast with Rule 1 (see **11.51**), estoppel appears to have no significant role to play when a Rule 2 constructive trust is divined from the common intention of the parties. The latter operates in the absence of any express discussion or assurance, whereas, estoppel requires some form of encouragement or assurance. In practice, therefore, they exist in mutually exclusive spheres. When the common intention to share is inferred, and the claimant has made a direct contribution to the purchase of the property, this is constructive trust territory and the rights of the parties will be determined according to the implied bargain reached between them. If, however, no direct contributions are made by the claimant, the Rule 2 constructive trust is unavailable. In those circumstances, and because detrimental reliance for estoppel purposes is not limited solely to financial contributions,[31] an estoppel might arise to prevent the other party from

---

[26] *Oxley v Hiscock* [2004] 3 W.L.R. 715.
[27] *Hammond v Mitchell* [1991] 1 W.L.R. 1127.
[28] See Neuberger J. in *Mortgage Corp v Shaire* [2001] Ch. 743 at 750.
[29] *Passee v Passee* [1988] 1 F.L.R. 263 where money was spent by one co-owner on re-roofing, central heating, double glazing and re-wiring.
[30] *Oxley v Hiscock* [2004] 3 W.L.R. 715.
[31] See *Jennings v Rice* (2003) 1 P. & C.R. 100 where the detriment was unpaid labour and caring duties.

unconscionably denying a representation or encouragement. These are sometimes referred to as "unilateral mistake" cases.[32]

Reform

The Law Commission concluded in its discussion paper that the current requirements for establishing the existence of a beneficial interest, "are not ideally suited to the typical informality of those sharing a home. We feel that to demand proof of an intention to share the beneficial interest in the home can be somewhat unrealistic, as people do not tend to think about their home in such legalistic terms. The emphasis upon financial input towards the acquisition of the home fails to recognise the realities of most cohabiting relationships".[33]   **11.59**

The Law Commission lamented also that the present system can cause lengthy and expensive litigation. The Commission attempted to provide an alternative scheme to ascertain whether a person had a beneficial interest (and, if so, to what extent) in the family home. The new scheme was, however, to be abandoned by the Commission because it failed to offer a viable alternative. Subsequently, a new scheme was championed by the Law Commission and this formed the recommendations of its 2007 report.

The rejected property approach

The Law Commission's now abandoned "property law scheme" was designed to apply only in the absence of a "valid express arrangement" between the parties. This allusion to validity presumably means when there is a "valid" declaration of an express trust which accords with the writing formalities as prescribed in s.53(1)(b) of the Law of Property Act 1925. Nevertheless, the Commission reveal an inconsistency by sometimes mysteriously dropping the "valid" label and speaking solely in terms of an express declaration of beneficial entitlement. It is, therefore, not entirely clear what the Commission intended.   **11.60**

As regards other situations, the scheme would jettison implied trusts and proprietary estoppel, would take no regard of a change of position and would create, "a statutory default scheme for the ascertainment and quantification of beneficial ownership which would offer greater certainty, clarity and consistency".[34] The acquisition of a beneficial interest in the shared home under this scheme would be pursuant to a "statutory trust". In outline, the conditions for this statutory trust would be that:

- two or more persons are living together;

---

[32] See Lord Walker in *Cobbe v Yeoman's Row Management Ltd* [2008] 1 W.L.R. 1752 at 1777.
[33] "Sharing Homes: A Discussion Paper" (2002) Law Com. 278, para.2.112; see generally, C. Rotherham, "The Property Rights of Unmarried Cohabitees: The Case for Reform" [2004] Conv. 268. This sentiment was echoed in the Law Commission "Cohabitation: The Financial Consequences Report of Relationship Breakdown" (2007) Law Com No.307 at para.2.16.
[34] Law Com. 278, para.3.4(3).

- there would be only limited exclusions (e.g. relating to employees, minors, lodgers and tenants) to the general rule that all who share a home will be caught by the scheme;

- at least one of them should have a legal or beneficial interest in the home upon which a statutory trust could be based;

- the claim must be made against a person who could have granted a proprietary interest in favour of the claimant;

- the claimant must have made a financial contribution whether direct or indirect to the acquisition, improvement or retention of the family home. In the alternative, the claimant must have made non-financial contributions to the construction or improvement of the home or to the parties' joint lives (e.g. by homemaking and caring services);

- the share awarded will be proportionate or pro rata to the contribution as ascertained;

- beneficiaries under the statutory trust would be able to protect their interests against third party purchasers by registering them at the Land Registry; and

- the beneficial interest will arise at the time that the contribution is first made.

11.61 The Law Commission disowned its own provisional scheme primarily because it was ill-thought out, disregarded the intentions of the parties and potentially offered an undue advantage for the sharing non-owner. It was also unclear whether the best way forward was to make the scheme retrospective or prospective only in effect and, if the former was chosen, whether it would contravene the European Convention on Human Rights. The Law Commission concluded, "The property law scheme does not go far enough in remedying injustices which arise under the current law, but creates new ones of its own. It is not, therefore, one which we can even provisionally propose".[35]

The difficulties associated with discerning a common intention from contributions made when there has been no discussion at all of co-ownership have prompted other jurisdictions to search for alternative solutions. For example, in the USA and Canada the courts have promoted allocation of shared property on the basis of good faith and unjust enrichment. These so-called "remedial constructive trusts" operate without regard to the parties' intentions and, instead, offer a broad based discretion in the court to counter unjust enrichment. Hence, if X (the legal owner) would be unjustly enriched if he was to retain the entire beneficial interest in the property, the court will subject X to an equitable duty to hold on trust for, say, Y. Y's contributions may be financial or of a household and caring nature. The shift of emphasis is that the North American courts will look to the benefit received by X and not focus on the detriment suffered by Y.

---

[35] Law Com. 278, para.3.100.

A relationship approach

As an alternative to a property based approach, the emphasis could be to focus upon **11.62** the nature of the parties' relationship and to consider what rights (if any) should be accorded to that relationship. This style of approach found some favour with Lord Walker in *Stack v Dowden* who predicted that, "any new legislation is likely to give the court new statutory discretions comparable to (but probably less far reaching than) those exercisable under the Matrimonial Causes Act 1973 (as amended). The law would then become more flexible (and so better able to avoid injustice)...."[36] In Australia, legislation that regulates the rights and obligations of those in relationships is widespread. The court is usually given a wide discretion to adjust property rights according to what is fair and equitable having regard to the direct and indirect contributions made by the parties. Australia, however, treats married couples differently from unmarried couples in that as regards the former the court can take into account the future needs of the spouses. In New Zealand, however, the distinction between the married and the unmarried is not drawn.

 Some jurisdictions (e.g. the Scandinavian countries, France, Belgium and the Netherlands) have for some time permitted unmarried couples to register their relationships as a form of "partnership" which attributes similar rights and obligations as that of marriage. This idea has now been imported into the United Kingdom, but only in relation to same-sex couples, by the Civil Partnership Act 2004. This legislation makes provision for property and financial arrangements on dissolution of the partnership. It is designed to equate the rights and obligations of parties within a registered same-sex relationship with those operating within the framework of a heterosexual marriage. For example, s.65 expressly makes the financing of substantial improvements to real or personal property a means by which the contributing party can acquire a beneficial interest. This has applied to married couples since s.37 of the Matrimonial Proceedings and Property Act 1970. The concept of registered partnerships, moreover, offers no solace for those who fail to make any formal provision concerning their relationship.

The Law Commission's new scheme

In its 2006 Consultation Paper, the Commission provisionally recommended a novel **11.63** and generally applicable scheme to redistribute family assets which operated to eligible cohabitants with children. The parties could, however, opt out of the scheme if they so wished. These proposals (albeit in a much modified form) formed the basis of the Commission's 2007 Report. The Report acknowledged that the current law was markedly deficient and that the allocation of property rights between cohabitants should no longer be dependent on the application of inflexible property principles. As it acknowledged, "The general law, therefore, is not equipped to provide a comprehensive

---

[36] [2007] 2 A.C. 432 at 445.

solution to problems arising on separation, responding to the economic consequences of the parties' contributions to their relationship."[37]

Although the Commission's own solution is by no means comprehensive, it does improve the lot of those cohabitants who qualify under the proposed scheme. The ambition is laudable, "Such a system would help individual cohabitants and their children. It would provide economically vulnerable members of society with the private means to rebuild their lives and ensure a fairer division of assets on relationship breakdown."[38]

11.64   In outline, eligibility under the scheme is as follows:

- the parties must have lived as a couple in a joint household;

- they must not be married or in a civil partnership;

- they must either have children of their own or (if none) have lived together for a continuous period of two years before their separation. The latter will only be dispensed with in exceptional circumstances;

- the parties must not have contracted out of the scheme. If they have, their entitlements will be governed by the old law, and

- the claim must be brought within two years of the parties' separation. The court will have the power to extend this period only in exceptional circumstances.

Once the claimant has satisfied the qualifying conditions

- the relief to be granted is at the court's discretion;

- the court will exercise its discretion with regard to listed criteria, including the welfare of any children, the needs and obligations of the parties and the conduct of the parties;

- the court will have a wide range of orders that it can make (not periodic maintenance payments though), and

- the order will be based upon the economic impact of cohabitation and qualifying contributions made by the parties. The latter are not limited to financial contributions.

GUIDE TO FURTHER READING

S. Bridge, "The Property Rights of Cohabitants—Where Do We Go From Here?" [2002] Fam. Law 743.

P. Clarke, "The Family Home: Intention and Agreement" [1992] 22 Fam. Law 72.

---

[37] (2007) Law Com 307 at [2.16].
[38] (2007) Law Com 307 at [1.4].

T. Etherton, "Constructive Trusts: A New Model for Equity and Unjust Enrichment" (2008) C.L.J. 265.

P. Ferguson, "Constructive Trusts—A Note of Caution" [1993] 109 L.Q.R. 114.

S. Gardner, "Rethinking Family Property" (1993) 109 L.Q.R. 263.

A. Lawson, "The Things we do for Love: Detrimental Reliance and the Family Home" (1996) Legal Studies 218.

Chapter 12

THE APPOINTMENT, RETIREMENT AND REMOVAL OF TRUSTEES

The trustee is the pivotal character in the trust relationship. Although it is possible to **12.01** have a trust without there being a settlor (as with implied trusts) or a beneficiary (as with purpose trusts), there can be no trust without the presence of a trustee. At the heart of a trust is the vesting of legal title to the trust property in the trustee. Hence, the trustee acquires all the rights and powers relating to that property, subject to his labouring under an obligation to use the property in a prescribed manner. The trustee is the representative of the trust. It is the trustee who has the power to deal with trust property and to make investments. It is the trustee who is responsible to carry out the terms of the trust and to exercise any discretion and powers that have been given to him. The operation of the trust, the achievement of the settlor's intentions and the promotion of beneficiary's interests, therefore, rest heavily upon the shoulders of the trustee. The obligations are onerous and the consequences for breach of trust are severe. Not everyone is equipped or will agree to act as a trustee.[1] The characteristics of a trustee are, as Pettit puts it, "integrity, a willingness to spend time and trouble on trust affairs, the ability to get on with co-trustees and beneficiaries; knowledge of financial matters, business acumen and common sense".[2]

This chapter introduces the reader to the types of trustee that may exist and to consider how trustees are appointed, both initially and by way of replacement. It will also examine the ability of a trustee, who no longer wishes to continue to act in that capacity, to retire voluntarily from his office and explain how a trustee can be compulsorily removed from office. Finally, this chapter will consider the ability of a trustee to delegate his powers and discretions without ceasing to hold the office of trustee.

---

[1] Hence, the rule is that no one can be compelled to undertake a trust: *Robinson v Pett* (1734) 3 P Wms 251. It is, of course, possible that an individual could be saddled unwillingly with the role under a constructive or resulting trust.

[2] P.H. Pettit, *Equity and the Law of Trusts*, at p.364.

TYPES OF TRUSTEE

Ordinary trustees

12.02   The general rule is that any individual, limited company or corporation may act as a trustee. An individual can act as a co-trustee with a corporation and a corporate trustee can act as co-trustee with another corporate body. Put simply, if you can hold property, you can be a trustee. For example, the Crown can in principle be a trustee[3] as can a local authority. There is, moreover, no problem with a foreigner holding as trustee (unless the trust property is a ship[4]). In contrast, an unincorporated association or a society cannot assume the office of trustee because such an entity does not have the legal personality to hold property. Instead, it is the members as individuals who have legal recognition, the property of the association held in accordance with the contract between them. Those convicted of crimes of dishonesty and bankrupts cannot usually be trustees of charities.[5] A minor cannot, moreover, be expressly appointed as a trustee and any attempt to do so will be void.[6] Nevertheless, a minor can become a trustee under a trust of personalty arising by implication or by operation of law. This was demonstrated in *Re Vinogradoff*[7] where a grandmother transferred £800 of War Loan Stock into the names of herself and her granddaughter. At the time, the granddaughter was only four years old. It was held that the child became a trustee holding the property on a resulting trust for the grandmother.[8] As a child cannot hold a legal estate in land,[9] the same outcome is impossible with implied trusts of land.[10]

An ordinary trustee will not usually be able to claim remuneration for the performance of his functions. This rule gives way when payment is authorised by the trust instrument or the trustee is either a trust corporation or is in the business of trust management and administration. In practice, a professional trustee (a solicitor or accountant) will undertake the task only when express provision is made for remuneration.

12.03   The number of trustees that can be appointed is, with one exception, unlimited. While there must be at least one trustee, there is no cap placed upon the maximum number permissible. The exception referred to concerns trusts of land where a maximum of four trustees only are allowed to hold legal title.[11] If more than four are named, the first four named who are willing and able to act will be the trustees. Obviously, it is inconvenient to have too many trustees and uncommon to have in excess of four. The potential downside of having a sole trustee is that the opportunities for fraud and maladministration are increased. For some purposes, moreover, a two-trustee rule operates. These include capital money arising from land which must be paid to (or at the

---

[3] See *Civilian War Claimants Association Ltd v R.* [1932] A.C. 14.
[4] Aliens have a limited ability to own such vessels: see s.17 of the Status of Aliens Act 1914 (as amended).
[5] Section 72 of the Charities Act 1993.
[6] Section 20 of the Law of Property Act 1925.
[7] [1935] W.N. 68.
[8] The presumption of advancement (i.e. gift) did not apply here because it was not a parent child situation and the grandmother did not stand in loco parentis to the girl.
[9] Section 1(6) of the Law of Property Act 1925.
[10] See *Newham LBC v Ria* Unreported January 15, 2004.
[11] Section 34(2) of the Trustee Act 1925.

direction of) at least two trustees[12]; a valid receipt for capital money must be given by at least two trustees[13]; and the process through which trust interests in land are overreached by a purchaser requires the involvement of at least two trustees.[14]

Trust corporations

Trust corporations play a major role in the administration of trusts. They can act jointly with ordinary trustees or, as is more usual, they can act as a sole trustee. Their size, longevity, financial stability and expertise place them in an advantageous position when compared with an ordinary trustee. The most recognisable trust corporations are large banks and insurance companies that have trust departments. Such corporations are, moreover, usually well equipped economically to make good any breach of trust. It is crucial to appreciate that a trust corporation is a very different creature than a mere corporate trustee. A trust corporation enjoys a special status and has powers and rights that an ordinary company trustee does not have. For example, a trust corporation may itself give a good receipt for capital money under a trust of land. As shown, the involvement of two trustees is normally required for an effective receipt for capital money to be given to a purchaser. Traditionally, a trust corporation was in the same position as an ordinary trustee and, thereby, only able to levy a charge if there were (as is usual) express arrangements made to do so. Since s.29 of the Trustee Act 2000, however, a trust corporation is able to charge a "reasonable remuneration" for its services. The downside is that the involvement of a trust corporation will not come cheaply.

    The status of a trust corporation is reserved for a body corporate that carries out the business of acting as a trustee and, moreover, satisfies certain conditions. These conditions[15] are that the company must:

- be expressly authorised by its constitution to carry out the business of acting as a trustee;

- have an issued share capital of not less than £250,000 (or its foreign equivalent) of which at least £100,000 (or its foreign equivalent) must be paid up in cash;

- have been incorporated in a European Union country; and

- operate from a place of business located within the United Kingdom.

In addition to these commercial trust corporations, a number of other bodies are afforded the status of a trust corporation by primary and secondary legislation. The meaning has been extended to include the Public Trustee or a corporation either appointed by the court to be a trustee or entitled under the Public Trustee Act 1906 to act as a custodian trustee. The definition also includes the Treasury Solicitor, the

12.04

12.05

---

[12] Section 27(2) of the Law of Property Act 1925.
[13] Section 14(2) of the Trustee Act 1925.
[14] Section 2(1) of the Law of Property Act 1925.
[15] See the Public Trustee (Custodian Trustee) Rules 1975 (SI 1975/1189).

Official Solicitor and other bodies as prescribed by the Lord Chancellor. These entities are, thereby, given the various privileges that extend to trust corporations.

Judicial trustees

12.06 A judicial trustee is a person or corporation appointed as trustee by the High Court under s.1(1) of the Judicial Trustees Act 1896[16] and in circumstances where the supervision of the court is required.[17] This appointment is at the discretion of the court[18] and is not to be confused with the appointment by the court of an ordinary trustee under s.41 of the Trustee Act 1925 (see **12.22**). Although the appointment of a judicial trustee is usually made following the application of an existing trustee or a beneficiary, it can be made at the behest of the settlor when creating a trust. The court can appoint any fit and proper person (e.g. a solicitor, bank or accountant) and, in the absence of a nomination or a suitable candidate, may appoint a court official so to act.[19] The appointment of a judicial trustee is usually made in circumstances where the administration of the trust by ordinary trustees has broken down in some way. This could occur where, for example, there has been major mismanagement[20] or misconduct,[21] the administration of the trust has become extraordinarily problematic or the trust is facing complex litigation.[22] The court will usually not appoint a judicial trustee when the person having a power to appoint trustees has nominated trustees willing to act.[23] Not surprisingly, the procedure is invoked infrequently. Instead, the tendency is to appoint a professional, corporate trustee to sort matters out.

Once appointed, the judicial trustee will work closely with, and under the supervision of, the court.[24] The judicial trustee will usually be appointed as the sole trustee, but might act jointly with a private trustee.[25] Although the judicial trustee is essentially in the same position as any other trustee, he is throughout an officer of the court. This entails that he can obtain directions informally from the court (i.e. without making a formal application) when necessary. Unless it is a court official that is appointed, the judicial trustee will provide the court with a financial guarantee in order to protect the beneficiaries from loss arising from the performance of his duties. The judicial trustee is, however, allowed to charge for his services and the court will determine the amount of remuneration, which is paid from the coffers of the trust fund.

---

[16] This is supplemented by the Judicial Trustee Rules 1983 (SI 1983/370).
[17] *Re Ridsdel* [1947] Ch. 597.
[18] Hence, an application can be refused: see *Re Chisolm* (1898) 43 S.J. 43.
[19] Section 1(3) of the 1896 Act.
[20] *McDonald v Horne* (1993) *The Times*, October 12.
[21] *Re Ratcliff* [1898] 2 Ch. 352. There the court declined to appoint because there was no misconduct on the part of the existing trustee.
[22] *Re Diplock* [1948] Ch. 465.
[23] *Re Chisolm*, (1898) 43 S.J. 43.
[24] See *Re Ridsel* [1947] Ch. 597.
[25] *Re Martin* [1900] W.N. 129.

The Public Trustee

The Public Trustee is an office established by the Public Trustee Act 1906. It is styled as **12.07** a "corporation sole" (i.e. it is a trust corporation with perpetual succession that may sue or be sued like any other corporation).[26] The Public Trustee can be appointed by the court to be a new or additional trustee. He can, therefore, act either alone or in conjunction with other trustees.[27] The Public Trustee may be appointed as an ordinary trustee, a custodian trustee (see **12.08**) or as a judicial trustee (see **12.06**).[28] If the Public Trustee is to act as an ordinary trustee, the appointment can be made expressly by a settlor/testator when the trust is created. As to the subsequent appointment of a Public Trustee, this cannot be excluded by the trust instrument[29] and can be made on the application of the settlor, a trustee, a beneficiary or the person nominated expressly by the trust instrument to appoint trustees. In default, the court can of its own volition appoint the Public Trustee. An attraction of using the Public Trustee is that the Lord Chancellor will compensate individuals in respect of liability for breach of trust. The Public Trustee may charge fees on a scale set by the Lord Chancellor.[30]

The office of Public Trustee was created to administer small estates and to help people who might otherwise have difficulty finding someone prepared to act as a trustee (e.g. until the Administration of Funds Act 1986 the Public Trustee enjoyed a role in the management of a mental patient's estate). A further role relates to the holding of the property of a person who has died without a will (i.e. intestate), pending the appointment of an administrator of the deceased's estate by the court.[31] Although the Public Trustee may refuse to act, such refusal cannot be based solely upon the ground of the small value of the trust property.[32] In addition the Public Trustee cannot, as a general rule, accept any trust that involves the carrying on of any business and can never administer charitable trusts.[33] The main role of this public sector service is, therefore, to provide a trustee of last resort for small private trusts.

Custodian trustees

The Public Trustee, the Official Custodian for Charities and trust corporations[34] are **12.08** authorised to act as custodian trustees. An individual cannot act in this capacity. The appointment of a custodian trustee is made either by the court, the creator of the trust or the person having power to appoint a new trustee.[35] This type of trustee is different

---

[26] Section 1(2) of the 1906 Act.
[27] Section 2(2) of the 1906 Act.
[28] Section 2(1) of the 1906 Act.
[29] Similarly, a provision which prohibits the exercise of discretion by fewer than two trustees will be overridden when the public trustee becomes the sole trustee: *Re Duxbury's ST* (1945) 1 W.L.R. 425.
[30] Section 2(1)(a) of the Public Trustee (Liability and Fees) Act 2002.
[31] Section 14 of the Law of Property (Miscellaneous Provisions) Act 1994.
[32] Section 2(3) of the 1906 Act.
[33] Sections 2(4), 2(5) of the 1906 Act.
[34] Accordingly, in *Re Brooke Bond & Co Ltd* [1963] Ch. 357, an insurance company was appointed the custodian trustee.
[35] Section 4(1) of the 1906 Act.

from the usual managing trustees. The custodian trustee takes custody of the trust property and documents of title while the managing trustees, who have free access to the property and documents, take care of the day to day running of the trust.[36] The custodian trustee must comply with the directions of the management trustees. Accordingly, it takes instructions from the managing trustees and not the beneficiaries. Nevertheless, as with any trustee, the custodian trustee owes a fiduciary duty to the beneficiaries. A custodian trustee cannot at the same time be a managing trustee.[37] Hence, if the sole managing trustee dies, the custodian trustee cannot take his place without first giving up the role of custodian trustee.[38] In addition, in determining the number of trustees for the purposes of the Trustee Act 1925, the custodian trustee is discounted from the calculation. The custodian trustee is not, however, a bare trustee and has duties to perform relating, for example, to the receipt and paying out of income and capital of the trust.[39] The advantage of appointing the comparatively passive custodian trustee is that, with large trusts, there can be changes made to the identity of the managing trustees without the need to vest the trust property in them.[40] This may involve considerable savings in expense, time and effort.

Not surprisingly, the custodian trustee can charge fees.[41] The appointment may be terminated by the court on the application of either the custodian trustee himself, a managing trustee or a beneficiary. Such removal will occur when the court is satisfied that it is the general desire of the beneficiaries or it is otherwise expedient to do so.[42]

APPOINTMENT OF TRUSTEES

12.09 Trustees may be appointed both on the creation of a trust and during its continuance, whether as replacement for an existing trustee or in addition to the existing trustees. The appointment is usually made by deed without the involvement of the court. Indeed, it is only in exceptional circumstances that the court will appoint a trustee.

The original trustees

12.10 The settlor or the testator usually appoints the original trustees at the time the trust is set up. If it is an inter vivos (i.e. a lifetime) trust, it is common for the trustees to be parties to the trust deed and for this instrument to transfer the trust property to them. With a lifetime trust, it is possible that the settlor might appoint himself as a trustee. In the case of a testamentary trust, understandably, that is not possible. In such circumstances, the executors of the deceased's will might be the same individuals who are nominated to act as trustees. If not, the executors will hold the property on trust for the

[36] Section 4(2)(a)–(c) of the 1906 Act.
[37] *Arning v James* [1936] Ch. 58.
[38] *Re Squire's Settlement* (1946) 115 L.J. Ch. 90.
[39] The duties, rights and liabilities of a custodian trustee are set out in s.4(2) of the Public Trustee Act 1906.
[40] See *Bankes v Salisbury Diocesan Council of Education* [1960] Ch. 631.
[41] Section 4(3) of the 1906 Act.
[42] Section 4(2) of the 1906 Act.

named trustees until the deceased's estate is wound up. The personal representative will then assent that the nominated trustees hold the property on trust.

If there is appointed more than one trustee, the trustees hold the trust property as joint tenants. As it is the legal estate that the trustees hold, there can be no severance of this joint tenancy into a tenancy in common. This entails that, if one of their brethren dies, the survivors retain the same duties and powers as before.[43] The trust property accrues by virtue of the right of survivorship to the living trustees.[44] The process will continue until there is only one trustee remaining. On the death of the last surviving or sole trustee, the personal representatives of that trustee (or, if he dies intestate, the Public Trustee) will hold the property on trust until replacement trustees are appointed.[45] On appointment of a new trustee(s), a personal representative automatically ceases to have the capacity to continue to act as trustee.[46]

As regards an inter vivos trust, there can be no valid trust if the trust is not completely constituted. Accordingly, if there are no original trustees named or they are dead by the time the trust is to take effect, the trust must necessarily fail. Simply put, there is no one in whom the legal title to the trust property can vest. With a testamentary trust the problem is less acute as the personal representatives of the deceased will always hold as trustees until replacement trustees are appointed.[47]

12.11

It is a very different situation that arises once the trust has been perfectly constituted. The trust will not subsequently be allowed to fail.[48] Hence, the death of an existing sole trustee will not prevent the continuation of the trust.[49] This accords with the equitable maxim that "the court will not allow a trust to fail for want of a trustee".[50]

Disclaimer

As indicated, an individual who has been appointed as trustee and has not yet accepted the role may disclaim the responsibility. Disclaimer by the intended trustee must, therefore, occur before he does any act indicating his acceptance, such as bringing legal action in the name of the trust[51] or giving directions as to the sale of trust property.[52] Accordingly, the trustee should disclaim as soon as is possible and before acting in relation to the trust property. For example, in *James v Frearson*[53] a person was named in a will as an executor and trustee. He was present when the property was sold at the behest of the other trustees and requested information concerning the deceased's financial accounts. These acts were held to constitute acceptance of trusteeship. A similar approach was adopted in *Conyngham v Conyngham*[54] where the nominated

12.12

---

[43] Section 18(1) of the Trustee Act 1925.
[44] *Warburton v Sandys* (1845) 14 Sim. 622.
[45] Section 18(2) of the Trustee Act 1925; ss.1, 3 of the Administration of Estates Act 1925.
[46] *Re Routledge's Trust* [1909] 1 Ch. 280.
[47] See *Re Smirthwaite's Trusts* (1871) L.R. 11 Eq. 251.
[48] *Jones v Jones* (1874) 31 L.T. 535.
[49] Section 18(2) of the Trustee Act 1925.
[50] See, for example, *Sonley v Clock Makers Co* (1780) 1 Bro. C.C. 81.
[51] *Montford v Cadogan* (1810) 17 Ves. 485.
[52] *James v Frearson* (1842) 1 Y. & C. Ch. Cas. 370.
[53] (1842) 1 Y. & C. Ch. Cas 370.
[54] (1750) 1 Ves. Sen. 522.

trustee received rents from the occupier of the trust property and was therefrom unable to renounce the office of trusteeship.

When disclaiming a trust it is advisable, albeit not essential, to do so expressly by deed.[55] The presence of a deed will offer clear and certain evidence of the disclaimer. Disclaimer can also occur by implication from conduct (e.g. by apathy and inaction[56]). It is, however, impermissible to disclaim part only of the trust.[57] Once the role has been disclaimed, the individual cannot subsequently have a change of heart. Once an individual accepts the role, however, there can no longer be a disclaimer.[58] The trustee must then elect to retire which, as will become clear, is a very different matter. If the trustee disclaiming is the intended sole trustee, the trust property will result back to the settlor or his personal representatives. If there are other intended trustees, the property will remain vested in them and no resulting trust will arise.

12.13   As mentioned, the general rule is that a trust (once constituted) will not fail for want of a trustee. If an existing trustee later refuses to act then the trust continues[59] and new trustees will be appointed.

New trustees

12.14   As soon as the trust is created, the settlor has no automatic right to appoint future trustees. The authority to appoint replacement trustees can arise either from an express power, a statutory power or on the order of the court.

As to express powers, the trust instrument may reserve for the settlor or some other person the power to appoint new trustees. This is a common practice and will dictate the terms and mode of the appointment. As demonstrated in *Re Higgingbottom*,[60] this is the primary right to make an appointment. There the existing trustee had the power to appoint new trustees and this right took priority over the wishes of a large number of the beneficiaries. Nevertheless, the appointor should communicate with the beneficiaries and take on board their views even though there is no obligation to act on them.[61] The court will not usually interfere with the appointment process.[62] There are, however, potential pitfalls associated with express powers of appointment. If two or more persons are given the power to exercise it jointly, following the death of one of them the power will not be exercisable by the survivor.[63] Similarly, where two or more persons have the power, but cannot agree as to who should be appointed, the power is likely to be frustrated.[64] The ability to exercise the express power may, moreover, be curtailed by the attachment of conditions. For example, in *Re Wheeler*[65] the power was

---

[55] *Re Schar* [1951] Ch. 280.
[56] See *Re Clout & Frewer's Contract* [1924] 2 Ch. 230.
[57] *Re Lord and Fullerton's Contract* [1896] 1 Ch. 228.
[58] *Re Sharman's WT* [1942] Ch. 311.
[59] An exception to this rule arises when the trust is made conditional upon certain people acting as trustees: *Re Lysaght* [1966] Ch. 191.
[60] (1892) 3 Ch. 132.
[61] *O'Reilly v Alderson* (1849) Hare 10.
[62] *Re Hodson's Settlement* (1851) 9 Hare 118.
[63] *Re Harding* [1923] 1 Ch. 182.
[64] *Re Sheppard's ST* [1888] W.N. 234.
[65] [1896] 1 Ch. 315.

given to named donees to appoint a replacement trustee if one of the existing trustees became "incapable". One trustee became bankrupt and disappeared. The question was whether a new trustee could be appointed by the named donees. As bankruptcy did not make the trustee "incapable" (it merely made him "unfit"), the donees did not have the power to replace him. Similarly, if the power is to be exercised by deed, it cannot be exercised by a will. Furthermore, it is arguable that the donee of the power to appoint cannot nominate himself as the new trustee as this would be an improper exercise of a fiduciary power of selection.[66]

If the trust instrument does not cater for the appointment of new trustees, there are, **12.15** as indicated, further ways in which replacements may be appointed:

- under the statutory power afforded by s.36 of the Trustee Act 1925 to appoint replacement and/or additional trustees;

- by virtue of the more limited statutory power of beneficiaries to appoint under ss.19, 20 of the Trusts of Land and Appointment of Trustees Act 1996; and

- as a last resort, the court can appoint new trustees under s.41 of the Trustee Act 1925.

Method 1: s.36(1) of the Trustee Act 1925

Subject to its exclusion in the trust instrument,[67] s.36(1) applies to all trusts and allows **12.16** for new, replacement trustees to be appointed in writing[68] (but not by will[69]). The appointor may appoint himself under this provision. As the appointment has to be "in place of" a retiring trustee, the appointment of one new trustee will never be sufficient to discharge two retiring trustees.[70] The other trustee must, accordingly, retire under the machinery provided for by s.39 (see **12.28**). One trustee can, therefore, only replace another trustee. The power is, however, exercisable only on the occurrence of one or more of seven eventualities.[71] These eventualities are set out in s.36 and are where a trustee (whether an original trustee or not):

- has died and this includes where a trustee was nominated in a will, but has predeceased the testator: s.36(8);

- has, for whatever reason, remained outside the United Kingdom for a continuous period of more than 12 months.[72] Where the trust is designed to operate

---

[66] *Re Skeat's ST* (1889) 42 Ch. D. 522; cf. *Re Sampson* [1906] 1 Ch. 435.
[67] Contracting out is catered for by s.69(2) of the Trustee Act 1925.
[68] Normally a deed is executed to obtain the benefit of the vesting provisions set out in s.40 (see below).
[69] *Re Parker's Trusts* [1894] 1 Ch. 707. C/f retirements under s.39 which are required to be by deed (see **12.28**).
[70] *Adam & Co International Trustees Ltd v Theodore Goddard* (2000) W.T.L.R. 349. F. Barlow [2003] Conv. 15, however, criticises this limitation as unsound and unjustifiable.
[71] The court will interfere only if the appointment is viewed as being so inappropriate that it would not have been countenanced by a reasonable trustee: *Richards v Mackay* [1990] 1 O.T.P.R. 1.
[72] If the trustee returns to the UK for a period (however short) within the 12 month time frame, s.36 does not apply: *Re Walker* [1910] 1 Ch. 259 (one week's return).

abroad, the trust instrument should exclude the operation of this aspect of s.36(1);

- has expressed the wish to be discharged from the trust or part of the trust;

- has refused (this includes a disclaimer[73]), has become unfit to act as trustee (e.g. due to dishonesty[74] or bankruptcy[75]) or has become incapable of acting as trustee (e.g. through illness, old age or mental disorder[76]);

- is an infant. As a minor cannot be an express trustee, this applies only when the minor is a trustee under a resulting or constructive trust;

- has been removed under a power contained in the trust instrument (s.36(2))[77]; and/or

- is a corporation that has been dissolved (s.36(3)).

12.17　The aim of s.36 is not only to enable the appointment of a new trustee without a court order, but also to ensure that there will be someone who has the ability to exercise the power if necessary. It sets out in s.36(1)(a)–(b) a hierarchy of persons who may exercise the power to appoint. If there is no one able and willing to exercise the power in the first category, the power devolves to those in the second category and so on. If there is no person able and willing to act, the s.36 power necessarily becomes redundant.

The following characters in the following pecking order have the ability to engage s.36. First, the person having an express power to appoint new trustees given by the trust deed. There is no need for the power to refer to the statutory scheme. If this express right to appoint is limited to some only of the eventualities listed above (see **12.16**), the donee of that power is not to be treated as the nominated person as far as the other non-specified eventualities contemplated by s.36 are concerned.[78]

12.18　Second in line are the "surviving or continuing" trustees (i.e. the existing trustees). Some gloss is applied to the meaning of "continuing trustees" by s.36(8) and this provides that the term includes a refusing or retiring trustee (but not a trustee removed against his will[79]) who is willing to act for these purposes. This caters for a retiring trustee to nominate his successor. Indeed, it is standard practice for refusing and retiring trustees to become involved in the appointment of replacement trustees. Although the concurrence of the refusing or retiring trustee is usually necessary for a valid appointment, this rule gives way when he is unwilling to nominate. In the latter scenario, the trustee's participation is not essential.[80]

Thirdly, the personal representatives of the last surviving trustee. These include those

[73] *Noble v Meymott* (1841) 14 Beav. 19.
[74] *Turner v Maule* (1850) 15 Jur. 761.
[75] See *Re Barker's Trust* (1875) 1 Ch. D. 43.
[76] See *Re Watt's Settlement* (1872) L.R. 7 (Ch).
[77] It is important to appreciate that s.36 does not give the court the power to remove a trustee.
[78] *Cecil v Langdon* (1884) 28 Ch. D. 1.
[79] *Re Stoneham's ST* [1953] Ch. 59 where a trustee was removed because he had been outside the UK for more than 12 months.
[80] *Re Coates to Parsons* (1886) 34 Ch. D. 370.

who have proved the will of the dead trustee and those who have become the administrators of a trustee dying intestate (s.36(4)).[81]

Appointment of additional trustees

Traditionally, and unless the trust instrument provided to the contrary, a new trustee could only be appointed when there was a vacancy. Section 36(6) of the Trustee Act 1925, however, caters generally for the appointment in writing of additional trustees (i.e. without any replacement). The appointment may be made by the person nominated by the trust instrument to appoint new trustees or, if there is no such person able and willing to act, the trustee(s) for the time being.[82] An additional trustee can be appointed even when the existing trustee is a trust corporation. Unlike under s.36(1), it is thought that the appointor cannot appoint himself as an additional trustee.[83] Section 36(6), however, only permits an additional appointment when there are no more than three existing trustees (i.e. the general rule is that the number of trustees cannot be increased beyond four).[84] While as regards trusts of personalty the trust instrument may increase the number, the maximum ceiling for trusts of land must always remain at four trustees.[85]

12.19

Method 2: The Trusts of Land and Appointment of Trustees Act 1996

Where all the beneficiaries are sui juris (i.e. of full age and capacity) they may act in unison and direct the current trustees to appoint in writing any person(s) of the beneficiaries' collective choosing as trustee(s). The appointment is, thereby, effected by the existing trustees. This power is afforded to the beneficiaries by s.19(1) of the 1996 Act and applies retrospectively to trusts of all types of property. This was not a power previously available to the beneficiaries.[86] The written direction must be given to the existing trustees or, if there are none remaining, the direction must be given to the personal representative of the last surviving trustee. The power can be excluded in the trust instrument, for example, when a power to appoint trustees is vested in someone nominated for the purpose in the trust instrument. Hence, it is designed to apply only when the trust instrument makes no provision for the appointment of new trustees.

12.20

The direction can be made in tandem with a direction to some or all of the trustees to retire (s.19(2)). Unlike the power granted under s.36 of the Trustee Act, the appointment of new trustees under s.19 is not tied to such occurrences as death, unfitness, incapacity and the like. The power can, moreover, be exercised as often as the

---

[81] Section 36(5) provides that a sole executor intending to renounce probate (i.e. wishes to cease acting as a personal representative) shall have the power to appoint trustees until the time that probate is renounced.
[82] Including the donee of a lasting power of attorney to which trustee functions have been delegated under the Trustee Delegation Act 1999.
[83] *Re Power's ST* [1951] Ch. 1074.
[84] This rule does not apply to charitable trusts.
[85] Section 34 of the Trustee Act 1925.
[86] *Re Brockbank* [1948] Ch. 206 (it was then necessary for the beneficiaries to terminate the trust and create a new one appointing the chosen trustees themselves).

beneficiaries may deem appropriate. The beneficiaries may give joint or separate directions, but must nominate the same individual(s) for appointment or retirement.[87]

12.21 Section 20 of the 1996 Act deals with the situation where a trustee is rendered incapable of carrying out his office by reason of a mental disorder and there is no person willing or able to appoint a replacement under an express power of appointment or under s.36. In this situation, s.20 enables the beneficiaries of full age and capacity in unison to direct the appointment of a replacement trustee. Section 20(2) requires that the direction be given to a representative of the incapacitated trustee (i.e. a receiver, an attorney or a person authorised for the purpose under the Mental Capacity Act 2005). Again this provision can be excluded in the trust instrument.

Method 3: appointment by the court

12.22 The court has both an inherent and a statutory jurisdiction[88] to appoint replacement or additional trustees. The inherent jurisdiction is keyed in to the general role of the court to supervise trusts and trustees.[89] Although this jurisdiction remains intact, in the light of statutory developments its exercise will be rare.[90] The additional jurisdiction given by s.41 of the Trustee Act 1925 appears sufficiently wide to cater for most (if not all) eventualities.[91]

Under s.41, the court has a broad, discretionary power to appoint new trustees in circumstances where it is "inexpedient, difficult or impracticable so to do without the assistance of the court".[92] It does not have to be "necessary" for the court to act. As mentioned, the appointment might be of an additional trustee or a replacement trustee.[93] An order can be made on the application of either a trustee or beneficiary.[94] The court will not usually make an appointment when there is an express power in the trust instrument or where one of the other statutory powers can be employed.[95] If it does act, the court will not appoint someone against the wishes of the person who has a power to appoint.[96] Accordingly, the s.41 power tends to be exercised only in situations where there is doubt as to whether a trustee is "unfit" or "incapable" to act.[97] It has, however, been employed in circumstances where the trustee has emigrated,[98] when there is no one

---

[87] Section 21(1),(2).
[88] First afforded by the Trustee Act 1850.
[89] *Buchanan v Hamilton* (1801) 5 Ves. 722.
[90] It might, for example, be employed to remove a trustee against his will or to remove a donee of a fiduciary power: *Bridge Trustees Ltd v Noel Penny Turbines Ltd* [2008] EWHC 2054 (Ch).
[91] In the *Bridge Trustees Ltd* [2008] EWHC 2054 (Ch) above the person to be replaced was not a trustee proper because the trust property was not vested in him. Accordingly, s.41 did not apply to this appointment.
[92] In *Polly Peck International Plc v Henry* (1999) 1 BCLC 407, it was held that it could not be expedient to appoint a trustee if it was also not expedient to pay that trustee. The trust instrument provided that the trustees were not to receive remuneration or to claim for expenses.
[93] The consent of the trustee who is to be replaced is, understandably, not necessary: *Re Henderson* [1940] Ch. 764.
[94] Section 58 of the Trustee Act 1925.
[95] *Re Gibbon's Trust* (1882) 45 L.T. 756.
[96] *Re Brockbank* [1948] Ch. 206.
[97] In *Re Phelp's ST* (1885) 31 Ch. D. 351, for example, the trustee was aged, deaf and careering towards senility; see also, *Re Lemann's Trusts* (1883) 22 Ch. D. 633 as a further case where the trustee was aged and incapable.
[98] *Re Bignold's ST* (1872) 7 Ch. App. 223.

who has the power to make an appointment or where the intention is to increase the number of trustees beyond four.[99]

The court enjoys the discretion as to whom to appoint as trustee. The court has, however, deemed certain types of person to be unsuitable for appointment. For example, a beneficiary will not normally be appointed[1] nor will some person resident outside the jurisdiction.[2] A close relative of one of the parties interested in the trust will, moreover, usually make an unsatisfactory appointment.[3] This caution seemingly extends also to a solicitor acting for the beneficiary or the trustee.[4] In addition, the court will try to ensure that there is appointed more than a sole trustee.[5]

12.23

As regards suitable candidates, the court will exercise its discretion according to well-established principles:[6]

- it will have regard to the settlor's wishes (e.g. the settlor may have stated whom he does not want to be a trustee);

- it will not appoint a trustee against the wishes and interests of some of the beneficiaries;[7]

- it will not appoint a person excluded from being a trustee under s.36(1) (e.g. a person under a mental disability or permanently living abroad);[8]

- it will be reluctant to appoint a beneficiary as trustee because of a possible conflict in interest;[9]

- it will have regard to whether the proposed appointment will promote or, instead, impede the carrying out of the trust. For example, if the existing trustees refuse to work with the person who the court intends to appoint, this conflict would potentially jeopardise the effective running of the trust;[10]

- it will not, unless there has been incompetence or malpractice, appoint a new trustee if this would inflict financial loss on the existing trustee[11]; and

- it will not exercise its discretion simply to engineer the avoidance of tax (e.g. to appoint foreign trustees who are not liable to UK tax).[12]

---

[99] It is to be recalled that s.36(6) does not allow an additional trustee when the appointment would increase the number beyond four trustees.
[1] *Forster v Abraham* (1874) L.R. 17 Eq. 351.
[2] *Re Weston's Settlements* [1969] 1 Ch. 223.
[3] *Wilding v Bolder* (1855) 21 Beav. 222.
[4] *Re Norris* (1884) 27 Ch. D. 333.
[5] *Viscountess D'Adhemar v Bertrand* (1865) 35 Beav. 19.
[6] See *Re Tempest* (1866) L.R. 1 Ch. App. 485.
[7] *Re Parson's* [1940] Ch. 973.
[8] *Re Windeatt's WT* [1969] 1 W.L.R. 692.
[9] *Re Knowle's Settled Estates* (1884) 27 Ch. D. 707.
[10] See *Re Badger* [1915] W.N. 166 where an appointment of an additional trustee was declined because it conflicted with the wishes of a sole trustee.
[11] See *Re Pauling's Settlement (No.2)* [1963] 576 where the removal of the trustees would have deprived them of security for the costs that might be payable to them if litigation with the beneficiaries was successful.
[12] *Re Whitehead's WT* [1971] 1 W.L.R. 833.

Vesting of trust property

12.24 On the appointment of a new trustee under s.36 or s.41 of the Trustee Act 1925, or by direction of the beneficiaries under the Trusts of Land and Appointment of Trustees Act 1996, the new trustee has the same powers, authorities and discretions as the original trustee.[13] Accordingly, he may in all respects act as if he had been originally appointed under the trust instrument. It is, however, vital that the trust property becomes vested in the new trustee and this is so whether or not he is a sole trustee or is acting jointly with other continuing trustees.

Vesting can occur by means of the former or continuing trustees transferring title to the trust property to the new trustee. The appropriate method of achieving this depends upon the nature of the trust property. For example, legal title to land requires a deed of conveyance; shares require a completed transfer form and registration of the transaction; and chattels require physical delivery with intention to transfer.[14] This type of formal transfer is not, however, always necessary as automatic vesting in relation to existing trusts is facilitated by s.40 of the Trustee Act 1925.

12.25 Section 40(1) offers a short cut and provides that automatic vesting can occur when the new trustees are appointed by deed (which explains why this is the usual practice).[15] If the deed contains a declaration that the property shall vest in the new trustees (i.e. a "vesting declaration"), vesting of title will occur without any conveyance or other transfer. In such cases, the deed of appointment will itself operate to vest the property in the new trustees. If the deed does not contain an express vesting declaration, the declaration may be implied, subject to any provision in the deed of appointment to the contrary.[16]

There are, however, important exceptions to the operation of s.40 and in such circumstances title to the property must be transferred by the usual method appropriate to that property. These exceptions concern the following types of property:

- land conveyed by way of mortgage as security for a loan of trust money. This means that, where trust money is invested in the mortgage of land, on the appointment of new trustees automatic vesting does not occur. Instead, there must be a separate, formal transfer of the mortgage term to the new trustee;[17]

- land held under a lease or sub-lease that contains a covenant against assignment without consent, unless the consent has been obtained before the execution of the deed. This exemption prevents the appointment of a trustee causing an inadvertent breach of covenant against assignment and giving rise to a forfeiture of the lease;

---

[13] Sections 36(7), 43 of the Trustee Act 1925.
[14] See **3.04**.
[15] It does not apply where the property is held by personal representatives: *Re Cockburn's WT* [1957] 3 W.L.R. 212.
[16] Similar provisions are to be found in s.40(2) and these operate to vest trust property in the continuing trustees on the discharge of a trustee.
[17] *London & County Bank v Goddard* [1897] 1 Ch. 642.

- stocks and shares. This exception recognises that the legal title to shares can only be effected by registration with the relevant company;[18] and

- registered land. Section 27 of the Land Registration Act 2002 requires that the deed of appointment/retirement must be registered so that the change of registered proprietor can be duly recorded.

The court has a wide jurisdiction to make vesting orders by virtue of ss.45–56 of the **12.26** Trustee Act 1925. These overlap with s.40 in that vesting orders can be made either when the appointment is made under a statutory or express power or when made by the court. Nevertheless, the court's powers become relevant where the appointment is not made by deed or one of the exceptions to s.40 applies. Similarly a vesting order would be appropriate when it has proved difficult or impossible to obtain an express formal transfer of the legal title from the former trustees or, as regards the assignment of leases, the consent of the landlord.

RETIREMENT AND REMOVAL OF TRUSTEES

Once the office of trusteeship is accepted, the understanding is that it is a life long **12.27** appointment. This can cause difficulties when, say, the trustee and the beneficiaries are engaged in disagreement. Understandably, there exist ways in which a trustee can be compelled to retire or may of his own volition retire from the office. It is, however, to be appreciated that retirement does not guarantee freedom from liability. Not surprisingly, trustees will remain liable for breaches of trust that occurred during their trusteeship. As to future breaches, the retiring trustee is less vulnerable. The general rule is that retirement brings with it a discharge from further responsibility and liability under the trust. Nevertheless, trustees who retire knowing that that this will facilitate a breach by their successors or the continuing trustees will be jointly liable for future associated loss.[19]

The prospect of continuing liability explains why, on retirement, the trustee may seek a formal release by the beneficiaries of his liability in relation to the trust. On retiring in favour of new trustees, such a release is not available unless expressly permitted in the trust instrument. In contrast, if the trust is being wound up, the trustee can insist upon a release.[20] If a release is granted, it is effective only in so far as the beneficiaries are aware of the material facts.

[18] Note that s.40 cannot apply to "so called bearer" securities. Section 18 of the Trustee Act 2000, however, requires the trustees to appoint a custodian of bearer securities.
[19] *Head v Gould* [1898] 2 Ch. 250.
[20] *Tiger v Barclays Bank* [1952] 1 All E.R. 85.

Voluntary retirement

12.28 A trustee may retire only in one of five ways. Outside these five methods, a purported voluntary retirement is void and the trustee will continue to hold office.[21] Retirement may arise in the following ways:

- by virtue of a special power in the trust instrument. If express provision is made for retirement, the trustee can, of course, exercise that power. Although once customary, nowadays such a facility is rare and, because of the Trustee Act 1925, unnecessary;

- under s.36(1) of the Trustee Act 1925. As discussed above, retirement under s.36 can occur only when a replacement trustee is being appointed (see 12.16) and this retirement may relate to either the whole of the trust or merely part of the trust;

- under s.39 of the Trustee Act 1925.[22] This statutory escape is not, however, dependent upon the appointment of a replacement trustee. Section 39(1) allows a trustee to retire from the whole of the trusts (and not merely part) if there will remain at least two other trustees or a trust corporation in office. It is also necessary that the remaining trustees consent to the retirement and that the consent of any person who has an express power to appoint trustees has been obtained.[23] Section 39 requires that the retirement be made in deed form;

- with the consent of all the beneficiaries who must all be of full age and capacity. If this occurs, the trustee will not be liable for anything that happens in post-retirement times. If there is an infant beneficiary, therefore, no effective discharge can arise in this way; and

- by virtue of an order of the court. The court has a statutory jurisdiction under s.41 of the Trustee Act 1925 to discharge a trustee when it replaces him with a new appointment (see 12.22). The court also enjoys an inherent jurisdiction to discharge a trustee without nominating any replacement.[24] This is useful when the consent of the other trustees cannot be obtained for the purposes of s.39. Provided that there will be remaining at least one continuing trustee or a suitable replacement has been found, the court will usually accede to the trustee's wish to retire.[25] Costs of the procedure will normally be borne by the retiring trustee. If there is no continuing trustee, the court will postpone the discharge but, although the trustee will remain in office, he will be effectively relieved of responsibility.[26]

---

[21] *Mettoy Pension Trustees v Evans* [1990] 1 W.L.R. 1587.
[22] Previously, this was possible under the auspices of the Conveyancing Act 1881.
[23] These conditions do not apply when one of the remaining trustees is the Public Trustee: s.6 of the Public Trustee Act 1906.
[24] *Courtenay v Courtenay* (1846) 3 Jo. & La. T. 533.
[25] *Re Chetwynd's Settlement* [1902] 1 Ch. 692.
[26] *Courtenay v Courtenay* (1846) 3 Jo. & La. T. 533.

Compulsory removal

As a measure of last resort, a trustee may be removed against his wishes if there is the   **12.29**
power to do so contained in the trust instrument itself. This would be a fiduciary power
to remove and would, therefore, have to be exercised to promote the interests of the
beneficiaries. In such instances, the terms of any such power must be strictly complied
with.[27] As shown removal may also occur either under s.36 of the Trustee Act 1925 on
the appointment of a replacement trustee[28] or following an order of the court issued
under the statutory jurisdiction afforded by s.41 of the same Act. Removal against the
trustee's wishes can, however, arise in two further ways. The first method of removal,
which operates without the need to appoint a replacement, is by virtue of ss.19–21 of
the Trusts of Land and Appointment of Trustees Act 1996. The second means is via the
court's inherent jurisdiction to remove a trustee compulsorily.

Removal under the 1996 Act

A trustee must retire from his office if directed to do so in writing (there need not be a   **12.30**
deed) by the beneficiaries under s.19 of the Trusts of Land and Appointment of
Trustees Act 1996.[29] The direction may be made by all the beneficiaries jointly or be
given by each of them. The retirement must itself be made by deed. The retiring trustee
and the continuing trustees must then do whatever is necessary to vest the trust
property in any new trustee. If the trustee refuses to execute a deed of retirement, the
court has the ability to order the execution of the deed on the trustee's behalf.[30]

Once given, any beneficiary may withdraw the direction in writing and, as s.19
requires unanimity, the process will thus fail.[31] The direction may, either instead or in
addition, require the retiring trustee to appoint a successor. If it is purely a retirement
direction, it must be served on the retiring trustee(s). If it includes a direction to
appoint, the direction must be served on each of the current trustees.[32]

Section 19 operates only in specified circumstances. First, there must be no person   **12.31**
nominated by the trust instrument who has the power to appoint new trustees. The
statutory provision is not activated even though the donee of any such power is
unwilling to make the appointment or is incapable of exercising the power. If the donee
is deceased, however, the precondition is satisfied because there is no longer a nominated person in existence.

Secondly, all the beneficiaries must be of full age (18 years old and above) and full
capacity and they must act in unison (s.19(1)(a)–(b)). Albeit uncertain, this should be
taken to include beneficiaries under a discretionary trust. This interpretation would rest
easily with the collective ability of the beneficiaries of a discretionary trust, under the

---

[27] *Von Knieriem v Bermuda Trust Co* (1994) 1 BOS 116.
[28] Removal being justified on the grounds that the trustee has been outside the UK for a continuous period of
12 months or that the trustee refuses or is unfit to act or is incapable of acting.
[29] The operation of s.19 may, however, be excluded in the trust instrument.
[30] Section 39 of the Supreme Court Act 1981.
[31] Section 21(1).
[32] Section 19(2)(b).

rule in *Saunders v Vautier*,[33] to terminate the trust. Section 19 should enable such beneficiaries to appoint and/or retire trustees without the need to wind up the trust.

Thirdly, the trustee in receipt of such a direction must retire in circumstances where there will be at least two other trustees or a trust corporation remaining and either a replacement is to be appointed or the continuing trustees consent.

Fourthly, it is also necessary that reasonable arrangements be made for the protection of the retiring trustee's rights in connection with the trust. A trustee might have rights of reimbursement or indemnity for expenses incurred in relation to the trust and may need to take action to ensure that he can enforce those rights. He may also need to guard himself against taxation liabilities for which he could be held responsible after his retirement. In a similar vein, he may have incurred contractual liabilities to third parties in dealing with the trust property. Such possibilities explain why s.19(3) provides that the trustee shall be under an obligation to execute a deed of retirement only after reasonable arrangements have been made for the protection of his interests.

Removal under the court's inherent jurisdiction

12.32   The High Court enjoys an inherent jurisdiction to control the administration of a trust and the actions of the trustee. The overarching duty is to see that trusts are properly executed. To this end, the court may remove a trustee on the application of any beneficiary. Indeed, it can remove a trustee of its own volition during proceedings.[34] The inherent jurisdiction is particularly useful when there is a dispute as to the facts and/or no replacement is to be made.[35] For example, in *Letterstedt v Broers*[36] a beneficiary made a number of allegations of misconduct against the trustees and asked for their removal. Although the allegations were unfounded, he succeeded in his application. It was held that the duty of the court was to ensure the proper execution of the trust.[37] Even if the facts are disputed, or the trustees can disprove the allegations, they may still be removed if there is disharmony as to the manner in which the trust is to be administered.[38]

12.33   The welfare of the beneficiary is the paramount concern and the court must, therefore, evaluate whether the trustee's continuance in office would be prejudicial to the interests of the beneficiaries.[39] Accordingly, the court can consider the expense to the trust of a change of trustees and, even where there has been a minor breach of trust, decide against removal. Such occurred in *Re Wrightson*[40] where the test advocated was whether the trust property could safely be left in the control of the trustees. This demonstrates that not every error on the part of the trustee will be viewed as a ground for removal. It

---

[33] (1841) 4 Beav. 115.
[34] *Re Wrightson* [1908] 1 Ch. 789.
[35] If no such dispute exists and a replacement trustee is to be appointed, the court will tend to exercise its statutory power under s.41 of the Trustee Act 1925.
[36] (1884) 9 App. Cas. 371.
[37] In *Jones v Firkin-Flood* [2008] EWHC 2417 (Ch), four trustees were removed on the basis of their collective unfitness to be trustees.
[38] See *Re Consiglio Trusts* [1973] 3 OR 326, where all the trustees were removed and replaced by a trust corporation.
[39] *E v E* [1990] 2 F.L.R. 233; *Walker v Walker* Unreported January 30, 2007.
[40] [1908] 1 Ch. 789. There the trustees made unauthorised investments and were in breach of trust.

also emphasises that a trustee cannot be removed merely at the whim of a beneficiary.[41] Reasonable cause must be established to justify the removal.[42] For example, a case for removal was made out in *Cowan v Scargill*[43] in circumstances where the trustees persisted with an investment policy that was not in the best interests of the beneficiaries. The court felt that the trustees were endangering trust funds. Similarly, a trustee who sets up a rival business to the trust might not be in breach of trust and yet the conflict of interest could be a ground for his removal.[44] Other more mundane examples include where the trustee refuses to act,[45] has mismanaged the trust,[46] committed a criminal offence,[47] or has been adjudged bankrupt.[48]

DELEGATION OF TRUSTEESHIP

The general rule is that, while a trustee can delegate ministerial and administrative functions,[49] he cannot delegate his powers and discretions to a third party or, indeed, another trustee.[50] This principle is known as *delegatus non potest delegare*. As the role of trustee involves a high degree of personal trust, confidence and judgment, the settlor may have selected the trustee on the basis of his personal characteristics and beliefs. In the absence of an express power given in the trust instrument, a trustee cannot, therefore, delegate his discretion to select who gets what under the auspices of a discretionary trust or as to how the trust fund is to be invested. At common law, any attempt to do so will be ineffective.[51]   **12.34**

Exceptions to the rule against delegation do exist and are to be found in s.25 of the Trustee Act 1925 (as amended) and s.1 of the Trustee Delegation Act 1999. These provisions deal with delegation by individual trustees. A further statutory incursion allows collective delegation by the trustees of land to a beneficiary and is to be found in s.9 of the Trusts of Land and Appointment of Trustees Act 1996. If the trustee delegates outside the parameters of an express power or a statutory provision, he will be liable as if he had acted personally.[52]

---

[41] See *Lee v Young* (1843) 2 Y. & C.C.C. 532.
[42] The judge, however, need not give reasons for making an order: *Re Edward's WT* [1981] 2 All E.R. 941.
[43] [1985] Ch. 270.
[44] *Moore v M'Glynn* [1894] 1 Ir. 74.
[45] *Palairet v Carew* (1863) 32 Beav. 564.
[46] *Ex parte Phelps* (1742) 9 Mod. Rep. 357. In *Walker v Walker*, Unreported January 30, 2007, the trustee favoured his own interests over those of the beneficiaries and maintained suspect accounts. He was removed from office by the court.
[47] *Re Danson* (1899) 48 W.R. 73.
[48] *Re Barker's Trusts* (1875) 1 Ch. D. 43.
[49] Section 11 of the Trustee Act 2000. This is, however, no new thing: see *A-G v Scott* (1750) 1 Ves. Sen. 413.
[50] *Re May* [1926] 1 Ch. 136.
[51] *Fry v Tapson* (1884) 28 Ch. D. 268.
[52] *Turner v Corney* (1841) 5 Beav. 517.

Section 25 of the Trustee Act 1925

12.35   Under s.25(1),[53] a trustee can delegate, by power of attorney,[54] any or all of his duties, powers and discretions vested in him as trustee. This applies whether the trustee is a sole trustee or one of joint trustees. The delegation cannot exceed a period of 12 months from the commencement date of the power.[55] This provision was designed to cater for the situation where, say, a trustee emigrates abroad or the trust property is situated on foreign shores. There are no restrictions upon the number of delegations that can occur and, since the Trustee Delegation Act 1999, delegation can be made in favour of anyone, including an existing trustee and a trust corporation.[56] The delegating trustee must, at the latest within seven days of the granting of the power of attorney, provide the other trustees and anyone else who has an express power to appoint new trustees with notice in writing.[57] The notice must state the terms of the power of attorney: its commencement date and duration, the identity of the donee, the reason for the delegation and the powers and discretions that are delegated. Once delegation has occurred, the donee is in the same position as the delegating trustee, except that the donee has no power to delegate. The delegating trustee is liable for the acts of the donee as if they were his own acts.[58]

Section 25 is seldom invoked and is used only when delegation is essential. This is largely to do with the continuing liability of the delegating trustee. Instead, trustees prefer collectively to appoint agents to undertake their functions. The trustees are liable only for an agent's actions if the trustees have themselves failed in their duty of care.[59] Accordingly, there is a markedly reduced threat of liability for the acts of an agent than is the case with an attorney. As Parker and Mellows comment, "Section 25 of the Trustee Act 1925 could therefore work in a completely unjust way, particularly since the donor is likely to have no more control over the donee than he would over an agent".[60]

Section 1 of the Trustee Delegation Act 1999

12.36   A further power of delegation arises under s.1 of the Trustee Delegation Act 1999. The power operates only where the delegating trustee has a beneficial interest in land held by the trust and when the provision is not excluded in the trust instrument. Put simply, it was designed to cater for an express trust of land where the trustees are also the beneficiaries. For example, a father, mother and son buy a house together. The title is conveyed into their joint names so that they hold the land on trust for themselves (whether as joint tenants or tenants in common). It might be that the parents are aged

---

[53] As amended by the Trustee Delegation Act 1999.
[54] This includes a lasting power of attorney, which is one that survives the incapacity of the trustee: s.6 of the Trustee Delegation Act 1999.
[55] Section 25(2).
[56] Section 25(3).
[57] Section 25(4).
[58] Section 25(7).
[59] Section 1 of the Trustee Act 2000.
[60] At p.636.

and unwell and wish to delegate their trust powers to their son. The advantages of s.1 are first, that it enables the parents to delegate without having to jump through the hoops set by the Trustee Act 1925. Secondly, it enables the parents to make effective provision for the disposal of the land where they fear the onslaught of senility or other mental incapacity. To this end, a lasting power of attorney is an option available to the parents.

Section 1 allows such a trustee to delegate indefinitely all trustee functions, relating to the land and income and proceeds of sale from land, by power of attorney. The delegating trustee remains liable for the actions of the donee, but the s.1 facility is not limited to a 12-month period. Trustees who are not also beneficiaries cannot take advantage of this facility and must delegate under the more restricted s.25 procedure. A trustee who has granted an existing power of attorney under that procedure cannot also take advantage of s.1 of the 1999 Act.[61]

Under both the s.25 and s.1 procedures, one trustee can delegate to another trustee **12.37** by virtue of a power of attorney. Two trustees, moreover, can delegate to the same donee. This creates a potential problem with trust interests in land, which can be overreached only on the payment of the purchase money to two trustees or a trust corporation. Section 7 of the 1999 Act makes it plain that this requirement is not satisfied when the payment is made to an attorney who is acting in the dual capacity of a trustee and donee or as a donee representing two or more trustees. A further trustee would have to be appointed in such circumstances.

Section 9 of the Trusts of Land and Appointment of Trustees Act 1996

Section 9(1) expressly enables trustees of a trust of land collectively to delegate their **12.38** powers, including the power of sale, to any beneficiary or beneficiaries of full age entitled with an interest in possession to the trust land. Delegation can only be of powers relating to land and not other trust property. The delegation must be by power of attorney given by all the trustees and may be revoked subsequently by any one of them. It ceases also on the appointment of a new trustee.[62] The delegation may be made for any period of time or indefinitely.[63] This cannot, however, be by way of an enduring power of attorney, which as indicated caters for permanent delegation when a trustee is mentally incapable.[64] Beneficiaries, to whom the powers have been delegated, have the same duties and liabilities as the trustees, but are not regarded as trustees for any other purpose.[65] They cannot sub-delegate their functions nor can they receive capital monies so as to overreach the equitable interest of any beneficiary. If the donee subsequently ceases to be a person beneficially interested in the land (e.g. his interest is bought out), his ability to exercise powers under the delegation also ceases.[66]

---

[61] Section 1(8) of the 1999 Act.
[62] Section 9(3).
[63] Section 9(5) of the 1996 Act.
[64] Section 9(6).
[65] Section 9(7).
[66] Section 9(4).

GUIDE TO FURTHER READING

F. Barlow, "The Appointment of Trustees: A Disappointing Decision" [2003] Conv. 15.

C. Bell, "Some Reflections on Choosing Trustees" (1988) *Trust Law and Practice* 86.

M. Clements, "The Changing Face of Trusts: The Trusts of Land and Appointment of Trustees Act 1996" [1998] M.L.R. 56.

N. Hopkins, "The Trusts of Land and Appointment of Trustees Act 1996" [1996] Conv. 411.

M. Jacobs, "Trustees—Obtaining an Effective Discharge on Retirement" [1986] *Trust Law and Practice* 16.

M. Jacobs, "To be or not to be … Trustee Act 1925, s.37(1)(c) Revisited Again" [1993] *Trust Law International* 73.

G.H. Jones, "Delegation by Trustees: A Reappraisal" [1959] M.L.R. 381.

Chapter 13

The Duties of a Trustee

At the heart of a trust lies the fact that, while the trustee may have legal title to the trust property, real entitlement rests with the beneficiaries. A trustee has no personal stake in the trust property, unless of course that trustee is also a beneficiary. Despite outward appearances, the trustee simply cannot deal with the property as if it were his own.[1] Instead, he labours under a variety of duties and obligations. Understandably, the trustee's actions are, therefore, policed and controlled and the parameters of the trustee's duties and powers closely regulated. The rights and responsibilities of the trustee are as prescribed by the trust instrument, imposed by equity and set out in statutory form. The extent of a trustee's duties also varies according to the nature of the trust, e.g. whether it is a constructive trust, a bare trust or a pension trust. There is, as Lord Browne-Wilkinson pointed out, "a mistaken assumption that all fiduciaries owe the same duties in all circumstances. That is not the case".[2] Not surprisingly, the more onerous duties fall upon the trustee of an express trust. The failure to discharge the duties of trusteeship may, of course, mean that the trustee will incur personal liability to the beneficiaries.[3]

13.01

The duties that may rest upon the shoulders of a trustee are onerous and diverse. As Millet L.J. stated in *Armitage v Nurse* "there is an irreducible core of obligations owed by the trustees to the beneficiaries and enforceable by them which is fundamental to the concept of a trust. If the beneficiaries have no rights enforceable against the trustees there are no trusts".[4] He continued, "The duty of the trustees to perform the trusts honestly and in good faith for the benefit of the beneficiaries is the minimum necessary to give substance to the trusts".[5] By way of an overview, the trustee's duties may be divided into three categories:

[1] *Frith v Cartland* (1865) 2 Hem. & M. 417.
[2] *Henderson v Merrett Syndicates Ltd* [1995] 2 A.C. 145 at 206.
[3] See *Williams v Barton* [1927] 2 Ch. 9.
[4] [1998] Ch. 241 at 253.
[5] [1998] Ch. 241 at 253, 254.

- the general duties owed by a trustee in relation to the running of the trust (i.e. the administrative and managerial obligations). The trustee must both hold and deal with the property in a fashion that furthers and protects the interests of the present and future beneficiaries. The overarching duty is, therefore, to administer the trust for the benefit of all the beneficiaries. In doing so, the trustee must act impartially and in the best interests of all the beneficiaries.[6] This requires that the trustee manage the trust in a way that safeguards the capital value of the property and generates an income for the beneficiaries.[7] Of course, the trustee is able to employ agents (e.g. an accountant or a solicitor) to carry out key administrative tasks;[8]

- the fiduciary duties that automatically arise from the relationship of trustee and beneficiary. As all trustees stand in a fiduciary relationship with the beneficiaries (which entails that the trustee must always act in utmost good faith), an obligation of loyalty and faithfulness is expected of a trustee.[9] The trustee is not, therefore, permitted to advance the interests of one beneficiary at the expense of another. Similarly, a trustee is not entitled to profit from his position or to place himself in a position where his interests conflict with those of the trust; and

- the duties that concern the distribution of capital and income in favour of the beneficiaries (i.e. the distributive or dispositive obligations of the trustee). The trustee will have to dispose of the trust property according to the directions of the settlor and must not distribute trust money to someone who is not entitled. If the trust is discretionary, the trustee must exercise his discretion sensibly and responsibly while taking on board relevant matters and disregarding irrelevant concerns.[10]

THE TRUSTEE'S DUTY OF CARE

13.02   Before considering the categories of duty owed by trustees it is perhaps useful to depict the standards against which a trustee's actions are to be measured. This is known as the trustee's "duty of care". Each trustee owes a duty to take care (i.e. to avoid loss and injury arising from their conduct in relation to the trust). At common law, unpaid (i.e. amateur) trustees were required to utilise such due diligence and care as would be expected of an ordinary prudent man of business.[11] A higher expectation, however, operated in relation to the duty to invest. As Lindley L.J. explained "The duty of a trustee is not to take such care only as a prudent man would take if he had only himself

---

[6] *Lloyds Bank v Duker* [1987] 3 All E.R. 193.
[7] In *Walker v Walker* Unreported January 30, 2007 the trustee failed to take reasonable steps to ensure that the trust income was optimized for the benefit of the beneficiaries.
[8] Section 11 of the Trustee Act 2000; cf. the more limited ability to delegate the role of trustee to a third party: see **12.34**.
[9] *Bray v Ford* [1896] A.C. 44.
[10] *Re Hastings-Bass* [1975] Ch. 25.
[11] *Speight v Gaunt* (1883) 9 App. Cas. 1.

to consider; the duty rather is to take such care as an ordinary prudent man would take if he were minded to make an investment for the benefit of other people for whom he felt morally bound to provide".[12] This approach prevented the trustee from engaging in a speculative investment.

With the emergence of paid (i.e. professional) trustees and corporate trustees, an additional and higher standard of care was devised. These mercenary trustees fell to be judged by the standards they professed and which had led to their employment as trustees. As Brightman J. put it, "a professional corporate trustee is liable for breach of trust if loss is caused to the trust fund because it neglects to exercise the special skill and care that it professes to have".[13] The objective standard applicable at common law, therefore, depended upon the presence of payment, the nature of the trustee and the special skills that he claimed.[14] As such, it was not the most straightforward test to employ and took no account of the subjective standard that the trustee would actually have adopted in relation to his own affairs.[15]

The common law duty of care has now been subsumed, albeit strictly speaking not entirely, by the Trustee Act 2000, which imposes a new duty of care on trustees. This new duty applies to the activities carried out by trustees as listed in Sch.1. The ambition was to produce a uniform duty that would apply across the spectrum of trustees' duties and, thereby, instil more certainty and consistency into the regulation of the trustee's behaviour. These listed activities include, for example, the making of investments,[16] the acquisition of land, the employment of agents, the taking out of insurance, the carrying out of valuations of the trust property and beneficial interests and the auditing of trust accounts. This prescription, therefore, encompasses all of the trustee's key functions. The list is not, however, exhaustive and omits reference to a trustee's functions concerning the custody and management of trust property other than land and the commencement and defence of legal proceedings by or against the trust. As regards the few activities that are not so listed, it is an inescapable conclusion that the common law yardstick will still operate. The statutory duty can be excluded[17] and this suggests that, in such cases, the common law duty will be reactivated.

Subject to exclusion by the trust instrument, s.1(1) blends the objective with the subjective. It requires a trustee to "exercise such care and skill as is reasonable in the circumstances". In determining what is reasonable, particular regard is to be had to:

- any special knowledge or experience that he has or holds himself out as having.[18] This necessitates that, unlike at common law, the personal characteristics of a trustee can assume relevance. Although the general intention was that the statutory standard would be higher than that set by equity, this may not always be the case. As Parker and Mellows speculate, "So it may be that a trustee who is unintelligent or unworldly owes a lower statutory duty of care, not just than that of a trustee who is neither but also than that of the prudent man of

13.03

---

[12] *Re Whiteley* (1886) 33 Ch. D. 347 at 355.
[13] *Bartlett v Barclays Bank Trust Co* [1980] Ch. 515 at 534.
[14] *Bray v Ford* [1896] A.C. 44.
[15] *Re Lord de Clifford's Estate* [1900] 2 Ch. 707.
[16] The power to invest is considered fully in Ch.14.
[17] Sch.1, para.7. Professional trustees will often exclude or modify the statutory duty.
[18] Section 1(1)(a).

business under the pre-existing law".[19] It is to be emphasised that the standard is geared not only to the expertise that the trustee actually has, but it also reflects the expertise that the trustee claims to have. The claim must somehow have been communicated to the settlor, an appointing trustee or the beneficiaries. The claim could emerge from conversations, publicity material, advertisements and the like; and

- whether the trustee acts in the course of a business or profession and, if so, any special knowledge or experience reasonably expected of such a person in the same business or profession.[20] This must entail that a higher standard of care is expected from a paid trustee who specialises in trust work than from, say, an accountant or a solicitor who acts as a trustee as part of his general practice.

13.04   As to the trustee's duty when investing, the Trustee Act 2000 is modelled upon the common law test (see **13.02**). The requirement is that the trustee must behave like a prudent person acting for others when making investments, reviewing investments and obtaining investment advice.[21] This can, however, be excluded or modified in the trust instrument.[22] The contemporary approach is as advocated by Hoffmann J. in *Nestle v National Westminster Bank* and is that modern trustees are entitled to be judged by the standards of the "portfolio theory".[23] This issue will be revisited in Ch.14.

Provided that the trustee crosses the minimum threshold applicable, he will not be liable for subsequent loss that occurs. The trustee is able to apply to the High Court for directions prior to the taking of any act that might compromise his position as trustee. If the trustee does not take such pre-emptive action, it is still possible to apply to the court for relief under s.61 of the Trustee Act 1925 (see further, **13.52**). This enables the court to exonerate (in whole or in part) a trustee who has acted honestly and reasonably and who ought fairly to be excused for the breach and the failure to obtain the directions of the court. Case law demonstrates that an unpaid trustee is more likely to be released from liability than his professional counterpart.[24]

Exemption clauses

13.05   It is common practice for an exemption clause to be present in the trust instrument that will operate to restrict the potential liability of a trustee for breach of trust. As the Law Commission pointed out in its Consultation Paper, "As the powers of trustees have increased ... so has the breadth of trustee exemption clauses. When coupled with the less restrictive approach recently adopted by the courts to the construction of exemption clauses, it can be strongly argued that the protection offered to beneficiaries, one of

---

[19] At p.640.
[20] Section 1(1)(b).
[21] Sch.1, paras 1, 2.
[22] Sch.1, para.7.
[23] Unreported June 29, 1988.
[24] *Re Pauling's ST* [1964] Ch. 303; *Re Rosenthal* [1972] 1 W.L.R. 1273.

the prime concerns of trust law, is weaker than in the past."[25] It is to be appreciated, however, that there can be no exclusion of liability arising from fraud or intentional wrongdoing.[26] In each case, the wording of the clause must be construed in order to determine whether liability for the conduct complained of was excluded. If there is dispute concerning the wording of such clauses, the interpretation to be given is one that does not favour the trustee.[27] An illustration as to the effects of an exclusion clause is to be found in *Barraclough v Mell*.[28] In that case, there was a trustee exemption clause which, in effect, made the trustee liable for breach of duty for his own personal acts when he knew that the relevant acts were wrongful or when he had no belief that the act was right and did not care if it was wrong.[29] The trustee misapplied trust money by paying £64,000 to the wrong beneficiaries. Although the trustee admitted negligence, she still sought to avoid liability under the exemption clause. The High Court concluded that, as she had genuinely thought that she was acting within the terms of the trust, she was protected by the exemption clause.

In *Armitage v Nurse*,[30] a clause that purported to exempt trustees from any liability to the trust unless it was caused by their own "actual fraud" was upheld. The Court of Appeal interpreted "fraud" as meaning "dishonesty" and requiring, at the least, an intention to pursue a course of action either knowing that it ran contrary to the interests of the beneficiaries or being recklessly indifferent as to its impact on them. This approach is interesting in that it allows a clause to exempt a trustee not only for ordinary negligence,[31] but also for gross negligence.[32] It also gives rise to the possibility that a trustee who knowingly acts outside his powers, but does so in the belief that this will promote the best interests of the beneficiaries, would be shielded from liability. All seems to turn upon how "fraud" is defined.[33] In *Nurse* Millett L.J. viewed this type of conduct as falling outside the understanding of "fraud". By way of stark contrast, in *Royal Brunei Airlines v Tan*[34] Lord Nicholls believed that such conduct would indeed be fraudulent because the trustees were taking a risk that they knew they had no right to take. It is suggested that the latter stance is likely to prevail and, therefore, trustees would be most unwise deliberately to take unauthorised action in the hope that they are protected by an exemption clause.

[25] "Trustee Exemption Clauses" (2003) Consultation Paper No.171 at p.vi. In *Bonham v Fishwick* [2008] EWCA Civ 373, for example, the clause exempted the trustees from all liability except in the case of "wilful and individual fraud or wrongdoing".
[26] See *Baker v JE Clark & Co (Transport) Ltd* [2006] EWCA Civ 464.
[27] *Wight v Olswang (No.1)* (1999) *The Times*, May 18. As Kitchen J. pointed out at first instance in *Bonham v Blake Lapthorn Linell* [2006] EWHC 2513 (Ch) at [1777] "A liability can be excluded only by clear and unambiguous words. Nevertheless, trustees accept office on the Terms of a document for which they are not responsible, and they are entitled to have the document fairly construed according to the natural meaning of the words used."
[28] [2005] EWHC 3387; (Ch).
[29] In *Bonham v Fishwick* [2008] EWCA Civ 373, Mummery L.J. expressed the view that a trustee who acted upon legal advice could not be accused of willful wrongdoing.
[30] [1998] Ch. 241.
[31] Nothing contentious there: see *Bogg v Raper* (1998) *The Times*, 22 April.
[32] cf. the position in Scotland where there can be no exclusion of liability for gross negligence: *Lutea Trustees Ltd v Orbis Trustees* [1998] S.L.T. 471.
[33] The difference between fraudulent breaches of trust and other types of breach is reflected also in the limitation period in which action must be commenced. Section 21 of the Limitation Act 1980 provides that there is no limitation period applicable to fraudulent breaches of trust: see *Berezovsky v Abramovich* [2008] EWHC 1138 (Comm).
[34] [1995] 2 A.C. 378 at 390.

13.06   In the Trust Law Committee Consultation Paper entitled "Trustee Exemption Clauses" (published in June 1999) it was proposed that a distinction should be drawn between lay trustees and professional trustees. While the existing law would essentially be preserved as regards the former, professional trustees would no longer be able to claim protection against negligence. The attitude is that professional trustees should always be expected to act with reasonable care and, in any event, are likely to be covered by liability insurance. As explained in the 1999 Consultation Paper, "There is much to be said for trust corporations and professional individuals paid for their services as trustees, (like solicitors, barristers and accountants) to accept the price of liability for negligence in acting as a paid trustee and to insure against such risk, with the premiums being reflected in the fees for the services provided".[35] Four years later, the Law Commission echoed this sentiment and agreed that, while exclusion clauses should not be abolished, there should be further regulation. It believed that the present law was too deferential to professional trustees. The Commission provisionally concluded that professional trustees should not be allowed to rely on exclusion clauses as regards negligent breaches of trust and to claim indemnity from the trust fund.[36] These proposals were, however, rejected in the Law Commission's subsequent report.[37] The Report warned of, ". . . dangers in taking an oversimplified view of the role of trustee exemption clauses"[38] and proposed a scheme of regulation ("a rule of practice") to be enforced by the relevant professional bodies. This rule of practice would apply only to paid trustees and would operate when the trustee caused a settlor to include an exemption clause. In such cases, the trustee must take, "such steps as are reasonable to ensure that the settlor is aware of the meaning and effect of that clause."[39] This promotion of settlor awareness is designed to respect settlor autonomy and to prevent a deleterious impact on both trustees and beneficiaries. It remains to be seen what will happen to these proposals.

ADMINISTRATIVE DUTIES

13.07   The trustee is subject to a range of duties that arise on appointment and continue for the duration of the trust. As will become clear these duties relate to the preservation and dealings with trust property, the managerial actions taken by trustees and the information to be given to beneficiaries. These include various types of obligation.

Duties on appointment

13.08   Upon accepting the office, the trustee is expected to ascertain the terms of the trust and to confirm that he has been validly appointed and that the trust property has been

---

[35] Trust Law Committee Consultation Paper (1999) at para.7.8.
[36] "Trustee Exemption Clauses" (2003) Consultation Paper No.171 at p.viii.
[37] "Trustee Exemption Clauses" (2006) Law Com. 301, Cm 6874.
[38] (2006) Law Com. 301, Cm 6874 at [3.41].
[39] (2006) Law Com. 301, Cm 6874 at [6.65].

vested in him.[40] As Kekewich J. put it, "I think that when persons are asked to become new trustees, they are bound to inquire of what the property consists that is proposed to be handed over to them, and what are the trusts. They ought also to look into the trust documents and papers to ascertain what notices appear among them of incumbrances and other matters affecting the trust".[41] The trustee will, therefore, be expected to study the contents of the trust instrument and the trust accounts and to identify any co-trustees, the beneficiaries, the nature of the trust and the trust assets.

To enable a new trustee to obtain basic information, an existing or retiring trustee can be required to produce any documents maintained which relate to the management of the trust. As Jenkins L.J. explained, "If a natural executor or trustee does, in fact, reduce his deliberations to writing, as, for instance, by recording them in a diary relating to the administration of the estate or trust, we see no reason in principle why he should not be required to produce it to his successor in office".[42] This entails that, if previously there had been meetings held between trustees, the new trustee will be entitled to see the recorded minutes of those encounters. Similarly, the new trustee will wish to read all correspondence and other documents related to the trust. In addition, a new trustee is advised to question an existing or retiring trustee and elicit information via that means. If the existing or retiring trustee is a corporation, the new trustee should also call for the internal memoranda of that company.

A new trustee is entitled to operate on the basis that an existing or retiring trustee has **13.09** carried out his functions properly[43] and need not conduct a detailed examination of past conduct.[44] In *Hallows v Lloyd*,[45] the trustees could not discover the existence of a marriage settlement from the trust documentation and, therefore, were not in breach of duty. They did not have derivative notice from the retiring trustee who knew of the settlement. Nevertheless, any suspicions that the trustee may have as to the prior administration of the trust should be investigated and, if necessary, appropriate steps taken against the party responsible (i.e. a former or current trustee).[46] These pre-liminary steps are necessary to shield the new trustee from liability.

Safeguarding trust property

If the trust was in existence before his appointment, a new trustee must ensure that he **13.10** understands the provisions of the trust and that the trust property has been properly invested.[47] Hence, if a trust investment has fallen in value and threatens to jeopardise the trust fund, the trustee should consider whether to reinvest elsewhere. Otherwise, he will be liable for the failure to review. In *Re Medland*,[48] for example, trust money was lent on mortgage, but the security for the loan had depreciated in value and now risked

[40] *Harvey v Oliver* [1887] 57 L.T. 239.
[41] *Hallows v Lloyd* (1889) 39 Ch. D. 686 at 691.
[42] *Tiger v Barclays Bank* [1952] 1 All E.R. 85 at 87.
[43] *Re Miller* [1978] L.S. Gaz. R. 454.
[44] *Harvey v Oliver*, [1887] 57 L.T. 239.
[45] (1889) 39 Ch. D. 686.
[46] *Re Straham* (1856) 8 De GM & G 291.
[47] *Nestle v National Westminster Bank* [1993] 1 W.L.R. 1260.
[48] (1889) 41 Ch. D. 476.

the interests of the trust. North J. held that the trustee should have deliberated whether or not to call in the mortgage.

Except where expressly allowed in the trust instrument, the trustee should never lend trust money or allow it to remain outstanding on an unsecured basis.[49] If the trust property includes chattels, the trustee should also obtain an accurate inventory. The trustee is expected to ensure that all securities and chattels are in safe custody.[50] As regards land, the trustee should ensure that it is secure and free from the adverse claims of a trespasser. Perhaps surprisingly, there appears to be no duty to insure the trust property.[51]

Calling in loans

13.11   The trustee should, moreover, ensure that, where part of the trust property is a loan due for repayment, this loan should be called in.[52] This action is required because of the general notion that the trustee must take all reasonable steps to safeguard trust assets. The danger for the trustee is that, if he allows the debt to become statute-barred under the Limitation Act 1980, he will assume personal liability for the ensuing loss to the trust. If necessary, therefore, the trustee must institute legal action to enforce repayment.[53]

The trustee who decides not to bring an enforcement action should ask the court for directions under s.57 of the Trustee Act 1925 that support the intended inaction.[54] If not, the trustee might show, by way of a defence, that he held a well-founded belief that any enforcement action would be pointless.[55] It is, however, no defence for the trustee to argue that he thought it somehow indelicate or inappropriate to ask for the loan to be repaid and to initiate recovery proceedings. This was demonstrated in *Re Brogden*[56] where the trustees decided not to sue on a £10,000 debt owed to the trust because they feared a crisis in the family of the beneficiary would ensue. This excuse was held to be an inadequate justification for the trustees' failure to enforce the debt and liability followed accordingly for breach of duty. As Fry L.J. put it:

> "A trustee undoubtedly has a discretion as to the mode and manner, and very often as to the time in which and at which he shall carry his duty into effect. But his discretion is never an absolute one; it is always limited by the duty—the dominant duty, the guiding duty—of recovering, securing, and duly applying the trust fund. And no trustee can claim any right of discretion which does not agree with that paramount obligation".[57]

---

[49] *Pickard v Anderson* (1872) L.R. 13 Eq. 608.
[50] *Re Miller's Deed Trusts* [1978] L.S. Gaz. 454.
[51] *Bailey v Gould* (1840) 4 Y. & C. Ex. 221; *Revenue & Customs Commissioners v the Peter Clay Discretionary Trust* [2008] 2 W.L.R. 1052.
[52] *M'Gachen v Dew* (1851) 15 Beav. 84.
[53] *Buxton v Buxton* (1835) 1 My. & Cr. 80.
[54] *Public Trustee v Cooper* [2001] W.T.L.R. 901.
[55] *Re Brogden* (1888) 38 Ch. D. 546.
[56] (1888) 38 Ch. D. 546.
[57] (1888) 38 Ch. D. 546 at 571. Lopes L.J. added, "No consideration of delicacy, and no regard for the feelings of relatives or friends, will exonerate him ..." (at 574).

In contrast, in *Ward v Ward* the court decided that the trustee acted reasonably in failing to sue a debtor who was also a beneficiary in circumstances where to bring an action would have financially ruined the debtor and impacted deleteriously upon other beneficiaries (his children).[58]

Joint control

The trust property ought to be placed in the joint control of all the trustees. It must be **13.12** kept distinct from the trustee's personal property or the property of any other trust. Accordingly, a new trustee should ensure that investments are in the names of all the trustees. If not, and where trust property is misapplied by a trustee, the co-trustees are potentially liable for any loss that arises.[59] For example, in *Lewis v Nobbs*,[60] the trust property included bearer bonds which were in the sole control of one trustee. When this trustee went off with the bonds in his custody, the other trustee was held liable because by his negligence he had facilitated the misappropriation. As Hall V.C. pointed out, "care should have been taken that there could not be any improper disposition . . . he is liable for the illegal dealing with the moiety of the bonds of his co-trustee".[61] In order to protect themselves, trustees are now given the right by the Trustee Act 2000 to appoint custodians of trust property and documents. Indeed, in relation to so-called "bearer securities" (i.e. securities which are not registered in the name of anyone), the trustees must appoint a custodian unless exempted by the trust instrument or by statutory provision. By their very nature, these securities cannot be placed in the names and joint control of the trustees.

The duty to provide accounts

The obligation to provide financial accounts is central to the relationship of trustee and **13.13** beneficiary.[62] It is the first duty of the trustee, as Plumer M.R. noted in *Pearse v Green*, "to be constantly ready with his accounts".[63] The motivation underlying this duty to account is that all beneficiaries have the opportunity to discover whether a breach of trust has occurred. Understandably, the trustee will appoint an agent (i.e. a qualified accountant) to prepare and maintain the trust accounts. Trustees who do not maintain proper accounts can be directed to do so by the court and may face liability for costs in those and future proceedings.[64] As Farwell J. observed, "beneficiaries have a right to

---

[58] (1843) 2 H.L. Cas. 777.
[59] *Rodbard v Cooke* (1877) 36 L.T. 504.
[60] (1878) 8 Ch. D. 591.
[61] (1878) 8 Ch. D. 591 at 595.
[62] See *Tiger v Barclays Bank* [1952] 1 All E.R. 85. As Deputy Judge Roger Kaye Q.C. put it in *Walker v Walker* Unreported January 30, 2007, "A trustee must keep accounts, provide them when required and provide to the beneficiaries all reasonable information as to the manner in which the trust estate has been dealt with" (at [249]).
[63] (1819) 1 Jac. & W. 135 at 140.
[64] *Re Skinner* [1904] 1 Ch. 289. This is so where there is either gross negligence or where the refusal to provide accounts is wholly indefensible.

expect the performance of their duty by executors, and not the less when one of them has power to make professional charges".[65]

Every beneficiary is entitled to inspect the trust accounts[66] and this rule applies equally to fixed and discretionary trusts[67] and whether or not the beneficiary's interest is in possession.[68] It appears that, if the beneficiary wants a copy of the accounts, it is to be paid for out of the pocket of that beneficiary.[69] The beneficiary may challenge the accounts and this is traditionally known as "falsifying" and "surcharging" accounts. "Falsifying" refers to the ability of the beneficiary to show that an entry in the accounts was erroneous and should be rectified (i.e. the falsification of accounts). In *Bonham v Blake Lapthorn Lindell*, Kitchen J. explained that falsification is, "the means by which that loss is made good. The trust is restored by disallowing the payment away of the funds in issue."[70] "Surcharging" concerns a credit entry which was omitted entirely and which should be included in the accounts. The trustee is under a duty to correct any errors detected in the accounts.

13.14   The trustee has the power to have the accounts audited by an independent accountant. There is, however, no duty upon a trustee of a private trust to take such action.[71] Section 22(4) of the Trustee Act 1925 imposes limitations upon the ability of the trustee to have the accounts audited at his own behest. It provides that, as a general rule, an audit cannot occur more than once every three years. The idea is that the expense to the trust fund should be minimised. The three-year rule gives way, however, when the nature of the trust or special dealings with trust property make it desirable to have more frequent audits.

Any beneficiary or trustee can, however, apply to the Public Trustee for an audit to be carried out under s.13 of the Public Trustee Act 1906. In *Re Oddy*, Parker J. noted the potential breadth of this provision:

> "Section 13, when carefully examined appears to be an exceedingly drastic enactment. It enables any trustee or beneficiary to apply for an audit of the whole accounts of a trust at any time whatever ... There is no limit backwards beyond which the audit is not to be extended, and, therefore, in a trust which has lasted 30 or 40 years it is open to a *cestui que trust* to go back to the very beginning, unless of course, the court otherwise orders ...".[72]

There are, however, two limitations on this statutory right to an audit. First, an audit cannot occur within one year of a prior audit. Secondly, an applicant runs the risk of having to pay the costs of the process himself. As Parker J. demonstrated, "The only penalty for insisting improperly for an investigation of the trust accounts is ... to order

---

[65] [1904] 1 Ch. 289 at 292.
[66] *Kemp v Burn* (1863) 4 Giff 348.
[67] *Murphy v Murphy* [1999] 1 W.L.R. 282.
[68] *Armitage v Nurse* [1998] Ch. 241. This duty is placed upon Charity Trustees by ss.41, 42 of the Charities Act 1993.
[69] *Ottley v Gilbey* (1845) 8 Beav. 602.
[70] [2006] EWHC 2513 (Ch) at [180].
[71] cf. the trustee of a charitable trust who, subject to certain conditions, is under an obligation to audit imposed by the Charities Act 2006. Similarly, under the Judicial Trustee Rules there is provision for an annual audit following the appointment of a judicial trustee.
[72] [1911] 1 Ch. 532 at 537.

the applicant to pay the costs of the audit".[73] Due to this fear of costs, the s.13 route is rarely followed.

The duty to provide information

Apart from the keeping of accounts, the trustees must be prepared to provide infor-   **13.15**
mation and documents to the beneficiaries as to the current state of the trust property and any dealings that have occurred in relation to it. The beneficiary is entitled to receive explanations as to what the trustees have been doing with the trust property (e.g. concerning income, investments and distributions). In particular, the trustees must be able to give full and accurate information as to the value of the trust fund.[74] There is, moreover, a positive duty to inform a beneficiary of full age and capacity of his entitlement under a fixed trust.[75] It is thought that the trustees are also under a duty to reveal their names and addresses to the beneficiaries.[76] The trustees need not, however, provide reasons for their decision whether or not to exercise their discretion in a particular way. Hence, in *Re Beloved Wilkes' Charity* when the trustees selected a boy to be educated at Oxford University they were entitled not to disclose the reasons underlying their selection.[77]

It is the duty of the trustees to produce trust documents (including, as shown, accounts) at the request of a beneficiary whether under a discretionary trust or a fixed trust.[78] The problem, of course, concentrates upon what is properly to be classed as a "trust document" in a particular case. In *Re Londonderry's Settlement*, Salmon L.J. admitted that, "The category of trust document has never been defined. Nor could it be—certainly not comprehensively by me".[79] He managed, however, to identify certain characteristics of a trust document and these were, first, that the document is to be in the possession of the trustees as trustees. Secondly, that the document is to contain information about the trust which the beneficiaries are entitled to know. Thirdly, that the beneficiaries are entitled to see such documents. It can, therefore, be said that a trust document is, essentially, one that is in the possession of the trustee in his capacity as trustee and which contains information about the trust.

The ability of the court to order such production emerges from its general super-   **13.16**
visory role. As Lord Walker put it in *Schmidt v Rosewood Trust Ltd*, "the more principled and correct approach is to regard the right to seek disclosure of trust documents as one aspect of the court's inherent jurisdiction to supervise, and if necessary to intervene in, the administration of trusts".[80] Lord Walker, thereby, rejected the view that a beneficiary has any proprietary right to see trust documents. He felt that the court had to engage in a balancing exercise, "Especially when there are issues as to

---

[73] [1911] 1 Ch. 532 at 538.
[74] *Re Tillott* [1892] 1 Ch. 86. There it was made clear by Chitty J. (at 89) that a trustee is not bound to give a beneficiary information about a share in which he has no interest.
[75] *Hawkesley v May* [1956] 1 QB 304.
[76] *Murphy v Murphy* [1999] 1 W.L.R. 282.
[77] (1851) 3 Mac. & G. 440.
[78] *Schmidt v Rosewood Trust Ltd* [2003] 3 All E.R. 76 where Lord Walker accepted that, "The right to seek the court's intervention does not depend on entitlement to a fixed and transmissible beneficial interest" (at 91).
[79] [1965] Ch. 918 at 938.
[80] [2003] 3 All E.R. 76 at 91.

personal or commercial confidentiality, the court may have to balance the competing interests of different beneficiaries, the trustees themselves and third parties. Disclosure may have to be limited and safeguards may have to be put in place".[81] For example, the court might order disclosure of only certain types of document, either completely or in a redacted form, and might limit the use which may be made of the documents disclosed whether by undertakings to the court or by arrangements for professional inspection. Although in principle an order can be made at the behest of a beneficiary under a discretionary trust, Lord Walker accepted the uncertain nature of this type of beneficial interest. He observed, "In many cases the court may have no difficulty in concluding that an applicant with no more than a theoretical possibility of benefit ought not to be granted any relief".[82]

The documents that a beneficiary may call for would include, for example, any trust diary maintained by the trustees which records their decisions, any other *aide-memoire* such as the minutes of meetings between the trustees and correspondence or written advice from an agent of the trustee. In *Re Cowin*, North J. admitted that this is not an absolute rule, "I do not say that he is entitled as of right, but only that he is entitled under the circumstances, because there might be a state of circumstances under which the right to production would not exist".[83]

13.17 The right to information is, therefore, subject to limitations. First, there is no right to see documents that are not classified as trust documents. As indicated, not all documents held by trustees are "trust documents". For example, as Harman L.J. observed in *Re Londonderry's Settlement*, "I cannot think that communications between individual trustees and appointors are documents in which beneficiaries have a ... right ... I do not think that letters to or from an individual beneficiary ought to be open to inspection by another beneficiary".[84] This limitation arises because the beneficiary's entitlement to "trust documents" is traditionally thought to be justified only on the ground that, as Lord Wrenbury explained, "They are in a sense his own".[85] Hence, there is no right to see advice provided by the trustee's solicitor which was paid for out of his own pocket and relates to proceedings waged against the trustee personally.[86] Nevertheless, the beneficiary will be able to see documents such as the trust instrument;[87] all instruments concerning a change in trustee; all receipts for payments made by or on behalf of the trustees;[88] and written legal advice as to the administration of the trust.[89]

Secondly, the right to see trust documentation does not extend to those documents that state the reasons why the trustees made particular decisions when exercising their discretionary powers. In *Schmidt v Rosewood Trust Ltd*, Lord Walker described this as, "the need to protect confidentiality in communications between trustees as to the exercise of their dispositive discretions, and in communications made to the trustees by other beneficiaries".[90] The classic demonstration of this was by the Court of Appeal in

---

[81] [2003] 3 All E.R. 76 at 97.
[82] [2003] 3 All E.R. 76 at 97.
[83] (1886) 33 Ch. D. 179 at 187. There the beneficiary sought title deeds and other documents.
[84] [1965] Ch. 918 at 934.
[85] *O'Rourke v Darbishire* (1920) A.C. 581 at 626.
[86] *Talbot v Marshfield* (1865) 2 Dr. & Sm. 549.
[87] *Ex parte Holdsworth* (1838) 4 Bing. N.C. 386.
[88] *Re Ellis* [1908] W.N. 215.
[89] *Devaynes v Robinson* (1855) 20 Beav. 42.
[90] [2003] 3 All E.R. 76 at 91.

Re Londonderry's Settlement.[91] There the beneficiary was refused access to documentation that would show why the trustees chose to distribute the fund in the way that they did. The trustees determined that it would not be in the interests of family harmony to disclose documents which included minutes and agendas of trust meetings and correspondence between the trustees and their agents and other beneficiaries. If they were compelled to do so, the rule that trustees do not need to disclose their reasons would be defeated and the trustees felt that they would be unable to do their job effectively. As Harman L.J. acknowledged, "they are protected for the special reason which protects the trustees' deliberations on a discretionary matter from disclosure. If necessary, I hold that this principle overrides the ordinary rule".[92] The upshot of this decision is, therefore, that in trust law the right to inspect documents does not extend to documents that the trustees desire to be private and which contain the reasons for their decisions.[93]

The *Londonderry* case, however, does nothing to prevent a trustee being ordered to disclose such documents in the course of civil proceedings that allege that the trustees have exercised their discretion in some improper fashion. Indeed, discovery of such documents was ordered in *Talbot v Marshfield*.[94] Writing extra-judicially, Megarry questioned whether the courts will, "permit the bonds of secrecy to be invaded by the simple process of commencing hostile litigation against the trustees? It is not easy to see how the courts can prevent this".[95] It is, however, apparent that the court will not order disclosure as part of a "fishing expedition" by the claimant, seeking to establish a case. The claimant must at least be able to demonstrate a prima facie case before disclosure of documents is ordered.

Thirdly, the right gives way in exceptional circumstances where the trustees decide that, in providing the requested information to a particular beneficiary, the interests of the beneficiaries as a whole will be compromised[96] and the administration of the trust prejudiced.[97] This is likely to arise when the trust concerns the running of a business and the beneficiary seeks commercially sensitive information. A disgruntled beneficiary can test the correctness of the trustee's refusal to disclose by seeking directions of the court.

Finally, as regards so-called "letters of wishes", further restrictions may apply. These "letters of wishes" are no more than guidance provided by a settlor to his trustees as to how they should exercise their powers and discretions. This guidance is important in that it must be taken into account when a trustee exercises his discretion and must be passed on to new trustees. In *Breakspear v Ackland*,[98] Briggs J. noted that the large increase in the use of wish letters went hand in hand with the increased popularity of discretionary trusts and that they were useful in terms of both flexibility for trustees and privacy for the settlor. He accepted also that there is an inevitable tension between the advantages of confidentiality and the advantages of disclosure. As to whether the

13.18

13.19

[91] [1965] Ch. 918.
[92] [1965] Ch. 918 at 938.
[93] See *Wilson v Law Debenture Trust Corp* [1995] 2 All E.R. 337. There Rattee J. held that the rule applied equally to a pension trust (where the beneficiaries purchase their interests) as to any other type of trust (where the beneficiaries are volunteers).
[94] (1865) 2 Drew. & Sm. 549. Disclosure is now governed by Pt 31 of the Civil Procedure Rules.
[95] R. E. Megarry (1965) 81 L.Q.R. 192 at 196.
[96] *Rouse v 100F Australia Trustees Ltd* [2000] W.T.L.R. 111.
[97] *Re Rabaiotti's 1989 Settlement* [2000] W.T.L.R. 953 (a Channel Islands case).
[98] [2008] 3 W.L.R. 698.

beneficiaries enjoy a right to inspect a letter of wishes, however, the answer appears to be in the negative. They seem to fall within the *Londonderry* range of documents that enjoy immunity as they intimate the reasons underlying the exercise of discretion by the trustees.[99]

The duty to act jointly

13.20   The general rule is that, where there are two or more trustees, they must act unanimously in that decisions have to be made jointly by all the trustees. The actions of a majority cannot bind the trust estate.[1] This rule flows from the fact that settlor has given all the trustees the collective and generally non-delegable duty to act in furtherance of the trust. Hence, no cognisance is usually taken of a majority decision and the acts of some trustees cannot bind others.[2] The notion underlying the requirement of unanimity is that it puts in place a safeguard for beneficiaries and militates against incautious action by the trustees.[3] As with any general rule, however, there exist limited exceptions:

- the trust instrument may expressly cater for majority or unilateral decision making;[4]

- the court may order that a majority decision be implemented;[5]

- the trustees may authorise one trustee to receive income when it is in the interests of convenience[6]; and

- majority action is permissible in relation to charitable trusts[7] and pension trusts.[8]

The law does not differentiate between an "active" and a "passive" (or "sleeping") trustee. Each is liable by virtue of the mere assumption of the office of trustee. Hence, a trustee will maintain liability even though the management of the trust has been left to a co-trustee. This also entails that a trustee who disagrees with the majority decision of his brethren might be well advised to stand firm and not bow to the predominant wish. In *Bahin v Hughes*,[9] for example, three trustees held property on trusts for Mrs Bahin for life with remainder to her children. One trustee made unauthorised investments and a loss arose. Mrs Bahin sued the three trustees and the "passive" trustees were held to be as liable as the "active" trustee. As Fry L.J. noted, "I can see no principle in law for

---

[99] *Breakspear v Ackland* [2008] 3 W.L.R. 698.
[1] *Luke v South Kensington Hotel Co* (1879) 11 Ch. D. 121.
[2] *Boardman v Phipps* [1967] 2 A.C. 46.
[3] *Naylor v Goodhall* (1877) 47 L.J. Ch. 53.
[4] *Re Butlin's ST* [1976] Ch. 251 (e.g. to cater for the illness or infirmity of a trustee).
[5] See *Cowan v Scargill* [1984] 2 All E.R. 750 where Megarry V.C. accepted that the particular inclinations of the majority could, in exceptional circumstances, be decisive as to investment policy.
[6] *Townley v Sherbourne* (1634) J. Bridg. 35.
[7] *Wilkinson v Malin* (1832) Cr. & J. 636.
[8] Section 32 of the Pensions Act 1995.
[9] (1886) 31 Ch. D. 390.

such a distinction".[10] As the investing trustee had acted honestly (albeit improperly), the other trustees were not even entitled to an indemnity from the "active" trustee. Fry L.J. explained that if it were otherwise, "each trustee will be looking to the other or others for a right of indemnity and so neglect the performance of his duties. Such a doctrine would be against the policy of the court in relation to trusts".[11] The "passive" trustees had neglected their duty by doing nothing. Cotton L.J. concluded that, "All the trustees were in the wrong, and everyone is equally liable to indemnify the beneficiaries".[12] The trustees were, therefore, jointly and severally liable to Mrs Bahin.[13]

The duty to consult

Subject to modification in the trust instrument, s.11 of the Trusts of Land and Appointment of Trustees Act 1996 relates to trusts of land and requires that the trustees should, as far as is practicable consult the beneficiaries of full age. In addition, and so far as is consistent with the general interest of the trust, trustees should give effect to the expressed wishes of the beneficiaries. If there is a divergence of opinion, the wishes of the majority, according to the value of their combined interest, should be followed. This duty can be excluded.   **13.21**

THE GENERAL FIDUCIARY DUTY

What is a fiduciary?

The trustee is not the only type of fiduciary. The classic examples of a fiduciary relationship are as between principal and agent, director and company, partner and co-partner and, of obvious importance for present purposes, trustee and beneficiary. A fiduciary relationship emerges where one party undertakes to act in relation to the property or affairs of another in circumstances that give rise to a relationship of trust and confidence. In *Bristol & West Building Society v Mothew*, Millett L.J. highlighted the defining characteristics of a personal fiduciary relationship, "The core liability has several facets. A fiduciary must act in good faith; he must not make a profit out of his trust; he must not place himself in a position where his duty and his interest may conflict; he may not act for his own benefit or the benefit of a third party without the informed consent of his principal".[14] Millett L.J. did not intend this to be an exhaustive list, but felt that it offered a useful indication of the nature of fiduciary obligations. He   **13.22**

---

[10] (1886) 31 Ch. D. 390 at 397, 398.
[11] (1886) 31 Ch. D. 390 at 398.
[12] (1886) 31 Ch. D. 390 at 396.
[13] The Civil Liability (Contribution) Act 1978 allows one trustee who has been held liable for breach of trust to claim a contribution from the other trustees. This is at the discretion of the court and available only when it is "just and equitable" to make such an order.
[14] [1998] Ch. 1 at 18.

also made the point that as regards a fiduciary who acts for two principals with potentially conflicting interests, he must serve each as faithfully and loyally as the other.

More recently, in *Sinclair Investment Holdings SA v Versailles Trade Finance Ltd*,[15] Arden L.J. noted that an obligation of loyalty lies at the heart of the fiduciary relationship and this entails that the fiduciary will relegate his interests and act solely in the interests of his principal. The categories of fiduciary are not closed and the mantle can be adopted expressly or impliedly by agreement. Arden L.J. explained, "in my judgment if it is alleged that a person who does not fall within the usual categories of a fiduciary relationship, such as trustee and director, made manifest his intention to enter into a fiduciary relationship—that is, to undertake to the other a duty of loyalty—there would be sufficient pleading of fiduciary relationship".[16] Nevertheless, she noted that there was a need for the relationship to relate to an item of property. This requirement explains why a fiduciary relationship might be specific and concern only an aspect of a party's relationship with another.

What is a fiduciary duty and how is it breached?

13.23   In *Bristol & West Building Society v Mothew*, Millett L.J. considered what was meant by the concept of a "fiduciary duty" and warned, "this branch of the law has been bedevilled by unthinking resort to verbal formulae ... The expression 'fiduciary duty' is properly confined to those duties which are peculiar to fiduciaries and the breach of which attracts legal consequences differing from those consequences upon the breach of other duties ... It is obvious that not every breach of duty by a fiduciary is a breach of fiduciary duty".[17] While acknowledging that there is no need for dishonesty on the part of a fiduciary, Millett L.J. explained, "The various obligations of a fiduciary merely reflect different aspects of his core duties of loyalty and fidelity. Breach of fiduciary duty, therefore, connotes disloyalty and infidelity. Mere incompetence is not enough".[18]

The core proposition that emerges is that a trustee may not profit from the office of trusteeship and must not allow self-interest to conflict with his duty to the trust.[19] As Lord Herschell explained in *Bray v Ford*, where a solicitor-trustee unsuccessfully claimed for costs from the trust fund in bringing a libel action for defamatory comments made against himself in his capacity as trustee of a college:

> "It is an inflexible rule of a Court of Equity that a person in a fiduciary position ... is not, unless otherwise expressly provided, entitled to make a profit; he is not allowed to put himself in a position where his interest and duty conflict ... human nature being what it is, there is a danger, in such circumstances, of the person

---

[15] [2005] EWCA Civ. 722; see also *Ultraframe (UK) Ltd v Fielding* [2006] F.S.R. 17 (re so-called "shadow directors")

[16] [2005] EWCA Civ 722 at [20]; see *Hageman v Holmes* [2009] EWHC 50 (Ch).

[17] [1998] Ch.1 at 16. There a solicitor acted for both the borrower and the lender in a mortgage transaction. The solicitor was held not to be in breach of a fiduciary duty to the lender because of an inadvertent and non-conscious failure to act with care.

[18] [1998] Ch.1 at 18.

[19] *Boardman v Phipps* [1967] 2 A.C. 46. As W. Bishop and D. Prentice observe, "The rules have been designed to operate prophylactically and place the maximum deterrent on a fiduciary benefiting from his position" ("Some Legal and Economic Aspects of Fiduciary Remuneration" [1983] M.L.R. 289 at p.309).

holding a fiduciary position being swayed by interest rather than by duty, and thus prejudicing those whom he was bound to protect. It has, therefore, been deemed expedient to lay down this positive rule".[20]

The profit and the conflict rules are best viewed as imposing mainly distinct, but sometimes overlapping, standards that tend to be strictly applied by the courts. The decided cases have focused upon when the trustee obtains an unauthorised remuneration, when the trustee acts in such a way as to benefit both himself and the trust and when the trustee acts solely for his own profit.[21]

Trustees' remuneration *payment.*

Until the Trustee Act 2000, the general rule was that the role of trustee had to be performed without remuneration or profit.[22] The underlying notion was that a trustee might undertake unnecessary work in order to receive payment and, hence, provide a potential conflict between interest and duty. As Chitty J. commented in *Re Barber*, "The difficulty would be in saying in each particular case that the business was not required to be done".[23] It is also thought that the professional services of an individual trustee are difficult to value and that, in any event, a person can always decline to accept the role of trustee. The argument runs that if the trustee voluntarily accepts the office then he cannot complain if he is not paid for his services. Traditionally, the onus was upon the trustee to show that there was an express charging clause[24] or some other legal validation for remuneration. Prior to the 2000 Act, justification might come from a variety of sources.

13.24

By virtue of contract

This would operate when the trustee has entered into a contract allowing payment directly with all the beneficiaries when all are of full age and capacity.[25] This need for unanimity reduces the potential for exploitation and unfairness. The consideration for this contract can be the performance by the trustee of existing or future services (but not past services).[26] Of course the contract can be set aside if it is induced either by undue influence, misrepresentation or duress.[27] Indeed, this occurred in *O'Sullivan v Management Agency & Music Ltd*[28] where a contract between a singer (the once famous Gilbert O'Sullivan) and his agent was avoided on the ground of undue influence.

13.25

---

[20] [1896] A.C. 44 at 51, 52.
[21] See *Ultraframe (UK) Ltd v Fielding* [2006] F.S.R. 17.
[22] *Robinson v Pett* (1734) 3 P. Wms. 249.
[23] (1887) 34 Ch. D. 77 at 81. This case concerned the profit costs of a solicitor-trustee.
[24] For example, in *Robinson v Pett* (1734) 3 P. Wms. 249 the executors were allowed to charge £100 for their services; see also, *Ellison v Airey* (1748) 1 Ves. Sen. 111.
[25] *Ayliffe v Murray* (1740) 2 Atk 58.
[26] *Williams v Roffey Brothers & Nicholls (Contractors) Ltd* [1990] 1 All E.R. 512.
[27] *Stilk v Myrick* (1809) 2 Camp. 317.
[28] [1985] 3 All E.R. 351.

By order of the court

13.26   Under the inherent jurisdiction to ensure the adequate administration of the trust, the court might award payment to a trustee. This will occur only when the services of the trustee are regarded as being of exceptional benefit to the trust.[29] As Fox L.J. acknowledged in *Re Duke of Norfolk's Settlement Trusts*, "In exercising that jurisdiction the court has to balance two influences which are to some extent in conflict. The first is that the office of trustee is, as such, gratuitous; the court will accordingly be careful to protect the interests of the beneficiaries against claims by the trustees. The second is that it is of great importance to the beneficiaries that the trust should be well administered".[30]

In *Foster v Spencer*,[31] for example, two trustees sought remuneration for past and future services designed to enhance greatly the development value of the trust property (a cricket ground). Paul Baker Q.C. sitting in the High Court allowed payment for the past services (but not the proposed future services because they did not call for any specific expertise). Payments for past services were justified on the basis that otherwise the beneficiaries would be unjustly enriched. Similarly, in *Perotti v Watson* a solicitor undertook the administration of an estate that in time became unexpectedly complex.[32] Although the services provided were not always of a high standard, the Court of Appeal allowed the solicitor to claim fees, albeit scaled down to 75 per cent to reflect the varying quality of those services.

13.27   Even when a charging clause has been inserted into the trust instrument, the court can employ its inherent powers to vary or increase the amount that can be charged. For example, in *Re Duke of Norfolk's Settlement Trusts*,[33] a trust corporation accepted the administration of the trust for a low annual fee. As trustee, it subsequently became involved in an extensive redevelopment project and was allowed an increase in remuneration because the duties became unexpectedly onerous. As Fox L.J. reasoned, "if the court has jurisdiction ... upon the application of a trustee to authorise remuneration though no such power exists in the trust instrument, there is no reason why the court should not have the power to increase the remuneration given by the instrument".[34] In the *O'Sullivan* case, and even though the contract was set aside, the court allowed the agent to recover some payment in acknowledgement of his role in advancing his client's career. An application for approval of remuneration was, however, rejected in *Guinness Plc v Saunders*.[35] The House of Lords emphasised that payment will not be permitted in circumstances where there is a possible conflict between personal interest and fiduciary duty. There a director of one company unsuccessfully claimed £5.2 million for advice and services provided in facilitating the take over of another company. His personal interests were in stark conflict with his fiduciary duty as a director. Lord Goff spoke of limiting the jurisdiction to cases, "where it cannot have the effect of encouraging

---

[29]   *Re Barbour's Settlement* [1974] 1 All E.R. 1188, where a bank's claim for an allowance failed as there was no benefit to the beneficiaries upon which it could be justified.
[30]   [1982] Ch. 61 at 79.
[31]   [1996] 2 All E.R. 672.
[32]   (2001) EWCA Civ. 116.
[33]   [1982] Ch. 61.
[34]   [1982] Ch. 61 at 78.
[35]   [1990] 1 All E.R. 652.

trustees in any way to put themselves in a position where their interests conflict with their duties as trustees".[36] He declined, however, to comment upon whether a director could claim an equitable allowance if the director was not also a trustee.

Special treatment of solicitors' profit costs in litigation work

A solicitor-trustee's costs of litigation are the subject of special treatment. According to   **13.28** the oft-criticised and curious rule in *Cradock v Piper*,[37] a solicitor-trustee is entitled to profit costs in litigation where he acts as solicitor on behalf of himself and a co-trustee or beneficiary in relation to trust affairs.[38] This is provided that the costs are no more than they would have been had he acted for the co-trustee alone. Although the reasoning underlying this distinction is somewhat unclear, the rule does not apply when a solicitor-trustee employs his firm to do non-litigious work.[39] It is thought that this distinction is to do with the difficulties of costing work that is not subject to judicial scrutiny.[40] Upjohn J. later described the *Cradock* rule as, "exceptional and anomalous and not to be extended ...".[41]

Overseas property

If the trust property is located abroad, and the law of the country where it is situated   **13.29** permits the remuneration of trustees, it appears that the trustees are entitled to keep any payments made. In *Re Northcote's WT*,[42] a testator left property both in England and the USA. The executor was obliged to obtain probate in the USA relating to the assets located there. Harman J. held that the executor could charge for those costs because there was no conflict of interest and duty.

Statutory authority

Remuneration is payable in those circumstances where Parliament has authorised its   **13.30** payment, for example, on the appointment by the court of a trust corporation (under s.42 of the Trustee Act 1925); on the appointment of a judicial trustee (under s.1(5) of the Judicial Trustees Act 1896) and on the appointment of the public trustee (under s.9 of the Public Trustee Act 1906).

With the emergence of professional trustees (such as banks, solicitors and accountants), the need for payment became more pronounced and the existing provisions

---

[36] [1990] 1 All E.R. 652 at 667.
[37] (1850) 1 Mac. & G. 664. This overruled the contrary authority of *Bainbrigge v Blair* (1845) 8 Beav. 588.
[38] The rule was reaffirmed in *Broughton v Broughton* (1854) 5 De G.M. & G. 160.
[39] See *Re Corsellis* (1887) 34 Ch. D. 675 where the solicitor was unable to recover costs for work done in passing receiver's accounts and granting leases.
[40] See *Broughton v Broughton*, (1854) 5 De G.M. & G. 160.
[41] *Re Worthington* [1954] 1 All E.R. 677 at 679.
[42] [1949] 1 All E.R. 442.

revealed as woefully inadequate. The Law Reform Committee in its 1982 Report concerning trustees' powers and duties highlighted such defects.[43] As Parry commented in 1984, "It is time to recognise that the changed social and economic circumstances in which trusts today operate call for increasing professionalism on the part of trustees. If a professional is appointed to undertake this function ... he should be entitled to reasonable remuneration for his services".[44] Of course, if the appointment of a professional trustee was anticipated by the settlor, a well-drafted charging clause could easily be included in the trust instrument. Nevertheless, in cases of uncertainty or ambiguity, the courts strictly construe such clauses. In *Re Chalinder & Herington*,[45] a clause which allowed the solicitor-trustee to claim for "all professional and other charges for his time and trouble" was held not to cover costs incurred in non-professional work.

13.31   Not surprisingly, difficulties arise when no express facility is reserved. This omission would effectively prevent a professional trustee from acting as an original or a replacement trustee. The reason is that when a trustee receives unauthorised remuneration he is liable to account to the trust and the money will be held by him on constructive trust. This was the problem that Pt V of the Trustee Act 2000 sought to address.[46] It is specifically catered for in ss.28–29 of the 2000 Act and these provisions operate in two situations:

- s.28 operates when there is an express charging clause in the trust deed. As regards trust corporations or trustees acting in "a professional capacity",[47] s.28 enables these trustees to claim remuneration under such a clause. This rule relaxes the strict construction previously given to charging clauses and applies even if a lay trustee could have effectively provided those services.[48] Although s.28 applies to trusts whenever created, it only covers services provided after the commencement date of the 2000 Act (1/2/2000). Section 28 can be excluded in the trust instrument;[49] and

- s.29 operates when there is no express provision made for remuneration.[50] Subsections (1)–(2) provide that a trust corporation and trustees (other than sole trustees) who act in a professional capacity are entitled to receive "reasonable remuneration". A reasonable remuneration is one that is reasonable for the provision of those services to the trust by the particular trustee.[51] It will reflect the time and trouble taken by the trustee. As with s.28, this provision applies to trusts whenever created[52] and to services that could otherwise have

[43] Law Reform Committee 23rd Report, "The Powers and Duties of Trustees" (1982) Cmnd 8733.

[44] N.B.M. Parry [1984] Conv. 275 at p.285.

[45] [1907] 1 Ch. 58.

[46] This does not apply fully to charitable trusts. The appropriate Secretary of State has the power to issue regulations for the provision of remuneration to such trustees: s.30.

[47] For these purposes, this requires the trustee to act in the course of a profession or a business that is connected with the management or administration of trusts: s.28(5).

[48] Section 28(2); cf. the former rule in *Re Chapple* (1884) 27 Ch. D. 584 where a solicitor-trustee was not allowed to claim for services of a non-professional character.

[49] Section 28(1).

[50] Section 29(5).

[51] Section 29(3).

[52] Section 33(1).

been provided by a lay trustee.[53] Despite the improvements offered by s.29, it remains best practice for the settlor to insert a comprehensive charging clause in the trust deed.

Directors' fees

Often a trustee will obtain remuneration as a director of a company connected with the trust. As shown in *Re Macadam*,[54] when the directorship was acquired because of his position as a trustee, the trustee is accountable to the trust for fees received. This rule does not apply, however, when the directorship was obtained independently of the trust. In *Re Gee*,[55] for example, the trustee became a director without any reliance upon trust votes and was able to retain the remuneration received. Similarly, as in *Re Dover Coalfield Extension Ltd*,[56] payments may be kept when the directorship was obtained before assuming the office of trusteeship. The rule, therefore, focuses upon preventing a serving trustee becoming a director and claiming a profit from acting as such. In that scenario, the possibility of self-advancement at the expense of the better interests of the trust is evident. The will or settlement may, however, authorise the trustee to keep any remuneration obtained from a directorship whenever obtained. As Jenkins L.J. admitted in *Re Llewellin's Will Trusts*, "there is no rule of equity which says that a testator, if so minded, may not provide that the trustees can hold salaried offices in companies which the testator's estate controls and receive the emoluments attached to those offices without liability to account ... indeed as a matter of business it is often a very sensible provision to make".[57]

13.32

Out of pocket expenses

Not surprisingly, a trustee is entitled to be reimbursed for out of pocket expenses properly incurred.[58] This does not, however, allow the trustee to claim interest in respect of any such outlay.[59] Reimbursement extends both to money spent and liabilities to pay that may arise. Any expenses claimed, however, must be reasonable and appropriate in the circumstances. Hence, in *Malcom v O'Callaghan*[60] the trustee's claim for expenses for frequent trips to Paris on trust business was disallowed because his presence there was not necessary. Mundane examples of recoverable expenditure include the payment of insurance premiums, fees paid to agents and money spent on repairs to trust property. A less obvious scenario arose in *Benett v Wyndham*[61] where a trustee

13.33

---

[53] Section 29(4).
[54] [1946] Ch. 73.
[55] [1948] Ch. 284.
[56] [1908] 1 Ch. 65.
[57] [1949] Ch. 225 at 227.
[58] Section 31(1) of the Trustee Act 2000. For example, this would include legal costs incurred by a trustee acting on behalf of the trust: *Close Trustees (Switzerland) SA v Vildosola* [2008] EWHC 1267 (Ch).
[59] *Foster v Spencer* [1996] 2 All E.R. 672.
[60] (1835) 3 Myl. & Cr. 52.
[61] (1862) 4 De G.F. & J. 259.

employed woodcutters to topple some trees on the trust land. Due to their negligence, a branch fell on a passing stranger causing injury. The trustee, as legal owner of the land, was successfully sued and had to compensate the victim. The trustee was able to claim the cost of the damages paid from the trust fund.

A trustee will be allowed his litigation costs if all the beneficiaries approve the action or the High Court grants leave to sue or to defend. The latter is known as a "Beddoe Order" and derives its name from the decision of the Court of Appeal in *Re Beddoe*.[62] An application for a Beddoe Order should be made in separate preliminary proceedings.[63] Where a Beddoe Order is not sought, the trustee will obtain costs only if the action was properly brought or defended for the benefit of the trust estate.[64] In other words, the trustee will be shielded where a Beddoe Order would have been made had the trustee applied for it.[65] As in *Beddoe*, trustees who act without the approval of the beneficiaries or the court run the risk that they may have to pay their own (and possibly also the other party's) costs themselves.[66] The failure to apply for a Beddoe Order does not amount to a breach of trust.[67]

Purchase of trust property

13.34   Traditionally, the prevention of a trustee from purchasing trust property was classified as merely one aspect of the trustee's duty not to profit from his position. The modern approach, however, is to view this type of purchase as being the subject of two distinct rules, namely, the "self-dealing" rule and the "insider dealing" rule (sometimes known also as the "fair dealing" rule).[68] As Megarry J. explained, "there are two rules: the consequences are different, and the property and the transactions which invoke the rules are different. I see no merit in attempting a forced union which has to be expressed in terms of disunity".[69] The former rule caters for purchases by a trustee of property that is legally owned by the trustees as a body. The latter rule deals with the situation where a trustee buys out a beneficiary's equitable interest under the trust. It is necessary to look at these rules in some detail.

The self-dealing rule

13.35   Where a trustee purchases trust property, for example, he buys the freehold or takes a lease of trust land,[70] the beneficiaries can subsequently set the transaction aside (i.e. it is

---

[62] [1893] 1 Ch. 547.
[63] *Alsop v Neary* [1995] 1 All E.R. 431.
[64] *Holding & Management Ltd v Property Holding & Investment Trusts Plc* [1990] 1 All E.R. 938.
[65] *McDonald v Horn* [1994] P.L.R. 33. The burden lies on the trustee to show that the costs were properly incurred.
[66] See *Singh v Bhasin* (1998) *The Times*, August 21, where the trustee acted unreasonably in defending an action and could not, therefore, claim the costs of that litigation from the trust.
[67] *Bonham v Blake Lapthorn Linnel* [2006] EWHC 2513 (Ch). The order is designed merely to protect the trustee.
[68] See *Tito v Waddell (No.2)* [1977] Ch. 106 at 240, 247–249.
[69] [1977] Ch. 106 at 240.
[70] *AG v Earl of Clarendon* (1810) 17 Ves. 491.

voidable at the behest of the beneficiaries[71]). The notion is that the trustee should not profit from his office and it reflects the possibility that the trustee might not give the best price obtainable.[72] This self-dealing rule applies to all types of property and the transaction can be set aside as against the trustee as well as against any purchaser from the trustee who has notice of the breach of trust.[73] The rule would be invoked when, for example, a co-trustee buys trust property from himself and the other trustees. Matters are, understandably, different when it is a sole trustee who purports to sell. In this instance, the transaction is necessarily void ab initio.[74] The trustee cannot intelligibly be said to buy property from himself.[75]

The self-dealing rule gives way when the purchase is authorised by Parliament[76] or in the trust instrument. In *Sargeant v National Westminster Bank Plc*, the sale of certain farms to the trustees was expressly permitted by the settlor and the transactions were upheld.[77] As Nourse L.J. admitted, "the rule is expressed by saying that a trustee must not put himself in a position where his interest and duty conflict. But to express it that way is to acknowledge that if he is put there, not by himself, but by the testator or settlor under whose dispositions his trust arises, the rule does not apply".[78]

A transaction is tainted by the self-dealing rule even in the absence of unfairness or sharp practice[79] and regardless of whether or not the trustee makes a profit.[80] The rule applies even if the trustee bought the property at public auction.[81] The operation of the rule is well illustrated in *Wright v Morgan*[82] where the trustee took an assignment of an option to purchase trust property (land and the stock thereon) at a valuation to be provided by another trustee. The Privy Council held that, despite the air of an independent valuation, there was a still conflict of interest and duty.

13.36

As the underlying ethos is that the trustee's interests must not collide with his fiduciary duty, the rule has no application if the contract to sell or the sale itself occurred before assuming the role of trustee.[83] Similarly, a person who at the outset disclaims the role of trustee may make an effective purchase[84] and it appears that a bare trustee with no active duties to carry out also falls outside the scope of the rule.[85] In *Holder v Holder*,[86] a son was appointed as one of the executors under his father's will. He attempted to renounce his executorship and announced his intention to buy part of the estate (a farm) at public auction. Although he acquired the farm at a fair price, a beneficiary under the will sought to have the sale set aside. The Court of Appeal could

---

[71] *Campbell v Walker* (1800) 5 Ves. 678; see *Walker v Walker* Unreported January 30, 2007 where a lease to a trustee was set aside under the self-dealing rule.

[72] The self-dealing rule cannot apply when there is no trust relationship with the property; *Hollis v Rolfe* [2008] EWHC 1747 (Ch).

[73] *Aberdeen Town Council v Aberdeen University* (1877) 2 App. Cas. 544.

[74] *Franks v Bollans* (1868) 3 Ch. App. 717.

[75] See *Rye v Rye* [1962] A.C. 496.

[76] For example, s.68 of the Settled Land Act 1925 enables the tenant for life to purchase trust property.

[77] (1990) 61 P. & C.R. 518.

[78] (1990) 61 P. & C.R. 518 at 519.

[79] *Dyson v Lum* (1866) 14 L.T. 588.

[80] *Ex parte Lacey* (1802) 6 Ves. 62.

[81] *Lister v Lister* (1802) 6 Ves. 631.

[82] [1926] A.C. 788.

[83] *Vyse v Foster* (1874) L.R. 7 H.L. 318.

[84] *Stacey v Elph* (1833) 1 My. & K. 195.

[85] *Parkes v White* (1805) 11 Ves. 209.

[86] [1968] 1 All E.R. 665.

see no sufficient conflict of interest and duty to activate the rule against self-dealing and upheld the transaction. It was important that the son had never become actively involved in the administration of his father's estate, had not acquired any special knowledge in his capacity as executor and had exerted no pressure on the other executors as to the sale or the timing of sale.

13.37 Not surprisingly, the self-dealing rule cannot be sidestepped by the trustee retiring in order to purchase trust property.[87] The rule will cease to apply, however, after a long period of retirement.[88] The rule cannot be circumvented by the trustee employing a nominee company to act on his behalf,[89] selling to his children,[90] selling to his wife,[91] transferring the property into the name of a partnership between the trustee and others[92] or acting as the agent for a third party.[93] In *Campbell v Walker*,[94] an apparent conflict emerged when the trustee attempted to sell to a party who was, in reality, a trustee for the selling trustee. The rule bites also when the trustee sells to a business partner, but only when there is some benefit (direct or indirect) for the trustee.[95] In contrast, where the trust property is sold bona fide to a third party, there is nothing to prevent a trustee from subsequently purchasing the property from the new owner.[96]

The advisable course for a trustee who seeks to purchase trust property from his co-trustees is to apply to court for approval of the sale. Such leave will be given when the transaction is to the manifest advantage of the beneficiaries[97] and usually only with the consent of the beneficiaries.[98] It is, therefore, recommended that, in all cases, the purchasing trustee obtain the beneficiaries' informed consent to the proposed transaction.[99]

The insider dealing (fair dealing) rule

13.38 A different approach is adopted when the trustee or other fiduciary intends to purchase the equitable interest of a beneficiary, for example, when the trustee wishes to buy out the beneficiary's interest in land. Whereas the self-dealing rule is based upon the relationship between the parties, the fiduciary rule against insider dealing is framed around the conduct of the trustee. In order for the sale to be effective, the transaction must be fair and honest. This means that the consideration provided must be adequate,[1] there must be no undue influence exerted by the trustee and the beneficiary must be given full

---

[87] *Holder v Holder* [1968] 1 All E.R. 665.
[88] In *Re Boles & British Land Co's Contract* [1902] 1 Ch. 244, Buckley J. held that a trustee who had retired 12 years before the purchase was able to buy trust property as there was no evidence that there was any longer a potential conflict of interest and duty.
[89] *Silkstone & Haigh Moore Coal Co v Edey* [1900] 1 Ch. 167.
[90] *Gregory v Gregory* (1815) Jac. 631.
[91] *Ferraby v Hobson* (1847) 2 Ph. 255.
[92] *Re Thompson's Settlement* [1986] Ch. 99. There the trustees granted a lease to a company and partnership of which the trustees were directors and partners.
[93] *Ex parte Bennett* (1805) 10 Ves. 381.
[94] (1800) 5 Ves. 678.
[95] *Ex parte Moore* (1881) 45 L.T. 558.
[96] See *Whitcomb v Minchin* (1820) 5 Madd. 91.
[97] *Farmer v Dean* (1863) 32 Beav. 327.
[98] *Tennant v Trenchard* (1869) 4 Ch. App. 537.
[99] *Randall v Errington* (1805) 10 Ves. 423.
[1] *Dougan v MacPherson* [1902] A.C. 197.

and accurate information about the extent of the beneficial interest to be bought.[2] As Megarry J. observed in *Tito v Waddell (No.2)*, "the fair dealing rule is essentially a rule of equity that certain persons (including trustees) are subject to certain consequences if they carry through certain transactions without, where appropriate, complying with certain requirements".[3]

The purchase of a minor's interest will, for obvious reasons, usually fall foul of the fair dealing rule.[4] It is also a relevant factor if it is the beneficiary who initiated the sale. In *Coles v Trecothick*,[5] for example, the sale was upheld in circumstances where the beneficiary took control of the sale by auction. The beneficiary had chosen both the venue and the auctioneer and, moreover, was content with the price obtained on the sale. As Lord Eldon explained, a trustee may buy from a beneficiary provided that, "there is a distinct and clear contract, ascertained to be such after a jealous and scrupulous examination of all the circumstances, proving that the *cestui que trust* [the beneficiary] intended the trustee should buy; and there is no fraud, no concealment, no advantage taken, by the trustee of information acquired by him in the character of trustee".[6] In *Morse v Royal*,[7] an ex-army officer sold his interest to the trustee. There was no concealment or deceit by the trustee. When the property went up in price, the beneficiary, who had pressed the trustee to buy the property, regretted the sale and sought to have it set aside. The beneficiary was unsuccessful in his action.

In contrast, in *Dougan v Macpherson*[8] two brothers were beneficiaries under a trust. One brother was also a trustee. The trustee purchased his brother's beneficial interest without disclosing to him a valuation report of the trust estate. The beneficial share was worth much more than the trustee paid for it. The transaction here was set aside. As the Earl of Halsbury L.C. concluded, "it is to my mind an absolute novelty to hear it gravely argued that such a transaction as that can stand".[9] Lord Ashbourne observed, "It was the absolute and obvious duty of the defender in this case, if he thought he could maintain the transaction upon which he had entered, to have present in his mind the distinct duty which he owed to his brother".[10]

13.39

Incidental profit

In light of the rule that a trustee may not put himself in a position where his interest and duty conflict, the derivation of a direct profit by a trustee clearly contravenes the fiduciary relationship existing with the beneficiaries. Unless authorised by the trust instrument, the beneficiaries, the court or Parliament, a trustee is under a strict duty to account for any profits made by exploiting trust property or the office of trustee. For

13.40

---

[2] *Randall v Etherington* (1805) 10 Ves. 427.
[3] [1977] Ch. 106. For example, the rule does not apply when the sale is by an independent person acting in pursuance to a court order: *Bank of Scotland v Neath Port Talbot County B.C.* [2008] B.C.C. 376.
[4] See *Sanderson v Walker* (1807) 13 Ves. 601.
[5] (1804) 9 Ves. 234.
[6] (1804) 9 Ves. 234 at 247.
[7] (1806) 12 Ves. 355.
[8] [1902] A.C. 197.
[9] [1902] A.C. 197 at 202.
[10] [1902] A.C. 197 at 203, 204.

example, in *Williams v Barton*[11] the trustee worked as a clerk to a stockbroker. His salary was partly commission based. He instructed the stockbroker to act on behalf of the trust and was then liable to account for the commission he earned in respect of that business. As Russell J. acknowledged, "the case falls within the mischief which is sought to be prevented by the rule. The case is clearly one where his duty as trustee and his interest in an increased remuneration are in direct conflict".[12] The profit arose out of and by reason of his trusteeship.

In modern times, the means by which a trustee can make a direct profit from his position are various. It is, therefore, convenient to categorise the common scenarios that may emerge where a conflict of interest and duty will emerge.

Sale of property to the trust

13.41   A sale by the trustee of property to the trust is apt to be set aside by the beneficiaries in circumstances where the trustee did not fully disclose the nature of his interest in the property sold. The honesty of the trustee and the fairness of the consideration paid are irrelevant factors.[13] Indeed, a sale may be set aside even if it was negotiated prior to the vendor assuming the role of trustee. The same principle operates where the trustee runs a business that trades with a business carried out by the trust.

Competing with the trust

13.42   The general rule is that a trustee and other fiduciaries may not enter into business competition with the trust.[14] In *Re Thomson*,[15] the trustee claimed the right to carry on a yachtbroker's business in the same town as a similar business operated by the trust. The trustee's commercial activities were reined in by Clauson J. on the basis that business competition within the same locality was unavoidable. He explained:

> "The rule of universal application is that an executor and trustee having duties to discharge of a fiduciary nature towards the beneficiaries under the will—in this particular case the duty of a fiduciary nature was to carry on the business of the testator to the best advantage of the beneficiaries—he shall not be allowed to enter into any engagement in which he has or can have a personal interest conflicting, or which may possibly conflict, with the interests of those whom he is bound to protect".[16]

---

[11] [1927] 2 Ch. 9.
[12] [1927] 2 Ch. 9 at 12.
[13] *Gillett v Peppercone* (1840) 3 Beav. 78.
[14] *Balston Ltd v Headline Filters Ltd* [1990] F.S.R. 385 (competitive tendering for the business of a client of the company of which he had been a director).
[15] [1930] 1 Ch. 203.
[16] [1930] 1 Ch. 203 at 215.

Several observations may be made about this rule. First, the specialist nature of the businesses in *Thomson* may exert some significance in that it highlights the inevitability of conflict. Clauson J. placed great emphasis upon the nature of a yacht agent's business and limited his decision to the business operated on the facts before him.[17] It is unclear whether the same rule would apply to a general business carried out by the trustee. For example, it is doubtful whether the court would prevent the trustee opening up a rival greengrocer's shop in the same town. Unless the shops are in close proximity, there appears to be no meaningful conflict of interest and duty that could justify such drastic action.[18]

Secondly, the trustee in the *Thomson* case commenced his rival business after accepting the office of trustee. If the conflicting business of the trustee was in existence prior to his appointment, the outcome would depend upon whether the settlor knew of the trustee's business. Presumably, if the settlor did possess such knowledge then the trustee will be allowed to continue with his commercial activity until a real and meaningful conflict of interest and duty emerges.

Thirdly, the rule appears to apply more strictly to trustees than other types of fiduciary (e.g. company directors). In *Island Export Finance Ltd v Umunna*,[19] it was held by the High Court that, although his fiduciary duties did not end upon his resignation, a former director could enter a competing business provided that he did not exploit a maturing business opportunity of his former company.[20] The company was not actively seeking such contracts when he resigned or, indeed, when he later obtained the contracts for himself. There was, moreover, no improper use by him of confidential information acquired while he was a director.[21] All turns upon the facts of a particular case. As Etherton J. explained in *Shepherds Investments Ltd v Walters*, "It is obvious, for example, that merely making a decision to set up competing business at some point in the future and discussing such an idea with friends and family would not of themselves be in conflict with the best interests of the company and the employer. The consulting of lawyers and other professionals may, depending on the circumstances, equally be consistent with a director's fiduciary duties and the employee's obligation of loyalty. At the other end of the spectrum, it is plain that soliciting customers of the company and the employer or the actual carrying on of a trade by a competing business would be in breach of the duties of a director and the obligations of an employee. It is the wide range of activity and decision making between the two ends of the spectrum which will be fact sensitive in every case."[22]

13.43

---

[17] [1930] 1 Ch. 203 at 213, 216.
[18] See *Moore v M'Glynn* [1894] 1 Ir. R. 74. If the trustee was allowed to continue his business, however, he may be required to resign or be removed from office.
[19] [1986] BCLC 460.
[20] See also *Framlington Group Plc v Anderson* [1995] 1 BCLC 475; *Foster Bryant Surveying Ltd v Bryant* [2007] EWCA Civ 200.
[21] cf. *British Midland Tool Ltd v Midland International Tooling Ltd* [2003] 2 BCLC 523.
[22] [2006] EWHC 836 (Ch) at [108].

Renewal of trust lease

13.44   This aspect of the non-profit rule is illustrated by *Keech v Sanford*[23] where a trustee of a lease of Romford Market applied for its renewal for the benefit of an infant beneficiary. The landlord refused to renew the lease in favour of the beneficiary, but agreed to renew the lease in the trustee's own favour. In the genuine knowledge that a lease renewal would not be granted to the beneficiary, the trustee went ahead and took the grant. The infant then sought to have the lease assigned to him. Although there was no question of fraud, Lord King L.C. concluded that the trustee held the lease on constructive trust for the infant and that he had to account for profits received. The underlying reason was that there would be less incentive on the trustee to press for a renewal for the trust if he knew that he would benefit by a refusal. As Lord King L.C. put it, "I very well see, if a trustee, on the refusal to renew, might have a lease for himself, few trust estates would be renewed to the *cestui que use;* though I do not say that there is a fraud in this case, yet he should have rather let it run out, than to have had the lease himself ... for it is very obvious what would be the consequences of letting trustees have the lease, on refusal to renew to *cestui que use*".[24]

The rule in *Keech v Sanford*, however, applies only when it is the trustee (or some other fiduciary) who obtains the benefit. As Lord King L.C. acknowledged, "the trustee is the only person of all mankind who might not have the lease".[25] In *Re Biss*,[26] for example, a yearly tenant of a shop died intestate and a renewal was refused to his widow. Although one of their children subsequently obtained a renewal, he was entitled to keep the lease for himself. No fiduciary duty was owed to the estate.

Abuse of position: bad faith

13.45   Understandably, where the trustee has acted in bad faith, and by doing so made a profit, he will have to account for that profit. In *Reading v A-G*,[27] an army sergeant earned £19,000 by transporting smuggled goods in an army vehicle and while in army uniform. The profit was confiscated and, on his release from prison, he took action for its return. His action failed because he was a fiduciary and was liable to account for the profits to the Crown. Lord Normand commented, "he owes to the Crown a duty as fully fiduciary as the duty of a servant to his master or of an agent to his principal, and in consequence that all profits and advantages gained by the use or abuse of his military status are to be for the benefit of the Crown".[28] A similar approach was adopted in *A-G for Hong Kong v Reid*[29] where a fiduciary accepted bribes during the course of his employment by the Crown. It was held that the Crown was able to claim the property acquired by the bribes (three houses) even though the houses were now of a higher value

---

[23] (1726) Sel. Cas. Ch. 61.
[24] (1726) Sel. Cas. Ch. 61.
[25] (1726) Sel. Cas. Ch. 61.
[26] [1903] 2 Ch. 40.
[27] [1951] A.C. 507.
[28] [1951] A.C. 507 at 517.
[29] [1994] 1 A.C. 324.

than the bribes received. In *Islamic Republic of Iran Shipping Lines v Denby*,[30] a solicitor accepted a cash inducement from the opposing side to settle a case initiated by his client. It was held that the solicitor was liable to pay the money received to his client. In *English v Dedham Vale Properties*,[31] agents were held liable to account for profits when they allowed Ms English to sell her property to them for £7,750 without her knowing that the agents had previously applied for planning permission. The agents were treated as fiduciaries and they should have disclosed the application before the contract was entered.

Abuse of position: good faith

In the above cases there was clearly bad faith shown by the fiduciary, but this is not a **13.46** necessary requirement before a fiduciary is compelled to account for abuse of position. For example, in *Industrial Development Consultants Ltd v Cooley*[32] a managing director of a company had been negotiating a contract with the Eastern Gas Board. The Gas Board did not wish to enter into any dealings with the company, but it was prepared to enter a contract with the managing director privately. Consequently, he terminated his association with the company on the false basis of illness and signed the contract with the Gas Board. The first issue was whether he was a fiduciary and Roskill J. answered this in the affirmative, "The defendant had one capacity and one capacity only in which he was carrying on business at the time. That capacity was as managing director of the plaintiffs".[33] The second issue concerned whether he was in breach of fiduciary duty. Although a contract between the company and the Gas Board would never have come to fruition, its former managing director had to account to the company for the benefit of the contract he had personally entered. Roskill J. observed, "he was guilty of putting himself into the position in which his duty to his employers ... and his own private interests conflicted and conflicted grievously".[34] The conflict was that he had negotiated the contract in the company's time and had a platform for negotiation with the Gas Board because of his association with the company. Roskill J. explained, "Information which came to him while he was managing director and which was of concern to the plaintiffs and relevant for the plaintiffs to know was information which it was his duty to pass on to the plaintiffs".[35] Instead, he guarded the information for his own personal profit. Roskill J. continued, "if the defendant is not required to account he will have made a large profit as a result of having deliberately put himself into a position in which his duty to the plaintiffs who were employing him and his personal interests conflicted".[36]

Two of the most illustrative cases concerning the abuse of position by a fiduciary are

[30] [1987] 1 Lloyds Rep. 367.
[31] [1978] 1 All E.R. 382.
[32] [1972] 1 W.L.R. 443.
[33] [1972] 1 W.L.R. 443 at 451.
[34] [1972] 1 W.L.R. 443 at 453.
[35] [1972] 1 W.L.R. 443 at 451. Cf. acquisition by directors of a general fund of knowledge which can be exploited subsequently in a new position: *CMS Dolphin Ltd v Simonet* [2001] 2 BCLC 704.
[36] [1972] 1 W.L.R. 443 at 453.

Regal (Hastings) Ltd v Gulliver[37] and *Boardman v Phipps*.[38] In *Regal (Hastings) Ltd v Gulliver*, Regal operated a cinema and wished to buy two further motion picture theatres in the vicinity. The directors determined to set up a subsidiary company which would acquire the leases to the other cinemas. The idea was that Regal would then sell its interest in all three venues as a going concern. Unless the subsidiary company had a paid up capital of at least £5,000, the landlord of the two cinemas demanded a financial guarantee from the directors. The directors were reluctant to offer a personal guarantee and elected for the alternative course. As Regal could fund only £2,000 of the required £5,000, the directors decided to club together and to raise the shortfall themselves in return for a share issue. The leases were duly acquired, but Regal did not sell its business interest. Instead, the directors sold their shares in both Regal and the subsidiary company and made a substantial profit. A new board of directors was appointed and the board sought an account of the profits personally made from the sale of the shares in the subsidiary company. The directors argued that they had acted in good faith and had secured a benefit for Regal in the process. Reversing the decision of the Court of Appeal, the House of Lords held that the directors were liable to account for the profits made. Lord Russell explained:

> "The rule of equity which insists on those, who by use of a fiduciary position make a profit, being liable to account for that profit, in no way depends on fraud, or absence of *bona fides;* or upon such questions or considerations as whether the profit would or should otherwise have gone to the plaintiff, or whether the profiteer was under a duty to obtain the source of the profit for the plaintiff, or whether he took a risk or acted as he did for the benefit of the plaintiff, or whether the plaintiff has in fact been damaged or benefited by his action. The liability arises from the mere fact of a profit having, in the stated circumstances, been made. The profiteer, however honest or well intentioned, cannot escape the risk of being called to account".[39]

13.47 The outcome of this decision was to provide the new purchasers of Regal and its subsidiary with a windfall bonus because they were able to recoup some of the money that had been spent on acquiring the businesses. Nevertheless, as Lord Porter acknowledged, "the principle that a person occupying a fiduciary relationship shall not make a profit by reason thereof is of such vital importance that the possible consequence in the present case is in fact as it is in law an immaterial consideration".[40] Lord Wright stated that the directors should have, "let the opportunity pass".[41] Viscount Sankey reiterated the traditional line, "no-one who has duties of a fiduciary nature to perform is allowed to enter into engagements in which he has or can have a personal

---

[37] [1942] 1 All E.R. 378.
[38] [1967] 2 A.C. 46.
[39] [1942] 1 All E.R. 378 at 386. This strict approach has, however, been rejected by both the Supreme Court of Canada in Canada *(Peso Silver Mines v Cropper* (1966) 58 D.L.R. (2d) 1) and the High Court of Australia *(Consul Development v DPC Estates* (1975) 132 C.L.R. 373). Both jurisdictions favour a more flexible approach in keeping with modern times.
[40] [1942] 1 All E.R. 378 at 394.
[41] [1942] 1 All E.R. 378 at 394.

interest conflicting with the interests of those whom he is bound to protect. If he holds any property so acquired as trustee, he is bound to account for it ... ".[42]

By way of an aside, Lord Russell believed that this liability to account could have been sidestepped had the trustees obtained the prior approval of Regal's shareholders to the purchase of the shares in the subsidiary company. Following *Queensland Mines v Hudson*, it is arguable that ratification might be effective even when coming from the board of directors provided that the fiduciary is not a controlling shareholder of the company.[43]

13.48 In *Boardman v Phipps*, a testator set up a trust for the benefit of his widow and children. The trust solicitor was Mr Boardman. In time, Mr Boardman became concerned about a trust investment in an ailing private company. He concluded that the only way to protect the trust investment was for the trust to obtain a majority shareholding in the company and to appoint a new management. As the trustees were unwilling to do this, he and one of the beneficiaries (Tom Phipps) went off and bought the outstanding shares themselves. During the phase leading up to the take-over Mr Boardman had claimed to represent the trust and had obtained information that was not available to the public at large. With the support of two of the three trustees, the pair took control of the company. As a consequence, the trust benefited by £47,000. Mr Boardman and the beneficiary made a profit in the region of £75,000. One of the other beneficiaries (John Phipps) claimed that the profit had been made by the use of information that had been acquired by the pair while acting on behalf of the trust and in a fiduciary capacity. The claim, which was based on the principle enunciated in the *Regal (Hastings)* case, succeeded before the House of Lords by virtue of a majority decision.[44]

It was concluded by Lords Guest, Cohen and Hodson that the rule in *Keech v Sandford* (see **13.44**) operated in the present case. As both Mr Boardman and the beneficiary were fiduciaries and, as they had made a profit from speculating with trust property (i.e. trust information and contacts), they were liable to account to the trust for the profit made. It was immaterial that the pair had acted honestly in a fashion that was of great benefit to the trust. Lord Cohen felt that Mr Boardman would have been incapable of giving independent advice to the trust if it had been sought as he was himself negotiating privately for the purchase of shares.[45] Put shortly, there was a conflict between his interest and his duty. While the reasoning of the majority is convincing as regards Mr Boardman, it does not sit as comfortably with the position of Tom Phipps. It could be argued that, as the latter acquired the information in his capacity as beneficiary, he was not a fiduciary and, hence, there was no conflict of interest and duty.

13.49 Viscount Dilhorne and Lord Upjohn were the dissenting voices in *Boardman v Phipps*. Lord Upjohn concluded that the "no conflict" rule should not be applied strictly and automatically and that it should be tempered by the concept of reasonableness, "In my view it means that the reasonable man looking at the relevant facts and circumstances of the particular case would think that there was a real sensible

[42] [1942] 1 All E.R. 378 at 381.
[43] (1977) 18 A.L.R. 1 (PC). There the Board of Directors waived a fellow directors breach of duty in exploiting a business opportunity for personal gain; cf. *Cook v Deeks* [1916] 1 A.C. 554.
[44] Mr Boardman was, however, allowed a financial payment for his valuable services.
[45] [1967] 2 A.C. 46 at 103, 104.

possibility of conflict; not that you could imagine some situation arising which might, in some conceivable possibility in events not contemplated as real sensible possibilities by any reasonable person, result in a conflict ...".[46] Viscount Dilhorne advocated an alternative test to be applied when considering the liability of a fiduciary to account for a profit. In his eyes, it should be shown that the fiduciary made a profit within the scope and ambit of his duty and in circumstances where there was a real and sensible possibility of conflict between interest and duty. He commented, "On the facts of this case there was not, in my opinion, any conflict or possibility of a conflict between the personal interests of the appellants and those of the trust".[47] Although Viscount Dilhorne's test does not represent the present state of the law, it is attractive in that it would instil flexibility and alleviate the harshness of outcome as occurred in *Boardman v Phipps*.

13.50   Lord Upjohn took the view that "knowledge" was not property in the strict sense and should be regarded as such only when the use of it is injurious to the trust.[48] On the facts, he concluded that it was not injurious and felt that the majority decision of the House was unreasonable and inequitable.[49] Viscount Dilhorne agreed and admitted that the information gathered here was of no value to the trust.[50]

DISTRIBUTIVE DUTIES

13.51   After the payment of all debts of the trust, the basic duty of the trustee in relation to the distribution of remaining trust property (i.e. income and capital) is to hand over the property to the proper persons in accordance with the directions contained in the trust instrument. Once this is done, and following the timely presentation of final accounts[51] and the disclosure of any breaches of trust,[52] the trustee will seek a formal discharge by the beneficiaries.[53] The release is usually by deed and paid for out of the trust fund.

The trustees must take this distributive responsibility seriously as, if there is an unauthorised allocation, it will amount to a breach of trust and the trustee will not be released from liability even if he acted following legal advice. It is for the aggrieved beneficiary to decide whether to sue the trustee or, instead, to follow the money into the hands of the wrongful recipient. For example, in *Eaves v Hickson*[54] the trustees wrongly paid money to beneficiaries on the strength of a forged marriage certificate which led the trustees to believe falsely that the recipients were legitimate children and entitled under the trust. The trustees were required to account to the rightful beneficiary for such payments. Similarly, in *Re Hulkes*[55] the trustees adopted an honest, but mistaken,

---

[46] [1967] 1 A.C. 46 at 124.
[47] [1967] 2 A.C. 46 at 88.
[48] [1967] 2 A.C. 46 at 128.
[49] [1967] 2 A.C. 46 at 133, 134.
[50] [1967] 2 A.C. 46 at 91.
[51] *Wedderburn v Wedderburn* (1838) 4 My. & Cr. 50.
[52] *Cole v Gibson* (1750) 1 Ves. Sen. 507.
[53] *King v Mullins* (1852) 1 Drew. 311.
[54] (1861) 30 Beav. 136.
[55] (1886) 33 Ch. D. 552.

meaning of the trust instrument and, as a result, paid sums to the wrong beneficiaries. The trustees were again held to be liable.

It is to be appreciated that the court enjoys the discretion to relieve a trustee of personal liability (e.g. for an irregular distribution) afforded by s.61 of the Trustee Act 1925. This applies to all breaches of duty by a trustee. The discretion will, however, be exercised only in circumstances where it appears to the court that the trustee has acted honestly and reasonably and, moreover, ought fairly to be exonerated (in whole or in part) for the consequences of the breach of trust or the failure to obtain directions. Although in *Barraclough v Mell* the trustee was shielded behind the very wide terms of the exclusion clause, Deputy Judge John Behrens added that he would have refused relief to the trustee under s.61, "Her conduct was in my view grossly negligent. Whilst I think she has acted honestly I do not think that she has acted reasonably. Nor do I think she ought fairly to be excused for the breach of trust".[56] In *Re Evans (Deceased)*,[57] a daughter distributed her father's estate on the basis that her brother was dead. He reappeared four years later and claimed that his sister (as trustee) was in breach of trust. The court granted the trustee partial relief against her brother's claims. Although each case will turn upon its own facts, the primary focus will be upon whether the trustee acted reasonably or not.[58] On the facts of *Evans*, the trustee had acted honestly, but had not acted reasonably.

There exist several ways in which a trustee can shield himself from the perils of adverse claims. First, if the trustee makes an overpayment to a beneficiary, he may recoup the overpayments by deducting the amount from any future payments made to that beneficiary. This occurred in *Re Ainsworth* when the executors wrongly paid legacy duty out of capital and not from income.[59] Secondly, there are opportunities to involve the court in the distribution process:

- if it is unclear whether someone is entitled or not, the safest course is for the trustee to apply to the court for directions.[60] Provided those directions are adhered to, the trustee will be protected from ensuing liability. As Megarry put it, "It is well settled that trustees confronted by a particular problem may surrender their discretion to the court, and so be relieved of the agony of decision and the responsibility for the result".[61] The Law Reform Committee, however, recognised that the costs of going to court for directions are sometimes out of all proportion to the amount of money at stake.[62] In such circumstances, the Committee recommended that trustees should be allowed to take the advice of counsel and to distribute on the basis of that advice if proceedings are not commenced by a beneficiary within three months of receiving a copy of counsel's opinion;

13.52

---

[56] Unreported December 1, 2005.
[57] [1999] 2 All E.R. 777.
[58] *Chapman v Browne* [1902] 1 Ch. 785. In *Kemp v Sims* Unreported July 22, 2008 a trustee was denied relief under s.61 because he was a qualified lawyer.
[59] [1915] 2 Ch. 96.
[60] See *Re Allen-Meyrick's WT* [1966] 1 W.L.R. 499 where the trustees did not agree as to the application of trust income.
[61] R.E. Megarry (1966) 82 L.Q.R. 306 at p.307.
[62] Law Reform Committee 23rd Report, "The Powers and Duties of Trustees" 1982 Cmnd. 8733.

- under s.63 of the Trustee Act 1925, a trustee who is in doubt as to who is entitled is permitted to pay the trust fund into court and, on the issue of a receipt by the court, is then discharged from liability. Although the payment into court will mark the retirement of the trustee,[63] he will remain liable for past breaches of trust and be responsible for any trust money that comes to him in future. A new trustee can then be appointed by the court or the person nominated as appointor by the trust instrument. The disadvantage attached to this process is that, unless the trustee has reasonable cause for the payment into court, he is likely to be made liable for costs.[64] The trustee's doubts have to be bona fide and be such that they would concern a practical lawyer.[65] Although the general rule is that, where there is more than one trustee, they must act jointly (see **13.20**), by way of an exception s.63 allows a majority decision to pay money into court; and

- if there is the real possibility of an undiscovered beneficiary, the trustee can apply for a "Benjamin order", which takes its name from *Re Benjamin*,[66] that authorises the distribution of trust property. The onus then shifts from the trustee to those beneficiaries who receive a distribution, and it is they who usually will be required to provide some security so that any later discovered claimant will not be deprived of his entitlement.

13.53   Thirdly, the trustee may take advantage of s.27 of the Trustee Act 1925 (as amended). This allows a trustee to advertise publicly in order to discover the existence of potential claims under the trust, whether it is fixed or discretionary. Under s.27, the trustee must advertise in the London Gazette, in a local newspaper and anywhere else as directed by the court. Those advertisements must invite interested parties to forward to the trustees their personal details within a stated time limit. The time limit for claims must allow at least two months from the publication of the last advertisement within which a response is to be given. On the lapse of the stated time limit, the trustee can distribute the property to the beneficiaries of whom he is aware whether as a result of the advertisements or otherwise.[67] Provided that the conditions of s.27 are satisfied, the trustee will not be liable for breach of trust to any beneficiary of whom he has no notice (e.g. the assignee of a beneficial interest who has not notified the trustee of the transaction[68]). The concept of notice is, therefore, pivotal to the operation of s.27. If the statutory prescription is followed and there is an absence of notice (whether in actual, constructive or imputed form), the trustee will be in the same position as if he had administered the estate under the directions of the court. This ability cannot be modified or excluded in the trust instrument.[69] Section 27(2)(a) expressly preserves the right of an aggrieved beneficiary to trace the property into the hands of a person who has received it.

---

[63] *Re Williams' Settlement* (1858) 4 K. & J. 87.
[64] *Re Giles* (1886) 34 W.R. 712; see A.J. Hawkins (1968) 84 L.Q.R. 65.
[65] *Re Knight's Trusts* (1859) 27 Beav. 45.
[66] [1902] 1 Ch. 723. There the beneficiary was presumed to be dead, but not declared to be dead.
[67] Section 28 of the Trustee Act 1925 provides that notice acquired in the capacity as trustee of another trust does not, absent the trustee's fraud, count for these purposes.
[68] As required by s.137 of the Law of Property Act 1925.
[69] Section 27(3).

GUIDE TO FURTHER READING

W. Bishop and D. Prentice, "Some Legal and Economic Aspects of Fiduciary Remuneration" [1983] M.L.R. 289.

J. Lowry, "Directorial Self-Dealing: Constructing a Regime of Accountability" 48 N.I.L.Q. 211.

J. Lowry, "*Regal (Hastings)* Fifty Years On: Breaking the Bonds of the *Ancien Regime?*" 45 N.I.L.Q. 1.

P. Matthews, "The Efficacy of Trustee Exemption Clauses in English Law" [1989] Conv. 42.

N.D.M. Parry, "Remuneration of Trustees" [1984] Conv. 275.

Chapter 14

TRUSTEES' POWERS: INVESTMENT, MAINTENANCE AND ADVANCEMENT

As demonstrated in the previous chapter the trustee labours under a variety of duties as **14.01** imposed by the trust instrument, equity and statute. By way of a correlative, the trustee is afforded a wide range of administrative powers. Some of these powers concern how the trustees may deal with the trust property, while others may focus upon how the trustees deal with the beneficiaries. The starting point is that trustees have all the powers of a legal owner of the property and that such powers can be exercised only by the trustee and not by an equitable owner.[1]

Although for the purposes of this chapter, the key powers of investment, maintenance, advancement will be considered in detail, it is to be appreciated that there is a variety of other powers that may be exercised by a trustee. At the outset, it is useful to provide illustrations of such powers. This may be done by a cursory examination of Pt II of the Trustee Act 1925 as this offers a short catalogue of powers. Subject to exclusion or modification in the trust instrument,[2] these powers include:

- the s.12 power to sell the whole or a part of the property at public auction;

- the s.14 power to give a purchaser a good receipt for money paid (except when the property is land in which case the receipt must be by at least two trustees or a trust corporation);

- the s.15 power to compound liabilities by, for example, the payment of debts, accepting security for debts, allowing time for payment of debts and compromising or settling any debt;

---

[1] *Schalit v Joseph Nadler Ltd* [1933] 2 K.B. 79 (the beneficiary unsuccessfully sought to exercise the remedy of distress instead of the trustee landlord).
[2] Section 69(2).

- the s.16 power to raise money by the sale or mortgage of trust property. This operates when the trustee is authorised to pay or apply capital money for any purpose or in any manner. This power has been limited to those cases where the money is required either to preserve assets or to advance capital[3]; and

- the s.19 power to insure trust property.[4] This enables a trustee to insure fully the trust property against risk of loss and damage. The insurance premiums can be met from the trust fund. It is to be appreciated that there is no power to take out life assurance and, thereby, protect against the ravages of inheritance tax on the death of a beneficiary.

THE POWER TO INVEST

14.02   The investment of trust funds is a major aspect of the administration of trusts and will be a feature of all but the most primitive of trusts. In particular, if the subject matter of the trust is money (as opposed to, say, a house) the trustee will be under a duty to invest the trust fund to the advantage of the beneficiaries. Investment is an attractive option as it should shield the trust fund from the depreciating effects of inflation (which is especially desirable where the trust is designed to run for a number of years). Investment of capital should also ensure that there is an income stream from which interim payments can be made to the beneficiaries (which is especially pertinent where there is a beneficiary who enjoys merely a life interest). Although there is usually a duty to invest, the trustee is not given an unbridled ability to invest as he wishes. The choice of investment is governed by the administrative power to invest. This power is subject to regulation by Parliament, the courts and the trust instrument.

The first port of call is to examine the trust instrument. Not surprisingly, in many contemporary trusts there will be found an express investment clause. This will reflect the vision of the settlor as to how trust property is to be invested for the better advantage of the beneficiaries. If no express power of investment is contained in the trust instrument, the trustee is given a statutory power to invest which is now to be found in the Trustee Act 2000.[5]

Express powers

14.03   As mentioned, a common practice is to insert an express investment clause into the trust instrument. Although such a clause may operate to narrow the field of investments open to a trustee,[6] it is usual for it to broaden the choice beyond that which is permissible under statute.[7] By way of a simple example, such a clause might allow the trustees, "to invest in or upon such investments as to them may seem fit and as if they

---

[3] *Re Suenson-Taylor's Settlement* [1974] 3 All E.R. 397.
[4] Amended by s.34(1) of the Trustee Act 2000.
[5] This repealed the more limited power previously contained in the Trustee Investments Act 1961.
[6] See *Re Hill* [1914] W.N. 132, where a power was given to invest in specified investments only and no others.
[7] See the aptly named *Re Power* [1947] Ch. 572, where the clause allowed the trustee to invest in land.

were the absolute owners of the fund". This type of wide power is intended to offer the trustees the utmost flexibility as to how and where they may invest trust money. As will become clear, this does not give a trustee carte blanche to do exactly what he wishes. The trustee throughout remains subject to the general duty to take care and the other duties now imposed by the Trustee Act 2000. Although the trustee's statutory power to invest has been greatly extended by the 2000 Act, it is still possible for an express power to confer more freedom of choice and action than its statutory counterpart.

An express power must be carefully drafted so as to be clear, understandable and capable of enforcement.[8] Traditionally, the clause is to be construed strictly with the onus upon the trustee to establish that the investment is within its scope.[9] Hence, in *Bethell v Abraham*[10] a clause offered the trustees a wide discretion to change investments "from time to time". Jessell M.R. held that this did not enable the trustees to make certain speculative and substantive investments of a type substantially different from the investments chosen by the settlor before his death. Nevertheless, and as demonstrated in *Re Harari's ST*,[11] the court will strive to give an investment clause a plain and ordinary meaning. In that case, the settlor gave his trustees the power to invest trust money "in or upon such investments as to them may seem fit". Existing investments included certain Egyptian bonds and securities which, at the time, were not authorised investments. The court had to determine whether the express power was to be limited to the statutorily permitted range of investments or whether the trustees could lawfully invest outside that limited range. Jenkins J. could see no justification for reading into the clause such a restriction and added, "I think the trustees have power, under the plain meaning of those words, to invest in any investments which ... they 'honestly think' are desirable investments ...".[12]

Statutory regulation

Until the eighteenth century, there had been little fetter placed upon the ability of a trustee to invest trust money. There was no statutory regulation and no effective guidance from the courts. Trustees were allowed to invest in any manner that was deemed appropriate. This laissez faire approach, however, came to an abrupt end with the misguided speculation of trustees in the South Sea Company and other high risk ventures. The so-called "bursting of the South Sea bubble", as well as the financially draining Napoleonic wars, promoted a response from the Court of Chancery. While the Court of Chancery restricted the types of investment that the trustee could select without express authorisation in the trust instrument (i.e. it frowned upon commercial speculation), it encouraged investment in government stock by offering trustees immunity from ensuing liability for breach of trust.[13] Prior to the modern Trustee Acts,

14.04

---

[8] See *Re Kolb's WT* [1962] Ch. 531, where a provision allowing investment in "blue chips" was void for uncertainty.
[9] As will be discussed in Ch.15, the trustees may apply under the Variation of Trusts Act 1958 for the investment clause to be widened: *Trustees of the British Museum v AG* [1984] 1 W.L.R. 418.
[10] [1873] L.R. 17 Eq. 24.
[11] [1949] 1 All E.R. 430.
[12] [1949] 1 All E.R. 430 at 434.
[13] *Pocock v Reddington* (1801) 5 Ves. 800.

the trustee's power to invest outside the terms of an express power remained limited. The emphasis was then upon the preservation of the trust fund rather than the maximisation of benefit for the beneficiaries. Indeed, trustees could not invest in stock of a private company or Bank of England stock, lend money on security or invest in mortgages.[14]

The nineteenth century and the advent of industrialism brought a need for a broader view of trustee investment. This was satisfied to a small extent by the Law of Property Amendment Act 1859 which allowed investment in stocks of the Bank of England, the Bank of Ireland and the legendary East India Co. These powers were extended piecemeal by further legislation. The range of authorised investment, however, still excluded major classes of stock and focussed largely upon safe, fixed rate investments. The next significant developments were the Trustee Investments Act 1889 and Trustee Act 1893 which brought with them a greater freedom to invest in railway stock, local authority stock and public utility stock. In 1925, the government considered whether to widen the range of trustee investment, but concluded that the cautious approach remained the best way forward. A gradual defrosting process was to continue, with further stocks added incrementally to (and, indeed, sometimes removed from) the list of permissible investment, until the Trustee Investments Act 1961.

14.05 In post-World War II times, the nature of the trust changed dramatically. Moving away from strict settlements under which there were successive interests (i.e. tenant for life and remainderman), trusts became employed to redistribute family property in a tax efficient manner. In addition, the vehicle of the trust was hijacked to facilitate investment in unit trusts and to provide pension trusts for employees. The ambitions of the trustee necessarily shifted in the wake of these changes. In short, the emphasis is now placed upon generating the best financial returns for beneficiaries. With the emergence of inflation, coupled with the realisation that government stock was declining in value at a time when the shares of large industrial companies were increasing in worth, the clamour for greater investment powers intensified. The Trustee Investments Act 1961 was designed to cater for these modern developments.

The 1961 Act introduced a new scheme of trustee investment. The ambition was to provide a compromise between the competing objectives of safety and flexibility. The Act prescribed three classes of authorised investment which were to limit the trustee's power. The first category was styled as "narrower range investments not requiring advice." This comprised of a limited band of investment that the trustee could make at any time and without consultation. It included such cautious investments as National Savings Certificates, Post Office savings accounts, bank deposits and defence bonds. The second category was described as "narrower range investments that required advice." This included government stock and the stock of nationalised industries. The third category was termed as "wider range investments requiring advice" and these concerned securities and shares of UK companies and UK unit trusts. There was no power to invest in land.

14.06 The 1961 Act also introduced changes to procedure. Although a trustee could invest exclusively in narrow range investments, when making wider range investments the trustee was originally required to divide the trust fund into two equal parts. One part only could then be invested in the wider range, with the other part remaining in

---

[14] See *Ex parte Calthorpe* (1785) 1 Cox 182.

narrower range investments.[15] In the making of (and changing of) wider range investments, moreover, the trustee was required to obtain proper written advice from a
qualified person as to the wisdom of the proposed dealings. The trustee also was to have
regard to the need to diversify the investments and to evaluate their suitability for the
trust. In 1982, the Law Reform Committee described the 1961 Act as "tiresome,
cumbrous and expensive in operation with the result that its provisions are now seen to
be inadequate".[16] The Committee appreciated that, in a large number of instances, the
1961 Act was modified or excluded in the trust instrument. Not surprisingly, the
Committee recommended that the 1961 Act should be repealed and replaced by a new
statutory code. It rejected the suggestion that trustees should enjoy a general freedom to
invest, subject only to the requirement of sound prudent management. Instead, it
favoured a formal scheme that categorised investments into those that could be made
without advice and those which could be made only subsequent to advice being taken.
The Committee did not see the justification of retaining restrictions upon the proportions of the trust fund that might be invested in either of these categories.

The Trustee Act 2000

Unless the trust instrument contains an express investment clause, the power to invest is   **14.07**
now widened and regulated by Pt II of the Trustee Act 2000. This regulation is retrospective in application.[17] The so-called "general power of investment" is set out in
s.3(1) which authorises the trustee to make "any kind of investment that he could make
if he were absolutely entitled to the assets of the trust". The statutory power can,
however, be modified or excluded in the trust instrument.[18] An investment for these
purposes requires an anticipation of profit or income (e.g. granting a mortgage on terms
that it will be repaid with interest) and "investments of the trust" refers to "the assets of
the trust" or "the trust fund".[19] This power does not extend to investments in land
(except loaning money by way of mortgage) as the power to invest in land is specifically
governed by s.8. Unlike its predecessor, the new Act does not restrict the trustees to
listed investments. Instead, the power is broadened to facilitate any investment. As will
be discussed in **14.14**, the trustee labours under the duty of care as prescribed in s.1 of
the 2000 Act.

Standard investment criteria and reviews

Trustees when exercising the statutory power of investment are required to have regard   **14.08**
to what are styled "standard investment criteria".[20] Section 4(3)(a) requires the trustees

---

[15] This was later modified to allow a trustee to invest as little as 25 per cent in the narrow range with
potentially 75 per cent of the trust fund being invested in the wider range.
[16] *The Powers and Duties of Trustees* (1982) Cmnd 8733 at para.3.17.
[17] Section 7(1).
[18] Section 6(1). It cannot be limited or excluded in a trust instrument created before August 3, 1961 (i.e. the
coming into force of the Trustee Investments Act 1961).
[19] See *Gregson v HAE Trustees Ltd* [2008] EWHC 1006 (Ch).
[20] Section 4(1).

when making any investment or reviewing existing investments to have regard to the suitability of particular investments. This will involve consideration of the extent to which the investments are appropriate in light of the nature of the trust and the needs of the beneficiaries. Section 4(3)(b) also emphasises the need for diversification and this is designed to ensure that there will be a range of investments and a minimisation of investment risk.

The trustees are obliged by virtue of s.4(2) to carry out periodic reviews of the investment portfolio and, if necessary, vary the investments. The duty to review applies equally to an investment which is settled on a trustee and one which is purchased by a trustee in the exercise of his powers.[21] This requirement was imposed at common law by virtue of cases such as *Bartlett v Barclays Bank Trust Co Ltd*.[22] A trustee who fails to carry out periodic reviews will be in breach of trust. For most purposes, an annual review carried out at the end of each tax year will be appropriate.

Taking advice

14.09   Section 5 requires the trustees to obtain and consider proper investment advice from a suitable source before exercising any power of investment or before reviewing the existing investments of the trust. The need to take advice is not limited to investment under the statutory power, but applies also to any investment under an express power. The rule requiring advice only gives way when it would be reasonable to proceed without such advice (e.g. if the investment is small or the investments proposed are low risk).[23]

Section 5(4) states that the advice must come from "a person who is reasonably believed by the trustee to be qualified to give it by his ability in and practical experience of financial and other matters relating to the proposed investment". The adviser must be licensed under the Financial Services and Markets Act 2000. Hence, the source could be an expert trustee or an outside adviser. Although trustees are not obliged to follow the advice received, if they decline to do so they run the risk of personal liability for any resultant loss.

Delegation

14.10   As the investment of trust funds is a complex and potentially risky venture, it is a desirable practice that the task should be delegated to someone with the necessary skills and expertise (e.g. an asset manager). Until the enactment of the Trustee Act 2000, the rule was that the trustee could delegate only administrative functions. This entailed that the trustee could not delegate discretions relating to which investments should be made and when those investments should be changed.[24] This unsatisfactory state of affairs has been remedied by the 2000 Act which allows the delegation of investment discretions.

---

[21] *Gregson v HAE Trustees Ltd* [2008] EWHC 1006 (Ch).
[22] [1980] 1 All E.R. 139.
[23] Section 5(3).
[24] An exception to this rule, however, applied in relation to pension trusts: s.34 Pensions Act 1995.

Section 15, however, imposes some special restrictions on this newly given power to delegate. It provides that the employment of the investment manager be in writing or, at the least, evidenced in writing. Section 15 also requires the trustee to draft a policy document which details how the asset manager is to go about his business. This policy statement will provide a set of trust objectives that the agent must follow. When appropriate, the statement can be revised by the trustee at a later date.

Investment in land

As mentioned, traditionally the trustee could not purchase land as an investment. This **14.11** rule gave way in the face of express authority in the trust instrument or when such investment was permitted by s.6 of the Trusts of Land and Appointment of Trustees Act 1996. As to express authority, land could only be acquired for the purposes of generating an income for the trust[25] and not, say, to provide rent-free accommodation for a beneficiary.[26] The 1996 Act, however, operates with a different ethos. This allows trustees of land (not personalty) to purchase land for occupation by a beneficiary or for any other purpose. Accordingly, a house might have been acquired initially for resale at a profit, but subsequently the trustee may decide instead to allow the beneficiary to reside therein.

Section 8 of the Trustee Act 2000 is modelled upon the 1996 Act provision and allows the trustee of personalty to purchase freehold or leasehold land as an investment, for occupation by a beneficiary or for any other reason. It does not have to be intended to generate a rental income. It might, therefore, simply be purchased to provide a home for a beneficiary. On acquiring land, the trustee under both schemes has the same powers as would an absolute owner and this allows the trustee to sell, mortgage, lease or otherwise deal with the land. The application of s.8 can be excluded in the trust instrument and, if not so excluded, operates regardless of when the trust was created.

Investing in mortgages of land

Section 3 of the 2000 Act permits the trustee to invest in land by means of providing a **14.12** loan secured on the land (i.e. the granting of a mortgage). The mortgage may be legal or equitable. Understandably, private mortgages are now uncommon. Mortgage funds are in modern times provided by banks, building societies and other lending institutions. For the trustee the grant of a mortgage is not an attractive form of investment. Instead, investment in stocks and shares is the preferred option. Some guidance to the trustee who wishes to grant a mortgage is to be found in s.8 of the Trustee Act 1925. This sets standards which the trustee should (but is not obliged to) follow. Section 8 deals with issues of value and is not concerned with whether the investment by way of mortgage is prudent. It states that:

---

[25] *Re Wragg* [1919] 2 Ch. 58.
[26] *Re Power* [1947] Ch. 572. There was no income stream from the property so it could not be said to be an investment at all.

- the trustee should not lend a sum greater than two-thirds of the value of the property;

- the trustee should obtain a valuation report from a surveyor or valuer; and

- the trustee should grant the mortgage on the advice of the surveyor or valuer.

In circumstances where a trustee complies with the statutory guidance, he will be protected as regards any loss that arises from an incorrect valuation of the mortgaged property. If he does not follow such steps, however, the trustee will be liable for loss which is suffered by the trust estate by reason of his failure to do so.[27] Accordingly, if the trustee lends more than two-thirds of the value of the security, the trustee's liability will (if otherwise the mortgage is a proper investment) be scaled down to the excess sum with interest. In *Shaw v Cates*,[28] the maximum advance authorised was £3,400, but the trustee advanced £4,400. The trustee's liability was capped at making good the £1,000 excess with interest.

The trustee's duty of care

14.13 At common law, the duty of care placed upon a trustee when investing trust funds was higher than that imposed on him when carrying out his other administrative functions. The general yardstick was that that the trustee must invest the trust property wisely acting as an ordinary prudent man making investments. At the Court of Appeal stage in *Learoyd v Whiteley*, Lindley L.J. explained that, "The duty of a trustee is not to take such care only as a prudent man would take if he had only himself to consider; the duty rather is to take such care as an ordinary prudent man would take if he were minded to make an investment for the benefit of other people for whom he felt morally bound to provide".[29] The distinction is framed around the acceptance that a prudent man of business might still invest in risky ventures. As Lord Watson commented in the House of Lords in *Learoyd v Whiteley*, "businessmen of ordinary prudence may, and frequently do, select investments which are more or less of a speculative character; but it is the duty of trustees to confine themselves to the class of investments which are permitted by the trust, and likewise to avoid all investments of that class which are attended with hazard".[30] This test was, however, to prove ill-suited to developing investment practices. The objective standard of a prudent businessman became relatively meaningless in a complex commercial environment where businessmen display varying degrees of skill and aspire to different objectives. A further gloss was added by Hoffmann J. at first instance in *Nestle v National Westminster Bank Plc*.[31] He advocated what is known as the "portfolio theory" which entails that, as trustees will often introduce an element of diversity to their investment portfolio, they are to be judged on their overall performance and not on the failure or success of a particular investment.

---

[27] *Re Solomon* [1912] 1 Ch. 261, where Warrington J. surveyed the relationship between the valuer and the trustee.
[28] [1909] 1 Ch. 389.
[29] (1886) 33 Ch. D. 347 at 355.
[30] (1897) L.R. 12 A.C. 727 at 733.
[31] Unreported June 29, 1988.

Hoffmann J. observed, "... modern trustees acting within their investment powers are entitled to be judged by the standards of the current portfolio theory, which emphasises the risk level of the entire portfolio rather than the risk attaching to each investment taken in isolation".[32]

As discussed in Ch.13, the standard of care expected of a trustee has been redefined in s.1 of the Trustee Act 2000. This overhauled duty is not limited merely to investment and extends widely to such diverse functions as, for example, the acquisition of land, the entering into arrangements to appoint agents and nominees, the exercise of powers of compromise and insurance and the valuation of trust property.

Subject to exclusion in the trust instrument, s.1 provides that the trustee must exercise such care and skill as is reasonable in the circumstances having regard first, to any special knowledge or experience that he has or holds himself out as having. This instils a subjective element into the test. Secondly, and if he acts as trustee in the course of a business or profession, regard must be had to any special knowledge or experience that it is reasonable to expect of a person acting in the course of that business or profession. This instils an objective element into the test. The standard of care prescribed in the 2000 Act confirms that a professional trustee is expected to show a higher degree of care than a lay trustee. A lay trustee who makes investments will, therefore, be judged against a different standard of reasonableness than will his professional counterpart. Hence, as is evident from *Bartlett v Barclays Bank Trust Co Ltd*, a trust company with specialist staff will be judged on a different level to an unpaid, family trustee.[33] This case was in its time described by Schindler as marking, "a radical departure from the single standard of competence expected from trustees".[34]

14.14

In the *Bartlett* case, the trustee Bank allowed a management company to invest trust money in two ambitious development projects which were described by Brightman J. as, "a gamble and not, on the evidence I have heard, a very good gamble".[35] The Bank did not ask for or receive much information about the transactions. Subsequently, the beneficiaries sued the Bank as trustee for breach of trust for the substantial losses that were incurred by the failure of the two projects. The Bank attempted to shield itself behind the management company, claiming that it should be entitled to rely on the expertise and skills of the company's experienced board of directors. Brightman J. accepted that there is an element of risk inherent in any investment, but noted that, "The distinction is between a prudent degree of risk on the one hand, and hazard on the other".[36] This was such a hazardous investment that it should not have been made without express authorisation in the trust instrument. The judge considered the Bank's position as if, first, it had been an ordinary trustee and, secondly, as a specialist trustee. The Bank had failed in its duty whether it was judged by the standard of the prudent businessman or the skills of a trust corporation. In relation to the former, Brightman J. determined that such a trustee, as a prudent man of business, would have been more proactive and sought out more information about the activities of the management company. The Bank should have overseen the company's use of the trust money. The

[32] Unreported June 29, 1988.
[33] [1980] 1 All E.R. 139.
[34] G.A. Schindler [1980] 44 Conv. 155 at p.158; see also, P. Pearce and A. Samuels, "Negligent Investment by Trustees" [1983] Conv. 127.
[35] [1980] 1 All E.R. 139 at 147.
[36] [1980] 1 All E.R. 139 at 150.

judge, however, concluded that the Bank was an expert trustee and, therefore, plainly owed a higher level of care. Brightman J. explained:

> "A trust corporation holds itself out in its advertising literature as being above ordinary mortals. With a specialist staff of trained trust officers and managers with ready access to financial information and professional advice, dealing with and solving trust problems day after day, the trust corporation holds itself out, and rightly, as capable of providing an expertise which it would be unrealistic to expect and unjust to demand from the ordinary prudent man or woman who accepts, probably unpaid and sometimes reluctantly from a sense of family duty, the burdens of trusteeship ... a professional corporate trustee is liable for breach of trust if loss is caused to the trust fund because it neglects to exercise the special care and skill which it professes to have".[37]

Dog Leg Claims

14.15 A phenomenon known as a "dog leg claim" has emerged in the context of trustee companies and the potential liability of their directors to beneficiaries. This was demonstrated in *Gregson v HAE Trustees Ltd*[38] where the beneficiary, Ms Gregson alleged that the trustee company, HAE Trustees Ltd, was in breach of duty in failing to review the need to diversify the investments of the settlement. As the trustee company had no assets, the real targets of the action were its directors. Ms Gregson asserted that the directors were in breach of their duty of care to HAE Trustees Ltd and that the claims of the company were part of the trust property of the settlement. By analogy with trust advisers (such as solicitors and valuers), she argued that the directors in performing their duties to the company were necessarily performing the company's duties to avoid losses to the trust and that the relevant obligations of the directors formed part of the trust property itself. Under s.174 of the Companies Act 2006, however, the duties of a director are owed to the company and not to the beneficiaries of the settlement. The duty owed by the directors was to avoid loss to the company and it was a misunderstanding to say that the duty extends to third parties. Deputy Judge Robert Miles Q.C. concluded, "the fact that the performance of the director's functions relates to trusts administered by the company does not mean that the duties of the directors can be defined as the avoidance of loss to the trust funds."[39] The directors stand in a fiduciary relationship to the company, but not to a third party with whom the company is dealing.[40] Hence, if a breach of trust is committed by the company, a beneficiary cannot maintain an action against the directors. This could not be side-stepped by a dog leg claim. As the Deputy Judge observed, "The dog leg claim, if valid, would for all practical purposes, circumvent the clear and established principle that no direct duty is owed by the directors to the beneficiaries."[41] In addition, there is no

---

[37] [1980] 1 All E.R. 139 at 152.
[38] [2008] EWHC 1006 (Ch).
[39] [2008] EWHC 1006 (Ch) at [58].
[40] *Bath v Standard Land Co Ltd* [1911] 1 Ch. 618.
[41] [2008] EWHC 1006 (Ch) at [46].

intelligible legal mechanism whereby the rights of the company against its directors could be said to be held on trust for the beneficiaries of the settlement. The directors are not appointed by the trustee in the course of the administration of the trust. Instead, they are appointed by the relevant organs of the company. In no sense were the directors engaged by the trustees of the trust. The Deputy Judge explained, "It may be that in performing their duties the directors of the trustee company are engaged in acts of administration of the trust, but it does not follow, in my judgment, that the directors have been appointed by the trustees, whether under their administrative powers or pursuant to their duties."[42]

Consecutive interests

As regards trusts with consecutive interests (i.e. where there is a tenant for life and a **14.16** remainderman), the trustees are under a duty to treat income and capital beneficiaries in an impartial manner.[43] This might be described as a duty to act fairly between all types of beneficiary. The trustee must, therefore, ensure that a fair balance is drawn between high income and high risk investments and those safer and less lucrative investments that will preserve the capital. As Hoffmann J. put it at first instance in *Nestle v National Westminster Bank Plc*, "The trustees must act fairly in making investment decisions which may have different consequences for different classes of beneficiaries."[44]

In the *Nestle* case, the settlor had left £54,000 in shares on trust for his widow for life and thereafter for his children and grandchildren. Eventually, his granddaughter (as remainderman) became entitled to the trust fund (then worth £269,000). The investment portfolio had throughout been managed by the Bank as trustee. The granddaughter claimed that the Bank was in breach of trust because it had mismanaged the trust investments by failing to diversify and to review the portfolio. She argued that, had the Bank not acted in an overly cautious manner, the fund should have been worth more than £1 million. In the Court of Appeal,[45] it was determined that the Bank was not in breach of trust. This was so even though it had misunderstood the scope of its investment powers, failed to conduct periodic reviews, did not diversify effectively and in the past had shown symptoms of what Staughton L.J. described as, "incompetence or idleness".[46] The trustee had nevertheless satisfied the required standard of care. By the undemanding standard of prudence, the Bank was not shown to have been in breach of its duty. Leggatt L.J. explained that the Bank's, "engagement was as a trustee, and, as such, it is to be judged not so much by success as by absence of proven default".[47] Staughton L.J. added that Ms Nestle failed because she was unable to show

---

[42] [2008] EWHC 1006 (Ch) at [50].
[43] See *Close Trustees (Switzerland) SA v Vildosola* [2008] EWHC 1267 (Ch) where the trustees sought to make a one-third retention of future income of life tenant in order to secure their anticipated legal costs. In rejecting the trustees' claim, Deputy Judge Mark Herbert observed; "the trustees and the court should not favour one party against the other…" (at [29]).
[44] Unreported June 29, 1988.
[45] [1994] 1 All E.R. 118; noted at [1993] Conv. 63 (A. Kenny).
[46] [1994] 1 All E.R. 118 at 133.
[47] [1994] 1 All E.R. 118 at 142.

that, "the trustees made decisions which they should not have made or failed to make decisions which they should have made".[48]

14.17   As to consecutive interests, in the *Nestle* case the trustee had attempted to balance the income needs of the tenant for life with the longer term capital interests of the granddaughter. It is for the trustee to reconcile this conflict of interest. As Staughton L.J. accepted, "At times it will not be easy to decide what is an equitable balance. A life tenant may be anxious to receive the highest possible income, whilst the remainderman will wish the real value of the trust fund to be preserved. If the life tenant is living in penury and the remainderman already has ample wealth, common sense suggests that a trustee should be able to take that into account, not necessarily be seeking the highest possible income at the expense of capital but by inclining in that direction".[49] The trustee has merely to maintain a fair, impartial and equitable balance between the two camps. Although this does not require the interests to be evenly balanced, the appellate court accepted that, where there are successive interests under a trust, at least 50 per cent of the investments should lie in ordinary shares issued by companies. The reasoning is that such investments tend to keep apace with inflation. It will suffice if, as here, those investments are in the "safest" (but often financially less rewarding) shares such as in banks and insurance companies.

Non-financial considerations

14.18   The duty of a trustee is to act in the best financial interests of the beneficiaries. This entails that the trustee must obtain the best rate of return available coupled with diversification of risks. This is so even where it is against the political, social or moral views of some of the beneficiaries. In *Cowan v Scargill*,[50] the investment policy of the mineworkers' pension fund was challenged. The fund was managed by 10 trustees, half of whom were appointed by the National Union of Mineworkers and the rest appointed by the Coal Board. The dispute concerned investments in foreign energy companies. The trustees appointed by the Trade Union objected to the investments on the ground that these companies were in direct competition with the domestic coal mining industry. The High Court held that the trustees had to act in the best financial interests of the beneficiaries and, hence, that they would be in breach of duty if they failed to invest in the overseas energy companies. The trustees, therefore, had to put aside their personal interest and views. Megarry V.C. considered the relevance of non-financial concerns:

> "Trustees may have strongly held social or political views. They may be firmly opposed to investment in South Africa or other countries, or they may object to any form of investment in companies concerned with alcohol, tobacco, armaments or many other things. In the conduct of their own affairs, of course, they are free to abstain from making any such investments. Yet under a trust, if investments of this type would be more beneficial to the beneficiaries than other investments, the

---

[48] [1994] 1 All E.R. 118 at 133, 134.
[49] [1994] 1 All E.R. 118 at 137.
[50] [1985] Ch. 270.

trustees must not refrain from making the investments by reason of the views that they hold".[51])

It has been argued by Farrar and Maxton that the stance adopted by Megarry J. is too rigid. "The pension scheme in question was not an ordinary private trust. It was an extraordinary trust with certain public characteristics set up under a scheme for nationalization. The object of the nationalization was to develop the industry in the national interest and safeguard the welfare of employees".[52] Perhaps this overstates the nature of the trust and overlooks the fact that the primary aim was to benefit individuals. It is, moreover, important to appreciate that ethical investment is not prohibited by the decision in *Cowan*. Even Megarry V.C. admitted, "I am not asserting that the benefit of the beneficiaries which a trustee must make his paramount concern inevitably and solely means their financial benefit ...".[53] It is still possible for the trust instrument to sanction ethical investment or to prohibit investment in certain companies. The beneficiaries, moreover, may collectively sanction such an investment policy and the trustees retain the ability to choose ethical investing when the financial returns will be equivalent to an alternative, "non-ethical" portfolio.[54]

As regards charitable trusts, however, a modified approach is adopted. The trustees are entitled to decline investments that run contrary to the objectives of that trust (e.g. investing in armament companies). As Nicholls V.C. put it in *Harries v Church Commissioners for England*, "There will be some cases, I suspect comparatively rare, when the objects of the charity are such that investments of a particular type would conflict with the aims of the charity. Much cited examples are those of cancer research companies and tobacco shares, trustees of temperance societies and brewery and distillery shares, and trustees of charities of the Society of Friends and shares in companies engaged in production of armaments".[55] Although logically the trustees could take this course even if it was to the financial detriment of the charity, this is unlikely to arise in practice. As Nicholls V.C. observed, "It is not easy to think of an instance where in practice the exclusion for this reason of one or more companies or sectors from the whole range of investments open to trustees would be likely to leave them without an adequately wide range of investments from which to choose a properly diversified portfolio".[56] The trustees cannot, therefore, totally disregard the financial implications of their restrictive decision making. As demonstrated in the *Harries* case, charitable trustees are not allowed to pursue a blanket policy of ethical investment if this would be detrimental to the value of the trust fund.

Investment and charitable trusts

The powers and duties of charitable trustees as regards investment are broadly similar to those of private trustees. Such powers will be prescribed either expressly in the trust

14.19

---

[51] [1985] Ch. 270 at 287, 288. He added at 288, "trustees may even have to act dishonourably (though not illegally) if the interests of their beneficiaries require it".
[52] J.H. Farrar and J.K. Maxton, "Social Investment and Pension Scheme Trusts" (1986) 102 L.Q.R. 32 at p.33.
[53] [1985] Ch. 270 at 288.
[54] See *Martin v City of Edinburgh DC* [1988] S.L.T. 329.
[55] [1992] 1 W.L.R. 1241 at 1246.
[56] [1992] 1 W.L.R. 1241 at 1246.

instrument or by legislation. Accordingly, charitable trustees have the general power of investment conferred by s.3 of the Trustee Act 2000 and this allows them to invest as if they were the absolutely entitled to the fund, subject to the standard investment criteria and the taking of expert advice. These provisions only assume relevance where the trust fund is so substantial that diversification of investment and the associated professional costs can be absorbed. Many charities, however, have such small trust funds that the prescription of the Trustee Act 2000 is unsuitable and inappropriate. To cater for such small funds, s.24 of the Charities Act 1993 permits the court and the Charity Commission to devise schemes ("common investment schemes") which allow participating charities to have their investments pooled under the control of management trustees appointed by the court.[57] The aim is to allow separate charitable trusts to be combined into one scheme. Section 24 provides that such a scheme can be devised on the request of two or more charities and this remains so even if the trustees are the same persons. As Wilberforce J. acknowledged in *Re University of London Charitable Trusts*, "The result of that would be that the university has power to consolidate any other charitable trusts of which the university might become trustee so as to be part of the combined pool without coming back to court ...".[58] By way of an alternative strategy, charitable trustees can apply for the authorisation of a "common deposit fund" which allows the funds to be pooled and placed in an interest bearing account.[59]

MAINTENANCE OF MINOR BENEFICIARIES FROM INCOME

14.20 Absent an express provision in the trust instrument or statute, trustees are not authorised to pay trust income or capital to a minor. The basic idea is that a person under the age of 18 years (unless married[60]) is legally incapable of giving a valid receipt for such payments. Similarly a minor's parents or guardian cannot give a receipt on the infant's behalf.[61] As to payments made from trust income for the maintenance and education of a minor beneficiary, however, a paternalistic approach has long been adopted. This is of obvious merit in the situation, say, where Fred leaves shares by will to his grandson, Jordan, conditional upon Jordan reaching 18 years of age. At Fred's death, Jordan is 14 years old. The trustees will retain the legal title to the shares until the contingency is met (i.e. Jordan reaches majority age). In the intervening period, those shares will attract dividend payments (i.e. they will generate income for the trust). If (and only if) Jordan is beneficially entitled to that intermediate income, the income can be employed (either at the discretion of the trustees or pursuant to a court order) to promote his welfare. The power to make such maintenance payments is claimed by the court under an inherent jurisdiction and is afforded to trustees either expressly in the trust instrument or by virtue of s.31(1) of the Trustee Act 1925.

[57] The rules regulating common investment schemes are largely unaffected by the Charities Act 2006.
[58] [1964] Ch. 282 at 285.
[59] Again this is largely unaffected by the Charities Act 2006.
[60] The capacity for a married minor to give a good receipt is afforded by s.21 of the Law of Property Act 1925.
[61] *Harvell v Foster* [1954] 2 All E.R. 736.

The court's inherent jurisdiction

The court claims an inherent jurisdiction to authorise payments from income to maintain or educate an infant beneficiary.[62] The inherent jurisdiction to apply trust income for the benefit of a minor beneficiary exists even where the minor's interest is contingent (e.g. conditional upon attaining 18 years of age) or is otherwise defeasible (e.g. by the exercise by the trustees of a power of appointment). As Pearson J. pointed out *Re Collins*, the underlying notion is that a testator who has put property on trust for children could not intend, "that these children should be left unprovided for or in a state of such moderate means that they should not be educated properly for the position and fortune which he designs them to have …".[63] He continued, "… to deprive the children for 21 years of all the income would be to make the property, when it comes to them, an injury rather than a benefit".[64] This inherent jurisdiction is remarkable as it permits the court to disregard the clearest wording of a testator's will in order to promote an outcome that, it is assumed, the testator would have wished for had he given any thought to the matter.[65] It is not, however, to be used to deflect the living parents' responsibility to look after their own children. Accordingly, and even if there is a substantial trust fund, the parent must shoulder the burden of maintaining the child and cannot shift that responsibility on to the child.[66] In the light of the emergence of express and statutory powers, this jurisdiction is now seldom exercised.

14.21

Express powers

Despite the existence of the inherent jurisdiction of the court to provide for minors, it became common for express provision to be made in professionally drafted trust instruments enabling trustees to use trust income for maintenance purposes. Tax considerations (particularly as regards inheritance tax) traditionally shape when and in what form an express power will appear. Understandably, the precise effect of an express clause turns upon the construction given to the words employed by the settlor. In *Re Peel*,[67] for example, the express provision was couched in such imperative language that the court concluded it to be a trust and not a power at all. Hence, the income had to be used for the maintenance of the minor beneficiaries and could not be accumulated. In *Re Borwick's Settlement*,[68] there was an express power, but it was drafted to exclude maintenance while the minor was in the custody and control of his father or while his father "had anything to do with the education or bringing up" of the minor.

14.22

[62] In rare circumstances, moreover, the jurisdiction has been employed to maintain an adult beneficiary: *Revel v Watkinson* (1748) 1 Ves. Sen. 93.
[63] (1886) 32 Ch. D. 229 at 232. The court authorised £2,000 a year in total for the maintenance and education of three minor beneficiaries.
[64] (1886) 32 Ch. D. 229 at 233.
[65] See the speech of Lord Morton in *Chapman v Chapman* [1954] A.C. 429 at 456, where he acknowledged that this was an exception to the general rule that the court cannot alter a man's will because it thinks it beneficial.
[66] *Douglas v Andrews* (1849) 12 Beav. 310.
[67] [1936] Ch. 161. The clause read, "upon trust to pay or apply the same in manner thereinafter provided to or for the benefit of the children".
[68] [1916] 2 Ch. 304.

This restriction was effective to narrow the scope of the trustee's power which could not be exercised unless the father abandoned all parental control over the infant.

If the court discerns the existence of a power to maintain then the trustees enjoy the discretion to make payments. There is no obligation to make an award. The trustees must, therefore, honestly decide whether or not to exercise the power and make the payment to the parent or guardian of the minor.

14.23 In reaching their decision, the trustees must have regard to the interests of the minor and not take on board the interests of the settlor or anyone else (e.g. the infant's parents). Although the exercise of the power (say, to pay for school or medical fees) may in its wake be of incidental benefit to a parent, this does not prevent the trustees exercising their power. As Lightman J. commented in *Fuller v Evans*, "I find it very difficult to read the settlement as paralysing the trustees in this situation, barring them from exercising the powers conferred on them merely because a by-product of their exercise is an advantage to the settlor".[69] He concluded, "If the trustees reach the conclusion that it is in the best interests of the beneficiaries to make such provision out of trust funds, they are free to do so".[70]

In addition, and as demonstrated in *Wilson v Turner*,[71] the trustees have to make a separate decision each time that payment is claimed or made. There the trustees handed over the entire income of the trust fund to the father during the infancy of the minor beneficiary without periodically considering the continuing merits of the minor's claim and, thereby, exercising their discretion.[72] The money was recoverable from the father's estate. Similarly, the trustees cannot decide upon a blanket refusal ever to make a maintenance payment. If they do so, the beneficiary can apply to court for an appropriate order.[73] In the light of the statutory power to maintain (considered immediately below), an express power is no longer a necessary feature of the trust instrument. Those that remain, however, are usually modelled upon the statutory power with customised features as are desired by the settlor.

The statutory power

14.24 Parliament has, since Lord Cranworth's Act 1860, demonstrated a concern for infants and allowed trustees to make payments for the "maintenance or education" of minors. There has never been a statutory power to maintain adult beneficiaries. The current and wider statutory power is to be found in s.31 of the Trustee Act 1925 and, subject to exclusion or modification in the trust instrument,[74] this automatically applies to all trusts coming into operation after 1925.[75] The statutory power applies whether the trust is established by will or is an inter vivos (i.e. a lifetime) trust and operates regardless of

---

[69] [2000] 1 All E.R. 636 at 638.
[70] [2000] 1 All E.R. 636 at 639.
[71] (1883) 22 Ch. D. 521.
[72] See also, *Re Greenwood* (1911) 105 L.T. 509.
[73] *Stopford v Lord Canterbury* (1840) 11 Sim. 82.
[74] *Re Turner's WT* [1937] Ch. 15. There the Court of Appeal emphasised that s.31 bestowed a power and did not impose a duty.
[75] Section 31(5). Earlier trusts will be governed by the Conveyancing Act 1881.

the nature of the property.[76] Its purpose is, "to simplify the task of the draftsman of a trust instrument and to fill gaps which he might unwittingly leave in the disposal of trust income".[77] Unfortunately, s.31 is difficult to navigate and, as Lord Evershed M.R. admitted in *Re Vesty's Settlement*, "The language ... I confess, is by no means easy to follow, nor does it seem to me that the section has been put together in a way which makes the task of apprehending its effect as easy as might be".[78]

Section 31(1) provides that, "trustees may, at their sole discretion, pay to his parent or guardian, if any, or otherwise apply for or towards his maintenance, education or benefit, the whole or such part of the income of that property as may, in all the circumstances, be reasonable ...". Hence, the trustees could pay, say, fees directly to a school. The section adds that the discretion is unaffected by there being another fund applicable for the maintenance of the minor or the existence of someone bound at law to provide for the minor's maintenance and education. The rider is attached by s.31(1) that, if the trustees are aware of another trust fund available for the maintenance of the minor, a principle of proportionality applies. This entails that, as far as is practicable and unless the court directs otherwise, a proportionate part of each fund should be used for maintenance purposes. The trustees of the respective funds should, if possible, reach agreement concerning the proportion to be paid from each fund.

A contrary intention?

As indicated, the statutory power can be modified or even dispensed with entirely, **14.25** whether expressly or by implication.[79] An example of such modification would be when the trustees are expressly given an absolute discretion, as opposed to the statutory temperance afforded by the concept of "reasonableness". In *Re Delamere's ST*,[80] for example, the trust instrument provided that the income of the trust was to be held for the settlor's grandchildren in "equal shares absolutely". While they were minors, the sum of £120,000 had been accumulated in income. Even though the settlor probably had no notion of the existence of s.31, the use of the word "absolutely" displaced its operation because it made clear that the children's interests were indefeasible.[81] In order to avoid this potential trap, Slade L.J. proffered some advice for those drafting settlements, "In many cases the draftsman may well be advised out of caution either expressly to provide that the section is to apply with or without stated modifications or expressly to exclude its application altogether".[82]

A further example of how the statutory power may be excluded is to be found in *Re Erskine's ST* where the settlor made provision for the income to be accumulated.[83] Although the direction was void for offending the perpetuity period (see **4.45**), this otherwise ineffective provision demonstrated an intention to exclude the s.31 power to

---

[76] *Stanley v IRC* [1944] K.B. 255.
[77] *Re Delamere's ST* [1984] 1 All E.R. 584 at 592 per Walker L.J..
[78] [1950] 2 All E.R. 891 at 897.
[79] This is permitted by s.69(2).
[80] [1984] 1 All E.R. 584.
[81] For a criticism of this decision see R. Griffith [1985] Conv. 153.
[82] [1984] 1 All E.R. 584 at 592.
[83] [1971] 1 All E.R. 572.

maintain. Stamp J. explained, "Income cannot at one and the same time be both accumulated in accordance with a direction . . . and dealt with under s.31".[84] In short, as Lord Evershed M.R. put it, "it suffices to make the statutory power . . . inapplicable if, on a fair reading of the instrument in question, one can say that such application would be inconsistent with the purport of the instrument".[85] The overriding rule is that the settlor's expressed intentions are paramount.

Entitlement to income

14.26   Section 31 offers the trustees a broad, discretionary power to apply trust income for the benefit of a minor (but not an adult) beneficiary. This power may be exercised as regards any trust interest whether or not it has vested or remains contingent.[86] All that is required by virtue of s.31(3) is that the trust interest carries the entitlement to intermediate income (i.e. income generated between the date that the gift is made and the date that it vests in the beneficiary). Not all gifts, however, carry this entitlement to income.[87] Nevertheless, this is a necessary requirement in the light that statutory maintenance is payable only from income. For example, a trust of shares for Jordan if he reaches the age of 18 will vest only when Jordan reaches majority age. In the intervening period, he has what is described as a "contingent" interest. Whether or not the trust was created inter vivos or by will, Jordan will be entitled to any intermediate income (i.e. the dividends) and can, therefore, benefit from the statutory power to maintain.

As discussed below, the general rule remains that, subject to a contrary intention, vested gifts or inter vivos and testamentary contingent gifts will carry the intermediate income. A contrary intention might arise where, for example, there is a settlement that gives an adult a life interest and leaves the minor as the remainderman. The statutory power cannot then arise. The life tenant is entitled to income and there is nothing from which the infant remainderman can be maintained. Similarly, and as demonstrated in *Re Vesty's Settlement*,[88] if the minor is a beneficiary under a discretionary trust there is no entitlement to income sufficient to activate s.31. It also remains open for the settlor to direct that a party other than the minor is entitled to the income and, thereby, disarm s.31.

14.27   A vested interest will, subject to a contrary intention, carry the right to income.[89] Consider the example of a legacy of £100,000 to Jordan who is 14 years of age when the testator dies. Although the trustees will hold legal title to the capital sum until Jordan can give a valid receipt for it (on his reaching majority or entering into an earlier marriage), his interest has vested and he is entitled to the income.

As regards contingent interests, however, the rules are more complicated. Three key propositions emerge. First, an inter vivos contingent gift will carry the right to income.

---

[84] [1971] 1 All E.R. 572 at 574.
[85] *IRC v Bernstein* [1961] Ch. 399 at 413. There a trust for accumulation of income showed a conflicting intention to exclude the closely allied provision relating to advancement contained in s.32.
[86] See generally, A.M. Prichard [1973] C.L.J. 246.
[87] See generally, B.S. Ker (1953) 17 Conv. 275.
[88] [1950] 2 All E.R. 891.
[89] *Berry v Geen* [1938] A.C. 575.

A lifetime trust of shares for Jordan when he becomes 18 years old, for example, does not vest until that time is reached and, in the interim, remains a contingent interest. Secondly, s.175(1) of the Law of Property Act 1925 provides that a contingent testamentary disposition of real or personal property will usually carry the intermediate income. Accordingly, a legacy of land to benefit Jordan when he marries will bring with it the entitlement to income. Finally, and subject to delimited exceptions, a contingent pecuniary testamentary disposition will not usually carry the right to income. The gift is in suspense.[90] Take, for example, a legacy of £100,000 to Jordan when he reaches 18, if the general rule is followed, and as this is a pecuniary legacy (i.e. purely monetary), it does not fall within s.175(1) and attracts income only when it becomes payable and not during the intervening period.[91]

To complicate matters further, there are several exceptions to the general restriction **14.28** concerning pecuniary legacies. Such a contingent legacy will carry the income when:

- the legacy was given to a minor by his father (but not mother[92]) or some person standing in loco parentis.[93] As Ker points out, "The idea is simple; a father is under an obligation to maintain his child and is therefore presumed to intend the income of the gift to be paid for his child's maintenance until the contingency happens".[94] The contingency, however, has to be of the minor reaching 18 years (not, say 30 years)[95] or making an earlier marriage.[96] In addition, there must be no other fund available for the infant's maintenance. In *Re West*,[97] an aunt made two distinct provisions for her niece's welfare. First, a contingent pecuniary legacy of £900 and, secondly, a separate provision for maintenance. It was held that the availability of this other source prevented the niece being entitled to income of the £900 legacy;

- the will demonstrates an intention (whether expressly or by implication) that the beneficiary should be maintained out of the testator's bounty. There is no need for any special relationship here nor does the legacy have to be contingent upon attaining majority or earlier marriage. In *Re Churchill*,[98] for example, the testatrix gave a pecuniary legacy to her grandnephew. She directed her trustees to pay money "towards the advancement in life or otherwise for the benefit" of the legatee. The court determined that this demonstrated a sufficient intention for the s.31 power to maintain to operate;[99] and

- the testator has directed (whether expressly or by implication) that the pecuniary legacy be put aside to be available to the infant legatee as soon as the contingency occurs. For example, a gift of £100,000 to Jordan on reaching 18

---

[90] *Re George* (1877) 5 Ch. D. 837.
[91] *Re Raine* [1929] 1 Ch. 716.
[92] *Re Eyre* [1917] 1 Ch. 351.
[93] This would include a mother: *Re Eyre* [1917] 1 Ch. 351.
[94] (1953) 17 Conv. 275 at p.277
[95] *Re Abrahams* [1911] 1 Ch. 108.
[96] See Farwell J. in *Re Jones* [1932] 1 Ch. 642 at 649, 651.
[97] [1913] 2 Ch. 345.
[98] [1909] 2 Ch. 431.
[99] See also, *Re Selby-Walker* [1949] 2 All E.R. 178, where the trustees had the power to apply the legacy so as to promote the education of the legatee.

years of age. This ring fencing of the £100,000 shows the intention for Jordan to have the accretions earned meanwhile.[1]

Maintenance, education or benefit

14.29   This statutory expression alludes to recurring expenditure and is of wide ambit. In addition to any run-of-the-mill living expenses, it may embrace the purchase of a house in which the minor beneficiary can live or a share in a business partnership for the minor.[2] It can also include the payment of the beneficiary's debts.[3] Income may be employed to pay past maintenance expenses and, albeit exceptionally, it might be used to make donations to charity.[4] The money can be employed for school fees and medical expenses and might be properly used to provide a holiday for the minor.

Decision making

14.30   Unless the minor is married, the payments may be made to the parent or guardian of the minor. The payments made may exhaust the entire trust income and (unlike with the inherent jurisdiction) are not affected by the legal liability of a parent to maintain the minor beneficiary. The trustees are directed by s.31(1) to, "have regard to the age of the infant and his requirements and generally to the circumstances of the case, and in particular to what other income, if any, is applicable for the same purposes". The trustees must focus upon the best interests of the minor beneficiary and these will vary according to the age of the minor and his family circumstances. The trustees should, as Cotton L.J. explained in *Re Lofthouse*, "take into account that the father is not of sufficient ability properly to maintain his child, and that it is for her benefit not merely to allow him enough to pay her actual expenses, but to enable him to give her a better education and a better home. They must not be deterred from doing what is for her benefit because it is also to the father, though, on the other hand, they must not act with a view to his benefit apart from hers".[5]

Provided that the trustees act in a bona fide and prudent manner and periodically direct their minds to whether or not the power should be exercised, the court will not interfere.[6] As discussed above (see **14.23**), the trustees, however, cannot make a blanket decision never to pay maintenance or pay over the entire trust fund to the beneficiary's parents for them to decide how best to use the money. As it is a power, the trustees cannot be compelled to pay maintenance. Short of making a payment under its inherent jurisdiction, all the court can do is direct a trustee to consider whether or not to make a payment.

[1] In *Re Medlock* (1886) 55 L.J. Ch. 738 the testator segregated a sum of £750 to be divided between three people on their attaining 21 years. This was a definite fund that was divorced from the remainder of the estate.
[2] *Re Heyworth's Contingent Reversionary Interest* [1956] Ch. 364.
[3] A possibility recognised in *Re Spencer* [1935] Ch. 533.
[4] *Re Walker* [1901] 1 Ch. 879. This was, as Farwell J. noted at 887, "keeping up the reputation of the family and estate . . .".
[5] (1885) 29 Ch. D. 921 at 932.
[6] *Re Bryant* [1894] 1 Ch. 324.

Ceasing to be a minor

The power to maintain ceases when the beneficiary attains the age of majority. The **14.31** primary issue then concerns what is to happen to the surplus income. The now adult beneficiary will be entitled either to all the income or none of it. Section 31(1) deals with the scenario where the beneficiary attains 18 years of age.

First, if in accordance with the terms of the trust, the beneficiary acquires a vested interest (in income or capital) on attaining majority[7] there is little problem. Understandably, the beneficiary becomes entitled to the unused income.

Secondly, where the beneficiary attains the age of majority, but still only has a **14.32** contingent interest in the trust property, s.31(1)(ii) obliges the trustees to pay the income to the beneficiary until his interest either vests or fails. This provision accelerates the beneficiary's interest, as, in its absence, he would not be entitled to the income until the contingency was satisfied. Any maintenance paid is not recoverable from the beneficiary (or his estate) if the contingency is not met. Take, for example, a trust of shares for the benefit of Jordan when he reaches the age of 21 years. Although now 18 years old, Jordan's interest remains contingent until he achieves the greater age of 21 years. His interest will vest if and when he becomes 21 years old. The gift, of course, fails if the contingency is not satisfied. Nevertheless, Jordan will entitled to the intermediate income.

This facilitating rule, however, gives way in the face of a contrary direction in the trust instrument. In *Re McGeorge*,[8] the testator bequeathed land to his daughter. The bequest was not to take effect until after his wife's death. The 21-year old daughter claimed the income. Cross J. held that she was not entitled to maintenance from the income because the gift was deferred (i.e. it was limited to take effect only on a future specified event). This deferral indicated a contrary intention and she was not entitled to the interim income. Similarly, if the settlor has directed that the surplus income was to be accumulated, the beneficiary has no entitlement to the income produced until the interest vests. In *Re Turner's WT*,[9] the interest was contingent upon the beneficiaries attaining 28 years of age. The settlor had directed the trustees to accumulate surplus income. The beneficiaries that reached majority age were not entitled to claim the income generated prior to their becoming 28 years old.

Entitlement to accumulated income

Subject to a contrary intention in the trust instrument, and until the beneficiary reaches **14.33** majority age, s.31(2) provides that the trustees must accumulate and invest the income that has not been applied for the maintenance of the beneficiary. This has the effect of, as Lord Greene M.R. observed in *Stanley v IRC*, "engrafting upon the vested interest originally conferred on the infant by the settlement or other disposition a qualifying trust of a special nature which confers on the infant a title to accumulations if, and only

---

[7] Or by previous marriage if that is the prescribed contingency.
[8] [1963] 1 All E.R. 519.
[9] [1936] 2 All E.R. 1435.

if, he attains [the age of majority] or marries".[10] During the infancy of the beneficiary, however, the accumulated income may also be used for maintenance purposes.[11] A thorny and technical issue concerns the entitlement to any surplus accumulated income once the beneficiary achieves the age of 18 years or marries under that age.

First, s.31(2)(i)(a) provides that, if the interest vests upon majority or previous marriage (as appropriate), the beneficiary is entitled to the accumulated income.

Secondly, s.31(2)(i)(b) provides that the right to accumulated income also arises where, on attaining the age of 18 years or earlier marriage, the beneficiary has become entitled to the trust property (i.e. the capital) "in fee simple, absolute or determinable, or absolutely, or for an entailed interest". The reference to "fee simple" exclusively applies to trusts of land whereas the allusion to "absolutely" concerns trusts of personalty. The words "for an entailed interest" extend to both realty and personalty. In *Re Sharp's ST*,[12] the High Court held that, when the beneficiaries were entitled to capital (personalty) on attaining majority age, they were not entitled to accumulated income as they were not "absolutely" entitled. This was because the settlor had given the trustees an overriding power of appointment and this prevented the beneficiaries from having complete beneficial ownership of the property. Their interest could be defeated if the power was exercised. Pennycuick V.C. identified the anomaly that a beneficiary with a determinable interest in realty will qualify for accumulated income under s.31(2)(i)(b) whereas a beneficiary having a similar interest in personalty will not.[13] Although he criticised the distinction, "as little short of disgraceful to our jurisprudence",[14] it was too well established to be disturbed.

Thirdly, in any other case s.31(2)(ii) requires that the accumulated income be added to the capital of the property from which it was derived. Hence, if an interest in the capital devolves to Jordan on reaching 21 years, he will not be able to claim the accumulated income when he reaches 18 years of age. It will instead be an accretion to the capital to which he will become entitled in three years time. In a like vein, if Jordan was given merely a life interest then any surplus accumulated income (in the guise of capital) must belong to the remainderman.

ADVANCEMENT FROM CAPITAL

14.34   As shown, maintenance concerns the trustee's ability to use trust income to promote the welfare of a minor beneficiary by defraying recurrent expenditure. The power of advancement, however, caters for the deployment of part of the trust capital to benefit permanently a minor or adult beneficiary before his entitlement under the trust has vested. The key distinction between the two powers, therefore, lies with the source of the funds given to the beneficiary. Other differences are that advancement is not geared to the age of the intended recipient[15] and is designed primarily to make particular,

---

[10] [1944] K.B. 255 at 261.
[11] Section 31(2)(ii).
[12] [1973] Ch. 331 at 340.
[13] [1973] Ch. 331 at 340.
[14] [1973] Ch. 331.
[15] For example, in *Hardy v Shaw* [1975] 2 All E.R. 1052, advancement was made to a middle aged beneficiary.

permanent and substantial long term provision for a beneficiary rather than to meet the payment of day-to-day expenses.

The trustee's ability to make advance payments from capital will arise either from an express power in the trust instrument or under s.32 of the Trustee Act 1925. These sources will, in due course, be considered in turn. At the outset, however, it is perhaps useful to consider the circumstances in which the power of advancement has been utilsed:

- to buy premises for a beneficiary to set up business as a doctor.[16] In *Re Kershaw's Trusts*,[17] the trustees were able to advance £5,000 to set the husband of the beneficiary up in business in England because it was in the interests of the beneficiary wife that he remain in this country and not set up business abroad. As Malins V.C. observed, " ... in such a case what is for the benefit of the husband is for the benefit of the wife"[18];

- to provide a dowry on the marriage of a woman;[19]

- to purchase a commission in the armed forces;[20]

- to pay the beneficiary's emigration costs;[21]

- to discharge the beneficiary's debts[22] and this is so even if it is without the consent of the beneficiary;[23]

- to finance improvements to land;[24]

- to minimise the beneficiary's tax liability to death duty and surtax;[25]

- to promote a legal career at the Bar;[26] and to allow the beneficiary to fund a sub-trust/new settlement in favour of, say, his wife and children.[27] As Farwell J. commented, "To some extent it would be to benefit objects other than the objects of the power, because the wife and children might be the persons to benefit. But I cannot doubt that it would be for the plaintiff's benefit that some provision should be made for them".[28]

---

[16] *Re William's WT* [1953] 1 Ch. 138. Danckwerts J. would have upheld the advance even if it had been to provide a home without a surgery for the doctor/beneficiary.
[17] (1868) L.R. 6 Eq. 322.
[18] (1868) L.R. 6 Eq. 322 at 323.
[19] *Lloyd v Cocker* (1860) 27 Beav. 645.
[20] *Lawrie v Bankes* (1858) 4 K.&J. 142.
[21] *Re Long's ST* (1868) 38 L.J. Ch. 125.
[22] *Marshall v Crowther* (1874) 2 Ch. D. 199.
[23] See *Pilkington v IRC* [1962] 3 All E.R. 622; but note the view of Pennycuick J. in *Re Clore's ST* [1966] 2 All E.R. 272 at 275 that, in relation to a charitable donation "It is not open to trustees to pay away the beneficiary's prospective capital over his head or against his will in discharge of what they consider to be his moral obligation".
[24] *Re Walker's Settled Estate* [1894] 1 Ch. 189 (the rebuilding of an old mansion house).
[25] *Pilkington v IRC* [1962] 3 All E.R. 622.
[26] *Roper-Curzon v Roper-Curzon* (1871) L.R. 11 Eq. 452.
[27] *Re Halsted's WT* [1937] 2 All E.R. 570; see generally D.W.M. Waters, "The Creation of Sub-Trusts under a Power of Advancement" [1959] 23 Conv. 27.
[28] [1937] 2 All E.R. 570 at 571.

14.35   For example, Fiona is the beneficiary under a trust of £100,000, which is contingent upon her becoming 35 years of age. Now at the age of 30 years, Fiona wishes to open a hairdressing salon, but has insufficient funds to buy the necessary premises and equipment. Maintenance from income is unavailable as she is an adult and, in any event, it is unlikely that sufficient income will be generated to finance such a project. Hence, an advance payment from capital before she reaches the magic age of 35 years is the option that Fiona might pursue.

Benefit?

14.36   Although in the above example, the "needy" beneficiary (Fiona) might be directly helped out by an advance from capital, it would be naïve to think that this is the only purpose underlying the exercise of the power of advancement. As with maintenance, it is often used as a tax-saving device and the premature movement of capital might be employed to reduce the beneficiary's prospective liability to such duties.[29] A good illustration of this is where capital is advanced to the remainderman in order to reduce the tax liability arising on the death of the tenant for life.[30]

The concept of "benefit" will embrace any use of the money which improves the material situation of the beneficiary. In *Re Clore's ST*[31] the trustees, as part of a tax-saving scheme, used one-seventh of the trust capital to make large donations to a family charitable foundation. Pennycuick J., however, accepted that the improvement of the material situation of the beneficiary was not confined to his direct financial situation, but could include the discharge of certain moral or social obligations, particularly providing for family and dependants. He noted also that the court has long recognised that a wealthy person is under a moral obligation to make donations to charity. Pennycuick J. reasoned, moreover, that it is to the donor's material advantage that the moral obligation be discharged out of the trust capital rather than from his own pocket. Nevertheless, he pointed out that the nature and amount of those donations must depend upon the circumstances, including the position in life of the intended donor, the amount of the trust fund and the amount of the donor's other resources. Quantum of the donation is a necessary ingredient in the proper exercise of the power to advance capital.

14.37   In these circumstances, therefore, a benefit can be discerned even when the advance proposed will operate to deprive the beneficiary of a material benefit currently available in order to promote a charitable cause. In *Re CL*,[32] the transaction approved the extinction of the beneficiary's interest in favour of her adopted children and a consequential saving on estate duty. In *Re Hampden's ST*,[33] an advance in favour of the beneficiary's children was of benefit as it relieved the beneficiary of the considerable obligation of making further provision for their future. There the approach adopted was that the capital must be dealt with in a way which, when viewed objectively, can

---

[29] *Pilkington v IRC* [1962] 3 All E.R. 622.
[30] *Re Ropner's ST* [1956] 1 W.L.R. 902.
[31] [1966] 2 All E.R. 272.
[32] [1969] 1 Ch. 587.
[33] [1977] T.R. 177.

fairly be said to be for the benefit of the donor and the donor subjectively believes it to be so. The proposed advance may be generous, but cannot be excessive. Accordingly, it cannot objectively be regarded as being to the benefit of a beneficiary with no resources to make an advance from capital of £500,000 in order to provide for his children.

The issues of quantum and reasonableness were returned to in *X v A* where Hart J. emphasised that there has to be the objective existence of a moral obligation.[34] It was not enough that the beneficiary subjectively believes it to be her moral obligation to give away to charity a substantial part of the capital (around £2.5 million). Hart J. accepted that, in distinguishing between the objective existence of a moral obligation on one hand and the beneficiary's own recognition of it on the other, "there is a danger of the court being cast adrift in an open sea".[35] Nevertheless, the answer had to be found in concrete examples provided by the decided cases and generally accepted norms applicable in the context of dealings with settled wealth. Hart J. concluded that, "No such case goes anywhere near recognising the existence of a moral obligation of the extent in question here". Accordingly, he could not see how this transaction could be said to benefit the wife:

> "It cannot be said that the proposed advance is relieving the wife of an obligation she would otherwise have to discharge out of her own resources if only because the amount proposed exceeds the amount of her own free resources. In any event the court has no reason to suppose that, in relation to her free assets, she will regard the advance as having discharged her moral obligation. The moral imperative informing her request to the trustees might logically be thought to apply to her own assets regardless of whether or not an advance is made out of the trust fund".[36]

Express powers

As indicated, a power to apply capital for the advancement or benefit of a minor or contingent beneficiary may be afforded expressly by the trust instrument. The precise extent of such power will turn upon the skills of the draftsman and the construction given by the court to the exact words employed.[37] An express power might be employed where the settlor regards the statutory power of advancement (see below) to be too limited. For example, the statutory power limits the proportion of the trust capital that can be advanced to a beneficiary. An express power might, therefore, be desirable in order to allow a greater proportion to be advanced to the beneficiary. It might also give a tenant for life a right to capital without the consent of the remainderman.[38] An express power might also overcome problems of classifying what expenditure should properly come from income and what should come from capital. Take, for example, routine repairs carried out to the beneficiary's house. The cost of such repairs should be

14.38

[34] [2005] EWHC 2706 (Ch).
[35] [2005] EWHC 2706 (Ch) at [43].
[36] [2005] EWHC 2706 (Ch) at [42].
[37] See generally, D.W.M. Waters [1958] 22 Conv. 413 at pp.417–428.
[38] *Re Marquess of Abergavenny's Estate Act Trusts* [1981] 2 All E.R. 643.

defrayed from income (i.e. via the power of maintenance). Nevertheless, it is open to the settlor to provide expressly that this expenditure be made from capital. Similarly, as will become clear, the statutory power does not apply to settled land. Hence, an express power of advancement would be appropriate as regards such settlements.

The statutory power

14.39 Prior to 1926, it was usual for there to be an express power of advancement inserted into the trust instrument. The statutory power of advancement is now to be found in s.32 of the Trustee Act 1925. This provides that, absent the finding of a contrary intention, every trust created after 1925[39] offers the trustees an absolute discretion to apply capital money for "the advancement or benefit" of a beneficiary. It does not matter whether the trust is inter vivos or testamentary in nature. The use of the word "benefit", therefore, widens the scope of the power to make payments.[40] In *Pilkington v IRC*, Viscount Radcliffe accepted that the term should be given a wide construction.[41] He commented, "I have not been able to find in the words of s.32 ... anything which in terms or by implication restricts the width of the manner or purpose of advancement".[42] He was of the opinion that s.32 offered the trustees the discretion to employ capital in any way that would improve the lot of a beneficiary.

Section 32 makes clear that this power applies where there is a minor beneficiary with a vested interest as well as where there is a beneficiary with a contingent interest (e.g. £100,000 to Fiona when she reaches 35 years of age). Hence, even though the contingency may never be satisfied (by Fiona failing to attain 35 years), the statutory power to advance capital to Fiona remains available during the interim period. Section 32 goes on to state that the power is exercisable even though the interest of the beneficiary is liable to be defeated by the exercise of a power of appointment or revocation or to be diminished by an increase in the class of beneficiary. An example of the latter would be where Fred leaves £100,000 on trust for any of his children who reach 35 years of age. Although when the trust is created Fred might have two children, it is possible that there might be future offspring who will live to the age of 35 years and satisfy the specified contingency. The existing children's interests are, therefore, capable of being diminished. Nevertheless, this does not affect the availability of the power of advancement.

Limitations to s.32

14.40 There are five limitations to the operation of s.32. First, s.32(1)(a) imposes what is known as the half-share rule. This entails that the money advanced cannot exceed, "altogether in amount one-half of the presumptive or vested share or interest of that person in the trust property". In the example, where Fiona is entitled to the £100,000 on

[39] Section 32(3).
[40] See generally, D.W.M. Waters [1958] 22 Conv. 413.
[41] [1962] 3 All E.R. 622; noted at [1963] 27 Conv. 65 (F.R. Crane).
[42] [1962] 3 All E.R. 622 at 627, 628.

reaching 35 years of age, the maximum amount in total that can be advanced under s.32 is capped at £50,000.[43] If the trust had been of £100,000 for the benefit of Fiona and Jordan upon attaining 35 years of age, however, Fiona's entitlement to an advance payment would have a ceiling of £25,000, that is, one-half of her presumptive share. A novel gloss on s.32 arose from the decision in *Re Marquess of Abergavenny's Estate Act Trusts*.[44] There the beneficiary was advanced the maximum one-half share of his trust interest. Subsequently, the capital value of the trust (mainly land) appreciated considerably and the beneficiary asked for a further advance. The trustees were willing to do this, but as a precaution sought directions from the High Court. Goulding J. felt that the answer was plain and held that there could be no further exercise of the statutory power because the one-half share had been exhausted at the time of the original advance. He concluded:

> "All that the settlor authorised has been done. It would to my mind be strange and unexpected if the object of the power as such retained an interest or possibility of interest in the fund still in settlement, so that he could require accounts from the trustees and demand reconsideration of his position whenever there should be an appreciation of assets ... There is no reason that I can see why such ... exposure to fortune, should be continued to the possible disadvantage of other beneficiaries after the limit has been reached".[45]

Albeit a little unconvincingly, Price defends this decision, "It would surely be undesirable to allow a beneficiary to obtain his or her full share at a given date and then to return and "milk" the trust fund of further sums as inflation or wise investment caused increases in the value of the fund. There could never effectively be an end to the exercise of such a power".[46] Price adds, "Trustees need to know easily when a power is exhausted".[47] The irony is that had the beneficiary initially obtained an advance of less than his half-share, he could subsequently have taken advantage of the increased value and received a greater advance overall. In order to retain flexibility, therefore, the beneficiary should never be paid his full share.

The one-half share rule is not, however, immutable in its operation. In *CD (a minor) v O*,[48] for example, Lloyd J. held that the one-half share rule could be varied by the court under the jurisdiction afforded by s.1 of the Variation of Trusts Act 1958.[49] This case concerned the proceeds of two life assurance policies that were held on trust for three minors in equal shares. The claimant's school fees had originally been paid from trust income (i.e. under the power of maintenance), but the income became exhausted with fees remaining to be paid. The trustees then resorted to making an advance payment from capital under s.32.[50] The claimant wanted her entire share in the capital to be available for these purposes and sought to sidestep the one half-share rule. Lloyd

---

[43] An application can, however, be made under the Variation of Trusts Act 1958 for this ceiling to be increased: see *CD (a minor) v O* [2004] 3 All E.R. 780.

[44] [1981] 2 All E.R. 643; noted at [1982] 46 Conv. 158 (J.W. Price).

[45] [1981] 2 All E.R. 643 at 646.

[46] [1982] 46 Conv. 158 at p.158.

[47] [1982] 46 Conv. 158 at p.159.

[48] [2004] 3 All E.R. 780.

[49] See Ch.15.

[50] An appropriate candidate for advancement payments: see *Re Harris' Settlement* (1940) 162 L.T. 358.

J. approved the requested extension of the statutory power of advancement. He was influenced by the fact that the trust instrument made no provision for the use of capital and income and that the claimant would, had it not been for her age, be entitled absolutely to her share. He noted also that the rule is commonly relaxed in modern trust instruments. Lloyd J. was satisfied that it would be for C's benefit for the limit imposed by s.32 of the 1925 Act on the application of the capital of the fund for her education to be lifted. The key question was whether, and on what basis, the court has power to achieve this result. He considered the source of this jurisdiction. Although in exceptional circumstances the variation could be justified under the court's inherent jurisdiction to provide for a minor,[51] Lloyd J. preferred to frame his decision around the Variation of Trusts Act 1958. Alluding to s.1 of that Act, he concluded that the whole fund, as well as C's fund separately, was "property ... held on trusts arising ... under any will, settlement or other disposition". The court allowed the entire capital fund to be used for advancement purposes under the 1958 Act because it was satisfied that the proposed variation of the trusts was for the benefit of the relevant beneficiary.

14.41 The second limitation is that s.32 allows the trustees to make payments out of "capital". "Capital" for these purposes is limited to personalty (e.g. money and securities) and realty that is subject to a trust of land under the Trusts of Land and Appointment of Trustees Act 1996. Its meaning does not extend to settled land or the proceeds of sale of settled land.[52]

The third limitation is that s.32(1)(b) imposes an obligation on the beneficiary to account for money advanced when he "becomes absolutely and indefeasibly entitled to a share in the trust property". Hence, the money is to be deducted from the beneficiary's eventual share under the trust. This is sometimes known as "hotchpot" and, being designed to ensure equality of distribution between the beneficiaries, operates to give effect to the settlor's presumed intentions. For example, where Fiona is advanced £25,000 under a settlement of £100,000 for herself and Jordan she must deduct that payment from her eventual entitlement under the trust. Hence, Fiona will subsequently receive a further £25,000 and Jordan will receive £50,000. At the present time, this rule makes no allowance for inflationary tendencies, as the property is valued as at the time the advance is made. The Law Reform Committee recommended that the calculation should be based upon fractional distributions of entitlement and not geared to the cash sums advanced.[53] Unfairness might arise under the present law because, as the Committee explained, "The result might well be that the beneficiary who has received part of his share by way of advancement will, in fact, in the long run, receive a larger portion of the whole fund than would be expected given the value of his initial, undivided, share".[54]

14.42 The fourth exception is that s.32(1)(c) provides that no payment shall be made to prejudice any interest prior to that of the beneficiary's interest. For example, take the situation were property is held on trust for Noel for life with remainder to Rhonda. If sums from capital were advanced to Rhonda while Noel was still with us, it would reduce the fund from which Noel's income was to be derived. It would, thereby, prejudice her prior interest. Not surprisingly, the Act only allows such advances when Noel

---

[51] See *Chapman v Chapman* [1954] 1 All E.R. 798.
[52] Section 32(2) (as amended).
[53] The Law Reform Committee, "The Powers and Duties of Trustees" (1982) Cmnd. 8733, paras 4.43–4.47.
[54] (1982) Cmnd. 8733 at para.4.43.

is of full age and gives written consent to the payment. The court will be slow to infer any contrary intention on the part of the settlor. In *Henly v Wardell*,[55] a trust was established under which the testator gave his widow a life interest with remainder to his two sons. The trust instrument gave the trustees an "absolute and uncontrolled" discretion to advance capital to the benefit of the testator's children. The court had to consider whether the latter provision was sufficient to override the need for the life tenant's written consent to an advance from capital. On a proper construction of the instrument, it was held that the word "uncontrolled" was not strong enough to disarm s.32(1)(c). The modification instead was merely to enlarge the provision so that the whole of a beneficiary's share could be advanced if the trustees thought fit. It did not do away with the need for the consent of the life tenant. Indeed, it was unlikely that the testator would have wished for his sons to have the capital at his widow's expense.

Finally, the section gives way in the face of a contrary intention.[56] This means that the power can be excluded either expressly by an appropriate declaration in the trust instrument or by implication. As regards the latter option, this occurred in *Re Evans' Settlement* where the trust instrument stated that the trustees were to have a power to advance capital up to a specified amount.[57] As this contradicted the statutory half-share rule (see **14.40**), the intention was that s.32 was not to apply. In *Re Craven*,[58] the express power was limited by a clause that permitted advancement only for specified purposes. The limitation imposed was sufficient to prevent the application of the wider statutory power. Similarly, the Court of Appeal in *IRC v Bernstein*[59] concluded that a trust, under which income was to be accumulated income during the settlor's lifetime, demonstrated the intention to exclude s.32.

Discretion

As the notion of "benefit" is now divorced from the concept of "need", the trustees **14.43**
have to take special care to ensure that their discretion is exercised properly. Trustees, of course, have always been liable for negligently making an advance. In *Simpson v Brown*,[60] on coming of age a beneficiary successfully recovered from his trustee money that had been advanced to provide the beneficiary with an apprenticeship with a chemist. The problem was that the chemist was unqualified and, therefore, unable to provide the beneficiary with the appropriate training. Beyond this, however, a trustee who could show that the advancement was to alleviate a "need" of the beneficiary would generally be shielded.[61] Different considerations necessarily apply when the advancement is instead to confer a benefit. More is expected from a trustee when making an advance to benefit the beneficiary rather than to assuage his need.[62] The trustees are expected to take on board all relevant considerations and determine that it

---

[55] (1988) *The Times*, January 29.
[56] Section 69(2).
[57] [1967] 3 All E.R. 343.
[58] [1937] Ch. 431.
[59] [1961] Ch. 399.
[60] (1864) 11 L.T. 593.
[61] See *Re Brittlebank* (1881) 30 W.R. 99.
[62] See D.W.M. Waters [1958] 22 Conv. 413, pp.431–434.

is a proper case for advancement. The court can, therefore, prevent trustees from an exercise of discretion that is wrong or unreasonable. As Lindley L.J. pointed out in *Hampden v Earl of Buckinghamshire*, "A honest trustee may fail to see that he is acting unjustly towards those whose interests he is bound to consider and to protect; and, if he is so acting, and the Court can see it although he cannot, it is in my opinion the duty of the Court to interfere".[63] If, however, there is no injustice, the court will not readily interfere. This was demonstrated in *Re Charteris* where there was an allegation that trustee's unreasonably exercised a discretion to postpone the payment of a legacy.[64] Swinfen-Eady L.J. concluded that this was a proper exercise of discretion as the trustees had acted fairly and properly in the general interest of the estate, and in the interests of all the beneficiaries.

Continuing supervision

14.44   Regardless of the terms of the power of advancement, on exercising the discretion the trustees must ensure that the funds advanced are actually used for the purposes stated by the beneficiary. This continuing responsibility was highlighted in *Re Pauling's ST*[65] where the trustees (Coutts & Co) advanced numerous capital sums to beneficiaries from their presumptive share. Although nominally for the benefit of their children, the capital was really used to finance the luxurious lifestyle of their parents. The children were of full age and did not complain about the manner in which the money was used. It was presumed, however, that they were under the undue influence of their parents. The belief of the trustees was that they had acted lawfully in making the advances to the children and what the children did with the money was not their concern. Subsequently the children succeeded in suing the trustees for breach of trust in making improper advances. The Court of Appeal concluded that the power had been improperly exercised and that, as the payments had been made for a particular purpose, the trustees had an obligation to inquire as to the actual use of the money. Willmer L.J. reading the majority judgment made clear that what the trustees cannot do, "is to prescribe a particular purpose, and then raise and pay the money over to the advancee leaving him or her entirely free, legally and morally, to apply it for that purpose or to spend it in any way he or she chooses, without any responsibility upon the trustees even to inquire as to its application".[66] The trustees had to pay the money back into the trust fund. The moral is that a trustee must not abandon the beneficiary to his own folly.

If, as opposed to a direct payment, the money is to be paid to an agent of the beneficiary, the trustee must ensure that the agent is authorised. On payment to an unauthorised agent (e.g. one with a forged power of attorney), the general rule is that (barring ratification, estoppel or contributory negligence) the trustee will remain liable to the beneficiary.[67]

---

[63] [1893] 2 Ch. 531 at 544.
[64] [1917] 2 Ch. 379.
[65] [1963] 3 All E.R. 1.
[66] [1963] 3 All E.R. 1 at 8.
[67] *Welch v Bank of England* [1955] 1 Ch. 508.

GUIDE TO FURTHER READING

B.S. Ker, "Trustees' Powers of Maintenance" [1953] 17 Conv. 273.
A.M. Prichard, "Acceleration and Contingent Remainders" [1973] C.L.J. 246.
D.W.M. Waters, "The 'New' Power of Advancement" [1958] Conv. 413.

Chapter 15

VARIATION OF TRUSTS

The working rule is that the terms of a properly constituted trust are to be followed **15.01** strictly. The trustees are obliged to apply the property in accordance with the terms of the trust and, if they do not do so, are potentially liable for breach of trust. As Romer L.J. put it, "As a rule, the court has no jurisdiction to give, and will not give, its sanction to the performance by the trustees of acts with reference to the trust estate which are not, on the face of the instrument creating the trust, authorised by its terms".[1] This rule of strict fidelity is, however, subject to exceptions and these recognise that, as a trust may last for many years, it is likely that, in time, the original terms might become tired, unreasonable and undesirable. This might occur in relation to the original management and administrative provisions of the trust or, indeed, might focus upon the beneficial interests as originally allocated by the settlor.

A variation of the trust terms might be catered for by the settlor giving to the trustees a power to amend a trust. This is a common feature of modern pension trusts. It might be described as a power to amend or might adopt the form of a power to add to, vary, modify or alter the terms of the trust. If such ability is given by the trust instrument, the court will be vigilant to ensure that it is properly exercised for the purpose for which it was granted and as intended by the settlor.[2] As Lord Steyn commented in *Society of Lloyds v Robinson*, "This principle is closely linked with the general proposition that the power must not be exercised beyond the reasonable contemplation of the parties ...".[3] Accordingly, any restrictions on the power of amendment must be complied with. For example, if the power is expressed to allow only administrative or managerial changes, it cannot be employed to vary the beneficial interests under the trust.

Beyond the presence of an express power, only in limited circumstances will the law **15.02** allow the terms of a trust to be varied. First, it is possible that the beneficiaries might collectively authorise a variation. Secondly, and where the beneficiaries are not sui juris

---

[1] *Re New* [1901] 2 Ch. 534 at 544.
[2] *Hole v Garnsey* [1930] A.C. 472.
[3] [1999] 1 W.L.R. 756 at 766.

or unanimous, an application for variation can be made to the court. If the latter course is followed, a variation might be ordered under the court's inherent jurisdiction or its statutory jurisdiction. The primary example of Parliamentary intervention in this area takes the form of the Variation of Trusts Act 1958. Such inroads upon the sanctity of the trust instrument once again illustrate that the clearest expressed intentions of a settlor are most certainly not sacrosanct.[4]

CONSENSUAL VARIATION

15.03   The general ability of beneficiaries to redraft the trust emerges from the rule in *Saunders v Vautier*[5] which was concerned with the premature termination of the trust by the beneficiaries. Once it was accepted that the beneficiaries could end a trust, it followed naturally that the rule in *Saunders v Vautier* could instead be employed to vary the terms of a continuing trust. Hence, it offers a prime example of when the current interests of the beneficiaries take priority over the original prescription of the settlor. The trustees are protected as the beneficiaries have authorised the deviation and are, thereby, unable to pursue successfully an action for breach of trust.[6]

The modification contemplated here will usually involve a recasting of the beneficial interests and be motivated by tax considerations, especially the fear of inheritance tax. It is also thought that a variation of an existing trust is not a disposition for the purposes of Capital Gains Tax, whereas the revocation of the existing settlement and the creation of a new one is most definitely a taxable disposal. The overriding goal is, therefore, usually to minimise potential fiscal liabilities. As Lord Denning M.R. acknowledged in *Re Weston's Settlements*, "Nearly every variation that has come before the court has tax avoidance for its principal object: and no one has ever suggested that this is undesirable or contrary to public policy".[7]

15.04   Under the rule in *Saunders v Vautier* a beneficiary who is of full age (i.e. 18 years and above), of sound mind and entitled to the entire equitable interest can direct the trustees to transfer the trust property to him and, thereby, put a premature end to the trust.[8] The rule will also allow two or more beneficiaries who are absolutely entitled to the trust assets to require an outright transfer of their shares.[9] Indeed, Walton J. considered it to be, "trite law that persons who between them hold the entirety of the beneficial interests in any particular trust fund are as a body entitled to direct the trustees how that fund is to be dealt with ...".[10]

The facts of *Saunders v Vautier* concerned a testator who bequeathed £2,000 of East India stock upon a fixed trust for Mr Vautier, with a direction that the dividends were to be accumulated until Mr Vautier achieved 25 years of age. On reaching 21 years,

---

[4] This is evident also in the context of charitable trusts with the scope for variation afforded by the cy-près doctrine: see Ch.8.
[5] (1841) 4 Beav. 115.
[6] *Re Pauling's ST* [1963] 3 All E.R. 1.
[7] [1969] 1 Ch. 234 at 245.
[8] See also, *Tod v Barton* [2002] 4 ITELR 715, where the two beneficiaries (a charity and the testator's son) agreed to end the trust prematurely.
[9] *Stephenson v Barclays Bank* [1975] 1 All E.R. 625.
[10] *Stephenson v Barclays Bank* [1975] 1 All E.R. 625 at 637.

however, Mr Vautier claimed to be entitled to the entire trust fund. It was held that, although it was the settlor's intention that enjoyment be postponed until Mr Vautier reached 25 years, the interest vested on his reaching majority (then 21 years). He was entitled to have the property transferred to him. Lord Langdale M.R. explained, "where a legacy is directed to accumulate for a certain period, or where the payment is postponed, the legatee, if he has an absolute indefeasible interest in the legacy, is not bound to wait until the expiration of that period, but may require payment the moment he is competent to give a valid discharge".[11] Accordingly, as Swinfen Eady M.R. put it in *Re Nelson*, "where there is what amounts to an absolute gift, that absolute gift cannot be fettered by prescribing a mode of enjoyment".[12]

Subsequently, the rule was extended so that it could be applied collectively. If there is more than one beneficiary, the conditions as to age and mental capacity must be satisfied by each, they must act unanimously, and together they must be entitled to the entire beneficial interest. The rule in *Saunders v Vautier* has no application, therefore, when one beneficiary refuses to join in, is underage or is mentally unequipped to make his own decisions. **15.05**

The rule in *Saunders v Vautier* applies equally to discretionary trusts. The operation of the rule in this sphere was demonstrated in *Re Smith*.[13] There the Public Trustee held a fund on a discretionary trust to pay any part of the income or capital for the benefit of Mrs Aspinall. Any surplus income was to be accumulated and the fund remaining at Mrs Aspinall's death was to pass to her children in equal shares. Mrs Aspinall was alive when all her children reached majority age. Subsequently, Mrs Aspinall and her children mortgaged their trust interests to the Legal and General Assurance Co. The mortgagee sought payment of the whole income by the trustees until the mortgage was paid off. Romer J. held that the Public Trustee was obliged to utilise the income in this way. The key factor was that Mrs Aspinall and her children were together entitled to the whole fund. It did not matter that that the Public Trustee enjoyed a discretion vested in it as to what sums Mrs Aspinall would receive and whether this would be funded from capital as well as from income. The beneficiaries were collectively entitled to require the trustee to hand over the fund to them.

The following propositions can be distilled from *Re Smith* and all turn upon the nature of the beneficiary's equitable ownership of the trust property. **15.06**

First, if the trustees have the discretion to apply the whole or part of a fund to or for the benefit of a particular person, that person cannot come to the trustees and demand the fund. This is because the whole fund has not been dedicated to that person and his entitlement is only to so much as the trustees think fit to afford to him.

Secondly, where the entire fund is available to be applied for the benefit of a particular person there is nothing to prevent that person claiming the whole trust fund. The fact that the trustees enjoy the discretion as to the method in which the whole fund was to be applied for the benefit of that person makes no difference.

Thirdly, where the trustees have the discretion whether to apply the whole or part of the fund for the benefit of one person, but are obliged to apply the rest of the fund for the benefit of a second named person, collectively the beneficiaries can claim the fund. **15.07**

---

[11] (1841) 4 Beav. 115 at 116.
[12] [1928] Ch. 920 at 921.
[13] [1928] Ch. 915.

They are together the sole objects of a discretionary trust and between them are entitled to the entire fund. As Romer J. commented, "in such a case as that you treat all the people put together just as though they formed one person, for whose benefit the trustees were directed to apply the whole of a particular fund".[14]

The situations in which a consensual rearrangement of beneficial interests might be sought traditionally arose around consecutive trust interests. A classic example is that of a life tenant and a remainderman. Although there are various permutations possible, the following illustrate the methods through which beneficial interests can be varied by agreement:

- the surrender by a life tenant of his interest to the remainderman (i.e. the person entitled to the shares on the death of the life tenant). For example, Adrienne sets up a trust in shares which gives Rhonda a life interest with remainder to Trevor. If Rhonda decides to sell her life interest to Trevor, she will be surrendering her interest up to Trevor;

- the surrender by the remainderman of his interest to the life tenant. This would occur when it is Trevor who disposes of his remainder interest to Rhonda;

- the disclaimer of a life interest created by will;

- the release of an annuity created by will; and

- the division of the trust fund between the life tenant and the remainderman. This would arise where Rhonda and Trevor agree to allocate the shares between them and put an end to the trust.

THE COURT'S INHERENT JURISDICTION

15.08 As made clear, consensual variation cannot occur if unanimity is absent or the beneficiaries are not all adults and of sound mind. If, for example, the trust is designed to benefit children or, as yet, unborn beneficiaries the rule in *Saunders v Vautier* is rendered inoperative. In such circumstances, therefore, variation can occur only following the authorisation of the court. A variation can be justified under the, admittedly limited, inherent jurisdiction of the court. The parameters of this jurisdiction remain as charted by the House of Lords in *Chapman v Chapman*.[15] There it was made clear that apart from compromise (see **15.11**) and maintenance (see **15.13**), the court's inherent powers of variation extend only to management and administrative matters. As Marshall explains, "This decision makes it clear that the court does not possess plenary powers to alter a trust because alteration is thought to be advantageous to beneficiaries who are infants or not yet born, even though paradoxically, such beneficiaries could of their own volition and without the assistance of the court have made the desired alteration, had they been *in esse* and *sui juris*".[16]

---

[14] [1928] Ch. 915 at 919.
[15] [1954] A.C. 429; noted by J.D.B. Mitchell [1954] 17 M.L.R. 473.
[16] O.R. Marshall, "Deviations from the Terms of a Trust" [1954] M.L.R. 17 420 at p.420.

In the *Chapman* case, the House was, put simply, invited to rewrite the trust interests in order to avoid death duties. The House concluded that it had no power to vary the trust in the circumstances before it. Indeed, this restrictive stance provided the momentum behind greater statutory intervention, namely the Variation of Trusts Act 1958. Lord Morton justified his decision by invoking a policy argument:

> "if the Court had power to approve, and did approve, schemes such as the present scheme, the way would be open for a most undignified game of chess between the Chancery Division and the legislature. The alteration of one settlement for the purposes of avoiding taxation already imposed might well be followed by scores of successful applications for a similar purpose by beneficiaries under other settlements. The legislature might then counter this move by imposing fresh taxation upon the trusts as thus altered. The beneficiaries would then troop back to the Chancery Division ... So the game might go on, if the judges of the Chancery Division had the power which the appellants claim for them, and if they thought it right to make the first move".[17]

The upshot of this approach was that the courts had to pay more respect to the expressed intention of the settlor and that the possibilities of varying trusts for tax saving purposes were greatly diminished. Lord Morton did, however, identify the limited circumstances in which the court can invoke its inherent jurisdiction to vary the terms of a trust.[18] These are:

- salvage and emergency;
- compromise; and
- maintenance.

Salvage and emergency

The first occasion on which the inherent jurisdiction emerges is when the court sanctions some special managerial act in accordance with the so-called "salvage principles". The traditional notion is that, in an emergency, the court can sanction a transaction (e.g. the sale or mortgage of part of an infant's trust interest) in order that the trustees can raise money to carry out necessary repairs to land. The idea is that the beneficiary's inheritance can be preserved. This is, however, a limited jurisdiction. In *Re De Teissier's Settled Estates*,[19] Chitty J. refused to allow the money to be used to rebuild, repair and improve a mansion house because there were two life interests preceding that of the infant beneficiary. There was no suggestion that the life tenant in possession could not afford the works and it was clear that, if the works were carried out, it would be chiefly for the benefit of the current tenant in possession. Chitty J. concluded that, "unless the

15.09

---

[17] [1954] A.C. 429 at 468.
[18] [1954] A.C. 429 at 451. As will become clear, further statutory exceptions have subsequently emerged (e.g. s.57(1) of the Trustee Act 1925).
[19] [1893] 1 Ch. 153.

Court is firm in a matter such as this the Court will be flooded with similar applications".[20] This reticence is evident also in *Re Jackson*[21] where Kay J. felt it necessary to conduct a limited inquiry as to what repairs were absolutely necessary. There an infant was entitled to real estate in possession, but the property was in a very dilapidated condition. While expressing the view that the jurisdiction should be jealously exercised, he felt that it was in the infant's interests that the absolutely essential works be authorised. Hence, it is not sufficient that the repairs are merely desirable or beneficial.[22] Accordingly, in *Re Montagu*[23] the Court of Appeal declined to sanction a scheme to demolish and rebuild certain houses even though it was clearly in the interests of the tenant for life and his children (who enjoyed an interest in remainder) that it do so. As Lopes L.J. admitted, "That is not enough. If the buildings were falling down it would be a case of actual salvage and would stand differently".[24]

In *Re New*,[25] however, the salvage rules were extended into less conventional territory. There the trustees held legal title to shares in a particular company and, as an emergency matter, sought to become involved in the capital reconstruction of that company. As a result, the existing shares would be exchanged for new shares in the reconstructed company. This fell outside the trustees' powers of investment as set out in the trust instrument. The court sanctioned the transaction on the basis that it was analogous to the salvage cases. Romer L.J. explained:

> "In a case of this kind, which may reasonably be supposed to be one not foreseen or anticipated by the author of the trust, where the trustees are embarrassed by the emergency that has arisen and the duty cast upon them to do what is best for the estate, and the consent of all the beneficiaries cannot be obtained by reason of some of them not being *sui juris* or in existence, then it may be right for the Court, and the Court would in a proper case have jurisdiction, to sanction on behalf of all concerned such acts on behalf of the trustees...".[26]

Romer L.J. provided the further example of a testator who declared that land is to be sold by a stipulated date. If, due to an unforeseen change of circumstances sale by the prescribed time would prove ruinous to the estate, he felt that the court would authorise the trustees to postpone sale in order to effect a proper sale at a later time.[27]

15.10 *Re New* was later described by Cozens-Hardy L.J. in *Re Tollemache* as representing, "the high-water mark of the exercise by the court of its extraordinary jurisdiction in relation to trusts".[28] In *Re Tollemache*, the trustees sought permission to invest in a mortgage using trust money. They argued that it would benefit the life tenant by generating an increased income and would not prejudice the position of the remainderman. The court, however, refused to approve this unauthorised use of trust funds as it could not be said to be an emergency transaction. The clear inference to be drawn

---

[20] [1893] 1 Ch. 153 at 165.
[21] (1882) 21 Ch. D. 786.
[22] See *Conway v Fenton* (1888) 40 Ch. D. 512.
[23] [1897] 2 Ch. 8.
[24] [1897] 2 Ch. 8 at 11.
[25] [1901] 2 Ch. 534.
[26] [1901] 2 Ch. 534 at 545.
[27] [1901] 2 Ch. 534 at 545.
[28] [1903] 1 Ch. 955 at 956.

from *Re Tollemache* is that the salvage and emergency rule does not cater for a scheme designed directly to vary existing beneficial entitlements under the trust. Such variation may be a consequence, but it is not a justification.

Compromise

The second inroad is, as Lord Morton confirmed in the *Chapman* case, that the court enjoys an inherent jurisdiction to approve compromises reached on behalf of an infant beneficiary. In this context, it is important to note that the infant does not enjoy the legal capacity to enter the compromise of its own volition. This aspect of the court's inherent jurisdiction is, however, dependent upon there being a real dispute concerning the infant's interest under the trust and a real compromise of that dispute that is proposed.[29] The dispute might concern the powers of the trustees or the beneficial interests created under the trust. Hence, the court's approval may engineer a variation of beneficial entitlement. As Lord Cohen put it in *Chapman v Chapman*, "The very essence of a compromise is that it may give each party something other than that which the will or settlement would, on its true construction, confer on them".[30]   **15.11**

The *Chapman* case emphasised that a proposed exchange or bargain is not a compromise. A fictitious or manufactured dispute will not, moreover, operate to engage the jurisdiction. In *Re Powell-Cotton's Resettlement*,[31] there was an investment clause of uncertain meaning and a proposed new investment clause was approved by the adult and infant beneficiaries. As there was not really any dispute, the court was invited to accede to a compromise so as to resolve a doubt or difficulty. This it refused to do. Although Lord Evershed M.R. sought, "to avoid laying down any hard and fast rule",[32] he concluded, "it seems to me very doubtful, to say the least, whether it could be said that as between the beneficiaries in this case there is any dispute as to their rights".[33] Put simply, there was nothing to compromise. In *Mason v Farbrother*,[34] ambiguity again descended upon the extent of the trustees' power to invest as given by the trust instrument. In this case, however, the High Court held that a genuine difference of potential meaning allowed it to exercise its inherent jurisdiction at the behest of the trustees. This was so even though there was no contested dispute involving third parties. As Judge Blackett explained, "I do not think there need be open warfare before the court may approve a compromise, provided that there are genuine points of difference requiring determination or settlement".[35] In theory, the jurisdiction to vary exists even if the compromise will have the effect of reducing a beneficiary's eventual entitlement.

In the *Chapman* case, there was no such dispute and no suggestion of a compromise. All that was sought there was a simple rearrangement of existing and undisputed   **15.12**

---

[29] See *Re Lord Hylton's Settlement* [1954] 1 W.L.R. 1055.
[30] [1954] A.C. 429 at 472.
[31] [1956] 1 W.L.R. 23.
[32] [1956] 1 W.L.R. 23 at 27.
[33] [1956] 1 W.L.R. 23 at 28.
[34] [1983] 2 All E.R. 1078.
[35] [1983] 2 All E.R. 1078 at 1085. Nevertheless, the court preferred to utilise its jurisdiction under s.57 of the Trustee Act 1925 so as to insert a new investment clause.

interests. Lord Simonds noted, "It is the function of the court to execute a trust, to see that the trustees do their duty and to protect them if they do it, to direct them if they are in doubt and, if they do wrong, to penalise them. It is not the function of the court to alter a trust because alteration is thought to be advantageous to an infant beneficiary".[36]

Maintenance

15.13 The third example of where the inherent jurisdiction of the court arises is when the court awards maintenance from income that the testator has directed should be accumulated. The testator may make provision for his family, but might seek to postpone the enjoyment of the gift while the estate is increasing in value. As examined in Ch.14, the court will assume that the testator did not intend for his family to go short in the interim period and can override his express directions by ordering the payment of maintenance.[37] The court will, therefore, interfere with the accumulation. Any such order will necessarily result in a variation of the beneficial interests. The jurisdiction is not limited to urgent cases[38] and maintenance is not limited to minor beneficiaries.[39] In *Revel v Watkinson*, the Lord Chancellor expressed the following view, "she stands entirely in the light of a child unprovided for during that time, and at the mother's pleasure, and the court will not, in favour of a remainder man ... leave a daughter and heir at law to starve".[40]

STATUTORY JURISDICTION: MISCELLANEOUS PROVISIONS

15.14 Prior to the Variation of Trusts Act 1958, the statutory exceptions to the duty of the trustee not to depart from the terms of the trust were piecemeal and scattered across a number of Acts of Parliament. As these provisions (albeit in amended form) still retain validity in the post-1958 Act era, it is convenient to consider them at the outset in isolation from the Validation of Trusts Act. The provisions to be considered in turn are:

- s.53 of the Trustee Act 1925;
- s.57(1) of the Trustee Act 1925;
- s.64 of the Settled Land Act 1925;
- s.24 of the Matrimonial Causes Act 1973; and
- s.16 of the Mental Capacity Act 2005.

---

[36] [1954] A.C. 429 at 446.
[37] *Re Collins* (1886) 32 Ch. D. 229; *Havelock v Havelock* (1881) 17 Ch. D. 807.
[38] *Haley v Bannister* (1820) 4 Madd. 275.
[39] *Revel v Watkinson* (1748) 1 Ves. Sen. 93. There an adult daughter was entitled to maintenance during her mother's lifetime.
[40] (1748) 1 Ves. Sen. 93 at 95.

Section 53 of the Trustee Act 1925

Section 53 of the Trustee Act 1925 provides that, when an infant is beneficially entitled **15.15** to any property, the court may order certain dealings with the property with a view to the application of capital or income for the maintenance, education or benefit of that infant.[41] For example, the court may order that the property be conveyed for the infant's advantage or vest in any person the right to receive income or dividends from the property so as to further the interests of the infant. The statutory provision is wider than the inherent jurisdiction to maintain in that it allows for capital to be employed for these purposes and alludes to "benefit" and not merely to "maintenance". As Upjohn J. noted in *Re Heyworth*, "It covers not merely expenditure but capital investment such as the purchase of a house to live in or a share in a partnership, or even in some cases placing of money on deposit for an infant".[42] Accordingly, in *Re Meux's WT*[43] the court authorised dealings under which an infant's reversionary interest was sold to the tenant for life with the ambition of reducing estate duty and, thereby, advancing the interests of the infant beneficiary. It was central to the decision that the proceeds of sale were to be held on new trusts for the infant. This was viewed as a single transaction which was overwhelmingly to the benefit of the infant. In *Re Gower's Settlement*,[44] the court was invited to sanction the raising of money by a mortgage of the interest of an infant beneficiary under a settlement. The infant was a tenant in tail subject to a preceding life interest and the mortgage was to benefit the infant. The court authorised the dealing under s.53 even though the mortgage would take priority over the potential claims of remote beneficiaries. In *Re Bristol's SE*,[45] a transaction was authorised by Buckley J. so as to bar an entail and thus pave the way for an infant's subsequent application under the Variation of Trusts Act 1958. This was for the benefit of the beneficiary and amounted to an application of capital or income.

Section 53 does not, however, allow the court to vary the infant's actual beneficial interest under the trust. This was demonstrated in *Re Heyworth* where Upjohn J. refused to countenance a dealing under which the proceeds of sale of an infant's reversionary interest were to be given to the infant absolutely.[46] Upjohn J. explained:

> "The deed is not in the least degree entered into with a view to the application of, or for the purpose of applying, any capital or income of the infant for her benefit ... If I sanctioned this scheme on behalf of the infant I should be reading the section as though it empowered the court to convey the property of an infant whenever it was for her benefit. Unfortunately, the section only confers a more limited jurisdiction".[47]

[41] See O.R. Marshall, "The Scope of Section 53 of the Trustee Act 1925" [1957] 21 Conv. 448.
[42] [1956] 2 W.L.R. 1044 at 1048, 1049.
[43] [1958] Ch. 154.
[44] [1934] Ch. 365.
[45] [1964] 3 All E.R. 939.
[46] [1956] 2 W.L.R. 1044.
[47] [1956] 2 W.L.R. 1044 at 1049.

Section 57(1) of the Trustee Act 1925

15.16   Section 57(1) of the Trustee Act 1925 provides that trustees (other than trustees under the Settled Land Act 1925[48]) can be authorised to do any act, relating to the management or administration of trust property, which the court deems to be expedient. As demonstrated in *Re Salting*,[49] the statutory authorisation operates as if it was an overriding power inserted into the trust instrument. Nevertheless, Eve J. could not accept that the revised terms were to be treated as if they were originally in the trust instrument.[50] The underlying ethos is that trust property should be managed as effectively as possible in the best interests of the beneficiaries. The court will be invited to sanction specific dealings with the property that would otherwise be unauthorised and yet are to the overall advantage of the beneficiaries.[51] In *Re Mair*,[52] a scheme was approved under which the life interest given to two women was to be sold, primarily to enable one of them to pay her debts. The scheme involved the payment out of capital of a considerable sum to the two women.

Section 57(1) clearly overlaps with the narrower "salvage" jurisdiction (see **15.09**). Two major differences, however, emerge. First, the inherent jurisdiction is framed around the existence of an "emergency", whereas, s.57(1) is based upon the more generous concept of "expediency". Secondly, as regards the statutory jurisdiction there is no requirement that the reason for intervention be one that the settlor could not reasonably have foreseen.[53] Accordingly, s.57(1) offers greater scope than the salvage principles and has, for most practical purposes, subsumed the traditional jurisdiction.

15.17   Section 57(1) cannot, however, be operated merely to promote the position of one beneficiary at the expense of others. In *Re Craven's Estate (No.2)*,[54] the testatrix left her residuary estate on trust for several beneficiaries, including her son. The trustees were given an express power of advancement for the limited purpose of buying a business. The son sought to become a member of Lloyds, which required the payment of a deposit, and asked the court to vary the terms of the advancement provision under its s.57 jurisdiction. It was clear that the use of the money did not amount to the purchase of a business. Although it would clearly benefit the son, Farwell J. concluded that it would not be expedient to the other beneficiaries to allow part of the trust fund to be used in this unauthorised fashion. The court refused to sanction the variation. Farwell J. explained:

> "The word 'expedient' there quite clearly must mean, in my judgment, expedient for the trust as a whole. It cannot mean that however expedient it may be for one beneficiary, if it is inexpedient from the point of view of the other beneficiaries concerned the court ought to sanction the transaction. In order that the matter

---

[48] Section 57(4). Such trustees are offered an alternative and wider route under s.64 of the Settled Land Act 1925 (see **15.18**).
[49] [1932] 2 Ch. 57.
[50] [1932] 2 Ch. 57 at 64.
[51] See Lord Evershed M.R. in *Re Downshire's Settled Estates* [1953] Ch. 218 at 248.
[52] [1935] Ch. 562.
[53] *Re Downshire's Settled Estates* [1953] Ch. 218.
[54] [1937] Ch. 431.

may be one which is in the opinion of the Court expedient, it must be expedient for the trust as a whole".[55]

The provision is designed to promote the "management" and "administration" of property vested in the trustees. These terms, however, remain undefined in the Act and, although most proceedings occur in private and the decisions are unreported, it has been left for the courts to ascribe some meaning to these words. Section 57(1) has been utilised to authorise, for example, a modernisation of the trustees' investment powers,[56] the sale of settled chattels,[57] the sale of land where the necessary consents could not be obtained,[58] the widening of the investment powers of a charitable corporation,[59] the sale of a reversionary interest,[60] and the expedient partition of property.[61] Accordingly, s.57 is focused upon the supervision and control of trust property. It has nothing to do with the variation of beneficial interests (these are not vested in the trustees) or stimulating tax advantages. As Marshall concludes, "The object of the section is to enable the court to authorise specific dealings with the trust property which it might not have been able to do on the basis of salvage or emergency, but it was no part of the legislative aim to disturb the rule that the court will not rewrite a trust".[62]

Section 64 of the Settled Land Act 1925

Section 64 of the Settled Land Act 1925 affords the court a generous jurisdiction to authorise the tenant for life of settled land to carry out a wide variety of transactions as if he were the absolute owner. The transactions include "any sale, extinguishment of manorial incidents, exchange, assurance, grant, lease, surrender, reconveyance, release, reservation or other disposition, any purchase or other acquisition, any covenant, contract, or option and any application of capital money ... and any compromise or other dealing or arrangement ...".[63]   **15.18**

With the rider that the provision operates when the trust is of settled land,[64] this is a more flexible and much wider power than that offered under s.57(1) of the Trustee Act 1925. First, there is no requirement that the authorisation may only be of management and administrative actions. This was demonstrated in *Hambro v Duke of Marlborough* where variation of the beneficial interest of an adult beneficiary was proposed.[65] Section 64 merely requires that the transaction be for the benefit of either the settled land or the

[55] [1937] Ch. 431 at 436.
[56] *Mason v Farbrother* [1983] 2 All E.R. 1078.
[57] *Re Hope's WT* [1929] 2 Ch. 136. Three valuable family portraits were amongst the chattels concerned. Eve J. described the sale as, "beneficial to all parties interested, and indeed is almost unavoidable" (at 140).
[58] *Re Beale's ST* [1932] 2 Ch. 15. There the trustee in bankruptcy wished to sell, but the bankrupt refused his consent.
[59] *Re Shipwrecked Fishermen & Mariner's Benevolent Fund* [1959] Ch. 220.
[60] *Re Cockerell's ST* [1956] Ch. 372. The benefit sought here was the avoidance of death duties.
[61] *Re Thomas* [1930] 1 Ch. 194. This concerned the allocation (partition) of real and personal property held on trust amongst the beneficiaries.
[62] O.R. Marshall [1954] 17 M.L.R. 420 at p.425.
[63] Section 64(2).
[64] Accordingly, it has no application to a settlement of personalty or to trusts of land governed by the Trusts of Land and Appointment of Trustees Act 1996.
[65] [1994] Ch. 158.

persons interested under the settlement.[66] Secondly, under s.64 the court can vary beneficial interests in order to generate tax savings. In *Raikes v Lygon*,[67] Peter Gibson J. upheld the transfer of capital assets from one settlement to another in order to ensure the maintenance of a mansion house and its grounds. The key motivation behind the proposal was to mitigate foreseeable inheritance tax consequences. Nevertheless, this was a transaction within s.64 and the property which consisted of the settled land and those interested under the settlement were to be benefited. It was, moreover, a transaction that could have been effected by an absolute owner.

15.19   The types of transaction that are subject to s.64 are widely defined.[68] The section covers a conveyance by the tenant for life to trustees of a new settlement. This was demonstrated in *Hambro v Duke of Marlborough*[69] where the Duke (as tenant for life) and the trustees concluded that the Marquess of Blandford (the tenant in tail in remainder) was ill suited to managing the Blenheim Estates on the death of the Duke. This heir apparent displayed unbusinesslike habits and lack of responsibility. Against the wishes of the Marquess, they floated a scheme under which the estate would be transferred to trustees of a new trust. This redesigned trust would provide the Duke with the income for his life and, following his death, the estate would be held on protective trusts for the Marquess for life. Following the death of the Marquess, the estate was to be held on the trusts of the original settlement. Morrit J. held that this was a transaction within s.64 and this was so despite the opposition of the adult beneficiary. As Cooke comments, "The amusing point is that the 1925 legislation, which aimed to make land freely alienable, will be the means of keeping this estate intact for future generations".[70]

By way of a further example, in *Re Scarisbrick Resettlement Estates*[71] the sale of investments to raise £10,000 to facilitate the continued occupation of the tenant for life in a stately home (Scarisbrick Hall) and, thereby, assuring the preservation of the property was held to be a transaction for these purposes. As indicated, s.64 might also be employed to adjust existing beneficial interests in order to avoid tax liabilities, particularly those relating to inheritance tax.[72]

Section 24 of the Matrimonial Causes Act 1973

15.20   Section 24 of the Matrimonial Causes Act 1973 allows the High Court, when making an order of divorce or annulment of marriage, to make a property adjustment order.[73] This can operate to vary the trusts contained in any settlement that was made for the benefit of the parties to the marriage or the children of that marriage. This jurisdiction caters for the remoulding of beneficial interests.[74] In *Brooks v Brooks*,[75] a company pension

---

[66] If the land has been sold, s.64 has no application: see *Re Simmons* [1956] Ch. 125.
[67] [1988] 1 W.L.R. 281.
[68] See *Re Downshire's Settled Estates* [1953] Ch. 218.
[69] [1994] Ch. 158; noted at [1994] Conv. 492 (E. Cooke).
[70] [1994] Conv. 492 at p.495.
[71] [1944] Ch. 229.
[72] See *Raikes v Lygon* [1988] 1 W.L.R. 281.
[73] This applies also to registered same-sex partnerships under the Civil Partnership Act 2004.
[74] *Thomson v Thomson* [1956] P 384.
[75] [1996] 1 A.C. 375; noted at [1997] Conv. 52 (M. Thomas).

scheme of which the husband was the sole member was varied under s.24. Under the scheme, the husband had the power to surrender part of his pension so as to provide his wife with a deferred pension for life. On the company ceasing to trade, the pension fund was valued at £440,000. When looked at in the round, the House of Lords considered this to be a post-nuptial settlement that fell squarely within the statutory jurisdiction. The settlement was made after the marriage and contained the nuptial element of providing for the wife in her capacity as wife. Lord Nicholls explained, "The section gives the court power to vary a settlement. Inherent in this provision is the notion that the court's jurisdiction extends to all property comprised in the settlement. This includes any interest the settlor himself thenceforth may have in the settled property by virtue of his own settlement".[76] As Lord Nicholls further observed, "it is also implicit in the section that the court's power does not extend to property which is not part of the settled property".[77] This case, therefore, turned upon the fact that there was an express ability for the wife to benefit under the scheme and that there was only one member of that scheme. He cautioned that, "Not every pension scheme constitutes a marriage settlement".[78] The decision does not concern entitlement under the usual style of multi-member pension scheme. As regards this common type of pension scheme, so-called "pension splitting" on the breakdown of a marriage or same sex registered partnership is catered for by the Welfare Reform and Pensions Act 1999.

Section 16 of the Mental Capacity Act 2005

Section 16 of the Mental Capacity Act 2005 gives the Court of Protection the power to make a settlement of a patient's property. Section 16(7) allows the court to vary that settlement in such manner as it thinks fit in the best interests of the person (as defined in s.4) and with regard to the statutory principles listed in s.1. In *Re CWHT*,[79] the Court of Protection ordered that certain property of a patient be settled on trust. This gave the patient's sister a life interest with remainder for the patient's children and remoter issue. No power of revocation was reserved. Subsequently, the trust was varied during the lifetime of the patient so that the property was to be divided (i.e. a partition was effected) between tenant for life and the remaindermen.   **15.21**

THE VARIATION OF TRUSTS ACT 1958

As shown, the decision of the House of Lords in *Chapman v Chapman*[80] had the effect of narrowing the scope for the variation of trusts for the purposes of tax planning. It also left the law in an uncertain and unpalatable state. Indeed, Lord Simonds acknowledged that the way the law had developed might not be logical, but was not prepared to claim   **15.22**

---

[76] [1996] 1 A.C. 375 at 392.
[77] [1996] 1 A.C. 375 at 392, 393.
[78] [1996] 1 A.C. 375 at 396.
[79] [1978] Ch. 67. This concerned the equivalent provisions then contained in the Mental Health Act 1959.
[80] [1954] A.C. 429.

for the court, "a certain jurisdiction, merely because we think it ought to have it".[81] He continued, "It is for the legislature, which does not rest under that disability, to determine whether there should be a change in the law and what that change should be".[82] In response, during 1957 the Law Reform Committee was invited to consider whether the powers of the court to sanction variations of trusts should be widened. The Committee reported later in the year and unanimously recommended that the court should be given an extensive jurisdiction to authorise variations.[83] The Committee said of the *Chapman* decision that, "it has created distinctions between cases in which the trusts can be varied and cases in which they cannot be varied which have nothing to do with the merits of the proposed variations".[84] The recommendations of the Committee shortly afterwards became embodied in the Variation of Trusts Act 1958. The central ambition of the Committee was to restore the jurisdiction of the court to its pre-*Chapman* days. As it admitted, "In our view the only satisfactory solution of the problem is to give the Court the unlimited jurisdiction to sanction such changes which it in fact exercised in the years immediately preceding the decision in *Chapman v Chapman* ... Logically, there is no satisfactory stopping place short of an unlimited jurisdiction".[85]

The Committee rejected the view of Lord Morton that variation for tax purposes was analogous to an undignified game of chess between the court and the legislature. The Committee concluded that lawful tax avoidance was a legitimate strategy goal for the court to condone. Indeed, the majority of applications under the 1958 Act are framed so as to avoid tax that would arise if the existing provisions remained unaltered.[86]

The discretionary power

15.23   Section 1 of the Variation of Trusts Act 1958 confers on the court what Evershed M.R. in *Re Steed's WT* described as a, "very wide and, indeed, revolutionary discretion".[87] The court is afforded the discretionary power to approve "any arrangement (by whomsoever proposed, and whether or not there is any other person beneficially interested who is capable of assenting thereto) varying or revoking all or any of the trusts, or enlarging the powers of the trustees of managing or administering any of the property subject to the trusts". Section 1 makes clear that the discretion applies to trusts whether created by will or inter vivos and regardless of whether the subject matter is real or personal property. It is retrospective in effect and, therefore, operates in relation to trusts whenever established. It has also been accepted that the 1958 Act extends to property held on a bare trust, at least for a minor.[88] Accordingly, Lloyd J.

---

[81] [1954] A.C. 429 at 444.
[82] [1954] A.C. 429 at 444.
[83] "The Court's Power to Sanction Variation of Trusts" (1957) Cmnd 310.
[84] (1957) Cmnd 310 at para.9.
[85] (1957) Cmnd 310 at para.13.
[86] See, for example, *Re Clitheroe's ST* [1959] 3 All E.R. 789. In *Re Weston's Settlement* [1969] 1 Ch 223 Stamp L.J. explained that the court, "is not the watchdog of the Commissioners of Inland Revenue" (at 232).
[87] [1960] Ch. 407 at 420, 421.
[88] *CD (a minor) v O* [2004] 3 All E.R. 780.

concluded that the 1958 Act was not limited to where there is more than one beneficial interest.[89]

The 1958 Act does not affect the powers, already discussed, which the court already enjoyed under either its inherent jurisdiction or its pre-1958 statutory jurisdiction. As Mowbray put it, "The jurisdiction given by the new Act takes its place among other powers of the court to vary trusts. It differs from most of the other powers, however, in that it is a mere power to assent and (with few exceptions) no order made under the new Act can override the wishes of any beneficiary ascertained and capable of making up his own mind on the proposed variation".[90] In *CD (a minor) v O*,[91] it was emphasised that it is more appropriate that the court proceed under the 1958 Act if that is possible.

Any person interested can make an application, for example, a beneficiary, trustee or settlor. Nevertheless, the court can only approve an arrangement entered on behalf of the limited classes of beneficiary listed in s.1(1) (see **15.29**). Even then, with the exception of a discretionary beneficiary under a protective trust (i.e. a trust under which the beneficial interest is liable to be forfeited on the occurrence of some event), the court can only sanction the arrangement if it will work to the benefit of the person on whose behalf the application is made. Again apart from discretionary beneficiaries under a protective trust, the rule is that the court cannot agree on the behalf of ascertained beneficiaries who are *sui juris*. Hence, the court is unable to override any objection or the need for consent of such a beneficiary. The underlying design of s.1 is, therefore, to allow the court to approve arrangements on behalf of beneficiaries who cannot give consent themselves. Mummery L.J. considered that, "In relation to the members of the specified class who cannot act for themselves, the court is almost in the position of a 'statutory attorney' ...".[92] He appraised the 1958 Act as being, "a statutory expansion of the consent principle embodied in the rule in *Saunders v Vautier*".[93] Lord Reid explained in *Re Holmden's ST*:

15.24

> "The beneficiaries are not bound by the variations because the court has made the variation. Each beneficiary is bound because he has consented to the variation. If he was not of full age when the arrangement was made, he is bound because the court was authorised by the Act to approve of it on his behalf and did so by making an order. If he was of full age and did not in fact consent he is not affected by the order of the court and he is not bound. So the arrangement must be regarded as an arrangement made by the beneficiaries themselves. The court merely acted on behalf of or as representing those beneficiaries who were not in a position to give their own consent and approval".[94]

---

[89] This, however, contrasts with the observations of Eveleigh J. in *Allen v Distillers Company (Biochemicals) Ltd* [1974] QB 384.
[90] W.J. Mowbray, "Varying Trusts" [1958] 22 Conv. 373 at p.373.
[91] [2003] 3 All E.R. 780.
[92] *Goulding v James* [1997] 2 All E.R. 239 at 249.
[93] [1997] 2 All E.R. 239 at 247.
[94] [1968] A.C. 685 at 701.

Types of variation

15.25   The 1958 Act allows for administrative variations as well as variations affecting beneficial interests. It has been employed to authorise a wide range of changes. These include:

- the insertion of a power of advancement[95] and the modification of such a power;[96]

- the insertion of an accumulation period for income[97] and the termination of a trust for accumulation;[98]

- the widening of the investment powers of the trustees[99] and the substitution of one investment clause by another;[1]

- the addition of a clause which prevented the settlor or his wife from taking any benefit under a charitable trust and side stepped the potential tax liability of the settlor;[2]

- the variation of a settlement in which the applicant held a life interest[3] and the variation of a testamentary trust so as not to disadvantage the next generation of beneficiary;[4]

- the appointment of a Canadian Trust Corporation in place of the existing English trustees following the emigration of the beneficiaries under a marriage settlement;[5] and

- the enlargement of a protective life interest into a life interest free of the protective trusts.[6]

An arrangement?

15.26   The term "arrangement" was regarded by Lord Evershed M.R. in *Re Steed's WT* as, "deliberately used in the widest possible sense so as to cover any proposal which any person may put forward for varying or revoking the trusts".[7] Accordingly, Lord Evershed M.R. makes clear that the term is not limited to a scheme that is inter partes and worked out between two or more persons. Evans advances the following definition:

---

[95] *Re Lister's WT* [1962] 1 W.L.R. 1441.
[96] *CD (A Minor) v O* [2004] 3 All E.R. 780 where the application was intended to secure that, if necessary, the whole capital could be applied for advancement purposes.
[97] *Re Holt's Settlement* [1961] Ch. 100.
[98] *Re Tinker's Settlement* [1960] 1 W.L.R. 1011.
[99] *Re Coates' Trusts* [1959] 1 W.L.R. 375.
[1] *Re Byng's WT* [1959] 1 W.L.R. 379.
[2] *Re Robert's ST* (1959) The Times, February 27.
[3] *Re Oake's Settlement* [1959] 1 W.L.R. 502; *Ridgwell v Ridgwell* [2007] EWHC 2666 (Ch).
[4] *Re Cohen's WT* [1959] 1 W.L.R. 865.
[5] *Re Seale's Marriage Settlement* [1961] 3 W.L.R. 262.
[6] *Re Burney's ST* [1961] 1 W.L.R. 545.
[7] [1963] 3 All E.R. 759 at 762.

"an arrangement is any dealing with the trust property, or any disposition of the beneficial interests therein which are not sanctioned by nor contemplated in the trust instrument creating the trust".[8]

A major limitation has, however, emerged from the decision of Wilberforce J. in *Re Towler's ST*.[9] In this case, the arrangement emerged because of concerns by a mother over the financial recklessness and immaturity of a minor beneficiary. The proposal was to transfer the child's share of settled funds to trustees to hold on protective trusts for the child's lifetime with remainders over. The minor would otherwise have become absolutely entitled on reaching 21 years of age. The court refused to approve the arrangement as it would be tantamount to creating an entirely new trust and could not be viewed as a variation. Wilberforce J. explained, "the proposal goes much too far, because it is not confined to dealing in a beneficial way with the special requirements of this infant but seeks authorisation for a complete resettlement".[10] This was a sentiment later echoed by Megarry J. in *Re Ball's Settlement*:

> "If an arrangement changes the whole substratum of the trust, then it may well be that it cannot be regarded as merely varying that trust. But if an arrangement, while leaving the substratum, effectuates the purpose of the original trust by other means, it may still be possible to regard that arrangement as merely varying the original trusts, even though the means employed are wholly different and even though the form is completely changed".[11]

In the *Ball* case, Megarry J. felt able to approve an arrangement that preserved the general tenor of the existing trust even though the old trusts were remoulded by the disappearance of a life interest and the defining of the interests of the other beneficiaries. He added, "the differences between the old provisions and the new may, I think, fairly be said to lie in detail rather than in substance".[12] In *Re Towler's ST*, the court approved a revised arrangement under which the minor's right to capital should be deferred for a period, leaving her entitled to a life interest during the deferred period. It was a different and palatable way of achieving a broadly similar result.   **15.27**

On whose behalf?

It will be recalled that the 1958 Act empowers the court to approve arrangements on behalf of those beneficiaries who cannot give consent themselves. It does not operate as regards a beneficiary who is sui juris. It follows that, before an application is lodged, the consent of all adult and able beneficiaries should be obtained. Take, for example, a scenario where property is held on trust for Fiona and Jordan for life with remainder to Adrienne. Jordan is an infant. The trustees seek to divide the trust property so as to afford Adrienne a half share absolutely. The court can only approve the arrangement   **15.28**

---

[8] D.M.E. Evans, "The Variation of Trusts Act In Practice" [1963] 27 Conv. 6 at p.10.
[9] [1964] Ch. 158.
[10] [1964] Ch. 158 at 162.
[11] [1968] 2 All E.R. 438 at 442.
[12] [1968] 2 All E.R. 438 at 443.

on behalf of Jordan. The others (i.e. Fiona and Adrienne) will have to consent expressly to the remodelling of the beneficial interests. If either of the adult beneficiaries decline to consent, the general rule is that the arrangement will not be sanctioned or effective.[13] As Mowbray points out, "In this it differs from the court's other statutory powers, which are powers, if necessary, to override the wishes of some of the beneficiaries".[14] The fact that the arrangement if approved would override the wishes of the settlor is a consideration to be taken on board,[15] but it is merely one factor that can exert influence on the exercise of judicial discretion. Approving a variation that would defeat the testator's intentions, Pennycuick J. said in *Re Remnant's ST* that such intentions are, "a serious but by no means a conclusive consideration".[16]

In *Goulding v James*,[17] the testatrix, Mrs Froud, left her residuary estate on trust for her daughter, June, for life remainder to June's son, Marcus, provided that he attained the age of 40 years. If Marcus predeceased June (whether or not he reached 40 years of age) or died before reaching the stipulated age, Marcus' children living at his death would take the capital absolutely. The testatrix died in 1994, leaving an estate valued at £1.14 million. June and Marcus (who was still childless) applied to court for the approval of an arrangement which would recast the beneficial interests. The proposal was that June would have a 45 per cent interest, Marcus would have a 45 per cent interest and Marcus' as yet unborn children would have the remaining 10 per cent. This was demonstrated to be an improvement on the estimated value of the unborn children's contingent interests under the existing trust. The evidence also showed that the testatrix had never wanted June to get her hands on the capital. Nevertheless, the Court of Appeal approved the arrangement. Mummery L.J. recognised that the court must take care not to allow, "extrinsic evidence of the subjective wishes of Mrs Froud ... to outweigh considerations of objective and substantial benefit to the class on whose behalf the court is empowered to act".[18]

The four classes

15.29   There are four specified classes of beneficiary or potential beneficiary on whose behalf the arrangement may be made for the purposes of s.1. The first category includes any person having, directly or indirectly, a vested or contingent interest who by reason of infancy or other incapacity is incapable of assenting (s.1(1)(a)). This is a straightforward classification that embraces those too young to consent[19] and those of unsound mind who cannot consent.[20] Hence, a settlement made in favour of a beneficiary who becomes a mental patient can be varied under this paragraph as long as it is for his benefit.[21] By way of illustration, take the situation where property is held on trust for

---

[13] See the views of Buckley J. in *Re Suffert's Settlement* [1960] 3 All E.R. 561 at 563.
[14] W.J. Mowbray [1958] 22 Conv. 373 at p.375.
[15] *Re Steed's WT* [1960] Ch. 407.
[16] [1970] Ch. 560 at 567.
[17] [1997] 2 All E.R. 239; noted at [1997] 60 M.L.R. 719 (P. Luxton).
[18] [1997] 2 All E.R. 239 at 251.
[19] In *CD (a minor) v O* [2004] 3 All E.R. 780 the application was made on behalf of a 12-year-old girl.
[20] Section 1(6) states that this provision does not limit the powers of the Court of Protection.
[21] *Re CL* [1969] 1 Ch. 587.

Adrienne for life with remainder to Fiona. If either (or both) are infants or insane, para.(a) will then become engaged.

The second type of beneficiary is "any person unborn" (s.1(1)(c)). Such beneficiaries obviously cannot consent to a variation. A practical limitation was, however, imposed in *Re Pettifor's WT*[22] where it was held that it was unnecessary to seek approval on behalf of the unborn children of a 78-year-old woman. Pennycuick J. concluded, "It does not seem to me that protection against this impossible contingency is a matter which can properly be dealt with by way of variation of existing trusts".[23] He commented, "In the case of a woman in her seventies, not only would trustees be authorised to distribute a fund on that footing without any doubt or question, but the court would, I think, normally consider it an unnecessary waste of money to come to court and ask for leave so to distribute. Trustees can with complete safety and propriety deal with their funds on the basis that a woman of 70 will not have a further child".[24]

The third category includes any person[25] who has a discretionary interest under a protective trust[26] provided that the interest of the principal beneficiary (e.g. a life tenant) has not failed or determined (s.1(1)(d)). Put more simply, this caters for the variation of protective trusts. A protective trust is employed when the settlor wishes to protect property against an improvident beneficiary and/or the claims of his creditors. Traditionally, the settlor will give the beneficiary what is known as a "determinable life interest", which upon forfeiture is succeeded by a discretionary trust for a class of beneficiaries. Take, for example, a trust for "Fiona for life until she becomes bankrupt with remainder to be held on discretionary trusts for Jordan". Fiona has a determinable life interest, which will be forfeited on her becoming a bankrupt. Until that time, Jordan has a discretionary interest under a protective trust for the purposes of para.(d). The court may, for example, approve an arrangement on Jordan's behalf under which Fiona's protected life interest is enlarged to become an absolute life interest.[27] Alternatively, it might sanction an arrangement under which Fiona releases her life interest in favour of Jordan. It is irrelevant whether or not Jordan is an adult and, under para.(d), it does not matter that the arrangement might be to Jordan's disadvantage. As Danckwerts J. observed in *Re Turner's WT*, "the court may, if it likes, disregard the question whether any benefit is provided or not".[28]

Although there is no need to show benefit for the purposes of para.(d), it should not **15.30** be overlooked that the court's power is discretionary and the presence or absence of benefit may still play an important role. As Wilberforce J. commented in *Re Burney's ST*, "a specific and substantial benefit ... makes the arrangement as a whole appreciably more attractive of the court's discretionary approval".[29] The court must still consider the evidence and will require the applicant to make out a case to justify the variation of a protective trust. In *Re Baker's ST*, Ungoed-Thomas J. adjourned an

[22] [1966] Ch. 257.
[23] [1966] Ch. 257 at 260.
[24] [1966] Ch. 257 at 260.
[25] This includes unascertained or unborn persons: *Re Turner's WT* [1960] Ch. 122. Danckwerts J. admitted that the words 'any person' are "perfectly general" and embrace, "any person who might take under the provisions of a discretionary trust" (at 127).
[26] Defined by reference to s.33 of the Trustee Act 1925; see *Re Wallace's Settlements* [1968] 2 All E.R. 209.
[27] *Re Burney's ST* [1961] 1 W.L.R. 545.
[28] [1960] Ch. 122 at 127.
[29] [1961] 1 W.L.R. 545 at 550, 551.

application to convert a protected life interest into an absolute interest in both capital and income, stating, "evidence, including evidence of the financial position of the applicant and her husband, must be laid before the court to show to what extent the protective trusts continued to serve any useful purpose".[30]

The fourth and final categorisation is by far the most problematic. It is defined in s.1(1)(b) so as to include, "any person (whether ascertained or not) who may become entitled, directly or indirectly, to an interest under the trusts as being at a future date or on the happening of a future event a person of any specified description or a member of any specified class of persons ...". By way of a proviso, it goes on to exclude, "any person who would be of that description, or a member of that class, as the case may be, if the said date had fallen or the said event had happened at the date of the application to the court". This opaque provision does not lend itself well to ready interpretation and demands more detailed attention.

Deconstructing para.(b)

15.31 The allusion in s.1(1)(b) to the future ("who may become entitled") entails that those who already have an interest, whether vested or contingent, are outside the scope of para.(b). This was demonstrated in *Knocker v Youle*[31] where property was held on trust for the settlor's wife for life, with remainder to appointees under her will. In default of any such appointment, there was a gift over in favour of the settlor's son or, if the son was dead, to the settlor's four sisters living at the son's death or, if they were then dead, their issue who should reach 21 years of age. The settlor's wife and four sisters died prior to the application. Approval of an arrangement was sought on behalf of numerous individuals who were the issue of the four sisters. As some lived in Australia, it was thought to be impracticable to obtain each individual's consent. Warner J. was unable to sanction the arrangement because they already held contingent beneficial interests. The wording of para.(b) prevented the court giving its approval and the cousins' consent to the variation was necessary. As Warner J. concluded regretfully, "people in the position of cousins in this case have an interest that is extremely remote. None the less, it is an interest, and the distinction between an expectation and an interest is one which I do not think that I am entitled to blur".[32]

Among the classes that can fall within para.(b) are the prospective next of kin of a living person.[33] These persons do not enjoy even a contingent interest and, instead, have a mere hope of succeeding. As Buckley J. recognised in *Re Moncrieff's ST*,[34] such persons might become interested in the settlor's estate at a future date. This type of interest is sometimes referred to as a *spes successionis*. Similarly, the future spouse of an unmarried beneficiary may fall within para.(b).[35] Take, for example, where property is settled on Jordan for life with remainder to Jordan's wife, with remainders over. At a time when Jordan is an adult, but is unmarried, the court can approve an arrangement

---

[30] [1964] 1 W.L.R. 336 at 337.
[31] [1986] 2 All E.R. 914; noted at [1987] Conv. 144 (J.G. Riddall).
[32] [1986] 2 All E.R. 914 at 918.
[33] See *Re Suffert's Settlement* [1960] 3 All E.R. 561.
[34] *Re Moncrieff's ST* [1962] 1 W.L.R. 1344.
[35] *Re Clitheroe's ST* [1959] 3 All E.R. 789.

on behalf of his future unascertainable spouse. If it were otherwise no variation in that situation would be possible because the consent of an unknown future spouse is obviously impossible to obtain.

Matters are further complicated by the express and speculative exclusion in s.1(1)(b)   **15.32**
of any person who would be of that description or a member of the class if the future date/event had already occurred at the date of the application to the court. In *Re Suffert's Settlement*,[36] a 61-year old spinster was entitled to the income under a protective trust. After her death, the property was destined to go to her statutory next of kin (three cousins). She sought a variation under which a fund of £500 would be held on trust for her cousins with the remainder of the fund (some £8,300) to be held on trust for herself absolutely. One cousin consented to the application, but the others did not. She invited the court to approve the arrangement on behalf of the other two cousins as well as any unborn or unascertained persons who might become entitled. Buckley J. held that, while he could approve the variation on behalf of the unborn and the unascertainable, the court could not approve the arrangement on behalf of the two cousins. The cousins would have been entitled as next of kin had the tenant for life been dead at the date of the court application. The cousins had themselves to decide whether or not to consent.

In *Re Moncrieff's ST*,[37] property was assigned by the settlor, Mrs Parkin, to trustees to be held on trust for herself for life with remainder to such of her children as by deed or by will she should appoint. In default of appointment, the property was to be held on trust for her next of kin as if she died a widow and intestate. An application to court for approval of an arrangement was made by Mrs Parkin. At the date of the application, her next of kin was her adopted adult son, Alan. If he predeceased her, however, the next of kin would be her four infant cousins. The approval was sought on behalf of Alan and the cousins as persons who might "become entitled ... on the happening of a future event". On this occasion Buckley J. approved the arrangement on behalf of the cousins. Alan, however, fell outside para.(b) because of the proviso. He was the next of kin if at the date of the application Mrs Parkin was deceased. As to the cousins, "none of them would be within the class of next of kin if she died today".[38] Their interest depended not only upon the death of Mrs Parkin, but also on the demise of Alan. The arrangement could, therefore, become effective only with the consent of Alan.

Benefit

As mentioned earlier, with the exception of "discretionary beneficiaries" under pro-   **15.33**
tective trusts, the arrangement must be for the benefit of the persons on whose behalf approval is sought. Although the 1958 Act is silent on the matter, the court has adopted a broad view of what constitutes "benefit" for these purposes. Although most cases concern a financial (particularly tax) advantage, this is not the only factor that the courts will consider. As Megarry J. admitted in *Re Holt's Settlement*, "The word benefit

---

[36] [1960] 3 All E.R. 561
[37] [1962] 1 W.L.R. 1344.
[38] [1962] 1 W.L.R. 1344 at 1346.

... is ... plainly not confined to financial benefit, but may extend to moral or social benefit".[39] This theme was pursued also by Ungoed Thomas J. in *Re Van Gruisen's WT*:

> "The court is not merely concerned with this actuarial calculation ... The court is also concerned whether the arrangement as a whole, in all the circumstances, is such that it is proper to approve it. The court's concern involves, *inter alia*, a practical and business-like consideration of the arrangement, including the total amounts of the advantages which the various parties obtain and their bargaining strength".[40]

The court must, therefore, look at matters in the round and not focus unduly upon a balance sheet approach.[41] The prospect of financial gain is not always decisive nor, indeed, is it always necessary. Accordingly, the court will not sanction an arrangement, even though it might promise monetary savings, if it is not for the overall benefit of those on whose behalf the application is made. Financial advantage and benefit will, however, usually go hand in hand. As Lord Reid put it in *Re Holmden's* ST, "an arrangement which would avoid large payments of estate duty could hardly fail to be for the benefit of such an infant and potential beneficiaries".[42] Nevertheless, in *Re Weston's Settlements*,[43] the settlor sought approval of an arrangement under which property settled on his sons would be transferred from the existing English settlements to settlements based in the Channel Isles. The purpose was to avoid capital gains tax in the region of £163,000. Harman L.J. described the proposal as, "an essay in tax avoidance naked and unashamed".[44] The drawback was that the settlor's sons would have to take up residence in the Channel Isles. Even though they had already moved to Jersey some months earlier, the Court of Appeal held that the arrangement was not for the overall benefit of the children. As Lord Denning M.R. admitted, "There are many things in life more worthwhile than money. One of these things is to be brought up in this our England, which is still 'the envy of less happier lands'. I do not believe it is for the benefit of children to be uprooted from England and transported to another country simply to avoid tax ... Children are like trees: they grow stronger with firm roots".[45] Harman L.J. also voiced his concerns, "It seems to me unlikely that two wealthy young men of this sort will be content at the threshold of their lives to settle down in the island ...".[46] Accordingly, it was the judicially perceived welfare of the beneficiaries that was the important consideration. The decision of the Court of Appeal, as Harris observes, "is overtly based upon a rather surprising balancing of cash gains against non-cash losses".[47] In a more cynical vein, Baker ponders, "How is the court to know whether a

---

[39] [1968] 1 All E.R. 470 at 479.
[40] [1964] 1 All E.R. 843 at 844.
[41] See *Ridgwell v Ridgwell* [2007] EWHC 2666 (Ch) where the theoretical postponement of the children's interests was outweighed by the practical advantages associated with the tax savings to be made.
[42] [1968] A.C. 685 at 699.
[43] [1969] 1 Ch. 223; noted at [1969] 85 L.Q.R. 15 (P.V. Baker).
[44] [1969] 1 Ch. 223 at 246.
[45] [1969] 1 Ch. 223 at 245, 246. He commented, "I cannot help wondering how long these young people will stay in Jersey" (at 245).
[46] [1969] 1 Ch. 223 at 248.
[47] J.W. Harris [1969] 32 M.L.R. 320 at p.322.

person who has professed to go away for good has in reality only gone for a holiday at the expense of the revenue?"[48]

In *Re Seale's Marriage Settlement*,[49] however, the court felt able to approve the **15.34** exportation of an English trust to Quebec. Although this was to achieve tax advantages and involved child beneficiaries living in Canada, the court concluded that it was for their benefit. It avoided many administrative difficulties and financial disadvantages. The key influences were that the children already lived in Canada and had been brought up there by their parents.[50] It was a case of genuine and long standing emigration. As Lord Denning M.R. later commented in *Re Weston's Settlement*, "The family has emigrated to Canada many years before, with no thought of tax avoidance, and had brought up the children there as Canadians. It was very proper that the trust should be transferred to Canada".[51]

In *Re CL*,[52] the Court of Protection approved an arrangement on behalf of a 78-year-old widow who was a Mental Health Act patient. Under the arrangement the widow sacrificed her life interest, for no consideration, for the benefit of her daughters. The purpose was to reduce her estate's liability to tax, but there was no financial advantage to her personally. The benefit was a moral one. It appears that Cross J. was influenced by the fact that her income greatly exceeded her outgoings, that she was unlikely ever to be discharged from care and that this is what she would have wished for had she been of full mind.[53]

Albeit rare, it is also possible that the court might approve an arrangement that **15.35** operates to the financial disadvantage of the persons on behalf of whom it was sanctioned. Such was demonstrated in *Re Towler's ST*[54] where an application to postpone the vesting of a capital fund in a beneficiary was successful on the basis that the fund would otherwise be dealt with in a reckless fashion. It did not matter that the beneficiary would claim to be disadvantaged by the arrangement. In a like vein, in *Re Remnant's ST*[55] the High Court allowed the deletion of a forfeiture clause that was to operate on any of the beneficiaries becoming or marrying a Roman Catholic. Pennycuick J. acknowledged that this variation potentially worked to the financial disadvantage of the beneficiaries, but it was for their general benefit. He explained, "There are the non-financial considerations which seem to me to loom large in this matter" and added, "Obviously, a forfeiture provision of this kind might well cause very serious dissension between the families ...".[56] The usual rule of thumb, however, is that the court will not leave the beneficiary materially out of pocket as a result of the arrangement.[57]

---

[48] P.V. Baker [1969] 85 L.Q.R. 15 at p.16.
[49] [1961] 3 All E.R. 136.
[50] A similar approach was adopted in *Re Windeatt's WT* [1969] 2 All E.R. 324, as regards the exportation of a trust to Jersey where the beneficiaries had lived for 19 years.
[51] [1969] 1 Ch. 234 at 245.
[52] [1969] 1 Ch. 587.
[53] [1969] 1 Ch. 587 at 593.
[54] [1963] 3 All E.R. 759.
[55] [1970] Ch. 560; noted at [1971] 34 M.L.R. 96 (R.B.M. Cotterrell).
[56] [1970] Ch. 560 at 566.
[57] See *Ridgwell v Ridgwell* [2007] EWHC 2666 (Ch).

No benefit?

15.36   The general requirement that there must be a benefit has caused few applications to be unsuccessful. Even where there is the chance of disadvantage arising from foreseeable circumstances, the court will still be prepared to take the risk. In *CD (a minor) v O*,[58] for example, the court authorised the use of the whole trust fund for the purposes of advancement of a minor even though this might operate to accelerate her benefit and entail that the trust property never becomes vested in her. As Megarry J. explained in *Re Holt's Settlement*, "the court should be prepared to take a risk if the arrangement appears on the whole to be for their benefit".[59] This was, however, no new observation and had previously been made in *Re Cohen's WT*. In that case, Danckwerts J. admitted, "if it is a risk that an adult would be prepared to take, the court is prepared to take it on behalf of an infant".[60] The risk under the proposed arrangement there was that infants and unborn persons would benefit except in the unlikely scenario of one of the testator's three children predeceasing the testator's widow, who was aged 80 years. Indeed, writing extra-judicially, Megarry translated this as meaning that the arrangement must be shown, on a balance of probabilities, to be for the benefit of the person on whose behalf approval is requested.[61]

The risk should, moreover, be one that a prudent and well advised adult would be prepared to take. The exercise undertaken by the court is to weigh the benefits of the arrangement against the magnitude of the risk and the degree of potential loss. It might be that the arrangement will contain a provision requiring insurance against the unlikely prospect of loss arising. On this point, Megarry commented:

> "Only if the credit balance on such a reckoning is sufficiently great ought insurance to be dispensed with. Even so, it is suggested that the principle of insurance ought to be the rule rather than the exception. Certainly it seems improbable that the legislature envisaged the court as performing the function of a superior form of gambling expert, with the duty of certifying whether the odds are sufficiently good for infants and the unborn".[62]

15.37   It is, however, useful to consider a brace of cases in which the court felt that there was no benefit. In *Re Tinker's Settlement*,[63] the settlor gave property on trust for his son and daughter. If the son died before reaching 30 years of age, his share was to pass to the daughter for life with remainder to her children. The settlor applied to court to vary the trust so that, if the son died before reaching 30 years, his share would pass to the son's issue. The application was made on behalf of the unborn children of the daughter, but as the variation was entirely without benefit for those unborn it was destined to fail.

58 [2004] 3 All E.R. 780.
59 [1968] 1 All E.R. 470 at 480, where the arrangement was approved even though it might conceivably operate to the detriment of as yet unborn children.
60 [1959] 1 W.L.R. 865 at 868; noted at [1960] 76 L.Q.R. 22 (R.E. Megarry).
61 [1960] 76 L.Q.R. 22 at p.22.
62 [1960] 76 L.Q.R. 22 at p.23.
63 [1960] 1 W.L.R. 1011.

Russell J. observed, "I cannot think that I would be benefiting the daughter's children if I gave away half of that which they would come into if the son dies under 30".[64]

Similarly, in *Re Cohen's ST*[65] property was to be held on trust until the settlor's last surviving son died. At that point, the property was to be divided between the settlor's grandchildren and surviving issue of any deceased grandchild. By 1965, only one son survived. The son applied for the approval of a tax advantageous arrangement on behalf of unborn beneficiaries that would allow the trust fund to be distributed in June 1973. The application was rejected because it would operate to debar any issue of a grandchild born between June 1973 and the son's eventual death. The proposal, as Stamp J. acknowledged, "deprives him of any chance of taking ...".[66]

GUIDE TO FURTHER READING

O.R. Marshall, "Deviations from the Terms of a Trust" [1954] 17 M.L.R. 420.
O.R. Marshall, "The Scope of Section 53 of the Trustee Act 1925" [1957] 21 Conv. 448.
M. Mowbray, "Varying Trusts" [1958] 22 Conv. 373.

---

[64] [1960] 1 W.L.R. 1011 at 1013.
[65] [1965] 3 All E.R. 139. This is a different case and Cohen family from that previously considered.
[66] [1965] 3 All E.R. 139 at 141.

Chapter 16

SETTING TRUSTS ASIDE

Unless there is a power of revocation in the trust instrument, the general rule is that, **16.01** once a trust has been completely constituted, it cannot be revoked by the settlor or, indeed, by anyone else. Unless the settlor is also a trustee, the trust property moves outside his legal control. It is never to be forgotten that, in the eyes of equity, the true owners of the trust property are the beneficiaries. All general rules, however, must have their exceptions and so it is here. No trust that contravenes the law or undermines the principles of public policy will be upheld. In addition, so-called "sham trusts" and "illusory trusts" can be revoked. Similarly, a settlement may be set aside when such avoidance is catered for by statute. Parliamentary concern has focused upon trusts designed to put property unfairly beyond the reach of creditors, spouses and other members of the family. It is these three types of invalidating factor that will be examined in this chapter.

Although outside the scope of this chapter, it is to be appreciated that there exist other means by which a trust may be rendered void. These include, first, where the trust offends the rules against perpetuity and inalienabilty. These rules are considered in detail within Ch.4. Secondly, when the settlor was induced to make the settlement by reason of:

- Duress—duress comprises of any threat (usually physical or economic) that brings about a coercion of the will sufficient to vitiate consent. For example, in *Ayliffe v Murray*[1] a beneficiary executed a deed under duress. The deed was set aside because of the excessive pressure exerted on the beneficiary by his trustees.

- Mistake—in *Forshaw v Welsby*,[2] the settlor, during a period of illness, executed a deed of settlement that was not read to him and knew nothing of its contents. The court revoked the settlement on his recovery from illness. The mistake had tainted the very nature of the settlement.

---

[1] (1740) 2 Atk. 58.
[2] (1860) 30 Beav. 243.

- Misrepresentation—an illustration of this arises from *Re Glubb*.[3] There a charity innocently misrepresented to subscribers that it would be entitled to a substantial legacy if additional funds were donated to it. Unfortunately, the opportunity to obtain the legacy had passed and the court ordered that the charity return the sums obtained by its misrepresentation.

- Fraud—a settlement induced by the fraud of the beneficiary can be revoked by the settlor. Although fraud has proved elusive to exact definition, an example of where it operated to unravel a transaction is *Baker v Monk*.[4] There an infirm and illiterate woman executed a deed without understanding its nature. As she had been the victim of a fraud, the deed was set aside.

- Undue influence—this is to do with the application of improper pressure on an individual and is, therefore, wider than the concept of duress. The traditional approach is that a settlement of an improvident nature, which is entered into without independent legal advice and without a fully informed and free will, is liable to be avoided on the basis of undue influence.[5] The law relating to undue influence, and how it is to be proved, has been subject to major overhaul by the House of Lords in *Royal Bank of Scotland Plc v Etridge (No.2)*.[6]

Public Policy and Illegality

16.02   As previously indicated, a trust or gift that is regarded as being offensive to public policy or is otherwise unlawful will not be enforced.[7] Although it is outside the scope of this book to provide a comprehensive list of such events, it is possible to illustrate the role of public policy and illegality by considering the major examples of where trusts have failed or conditions struck out on this basis. As will become clear, in some cases the gift will be absolute and free from the condition while in others both the condition and the gift will be void. The outcome depends primarily upon whether the condition is a condition precedent or is a condition subsequent.[8] The former relates to a gift that is not to take effect until the condition occurs (e.g. a gift to X if she marries). The latter concerns a gift that vests at once, but is to be forfeited on the occurrence of some event (e.g. a gift to X on condition that she does not marry). A condition precedent that is illegal or against public policy will render the entire gift void. If it is a condition subsequent that is void, the gift will be valid freed from the condition attached.

[3] [1900] 1 Ch. 355.
[4] (1864) 33 Beav. 419.
[5] See *Allcard v Skinner* (1887) 36 Ch. D. 145.
[6] [2002] 2 A.C. 773.
[7] Perhaps surprisingly, the provisions contained in the Race Relations Act 1976 and the Sex Discrimination Act 1975 do not taint a discriminatory trust.
[8] See J.H.C. Morris (1947) 11 Conv. 218.

Trusts for illegitimate children

The traditional stance is that a trust to benefit a future illegitimate child is void.[9] The underlying notion is that such a trust is designed to encourage immorality. As regards a trust to benefit an embryonic or otherwise existing illegitimate child, the law takes a different approach and concludes that, as the immorality had already occurred, the trust is good.[10] In *Occleston v Fullalove*,[11] the testator left property for the benefit of his three illegitimate children. Two had been born at the date of the will and the other was *en ventre sa mere* (i.e. in an embryonic state). By a majority, the Court of Appeal upheld the trust as valid in relation to all three of the testator's offspring. There was no promotion of future immorality. The rule, therefore, applies to both inter vivos and testamentary trusts. Mellish L.J. explained:

16.03

> "If a man, at the commencement of an illicit intercourse with a particular woman could make a valid settlement on his expected illegitimate children, this would I think, manifestly encourage the immoral connection and discourage marriage, which the law favours ... Now if a will was so worded as to give a bequest to illegitimate children to be begotten after the death of the testator, I think it would be subject to the same objection as a settlement by deed".[12]

As regards settlements created after 1969, these are now governed by the Family Law Reform Act 1987 (as amended). This legislative intervention is based on the acceptance that, as Maugham J. put it "no useful purpose is served by penalizing illegitimate children, and that the true interests of public policy do not require innocent persons to be punished in that manner".[13] The Act, therefore, abolishes the iniquitous rule that a settlement benefiting an illegitimate child not in being is void. This about turn demonstrates that public policy is not set in stone and as Danckwerts L.J. acknowledged in *Nagle v Feilden*, "the law relating to public policy cannot remain immutable. It must change with the passage of time. The wind of change blows on it".[14]

Trusts in restraint of marriage

Trusts, conditions or gifts over that impose a general restraint of marriage are wholly void and this is so even when the total restraint is merely the *probable* outcome of the trusts or condition.[15] A trust to promote celibacy in an individual, therefore, will be void. This prohibition does not, however, apply to total restraints on second or subsequent marriages. In *Allen v Jackson*,[16] a condition in restraint of the second marriage

16.04

---

[9] *Medworth v Pope* (1859) 27 Beav. 71. This still applies to trusts made before January 1, 1970.
[10] *Ebbern v Fowler* [1909] 1 Ch. 578.
[11] (1874) 9 Ch. App. 147.
[12] (1874) 9 Ch. App. 147 at 171.
[13] *Re Hyde* [1932] 1 Ch. 95 at 98. His comment concerned the Legitimacy Act 1926.
[14] [1966] 1 All E.R. 689 at 696. The Court of Appeal was concerned with whether it was against public policy for a woman to hold a licence to train horses.
[15] *Lloyd v Lloyd* (1852) 2 Sim. (NS) 255. This is so whether the property is realty or personalty.
[16] (1875) 1 Ch. D. 399.

of the deceased's husband was held to be valid. James L.J. noted that this had long been the case with a provision that was designed to prevent a widow from remarrying and explained that this exception came about because her husband, "if she were a widow with children ... might think that his children would not be so well cared for and protected if his widow formed a second alliance and became the mother of a second family".[17] Nevertheless, he concluded that there was no justification for treating the second marriage of a man in a different manner, "The case before us seems to me to shew what immense mischief one would be doing if one were to introduce a different rule of law in the case of a widower to that in the case of a widow".[18]

A partial restraint of marriage does not, however, contravene notions of public policy. For example, a trust that prohibits the marriage to a particular person or class of person is not deemed to offend public policy.[19] In *Hodgson v Halford*,[20] a restriction as to religious faith (i.e. the interest would be forfeited if the children married a person not of the Jewish denomination) was upheld. A son who married a Christian, thereby, lost his share of the trust fund. Similarly, in *Jenner v Turner*[21] a disposition of land by a testatrix that was to be forfeited on her brother marrying anyone that was or had been a domestic servant was upheld. The brother married a former domestic servant and, thereby, sacrificed his interest in the property. As Bacon V.C. explained, "The condition is not in restraint of marriage generally, for it was open ... to choose a wife from the whole female world, except only that portion of it which comprises domestic servants".[22]

16.05   A trust or gift with a condition that requires a named party's consent to the marriage is also acceptable. In *Re Whiting's Settlement*,[23] a mother made it a condition subsequent of a trust that her daughter's interest was to be forfeited if she married without the mother's consent. On this event, the property was to go to the Police Relief Fund. The Court of Appeal regarded the clause as valid and this was so even though the refusal of consent would prohibit marriage as effectively as the imposition of any general restraint. As Vaughan Willimans L.J. acknowledged, "This branch of the law is one with which it is not very satisfactory to deal, and I cannot say that I think the mode in which it has been dealt with is very easy to weld into one consistent whole".[24]

It is also to be appreciated that a provision that the trust or gift is to exist only until marriage is perfectly valid. In *Re Lovell*,[25] a testator was living with his mistress who had been deserted by her husband. The testator bequeathed to her an annuity of £750 provided that she did not return to her husband, did not remarry and lived "a clean moral and respectable life". The bequest did not offend public policy because it was neither an inducement to maintain the separation from her husband nor operated to deter remarriage. It was designed instead to provide for her until such an eventuality occurred. Although at first sight curious, the long standing logic is that such a provision creates merely a determinable interest (i.e. a limitation) and is not construed as a

---

[17] (1875) 1 Ch. D. 399 at 403.
[18] (1875) 1 Ch. D. 399 at 403.
[19] e.g. not to marry an Irish woman.
[20] (1879) 11 Ch. D. 959.
[21] (1880) 16 Ch. D. 188.
[22] (1880) 16 Ch. D. 188 at 197.
[23] [1905] 1 Ch. 96.
[24] [1905] 1 Ch. 96 at 115.
[25] [1920] 1 Ch. 122.

bequest upon a condition that operates as a penalty on the event of marriage. Whereas the latter will be void, the former interest determines according to its terms and is unaffected by notions of unlawfulness. In other words, it is not against public policy to provide for someone prior to that person's marriage.

Conditions violating marital harmony

The approach of the court to the sanctity of marriage is encapsulated in the judgment of   **16.06**
Turner L.J. in *Hope v Hope* where he said:

> "There is nothing which the courts of this country have watched with more anxious jealousy, and I will venture to say, with more reasonable jealousy, than contracts which have for their object the disturbance of martial relations. The peace of families—the welfare of children, depends to an extent almost immeasurable, upon the undisturbed continuance of those relations . . .".[26]

In the scenario where a husband and wife have elected to separate and, subsequent to that decision, enter into a deed of separation the terms of that agreement will, however, remain valid.[27] The key factor is that the trust contained in the separation agreement does not encourage the separation, but instead is a consequence of the break down of the relationship. The separation has already been decided upon and is, thereby, viewed as inevitable. If the parties do not then separate, the trusts will be void as the condition underpinning them has failed.[28] This is to be distinguished from a trust that is established by a husband and wife, while living together, in contemplation of their future separation. As such a trust might generate a separation that would not otherwise occur, the trust will be void. In *Re Moore*,[29] for example, a provision for weekly maintenance made by a testator for his sister "during such time as she may live apart from her husband" was entirely void. As Bowen L.J. concluded, "There can be no question that the object of this gift was to promote separation, an object which is against the policy of the law . . .".[30] This was not an absolute gift subject to a void condition. Although she later separated from her husband, the funds were unavailable to her. As Bowen L.J. lamented, "One regrets taking away a dead man's bounty from the object of it under the very circumstances in which he intended her to have it, but we must not depart from the law".[31]

This rule does not apply to ante-nuptial settlements that deal with the aftermath of divorce. As Denning L.J. observed in *Egerton v Egerton*, "A settlement which contains provisions for what should happen in the event of divorce is not contrary to public policy".[32]

---

[26] (1857) 8 D. M. & G. 731 at 744.
[27] *Wilson v Wilson* (1848) 1 H.L. Cas. 538.
[28] *Bindley v Mulloney* (1869) L.R. 7 Eq. 343.
[29] (1888) 39 Ch. D. 116.
[30] (1888) 39 Ch. D. 116 at 131.
[31] (1888) 39 Ch. D. 116 at 132, 133.
[32] [1949] L.J.R. 1683 at 1684.

16.07   The effect of the provision has to be evaluated in each case. At one extreme, a condition attached to a legacy to a married woman that she should separate from her husband must necessarily be invalid.[33] In *Re Caborne*,[34] a testatrix left her residuary estate to her son subject to a proviso that reduced the gift so long as he remained married to his wife. The gift was to become absolute if the wife should predecease him or the marriage otherwise be ended. The condition was struck out as being against public policy. As Simonds J. admitted, "I re-assert the sanctity of the marriage bond and with it the importance of maintaining the integrity of family life, and, therefore, denounce and declare void a provision which is designed or tends to encourage an invasion of that sanctity".[35] Similarly, in *Re Johnson's WT*[36] the residue of the testator's estate (some £11,000) was left to his daughter for life. The problem was that the legacy was subject to a proviso that reduced her entitlement to a comparatively meagre £50 p.a. so long as she was married and living with her husband. She was to be entitled to the entire income on the termination of the marriage or on separation. The proviso was void and disregarded because it encouraged the breakdown of marriage. It was irrelevant that the testator had been concerned to protect his daughter against her untrustworthy and disliked husband. The proviso was, as Buckley J. concluded, "an incentive to the break-up of a marriage that the court will not assist in any way".[37] She was entitled to the gift without the strings that her father sought to attach.

By way of contrast, a trust to benefit a deserted wife so long as she remained abandoned by her husband was upheld in *Re Charleton*.[38] This did not encourage marital breakdown, but was instead designed to provide for the welfare of the wife because her husband had left. As shown, in *Re Lovell*[39] the object was not to induce the woman to maintain the separation from her husband, but to care for her until she returned or remarried. In a like vein, in *Re Hope Johnstone*[40] a trust set up by a husband in favour of a wife for as long as she lived with him, with a gift over to the husband if she ceased to live with him, was held valid. Of this provision, Kekewich J. observed, "That seems to be a provision rather in favour of morality than against it, rather to secure the continuance of cohabitation than to encourage a severance".[41] It was a limitation and not a gift defeasible by the performance or non-performance of a void condition. Hence, the wife, who was no longer cohabiting with her husband, was not entitled under the trust he had previously declared.

16.08   The key factor is whether or not the purpose of the gift is construed as encouraging divorce or separation. If the court discerns a different motive then the gift will be upheld. In *Re Thompson*,[42] the testator provided that his daughter would receive an annuity of £300 while she remained married to her present husband. The testator intensely disliked his son-in-law. If she became a widow, divorced or remarried, however, she would be entitled to the entire income of the estate. It was held that the

---

[33] *Wren v Bradley* (1848) 2 De. G. & Sm. 49.
[34] [1943] Ch. 224.
[35] [1943] Ch. 224 at 228.
[36] [1967] Ch. 387.
[37] [1967] Ch. 387 at 396.
[38] [1911] W.N. 54.
[39] [1920] 1 Ch. 122.
[40] [1904] 1 Ch. 470.
[41] [1904] 1 Ch. 470 at 478.
[42] [1939] 1 All E.R. 681.

provision was not contrary to public policy. The object was merely to prevent the money falling into the hands of the spendthrift husband. It was not to induce a separation.

Conditions undermining parental duties

If a trust contains a condition that is framed to separate a parent from a child, the condition will be void as it offends public policy.[43] As demonstrated in *Re Piper*,[44] this is regardless of whether the parents are still married. There a condition precedent was attached to a legacy that prevented children from living with their father. This non-residence condition was invalidated even though, at the time of the will, the parents had divorced. The gift, therefore, took effect without the offending provision. A further illustration of this invalidating tendency emerges from *Re Sandbrook*[45] where the testatrix left her estate on trust for her two grandchildren. It was a condition that, if one or both lived with their father, was in his custody, control or guardianship or under his direct influence, the interest should be forfeited. The condition was struck out on the basis of both uncertainty and public policy and the remainder of the gift upheld as valid. The condition, as Parker J. acknowledged:

> "is inserted in the will with the direct object of deterring the father of these two children from performing his parental duties with regard to them, because it makes their worldly welfare dependant upon his abstaining from doing what it is certainly his duty to do, namely, to bring his influence to bear and not give up his right to custody, the control and education of his children".[46]

16.09

Other cases decided upon this basis include *Re Morgan* where the bequest was to grandchildren on condition of them living with their mother if the parents separated.[47] The condition was dispensed with on the ground of public policy. A more indirect condition that was designed to prohibit an infant's residence abroad was invalidated in *Re Boulter* because, as the father was seeking employment overseas and the mother was a German national, it tended for the possible separation of child and parent.[48] Sargant J. explained, "It seems to me that the whole tendency of this provision is one which in many sets of circumstances ... might have a very prejudicial effect indeed on the position of the infants and upon the judgment that has to be exercised by their parents for their benefit".[49]

A more contentious gloss was applied in *Re Borwick* where a condition subsequent was imposed to the effect that a child beneficiary would forfeit his interest if he "be or become a Roman Catholic or not be openly and avowedly Protestant".[50] It was held

16.10

---

[43] *Re Sandbrook* [1912] 2 Ch. 471.
[44] [1946] 2 All E.R. 503.
[45] [1912] 2 Ch. 471.
[46] [1912] 2 Ch. 471 at 476.
[47] (1910) 26 T.L.R. 398.
[48] [1922] 1 Ch. 75.
[49] [1922] 1 Ch. 75 at 84.
[50] [1933] Ch. 657.

that this condition was void as it restrained and hampered their parents in the performance of their parental duties.[51] Bennett J. observed that, "The parents' duty is to be discharged solely with a view to the moral and spiritual welfare of their children, and ought not to be influenced by mercenary considerations affecting the infant's worldly welfare".[52] This strict approach has, however, been diluted by the House of Lords in *Blathwayt v Lord Cawley*.[53] There the House upheld a forfeiture clause which was to operate on a male descendant becoming a Roman Catholic. Lord Wilberforce emphasised that not every condition, which might affect or influence the child rearing process, will be void. He concluded, "To say that any condition which in any way might affect or influence the way in which a child is brought up, or in which parental duties are exercised [is invalid] seems to me to state far too wide a rule".[54] The House signalled that a condition as to religious persuasion is not void simply because it makes parents choose between the path of money or spirituality for their child. As Lord Wilberforce added, "After all, a choice between considerations of material prosperity and spiritual welfare has to be made by many parents for their children—and, one may add, by judges in infants' interests—and it would be cynical to assume that these cannot be conscientiously and rightly made".[55] Lord Fraser made the distinction that, "deterring a father from performing his parental duty and from exercising any control at all over his children seems to me quite different from influencing him to exercise his authority in a particular way, as the will in the present case might tend to do".[56]

Accordingly, the current state of the law appears to be that, while a condition that prevents a parent from carrying out his parental duty is void, a condition which merely influences the way in which that duty is performed remains valid.

NAME AND ARMS CLAUSES

16.11   Although a quaint and old-fashioned notion (they date back to at least 1787), it is possible that a name and arms clause may be inserted into a trust. This will usually operate to require the bride on marriage to "take, use and bear on all occasions" her maiden name and her family coat of arms. The courts have had to consider on a number of occasions whether such a clause is void as running contrary to public policy. No objection to such clauses emerged until post-World War II when, as Wilberforce J. observed, "From 1945 onwards a wind of change of increasing force developed against them".[57] Indeed, such a clause was, in *Re Fry*, held to be void on the grounds of public policy.[58] Vaisey J. was of the opinion that, "the use of different surnames by a man and his wife cannot fail to be productive of many embarrassments and inconveniences, not

---

[51] See also, *Re Tegg* [1936] 2 All E.R. 878 where a condition that a child was not to be sent to any Roman Catholic school for education was void because it fettered the parents' judgment as to what was in the best interests of the child.
[52] [1933] Ch. 657 at 666.
[53] [1975] 3 All E.R. 625.
[54] [1975] 3 All E.R. 625 at 637.
[55] [1975] 3 All E.R. 625 at 637.
[56] [1975] 3 All E.R. 625 at 649, 650.
[57] *Re Howard's WT* [1961] Ch. 507 at 516. In *Re Neeld* [1962] Ch 643, Upjohn L.J. observed that, "this wind was but a light, fickle and variable breeze" (at 680).
[58] [1945] Ch. 348; see also, *Re Kersey* [1952] W.N. 541.

only to themselves, their children and relatives, but to their friends and acquaintances, and indeed to society generally".[59] A different judicial approach was, however, adopted in *Re Howard's WT*.[60] There Wilberforce J. saw no policy justification for invalidating a name and arms clause which applied to men. In the light of previous authority, however, he did feel that a clause that was applicable to a married woman would still be against public policy.[61] This has subsequently been held to be an untenable distinction by the Court of Appeal in *Re Neeld*.[62] Hence, the name and arms clause no longer offends public policy.[63]

ILLEGALITY

The general rule is that the court will not come to assist anyone who seeks to enforce a   **16.12**
trust set up for an illegal purpose. In light of the traditional stance that private purpose trusts are void,[64] there are few examples of trusts avoided on this basis. Nevertheless, as Harman L.J. noted in *Re Pinion*, a trust to set up a school for prostitutes and pickpockets would necessarily be void.[65] Similarly, a trust to evade (as opposed to avoid) tax will be invalid.[66] The traditional response is that, as regards illegal purpose trusts, the court will not aid the beneficiary or assist a settlor that seeks to recover the property in issue. As Truro L.C. commented, "Those who violate the law must not apply to the law for protection".[67]

The primary example of an illegal purpose trust is to be derived from *Re Great Berlin Steamboat Co*.[68] In this case, an individual paid £1,000 into the company's bank account. The aim was to mislead others as to the credit worthiness of the company. In short, it was for a fraudulent purpose. Although it was agreed that the money was to be held on trust, the company spent some of it without the individual's consent. The company was later wound up and the individual sought to recover the remaining balance of some £99. The Court of Appeal declined to offer any assistance. Cotton L.J. reasoned, "He left the money at the bank as long as the possibility of carrying out the illegal purpose continued, and it is now too late for him to reclaim it".[69]

In 1999, the Law Commission published a Consultation Paper concerning the effect   **16.13**
of illegality on contracts and trusts.[70] The Commission identified the forms that an illegal trust might adopt. These are:

- a trust which it would be legally wrongful to create or to enforce;

---

[59] [1945] Ch. 348 at 354.
[60] [1961] Ch. 507.
[61] [1961] Ch. 507 at 523, 524.
[62] [1962] Ch. 643.
[63] See also *Blathwayt v Lord Cawley* [1975] 3 All E.R. 625.
[64] See Ch.6.
[65] [1965] Ch. 85 at 105.
[66] See *Sekhon v Alissa* [1989] 2 F.L.R. 94.
[67] *Benyon v Nettleeld* (1850) 3 Mac. & G. 94 at 102.
[68] (1884) 26 Ch. D. 616.
[69] (1884) 26 Ch. D. 616 at 620.
[70] *Illegal Transactions: The Effect of Illegality on Contracts and Trusts* (1999) Law Com. C.P. No. 154.

- a trust which is created in order to facilitate fraud or some other legal wrong or which arises as a consequence of an arrangement with such objectives in mind;

- a trust which is created in return for the commission of a legal wrong or the promise to commit a legal wrong;

- a trust which, whether expressly or by implication, requires the beneficiary to commit a legal wrong or is intended to do so; and

- a trust which is otherwise contrary to public policy at common law.

There are, however, qualifications to the general rule that the court will not come to the aid of a party to an illegal purpose trust. First, the illegality may be overlooked when the illegal purpose has not been performed and has been abandoned. The judicial logic appears to be that the court should come to the assistance of the frustrated fraudster because, if it did not, it would be tantamount to facilitating the fulfilment of the illegal purpose. In *Symes v Hughes*,[71] Mr Symes was in financial difficulties and transferred leasehold property to his trustee with a view to defeating his creditors. Some 30 months later, Mr Symes was adjudged bankrupt and he achieved an arrangement with his creditors whereby he would recover the leasehold property in order to discharge his debts. Mr Hughes, however, claimed to have had the leases assigned to him by the trustee and argued that the court should not come to the aid of Mr Symes because of the fraudulent purpose underpinning the trust. The Court of Appeal held that Mr Symes was entitled to have the leases reconveyed to him. Romilly M.R. explained:

> "where the purpose for which the assignment was given is not carried into execution, and nothing is done under it, the mere intention to effect an illegal object when the assignment was executed does not deprive the assignor of his right to recover the property from the assignee who has given no consideration for it ... it is clear in the present case that no harm has been done to any creditor, and, in fact, the suit is now being prosecuted for the purpose of enabling the creditors to recover something".[72]

The second qualification is where there is a genuine gift between the parties to an unlawful or immoral relationship. Such is illustrated by *Ayerst v Jenkins*[73] where a widower who, prior to participating in a ceremony of marriage with his deceased wife's sister, created a settlement of 26 shares in her favour. Ten years after the "groom's" death, his trustee sought to set the settlement aside on the basis that it was founded upon bad and illegal consideration. The problem was that, at that time, marriage to a deceased wife's sister was prohibited by Parliament and contrary to public policy. Selbourne L.C. refused to set aside the settlement, "the voluntary gift of part of his own property by one *particeps criminis* to another, is in itself neither fraudulent nor prohibited by law ...".[74] He drew the distinction between when there was (as here) a

---

[71] (1870) L.R. 9 Eq. 475.
[72] (1870) L.R. 9 Eq. 475 at 479.
[73] (1873) 16 Eq. 275.
[74] (1873) 16 Eq. 275 at 283.

voluntary gift which was valid and irrevocable and when there was a covenant or bond
for an illegal consideration which has no effect at law.

The third qualification is where the party claiming is not the fraudulent party, but is   **16.14**
claiming through him. For example, a creditor of a deceased settlor might be able to
recover the property that was settled by virtue of an illegal purpose trust.[75] As Eldon
L.C. noted in *Mucklestone v Brown*, "there is a great difference between the case of an
heir coming to be relieved against the act of his ancestor in fraud of the law and of a
man coming upon his own act under such circumstances".[76]

Finally, where only part of the trust is unlawful, and it is possible to determine the
amount of money attributable to the illegal element, the lawful part may still be
enforced.[77] If such financial segregation is not possible, however, the entire trust must
fail.[78]

SHAM AND ILLUSORY TRUSTS

A trust that at face value appears perfectly valid may be set aside if it is a sham trust or   **16.15**
an illusory trust. The court will look at the reality and substance of the purported
transaction. It will determine whether the settlor has given the false impression that a
trust has been created. The term "sham", as Diplock L.J. explained in *Snook v London
and West Riding Investments Ltd*, "means acts done or documents executed by the
parties to the 'sham' which are intended by them to give to third parties or to the court
the appearance of creating between the parties legal rights and obligations different
from the actual rights and obligations (if any) which the parties intend to create".[79]
Accordingly, if the settlor retained the full beneficial interest and did not pass any
interest in the property to the proclaimed beneficiaries, the "trust" is a mere fiction, i.e.
sham. It will give rise to no legal obligations or rights.[80]

In *Midland Bank Plc v Wyatt*,[81] for example, a settlor underwent the pretence of
declaring a trust in favour of his wife and daughters. This was a ploy to put the property
beyond the reach of the Bank. A similar approach was adopted by Munby J. in *Re W*,
"the court will not allow itself to be bamboozled by husbands who put their property in
the names of close relations in circumstances where, taking a realistic and fair view, it is
apparent that the recipient is a bare trustee and where the answer to the real question—
whose property is it?—is that it remains the husband's property."[82] It was held that the
trust was a sham and that the Bank could lay claim to the property.

---

[75] *Miles v Durnford* (1852) 2 De. G.M. & G. 641.
[76] (1801) 6 Ves. 52 at 68.
[77] *Re Vaughan* (1886) 33 Ch. D. 187, which concerned the severance of charitable objects from non-charitable objects in order to prevent the failure of the entire trust.
[78] *Re Porter* [1925] Ch. 746. This concerned a trust to maintain a Masonic temple which failed as it was a private purpose trust. Although there was provision for the balance to be used for charitable purposes, this could not be ascertained and, therefore, the entire trust failed.
[79] [1967] 1 All E.R. 518 at 528. Of course, there has to be demonstrated some proper basis for overturning the translation. As Munby J. put it in *A v A* [2007] EWHC 99 (Fam) at [17], "the court cannot grant relief merely because the ... arrangements appear to be artificial or even 'dodgy'."
[80] *Kali v Chawla* [2007] EWHC 2357 (Ch).
[81] [1995] 1 F.L.R. 697.
[82] [2000] 2 FLR 927 at 938.

Illusory trusts

16.16   A further exception to the rule that a constituted trust cannot be revoked takes the form of so-called "illusory trusts". Although properly to be viewed as a particular type of "sham trust", the illusory trust concerns the transfer of property to trustees merely as a convenient mode of paying the settlor's debts.[83] As Sheridan puts it, "The peculiar feature of this type of assignment is that, in general, the debtor is accorded a power of revocation although nothing is said about revocability in the trust instrument".[84] These assignments are also known as "deeds of arrangement". The transaction does not give rise to a real trust in that it passes no beneficial interest in the property to the creditors. The settlor, as Pepys M.R. admitted in *Bill v Cureton*,"proposes only a benefit to himself by the payment of his debts—his object is not to benefit his creditors".[85] Hence, the creditors have no right to complain as they are not injured by the revocation, have waived no right of action and are not executing parties to the deed of arrangement.

This is, however, to be contrasted with an arrangement that is, instead, designed to benefit the creditors. In this latter scenario, an irrevocable trust can be created if that accords with the settlor's intentions.[86] The difficulty for the court is to determine which side of the divide a particular transaction falls. The forensic approach adopted by the court is as described by Turner V.C. in *Smith v Hurst*:

> "the motive of the party executing the deed may have been either to benefit his creditors or to promote his own convenience; and the Court there has to examine into the circumstances for the purpose of ascertaining what was the true purpose of the deed; and this examination does not stop with the deed itself, but must be carried on to what has subsequently occurred, because the party who created the trust may, by his own conduct, or by the obligations which he has permitted his trustee to contract, have created an equity against himself".[87]

16.17   In relation to an illusory trust, as no beneficial interest passes the trustees hold the property on resulting trust for the settlor.[88] They are the settlor's agents and they are to apply the property according to his directions and for his benefit. The creditors, as Shadwell V.C. observed in *Garrard v Lord Lauderdale*, "are merely persons named there for the purpose of showing how the trust property under the voluntary deed shall be applied for the benefit of the volunteers".[89] The settlor, therefore, retains control and power and the creditors have no say in what happens to the property set aside.[90]

An example of where an illusory trust might be employed is to be found in *Cornthwaite v Frith*.[91] There the debtor was to spend some time abroad and found it convenient to set up an arrangement by which he would transfer property to his agents

---

[83] *Garrard v Lord Lauderdale* (1830) 3 Sim. 1.
[84] L.A. Sheridan, "Trusts for Paying Debts" [1957] Conv. 280 at p.280.
[85] (1835) 2 My. & K. 503 at 511.
[86] *Mackinnon v Stewart* (1850) 1 Sim. 76.
[87] (1852) 10 Hare 30 at 47.
[88] *Smith v Hurst* (1852) 10 Hare 30.
[89] (1830) 3 Sim. 1 at 12.
[90] *Ellis & Co v Cross* [1915] 2 K.B. 654.
[91] (1851) 4 De. G. & Sm. 552.

on the understanding that they would sell the property and discharge his debts from the proceeds of sale. Knight Bruce V.C. held that the creditors could make no direct claim against the property. The arrangement did not create a deed of trust in favour of the creditors. Instead, it created a general agency whereby his agent could discharge his debts. This entailed that the settlor was free to revoke or vary the agent's mandate and, indeed, could at any time call for the property to be transferred back to him.

A noteworthy feature is that an arrangement that starts out life in the guise of a **16.18** revocable, illusory trust might metamorphose into an irrevocable and enforceable trust in favour of the creditors.[92] This has occurred in the following examples. First, it occurs where the settlor provides that the arrangement is to take effect following his death.[93] The logic here is that, as it was only the settlor that could countermand the trustee's instructions, the arrangement has now become irrevocable. Accordingly, the deceased's next of kin cannot lay claim to this property. If the arrangement is, instead, to pay debts both during the lifetime and after the death of the settlor, it would appear that it becomes irrevocable only following the death of the debtor.[94]

A second illustration is where the creditor is a party to the deed of arrangement and executes the deed, the deed is irrevocable as against him. The creditor becomes a beneficiary and can call upon the trustee to account. As Cranworth V.C. explained, "A valid trust is created in his favour; and the relation between the debtor and trustee is no longer that of mere principal and agent".[95]

Thirdly, where the deed is communicated to any of the creditors,[96] and they assent **16.19** and act to their detriment in reliance upon the arrangement, the deed cannot be revoked as against those creditors. For example, in *Harland v Binks*[97] it was demonstrated that, if a creditor assented to a trust for the payment of a debt and indicated that he would rely on the trust and not the debt, the trust becomes irrevocable. The election is the requisite detrimental act. The assent may be expressed or be discerned from some act that amounts to acquiescence.[98] It is not necessary that the debtor knows of the creditor's assent or acquiescence.[99]

Fourthly, the conduct or language of the settlor may demonstrate the intention to create an enforceable trust. In *News Trustee v Hunting*,[1] a deed was executed two days before the bankruptcy of the transferor. The purpose was that the property could be used to raise money so as to remedy several breaches of trust committed by the transferor. The intention was to create a valid trust in favour of those from whom he

---

[92] Note, however, the additional restrictions imposed by the Deeds of Arrangement Act 1914 appertaining to the need to register most deeds of arrangement and to obtain the written consent of the majority of creditors in some circumstances.
[93] *Re Fitzgerald's ST* (1888) 37 Ch. D. 18.
[94] *Montefiore v Browne* (1858) 7 H.L. Cas. 241.
[95] *Mackinnon v Stewart* (1850) 1 Sim. 75 at 89, 90.
[96] The creditor need not see the deed and it suffices that its existence is made known to the creditor (e.g. in correspondence with the trustees): *Re Baber's Trusts* (1870) L.R. 10 Eq. 554.
[97] (1850) 15 Q.B. 713.
[98] *Field v Lord Donoughmore* (1841) 1 Dr. & War. 227.
[99] *Siggers v Evans* (1855) 5 El. & Bl. 367.
[1] [1897] 2 Q.B. 19.

had previously misappropriated money. It was to shield himself against criminal action as regards his breaches of trust. Put simply, there was nothing illusory about this trust.

TRUSTS TO DEFEAT CREDITORS

16.20   Since the innovation of the trust, settlors have attempted to employ the concept as a means of putting property beyond the grasp of potential creditors. The transfer of property to trustees on trust for named family members generally has the effect of negating the settlor's interest in those assets. Consequently, those assets will be shielded from the claims of the settlor's creditors. When the beneficiary is a close family member (e.g. the wife), it is the settlor who will usually retain the physical enjoyment of the property. The self-serving attitude that pervades such transactions is evident. It is, as Jessell M.R. summed up, "If I succeed in business, I make a fortune for myself. If I fail, I leave my creditors unpaid. They will bear the loss".[2] Not surprisingly, Parliament has taken steps to protect creditors from the consequences of this type of debt evasion. It has long done so by imposing restrictions upon the use of trusts for these purposes.[3] Outside such legislative restrictions, however, a trust can be employed effectively to sidestep a creditor's claims. Indeed, the use of offshore trusts (often situated in the Channel Isles) is usually to achieve the protection of assets against adverse claims, whether by a private creditor or the Inland Revenue.

The present law is to be found within the Insolvency Act 1986. This chapter will now examine the jurisdiction of the court to set aside transactions that are at an undervalue and operate unfairly to disadvantage creditors. Albeit governed by different statutory provisions and different rules, the court has a jurisdiction to do so where the transferor remains solvent or when he is subsequently adjudged bankrupt. These possibilities will be considered in turn.

Transactions defrauding creditors

16.21   Other than on the bankruptcy of the debtor, a transaction at an undervalue may only be set aside under the auspices of ss.423–425 of the 1986 Act. Under these latter provisions there is no need that the transferor be insolvent.[4] Although the provisions can be invoked by a trustee in bankruptcy or liquidator, the overwhelming majority of applications are made by individual creditors. There are three conditions underlying the s.423 jurisdiction:

- the transaction has to involve a significant undervalue;

---

[2] *Re Butterworth* (1882) 19 Ch. D. 588 at 598.
[3] The initial regulation was contained in the Statute of Elizabeth 1571.
[4] If the transferor is adjudged bankrupt before the s.423 application is made, leave of the court is required: see *Geoffrey v Torpy* [2007] EWHC 919 (Ch).

- the purpose of the transaction must be either to place assets beyond the reach of a person who is making, or may in future make, a claim against the transferor[5] or to prejudice in some other way the interests of such a person in relation to any present or future claim made against the transferor.[6] The evidential burden lies, of course, with the applicant and, despite the recommendation of the Cork Committee,[7] there is no evidential presumption available to assist the applicant. Nevertheless, as admitted in *Midland Bank Plc v Wyatt* by Deputy Judge Young, "the more hazardous the business being contemplated is, the more readily the court will be satisfied of the intention of the settlor or the transferor";[8] and

- the claimant must demonstrate that he is a victim of the transaction and this is adjudged as at the time of the application and not the transfer.[9] The victim will usually be a creditor of the transferor, but could, instead, be a non-creditor who is in litigation with the transferor[10] or who has a cause of action against the transferor.[11] Indeed, a person can be a victim even though as was not in the transferor's mind when the translation was entered.[12]

As mentioned, there is no requirement that a debt exists at the time of the transaction. For example, a wealthy individual might make a settlement in favour of his wife prior to embarking upon a high-risk venture with a view to putting the property beyond the claims of future creditors.[13] The transaction is clearly vulnerable to being set aside. There is, moreover, no time limit beyond which the transaction is immune for these purposes.[14] The attraction of the s.423 route is outlined by Keay:

"It is a trite point that creditors often do not fare well when distributions are made by bankruptcy trustees or liquidators out of the estates of insolvents. So any action, other than the initiation of formal insolvency proceedings, will usually be worth considering. One possible option that creditors might consider, if they are aware that a debtor ... has disposed of any assets improperly at an undervalue, is to seek relief under s.423 of the Insolvency Act 1986".[15]

---

[5] It is not necessary to show that the intention was to put assets beyond the reach of the particular s.423 applicant: *Jyske Bank (Gibraltar) Ltd v Spjeldnaes (No.2)* [1999] 2 BCLC 101.
[6] See *Midland Bank Plc v Wyatt* [1995] 1 F.L.R. 697 where the transfer was attempted so as to prevent the bank making future claims against the matrimonial home.
[7] The Insolvency Law Review Committee Report, "Insolvency Law and Practice" (1982) Cmnd 8558, para.1215.
[8] [1995] 1 F.L.R. 697 at 709.
[9] *Pinewood Joinery v Starelm Properties Ltd* [1994] 2 BCLC 412.
[10] *Pinewood Joinery v Starelm Properties Ltd* [1994] 2 BCLC 412.
[11] *Moon v Franklin* (1990) *The Independent*, June 22.
[12] *Sands v Clitheroe* [2006] B.P.I.R. 1000.
[13] See *Re Butterworth* (1882) 19 Ch. D. 588, where a successful baker went into business as a grocer which, it turned out, was ill suited to his abilities.
[14] The Limitation Act 1980 does, however, apply to s.423 actions: *Hill v Spread Trustee Co Ltd* [2007] 1 W.L.R. 2402; *Giles v Rhind* [2008] EWCA Civ 118.
[15] A. Keay, "Transactions Defrauding Creditors: The problem of Purpose under s.423 of the Insolvency Act" [2003] Conv. 272 at p.272.

What can the court do?

16.22   Once satisfied that the transaction meets the above stated requirements, the court may make such order it thinks fit from a range set out in ss.423(2) and 425 of the 1986 Act. The court will do its best to restore the status quo ante and to protect the interests of those who were prejudiced or are potentially prejudiced by the transaction. These orders include, but are not limited to:

- setting the transaction aside either in whole or in part;

- requiring any property transferred to be vested in any person, either absolutely or for the benefit of all the victims of the transaction;

- requiring any property representing the proceeds of sale of the property to be so vested; and

- requiring any person who has received benefits from the transferor to pay to any other person such sums as the court may direct.

And third parties?

16.23   To be effective, it is necessary that the powers of the court can be exercised against third parties. This is explicitly recognised in s.425(2) which states that an order made may affect the property of, or impose an obligation on, a third party whether or not that person was a party to the impugned transaction. Obviously, the immediate transferee is most at risk from the transaction being unravelled. As regards subsequent transferees, however, they are protected provided that the transaction was entered in good faith, for value and without notice of the circumstances which made s.423 applicable in the first place. The same defence is available to a person who has acquired a benefit under the impugned transaction.

Purpose and motive

16.24   There is no requirement that the transferor must act dishonestly[16] and a transaction can be impugned even if the transferor was following legal advice.[17] It is the purpose of entry into the transaction and not the agreement itself that is the central issue.[18] It is not even necessary that a s.423 purpose be the predominant motive underlying the transaction. As Evans-Lombe Q.C. noted, the provision would be frustrated, "if it were possible successfully to contend that if the owner was able to point to another purpose, such as the benefit of his family, friends or the advantage of his business associates, the

---

[16] *Midland Bank v Wyatt* [1995] 1 F.L.R. 696.
[17] See *Arbuthnot Leasing International Ltd v Havelet Leasing Ltd (No.2)* [1990] BCC 636.
[18] As was made clear in *Hill v Spread Trustee Co Ltd* [2007] 1 W.L.R. 2402, s.423 requires the person entering the transaction to have a particular purpose. It is not sufficient to show that the transaction has a particular result.

section could not be applied".[19] Accordingly, the fact that it was also his intention to benefit a third party does not prevent the operation of s.423. Arden L.J. developed this theme further in *IRC v Hashmi*:

> "it will often be the case that the motive to defeat creditors and the motive to secure family protection will co-exist in such a way that even the transferor himself may be unable to say what was uppermost in his mind ... for something to be a purpose it must be a real substantial purpose; it is not sufficient to quote something which is a by-product of the transaction under consideration, or to show it was that it was simply a result of it ... or an element which made no contribution of importance to the debtor's purpose of carrying out the transaction ... trivial purposes must be excluded".[20]

Hence, it is sufficient if the ambition of the transferor is to deprive creditors of speedy access to property that would otherwise be applicable for their benefit. In certain circumstances, the intention to put assets beyond the creditors' reach will readily be inferred by the court. As Schiemann L.J. put it in *Barclays Bank Plc v Eustice*, "when action by the creditor was clearly anticipated by the debtor and that these transfers were at an undervalue and that what remains in the hands of the debtor barely if at all covers the debt, there is in my judgment a strong prima facie case that the purpose of the transactions was to prejudice the interests of the creditor".[21] The court must make its determination, as Deputy Judge Evans-Lombe Q.C. observed in *Chohan v Saggar*, "bearing in mind the mischief against which the section ... is aimed".[22] Hence, in *Fagan v Papanicola*[23] the transfer was designed to avoid divorce proceedings and fell outside s.423.

What is an undervalue?

It is to be appreciated that a transaction entered for adequate consideration is not a **16.25** transaction at an undervalue and, thereby, falls outside the statutory machinery. In that scenario, it matters not that the transaction was actually designed to defeat creditors.

A transaction at an undervalue is defined in s.423(1) as being either a gift, a transaction in consideration of marriage[24] or a transaction for consideration which, in terms of money or money's worth, is "significantly less than" the equivalent value of the property transferred. In some cases, the task is straightforward. Obviously, this is particularly so with the gift and the marriage transactions. In *Moon v Franklin*,[25] for example, a husband, facing legal proceedings, made a substantial gift to his wife. The

---

[19] *Chohan v Saggar* [1992] B.C.C. 306 at 321.
[20] [2002] WTLR 1027 at 1035. It is, therefore, a substantial purpose test that is to be applied rather than the stricter dominant purpose test that courted favour in earlier times (see *Lloyds Bank Ltd v Marcan* [1973] 1 W.L.R. 1387).
[21] [1995] 1 W.L.R. 1238 at 1248.
[22] [1992] B.C.C. 306 at 321.
[23] Unreported November 20, 2008.
[24] Obviously this has no application to transactions by a body corporate.
[25] (1990) *The Independent*, June 22.

purpose was to prevent the property being affected by the outcome of the case. The court rejected an argument that the gift was an expression of gratitude for the services rendered by the wife and set aside the gift under s.423. The most difficulty lies with those cases when consideration is given and the court has to compare in monetary terms the value of the consideration provided by both parties.[26]

16.26   In *Re Kumar*[27] the wife agreed to take sole responsibility for the mortgage in return for acquiring her husband's share in the matrimonial home. Although she gave consideration for the transaction, Ferris J. calculated that the obligations undertaken were worth much less than the value of the husband's share. As the consideration she gave was significantly less than that given by her husband, the transaction was at an undervalue and set aside in favour of his creditors. This shows that, in assessing whether a transaction is at an undervalue, the court must view the transaction in its entirety.

A similar approach was adopted in *Agricultural Mortgage Corporation Plc v Woodward*.[28] There a farmer, whose farm was subject to a £700,000 mortgage, granted a tenancy to his wife at the full rental value (£37,250) in order to ensure that the mortgagee would be unable to take possession when he defaulted on the mortgage. The tenancy was set aside on the basis that the wife would obtain benefits under the transaction beyond those that she had paid for. Those benefits were that she would be able to retain her home, allowed to operate the family business free from the claims of the husband's creditors and in a position to hold the mortgagee to ransom. The latter arose because the tenancy reduced the value of the mortgagee's security by more that 50 per cent and offered her a high surrender value (or ransom value) if the mortgagee was to buy her out. As she had paid nothing for such additional benefits, the transaction was at an undervalue and the tenancy set aside.[29] Sir Christopher Slade concluded, "when the transactions are viewed as a whole, the benefits which the first defendant thereby conferred on her were significantly greater in value, far greater in value, in money or money's worth than the value of the consideration provided by her. To hold otherwise would seem to me to fly in the face of reality and common sense".[30]

Who may apply?

16.27   Section 424 lists the persons who may apply to court for an order under s.423. The rider is attached by s.424(2) that, regardless of which party makes the application, it is treated as being made on behalf of every victim of the transaction (i.e. it is a class action under which the actual applicant obtains no priority).[31] The persons who can make an application are:

---

[26] See *Williams v White* Unreported July 27, 2007 there Judge Behrens said by way of obiter that a shortfall of 4.09 per cent would not be significant.

[27] [1993] 1 W.L.R. 224.

[28] (1995) 70 P. & C.R. 53.

[29] In *Barclays Bank v Eustace* [1995] 1 W.L.R. 1238 the "ransom point" was decisive in showing that the transferee obtained more than was paid for when he took the tenancy of a farm.

[30] (1995) 70 P. & C.R. 53 at 64.

[31] *Dora v Simper* [2000] 2 BCLC 561.

- (where the debtor has been adjudged bankrupt or it is a company that is being wound up or as regards which an administration order is in force), the official receiver, the trustee of the bankrupt's estate, the liquidator, the administrator or, with leave of the court, a victim of the transaction;

- (where there exists a voluntary settlement (i.e. compromise) made between the debtor and his creditors), the supervisor of the voluntary agreement or any person who is a victim of the transaction; or

- in any other case, a victim of the transaction.

Additional provisions on bankruptcy

The Insolvency Act 1986 contains a number of further provisions that operate on the **16.28** bankruptcy of a debtor and which enable the court to set aside transactions made at an undervalue (s.339) or by way of preference (s.340). The basic aim is to facilitate the trustee in bankruptcy in recovering the bankrupt's property for the benefit of creditors. These provisions co-exist with those dealing with undervalue transactions independently of bankruptcy. As will become clear, the two sets of provisions are similar, but are not identical. The trustee in bankruptcy will, however, usually prefer this route rather than instituting proceedings under s.423 because there is no need to show intention to defeat a creditor by an undervalue transaction. As Miller comments of these provisions, "They are an integral part of the insolvency code which is directed at securing *pari passu* distribution amongst the insolvent's creditors. They apply only to transactions within a limited period before insolvency and the intention of the insolvent is irrelevant. The rationale of s.423 . . . is quite different being directed at improper, if not dishonest, conduct by a debtor vis-à-vis a creditor or creditors".[32]

The orders that can be made resemble those available under ss.423, 425 (see **16.22**) and the overarching goal is the same, that is, to restore the position to what it would have been had the transaction not taken place.[33] The treatment of third parties is similar, that is, no order can be made against a bona fide purchaser for value without notice (see **16.23**).[34] There are, however, some differences between s.423 and the bankruptcy provisions. First, these provisions operate subsequent to the bankruptcy of the transferor. Secondly, they only allow an application to court by the trustee of the bankrupt's estate. Thirdly, they may only invalidate transactions that were entered into within specified periods prior to bankruptcy (this is known as the "relevant time"). Fourthly, and as mentioned above, in relation to an undervalue transaction there is no reference to any intention to be held by the transferor. Finally, whereas s.423(2) allows the court to protect the interests of persons who are victims of the transaction, there is no equivalent provision in s.339.

---

[32] G. Miller, "Transactions Prejudicing Creditors" [1998] Conv. 362 at pp.363 and 364.
[33] Section 342.
[34] Section 342(2).

Undervalue and creditor's preference

16.29   The meaning of "undervalue" is as considered above (see **16.25**). This entails, for example, that a trustee in bankruptcy of the husband may claim the wife's share in the matrimonial home to the extent that she did not contribute towards its purchase.[35] The 1986 Act also caters for a property adjustment order made in divorce proceedings to be overturned by one party's trustee in bankruptcy.[36] In *Re MC Bacon Ltd*,[37] the company granted a debenture in favour of its bank to secure an overdraft facility. Millett J. refused to classify this as an undervalue transaction because the granting of the debenture was not a gift and, in any event, did not involve the company suffering any loss or parting with something of value. He noted, "That gives the game away. The applicant's real complaint is not that the company entered into the transaction at an undervalue but that it entered into it at all".[38]

A "preference" arises where the debtor places one of his creditors or a guarantor in a more favorable position, should the debtor's bankruptcy ensue, than would otherwise have been the case. Accordingly, it strikes at a transaction that improves the position of one creditor above those of others. Section 340 allows the court to make any order as it thinks fit for restoring the position to what it was prior to the preference. It is a pre-condition that the debtor was influenced in deciding to give the preference by a desire to better the creditor's position in the event of the debtor's bankruptcy. It has been decided that, if the preferential transaction is entered into because of economic necessity, it is not to be regarded as being influenced by a desire to give the creditor a preference.[39] The requisite influence will, however, be presumed, unless the contrary is shown, where the preference is given to an "associate". For these purposes an "associate" includes family members, partners, employers, employees and related companies.[40]

Timing of the transaction: undervalue cases

16.30   As regards a transaction (including a preference) made at an undervalue, s.341 prescribes a two-tier time limit. First, it provides that the standard period is two years, which put simply means that, if a bankruptcy petition is presented within two years of an undervalue transaction, an order can be made in respect of it.

Secondly, an increased period of five years applies where the debtor was insolvent at the time of the transaction. For these purposes, "insolvency" is defined in s.341 as meaning either that the debtor is unable to pay his debts as they fall due or that the value of his assets is less than the amount of his existing liabilities. As regards the latter calculation regard must be had to the debtor's possible and prospective liabilities. As

---

[35] *Re Densham* [1975] 1 W.L.R. 1519.
[36] Sch.14; see *Re Flint* [1993] Ch. 319.
[37] [1990] BCLC 324.
[38] [1990] BCLC 324 at 340.
[39] *Re MC Bacon Ltd* [1990] BCLC 324.
[40] Section 435.

regards an undervalue transaction with an associate (see above), it is a rebuttable presumption that the debtor was insolvent at the time of the transaction.

Timing of the transaction: giving a preference

In relation to a preference, different time limits apply. The standard period afforded by s.341 is six months. Accordingly, the general rule is that the court can make an order concerning a preference (which is not also at an undervalue) given within the six months preceding the bankruptcy petition. This rule gives way when it can be shown that the individual was solvent at the time without taking into account the property included in the preference.   **16.31**

If the preference is given to an associate, the court can make an order relating to a preference given in the two years preceding the bankruptcy petition unless the individual was (discounting the property included in the preference) solvent at the time.

Transactions by companies

The above provisions, which operate on bankruptcy, extend only to transactions by individuals. Similar provisions that apply to transactions by bodies corporate are to be found in ss.238 and 239 of the Insolvency Act 1986. There are, however, differences between the two sets of rules and these will now be considered.   **16.32**

As to undervalue transactions, s.238 limits the ability of the court to make an order. It states that no order will be made when the court is satisfied that the company entered into the transaction in good faith for the purpose of carrying out its business and, at the time, there were reasonable grounds for believing that the company would be benefited by the transaction.[41] In addition, a transaction may be set aside only if the company was unable to discharge its debts at the time of the transaction or became unable to do so as a consequence of the transaction. The time requirement here is that the transaction must have been entered with a period of two years prior to the insolvency of the company.

In relation to transactions by way of preference, under s.239 the general rule is that the preference must have been given within six months prior to the insolvency, but this period is enlarged to two years if the preference was given to a party connected with the company. As with transactions at an undervalue, the transaction will be unravelled only if the company was unable to pay its debts at the time it was entered or ceased to be able to do so because of the transaction.   **16.33**

---

[41] See *Clements v Henry Hadaway Organisation Ltd* [2007] EWHC 2953 (Ch).

FAMILY CLAIMS

16.34   In the same way as a debtor might seek to transfer property in order to put it beyond the reach of creditors, it is possible that a transaction is designed to place property outside the grasp of a spouse or other dependant. Statutory restrictions have, not surprisingly, been imposed on the ability of a transferor to avoid maintenance and to sterilise his estate against claims for financial provision. Two incursions upon the freedom of a property owner to deal with property are to be found in the Matrimonial Causes Act 1973 and the Inheritance (Provision for Family and Dependants) Act 1975. The former, as the name suggests, applies to claims made in the course of matrimonial proceedings. The latter concerns the rights of dependants upon the death of the person who provided for them.

Section 37 of the Matrimonial Causes Act 1973

16.35   Section 37 protects one spouse (including a former spouse) against dealings by the other that may deplete the assets available for the funding of financial relief under the 1973 Act.[42] As Purchas L.J. acknowledged in *Kemmis v Kemmis*, "The clear purpose of s.37 is to give a power to the court to prevent a party acting to diminish the assets of the family which would otherwise be available for consideration by the court when making orders for financial relief".[43] If the transaction has not yet been made, the court can prevent it taking place. This is so even if the property is situated abroad. In *Hamlin v Hamlin*, for example, the property was a villa in Spain.[44] If the transaction has occurred, the transaction is classified as a "reviewable disposition" and may be set aside by the court.

There are several qualifications to the operation of s.37. First, an application under s.37 can be made only after proceedings for financial relief have been commenced. Nevertheless, it can catch transactions that were made at an earlier date.

16.36   Secondly, the court may intervene when one spouse is to make or has made a transfer or other disposition (e.g. the declaration of a trust)[45] with the subjective intention of reducing the capital source from which financial relief can be awarded. The requisite intention will be presumed when the transaction occurs within three years preceding the application for financial relief. It is then up to the transferor to rebut this evidential presumption.[46] Outside the three-year period, however, the applicant must prove affirmatively that this was the other spouse's subjective intention. In *Kemmis v Kemmis*, Purchas L.J. observed that, although there is no limit as to the retrospective effect of s.37, the task of showing the necessary intention, "will become increasingly difficult with the passage of time".[47]

Thirdly, s.37(4) offers a defence to a third party caught in the cross fire between

[42] This also applies to same sex registered partnerships under the Civil Partnership Act 2004.
[43] [1988] 1 W.L.R. 1307 at 1315. There the issue was whether the husband had procured a mortgage over the matrimonial home with the intention of defeating the wife's claim for financial relief.
[44] [1985] 2 All E.R. 1037.
[45] Section 37(6) of the 1973 Act.
[46] See *Shipman v Shipman* [1991] 1 F.L.R. 250.
[47] [1988] 1 W.L.R. 1307 at 1315.

husband and wife.[48] This provides that a transaction cannot be set aside when made for valuable consideration (other than marriage) to a bona fide purchaser without notice of any intention to defeat the matrimonial claim. For these purposes the concept of "notice" embraces the actual, constructive and imputed varieties.[49] In *Green v Green*[50] the husband and wife sold part of the grounds of their matrimonial home to a company which, in turn, charged the land to a bank as security for certain advances. She received no part of the proceeds of sale. The marriage broke down and the wife sought financial relief. She applied to have the transfer to the company set aside under s.37. As the bank had no notice of the husband's intention, the court refused to set aside the transaction and to deprive the bank of its statutory defence. By way of contrast, in *Sherry v Sherry*[51] a friend of the husband bought several properties at an undervalue. The purchaser knew that the couple were experiencing marital difficulties and that the husband feared that the wife would lay claim to his property. The purchaser was held to have constructive notice of the husband's intention and could not, therefore, rely upon the s.37(4) defence.[52] The moral of this case is that a third party, who is aware of the matrimonial difficulties between husband and wife, should make full enquiries of the other spouse before dealing with the selling spouse.

The Inheritance (Provision for Family and Dependants) Act 1975

In order to ensure that a surviving spouse or same sex registered partner and/or surviving dependants are provided for, the 1975 Act gives the court a broad, discretionary jurisdiction to make an award to an applicant.[53] Section 2 empowers the court to allocate part of the deceased's estate to make reasonable financial provision for a surviving spouse or same sex registered partner, former spouse or same sex registered partner who has not remarried or entered into a new registered partnership,[54] cohabitant,[55] child and other person who was, at the time of the death, maintained wholly or partly by the deceased.[56] The court is directed by s.3 to a number of factors which it must take into account. These include the present and future financial resources and needs of the applicant; any obligations and responsibilities which the deceased owed to the applicant; the size and nature of the estate; the conduct of the parties and any physical and mental disability of the applicant. The order will override the provisions of the will or the operation of the intestacy rules. Oliver J. described the approach that the court should adopt, "so these matters have to be considered at two stages—first in

16.37

---

[48] See J. Fortin, "Can She Avoid His Diverting Ploys" [1989] Conv. 204.

[49] *Kemmis v Kemmis* [1998] 1 W.L.R. 1307.

[50] [1981] 1 All E.R. 97.

[51] (1991) 1 F.L.R. 307.

[52] See J. Fortin, "The Diversions of a Fugitive Husband" [1991] Conv. 370.

[53] See generally, C. Sachs [1985] Conv. 258; [1990] Conv. 45.

[54] This is qualified by s.15 (as amended) which allows the court to order in "clean break" matrimonial proceedings that a spouse shall not make a claim on the death of the other spouse. This also applies to same sex registered partnerships.

[55] Provided that they have lived in the same household for the two years preceding death, the cohabitant does not have to show dependency: s.1 of the Law Reform (Succession) Act 1995; see *Baynes v Hedger* [2008] EWHC 1587 (Ch).

[56] As to the meaning of "dependency" see S. Bridge, "Money for Nothing? Family Provision in Dire Straits" (1991) C.L.J. 42.

determining the reasonableness of such provision (if any) as has been made by the deceased for the applicant's maintenance and, secondly, in determining the extent to which the court should exercise its powers under the Act if, but only if, it is satisfied that reasonable provision for the applicant's maintenance has not been made".[57]

Sections 10 and 11 of the 1975 Act cater for the possibility that the deceased may have given away property prior to death with the intention of not providing for his spouse (or registered partner) and dependants. The Act puts in place anti-avoidance machinery by giving the court the power to require the donee to make available a sum of money up to, but not in excess of, the value of the gift received. Except as to cash, the valuation is at the date of the death of the donor. This power, however, arises only when the gift was made within six years before the donor's death and was made with the intention of defeating an application for financial provision under the 1975 Act.[58] This intention, which need not be the donor's sole or dominant motive, must be demonstrated before the statutory machinery can be employed.[59] In *Re Dawkins*,[60] a husband left his entire estate to his daughter. Indeed, he had transferred the matrimonial home to her for £100 during his lifetime. His widow made a successful claim under the 1975 Act. As Bush J. concluded, when the deceased transferred to house to his daughter, "he did so with the intention, though not necessarily the sole intention, of preventing an order for financial provision being made under the Act, or reducing the amount of the provision which might otherwise have been granted...".[61]

Guide to Further Reading

J. Fortin, "Can she Avoid his Diverting Ploys" [1989] Conv. 204.

J. Fortin, "The Diversions of a Fugitive Husband" [1991] Conv. 370.

A. Keay, "Transactions Defrauding Creditors: The Problem of Purpose under s.423 of the Insolvency Act" [2003] Conv. 272.

G. Miller, "Transactions Prejudicing Creditors" [1998] Conv. 362.

L.A. Sheridan, "Trusts for Paying Debts" (1957) 21 Conv. 280.

---

[57] *Re Coventry* [1980] 1 Ch. 461 at 469; affirmed on appeal [1980] 1 Ch. 478.
[58] Section 10(2).
[59] Section 12.
[60] [1986] 2 F.L.R. 360.
[61] [1986] 2 F.L.R. 360 at 366.

Chapter 17

Breach of Trust and Associated Remedies

Breach of Trust

As considered in Ch.13, a trustee assumes a range of duties and responsibilities, breach **17.01** of which exposes him to liability in an action by the beneficiary. This chapter focuses on possible breaches of duty and the range of remedies that a beneficiary may pursue of both a personal and proprietary nature. Analysis of the case law on breach of trust will produce many examples of breach in a variety of different circumstances. It is difficult, therefore, to lay down any exhaustive list of possible breaches that will give rise to trustee liability. Confronted with this difficulty in *Armitage v Nurse*, Millett L.J. explained:

> "Breaches of trust are of many different kinds. A breach of trust may be deliberate or inadvertent; it may consist of an actual misappropriation or misapplication of the trust property or merely of an investment or other dealing which is outside the trustees' powers; it may consist of a failure to carry out a positive obligation of the trustees or merely of a want of skill and care on their part in the management of the trust property; it may be injurious to the interests of the beneficiaries or be actually to their benefit".[1]

A trustee who commits a breach of trust is obliged to restore to the trust estate the assets that have been lost in breach.[2] Where this is not possible, (e.g. where an asset has been misapplied or falls into the hands of a bona fide purchaser) the liability of the trustee extends to the restorative payment of sufficient sums to the value of the

---

[1] [1997] 3 W.L.R. 1046 at 1053.
[2] Historically, the Courts of Equity did not award damages, but instead ordered the defaulting trustee to restore the trust estate: see *Nocton v Lord Ashburton* [1914] A.C. 932.

misapplied assets. Alternatively, a beneficiary may seek recompense for loss caused by the failure of a trustee to perform his duties with requisite care and skill. The question arises in any given case as to the availability of what is termed "equitable compensation".[3] As will become clear, categorisation of breach assumes importance in determining the applicable remedy.

An introduction to trustee liability

17.02   Generally, a trustee is liable for his own breach of trust and not for the breach of his co-trustees.[4] He may not, however, stand by and watch a breach of trust be committed or, without question or inquiry, leave the carrying out of duties in the hands of a co-trustee.[5] The nature of this liability is compensatory, i.e. to make good any loss to the trust.[6] Logically, no liability is incurred for breaches occurring prior to appointment to the position of trustee.[7] On appointment, however, a trustee should familiarise himself with the terms of the trust and ensure that trust property has been vested in him appropriately.[8] Should he become aware of a pre-existing breach, the new trustee is obliged to begin proceedings against its perpetrators unless there are grounds to suggest that such action would be useless or wasteful.[9] In the absence of knowledge or reason to suspect that a breach of trust has occurred, a newly appointed trustee is entitled to assume that no breach has, in fact, taken place.[10] A retiring trustee will remain liable for breaches committed by him during his term in office. Liability may be released be those trustees who continue to act or by beneficiaries. At all times, a trustee must be mindful of his responsibilities to the trust. As Kekewich J. detailed in *Head v Gould*:

> "It is the duty of trustees to protect the funds intrusted to their care, and to distribute those funds themselves or hand them over to their successors intact, that is, properly invested and without diminution, according to the terms of the mandate contained in the instrument of trust. This duty is imposed on them as long as they remain trustees and must be their guide in every act done by them as trustees. On retiring from the trust and passing on the trust estate to their successors . . . they are acting as trustees, and it is equally incumbent on them in this ultimate act of office to fulfil the duty imposed on them as at any other time. If therefore they neglect that duty and part with the property without due regard to it, they remain

---

[3]   See S.B. Elliott, J. Edelman, "Money Remedies Against Trustees" (2004) 18 Tru. L. I. 116, for a breakdown of compensation claims into substitutive performance claims (i.e. claim for a money payment as a substitute for performance of trustees' obligations to deliver trust assets *in specie*) and reparation claims (i.e. claims for a money payment to make good the damage caused by a breach of trust). This categorisation is accepted in Hayton and Marshall at p.707.

[4]   *Townley v Sherbourne* (1643) Bridg. 35.

[5]   *Bahin v Hughes* (1886) 31 Ch. D. 390.

[6]   "The trustee is liable to place the trust estate in the same position it would have been in if no breach had been committed" (*Re Dawson* [1966] 2 NSWLR 211 at 215).

[7]   *Re Strahan* (1856) 8 De. G. M. & G. 291.

[8]   *Re Forest of Dean Coal Co* [1878] 10 Ch. D. 450.

[9]   For example, where a trustee cannot be traced: see *Re Forest of Dean Coal Co* [1878] 10 Ch. D. 450.

[10]   *Re Strahan* (1856) 8 De. G. M. & G. 291.

liable and will be held by the Court responsible for the consequences properly traceable to that neglect".[11]

Liability for breaches committed subsequent to retirement will be rare, but will arise where the retirement itself was geared or motivated to facilitate a breach of trust or to avoid involvement in a case of breach. In addition, liability will be incurred where a retiring trustee anticipates that his retirement will facilitate a breach of trust and where he foresaw (or ought to have foreseen) that a breach of trust would, indeed, occur.

Liability of trustees to account

The duty to provide accounts is discussed in detail in chapter 13.[12] The starting point in understanding a trustee's liability lies in the trustee's obligation to account for his stewardship of the trust. As Lindley L.J. commented in *Low v Bouverie*, "The duty of the trustee is properly to preserve the trust fund, to pay the income and the corpus to those who are entitled to them respectively, and to give all his *cestuis que trust* on demand information with respect to the mode in which the trust fund has been dealt with and where it is".[13] A beneficiary's challenge to the account is known as "falsifying" or "surcharging" the account. To falsify is to show that that an entry is erroneous and to disallow the payment away.[14] Surcharging is concerned with the omission of an entry which should be included. The trustee is under a duty to correct such errors. As Millett explained (in an extrajudicial capacity):

17.03

> "the primary remedy of the beneficiary ... is to have the account taken, to surcharge and falsify the account, and to require the trustee to restore to the trust estate any deficiency that may appear when the account is taken. The liability is strict ... If the beneficiary is dissatisfied with the way in which the trustee has carried out his trust—if, for example, he considers that the trustee has negligently failed to obtain all that he should have done for the benefit of the trust estate, then he may surcharge the account. He does this by requiring that the account be taken on the footing of wilful default ... The trustee is made to account, not only for what he has in fact received, but also for what he might with due diligence have received ... Where the beneficiary complains that the trustee has misapplied trust money, he falsifies the account, that is to say, he asks for the disbursement to be disallowed. If, for example, the trustee lays out trust money on an unauthorised investment which falls in value, the beneficiary will falsify the account by asking the court to disallow both the disbursement and the corresponding asset on the other side of the account. The unauthorised investment will then be treated as having been bought with the trustee's own money and on his own behalf. He will be required to account to the trust estate for the full amount of the disbursement—

[11] [1898] 2 Ch. 250 at 268.
[12] See **13.13**.
[13] [1891] 3 Ch. 82 at 99. Recently, in *Walker v Walker* Unreported January 30, 2007, Deputy Judge Roger Kaye QC explained that the trustee must, "keep accounts, provide them when required and provide to the beneficiaries all reasonable information as to the manner in which the trust estate has been dealt with".
[14] See *Bonham v Blake Lapthorn Linell* [2006] EWHC 2513 (Ch) at [180].

not for the amount of the loss. That is what is meant by saying that the trustee is liable to restore the trust property; and why the common law rules of damage and remoteness are out of place".[15]

Not every breach will result in a financial loss to the beneficiary. Consider, for example, a trustee who misapplies trust property in a lucrative investment. As to the case where a profit had been generated, Lord Millett continued:

"If the unauthorised investment has appreciated in value, then the beneficiary will be content with it. He is not obliged to falsify the account which the trustee renders; he can always accept it. (It goes without saying that the trustee cannot simply 'borrow' the trust money to make a profitable investment for his own account and then rely on the fact that the investment was unauthorised to avoid bringing the transaction into the account. He must account for what he has done with the trust money, not merely for what he has properly done with it). Where the beneficiary accepts the unauthorised investment, he is often said to affirm or adopt the transaction. That is not wholly accurate. The beneficiary has a right to elect, but it is really a right to decide whether to complain or not".[16]

17.04   It is clear, therefore, that the account is either falsified (and the trustee must restore the value of the misapplied assets) or surcharged (where the trustee is made liable on the footing of wilful default), but the trustee must compensate the trust for any losses incurred. It is conceivable, therefore, that a beneficiary may have two potential avenues of redress, from which one remedy must be elected. For example, it may be open to a beneficiary to seek an account of profits made by a trustee or seek equitable compensation for a simultaneous loss sustained as a result of being deprived of the property. Lord Nicholls considered this position, in *Tang Man Sit (Personal Representatives) v Capacious Investments Ltd.*[17] He outlined the circumstances in which the beneficiary must elect a remedy:

"Faced with alternative and inconsistent remedies a plaintiff must choose, or elect, between them. He cannot have both. The basic principle governing when a plaintiff must make his choice is simple and clear. He is required to choose when, but not before, judgment is given in his favour and the judge is asked to make orders against the defendant. A plaintiff is not required to make his choice when he launches his proceedings. He may claim one remedy initially, and then by amendment of his writ and his pleadings abandon that claim in favour of the other. He may claim both remedies, as alternatives. But he must make up his mind when judgment is being entered against the defendant. Court orders are intended to be obeyed. In the nature of things, therefore, the court should not make orders which would afford a plaintiff both of two alternative remedies".[18]

---

[15] P. Millett, "Equity's Place in the Law of Commerce" (1998) 114 L.Q.R. 214 at p.224.
[16] P. Millett, "Equity's Place in the Law of Commerce" (1998) 114 L.Q.R. 214 at p.226.
[17] [1996] 1 All E.R. 193.
[18] [1996] 1 All E.R. 193 at 197.

In addition, and, although a personal action against the trustee is an immediate avenue for redress for a beneficiary, it is clear that a variety of alternatives exist. These alternative options will be considered, say, where the trustee is insolvent and a personal remedy will be fruitless. As will be discussed in this chapter, the beneficiary may pursue a proprietary claim to the assets or their traceable proceeds in the hands of a third party. This will involve identification of property by employing the evidentiary process of following[19] or tracing[20] the movement of property or its proceeds away from the trust and the selection of an appropriate remedy such as a charge over the third party's assets. As has been discussed in Ch.10, a personal action may be available against third parties who knowingly receive trust property or dishonestly assist in a breach of trust.

EQUITABLE COMPENSATION

It is on the basis of the liability to account that a trustee who makes an unauthorised distribution of trust property is required to replenish the trust fund to the extent that it has diminished through the breach of trust. The nature of the obligation is restorative and, accordingly, the principles differ from those applicable to assessment of damages at common law. Although, as will be demonstrated, a causal link is required as between the breach of trust and the loss to the estate, the common law principles of foreseeability and remoteness are not applied. As Capper acknowledges, the approach to calculating equitable compensation in these circumstances is to, "look back to the breach to see if the loss can be traced to it. This contrasts with contract and tort where one looks forward from the acceptance of contractual risks or the breach of duty and asks whether the loss occurring was foreseeable".[21]
17.05

Measure of damages

The general principles governing the award of equitable compensation were scrutinised and reviewed by the House of Lords in *Target Holdings Ltd v Redferns*.[22] In a move away from the traditional approach of strict liability for breach of trust, the effect of the decision was to narrow the liability of fiduciaries to make good only that loss, which, in light of hindsight and common sense, can be said to have been *caused* by the breach. Here Lord Browne-Wilkinson pondered the divide between law and equity as to the appropriate measure of damages to be employed. He explained:
17.06

> "At common law there are two principles fundamental to the award of damages. First, that the defendant's wrongful act must cause the damage complained of. Second, that the plaintiff is to be put 'in the same position as he would have been in if he had not sustained the wrong for which he is now getting his compensation or

---

[19] See **17.35**.
[20] For a discussion of the common law and equitable rules see **17.39** and **17.43** respectively.
[21] D. Capper, "Compensation for Breach of Trust" [1997] Conv. 14 at 20.
[22] [1996] 1 A.C. 421.

reparation' . . . Although, as will appear, in many ways equity approaches liability for making good a breach of trust from a different starting point, in my judgment those two principles are applicable as much in equity as at common law. Under both systems liability is fault-based: the defendant is only liable for the consequences of the legal wrong he has done to the plaintiff and to make good the damage caused by such wrong. He is not responsible for damage not caused by his wrong or to pay by way of compensation more than the loss suffered from such wrong. The detailed rules of equity as to causation and the quantification of loss differ, at least ostensibly, from those applicable at common law. But the principles underlying both systems are the same".[23]

It is instructive to consider the facts as to which the Court of Appeal and the House of Lords responded with divergent approaches. Target Holdings (a mortgage lender) sought to provide a loan of around £1.5 million to Crowngate secured against a property it believed to be valued at £2 million. Target Holdings paid loan moneys to Redferns solicitors on trust to facilitate the acquisition. In breach of trust, Redferns paid away the sums received, not to Crowngate the prospective purchaser, but to an intermediary company in a series of purchases that would lead to Crowngate. In due course, however, the transaction was completed as intended and Target Holdings received a charge over the property as security for the loan. Unfortunately, however, the value of the property had been artificially inflated by the series of sales between the connected companies. When Target Holdings sought to enforce the security, it discovered that the property was worth only a fraction of the original loan. Against a property believed to be valued at £2 million, sale achieved only £500,000. In the light that Crowngate was insolvent, Target Holdings brought proceedings against Redferns claiming their entire loss of £1.5 million less the £500,000 achieved on sale.

17.07   The Court of Appeal identified a breach of trust, which occurred when Redferns made an improper and unauthorised payment of trust moneys to the intermediary company (i.e. a stranger to the trust). As a result, the trust estate suffered an immediate loss. Subsequent events, which reduced the loss suffered, were irrelevant save for imposing on the beneficiary an obligation to discount any benefit he subsequently received. The Court of Appeal drew a distinction between a case of administrative failure where it is necessary to wait to establish what loss, if any, is occasioned by the breach[24] and the case of a wrongful payment of trust moneys to a third party. The appellate court held, "there is an immediate loss, placing the trustee under an immediate duty to restore the moneys to the trust fund".[25] Accordingly, on the facts, the Court of Appeal held that no inquiry was necessary to establish whether the loss would have resulted notwithstanding the breach of trust. Summary judgment was ordered.

The House of Lords reversed the Court of Appeal decision giving the solicitors leave to defend on the basis that Target Holdings had sustained, "no compensatable loss flowing from the breach of trust".[26] On the facts, it was clear that the transaction would have gone ahead even if there had been no breach of trust. There was, therefore, no

---

[23] [1996] 1 A.C. 421 at 432.
[24] The assessment of compensation takes place at the date of trial.
[25] [1994] 1 W.L.R. 1089 at 1103 per Peter Gibson L.J.
[26] [1996] 1 A.C. 421 at 440.

causal link between the breach of trust and the loss occasioned to the trust fund. It was not possible, as the Court of Appeal had held, to "stop the clock" at the date the moneys were paid away as though events that occurred between the date of breach and the date of trial were irrelevant in assessing the loss suffered by reason of the breach.

As regards the approach adopted in *Target Holdings*, it is worthy of comment that **17.08** Lord Browne-Wilkinson endeavoured to forge a distinction between principles of trust law developed in the context of traditional trusts and those principles that might be employed in relation to bare trusts in the commercial context. In essence, he highlighted that in *Target Holdings* the solicitors held money on bare trust for their client as part of a conveyancing transaction, with the consequence that in a case of breach there was no sense in restoring the trust estate. Rather the appropriate remedy was the payment of compensation to the beneficiary. By contrast, in the context of traditional family trusts, principles had developed in equity to cater for the safeguard of a number of bene-ficiaries, perhaps, entitled in succession. He warned that it is, "wrong to lift wholesale the detailed rules developed in the context of traditional trusts and then seek to apply them to trusts of quite a different kind".[27] Emphasising that the trust has become an important device in commercial and financial dealings, he claimed:

> "The fundamental principles of equity apply as much to such trusts as they do to the traditional trusts in relation to which those principles were originally for-mulated. But in my judgment it is important, if the trust is not to be rendered commercially useless, to distinguish between the basic principles of trust law and those specialist rules developed in relation to traditional trusts which are applicable only to such trusts and the rationale of which has no application to trusts of quite a different kind".[28]

The apparent scope of the *Target Holdings* causation principles has excited some debate. Nolan, for example, argues that the case, "has not done a great deal to clarify the rules of causation employed in equity".[29] A similar confusion was expressed by Sir Peter Millett, when he objected that, "It is difficult to know what to make of this . . . Is it seriously to be supposed that the result in *Target Holdings Ltd v Redferns* would be different if the trust in question had been a traditional trust?"[30] Indeed Millett puts forward the proposition that the *Target Holdings* case might have been decided on the basis of the trustee's liability to account, that is, that the unauthorised use of the trust money entitled the claimant to falsify the account. No argument to this effect was considered (proceedings were, in fact, brought for professional negligence as the clai-mant only later became aware of the breach of trust). In any event, it transpired that the defendant solicitors complied, eventually, with their instructions and obtained the authorised security. It follows, therefore, that had this approach been applied, the outcome would have been the same as that reached by Lord Browne-Wilkinson via a different route. As Millett explained:

---

[27] [1996] 1 A.C. 421 at 435.
[28] [1996] 1 A.C. 421 at 435.
[29] R. Nolan, "A Targeted Degree of Liability" [1996] LMCLQ 161 at p.164.
[30] P. Millett, (1998) 114 L.Q.R. 214 at p.224.

"The plaintiff could not object to the acquisition of the mortgage or the disbursement by which it was obtained; it was an authorised application of what must be treated as trust money notionally restored to the trust estate on the taking of the account. To put the point another way; the trustee's obligation to restore the trust property is not an obligation to restore it in the very form in which he disbursed it, but an obligation to restore it in any form authorised by the trust".[31]

17.09   The application of general principles was again raised in *Swindle v Harrison* where *Target Holdings* was followed.[32] Mark Harrison convinced his mother to mortgage her house to provide the purchase money for a hotel that they would together operate as a restaurant business. Mrs Harrison arranged the mortgage loan and, in the mistaken belief that a further brewery loan would enable her to meet the full purchase price, she instructed her solicitors to exchange contracts. Unfortunately, she was not able to obtain further finance and looked certain to lose her deposit. One day before the date for completion, her solicitor (Mr Swindle) came to the rescue. He arranged a bridging loan to enable her to complete, secured by a first charge on the hotel property. He failed to disclose, however, that his firm would obtain a hidden profit from the transaction and that he had known from the outset that the brewery loan would be refused. The Harrisons' business met with little success. It followed that the house was repossessed and the solicitors sought to enforce their charge. Mrs Harrison alleged a breach of fiduciary duty and claimed, by way of compensation, the value of her lost equity.

As discussed above, in order to obtain compensation for breach of trust, Mrs Harrison had to show that the loss she had suffered was caused by the defendant's breach of duty. On the facts, however, it was clear that her losses stemmed from her own decision to expose her home to risk, since she would have accepted the loan in order to complete the purchase of the hotel even if full disclosure had been made.[33] As she would have lost the value of the equity in her home, the Court of Appeal was clear that her loss was not recoverable. Accordingly, the appeal was dismissed. *Swindle v Harrison* also demonstrates that different principles apply where the breach of fiduciary duty equates with fraud. Where, for example, a fiduciary makes a deliberate misrepresentation or fails to disclose a material fact, the claimant is entitled to rescission of the agreement and an account of profits.[34] The Court of Appeal noted that in the instant case, there had been no allegation or finding that the breach of fiduciary duty was the equivalent of fraud. Absent proof of fraud, it is the principle in *Target Holdings* that applies. The claimant must show that but for the breach she would not have proceeded in her course of action. Unfortunately, she failed.

[31] (1998) 114 L.Q.R. 214 at p.217.
[32] [1997] 4 All E.R. 705.
[33] In the words of Mummery L.J., "The loss which she had suffered did not flow from that breach of fiduciary duty. It flowed from her own decision to take the risk involved in mortgaging her own home to finance her son's restaurant business at the hotel" ([1997] 4 All E.R. 705 at 735).
[34] See M. Conaglen (2003) 119 L.Q.R. 246.

The trustee who acts without due care

In *Bristol & West Building Society v Mothew*,[35] Millett L.J. appears to promote a **17.10** distinction between categories of breach based on breach of fiduciary duty and other breaches of duty committed by a fiduciary.[36] It seems that the restorative approach to equitable compensation applies where there has been a breach of fiduciary duty, i.e. a breach of proscriptive duties which rest upon an obligation of loyalty.[37] As Millett L.J. observes, "The expression 'fiduciary duty' is properly confined to those duties which are peculiar to fiduciaries and the breach of which attracts legal consequences differing from those consequent upon the breach of other duties".[38] Accordingly, "not every breach of duty by a fiduciary is a breach of fiduciary duty".[39] Consider, for example, the solicitor (a fiduciary) who fails to act with the requisite skill in the course of his duties. Here, there is no reason to depart from the principles applicable in the assessment of common law damages for breach of contract or duty of care. As Millett L.J. argues:

> "Although the remedy which equity makes available for breach of the equitable duty of skill and care is equitable compensation rather than damages, this is merely the product of history and in this context is in my opinion a distinction without a difference. Equitable compensation for breach of the duty of skill and care resembles common law damages in that it is awarded by way of compensation to the plaintiff for his loss. There is no reason in principle why the common law rules of causation, remoteness of damage and measure of damages should not be applied by analogy in such a case. It should not be confused with equitable compensation for breach of fiduciary duty, which may be awarded in lieu of rescission or specific restitution".[40]

In conclusion, therefore, it may be seen that there are different measures for equitable compensation depending on the aim of the compensation. If deemed a necessary substitute for property misapplied or awarded instead of specific restoration of the fund, compensation is assessed in accordance with equitable principles. Where there is no misapplication of property and the breach cannot be falsified, compensation must be assessed by reference to loss that is occasioned thereby. Here it is inevitable that the concepts of remoteness, foreseeability and causation may assume significance, for example, in the case of a failure to act with due care or skill. It is instructive to consider a range of situations in which the general rules described above may be applied. These include:

---

[35] [1998] Ch. 1.
[36] See chapter 13 for a discussion of fiduciary duty.
[37] As Millett L.J. outlines [1998] Ch. 1 at 18, "The distinguishing obligation of a fiduciary is the obligation of loyalty. The principal is entitled to the single-minded loyalty of his fiduciary. This core liability has several facets. A fiduciary must act in good faith; he must not make a profit out of his trust; he must not place himself in a position where his duty and his interest may conflict; he may not act for his own benefit or the benefit of a third person without the informed consent of his principal. This is not intended to be an exhaustive list, but it is sufficient to indicate the nature of fiduciary obligations. They are the defining characteristics of the fiduciary".
[38] [1998] Ch. 1 at 16.
[39] [1998] Ch. 1 at 16.
[40] [1998] Ch. 1 at 17.

- unauthorised investments;
- authorised investments;
- profit;
- interest, and
- set-off.

Unauthorised investments

17.11   Trustees involved in the purchase of unauthorised investments are exposed to liability to replenish the trust for the loss that has occurred together with any adjustment necessary to replace the unauthorised investment with authorised investments.[41] In *Knott v Cottee*,[42] a trustee made an unauthorised investment in Exchequer bills. In 1846, the bills were sold at a loss by order of the court. In 1848, when sale would have produced a profit, the court declared that the investment was improper. Holding the trustee liable for the difference between the two prices, Romilly M.R. commented, "The case must either be treated as if these investments had not been made, or had been made for his own benefit out of his own monies, and that he had at the same time retained monies of the testator in his hands".[43] In *Re Massingberd's Settlement*,[44] trustees procured a sale of authorised investments and re-invested the proceeds in unauthorised mortgages. Although all of the money was recovered, the authorised investments had risen in value. Accordingly, the trustees were liable to replace the sold investments or replenish the trust estate to the equivalent value.

This category also includes examples of improper retention of trust property. In *Fry v Fry*,[45] trustees were instructed to sell the testator's house as soon as convenient following the death of the testator. Although an initial offer for the property was made and rejected, no sale of the property was achieved in the lifetime of the trustees. The trustees' estates were held to be liable for the difference in price between the current value of the property and the price that would have been achieved had the property been sold at the appropriate time.

Authorised investments

17.12   Under s.5 of the Trustee Act 2000, a trustee must obtain and consider proper advice regarding the investment of trust property before exercising any power of investment however conferred. A failure to invest within a reasonable period of time, however, will constitute a breach of the trustee's statutory duty of care.[46] Where the failure to invest is

---

[41]   It is, of course, open to beneficiaries of full capacity to adopt the unauthorised investment.
[42]   (1852) 16 Beav. 77.
[43]   (1852) 16 Beav. 77 at 79.
[44]   (1890) 63 L.T. 296.
[45]   (1859) 28 L.J. Ch. 591.
[46]   Trustee Act 2000, Sch.1, para.1.

as regards one specified investment, the trustee will be liable to provide the amount of the specified investment as would have been obtained with trust funds at the time at which the investment ought to have been made.[47] More frequently, however, trustees have a choice as to the investments purchased. In this case and, where no investment is made at all or, regard has not been had to the true scope of investment powers, the traditional approach is that liability extends only to the replacement of the trust fund. The basis of this rule is that in the absence of evidence as to the investment that would have been chosen, there is simply no other sum against which the trustee's liability should be measured. In *Nestlé v National Westminster Bank Plc*, however, Staughton and Dillon L.JJ. promote a sensible and modern working alternative whereby a trustee would be liable, "to make good to the trust fair compensation—and not just the minimum that might just have got by without challenge—for failure to follow a proper investment policy".[48]

Profit

A trustee may not make a profit out of the trust. As Lord Russell explained in *Regal*   **17.13**
(Hastings) Ltd v Gulliver:

> "The rule of equity which insists on those, who by use of a fiduciary position make a profit, being liable to account for that profit, in no way depends on fraud, or absence of bona fides; or upon such questions or considerations as whether the profit would or should otherwise have gone to the plaintiff, or whether the profiteer was under a duty to obtain the source of the profit for the plaintiff, or whether he took a risk or acted as he did for the benefit of the plaintiff, or whether the plaintiff has in fact been damaged or benefited by his action. The liability arises from the mere fact of a profit having, in the stated circumstances, been made. The profiteer, however honest and well-intentioned, cannot escape the risk of being called upon to account".[49]

Where an improper investment generates a profit, it will be held by the trustee as part of the trust property.[50] If trust funds have been ploughed into the trustee's trade or business, he will be held to account for profits or, if preferable to the beneficiary, the sums involved plus compound interest. In *Vyse v Foster*[51] James L.J. explained of the trustee that where, "improper dealing consists in embarking or investing the trust money in business, he must account for the profits made by him by such employment in such business".[52]

---

[47] *Byrchall v Bradford* (1822) 6 Madd. 235.
[48] [1993] 1 W.L.R. 1260 at 1268 per Dillon L.J.
[49] [1942] 1 All E.R. 378 at 386; see **13.46**.
[50] As Lord Browne-Wilkinson noted in *Target Holdings Ltd v Redferns* [1996] 1 A.C. 421 at 443, "A carping beneficiary could insist that the unauthorised investment be sold and the proceeds invested in authorised investments: but the trustee would be under no liability to pay compensation either to the trust fund or to the beneficiary because the breach had caused no loss to the trust fund".
[51] (1872) L.R. 8 Ch. 309.
[52] (1872) L.R. 8 Ch. 309 at 329.

Interest

17.14   A trustee who misapplies trust funds in breach of trust will be liable not only to replenish the trust fund but also to do so with interest from the date of the mis-application.[53] As Buckley L.J. explained in *Wallersteiner v Moir (No.2)*, "This is on the notional ground that the money so applied was in fact the trustee's own money and that he has retained the misapplied trust money in his own hands and used it for his own purposes".[54] It is a discretionary matter for the court to determine the rate of interest applied. In *Attorney-General v Alford*,[55] the policy of the court was summed up by Lord Cranworth L.C. who suggested, "What the Court ought to do, I think, is to charge him only with the interest which he has received, or which it is justly entitled to say he ought to have received, or which it is so fairly to be presumed that he did receive that he is estopped from saying that he did not receive it".[56] Accordingly, the usual practice is to charge the trustee with simple interest only. If, however, the money has been used in the furtherance of a trade, compound interest will be charged.[57] The justification for charging compound interest, "normally lies in the fact that profits earned in trade would be likely to be used as working capital for earning further profits".[58]

Set-off of profit against loss

17.15   As a general rule, where a trustee is liable in respect of distinct breaches of trust, one of which has resulted in a loss and the other in a profit, the trustee is not entitled to set off the profit against the loss.[59] In *Bartlett v Barclays Bank Trust Co Ltd*,[60] however, there appears to have been a softening of this general approach. There, the Bank had neglected its duty as trustee to ensure that it received sufficient information as regards the investment activities of a board of company directors. Two property development projects were highlighted: the "Guildford" project (which was successful), and the "Old Bailey" project (which was unsuccessful and described by Brightman J. as, "imprudent and hazardous and wholly unsuitable for a trust").[61] Brightman J. reflected on the development of authority and decided that the cases were not easy to reconcile. Nonetheless, he permitted the profit to be set off against a loss because both the profit and the loss arose out of the same course of speculative investment. He claimed:

> "The relevant cases are, however, not altogether easy to reconcile. All are cen-
> tenarians and none is quite like the present. The Guildford development stemmed
> from exactly the same policy and (to a lesser degree because it proceeded less far)

---

[53]   Historically interest was awarded at a rate of four per cent: see, for example, *Hall v Hallet* (1784) 1 Cox Eq. Cas 134.
[54]   [1975] Q.B. 373 at 397.
[55]   (1855) 4 De. G. M. & G. 843.
[56]   (1855) 4 De. G. M. & G. 843 at 851.
[57]   *Burdick v Garrick* (1870) 5 Ch. App. 233.
[58]   Per Buckley L.J. in *Wallersteiner v Moir (No.2)* [1975] QB 373 at 397.
[59]   *Dimes v Scott* (1828) 4 Russ. 195.
[60]   [1980] Ch. 515.
[61]   [1980] Ch. 515 at 534.

exemplified the same folly as the Old Bailey project. Part of the profit was in fact used to finance the Old Bailey disaster. By sheer luck the gamble paid off handsomely, on capital account. I think it would be unjust to deprive the bank of this element of salvage in the course of assessing the cost of the shipwreck. My order will therefore reflect the bank's right to an appropriate set-off".[62]

LIABILITY OF TRUSTEES INTER SE

Co-trustees who have acted in breach of trust are jointly and severally liable to beneficiaries.[63] Accordingly, a beneficiary may seek to recover a loss in its entirety from any one or more individual trustees or all of the trustees jointly. As between trustees, where any one trustee is compelled to pay more of his share of the liability for a breach of trust, he is entitled in equity to enforce an equal contribution from his complicit co-trustees.[64] As A. L. Smith L.J. put it in *Chillingworth v Chambers*, "As between two trustees who are in *pari delicto*, the one who has made good a loss occasioned by a breach of trust for which the two are jointly and severally liable may obtain contribution to that loss from the other".[65] Historically, the rules of equity ensured that a passive trustee could not, through inactivity evade the liability incurred by an active trustee who acted honestly, but fell into error. This principle was aptly prescribed by Cotton L.J. in *Bahin v Hughes*, where he claimed that it, "would be laying down a wrong rule to hold that where one trustee acts honestly, though erroneously, the other trustee is to be held entitled to indemnity who by doing nothing neglects his duty more than the acting trustee".[66]

The capacity to recover contribution from co-trustees now rests on a statutory basis. The Civil Liability (Contribution Act) 1978 confers on the court discretion as to the amount that can be recovered by one trustee against another. Section 2(1) highlights that the sums recoverable must be, "such as may be found by the court to be just and equitable having regard to the extent of that person's responsibility for the damage in question". It is open to the court, therefore, to depart from the equitable presumption of equal responsibility where the facts of the case demand. The Act does not, however cover cases where a trustee is not liable to contribute but, instead, is entitled to an indemnity against his own liability from his co-trustees.

Instances of indemnity might be usefully confined to three key categories:

17.16

17.17

- where one trustee alone is solely liable for a breach. Thus, in *Re Smith*, where in the course of a joint investment one trustee had acted dishonestly, Kekewich J. concluded, "The fact that he took a bribe is conclusive against him. Honesty seems to be out of the question after that; and I must hold that he is liable to make good the loss occasioned by the investment. I do not think that it is a case

---

[62] [1980] Ch. 515 at 538.
[63] See further **13.20**.
[64] *Fletcher v Green* (1864) 33 Beav. 426.
[65] [1896] 1 Ch. 685 at 707.
[66] (1886) 31 Ch. D. 390 at 396. As Fry L.J. perceived it, "the loss which has happened is the result of the combination of the action of Miss Hughes with the inaction of Mr Edwards" (at 398).

of joint and several liability".[67] This category, therefore, catches a variety of cases where one trustee alone has acted in a fraudulent manner;

- where a trustee is a solicitor on whose advice co-trustees have relied. Here, the court is cautious to ascertain the extent of the solicitor's control. As Kekewich J. warned in *Head v Gould*, a solicitor trustee is not bound to indemnify his co-trustee against loss, "merely because he was a solicitor, when that co-trustee was an active participator in the breach of trust complained of, and is not proved to have participated merely in consequence of the advice and control of the solicitor",[68] and

- where a trustee is also a beneficiary who participates in a breach of trust and obtains, as between himself and his co-trustee, an exclusive benefit. The trustee beneficiary must, in this case, indemnify his co-trustee to the extent of his interest in the trust estate, and not merely to the extent of the benefit he has received.[69]

CRIMINAL LIABILITY

17.18   The criminal liability of trustees who act in breach of trust is secured under the Theft Act 1968.[70] Hence, the dishonest appropriation of property (including land or anything forming part of it)[71] with the intention of permanent deprivation exposes a trustee to criminal sanction. Trust property, for the purposes of the Act belongs to, "any person having a right to enforce the trust".[72] This appears to include potential beneficiaries under a discretionary trust.

PROTECTION OF TRUSTEES

17.19   A trustee may take advantage of a wide range of defences to an action for breach of trust. It might be argued, for example, that another trustee committed the breach[73] or that a particular course of conduct was reasonable and that no breach has, therefore, been committed.[74] In addition, the principal defences relied upon by trustees to escape liability are as follows:

---

[67] [1896] 1 Ch. 71 at 77.
[68] [1898] 2 Ch. 250 at 265.
[69] *Chillingworth v Chambers* [1896] 1 Ch. 685.
[70] Historically, the trustee was considered to be the owner of the trust property with the consequence that a breach of trust did not infringe the criminal law.
[71] Under s.4(2)(a) a trustee may be deemed to steal land if, "he appropriates the land or anything forming part of it by dealing with it in breach of the confidence reposed in him".
[72] Section 5(2).
[73] On the ground that a trustee is not always liable for the acts or omissions of another trustee: *Townley v Sherborne* (1633) Bridg. 35.
[74] *Nestlé v National Westminster Bank Plc (No.2)* [1993] 1 W.L.R. 1260.

- the trustee exemption clause;
- the principle of consent;
- breach at the instigation of a beneficiary;
- entitlement to statutory relief, and
- limitation of actions.

Exemption clauses

A trustee may, by virtue of a provision in the trust instrument, claim relief from **17.20**
liability.[75] In *Armitage v Nurse*,[76] recent consideration was given to the scope of the so-
called "exemption clause" and its capacity to exclude liability for a trustee's negligence
in the course of his duties. The exemption clause in *Armitage* read, "No trustee shall be
liable for any loss or damage which may happen ... at any time or from any cause
whatsoever unless such loss or damage shall be caused by his own actual fraud ...".
Millett L.J. considered it, "apt to exclude liability for breach of trust in the absence of a
dishonest intention on the part of the trustee whose conduct is impugned".[77] As long as
he has not acted dishonestly, the trustee was free from liability for loss or damage to the
trust property, "no matter how indolent, imprudent, lacking in diligence, negligent or
wilful he may have been".[78]

In *Walker v Stones*,[79] further light was cast by Sir Christopher Slade in his effort to
distil a test of dishonesty. Three propositions emerge, each of which was derived substantially from the judgment of Rattee J. in the lower court. First, the deliberate
commission of a breach of trust is not necessarily dishonest.[80] Secondly, it is only
dishonest if the trustee committing it does so, "either knowing that it is contrary to the
interests of the beneficiaries or being recklessly indifferent whether it is contrary to their
interests or not".[81] Thirdly, Rattee J. described it as seemingly impossible to call a
trustee's conduct "dishonest" in any ordinary sense of that word, even if he knew he
was acting in breach of the terms of the trust, if he so acted in a genuine (even if
misguided) belief that what he was doing was for the benefit of the beneficiaries.[82] Sir
Christopher Slade was prepared to adopt this approach to the issue of the dishonesty of
a solicitor-trustee,[83] but subject to a key qualification. This third proposition would
apply save, "where the trustee's so-called 'honest belief', though actually held, is so

---

[75] See further **13.05**.
[76] [1997] 2 All E.R. 705.
[77] [1997] 2 All E.R. 705 at 710.
[78] [1997] 2 All E.R. 705 at 711.
[79] [2000] 4 All E.R. 412.
[80] [2000] 4 All E.R. 412 at 443.
[81] [2000] 4 All E.R. 412 at 443.
[82] Note *Bonham v Fishwick* [2008] EWCA Civ 373 where Mummery L.J. advanced the view that a trustee
acting upon legal advise could not be accused of willful wrongdoing.
[83] He accepted that the test of honesty may, "vary from case to case, depending on, among other things, the
role and calling of the trustee" ([2000] 4 All E.R. 412 at 443).

unreasonable that, by any objective standard, no reasonable solicitor-trustee could have thought that what he did or agreed to do was for the benefit of the beneficiaries".[84]

17.21   The law on trustee exemption clauses is frequently criticised.[85] In 2003, the Law Commission published a consultation paper which highlighted the inadequacy of the current position whereby a professional trustee can escape liability for breach of trust occasioned by his negligence and proposed that professional trustees should no longer be allowed to exclude this liability.[86] Millett L.J. himself conceded that, "it must be acknowledged that the view is widely held that these clauses have gone too far, and that trustees who charge for their services and who, as professional men, would not dream of excluding liability for ordinary professional negligence should not be able to rely on a trustee exemption clause excluding liability for gross negligence".[87] Nonetheless, the Law Commission has now changed its view. Instead, it proposes a rule of practice, that where a paid trustee causes a settlor to include a clause limiting liability, trustees must take such steps, "as are reasonable to ensure that the settlor is aware of the meaning and effect of the clause".[88] This radical shift of position has understandably angered some commentators. As Parker and Mellows laments, "this about turn was simply ludicrous and it is greatly to be regretted that the Law Commission allowed itself to be persuaded by the wholly self-serving arguments of the largely self-appointed representatives of professional trustees".[89]

Consent to a course of dealing

17.22   A trustee might seek to escape the prospect of liability for breach of trust by arguing that the beneficiary consented to, or acquiesced in, a given course of conduct. The classic statement of the principle of consent is that of Lord Eldon L.C. in *Walker v Symonds*:

> "it is established by all the cases, that if the *cestui que trust* joins with the trustees in that which is a breach of trust, knowing the circumstances, such a *cestui que trust* can never complain of such a breach of trust. I go further, and agree that either concurrence in the act, or acquiescence without original concurrence, will release the trustees: but that is only a general rule, and the court must inquire into the circumstances which induced concurrence or acquiescence".[90]

In essence, the court must be convinced that it is fair and equitable to deny a beneficiary a claim against the trustee. It must be shown that there was an exercise of independent judgment by a beneficiary in full knowledge of the facts. A beneficiary cannot be

---

[84] [2000] 4 All E.R. 412 at 443.
[85] In *Barraclough v Mell* [2005] EWHC 3387 at [89], Behrens J. pointed to "an area of law ripe for reform".
[86] Trustee Exemption Clauses (2003) Law Com. C.P. 171; see generally, P. Matthews, "The Efficacy of Trustee Exemption Clauses in English Law" [1989] Conv. 42.
[87] *Armitage v Nurse* [1997] 2 All E.R. 705 at 715.
[88] "Trustee Exemption Clauses" (2006) Law Com 301 at [6.65].
[89] Parker and Mellows, p.896.
[90] (1818) 3 Swan. 1 at 64; see generally, J. Payne, "Consent" in P. Birks, A. Pretto (eds) *Breach of Trust* (Oxford, Hart Publishing, 2002) at pp.297–318.

deemed to consent or acquiesce in conduct of which he has no knowledge or under-standing[91] or where consent has not been freely obtained,[92] or where consent is obtained from a minor.[93] The court is prepared to look at matters in the round. As Wilberforce J. put it in *Re Pauling's ST:*

> "the court has to consider all the circumstances in which the concurrence of the *cestui que trust* was given with a view to seeing whether it is fair and equitable that, having given his concurrence, he should afterwards turn round and sue the trustees: that, subject to this, it is not necessary that he should know that what he is concurring in is a breach of trust, provided that he fully understands what he is concurring in, and that it is not necessary that he should himself have directly benefited by the breach of trust".[94]

Accordingly, where a breach is known by trustees to be unauthorised, the availability of a defence will depend on whether the unauthorised nature of the transaction was communicated to the beneficiary. In the case of a negligent breach the beneficiary need not know that an act was unauthorised. As *Re Pauling's ST* suggests, the court will consider fully the fairest and most equitable result.[95]

Closely related to the defence of consent, a trustee may argue that conduct or words **17.23** after the breach should release a trustee from liability. Although delay in bringing a claim may, legitimately, point to the tenant's acquiescence or release post-breach, it is, of itself an insufficient ground to protect the trustee from liability. Comparatively less additional evidence is required to demonstrate acquiescence than release. In all cases, the court is guided by the same broad concepts of equity and justice on the facts of the case.

Breach at the beneficiary's instigation

Where a beneficiary instigates or requests a trustee to commit a breach of trust the court **17.24** enjoys a jurisdiction in equity to impound the beneficiary's interest, i.e. apply it as far as possible towards the provision of an indemnity for the trustee. Where a breach of trust is instigated or requested it is not necessary to show that the beneficiary was in receipt of a benefit.[96] The underlying motive of personal benefit is sufficient. This principle does not apply, however, where a beneficiary merely consents to or concurs in a breach of trust. Here a benefit derived by the beneficiary must be demonstrated.[97] As Romer L.J. identified in *Fletcher v Collis*, "If a beneficiary claiming under a trust does not instigate

---

[91] *Re Somerset* [1894] 1 Ch. 231.
[92] As the Court of Appeal emphasised in *Re Pauling's ST* [1964] Ch. 303 at 338, "a trustee carrying out a transaction in breach of trust may be liable if he knew, or ought to have known, that the beneficiary was acting under the undue influence of another, or may be presumed to have done so, but will not be liable if it cannot be established that he so knew, or ought to have known".
[93] *Lord Montford v Ladogan* (1816) 19 Ves. 635; note that a minor who misrepresents his age will not be permitted to deny the effectiveness of his consent.
[94] [1962] 1 W.L.R. 86 at 108.
[95] See also, *Holder v Holder* [1968] 1 All E.R. 665.
[96] *Trafford v Boehm* [1746] 3 Atk. 440.
[97] *Montford v Cadogan* (1816) 19 Ves. 635.

or request a breach of trust, is not the active moving party towards it, but merely consents to it, and he obtains no personal benefit from it, then his interest in the trust estate would not be impoundable in order to indemnify the trustee liable to make good loss occasioned by the breach".[98]

The statutory jurisdiction of the court to impound the beneficiary's interest is broader, at least to the extent that the receipt of a personal benefit is not an explicit consideration in the exercise of discretion. It is clear, nonetheless, that the provision will apply in the case of consent only where consent was secured in writing.[99] Section 62(1) of the Trustee Act 1925[1] provides:

> "Where a trustee commits a breach of trust at the instigation or request or with the consent in writing of a beneficiary, the court may, if it thinks fit, ... make such order as to the court seems just, for impounding all or any part of the interest of the beneficiary in the trust estate by way of indemnity to the trustee or persons claiming through him".

Two short points require attention. First, old cases remain a guide to the application of the statute. Accordingly, the court will refuse to impound a beneficiary's interest unless it can be shown that the beneficiary, whether by instigation or in concurrence, was aware that the proposed course of action would result in breach of trust. Secondly, the power to impound remains notwithstanding the appointment of a new trustee. As Wilberforce J. exclaimed in *Re Pauling's Settlement (No.2)*, "It seems to me to be an absurdity to suppose that there is a requirement, as a condition of exercising the right to obtain an impounding order, that the trustee, who *ex hypothesi* is in breach of trust, must remain a trustee in order to acquire a right of indemnity".[2]

Statutory relief

17.25 Section 61 of the Trustee Act 1925 confers on the court the power to relieve a trustee from personal liability. It reads:

> "If it appears to the court that a trustee ... is or may be[3] personally liable for any breach of trust ... but has acted honestly and reasonably, and ought fairly to be excused for the breach of trust and for omitting to obtain the directions of the court in the matter in which he committed such breach, then the court may relieve him either wholly or partly from personal liability for the same".

Applications for relief typically involve the trustee's payment of funds to an incorrect beneficiary or the entry into an unauthorised investment.[4] In all cases, the court is called

---

[98] [1905] 2 Ch. 24 at 32.
[99] The requirement of writing relates only to consent: *Re Somerset* [1894] 1 Ch. 231.
[1] Replacing the Trustee Act 1893 s.45.
[2] [1963] Ch. 576 at 584.
[3] Potential liability must relate to a past incident and not a future anticipated breach: *Re Rosenthal* [1972] 1 W.L.R. 1273.
[4] See *Perrins v Bellamy* [1898] 2 Ch. 521 (Judicial Trustees Act 1896 s.3).

upon to exercise its discretion judiciously. In *Marsden v Regan*, Evershed M.R. drew attention to, "the threefold obligation" on a trustee seeking relief, namely, "that he must show that he himself acted honestly and reasonably, and he must further satisfy the court that he ought 'fairly' to be excused".[5] Fairness here alludes to other people who may be affected. The burden of establishing honesty and reasonableness lies with the trustee.[6] As to fairness, the court enjoys a wide discretion to consider the facts of the case before it.

In *Re Evans*,[7] for example, an administratrix took out insurance to cover the share of a missing beneficiary (her brother) before effecting a distribution of her father's estate. She acted reasonably in taking legal advice and honestly in the belief that her brother was dead. Somewhat unexpectedly, her brother returned to claim his share. It transpired that the insurance covered only the capital sum to which the beneficiary was entitled. When he claimed for interest, the administratrix sought to employ s.61 as a defence to his action. Richard McCombe Q.C. was influenced by the judgment of Evershed M.R. in *Marsden v Regan*. He claimed that that authority, "clearly shows that to act on legal advice is not a 'passport to relief' under s.61, but that it is important to have regard to the nature of the estate, the circumstances of the defaulting representative and his or her actions in the light of the advice received".[8] On the instant facts Richard McCombe Q.C. identified a relatively small estate and that the administratrix was a lay person unaccustomed to problems of this nature. She had, at all times, been willing to abide by the advice of solicitors. Accordingly, her liability was excused to the extent that the claim could not be satisfied by assets she retained from the estate. As a matter of general principle, Richard McCombe Q.C. was no doubt influenced by the policy driven need to avoid discouraging personal representatives, particularly of small estates, from tackling difficult administration problems and without the expense of resort to the court. Not surprisingly, there is markedly less sympathy for professional trustees who receive payment for services.[9]

17.26

Limitation

In cases of breach of trust it is important that the beneficiary complies with the rules as to limitation of actions. Put simply, the beneficiary must sue within the permitted timeframe. The equitable nature of a claim for breach of trust exposes the claimant to a minefield of limitation rules, in essence an unpalatable mix of historical doctrine and complex statutory intervention. More particularly, in determining the permitted time

17.27

---

[5] [1954] 1 W.L.R. 423 at 435
[6] *Re Stuart* [1897] 2 Ch. 583.
[7] [1999] 2 All E.R. 777, noted by P. Kenny [1999] Conv 375 at p.376 as a, "sad little case tried over five days in the Chancery Division".
[8] [1999] 2 All E.R. 777 at 789.
[9] See, for example, *Re Rosenthal* [1972] 1 W.L.R. 1273.

limit, regard must be had both to the equitable doctrine of *laches*[10] and to the applicable provisions of the Limitation Act 1980.[11]

The Limitation Act 1980

Exclusions

17.28   Unusually, the natural starting point when examining the Limitation Act 1980 is not with the general rules as to limitation of actions, but instead with the exceptions to those rules. Section 21(1) outlines the circumstances in which a trustee will be unable to seek protection from the Act:

> "No period of limitation prescribed by this Act shall apply to an action by a beneficiary under a trust, being an action—
>
> (a) in respect of any fraud or fraudulent breach of trust to which the trustee was a party or privy; or
>
> (b) to recover from the trustee trust property or the proceeds of trust property in the possession of the trustee, or previously received by the trustee and converted to his use".

Paragraph (a) appears to be limited by the concept of dishonesty. In *Armitage v Nurse*, Millett L.J. confined its scope to, "cases of fraud or fraudulent breaches of trust properly so called, that is to say cases involving dishonesty".[12] By contrast, dishonesty is not a relevant factor for the purposes of para.(b) where trust property or its proceeds are in the hands of the trustee. In *Re Howlett*,[13] therefore, the trustee was considered to have retained possession of the trust property and the application of a period of limitation was, thereby, excluded.

17.29   It is important to note that s.21(1) requires a relationship of trustee and beneficiary to exist between the parties. Under s.38(1),[14] the words "trust" and "trustee" extend to include "implied and constructive trusts". It will be recalled, nonetheless, that in *Paragon Finance Plc v Thakerar*,[15] Millett L.J. supported a two-fold classification of constructive trusts. The first category is where constructive trusteeship arises because the constructive trustee has assumed fiduciary duties prior to the wrongful conduct complained of by the claimant. The second is where a constructive trust is imposed on the defendant as a direct result of his wrongful conduct rendering him personally liable

---

[10] See **17.32**. Under the Limitation Act 1980 s.36, "nothing in the Act shall affect any equitable jurisdiction to refuse relief on the ground of acquiescence or otherwise".

[11] The limitation rules are viewed by the Law Commission in (2001) Law Com. 270 "Limitation of Actions" at para.1.5 as, "unfair, complex, uncertain and outdated"; see also, W. Swadling, "Limitation" in P. Birks, A. Pretto (eds), *Breach of Trust* (Oxford, Hart Publishing, 2002) at p.344, where it is claimed that, "The current limitation regime for breach of trust is a mess".

[12] [1997] 2 All E.R. 705 at 719.

[13] [1949] Ch. 767 (occupation rent obtainable in respect of the trustee's continued possession of a wharf until his death).

[14] Applying the Trustee Act 1925 s.68.

[15] [1999] 1 All E.R. 400 (**10.07–10.08**).

to account. As regards the 1980 Act, this distinction is directly in point. Millett L.J. explained:

> "The importance of the distinction between the two categories of constructive trust lies in the application of the statutes of limitation. Before 1890 constructive trusts of the first kind were treated in the same way as express trusts and were often confusingly described as such; claims against the trustee were not barred by the passage of time. Constructive trusts of the second kind however were treated differently. They were not in reality trusts at all, but merely a remedial mechanism by which equity gave relief for fraud".[16]

Accordingly, it is only those who fall into the first class of constructive trusteeship that are exposed to perpetual liability. A personal action against a third party who dishonestly assists in a breach of trust must be brought with the conventional six-year limitation period because, although the label of constructive trustee is attached to the third party, he is not a constructive trustee within Millett L.J.'s first class.[17] By way of a contrasting example, in *JJ Harrison (Properties) Ltd v Harrison*[18] Chadwick L.J. held that a company director who obtained the company's property for himself by the misuse of the powers entrusted to him in his capacity as director was a constructive trustee within Millett L.J.'s first class of constructive trust. He argued that the director was vested with powers and duties to deal with the company property in the interests of the company. In that sense, he owed a fiduciary duty to the company in respect of those powers, the breach of which would be treated as a breach of trust. Chadwick L.J. held, therefore, that Mr Harrison was prevented by s.21(1)(b) of the 1980 Act from raising the defence of limitation. The appropriate remedy (in the light that the property had been sold) was an account of the value of the property and attendant profits.

Similarly, in *Gwembe Valley Development Co v Koshy*,[19] an action by a company **17.30** against a former managing director (for an account of profits secretly and dishonestly made from loan transactions with another company in which he had failed to declare an interest) was deemed to be an action for fraudulent breach of trust. Accordingly, it fell within s.21(1)(a) to which no limitation period applied.

General cases

Section 21(3) establishes the general rule that an action to recover trust property must **17.31** be brought within a period of six years from the date of the breach:

> "An action by a beneficiary to recover trust property or in respect of any breach of trust, not being an action for which a period of limitation is prescribed by any

---

[16] [1999] 1 All E.R. 400 at 409.
[17] *Cattley v Pollard* [2007] Ch 353; see *Statek Corp v Alford* [2008] EWHC 92 (Ch) at [125] per Evans-Lombe J for an alternative view.
[18] [2002] 1 BCLC 162; see also, *Bank of Credit and Commerce International (SA) v Saadi* [2005] EWHC 2256 (QB).
[19] [2004] 1 BCLC 131.

other provision of this Act, shall not be brought after the expiration of six years from the date on which the right of action accrued".

This statutory period of limitation does not apply to the exceptional circumstances outlined above or, moreover, to cases where trustees have breached the self-dealing or fair-dealing rules.[20] Where, however, a trustee can demonstrate that a breach was occasioned innocently, or by way of negligence, the applicable limitation period is the six year period outlined in s.21(3). In addition, the following considerations are relevant:

- in the case of a beneficiary with a future interest, a right of action is not deemed to have accrued until his interest falls into possession;

- under s.28, this limitation period is capable of extension where the person to whom the action accrues is under a disability.[21] In such cases, time will only begin to run when that disability ends;

- s.32 caters for an extension or exclusion of ordinary time limits in cases of fraud, concealment or mistake. Hence, s.32 applies to any action (for which a period of limitation is prescribed) based upon the fraud of the trustee, the trustee's deliberate concealment of a right of action or to cases where the action is for relief from the consequences of a mistake. In these delimited circumstances the period of limitation will not begin to run until the fraud, concealment or mistake has been discovered or could, with reasonable diligence, have been discovered; and

- s.22 provides an alternative time limit for actions in respect of claims to the personal estate of a deceased person. Here, subject to the s.21 exceptions, a limit of 12 years is provided.

Laches

17.32 A trustee might raise the defence of *laches* to establish that an acquiescent beneficiary knew of the existence of a breach of trust and delayed unacceptably in bringing his claim. As Lord Selbourne L.C. explained in *Lindsay Petroleum Co v Hurd*:

"the doctrine of *laches* in Courts of Equity is not an arbitrary or a technical doctrine. Where it would be practically unjust to give a remedy, either because the party has, by his conduct, done that which might fairly be regarded as equivalent to a waiver of it, or where by his conduct and neglect he has, though perhaps not waiving that remedy, yet put the other party in a situation in which it would not be reasonable to place him if the remedy were afterwards to be asserted, in either of these cases, lapse of time and delay are most material".[22]

---

[20] *Tito v Waddell (No.2)* [1977] Ch. 106; see **13.35** and **13.38**, respectively.
[21] Typically mental incapacity or infancy.
[22] (1874) L.R. 5 P.C. 221 at 239.

Indeed, the modern approach to the defence was detailed in *Frawley v Neill*[23] and endorsed by the Court of Appeal in *Green v Gaul*.[24] In *Frawley v Neill*, Aldous L.J. confirmed that:

> "The inquiry should require a broad approach, directed to ascertaining whether it would in all the circumstances be unconscionable for a party to be permitted to assert his beneficial right. No doubt the circumstances which gave rise to a particular result in the decided cases are relevant to the question whether or not it would be conscionable or unconscionable for the relief to be asserted, but each case has to be decided on its facts applying the broad approach".[25]

Of course, where an action falls within s.21(1) (discussed above), no statutory period of limitation applies. The current view (although not uncontested)[26] is that this does not prevent the trustee raising the defence of *laches*.[27]

ASSOCIATED REMEDIES

Having considered the liability of trustees in cases of breach of trust, it is now necessary to examine the availability of remedies to the claimant beneficiary. The primary focus of the remainder of the chapter is on the availability of proprietary remedies. Where property is misappropriated in breach of trust the beneficiary may chart its movement in order to recover the specific property or its traceable proceeds. The problem lies in ascertaining exactly what has happened to the property. Misappropriated property may remain in the hands of a dishonest trustee or it may pass into the hands of a third party, whether it be a bona fide purchaser, an innocent volunteer or a knowing recipient. Trust property may be exchanged for different property, it may become inextricably mixed with other property, such as in a bank account, or it may be dissipated altogether. Notwithstanding, obvious evidential difficulties, if beneficiaries can identify the trust property or its substitute or its inclusion in a mixture of trust property and other property, the beneficiary can assert a proprietary claim in respect of the loss occasioned to the trust.[28]

17.33

---

[23] *The Times*, April 5, 1999.
[24] [2007] 1 W.L.R. 591.
[25] *The Times*, April 5, 1999.
[26] See *Gwembe Valley Development Co. v Koshy* [2004] WTLR 97 at [140], where Mummery L.J. claimed: "The defence of *laches* is not available. As already explained no period of limitation is specified by the 1980 Act in respect of the cause of action for dishonest breach of fiduciary duty. The effect of s.21(1)(a) is that either as a result of direct application, or of analogy, there is no period of limitation applicable to that cause of action".
[27] *Green v Gaul* [2007] 1 W.L.R. 591.
[28] See, generally, L. Smith, *The Law of Tracing* (Oxford, Clarendon Press, 1997).

Proprietary or personal?

17.34 Consider the case of a trustee who wrongfully misappropriates trust property and uses it solely for the acquisition of a different asset for his own benefit. Here the beneficiary can either establish his beneficial ownership of the proceeds (i.e. the new asset) or bring a personal claim against the trustee for breach of trust secured by an equitable lien (charge) on the proceeds to secure restoration of the trust fund. Understandably, the beneficiary will choose the course of action most beneficial to him. The advantages of a proprietary claim lie on two fronts. First, a proprietary claim affords priority to the claimant in the event of the defendant's insolvency. Thus, whether the beneficiary asserts a claim to ownership of the asset itself or an equitable proprietary interest in its traceable proceeds, the trustee cannot claim that the asset forms part of his estate. The proprietary claim of a beneficiary to the trust property or its traceable proceeds can be maintained against the wrongdoer and anyone who derives title from him save for a bona fide purchaser for value without notice of the breach of trust.[29] As such, it is not relevant to the beneficiary that the trustee is insolvent. If the beneficiary is unable to trace the trust property into its proceeds, he will opt to pursue a personal claim against the trustee, although this claim will be unsecured.

Secondly, a proprietary claim will entitle the beneficiary to any appreciation in value generated from the appropriation of his asset. It would be improper to allow the trustee to benefit from the fruits of his misappropriation and illogical that anyone deriving title from him could assert a better title. Where there has been depreciation in the value of an asset, the claimant may choose, in addition, to embark on a personal action in order to recover the difference in value to the trust. In the alternative, he will opt for a personal claim from the outset.

Following or tracing?

17.35 Logically, there are two stages to the process of obtaining a remedy. The first is the identification of the trust property. This may be achieved by the process of "following" or "tracing". Lord Millett has recognised that following and tracing, "are both exercises in locating assets which are or may be taken to represent an asset belonging to the [beneficiaries] and to which they assert ownership".[30] He explains further that, "the processes of following and tracing are, however, distinct. Following is the process of following the same asset as it moves from hand to hand. Tracing is the process of identifying a new asset as a substitute for the old".[31]

The second step is the selection of an appropriate remedy to bring in respect of that property. Whether identification is achieved by the process of following or tracing,

---

[29] Equally where the beneficiary acquires a charge against the defendant's property, he will take priority over the claims of any unsecured creditors of the defendant.
[30] *Foskett v McKeown* [2001] 1 A.C. 102 at 127.
[31] [2001] 1 A.C. 102 at 127.

neither provides, by itself, a remedy.[32] At all times, the choice of remedies available to the claimant will depend on the circumstances of the case. For example, a constructive trust might be imposed, say, where property has been identified in the hands of the defendant, who has acted unconscionably.[33] An equitable charge or lien might be appropriate where trust money is used to provide part of the cost of acquiring an asset. This is because the claimant will be entitled a proportionate share of the asset (by equitable charge) or to enforce a lien to secure his personal claim for the amount of the misapplied money. Further, where the claimant's money has been used to discharge a mortgage on the defendant's land, the court may treat the land as subject to a charge by way of subrogation in favour of the claimant.[34]

Towards a unified process of tracing

Historically, different rules have applied to tracing at common law and in equity. The common law rules are characterised by a restrictive approach. Here, once trust property has become mixed with other property (e.g. in the bank account of the trustee or a third party), the beneficiary is no longer permitted to trace. As property obtained in breach of trust is frequently mixed in this way, the utility of common law tracing is evident in only delimited circumstances. As will be demonstrated, it is possible to "follow" an asset into the hands of a third party in order to achieve a recovery of the specific item or its "clean" substitute.[35] The common law rules also permit a claimant to follow an asset into a fund of property that contains the trust property (or its "clean" substitute) and any interest in its value that has accrued since the breach.[36]

In contrast, tracing in equity will assist a beneficiary in the establishment of a proprietary claim over property that has been mixed. It is the process by which a beneficiary can identify some property against which he can establish a new equitable proprietary right. Equity will allow the claimant to trace into a mixed fund and charge the fund. Equity does so in the light that the authentic trust property has been inextricably mixed with the property of the wrongdoer. Despite this seeming flexibility, it is a pre-requisite to equitable tracing that the claimant has some equitable interest in the property or that as between the parties there is a fiduciary relationship.[37] Although perfectly understandable from a historical perspective,[38] the need to establish the existence of a fiduciary relationship as a precondition to tracing has provided an

17.36

---

[32] As Lewison J noted in *Ultraframe v Fielding* [2005] EWHC 1638 (Ch) at [1464], "the tracing exercise must be carried out first. Only then can the court consider what rights (if any) the claimant has in the assets that have been identified as being trust property or their identifiable substitutes".

[33] *Westdeutsche Landesbank v Islington* [1996] A.C. 669.

[34] See *Boscawen v Bajwa* [1996] 1 W.L.R. 328.

[35] Whereas mixed substitutions occur where a new asset is acquired using a mixture of trust property and the defendant's assets, clean substitutions occur where the new asset is acquired solely with trust property: *Foskett v McKeown* [2001] 1 A.C. 102 at 130.

[36] *Jones (FC) & Sons v Jones* [1996] 3 W.L.R. 703.

[37] Note that tracing may occur in the context of other fiduciary relationships and is not strictly confined to claims between trustee and beneficiary: see *Re Hallett* (1880) 13 Ch. D. 696 at 709.

[38] As Fox L.J. claimed in *Agip (Africa) Ltd v Jackson* [1991] Ch. 547 at 566, "there must be a fiduciary relationship which calls the equitable jurisdiction into being".

unfortunate obstacle to the tracing process and, thereby, beset the logical development of the law towards a unified process for all claimants.

17.37 In past decades, judges and commentators alike have voiced regret that the law had failed to develop a single system of rules to determine the availability of proprietary claims. In particular, the lack of a unified process was a frequent topic for critical comment in the 1990s. As Millett L.J. observed in *Jones (FC) & Sons v Jones*, "There is no merit in having distinct and differing tracing rules at law and in equity, given that tracing is neither a right nor a remedy but merely the process by which the plaintiff establishes what has happened to his property and makes good his claim that the assets which he claims can properly be regarded as representing his property".[39] More recently, however, in *Foskett v McKeown* both Lord Millett and Lord Steyn spoke of a single set of tracing rules applicable to claimants in equity or the common law. Influentially, Birks has been a key proponent of the view that there is a unified regime for tracing which, "allows tracing to be cleanly separated from the business of asserting rights in or in relation to assets successfully traced".[40] He explained:

> "the modern law is equipped with various means of coping with the evidential difficulties which a tracing exercise is bound to encounter. The process of identification thus ceases to be either legal or equitable and becomes, as is fitting, genuinely neutral as to the rights exigible in respect of the assets into which the value in question is traced. The tracing exercise once successfully completed, it can then be asked what rights, if any, the plaintiff can, on his particular facts, assert. It is at that point that it becomes relevant to recall that on some facts those rights will be personal, on others proprietary, on some legal, and on others equitable".[41]

In *Foskett v McKeown*, Lord Steyn described this as a "crystalline analysis" stating, "I regard this explanation as correct. It is consistent with orthodox principle. It clarifies the correct approach to so-called tracing claims. It explains what tracing is about without providing answers to controversies about legal or equitable rights to assets so traced".[42] Similarly, Lord Millett was persuaded that:

> "Given its nature, there is nothing inherently legal or equitable about the tracing exercise. There is thus no sense in maintaining different rules for tracing at law and in equity. One set of tracing rules is enough ... There is certainly no logical justification for allowing any distinction between them to produce capricious results in cases of mixed substitutions by insisting on the existence of a fiduciary relationship as a precondition for applying equity's tracing rules. The existence of such a relationship may be relevant to the nature of the claim which the plaintiff can maintain, whether personal or proprietary, but that is a different matter".[43]

---

[39] [1996] 3 W.L.R. 703 at 712.
[40] "The Necessity of a Unitary Law of Tracing" in *Making Commercial Law, Essays in Honour of Roy Goode* (Oxford, Clarendon Press, 1997), at p.257.
[41] *Making Commercial Law* (Oxford, Clarendon Press, 1997) at p.258.
[42] [2001] 1 A.C. 102 at 113.
[43] [2001] 1 A.C. 102 at 129.

On the basis of *Foskett v McKeown*, there appears authoritative support for future courts to depart fully from the historical approach which was in favour of a robust application of different legal and equitable rules. In this light, it is surprising that in *Shalson v Russo*,[44] Rimer J. was not persuaded that he should regard *Foskett* as having decided that there is no longer any difference between the common law and equitable rules of tracing and that there was now no need to identify a fiduciary relationship as a precondition to tracing into a mixed fund. He claimed, "I do not regard *Foskett* as having decided that".[45] Admittedly, Lord Millett's remarks in *Foskett* are obiter. Having put forward his view, Lord Millett tellingly remarked, "This is not, however, the occasion to explore these matters further, for the present is a straightforward case of a trustee who wrongfully misappropriated trust money, mixed it with his own, and used it to pay for an asset for the benefit of his children. Even on the traditional approach, the equitable rules are available to the plaintiffs".[46] Hence, as Rimer J. properly identified, Lord Millett purposefully stopped short of deciding that the need to demonstrate a fiduciary relationship as a traditional precondition to tracing in equity should be regarded as overruled.

Rimer J. found that support for his view was strengthened having considered the **17.38** other speeches of the House in *Foskett*. Lord Hoffmann, for example, agreed with Lord Millett's speech, and he could not be deemed, thereby, to have decided any more on the point than Lord Millett. Similarly Lord Browne-Wilkinson agreed with Lord Millett's speech, but he expressly made clear that he did, "not want to enter into the dispute whether the legal and equitable rules of tracing are the same or differ".[47] Lord Hope did not deal at all with the point. Although Rimer J. accepted that Lord Steyn might be regarded as having adopted a more positive stance, the overall conclusion was clear, "it cannot be said that *Foskett* has swept away the long recognised difference between common law and equitable tracing".[48] Accordingly, the distinction between the legal and equitable rules must, at least for the present time, be maintained.

TRACING AT COMMON LAW

As indicated above, the process of tracing at common law establishes that trust **17.39** property has passed into the hands of a recipient in breach of trust. The beneficiary is, thereby, positioned to pursue a remedy that recognises his ownership of that property at common law. This may take the form of an action against the recipient for money had and received (misappropriated money) or for conversion (chattels). At its most simple, a beneficiary may be able to follow the specific property into the hands of the recipient, in which case he will seek a return of that specific property. In the alternative, a clean substitution of the original trust property may be traced. The claimant will trace his property into its product, "to assert his title to the product in place of his original

---

[44] [2003] EWHC 1637 (Ch).
[45] [2003] EWHC 1637 (Ch) at [104].
[46] [2001] A.C. 102 at 129.
[47] [2001] 1 A.C. 102 at 109.
[48] [2003] EWHC 1637 (Ch) at [104].

property".[49] For example, if money appropriated in breach of trust is used to pay the total purchase price of a number of shares, there has been a "clean" substitution of the money for the shares. Accordingly, the substitute property can be the subject matter of a common law claim. In *Lipkin Gorman v Karpnale Ltd*,[50] therefore, a firm of solicitors was able to trace money misappropriated from the firm's client account and gambled by a partner of the firm at the Playboy Club into the hands of the defendant recipient club owner. Although the solicitors had no proprietary interest in the money in their client account, at common law they were owners of the chose in action which arose through the indebtedness of the Bank to them. They were, thereby, able to trace their property into its direct product (the money drawn from the account) and follow it into the hands of the club owner. The rationale was, as Lord Templeman explained, "The club received stolen money by way of gift from the thief; the club, being a volunteer, has been unjustly enriched at the expense of the solicitors from whom the money had been stolen and the club must reimburse the solicitors".[51]

It is clear from this formulation of words that the House of Lords viewed the personal action for money had and received as achieving a form of restitution, i.e. a means of reversing the unjust enrichment of the recipient. To this, the Playboy Club had a defence that their payment of winnings in good faith constituted a "change of position" as a consequence of which the solicitors' firm should not be able to claim the entire shortfall. Lord Goff responded:

> "Whether change of position is, or should be, recognised as a defence to claims in restitution is a subject that has been much debated in the books. It is however a matter on which there is a remarkable unanimity of view, the consensus being to the effect that such a defence should be recognised in English law. I myself am under no doubt that this is right ... The time for its recognition in this country is, in my opinion, long overdue".[52]

Accordingly, the solicitors' firm was entitled to claim only the net winnings of the Playboy Club and not the total misappropriated in breach of trust.

17.40   The principle that the common law rules allow tracing into substitute assets has been said to derive from *Taylor v Plumer*.[53] There Sir Thomas Plumer gave money to a stockbroker for the purpose of buying exchequer bills. Contrary to instruction, the stockbroker instead used the money for buying American securities for his own purposes. Sir Thomas was able to trace his property into the securities held by the stockbroker so to defeat a claim made to them by the stockbroker's assignees in bankruptcy. As Lord Ellenborough C.J. explained:

> "It makes no difference in reason or law into what other form, different from the original, the change may have been made ... for the product of or substitute for the original thing still follows the nature of the thing itself, as long as it can be ascertained to be such, and the right only ceases when the means of ascertainment

[49] *Lipkin Gorman v Karpnale Ltd* [1991] 2 A.C. 548 at 573 per Lord Goff.
[50] [1991] 2 A.C. 548; noted at [1992] Conv. 124 (M. Halliwell).
[51] [1991] 2 A.C. 548 at 565.
[52] [1991] 2 A.C. 548 at 580.
[53] (1815) 3 M. & S. 562; see, for example, *Agip (Africa) Ltd v Jackson* [1990] Ch. 265 at 285 per Millett L.J.

fail, which is the case when the subject is turned into money, and mixed and confounded in a general mass of the same description".[54]

Although it has been shown that *Taylor v Plumer* was in fact decided on the rules of equity,[55] both *Lipkin Gorman v Karpnale Ltd*[56] and *Banque Belge pour L'Etranger v Hambrouck*[57] cite this case as authority for the proposition that tracing into exchanged assets was permissible at common law. In *Jones (FC) & Sons v Jones*,[58] Millett L.J. underlined the jurisdiction of the common law maintaining that Lord Ellenborough C.J. in *Taylor v Plumer*, "gave no indication that, in following assets into their exchange products, equity had adopted a rule which was peculiar to itself or which went further than the common law".[59] The principle, therefore, may be simply stated. Provided the trust property or its clean substitute is segregated and identifiable, i.e. it has not been mixed with other property, tracing at common law remains possible.

Common law tracing seemingly extends also to cases where the original property has been substituted and it is from the use of the new property that a profit is derived. The leading authority is that of *Jones (FC) & Sons v Jones*.[60] There the sum of £11,700 was loaned, lawfully, from the partnership account of a firm to Mrs Jones, the wife of one of the partners, who made a successful investment in potato futures. She returned a very healthy profit and proceeded to place the sum of almost £50,000 (comprising both capital and profit) in a bank account separate from all her other assets. It emerged that under the Bankruptcy Act 1914, the partnership was deemed to have been bankrupt before the payment to Mrs Jones. Accordingly, the partnership assets were to pass to the Official Receiver retrospectively. The Official Receiver and not Mrs Jones was, thereby, entitled to the original £11,700 at the point at which the loan was made. Although there was no question that the Official Receiver was entitled to recover the original amount, more difficulty surrounded the profits. Importantly, the rules of equitable tracing could not be employed to facilitate a claim in the light that no fiduciary relationship existed between the Official Receiver and Mrs Jones.[61] The court was left to consider solely the common law rules.

17.41 At common law, the appropriate remedy in such cases is an action for money had and received. Unfortunately, however, this would enable a claim for the original amount but not as to any profit.[62] Although at first glance, a claim to the original amount could be of little help to the Official Receiver's case, both Millett and Nourse L.JJ. swayed in his favour, albeit by different reasoning. Millett L.J. countenanced a proprietary claim to the entire sum on the basis that the property in issue had been retained in a separate bank account. He derived support from *Banque Belge pour*

[54] (1815) 3 M. & S. 562 at 575.
[55] L. Smith, "Tracing in *Taylor v Plumer*: Equity in the Court of King's Bench" [1995] LMCLQ 240.
[56] [1991] 2 A.C. 548.
[57] [1921] 1 K.B. 321.
[58] [1996] 3 W.L.R. 703.
[59] [1996] 3 W.L.R. 703 at 712.
[60] [1996] 3 W.L.R. 703.
[61] The pre-requisites of equitable tracing are discussed below (see **17.43**).
[62] As Fox L.J. explained in *Agip (Africa) Ltd v Jackson* [1991] Ch. 547 at 563, "Liability depends upon receipt by the defendant of the plaintiff's money and the extent of the liability depends on the amount received".

L'Etranger v Hambrouck[63] and the House of Lords in *Lipkin Gorman v Karpnale Ltd*,[64] and saw, "no reason for concluding that the common law does not recognise claims to substitute assets or their products".[65] He held the claimant entitled to the contents of the account stating that, "the fact that it included profits made by the use of that money is immaterial".[66] Undeniably, his approach marks an extension to the traditional understanding of the ambit of the common law rules.[67]

Nourse L.J. immediately acknowledged that they had gone further than the House of Lords in *Lipkin Gorman v Karpnale Ltd* to accept the proposition that, "the action for money had and received entitles the legal owner to trace his property into its product, not only in the sense of property for which it is exchanged, but also in the sense of property representing the original and the profit made by the defendant's use of it".[68] Interestingly, he agreed with the result, but by means of a broader justification. Focusing upon the personal action for money had and received, Nourse L.J. endorsed the view that the action "is a liberal action in the nature of a bill in equity".[69] Accordingly, he embraced an argument of conscience to deny Mrs Jones what would be unjust enrichment. As Nourse L.J. commented, "In my view the defendant cannot in conscience retain the profit any more than the original £11,700. She had no title to the original. She could not have made the profit without her use of it. She cannot, by making a profit through the use of money to which she had no title, acquire some better title to the profit".[70]

Loss of the right to trace at common law

17.42   Most cases of misappropriation of trust property require a claimant to trace into a mixed bank account, typically, where the defendant has mixed trust monies with other funds and insufficient funds remain to satisfy all claims. In such cases there is no scope for tracing at common law.[71] In the words of Lord Goff, "at common law, property in money, like other fungibles is lost as such when it is mixed with other money".[72] By way of example, in *Agip (Africa) Ltd v Jackson*,[73] the defendant accountants laundered the claimant's money through the bank accounts of a number of shell companies which were subsequently liquidated. The claimant's funds were transferred telegraphically from its bank in Tunis through the New York clearing system into accounts in London

---

[63] [1921] 1 K.B. 321.

[64] [1991] 2 A.C. 548.

[65] [1996] 3 W.L.R. 703 at 711.

[66] [1996] 3 W.L.R. 703 at 712.

[67] It is noteworthy that Millett L.J. had previously argued extra judicially that curtailment of the common law rules was appropriate, "A unified and comprehensive restitutionary remedy should be developed based on equitable principles, and attempts to rationalise and develop the common law action for money had and received should be abandoned" (P. Millett, "Tracing the Proceeds of Fraud" (1991) 107 L.Q.R. 71 at p.85).

[68] [1996] 3 W.L.R. 703 at 714.

[69] [1996] 3 W.L.R. 703 at 714, citing the words of Lord Mansfield C.J. in *Clarke v Shee and Johnson* (1774) 1 Cowp. 197 at 199.

[70] [1996] 3 W.L.R. 703 at 714.

[71] It appears that tracing into a substantially unmixed account is permissible: see *Banque Belge pour L'Etranger v Hambrouck* [1921] 1 K.B. 321.

[72] *Lipkin Gorman v Karpnale Ltd* [1991] 2 A.C. 548 at 572.

[73] [1991] Ch. 547.

controlled by the defendants. In the course of the complex transactions, therefore, the trust money was combined with other monies and changed into different currencies. As a partial remedy, the claimant sought to trace into the defendant's accounts. In the Court of Appeal, Fox L.J. held that, on the basis that mixing of the funds had occurred in the New York clearing system, common law tracing was unavailable. The rationale was highlighted by Millett J. in the High Court:

> "The money cannot be followed by treating it as the proceeds of a cheque presented by the collecting bank in exchange for payment by the paying bank. The money was transmitted by telegraphic transfer ... Nothing passed between Tunisia and London but a stream of electrons. It is not possible to treat the money received by Lloyds Bank in London or its correspondent bank in New York as representing the proceeds of the payment order or of any other physical asset previously in its hands and delivered by it in exchange for the money".[74]

The limitations of common law tracing are patently displayed in the case law. Although it is clearly possible in straightforward circumstances to trace cheques paid into bank accounts, the presence of telegraphic transfer, telexed instructions or the engagement of inter-bank clearing systems will obscure the identity of the original trust property with the consequence that tracing at law will fail. As will be demonstrated, such mixing is no barrier to tracing in equity. As in most cases mixing will have occurred, as mentioned previously, the common law rules maintain only a limited practical value. Nonetheless, where tracing in equity is unavailable to a claimant, an action at common law may be the only option.

TRACING IN EQUITY

The requirement of fiduciary relationship

It is frequently stated that a claimant is able to assert an equitable proprietary claim to the traceable proceeds of trust property only if he can demonstrate the existence of a fiduciary relationship. For example, in *Agip (Africa) v Jackson*, Millett J. claimed that the only restriction on the ability of equity to follow assets is the requirement that there must be some fiduciary relationship which permits the assistance of equity to be invoked. In *Re Diplock's Estate*, Caleb Diplock, who died in 1936, directed the executors under his will to apply his residuary estate, "for such charitable institution or institutions or other charitable or benevolent object or objects in England" as his executors should in their discretion select. Accordingly, his executors distributed £203,000 amongst 139 charitable institutions. Unfortunately, the gift was not exclusively charitable and was successfully challenged as an invalid charitable trust.[75] In addition to an action against the executors for misappropriation of the residuary estate, the next of kin sought to trace the property into the hands of the charities. In the Court

17.43

---

[74] [1990] Ch. 265 at 286.
[75] *Chichester Diocesan Fund v Simpson* [1944] A.C. 341.

of Appeal, it was held that, "equity may operate on the conscience not merely of those who acquire a legal title in breach of some trust, express or constructive, or of some other fiduciary obligation, but of volunteers provided that as a result of what has gone before some equitable proprietary interest has been created and attaches to the property in the hands of the volunteer."[76] As a matter of general principle, therefore, the holder of an equitable proprietary interest can trace property into the hands of a third party where a fiduciary relationship can be demonstrated.

This seeming precondition has been the subject of much criticism and confusion. In *Agip (Africa) v Jackson*, Millett J. viewed the requirement as resting on authority rather than principle. In particular, attention has been focused on cases such *Re Diplock's Estate* as authority for the proposition that the fiduciary relationship must be pre-existing. In *Box v Barclays Bank*, for example, Ferris J. evinced such an understanding when he observed that, "Equitable tracing is only available where there is an equity to trace, which requires that there must be an initial fiduciary relationship between the person claiming to trace and the party who is said to have misapplied that person's money".[77] Nonetheless, Millett J. was not of this view in *Agip (Africa) v Jackson*, when he claimed that, "it is not necessary that the fund to be traced should have been the subject of fiduciary obligations before it got into the wrong hands".[78] In his view, it is sufficient that the payment to the defendant itself gave rise to a fiduciary relationship.

17.44   Consequent to the need to establish a fiduciary relationship as a precondition to tracing in equity, the courts have strained to accept that fiduciary relationships exist in circumstances where fiduciary duties would not usually arise. This enthusiasm to discern a fiduciary relationship is, of course, motivated purely by the practical need to permit a claimant's use of the equitable tracing rules. The classic illustration is the thief who may be deemed to owe a fiduciary duty to his victim such that the victim can trace his property through a subsequent sale from which the proceeds have become mixed in a bank account.[79] The development of the law in this manner is patently unsatisfactory. As Hayton and Marshall express, "Instrumental findings of this sort debase the currency of the fiduciary concept".[80]

Nonetheless, development of the law is far from static. A discernible shift in thinking appears to have occurred in the House of Lords where, as indicated in *Foskett v McKeown*,[81] Lord Millett could see no logical justification for the insistence on a fiduciary relationship as a precondition to tracing. This goes beyond his adopted stance in *Bristol and West BS v Mothew*.[82] In *Mothew*, Millett L.J. (as he then was) bemoaned the "supposed rule that there must be a fiduciary relationship or retained beneficial interest before resort may be had to the equitable tracing rules".[83] Referring to his own

---

[76] *Re Diplock* [1948] Ch. 465 at 530. As will be discussed, they successfully brought a personal action to recover money from the charities [1951] A.C. 251, considered by the House of Lords.
[77] (1998) *The Times*, April 30.
[78] [1990] Ch. 265 at 290.
[79] See, for example, the view of Lord Templeman in *Lipkin Gorman v Karpnale Ltd* [1991] 2 A.C. 548 at 565.
[80] At p.802.
[81] [2001] 1 A.C. 102 at 128.
[82] [1998] Ch. 1.
[83] [1998] Ch. 1 at 23.

decision in *El Ajou v Dollar Holdings Plc*,[84] he admitted he had in the past been concerned to circumvent this rule the strict application of which "would have been productive of the most extraordinary anomalies. . .".[85] In *Mothew*, therefore, he voiced dissatisfaction, maintaining that as regards the pre-requisite to equitable tracing, "its existence continually threatens to frustrate attempts to develop a coherent law of restitution. Until the equitable tracing rules are made available in support of the ordinary common law claim for money had and received some problems will remain incapable of sensible resolution".[86] It may not be long before the higher courts revisit his more developed thinking as detailed in *Foskett*.

Equitable tracing rules in operation

The operation of the equitable tracing rules and consequent claims is best explained by a series of illustrations drawing on the typical contexts in which the rules will be invoked. For example, a claimant may simply need to show that trust property has been mixed with the property of the trustee, whether the mixing is physical or, more commonly, in a bank account. Logically, however, different rules are operative where the account contains the property of more than one trust fund or it contains both trust property and the property of an innocent volunteer. The detailed workings of these rules will now be considered.

17.45

Physical mixtures

Where trust property such as grain or oil is physically mixed with other property, it remains possible to divide the mixture into identical parts. Although it ceases to be clear exactly which part of the commingled mass belongs to each contributor, it is clear that the contribution of each contributor lies somewhere in the mixture. If some part of the mixture is consumed or dissipated, insufficient property remains to satisfy the claims of all contributors. In the case of wrongdoing, for example, where a trustee mixes trust property with his own property, the rules will operate in favour of the beneficiary as an innocent contributor.[87] Accordingly, the trustee will be deemed to use his own property first. Only when the beneficiary's claim is satisfied will the trustee be permitted to trace his own contribution to the mixture. By contrast, in the absence of wrongdoing, contributors share rateably, i.e. in proportion to their contributions.

Pro rata division is appropriate in the case of mixtures of fungibles such as money or oil. More problematic is the case where mixing of assets creates an entirely new product. Under the doctrine of specification, the prima facie conclusion must be the original asset has been destroyed and the ability to follow that asset is lost. This principle appears to give way where the mixing is carried out by a wrongdoer. In the Canadian

17.46

---

[84] [1993] 3 All E.R. 717 at 734, where he suggested that on rescission equitable title might revest in the representee retrospectively at least to the extent necessary to support an equitable tracing claim.
[85] [1998] Ch. 1 at 23.
[86] [1998] Ch. 1 at 23.
[87] See *Indian Oil Corporation Ltd v Greenstone Shipping SA (Panama)* [1987] 2 Lloyd's Rep. 286.

case of *Jones v De Marchant*,[88] a husband used 18 beaver skins belonging to his wife together with four skins of his own and made a fur coat as a present for his mistress. Although the mistress was an innocent volunteer who had no knowledge of the ownership of the skins, the wife was deemed entitled to recover the coat. It was clear that the mistress, as an innocent volunteer in receipt of misappropriated property, could stand in no better a position than the donor. The coat was a new asset created from the co-mingled skins of the claimant wife and her wrongdoing husband. Division of the coat into shares in proportion to the relative contribution was patently inappropriate. Accordingly, the facts gave rise to an, "all or nothing case" in which the coat should be assigned to one or other of the parties. As the wrongdoer carried out the mixing and it was by virtue of this mixing that the mistress acquired the asset, the maximum that the wrongdoer and his donee can ask for is pro rata division. Where this possibility is excluded, the beneficiary is entitled to the whole and should not be confined to enforcement of a lien.

Trustee's own money mixed with misappropriated trust money

17.47   Where there is competition as between a wrongdoing trustee and a beneficiary seeking to trace into the funds in a mixed bank account, there follows a "cherry picking" exercise[89] in which equity permits the beneficiary to elect the more beneficial of two rules that might be invoked. Take, for example, a trustee, Fred, who mixes £5,000 of his own money with £5,000 of trust money. Were he to proceed to squander £3,000 and then to invest £6,000 profitably, only £1,000 would remain in the account. Between the parties, the question arises as to the proportion of money dissipated, the proportion profitably invested and the proportion untouched in the account. Under the rule in *Re Hallett's Estate*,[90] it is presumed that if a trustee uses money from a fund in which he has mixed his own money with the trust money, he uses his own money first. The principle is that which Jessel M.R. famously declared, "Wherever it can be done rightfully, he is not allowed to say, against the person entitled to the property or the right, that he has done it wrongfully".[91] Accordingly, as the trustee has acted wrongfully, it is not open to him to assert that he lost anything other than his own money first.

In *Re Oatway*,[92] however, the trustee solicitor used funds from a bank account containing a mixture of his own and his clients' money to make a profitable investment in shares before proceeding to waste the rest of the funds. Joyce J. made clear that in these circumstances the trustee could not be deemed to spend his own money first. The claim of the beneficiary stood first in priority. As Joyce J. spelt out, "when any of the money drawn out has been invested, and the investment remains in the name or under the control of the trustee, the rest of the balance having been afterwards dissipated by him, he cannot maintain that the investment which remains represents his own money

---

[88] (1916) 28 D.L.R. 561.
[89] Per Rimer J. in *Shalson v Russo* [2003] EWHC 1637 (Ch) at [144].
[90] (1880) 13 Ch. D. 696.
[91] (1880) 13 Ch. D. 696 at 727.
[92] [1903] 2 Ch. 356.

alone, and that what has been spent and can no longer be traced and recovered was the money belonging to the trust".[93]

Looking again at the example above, Fred has wasted £3,000 and invested £6,000 at a profit. £1,000 remains in the account. Under the rule in *Re Hallett*, he would be deemed to spend his own money first. As to the beneficiary, in *Re Tilley's WT*, Ungoed-Thomas J. expressed the view, "that if, having regard to all the circumstances of the case objectively considered, it appears that the trustee has in fact, whatever his intention, laid out trust moneys in or towards a purchase, then the beneficiaries are entitled to the property purchased and any profits it produces to the extent to which it has been paid for out of trust money".[94] Accordingly, the beneficiary will look to trace into the property purchased from the mixed fund (and, thereby, the profit) before any claim to the sum that remains in the account.

17.48

Further clarification can be gleaned from *Foskett v McKeown*.[95] Here, Lord Millett described as a basic rule that where a trustee wrongfully uses trust money to provide part of the cost of acquiring an asset, the beneficiary is entitled at his option either to claim a proportionate share of the asset or to enforce a lien upon it to secure his personal claim against the trustee for the amount of the misapplied money. In *Foskett v McKeown*, Timothy Murphy took out a life assurance policy of £1 million and proceeded to pay the first two annual premiums out of his own funds. The next two premiums (from five in total) were paid from money held by Murphy as an express trustee for a group of purchasers who had paid substantial sums to Murphy pending the transfer to them of building land in the Algarve. Before his suicide in 1991, Murphy settled the life assurance policy on trust for his mother and his children. On his death the sum assured was paid to the trustees of the policy. The purchasers claimed that they were entitled to recover 40 per cent of the policy proceeds, i.e. a sum in proportion to the premiums paid. The beneficiaries argued that if the purchasers were entitled at all, it was to the amount of their premiums (with interest) and not to a pro rata share in the policy proceeds. By a majority, the House of Lords upheld the purchasers' claim to a pro-rata share on the basis that they could assert an equitable proprietary interest in the mixed fund.

It seems sensible and just that, as between the beneficiary and the wrongdoing trustee, the operation of the rules should overtly favour the beneficiary. In the case of the profitable investment, therefore, the beneficiary is entitled to claim a proportionate share in the asset. As Rimer J. explained in *Shalson v Russo*, "The justice of this is that, if the beneficiary is not entitled to do this, the wrongdoing trustee may be left with all the cherries and the victim with nothing".[96] In the example provided, the beneficiary can enforce a proprietary claim to a proportionate share of Fred's profitable investment, i.e. £5,000 plus profits.

17.49

---

[93] [1903] 2 Ch. 356 at 360.
[94] [1967] Ch. 1179 at 1193. On the facts, nonetheless, the trustee was deemed to have used her overdraft facility and not trust moneys towards the purchase of properties.
[95] [2001] 1 A.C. 102.
[96] [2003] EWHC 1637 (Ch) at [18].

Lowest intermediate balance

17.50   It should be noted that beneficiaries are able to trace only into what has been referred to as the lowest intermediate balance of the account. Consider where a trustee mixes £5,000 of his own money with £5,000 of trust money and proceeds to waste £7,000 of the entire fund. Even, if at some future date, the trustee replenishes the account, only £3,000 of the trust money can be traced. In the absence of evidence that the trustee intended to replace the claimant's funds, tracing can take effect against the lowest balance in the intervening period.[97] As Sargant J. emphasised in *Roscoe v Winder:*

> "in a case where the account into which the moneys are paid is the general trading account of the debtor on which he has been accustomed to draw both in the ordinary course and in breach of trust when there were trust funds standing to the credit of that account which were convenient for that purpose, I think it is impossible to attribute to him that by the mere payment into the account of further moneys which to a large extent he subsequently used for purposes of his own he intended to clothe those moneys with a trust in favour of the plaintiffs".[98]

This principle has been upheld in respect of the wrongful diversion of oil stocks in *Glencore International AG v Alpina Insurance Co Ltd.*[99] There Moore-Bick J. applied *Roscoe v Winder* claiming that, "an intention to transfer title cannot be inferred simply from the fact that a wrongdoer has added to a commingled bulk a quantity of his own goods ... sufficient to reverse the effect of previous wrongful withdrawals".[1]

Overdrawn bank accounts

17.51   The right to trace in equity is lost when trust funds pass into an overdrawn account.[2] As Rimer J. explained in *Shalson v Russo*,[3] this is simply because an overdrawn account is not an asset but a liability. "The consequence is that the claimant cannot show that his money has become represented by an asset into which it is possible to trace: all his money has done is to reduce a liability, and so has ceased to exist".[4] In *Bishopsgate Investment Management Ltd v Homan*,[5] therefore, no equitable tracing was available in respect of the improper payment of pension funds into an overdrawn account.

---

[97] See, for example, *Campden Hill Ltd v Chakrani* [2005] EWHC 911 (Ch) at [79].
[98] [1915] 1 Ch. 62 at 69. See also *BA Peters Plc* [2008] EWHC 2205 (Ch).
[99] [2004] EWHC 66 (Comm).
[1] [2004] EWHC 66 (Comm) at [18].
[2] *Re Goldcorp Exchange Ltd* [1995] 1 A.C. 74 at 104–105 per Lord Mustill; *Box v Barclays Bank* [1998] Lloyd's Rep. Bank 185 at 203 per Ferris J.
[3] [2003] EWHC 1637 (Ch).
[4] [2003] EWHC 1637 (Ch) at [140].
[5] [1995] Ch. 211.

Backwards tracing

The question arises as to whether beneficiaries might be permitted to trace backwards **17.52** through the payment of a debt using trust money, into an asset purchased with the borrowed funds. A simple example is of the trustee who uses £3,300 of his overdraft to buy a car and one day later pays the same sum into his account using misappropriated trust funds. The question arises as to whether a claimant to the misappropriated funds can trace through the repayment into the asset which is arguably intended to be purchased by the trust money. The Court of Appeal in *Foskett v McKeown*[6] considered this matter. There, Scott V.C. openly regarded it to be undecided:

> "I would wish, for my part, to make it clear that I regard the point as still open and, in particular, that I do not regard the fact that an asset is paid for out of borrowed money with the borrowing subsequently repaid out of trust money as being necessarily fatal to an equitable tracing claim by the trust beneficiaries. If, in such a case, it can be shown that it was always the intention to use the trust money to acquire the asset, I do not see why the order in which the events happen should be regarded as critical to the claim".[7]

At first instance in *Bishopsgate Investment Management Ltd v Homan*, Vinelott J. would not rule out the possible invocation of so called backwards tracing, arguing that proof that trust moneys were paid into an overdrawn account of the defaulting trustee might not always be sufficient to bar a claim to an equitable charge. In the Court of Appeal,[8] Leggatt L.J. was markedly less enthusiastic. Effectively ruling out such an application of the rules, he explained:

> "there can be no equitable remedy against an asset acquired before misappropriation of money takes place, since ex hypothesi it cannot be followed into something which existed and so had been acquired before the money was received and therefore without its aid. The concept of a 'composite transaction' is in my judgment fallacious. What is envisaged is (a) the purchase of an asset by means of an overdraft, that is, a loan from a bank, and (b) the discharge of the loan by means of misappropriated trust money. The judge thought that the money could be regarded as having been used to acquire the asset ... [but] there can ordinarily be no tracing into an asset which is already in the hands of the defaulting trustee when the misappropriation occurs".[9]

As against the conventional understanding of tracing as a process which allows a claimant to trace the value of specific assets through real time substitutions into specific, identifiable property, there is no room for backwards tracing. As Buckley L.J. identified in *Borden (UK) Ltd v Scottish Timber Products Ltd*, "it is a fundamental feature of the doctrine of tracing that the property to be traced can be identified at every stage of its

[6] [1998] Ch. 265.
[7] [1998] Ch. 265 at 283.
[8] [1995] Ch. 211.
[9] [1995] Ch. 211 at 221.

journey through life".[10] It is trite to restate that tracing is a process not a remedy in itself. It follows, however, that there is no room to import the concept of intention. As Ungoed-Thomas J. stated in *Re Tilley's WT*, "if, having regard to all the circumstances of the case objectively considered, it appears that the trustee has in fact, whatever his intention, laid out trust moneys in or towards a purchase, then the beneficiaries are entitled to the property purchased and any profits which it produces to the extent to which it has been paid for by the trust money".[11]

17.53   Similar logic might be employed to explain the discredited swollen assets theory as put forward in *Space Investments Ltd v Canadian Imperial Bank of Commerce Co (Bahamas) Ltd*.[12] There, Lord Templeman claimed obiter that beneficiaries could trace misappropriated trust money into all the assets of a bank without the need to point to the specific assets into which the value could be traced. The justification for this flexible approach was said to be that the trust money swelled the total assets held be the bank and that a claimant only needed to show that value had gone into the bank's general assets. As Lord Templeman explained, "equity allows the beneficiaries ... to trace the trust money to all the assets of the bank and to recover the trust money by the exercise of an equitable charge over all the assets of the bank ... that equitable charge secures for the beneficiaries and the trust priority over the claims of the customers ... and ... all other unsecured creditors".[13] Rejected in *Re Goldcorp Exchange Ltd* and also by the Court of Appeal in *Bishopsgate Investment Management Ltd v Homan*, it is clear that the tracing rules do not permit the claimant to move beyond specific identifiable property (into which the value of his assets have passed) to treat all of the defendant's assets as a large single fund in which trust assets have been mixed.

Mixed funds consisting of two trust funds or trust moneys with moneys of an innocent volunteer

17.54   The cases and illustrations above apply where there has been a mixture of trust money with the trustee's own money. Frequently, however, it is necessary to consider the position where a mixed fund contains property from two or more trust funds or where trust property has become mixed with the property of an innocent volunteer. In such cases, different rules apply to tracing claims.

Beneficiary against innocent volunteer

17.55   As regards the mixing of trust property with that of an innocent volunteer, the matter was duly considered in *Re Diplock's Estate*.[14] It will be recalled that this case concerned the distribution by executors of the testator's residuary estate to around 139 charities under a bequest later held by the House of Lords to be invalid. Accordingly, the

---

[10] [1981] Ch. 25 at 46.
[11] [1967] Ch. 1179 at 1193.
[12] [1986] 1 W.L.R. 1072.
[13] [1986] 1 W.L.R. 1072 at 1074.
[14] [1948] Ch. 46.

question arose as to how to balance the competing equitable claims of the beneficiary and the innocent volunteer. The answer provided by Lord Greene M.R. was that:

> "Where an innocent volunteer (as distinct from a purchaser for value without notice) mixes 'money' of his own with 'money' which in equity belongs to another person, or is found in possession of such a mixture, although that other person may not claim a charge on the mass superior to the claim of the volunteer, he is entitled, nevertheless, to a charge ranking *pari passu* with the claim of the volunteer".[15]

This principle is open to the criticism that it is unduly favourable to the innocent volunteer. Consider, for example, an innocent volunteer who purchases investments in part with trust money and in part with his own funds. He takes the proceeds of the investments and gambles away a large sum of money. As the proceeds are derived in part from trust money and in part from his own resources, he is deemed to have dissipated money rateably from the trust fund and his own funds. He is not presumed to spend his own money first. The potential for unfairness is even more pronounced where the mixing occurs in a current bank account. Where an account contains misappropriated funds from two or more trusts or there is a mixture of trust moneys and the money of an innocent volunteer, the court can elect to apply one of three different approaches. These are as follows:

- the "first in, first out" approach;

- proportionate shares, or

- the North American rolling charge.

First in, first out

The "first in, first out" rule established by *Clayton's case*[16] is the rule adopted traditionally where the property of different trusts has been mixed in a current or running bank account. The essence of the approach in *Clayton's case* is that when sums become mixed in a bank account, the withdrawals from that account are deemed to occur in the same order as the money was deposited. Historically, the rule achieved the most efficient means of balancing the respective interests of a banker and his customer in a bank account. What was an effective tool of accounting, however, quickly became regarded as the primary means to determine the distribution of property from a fund that is comprised of several beneficiaries' money or the money of an innocent volunteer where there is insufficient money to meet their respective claims.[17]

Even at first glance, it is clear that any rigid application of this rule is apt to produce arbitrary and unacceptable results. Consider a bank account into which £1,000 from

17.56

---

[15] [1948] Ch. 465 at 524.
[16] (1816) 1 Mer. 572.
[17] In *Barlow Clowes International v Vaughan* [1992] 4 All E.R. 22 at 33, Dillon L.J. recognised a "long-established general practice" of the courts in applying *Clayton's Case* in such circumstances.

Trust X is deposited, followed by £1,000 from Trust Y, followed by £1,000 from Trust Z. Imagine that £1,500 is withdrawn and invested profitably, whereas the remaining £1,500 in the account is dissipated. Under the rule in *Clayton's case*, Trust X would be entitled to trace the first £1,000 into the profitable investment. This opens the way to a full recovery of the value of the misappropriated funds and a claim to a proportionate share of the profit. Trust Y, by contrast, will recover only £500 and the proportion of the profit thereby generated. Purely on the basis of the timing of the deposit of moneys in the account, the rule in *Clayton's case* reduces the claim of Trust Y to half of the value it added to the account. Trust Z can recover nothing.

17.57   It should come as little surprise that the first in first out rule has attracted criticism. As Judge Learned Hand said in *Re Walter J Schmidt & Co, Ex p. Feuerbach:*

> "The rule in *Clayton's case* is to allocate the payments upon an account. Some rule had to be adopted, and though any presumption of intent was a fiction, priority in time was the most natural basis of allocation. It has no relevancy whatever to a case like this. Here two people are jointly interested in a fund held for them by a common trustee. There is no reason in law or justice why his depredations upon the fund should not be borne equally between them. To throw all the loss upon one, through the mere chance of his being earlier in time, is irrational and arbitrary, and is equally a fiction as the rule in *Clayton's case*. When the law adopts a fiction, it is, or at least it should be, for some purpose of justice. To adopt it here is to apportion a common misfortune through a test which has no relation whatever to the justice of the case".[18]

Notwithstanding, its frequent invocation, the rule in *Clayton's case* is merely a rule of convenience based on a presumption as to intentions.[19] In the words of Leggatt L.J. in *Barlow Clowes International v Vaughan*, "neither its acclaim nor its application has been universal".[20] Accordingly, as Woolf L.J. made clear, the modern approach is to apply the rule when it is convenient to do so and when its application can be seen to do broad justice having regard to the nature of the competing claims.[21]

Proportionality

17.58   As indicated above, the approach based on proportionality would entail that the available assets and moneys would be distributed rateably in proportion to the amounts contributed to the fund. This solution disregards the date at which investments were made. Instead, it is necessary to share the remaining assets on a proportionate basis among all contributors. The clear advantage of this approach lies in the capacity to minimise the potential for injustice where *Clayton's case* is applied. This principle of proportionate shares was adopted in the House of Lords in *Foskett v McKeown* where Lord Millett held that, "Where a beneficiary's claim is in competition with the claims of

---

[18] (1923) 298 F 314 at 316.
[19] *Re Diplock* [1948] Ch. 465 at 553 per Lord Greene M.R.
[20] [1992] 4 All E.R. 22 at 43.
[21] See generally M. Pawlowski, "The Demise of the Rule in Clayton's Case" [2003] Conv. 339.

other innocent contributors, there is no basis upon which any of the claims can be subordinated to any of the others. Where the fund is deficient, the beneficiary is not entitled to enforce a lien for his contributions; all must share rateably in the fund. The primary rule in regard to a mixed fund is that gains and losses are borne by the contributors rateably".[22] Accordingly, in the example cited above, Trusts X, Y and Z would claim equally between them.

Rolling charge

The North American solution is termed "the rolling charge". In the United States and Canada it has been adopted (where appropriate) in preference to the rule in *Clayton's case* as establishing a fairer and more equitable result.[23] As Woolf L.J. explained in *Barlow Clowes*, "This solution involves treating credits to a bank account made at different times and from different sources as a blend or cocktail with the result that when a withdrawal is made from the account it is treated as a withdrawal in the same proportions as the different interests in the account … bear to each other at the moment before the withdrawal is made".[24] It has the advantage that: **17.59**

> "each debit to the account, unless unequivocally attributable to the moneys of one depositor or source (e.g. as if an investment was purchased for one), should be attributed to all the depositors so as to reduce all their deposits pro rata, instead of being attributed, as under *Clayton's case*, to the earliest deposits in point of time. The reasoning is that if there is an account which has been fed only with trust moneys deposited by a number of individuals, and the account holder misapplies a sum from the account for his own purposes, and that sum is lost, it is fair that the loss should be borne by all the depositors pro rata, rather than that the whole loss should fall first on the depositor who made the earliest deposit in point of time".[25]

Consider, for example, a trustee who mixes £1,000 from Trust A with £1,000 from Trust B. He then gambles away £800. One day later, he adds £2,000 from Trust C. The balance of the account now stands at £3,200. If the "first in, first out" rule fell to be applied, Trust A would be disadvantaged, but both B and C could recover fully. By contrast, if losses were to be shared proportionately, a seemingly fairer outcome results. Trusts A, B and C would be entitled to a distribution of the balance in line with their respective contributions (i.e. 1:1:2). Trusts A and B can claim £800 each. Trust C can claim £1,600. The problem is that this rule ignores the timing of deposits into the account and withdrawals therefrom. It fails to distinguish cases where the claimant's money cannot have been dissipated because, physically, it had not, at the time of dissipation, entered the mixture from which the defendant extracted the funds. Nonetheless, the claimant is deemed to share rateably in the losses. Applying the rolling

---

[22] [2001] 1 A.C. 102 at 132.
[23] See, for example, the decision of the Ontario Court of Appeal in *Re Ontario Securities Commission and Greymac Credit Corp* (1986) 55 O.R. (2d) 673.
[24] [1992] 4 All E.R. 22 at 35.
[25] [1992] 4 All E.R. 22 at 27.

charge, however, the timing of deposits and withdrawals is factored in. In the example provided, C's money was not added until after the defendant loses £800. Under the rolling charge approach, only A and B should shoulder this loss in proportion to their respective contributions to the fund prior to the defendant's wasteful act. Accordingly, prior to the payment of £2,000 from Trust C into the account, the balance stands at £1,200. This is a balance to which A and B are entitled rateably (i.e. 1:1 ratio). Once Trust C's money is added to the account, a subsequent loss or gain will be shared in the same proportion as their interests bear to each other at the point at which the loss or gain was made (i.e. a 3:3:10 ratio).

17.60   Admittedly, on complex facts, the rolling charge will be difficult and expensive to apply.[26] In *Barlow Clowes*, for example, thousands of investors had contributed money to BCI. When the company went into liquidation, the question arose as to who was entitled to the remaining assets. Although the rolling charge was deemed to be fairest in the sense that claimants would share losses in proportion to their interest in the fund prior to each withdrawal, the method was deemed to be inapplicable. For example, Woolf L.J. noted that, "it might just be possible to perform the exercise", but he felt that, "the costs involved would be out of all proportion even to the sizeable sums which are here involved".[27] Accordingly, the rule in *Clayton's case* was re-affirmed as the rule of convenience in such cases. On the facts of *Barlow Clowes*, however, the rule in *Clayton's case* was not applied. The available assets were ordered to be distributed rateably to investors in proportion to their contributions to the fund.[28] A similar outcome was reached in *Commerzbank Aktiengesellschaft v IMB Morgan Plc*, where the rule in *Clayton's case* was deemed to be impracticable and unjust.[29] Albeit attractive in theory, the rolling charge is yet to displace the more traditional rules of equitable tracing in this context.[30]

The limits to tracing and equitable proprietary claims

17.61   Notwithstanding the operation of the rules of tracing, there is a variety of situations in which the capacity to trace is lost or it is clear that the claimant will be unsuccessful with his resulting claim. Key considerations are as follows:

- where misappropriated trust property falls into the hands of a bona fide purchaser for value without notice it ceases to be possible for a beneficiary to pursue a proprietary claim. Although, technically, it is possible to trace property into the recipient's hands, bona fide purchasers take free from the claims of beneficiaries. As demonstrated, no such defence is available to the volunteer who acts in good faith or otherwise;[31]

---

[26] See *Russell-Cooke Trust Co v Prentis* [2002] EWHC 2227 (Ch).
[27] [1992] 4 All E.R. 22 at 35.
[28] For Woolf L.J. this outcome had, "the virtue of relative simplicity and therefore relative economy and also the virtue of being in this case more just than the first solution [*Clayton's case*]. It would have the effect of sharing the pool of assets available proportionately among the thousands of investors in a way which reflected the fact that they were all the victims of a 'common misfortune'" ([1992] 4 All E.R. 22 and 35).
[29] [2005] 1 Lloyd's Rep 298 at 306.
[30] See, however, *Shalson v Russo* [2003] EWHC 1637 (Ch) where Rimer J. clearly preferred the rolling charge solution.
[31] See **17.55**.

- where trust property or its traceable value is consumed, dissipated or destroyed, the beneficiary will not succeed in making a proprietary claim. Typically, for example, a trustee or third party might gamble trust funds away, go on a holiday or pay off a debt. In such circumstances, a proprietary claim is destined to fail. As described above, money paid into an overdrawn bank account ceases to be identifiable[32] and it is not currently open to the beneficiary to trace backwards[33] or to argue that the assets of the bank have swollen and that trust funds must be located within the general assets of the bank.[34] Different considerations apply where a trustee uses trust money to effect improvements to land or to pay off a secured debt such as a mortgage. In the case of the former, the land will be charged with the payment to the claimant of a sum reflecting the extent to which the recipient's land has been improved by use of the misappropriated money. As to the latter, the beneficiary is permitted to trace into the discharged mortgage and acquire it as security for the unpaid money. The court may treat the land as subject to a charge by way of subrogation in favour of the claimant.[35] The claimant's position is said to be subrogated (i.e. substituted) to that of the original mortgagee, and

- the claim of a beneficiary may be met by the defence of change of position, i.e. that it is inequitable for a beneficiary to pursue his proprietary claim on the basis that a bona fide recipient's position has changed. Although this defence has only recently been recognised as applicable in the context of tracing,[36] consider the recipient charities in *Re Diplock*.[37] Where the charities, as innocent donees, had spent the claimant's money on improvements to their property, the Court of Appeal deemed it inequitable to permit the claimant to pursue a proprietary action. The charge, enforceable by sale, would have required the charities to sell their own property to meet the claims of the next of kin. It is, as yet, unclear how the restitutionary defence of change of position will mesh with the rules governing equitable proprietary claims. It is to be remembered that in *Foskett v McKeown*,[38] Lord Millett's rejected the link between equitable tracing and restitution and, thereby, kept separate the defences available in each context. He observed, "a claim in unjust enrichment is subject to a change of position defence, which usually operates by reducing or extinguishing the element of enrichment. An action like the present is subject to the bona fide purchaser for value defence, which operates to clear the defendant's title".[39]

---

[32] *Shalson v Russo* [2003] EWHC 1637 (Ch).
[33] See **17.52**.
[34] As argued by Lord Templeman in *Space Investments Ltd v Canadian Imperial Bank of Commerce Co (Bahamas) Ltd* [1986] 1 W.L.R. 1072; see **17.53**.
[35] *Boscawen v Bajwa* [1995] 4 All E.R. 769.
[36] *Lipkin Gorman v Karpnale Ltd* [1991] 2 A.C. 548.
[37] [1948] Ch. 465.
[38] [2001] 1 A.C. 102.
[39] [2001] 1 A.C. 102 at 129.

IN PERSONAM CLAIMS

17.62 It remains to examine the alternative claim made by the next of kin in *Re Diplock*.[40] It will be recalled that the personal representatives of the testator (whose residuary disposition was invalid) distributed his residuary estate to charity upon the footing that the disposition was, indeed, valid. In the Court of Appeal, it was held, subject to a principal qualification, that the next of kin could recover by means of a personal action in equity. In the light that the original wrong payment was due to the mistake of the personal representatives, the beneficiary's primary claim was against the personal representatives. Any in personam claim against those wrongly paid must be limited to the amount irrecoverable from the party responsible. Accordingly, it was held that the amount recovered from the executors must be apportioned among the charities in proportion to the grants they had received, so that the maximum recoverable from any individual charity by the next-of-kin would be rateably reduced.

In *Ministry of Health v Simpson*,[41] it fell to the House of Lords to consider the question of a direct claim in equity against the charities. The House of Lords endorsed the approach of the Court of Appeal upholding the right of an unpaid legatee to bring a personal action in equity against the persons to whom the estate had been wrongfully distributed. It is to be noted, nonetheless, that this principle may not extend to otherwise analogous cases in the context of execution of trusts. Indeed, Lord Simonds appears to indicate that the approach extends only to cases dealing with the administration of the deceased's estate. He claimed:

> "I think that it is important in the discussion of this question to remember that the particular branch of the jurisdiction of the Court of Chancery with which we are concerned relates to the administration of assets of a deceased person. While in the development of this jurisdiction certain principles were established which were common to it and to the comparable jurisdiction in the execution of trusts, I do not find in history or in logic any justification for an argument which denies the possibility of an equitable right in the administration of assets because, as it is alleged, no comparable right existed in the execution of trusts".[42]

GUIDE TO FURTHER READING

D. Capper, "Compensation for Breach of Trust" [1997] Conv. 14.

S.B. Elliott, J. Edelman, "Money Remedies Against Trustees" (2004) 18 Trust Law International 116.

P. Millett, "Equity's Place in the Law of Commerce" (1998) 114 L.Q.R. 214.

P. Millett, "Tracing and the Proceeds of Fraud" (1991) 107 L.Q.R. 71.

---

[40] [2001] 1 A.C. 102.
[41] [1951] A.C. 251.
[42] [1951] A.C. 251 at 265.

A.G. Mountford, "Tracing: An Examination of the Applicability of Tracing Principles Today" (1996) 70 A.L.J. 54.

M. Pawlowski, "The Demise of the rule in Clayton's Case" [2003] Conv 339.

L. Smith, "Tracing into the Payment of a Debt" [1995] C.L.J. 290.

Chapter 18

INJUNCTIONS

The remaining chapters are dedicated to an analysis of two principal equitable reme- **18.01** dies: the injunction and the order for specific performance. The focus of this chapter falls on injunctions. An injunction is issued to direct a person to commit or to refrain from committing a specified act. Like the order for specific performance, the injunction is an equitable and, therefore, discretionary remedy, developed largely in accordance with settled principles.[1] This chapter will evaluate the general jurisdiction of the court to grant an injunction, the nature of the remedy, the different types of injunction obtainable and the principles upon which judicial discretion is exercised. Due consideration will be given to the capacity of the court to award damages under Lord Cairns' Act in lieu of, or in addition to, the award of injunctive relief or specific performance. As regards either remedy, moreover, the failure to comply with an order of the court is a contempt of court ultimately punishable by imprisonment. Accordingly, the variety of means of enforcement at the disposal of the court also falls to be detailed in this chapter.

GENERAL ISSUES

Jurisdiction

The High Court jurisdiction to grant injunctions is now contained in s.37(1) of the **18.02** Supreme Court Act 1981.[2] It provides that, "The High Court may by order (whether interlocutory or final) grant an injunction ... in all cases in which it appears to the court to be just and convenient to do so". As with the remedy of specific performance, this

---

[1] Note that the power to grant an injunction may also be conferred upon the court by statute such as in the protection of copyright and patents: see, for example, Copyright Designs and Patents Act 1988.
[2] The jurisdiction of the county court is governed by s.38 of the County Courts Act 1984 (as amended).

discretion is exercised, "not by the caprice of the Judge, but according to sufficient legal reasons or on settled principles".[3] Being an equitable remedy, an injunction was originally obtainable only from the Court of Chancery. Subsequent statutory developments[4] saw a limited power to grant injunctions extend to the common law courts.[5] Thereafter, the effect of the Judicature Acts 1873 and 1875 was to vest in the High Court, the jurisdiction of the Chancery and the common law courts to grant injunctions.

There has been considerable and detailed discussion of the impact of these statutory developments, for example, whether s.25(8) of the Judicature Act 1873 enlarged the court's jurisdiction to embrace cases where no injunction would previously be granted[6] and likewise whether the 1981 Act enlarged the pre-existing jurisdiction.[7] A much-promoted view is that, "if no court had the power of issuing an injunction before the Judicature Act, no part of the High Court has power to issue such an injunction".[8] This restrictive approach has recent House of Lords approval in *Gouriet v Union of Post Office Workers* where, it was claimed that such provisions, "dealt only with procedure and had nothing to do with jurisdiction".[9] It is abundantly clear, nonetheless, that the approach of modern courts is flexible and responsive to changing times. As Lord Nicholls recognised in *Mercedes Benz A. G. v Leiduck*, "As circumstances in the world change, so must the situations in which the courts may properly exercise their jurisdiction to grant injunctions. The exercise of the jurisdiction must be principled, but the criterion is injustice. Injustice is to be viewed and decided in the light of today's conditions and standards, not those of yester-year".[10]

The protection of rights

18.03 In the enforcement of a claimant's private rights, it is a general requirement that a claimant show some legal or equitable cause of action. Equity will not intervene merely on the ground that there has been some perceived injustice to the claimant. As Lindley L.J. claimed in *Holmes v Millage*, "It is an old mistake to suppose that, because there is no effectual remedy at law, there must be one in equity".[11] In *Day v Brownrigg*,[12] for example, the claimants alleged that their house had been called "Ashford Lodge" for a period of 60 years and that the adjoining house belonging to the defendants had been called "Ashford Villa" for a period of 40 years. When the defendants altered the name of their house to the same name as the claimant's house, the claimants sought an injunction to restrain the inconvenience, annoyance and depreciation in value of their

---

[3] *Beddow v Beddow* (1878) 9 Ch. D. 89 at 93 per Jessel M.R.
[4] See Ch.1.
[5] See, for example, the Common Law Procedure Act 1854, s.79.
[6] As argued in *Cummins v Perkins* [1899] 1 Ch. 16 per Lindley and Chitty L.JJ.
[7] In *Chief Constable of Kent v V* [1983] Q.B. 34 at 42 Lord Denning M.R. argued that, "The section as it now stands plainly confers a new and extensive jurisdiction ... It is far wider than anything that had been known in our courts before".
[8] *North London Rly Co v Great Northern Rly Co* (1883) 11 Q.B.D. 30 at 36 per Brett L.J.
[9] [1978] A.C. 435 at 516.
[10] [1996] A.C. 284 at 308.
[11] [1893] 1 Q.B. 551 at 555.
[12] (1878) 10 Ch. D. 294.

property. The Court of Appeal refused injunctive relief. James L.J. explained, "This Court can only interfere where there is an invasion of a legal or equitable right. No such legal or equitable right exists ...".[13] More recently, in *Paton v Trustees of British Pregnancy Advisory Service*, it was held that a husband seeking to prevent his wife from aborting their child had, "no legal right enforceable in law or in equity to stop his wife having this abortion or to stop the doctors from carrying out the abortion".[14]

Notwithstanding such clear statements of principle, it is to be borne in mind that there is, on the part of many judges, a reluctance to accept that the statutory jurisdiction under s.37 is fettered by the pattern of historical intervention. Accordingly, it is possible to find support for the view that the power of the court should not be limited to "exclusive categories".[15] Such was the sentiment of Fox L.J. in *Bayer AG v Winter* when he observed, "Bearing in mind we are exercising a jurisdiction which is statutory and which is expressed in terms of considerable width, it seems to me that the court should not shrink, if it is of opinion that an injunction is necessary for the proper protection of a party to the action, from granting relief, notwithstanding it may, in its terms, be of a novel character".[16] In *Re Oriental Credit Ltd*, therefore, Harman J. granted an injunction ancillary to an order under s.561 of the Companies Act 1985 to prevent a the director of a company from leaving the jurisdiction prior to examination under the order. He claimed, "I had the power to make my order although it is not an order made in aid of a legal right or in protection of an equitable interest".[17] The grant of the injunction was deemed necessary to ensure that the order under s.561 was obeyed.

As to the enforcement of a claimant's public rights, the leading authority remains the House of Lords decision in *Gouriet v Union of Post Office Workers*.[18] There, a member of the public had sought an injunction to restrain a threatened disruption to postal communications between South Africa and England and Wales. This presented a difficulty for the claimant in that it is the Attorney-General who protects public rights either by an act on his own initiative or on behalf of a member of the public. In *Gouriet*, the Attorney-General refused to consent to a relator action and provided no justification for his refusal.

18.04

The House of Lords denied that the court has the jurisdiction to grant the injunction or that it had the power to review the exercise of the Attorney-General's discretion in any way. It reinforced the fundamental principle of English law that public rights can only be enforced in a civil action by the Attorney-General, as an officer of the Crown, representing the public. Save where statute provides otherwise, a private individual could only bring an action to restrain a threatened breach of the law where the threatened breach would infringe his private rights or inflict special damage upon him. Lord Wilberforce was adamant:

[13] (1878) 10 Ch. D. 294 at 305.
[14] [1979] Q.B. 276 at 281 per Sir George Baker P.
[15] Per Lord Goff in *South Carolina Insurance Co v Assurantie Maatschappij de Zeven Provincien NV* [1987] A.C. 24.
[16] [1986] 1 W.L.R. 497 at 502.
[17] [1988] 1 All E.R. 892 at 895.
[18] [1978] A.C. 435.

"The distinction between public rights which the Attorney-General can, and the individual (absent special interest) cannot seek to enforce, and private rights is fundamental to our law. To break it, as counsel for Mr Gouriet frankly invited us to do, is not a development in the law, but a destruction of one of its pillars".[19]

18.05   Further concerns were voiced in the House as to the use of the civil courts as a means of criminal law enforcement. It was accepted that instances of applications by Attorneys-General to the civil courts for aid in enforcing the criminal law are, "few in number and exceptional in character".[20] In the view of Viscount Dilhorne, it is appropriate that the criminal law is enforced in the criminal courts by the process of conviction and punishment of offenders and not in the civil courts. He accepted, however, that there may be circumstances where it is appropriate for an Attorney-General to seek an injunction to restrain the commission of a criminal act, not least where the penalties imposed for the offence are inadequate to deter its commission.[21] It is inevitable that such occasions will be rare. As Viscount Dilhorne put it, "It has been and in my opinion should continue to be exceptional for the aid of the civil courts to be invoked in support of the criminal law, and no wise Attorney-General will make such an application or agree to one being made in his name unless it appears to him that the case is exceptional".[22]

In personam

18.06   In granting an injunction, the court acts in personam. Equity fastens on the conscience of the defendant, "compelling the wrongdoing litigant himself to comply with the rule prescribed by equity".[23] The fact that a person is in residence abroad, i.e. outside the jurisdiction of the court, will not necessarily place him outside the reach of the court if service out of the jurisdiction can be achieved under the Civil Procedure Rules.[24] Generally, however, no injunction will be granted in respect of the title to, or possession of, land outside the court's jurisdiction.[25] Although the likelihood is that the order cannot be enforced and so it would be pointless to order an injunction, it seems that land presents something of a special case. The rule has never applied in relation to chattels in other jurisdictions. Further, in *R. Griggs Group Ltd v Evans*,[26] it was held that, absent any special local rule to the contrary, there is no reason why English courts cannot make orders in respect of in personam rights to foreign intellectual property, especially where the contract was governed by English law.

It is also worth noting that the injunction can be framed in surprisingly wide terms. It used to be said that, "you cannot have an injunction except against a party to the

---

[19] [1978] A.C. 435 at 482.
[20] [1978] A.C. 435 at 489 per Viscount Dilhorne.
[21] See, for example, *A-G v Sharp* [1931] 1 Ch. 121 (unlicensed carriage plying for hire in circumstances where the defendant intended to pursue his illegal activities).
[22] [1978] A.C. 435 at 491.
[23] *R. Griggs Group Ltd v Evans* [2005] Ch. 153 at 164 per Peter Prescott Q.C.
[24] CPR Pt 6.17.
[25] *Deschamps v Miller* [1908] 1 Ch. 856.
[26] [2005] Ch. 153, distinguishing *Tyburn Productions Ltd v Conan Doyle* [1991] Ch. 75.

suit".[27] The modern day approach of the courts is significantly changed and, moreover, it is markedly shaped by recent legislative developments. First, the Civil Procedure Rules provide the court with a procedural code, the overriding objective of which is to deal with cases justly.[28] Secondly, following the coming into force of the Human Rights Act 1998 the influence of European jurisprudence is increasingly manifest.[29] Accordingly, there is a growing array of examples of injunctions granted against unnamed defendants,[30] or even *contra mundum* (as against the world) legitimised on the basis of recent statutory developments.[31] In addition, injunctions are effective not only against persons to whom the order is directed, but also third parties who knowingly act in breach of the injunction resulting in impedance to, or interference with, the administration of justice.[32]

Failure to comply with an injunction

The next matter to consider is the enforcement of injunctions. Where a person fails to abide by the terms of an injunction, (or indeed an order for specific performance) he is liable for contempt of court.[33] Nonetheless, non-compliance can take a variety of forms and the court will weigh up a variety of considerations such as the conduct of the defendant and the history of the case before it decides on an appropriate course of enforcement. The range of penalties at the disposal of the court includes imprisonment, a writ of sequestration of property,[34] the provision of a fine or simply an order to pay costs. The ultimate sanction against the individual is, of course, committal to prison. The justification for imprisonment is evident on two levels. First, there is a punitive element based on the need to punish the defendant for his continuing disregard of the court. Secondly, there is a coercive element, whereby the court aims to force compliance with its order.[35] Accordingly where continuing imprisonment is deemed to have no further coercive effect, the court can cut short the term of imprisonment imposed on the contemnor.[36] The power to order release should be exercised sparingly because the value of the coercive element of a prison sentence is in jeopardy if it is clear to a

18.07

---

[27] Per Lord Eldon in *Iveson v Harris* (1802) 7 Ves. 251 at 257.

[28] For example, there is no requirement that a defendant must now be named: see *Bloomsbury Publishing Group Plc v News Group Newspapers Ltd* [2003] 1 W.L.R. 1633, considering CPR Pt. 3.10.

[29] As Dame Elizabeth Butler-Sloss noted in *Venables v News Group Newspapers Ltd* [2001] 1 All E.R. 908 at 939, "in light of the implementation of the 1998 Act, we are entering a new era, and a requirement that the courts act in a way which is compatible with the convention, and have regard to European jurisprudence, adds a new dimension to those principles".

[30] See, for example, *Bloomsbury Publishing Group plc v News Group Newspapers Ltd*, above, where an injunction was issued against, "the person or persons who have offered the publishers of The Sun, The Daily Mail and the Daily Mirror newspapers a copy of the book Harry Potter and the Order of the Phoenix by JK Rowling or any part thereof and the person or persons who has or have physical possession of a copy of the said book or any part thereof without the consent of the claimants".

[31] For example, to protect the confidentiality of information regarding the killers of Jamie Bulger: *Venables v News Group Newspapers Ltd*, above.

[32] See *A-G v Times Newspapers* [1992] 1 A.C. 191.

[33] Contempt of Court Act 1981.

[34] Usually in the case of corporations.

[35] See *Re Barrell Enterprises Ltd* [1972] 3 All E.R. 631.

[36] See generally, *Enfield London Borough Council v Mahoney* [1983] 2 All E.R. 901, where a landowner refused to handover a Saxon artefact to the local borough council.

contemnor that the court will order release if he is simply to state his intention not to comply. As Neuberger admitted in *Shalson v Russo*, "if it became known that the court would let a contemnor out of prison early whenever he made it clear that there was no possibility of his complying, then much of the value of the coercive element of a prison sentence would be at risk".[37]

18.08   Generally, committal to prison will be avoided in circumstances where the court has a viable alternative,[38] but it may be especially appropriate where an order of the court is met with unwavering defiance. Thus, in *Burton v Winters*,[39] a sentence of two years imprisonment, (the maximum term permitted by s.14(1) of the Contempt of Court Act 1981) was held to be justified because the claimant, in proceedings in trespass and nuisance against the defendants, persisted in attempts to build a wall on the defendant's land, ignoring the terms of an injunction against her.

A third party who aids and abets the breach of an injunction becomes an accessory and also liable for civil contempt.[40] The problems are somewhat different with regard to strangers. In the light that they are neither accessories to the breach nor party to the order, such third parties cannot be said to be in breach of an order of the court. As regards interim proceedings, however, an exception has evolved to the effect that third parties are in criminal contempt of court if they wilfully interfere with the adminis-tration of justice in the proceedings in which the order was made, notwithstanding that their actions were wholly independent of the defendant.[41] Intentional interference with the manner in which a judge is conducting a trial is a basis of criminal rather than civil contempt.[42] When a claimant brings an action to preserve an alleged right of con-fidentiality, for example, a third party who, with knowledge of the order, publishes the information and thereby destroys its confidentiality, will be in contempt of court.[43] This reasoning will apply in the case of an interim but not a final injunction[44] As Lord Phillips M.R. acknowledged in *AG v Punch*, "the offence lies not simply in the com-mission of the act prohibited by the order, but in the effect that the act has of interfering in the conduct of the trial".[45]

The award of damages in equity

18.09   Section 50 of the Supreme Court Act 1981 provides that, "Where the Court of Appeal or the High Court has jurisdiction to entertain an application for an injunction or specific performance, it may award damages in addition to, or in substitution for, an injunction or specific performance". This provision is a substantial re-enactment of

---

[37] [2002] EWHC 399 (Ch) at [20].
[38] *Danchevsky v Danchevsky* [1974] 3 All E.R. 934; see also, *Larkman v Lindsell*, (1985) *The Times*, November 30 where a property owner could have sought to enforce an order to vacate property by committal pro-ceedings, but the grant of a possession order was a reasonable alternative to secure compliance.
[39] [1993] 3 All E.R. 847.
[40] *Acrow (Automation) Ltd v Rex Chainbelt Inc* [1971] 3 All E.R. 1175. Of course, the defendant is always potentially liable for the actions of his agent.
[41] *A-G v Punch* [2003] 1 All E.R. 289.
[42] *A-G v Times Newspapers Ltd* [1991] 1 A.C. 191.
[43] [1991] 1 A.C. 191.
[44] See *Jockey Club v Buffham* [2003] Q.B. 462.
[45] [2001] Q.B. 1028 at 1055.

powers conferred on the court by Lord Cairns' Act (Chancery Amendment Act 1858) to award damages in addition to or in substitution for an injunction "in all cases in which the Court of Chancery has jurisdiction to entertain an application for an injunction".[46] The mischief at which this Act was addressed was, as noted by Turner L.J. that, "great complaints were constantly made by the public, that when plaintiffs came into a court of equity for specific performance the court of equity sent them to a court of law in order to recover damages so that parties were bandied about, as it was said from one court to another".[47]

The Act, therefore, facilitated the court of equity to award damages in cases where a court of law had done so previously as well as to award an injunction to prevent the continuance or repetition of the prohibited activity. Lord Cairns' Act is also the basis of the court's jurisdiction in cases where there is no right to damages at law, for example, where the breach in question is a breach of an equitable rather than a legal right[48] or where an injury is threatened and has not yet occurred. Where injury was merely threatened or apprehended, no damages could be recovered at law because, "such damages were given only in respect of a cause of action which had accrued at the date of the commencement of the action".[49] Nonetheless, equity could restrain a threatened breach with the issue of a *quia timet* injunction[50] and, accordingly, it lies open to the court to award damages in lieu of (or in addition to) the grant of an injunction or an order for specific performance.

It should be remembered that the award of damages is dependent on the court's **18.10** jurisdiction to grant an injunction (or to order specific performance) and this is so even if the court is likely to refuse relief. The claimant must show that he has a prima facie case for equitable relief. Where the claimant is unable to do so, there can be no award of damages under Lord Cairns' Act.

Damages in lieu of injunction

The reluctance of the court to award damages instead of an injunction is premised upon **18.11** the view that do so would allow the defendant to purchase the right to persist in committing a wrongful act. In *Shelfer v City of London Electric Lighting Co*, Lindley L.J. commented, "ever since Lord Cairns' Act was passed the Court of Chancery has repudiated the notion that the legislature intended to turn that court into a tribunal for legalizing wrongful acts; or in other words, the court has always protested against the notion that it ought to allow a wrong to continue simply because the wrongdoer is able to pay for the injury he may inflict".[51] Similarly, as Buckley J. emphasised in *Cowper v Laidler*, "The court has affirmed over and over again that the jurisdiction to give damages where it exists is not so to be used as in fact to enable the defendant to

---

[46] Chancery Amendment Act 1858 s.2.
[47] *Ferguson v Wilson* (1866) 2 Ch. App. 77 at 88.
[48] See *Baxter v Four Oaks Properties Ltd* [1965] Ch. 816 (restrictive covenant).
[49] *Leeds Industrial Co-Operative Society Ltd v Slack* [1924] A.C. 851 at 856 per Viscount Finlay.
[50] To restrain a threatened infringement of the claimant's rights (see **18.23**).
[51] [1895] 1 Ch. 287 at 315. Here, the Court of Appeal awarded injunctive relief where the defendant electricity company had caused structural damage to the claimant's property and nuisance to the claimant.

purchase from the plaintiff against his Will his legal right …".[52] Accordingly, the courts developed the practice of refusing to award damages in substitution for an injunction save for exceptional circumstances. Of the many attempts to draw guidelines, as to when damages in lieu are appropriate, the most cited is that made in *Shelfer v City of London Electric Lighting Co.*[53] A. L. Smith L.J. laid down what he described as "a good working rule"[54] that damages may be given in substitution for an injunction where:

> (i) the injury to the claimant is small,
>
> (ii) the injury is one which is capable of being estimated in money,
>
> (iii) the injury is one which can be adequately compensated by a small money payment, and
>
> (iv) the case is one in which it would be oppressive to the defendant to grant an injunction.

There is no shortage of critical discussion in the case law as to how the working rule in *Shelfer* ought to be applied. In *Fishenden v Higgs and Hill Ltd*, for example, Lord Hanworth M.R. doubted the wisdom in formulating specific rules. He described the prescription as the, "high-water mark of what might be called definite rules".[55] Romer L.J., moreover, was without any doubt that the discretion of the court could be fettered. He emphasised that, "Where the four conditions … are fulfilled, I do not doubt that a court will grant damages in lieu of an injunction, but it by no means follows that A. L. Smith L.J. intended to say or did say or in fact could say that in all cases in which those four conditions do not prevail, the injunction must be granted; he could not have intended to fetter the discretion imposed upon the court by Lord Cairns' Act".[56] Maugham L.J., too, questioned the scope of the rule, arguing that in was, "not a universal or even sound rule in all cases of injury to light".[57] On the facts of *Fishenden*, substantial damages were awarded to a claimant whose right to light was obstructed by the defendant's construction of a new building. Here, in particular, the conduct of the claimant militated against the provision of specific relief.

18.12   If many older authorities are overtly critical, modern courts appear generally ready to accept the longstanding influence of *Shelfer*. In *Jaggard v Sawyer*,[58] Millett L.J. accepted the legitimacy of the *Shelfer* guidelines, commenting that, "Laid down just 100 years ago, A. L. Smith L.J.'s test has stood the test of time".[59] He proceeded to single out the fourth limb of A. L. Smith L.J.'s rule as being of particular importance, stating that, "The outcome of any particular case usually turns on the question: would it in all circumstances be oppressive to the defendant to grant the injunction to which the plaintiff is prima facie entitled?"[60] Accordingly, on this basis, the Court of Appeal held

---

[52] [1903] 2 Ch. 337 at 341.
[53] [1895] 1 Ch. 287.
[54] [1895] 1 Ch. 287 at 322.
[55] (1935) 153 L.T. 128 at 138.
[56] (1953) 153 L.T. 128 at 141.
[57] (1953) 153 L.T. 128 at 144.
[58] [1995] 1 W.L.R. 269.
[59] [1995] 1 W.L.R. 269 at 287.
[60] [1995] 1 W.L.R. 269 at 288.

damages to be the appropriate course for the court. In a similar vein, in *Kennaway v Thompson*, the Court of Appeal acknowledged that, "The principles enunciated in *Shelfer's* case, which is binding on us, have been applied time and time again over the past 85 years".[61] On the facts, however, the first three limbs of A. L. Smith L.J.'s rule had not been met. Although damages were awarded at first instance, the Court of Appeal granted an injunction to restrict the noise generated by motorboat racing, which constituted nuisance to the claimant.

Two recent Court of Appeal decisions have provided clarification as to the appropriate approach of the court to awarding damages in lieu of injunction. In *Regan v Paul Properties*,[62] the claimant, Mr Regan had alleged that the defendant property developers had infringed his right to light when they erected, directly opposite to his property, a 16 unit development complete with penthouse. When Regan complained about the loss of light caused by the penthouse, the defendants relied on misleading legal advice (that there was no actionable injury) and continued with the development, undeterred. At first instance, it was accepted that nuisance was committed but that the appropriate remedy was an award of damages in lieu of injunction. Applying *Shelfer*, the trial judge was clear that all four elements of the A. L. Smith L.J test had been met and the claimant had not shown that he should not be left to a remedy in damages.   **18.13**

Somewhat surprisingly, the Court of Appeal found in Regan's favour. In doing so, the opportunity was taken to affirm some basic principles and to warn developers in future cases that an award of damages is by no means certain. Mummery L.J. noted that the claimant was prima facie entitled to an injunction because of the nuisance caused by the defendants. He emphasised, moreover, that damages in lieu of injunction was appropriate for exceptional cases only, i.e. the burden of proof did not lie with the claimant to convince the court not to award damages as the trial judge had directed. On the facts, the injury to light was not small. It could be estimated in money terms, but it could not be compensated by the payment of a small money sum. Further, as regards the oppression caused to the defendant should part of the building works be required to be dismantled, Mummery L.J. found that this was not, of itself decisive: "It is necessary to consider all the surrounding circumstances of the dispute and the conduct of the parties".[63] In contrast to Mr Regan, ("against whose conduct no criticism can be made and who acted on advice which was correct")[64] the defendants had taken a calculated risk to continue on the basis of advice which turned out to be wrong. According, as Mummery L.J. explained, the court could not be justified in, "denying him an injunction and effectively forcing him to accept compensation from the defendants for losing the light in respect of his home".[65]

This emphasis on the conduct of the parties has also been highlighted in *Jacklin v Chief Constable of West Yorkshire*.[66] Here, a police authority had begun construction work, the effect of which was to interfere with a landowner's right of access to his property. A delay of three years occurred before the claimant sought a mandatory injunction for the removal of the offending structures. Although this was not an   **18.14**

[61] [1981] Q.B. 88 at 93.
[62] [2006] 3 W.L.R. 1131.
[63] [2006] 3 W.L.R. 1131 at 1144.
[64] [2006] 3 W.L.R. 1131 at 1144.
[65] [2006] 3 W.L.R. 1131 at 1144.
[66] [2007] EWCA Civ 181.

exceptional case where damages in lieu may have been appropriate (there being no oppression caused to the defendant by the grant of injunctive relief), the Court of Appeal adopted a broad approach to determining oppression within the fourth *Shelfer* limb. As with *Regan*, the conduct of both parties came to the fore. Notably, Lloyd L.J. highlighted the court's distaste for unreasonable conduct, in that, "Mr Jacklin protested orally ... and did so before the police took any step involving any substantial or irrevocable expenditure or other irreversible action, and that the police proceeded in the face of that protest without taking steps to clarify the position or check their own deeds or ask for those of Mr Jacklin, in order to see for certain what the position was".[67]

Accordingly, both *Jacklin* and *Regan* demonstrate that although the *Shelfer* principles remain at the heart of the court's approach, there has been renewed enthusiasm at Court of Appeal level for the grant of injunctive relief. It appears no longer safe for defendants to rely on the oppression that would be caused by the grant of an injunction when their conduct throughout shows insufficient regard for the risk of infringement of the claimant's rights. As Richard Arnold QC acknowledged recently in *Site Developments (Ferndown) Limited v Barratt Homes Ltd*, "whether it would be oppressive depends on all the relevant circumstances existing as at the date the court is asked to grant an injunction ... [including] the conduct of the parties and the reality on the ground at the time that the question falls to be decided".[68]

Measure of damages in lieu

18.15 Determining the appropriate measure of damages under Lord Cairns' Act will usually involve the court in adopting the same measure of damages in equity as in an action at common law for breach of contract. In *Leeds Industrial Co-Operative Society v Slack*, however, Lord Sumner demonstrated that "No money awarded in substitution can be justly awarded, unless it is at any rate designed to be a preferable equivalent to an injunction and therefore an adequate substitution for it".[69] This statement appears to recognise a discretion to determine what damages are just and reasonable in the circumstances. This, perhaps, leaves open the question as to whether the same compensatory principle applies under Lord Cairns' Act as does when common law damages are sought. Accordingly, in *Wroth v Tyler*,[70] (where specific performance was refused) Megarry J. awarded damages for loss of bargain calculated at the date of assessment and not as at the date of breach of contract. He argued that the case was one that fell within the Lord Cairns' Act 1858 and the court had jurisdiction to give damages that would put the claimant into a position as good as though the contract had been performed. £5,500 was awarded. Common law damages would have been £1,500.

In *Johnson v Agnew*,[71] however, Lord Wilberforce emphasised that there is no difference between the measure of damages obtainable under Lord Cairns' Act and at common law. At first glance these views appear definitive. This is clearly so where

---

[67] [2007] EWCA Civ 181 at [45]
[68] [2007] EWHC 415 (Ch) at [64].
[69] [1924] A.C. 851 at 870.
[70] [1974] Ch. 30.
[71] [1980] A.C. 367.

damages are recoverable in respect of the same cause of action either at common law or under Lord Cairns' Act.[72] The question is more complex where the breach is one for which damages would not be recoverable at common law, but are available under Lord Cairns' Act. For example, damages may be awarded in lieu of an injunction to restrain a future or threatened breach or where the defendant is in breach of contract but the claimant has suffered no loss. *Wrotham Park Estate Co v Parkside Homes Ltd*,[73] provides an example of the latter. There a developer built houses in breach of covenant only to build in the layout described in the claimant's plans. The claimant sought an injunction, but omitted to seek interlocutory relief with the consequence that the houses were complete when the issue was tried. The claimant sought a mandatory order requiring the houses to be pulled down. Brightman J. declined and recounted the social and economic reasons that informed his decision.

"The erection of the houses, whether one likes it or not, is a fait accompli and the houses are now the homes of people. I accept that this fait accompli is reversible and could be undone. But I cannot close my eyes to the fact that the houses now exist. It would, in my opinion, be an unpardonable waste of much needed houses to direct that they now be pulled down and I have never had a moment's doubt during the hearing of this case that such an order ought to be refused".[74]

The claimant had suffered no financial damage as a result of the breach of the layout stipulation and the claimants' use of the estate was in no way impeded. Nominal damages were not, however, awarded. Brightman J. held that the claimants would be entitled to such a sum as they might reasonably have demanded in return for the relaxation in the covenant (five per cent of the developer's anticipated profit).[75]

The *Wrotham Park* principle fell to be reviewed in two subsequent Court of Appeal   **18.16** decisions. First, in *Surrey CC v Bredero Homes Ltd*,[76] the defendant property developer had, in breach of contract, supplemented his profits by building additional houses. Relying on the decision in *Wrotham Park*, the claimant sued for damages calculated to be such part of the profits made on the additional houses as would reflect a reasonable payment for the defendant's release from the covenant. The Court of Appeal awarded only nominal damages on the basis that the claimant could not establish loss. This was not a decision on Lord Cairns' Act and the decision in *Wrotham Park* was thereby distinguished. Secondly, and only two years later, the Court of Appeal in *Jaggard v Sawyer* adopted the contrary approach. Here the defendant erected a house in breach of covenant to which his only means of access was by way of trespass on a private road. The claimant sought an injunction. The Court of Appeal openly followed the *Wrotham Park* case. To avoid the undesirable consequence of an injunction, i.e. that the defendant's property would be landlocked, the claimant was awarded a sum that reflected

[72] See *Jaggard v Sawyer* [1995] 1 W.L.R. 269 at 291 per Millett L.J.
[73] [1974] 2 All E.R. 321.
[74] [1974] 2 All E.R. 321 at 337.
[75] See also *Tamares (Vincent Sq) Ltd v Fairpoint Properties (Vincent SQ) Ltd* [2007] 1 W.L.R. 2167 (measure of damages in right to light cases), where the court attempted to find what would have been a fair result of a hypothetical negotiation between the parties.
[76] [1993] 1 W.L.R. 1361.

what the defendant ought to have paid for the right of way and for release from the restrictive covenant.

In *AG v Blake*,[77] Lord Nicholls had cause to review the authorities on Lord Cairns' Act. He cited *Bredero* as a "difficult decision" which so far as it was inconsistent with *Wrotham Park*, the latter was to be preferred.[78] He concluded his analysis with the recognition that the *Wrotham Park* case "still shines, rather as a solitary beacon, showing in contract as well as tort damages are not always narrowly confined to recoupment of financial loss. In a suitable case damages for breach of contract may be measured by the benefit gained by the wrongdoer from the breach".[79]

TYPES OF INJUNCTIONS

18.17 Having considered by way of introduction some important general matters regarding injunctions, it is now necessary to address the variety of injunctions that are issued by the court and the differences between them. The following categories are considered:

- prohibitory or mandatory injunctions;
- perpetual or interim injunctions;
- mandatory injunctions and orders for specific performance;
- without notice injunctions, and
- *quia timet* injunctions.

Prohibitory or mandatory?

18.18 A prohibitory injunction is restrictive in nature and it requires the defendant to refrain from initiating or committing the prohibited act. For example, an injunction ordered to prevent the defendant from building an extension, will be prohibitory in nature.

A mandatory injunction, however, is positive in the sense that it requires the defendant to act. Such an injunction will be necessary where the prohibited act has been committed and an order restraining the defendant would be pointless. For example, where the defendant has begun to build his extension, an order restraining him from doing so will not be an effective remedy. A mandatory injunction will, however, require positive steps to ensure that the act be undone.[80] Accordingly, it is irrelevant that a mandatory order is couched in negative terms,[81] for example, that the defendant

---

[77] [2001] 1 A.C. 268, concerning whether the remedy of account was available for breach of contract.
[78] [2001] 1 A.C. 268 at 283.
[79] [2001] 1 A.C. 268 at 283.
[80] Usually evidenced by the need for expenditure on the part of the defendant.
[81] An injunction that is in substance mandatory should now be worded in positive terms: *Jackson v Normanby Brick Co* [1899] 1 Ch. 438.

"refrains from permitting the extension to remain". The action required is that he takes the positive steps necessary to demolish it.

Perpetual or interim?

A perpetual injunction simply means an injunction that (the court having heard the arguments put forward in full by both sides) finally settles or resolves the dispute between the parties.[82] Such injunctions are also referred to as "final" or "permanent". Interim injunctions (formally termed interlocutory injunctions) are granted pending the full hearing of the case and in circumstances where the claimant requires (until the case is heard in full) the immediate restraint of the defendant's proposed course of action. The object of an interim injunction is as Lord Wilberforce put it, "to prevent a litigant, who must necessarily suffer the law's delay, from losing by that delay the fruit of his litigation".[83] As will be discussed, the principles upon which an interim injunction is granted are specific to the role of that particular injunction and do not follow the general equitable considerations which underpin the grant and refusal of perpetual injunctions or, indeed, specific performance.

18.19

Mandatory injunction?

Both the mandatory injunction and the order for specific performance[84] compel the defendant positively to act in order that positive obligations will be enforced. Being part of the armoury of equitable remedies, both bring with them the same sanctions should the defendant fail to perform the stipulated positive act.[85] It is however possible to distinguish between them on two fronts. First, the grounds upon which specific performance will be refused are more numerous and far-reaching. As will be discussed, the court must test the justice and wisdom in compelling an unwilling defendant to perform his positive contractual obligations. The grant of an injunction requires no positive act unless, of course, the defendant has by his own wrongdoing initiated a course of action that requires a mandatory order to effect a return to the status quo.

18.20

Secondly, it has recently been emphasised by Lord Hoffmann that an order for specific performance is a final order, i.e. it is not available on an interim basis.[86] Clearly, this presents a restriction to the claimant where interlocutory relief is sought. In *Sky Petroleum Ltd v VIP Petroleum Ltd*,[87] however, the judgment of Goulding J. suggests that the matter is not so straightforward. There, the claimant applied for an interim injunction restraining the defendant company from failing to supply it with petrol. Goulding J. acknowledged that, if he granted the injunction, he would be specifically enforcing the contract until the date of the hearing. Nonetheless, he treated it as a claim

---

[82] It is not perpetual in the sense that it endures indefinitely.
[83] *Hoffman-La Roche & Co v Secretary of State for Trade and Industry* [1975] A.C. 295 at 355. See **18.33**.
[84] See Ch. 19.
[85] For example imprisonment, a fine or sequestration of assets: (see **18.07**).
[86] *Co-Operative Insurance Society Ltd v Argyll Stores (Holdings) Ltd* [1998] A.C. 1 at 18.
[87] [1974] 1 W.L.R. 576.

for specific performance and issued the injunction. On the basis that the contract with the defendant appeared to be the sole means by which the plaintiff could keep his business, damages was not a sufficient remedy.

Without notice injunctions

18.21 Where the interim relief sought is particularly urgent in nature, (i.e. that irreparable damage would be caused by following the usual procedure), an injunction may be applied for without notice. Such injunctions were previously referred to as ex parte, meaning in the absence of the party against whom the injunction is sought. The availability of injunctive relief under these circumstances is given sparingly and only where necessary[88] on the basis that "no order should be made to the prejudice of a party unless he has the opportunity of being heard in defence".[89] On occasion, however, the balance of justice will militate against the defendant where the need for immediate intervention outweighs his interest in being heard. In the context of family disputes, for example, a claimant will succeed only where there is a real immediate danger of serious injury or irreparable damage. Indeed, the more intrusive the order, the more the court will require by way of proof that the order is necessary and that it should be made in the form sought. For example, in *Harris v Moat Housing Group South Ltd*, Brooke L.J. emphasised, "It is one thing to restrain a defendant from what would in any event be anti-social behaviour for a short time until a hearing can be arranged at which both sides can be heard. It is quite another to make a 'without notice' order directing the defendant to leave their home immediately and banning them from re-entering a large part of the area where they live".[90] There, the Court of Appeal held that an anti-social behaviour injunction under the Housing Act 1996 excluding the appellant and her children from their home should not have been made on a without notice application. By way of a further example, in the context of patent infringement no without notice injunction will be granted unless there is real urgency. As between the without notice application and the hearing of the effective application, there must be an, "element of threatened damage that requires the immediate intervention of the court".[91] This requirement is more difficult to meet where an early effective hearing date is available.

Injunctions without notice are also available where service on the defendant cannot readily or easily be achieved and there is an immediate need to prevent a threatened act. In *Bloomsbury Publishing Ltd v Newsgroup Newspapers*,[92] injunctive relief was granted without notice against an unnamed individual to restrain the unauthorised publication of the fifth book in the "Harry Potter" series. The claimant had an arguable case that loss would be substantial (i.e. measurable in millions of pounds) and inflicted in a very short time. The recipient (who had tried to sell the book to three national newspapers) would be in no doubt that the injunction would be directed at him. The order was

---

[88] As Ormrod L.J. explained in *Ansah v Ansah* [1977] 2 All E.R. 638 at 642, "Orders made *ex parte* are anomalies in our system of justice which generally demands service or notice of the proposed proceedings on the opposite party".
[89] *Thomas A. Edison Ltd v Bullock* (1912) 15 C.L.R. 679 at 681.
[90] [2006] Q.B. 606 at 625.
[91] *Mayne Pharma (USA) Inc v Teva UK Ltd* [2004] EWHC 3248 at [14] per Pumfrey J.
[92] [2003] 1 W.L.R. 1633.

effective also against all those who, knowing of the order, assisted in attempts to sell the book.

Where granted, the injunction without notice is effective for only a limited period and subject to review on the defendant's application.[93] Particularly stringent rules apply to the claimant seeking an injunction without notice. A claimant is required to disclose all facts relevant to the exercise of judicial discretion and this extends to revealing any defences that might have been employed by the defendant if present. Should the claimant be in breach of duty to do so, the court will discharge the injunction and leave the claimant to apply again.   **18.22**

Quia timet injunctions

A *quia timet* injunction is issued to prevent an infringement of the claimant's rights where the infringement is threatened, but has not yet occurred. There must be an immediate threat to do something. In the words of Lord Buckmaster, "a mere vague apprehension is not sufficient to support an action for a *quia timet* injunction".[94] In *Drury v Secretary of State for the Environment, Food and Rural Affairs*,[95] where a possession order was sought against trespassers, the Court of Appeal considered that the court's jurisdiction to include an area of land because of a threatened or anticipated trespass was dependent upon the claimant showing entitlement to a *quia timet* injunction against the occupants. Unfortunately, the claimant failed to show, "convincing evidence of real danger of actual violation".[96] As Wilson J. explained, this danger might have been demonstrated by evidence of "an expression of intention to decamp to the other area ... a history of movement between the two areas from which a danger of repetition can be inferred ..." or evidence of, "such propinquity and similarity between the two areas as to command the inference of a real danger of decampment of one to the other".[97] In *British Telecommunications Ltd v One in a Million Ltd*,[98] furthermore, the registration of Internet domain names comprising the name or trademark of well-known companies was a threatened "passing off" and trademark infringement. The registration was patently calculated to infringe the plaintiffs' rights in future. Aldous L.J. drew attention to the general rule that a *quia timet* injunction will be issued in these circumstances only where the defendant has equipped himself with or intends to equip another with an instrument of fraud.   **18.23**

---

[93] It is open to the defendant to request a hearing at any time before the end of the period in order to have the injunction discharged or varied.
[94] *Graigola Merthyr C Ltd v Swansea Corporation* [1929] A.C. 344 at 353.
[95] [2004] 1 W.L.R. 1906.
[96] [2004] 1 W.L.R. 1906 at 1912 per Wilson J. See also, *Ministry of Agriculture Fisheries and Food v Heyman* (1989) 59 P. & C.R. 48 per Saville J.
[97] [2004] 1 W.L.R. 1906 at 1913.
[98] [1999] 1 W.L.R. 903.

PRINCIPLES GOVERNING THE GRANT OF FINAL INJUNCTIONS

18.24   Unlike the principles governing the grant of interim relief, the jurisdiction of the court as to the grant of final injunctions is based on settled equitable principles. As will be seen, similar principles guide the court in determining whether to order specific performance.

Adequacy of damages and other legal remedies

18.25   It was once declared by Lindley L.J. that, "the very first principle of injunction law is that prima facie you do not obtain injunctions to restrain actionable wrongs, for which damages are the proper remedy".[99] The test as to appropriateness of damages was hailed by Turner L.J. to be, "whether this is a case in which the remedy at law is so inadequate that the court ought to interfere, having regard to the legal remedy, the rights and interests of the parties, and the consequence of the court's interference".[1] Accordingly the court considers factors such as the danger of repetition (i.e. the need to relieve the applicant of the necessity of bringing a series of actions) or the damage done to the applicant and whether this was assessable in monetary terms. Nowadays, the central question appears to be when taking on board a fuller range of considerations whether it is more just to grant an injunction than to award damages.[2] Principally, the court may consider the following matters:

- the conduct of the claimant,
- equity will not act in vain,
- delay and acquiescence,
- hardship, and
- public interest.

Conduct of the claimant

18.26   Such maxims of equity as "he who comes to equity must come with clean hands" and "he who comes to equity must do equity" are prominent illustrations of equity's regard for proper conduct.[3] Naturally, therefore the gaze of equity falls on the conduct of the claimant. As an application of the clean hands principle, a claimant who has behaved unconscionably or improperly may be denied equitable intervention. Mere "general depravity" will not suffice.[4] The court will exercise its discretion only where there is a

---

[99] *London and Blackwell Rly Co v Cross* (1886) 31 Ch. D. 354 at 369.
[1] *AG v Sheffield Gas Consumers Co* (1853) 3 De G M & G 304 at 321.
[2] *Beswick v Beswick* [1968] A.C. 58 at 102; see further **19.12**.
[3] Also explored in the context of specific performance.
[4] Per Eyre C.B. in *Dering v Earl of Winchelsea* (1787) 1 Cox 318 at 319.

strong link between the poor conduct of the claimant and the relief sought, such that one has, "an immediate and necessary relation" to the other.[5] In *Littlewood v Caldwell*,[6] therefore, the wrongful removal of partnership books by the claimant led to the refusal of an injunction to a claimant in the midst of proceedings to dissolve the partnership.

By contrast, the maxim, "he who comes to equity must do equity" focuses on the claimant's future conduct. Accordingly, no injunction will be granted to a claimant unless he is ready, willing and able to carry out any contractual obligations owed to the defendant. Thus, in an action to restrain breach of covenant, Cozens-Hardy M.R. explained that, "the plaintiffs who are seeking equitable relief by way of injunction, cannot obtain such relief unless they ... are ready and able also to perform their part in future".[7]

Equity will not act in vain

This further equitable maxim can be employed to justify the refusal of the court to issue an injunction on the grounds of impossibility or futility of performance. In *Evans v Manchester, Sheffield and Lincolnshire Rly Co*,[8] it was impossible for the defendant to comply with the terms of an injunction to prevent further subsidence of the foundations of a canal and its banks because the extent of any further subsidence could not be foreseen. As Kekewich J. explained, "I think it would be wrong to enjoin a company or an individual from permitting that to be done which is really beyond his control ... in the sense that he cannot by any precaution or by any works with reasonable certainty [prevent further subsidence]" and comply with the order sought.[9] More recently, in *AG v Observer Ltd*,[10] the futility of continuing with existing injunctions led directly to the discharge of injunctions against national newspapers prohibiting the publication of confidential information. The worldwide publication of "Spycatcher" (Peter Wright's memoirs) had destroyed any secrecy as to its contents. As copies were readily available to any individual who wished obtain them, the injunction had ceased to serve any legitimate or useful purpose.

18.27

Delay and acquiescence

The related matters of delay and acquiescence have the capacity to influence any exercise of discretion by the courts. The former demands of a claimant that equitable relief is sought without unreasonable delay. The latter entails that the knowing failure to object to wrongdoing may prevent the claimant from seeking to object to it at some future juncture. Unfortunately, many of the authorities on the defence of delay are contradictory and inconsistent, some questioning whether at all delay can act as a bar

18.28

---

[5] (1787) 1 Cox 318 at 319; see also *Moody v Cox* [1917] 2 Ch. 71 at 87.
[6] (1822) 11 Price 97.
[7] *Measures Bros Ltd v Measures* [1910] 2 Ch. 248 at 254.
[8] (1887) 36 Ch. D. 626.
[9] (1887) 36 Ch. D. 626 at 639.
[10] [1990] 1 A.C. 109.

to relief. Recent authorities appear to stress that an "inordinate" delay would be required to prevent the grant of an injunction.[11]

A shorter period is sufficient to bar enforcement of rights in the case of acquiescence.[12] The defence of acquiescence arises where the claimant has assented to the acts of the defendant or has been passively inactive in a case where the defendant changes his position and violates the claimant's rights. In consequence, it may be unjust to grant relief. A classic statement of principle was provided by Lord Wensleydale that, "If a party, who could object, lies by and knowingly permits another to incur an expense in doing an act under the belief that it would not be objected to, and so a kind of permission may be said to be given to another to alter his condition, he may be said to acquiesce".[13] Thus, in *Sayers v Collyer*,[14] where a house was used for the sale of beer in clear breach of covenant, the claimant was denied an injunction on the grounds that he had knowledge of the breach for a period of three years and that he, himself, had purchased beer there. This was held to be a sufficient bar to any remedy.

18.29   Acquiescence may be an entire bar to all relief[15] or it may be a ground for inducing the court to give damages in lieu of injunction under Lord Cairns' Act. Thus, in the words of Fry L.J., "an amount of acquiescence less than what would be a bar to all remedy, may operate on the discretion of the Court and induce it to give damages instead of an injunction".[16] In *Shaw v Applegate*,[17] the claimant sought to enforce a covenant prohibiting the use of land as an amusement arcade. The claimant had been unsure as to whether the actions of the defendant were in breach of covenant. Although he began proceedings after a delay and failed to seek interlocutory relief, it was not "unconscionable or dishonest" for him to seek to enforce his rights. There was sufficient acquiescence to rule out the availability of an injunction in that the defendant had been lulled into a false sense of security by the claimant's delay and failure to apply for interlocutory relief when the action was commenced. The defendant had, furthermore, continued to build up his business. The proper course was, therefore, to award damages in lieu of an injunction.

No such acquiescence was evident in *Mortimer v Bailey*, where a mandatory injunction to pull down the defendant's extension was granted notwithstanding the claimant's failure to commence proceedings in a timely manner.[18] As Peter Gibson L.J. explined,

> "I would not characterise what occurred in this case as the claimants standing by while the extension was built. I accept that the claimants were slow to seek an interim injunction and left it far too late, and, as I have said, such delay is a relevant consideration in the exercise of discretion whether to grant a final injunction. But very shortly after work commenced, and with the completion of the extension still two months away, the defendants had been warned by the claimants

---

[11] *H. P. Bulmer Ltd & Showerings Ltd v Bolinger SA* [1977] 2 C.M.L.R. 625.
[12] *Sayers v Collyer* (1884) 28 Ch. D. 103 per Baggallay L.J.
[13] *Archbold v Scully* (1861) 9 H.L.C. 360 at 383.
[14] (1884) 28 Ch. D. 103.
[15] See *Gafford v Graham* (1999) 3 EGLR 75, where knowledge of a breach of a restrictive covenant coupled with a failure to complain for 3 years was a bar to all relief by virtue of acquiescence.
[16] *Sayers v Collyer* [1884] 25 Ch. 103 at 110.
[17] [1977] 1 W.L.R. 970.
[18] [2005] P. & C.R. 9; see G. Watt, [2005] Conv 14.

that if the construction continued proceedings would be brought against them ... They chose to rely on the advice of their legal advisers and to proceed with the construction. In so doing they took a gamble that it was unreasonable for the claimants to have refused consent. They lost that gamble".[19]

Hardship

Any element of hardship is a key consideration for the court where the injunction **18.30** sought is interim or mandatory in nature. In the case of an interim injunction, the rights of the parties have not yet been determined and it is appropriate that the court safeguard the defendant from potential hardship as he has not yet been found to be in breach of the claimant's rights. In the case of the mandatory injunction, the court inevitably guards against the hardship that may result from compelling the defendant positively to act (usually by expenditure). Here, there is an obvious risk that hardship to the defendant can outweigh the benefit to the claimant.[20]

Albeit less weighty, hardship remains a consideration where a final order is sought, but the principal question for the court concerns the adequacy of damages in the circumstances of the case. Where, however, disproportionate hardship will be caused to the defendant by the grant of an injunction than to the claimant in being confined to a remedy of damages, the court can, in its discretion, refuse to grant an injunction.[21] Generally, this discretion will be exercised only exceptional circumstances. The defendant's position must, of course, be weakened in cases where he knew he was acting in breach of the claimant's rights.[22]

Public interest

As will be discussed with regard to specific performance, considerations of public policy **18.31** impact upon the availability of equitable relief. Thus, in a breach of contract, the courts are loath to enforce private rights that conflict with public policy. A different emphasis appears to prevail where an injunction is sought to restrain commission of a tort. Indeed, the difficulties inherent in the exercise of judicial discretion came markedly to the fore in *Miller v Jackson*.[23] There, an established cricket ground was alleged to be a nuisance due to the frequency that cricket balls landed in the garden of a newly erected, nearby house. Both Geoffrey Lane and Cumming-Bruce L.JJ. accepted that the activity constituted nuisance, but they disagreed as to whether an injunction ought to be granted (the former in favour; the latter against). Lord Denning M.R. denied the presence of nuisance on the facts and agreed with Geoffrey Lane L.J. (but for different reasons) that the injunction should be refused. He argued that, even if the tort of nuisance had been committed, an injunction should be refused on the basis of the

---

[19] [2005] P. & C.R. 9 at [35].
[20] See **18.44** for a discussion of hardship in the context of interim mandatory orders.
[21] *Wood v Sutcliffe* (1851) 61 E.R. 303 at 305.
[22] *Smith v Smith* (1875) L.R. 20 Eq. 500 at 505.
[23] [1977] Q.B. 966.

greater public interest in, "protecting the environment by preserving our playing fields in the face of mounting development, and by enabling our youth to enjoy all the benefits of outdoor games".[24] As a statement of principle, he declared obiter that, "I am of the opinion that the public interest should prevail over the private interest".[25]

In light of the divergence of opinion, it is unsurprising that more recent courts have not felt bound by *Miller v Jackson*. Neither is it surprising that the views of Lord Denning M.R. have been singled out for attack. In *Kennaway v Thompson* Lawton L.J. criticised his conclusion holding that, "The statement of Lord Denning M.R. that the public interest should prevail over the private interest runs counter to the principles enunciated in *Shelfer's* case[26] and does not accord with the reasoning of Cumming-Bruce L.J. for refusing an injunction".[27] Accordingly, the Court of Appeal denied that the public interest in motor-boat racing could prevail over a claimant's right to quiet enjoyment of her property. The claimant in that case had sought an injunction to restrain the defendants from creating excessive noise in the pursuit of their chosen sport. Lawton L.J. highlighted the considerable public interest in the club and that the public attended in large numbers. On the basis of this public interest, the claimant was denied an injunction restraining all of the club's activities. Instead, the court decided on a form of order that made restrictions in the number and type of event, to the number of permitted racers and users and as to acceptable levels of noise. The effect was to protect the claimant from intolerable noise whilst at the same time allowing the club to organise activities about which the claimant could not legitimately complain. The Court of Appeal accepted that a balance must be achieved and that the question of public interest was one matter to be taken into account in performing that balancing function. Rarely will public interest be the decisive matter.

18.32   *Dennis v Ministry of Defence* emphasises that the effect of public interest will, "depend on the circumstances, not least the strength of the public interest in question".[28] Here, the claimants brought an action for a declaration[29] and damages in relation to nuisance and or interference with human rights, constituted by noise emanating from a nearby air force base. It was accepted that there was a strong and legitimate public interest served in the continuation of the training of RAF pilots. The court concluded, however, that the claimants should not bear the cost of the public benefit. Accordingly, although the declaration was refused on the ground of public interest, damages of £950,000 were awarded for loss of capital value together with past and future loss of use and amenity. In short, these cases serve to illustrate that the interest of the public and third parties generally can impact upon the remedy adopted, i.e. there are cases where it is not in the public interest to grant an injunction and damages are instead awarded.

[24] [1977] Q.B. 966 at 981.
[25] [1977] Q.B. 966 at 982.
[26] *Shelfer v City of London Electric Lighting Co* [1895] 1 Ch. 287.
[27] [1981] Q.B. 88 at 93.
[28] [2003] 2 EGLR 121 at 126.
[29] The appropriate remedy when an injunction is sought against the Crown.

PRINCIPLES GOVERNING THE GRANT OF INTERIM INJUNCTIONS

It will be recalled that the principles upon which the court will issue an interim injunction differ in their particularity and their origin from those that apply at the trial. At the interim stage, the court is not in a position to decide the case or to resolve uncertainty. Its role is to minimise the risk of injustice to the parties in circumstances where it is unclear that the claimant will succeed. As Lord Diplock put it, "It was to mitigate the risk of injustice to the plaintiff during the period before that uncertainty could be resolved that the practice arose of granting him relief by way of interlocutory injunction".[30]   **18.33**

The undertaking in damages

The grant of an interim injunction requires (unless the court otherwise orders) that the claimant enter into the "usual undertaking" that he will abide by any order as to damages which the court may make if it transpires that the claimant was not entitled to the interim injunction and the defendant has suffered damage thereby.[31] Its function is to aid the court, "in doing that which was its great object, viz abstaining from expressing any opinion upon the merits of the case until the hearing".[32] The court, however, has no power to compel a claimant to enter into an undertaking, but the claimant will be aware that the court will be reluctant to grant the injunction unless the undertaking is given. In *Bunn v BBC*,[33] for example, relief was sought to protect the confidentiality of a statement made to the police. Lightman J. admitted that an applicant's lack of means would not, "be a sufficient ground in itself to prevent him obtaining relief".[34] Conveniently, however, he was not required to test this on the facts. The applicant was barred by delay and the injunction would have been in vain as the statement was already in the public domain.   **18.34**

Although the undertaking is for the benefit of the defendant, the undertaking is made to the court. Accordingly, a failure to perform is a contempt of court and not a breach of contract. The court then enjoys the discretion as to whether to enforce the undertaking.[35] If it does so, the measure of damages is calculated as though the claimant had breached a contract with the defendant.[36] If there is doubt as to the capacity of the claimant to pay any damages, the court can require the claimant to deposit sums with

---

[30] *American Cyanamid Co v Ethicon Ltd* [1975] A.C. 396 at 406.
[31] CPR Pt 25.5(1). Equally, as a condition of refusing to grant the injunction, the court can require the defendant to make an undertaking that should the claimant succeed at trial, he will compensate the claimant for damage suffered.
[32] *Walkefield v Duke of Buccleugh* (1865) 12 L.T. 628 at 629 as cited by Lord Diplock in *American Cyanamid Co v Ethicon Ltd* [1975] A.C. 396 at 408.
[33] [1998] 3 All E.R. 552.
[34] [1998] 3 All E.R. 552 at 558.
[35] *Cheltenham & Gloucester v Ricketts* [1993] 1 All E.R. 1545.
[36] See the views of Lord Diplock in *Hoffmann La-Roche (F) & Co v Secretary of State for Trade and Industry* [1975] A.C. 295 at 361.

solicitors or to give security to the court. No undertaking is required from the Crown when it is seeking to enforce the law by means of a law enforcement action.[37] An undertaking will be extracted in cases where the Crown seeks to enforce its own proprietary or contractual rights.[38] In this respect, the Crown is placed in the same position as an individual as regards the usual undertaking in damages.

18.35   Until the decision in *American Cyanamid Co v Ethicon Ltd*,[39] it was understood that a claimant was required to show a strong prima facie case that he would succeed at trial and that damages would be an inadequate remedy.[40] In *American Cyanamid*, however, Lord Diplock criticised as unnecessary this seemingly accepted requirement. He was of the view that, "The use of such expressions as, 'a probability', 'a prima facie case', or 'a strong prima facie case' in the context of the exercise of a discretionary power to grant an interlocutory injunction leads to confusion as to the object sought to be achieved by this form of temporary relief".[41] His principles have been taken to lay down new guidelines as to the balancing function of the court in such cases. It is the "balance of convenience" that lies at the heart of the *Cyanamid* approach.

The American Cyanamid principles

18.36   The court must be satisfied that the claim is not frivolous or vexatious. In other words, there must be a serious issue to be tried.[42] Thereafter, the balance of convenience must be considered. The balance of convenience is not by any means a new consideration, but it is a most important element in the *Cyanamid* guidelines. The balance of convenience or "balance of justice"[43] is the result of weighing up respective risks that injustice may result from deciding the case in one way rather than the other in the face of incomplete evidence. In other words, it is a balancing exercise whereby the court determines how best it can minimise the risk of injustice to the parties. The court takes, "whichever course appears to carry the lower risk of injustice if it should turn out to be wrong".[44]

    The inadequacy of damages to each party is the primary focus. The process is as follows: If an injunction is not granted, the court will consider whether damages will be an inadequate remedy to compensate the claimant if he should succeed at trial. If damages can compensate, and the defendant is able to pay, the court will lean towards refusal of interim relief. If the loss to the claimant is not remediable,[45] the court will

---

[37] This involves proceedings brought by the Crown to prevent a subject from breaking the law and causing harm to the general public.

[38] *Hoffmann La-Roche (F) & Co v Secretary of State for Trade and Industry* [1975] A.C. 295.

[39] Which concerned a *quia timet* interlocutory injunction to restrain infringement of a patent; see P. Prescott (1975) 91 L.Q.R. 168.

[40] In *Stratford & Sons Ltd v Lindley* [1965] A.C. 269 at 323, for example, Lord Reid made reference to, "a sufficient prima facie case".

[41] [1975] A.C. 396 at 407.

[42] That is, that the claimant's case is not, for example, futile or misconceived.

[43] See *A-G v Barker* [1990] 3 All E.R. 257 per Lord Donaldson M.R.

[44] *Films Rover International Ltd v Cannon Films Sales Ltd* [1987] 1 W.L.R. 670 at 680 per Lord Hoffmann. As Jacob L.J notes in *SmithKline Beecham Plc v Apotex Europe Ltd* [2007] Ch. 71 at 83 "the expression 'wrongful injunction' is used, but in truth there is nothing wrongful about it. The decision whether or not to grant it is made on the basis of a necessarily incomplete picture".

[45] For example loss of trade caused by picketing the claimant's business: see *Hubbard v Pitt* [1976] Q.B. 142.

consider the possibility of granting the injunction. If an injunction is granted, the court must question whether the claimant would be in a position to compensate the defendant for any loss caused to him pending trial, if at trial the defendant was to succeed. If damages are an adequate remedy, the court will require from the claimant an undertaking in damages. Moreover, where damages will *not* compensate the claimant in circumstances where an interim injunction is wrongly refused, but *will* compensate the defendant if an interim injunction was wrongly granted, the court will favour the grant of an injunction, provided the claimant can make an undertaking in damages.

Frequently, however, damages are inadequate for both parties or there is doubt as to the adequacy of the respective remedies in damages.[46] In such cases, other aspects of the balance of convenience come into play. Although Lord Diplock considered it "unwise" to attempt to list the various matters to be taken into consideration in determining where the balance lies,[47] the court will address matters such as public interest[48] or the particular circumstances of the case.[49] Where these factors appear to be evenly balanced, Lord Diplock emphasised that it is, "a counsel of prudence to take such measures as are calculated to preserve the status quo",[50] that is, an interim injunction should not be granted.

18.37

Finally, Lord Diplock addressed the circumstances in which it may be appropriate to evaluate prospects of success. It will be recalled that, prior to *Cyanamid*, the assessment of the strength of each party's case was the most significant matter. The court was, understandably, reluctant to subject a claimant to the risk of irrecoverable loss by refusing injunctive relief in a case where it was felt that the client was likely to succeed at trial. Post-*Cyanamid*, it appears that the court should refrain from immediate recourse to this test. As is clear from the caution with which Lord Diplock discussed the issue, the court should assess the strength of the cases as a last resort and only where the strength of one party's case is evidently disproportionate to that of the other party. As Lord Diplock put it:

> "If the extent of the uncompensatable disadvantage to each party would not differ widely, it may not be improper to take into account in tipping the balance the relative strength of each party's case as revealed by the affidavit evidence adduced on the hearing of the application. This, however, should be done only where it is apparent upon the facts disclosed by evidence as to which there is no creditable dispute that the strength of one party's case is disproportionate to that of the other party. The court is not justified in embarking upon anything resembling a trial of

---

[46] Most cases will not be resolved at this stage because as Laddie J. explained in *Series 5 Software v Clarke* [1996] 1 All E.R. 853 at 863, "evidence relating to the adequacy of damages normally will be contradictory and there will be no possibility of resolving the differences by cross-examination". Cf. *Factortame Ltd v Secretary of State for Transport (No.2)* [1991] 1 All E.R. 70 at 118, where Lord Goff argued that, "At this stage … many applications for interim injunctions can well be decided".

[47] [1975] A.C. 396 at 408.

[48] Where the defendant is a public body, allegedly in breach of its statutory duty, the court will weigh up the interests of the general public in determining the balance of convenience: see *Smith v Inner London Education Authority* [1978] 1 All E.R. 411.

[49] For example, the courts are reluctant to grant an interim injunction in cases of industrial disputes or political decisions.

[50] [1975] A.C. 396 at 408.

the action upon conflicting affidavits in order to evaluate the strength of either party's case".[51]

Finally, and without elaboration, Lord Diplock accepts that special factors arising in the particular case can be considered.

The American Cyanamid approach considered

18.38 The *American Cyanamid* principles appear, at first glance, emphatic and constraining. In the face of such firm House of Lords' guidance, there seems little doubt as to the appropriate framework to be adopted in interim proceedings. It looks impossible to reconcile these principles with the previous practice of requiring the plaintiff to make a strong prima facie case. In short, *Cyanamid* relegates any assessment of the relative strengths of the cases as far as possible behind the need to assess the balance of convenience. Not surprisingly, it is a decision that has been met with criticism and consternation and to which there is a growing body of exceptions. Much judicial focus has fallen on the extent to which the court is bound to follow *Cyanamid* and the role of special factors, particularly whether their presence enables the court to move outside the balance of convenience to assess prospects of success or, alternatively, whether "special factors" are merely part of the balance of convenience.

In *Fellowes & Son v Fisher*,[52] the claimant firm of solicitors sought to restrain a breach of restrictive covenant in the contract of a former employee. The employee contended that the covenant was invalid. No interlocutory relief was granted. Browne L.J. accepted that the court was, "bound to follow and apply" the decision in *American Cyanamid*.[53] In the absence of evidence as to the adequacy of damages to either party, the balance of convenience favoured refusal of the interlocutory injunction. Sir John Pennycuick agreed, but regarded it as, "the most serious difficulty" that the prospects of success have been disregarded, "except as a last resort when the balance of convenience is otherwise even".[54] He pointed out that there are many classes of case, "where the prospect of success is within the competence of the judge hearing the interlocutory application and represents a factor which can hardly be disregarded in determining whether or not is just to give interlocutory relief".[55] Accordingly, he confessed to difficulty in arriving at a just conclusion without considering the prospects of success at trial. Both he and Browne L.J. felt unduly constrained to apply *American Cyanamid*. On the other hand Lord Denning M.R. found it impossible to reconcile the statements made by Lord Diplock in *American Cyanamid* with those in *JT Stratford & Son v Lindley*.[56] The latter was a House of Lords' decision that was not considered by Lord Diplock where all members of the House of Lords agreed that a claimant must establish a prima facie case. Lord Denning M.R. viewed the instant case as one of many individual cases that allowed the court to depart from *American Cyanamid* and to look to

---

[51] [1975] A.C. 396 at 411.
[52] [1976] Q.B. 122.
[53] [1976] Q.B. 122 at 138.
[54] [1976] Q.B. 122 at 141.
[55] [1976] Q.B. 142 at 185.
[56] [1965] A.C. 269.

whether a prima facie case was established. Alternatively, he considered the case to be one of "uncompensatable disadvantages" (where damages on either side would not be an adequate remedy), thus permitting consideration of the relative strength of the parties.

In *Hubbard v Pitt*,[57] Lord Denning M.R. again took the opportunity to argue that **18.39** special factors were not merely an aspect of the balance of convenience but permitted the court to move outside *Cyanamid* altogether. The case concerned a campaign against an estate agency in Islington that involved demonstrating and leafleting outside the claimant's office. At first instance, an injunction was granted restraining the picketing of the premises. This was upheld by a majority of the Court of Appeal. Stamp L.J. explicitly raised Lord Denning's interpretation of the role of "special factors" and admitted nonetheless that, "it appears to me clear beyond peradventure that Lord Diplock was there referring to special factors affecting the balance of convenience and not to special factors enabling the court to ignore the general principles there laid down".[58]

Both *Fellowes & Son v Fisher* and *Hubbard v Pitt* provide examples of cases where the Court of Appeal has felt constrained to follow (or in the case of Lord Denning to re-interpret) the House of Lords' guidelines. Other cases reveal markedly less concern that the discretion of the court has been patently restricted. As Kerr L.J. declared in *Cambridge Nutrition Ltd v BBC*, for example, "The *American Cyanamid* case contains no principle of universal application. The only such principle is the statutory power of the court to grant injunctions when it is just and convenient to do so. The *American Cyanamid* case is no more than a set of useful guidelines which apply in many cases. It must never be used as a rule of thumb, let alone a strait-jacket".[59] Similarly, Lord Goff has emphasised that the court should not feel shackled by *Cyanamid*. He claimed in *R. v Secretary of State for Transport ex parte Factortame Ltd (No.2)*:

"I do not read Lord Diplock's speech as intended to fetter the broad discretion conferred on the courts by s.37 of the Supreme Court Act 1981; on the contrary a prime purpose of the guidelines established ... was to remove a fetter ... that a party seeking an interlocutory injunction had to establish a *prima facie* case ... It is now clear that it is enough if he can show that there is a serious question to be tried. If he can establish that, then he has, so to speak, crossed the threshold; and the court can then address itself to the question whether it is just or convenient to grant an injunction".[60]

Perhaps the most interesting attempt to re-evaluate Lord Diplock's *Cyanamid* guide- **18.40** lines was provided by Laddie J. in *Series 5 Software v Clarke*.[61] This is another case where the perceived inconsistency between past practice and the *Cyanamid* guidelines came to the fore. Laddie J. was acutely aware that, as recently as four months before *Cyanamid* was decided, Lord Diplock, himself, had cited with approval the traditional

---

[57] [1976] Q.B. 142.
[58] [1976] Q.B. 142 at 185.
[59] [1990] 3 All E.R. 523 at 534.
[60] [1991] 1 All E.R. 70 at 118.
[61] [1996] 1 All E.R. 853.

need for the claimant to show a strong prima facie case.[62] He could not accept that Lord Diplock had radically changed his view in such a short space of time. Laddie J. was of the opinion, therefore, that there was, "no significant inconsistency" between *Cyanamid* and *La Roche* and that the prospects of success remained an important factor. He argued that there was nothing in what Lord Diplock said to suggest that it is not legitimate to look at the relative strength of the parties' cases. Although Lord Diplock appears to suggest that the court cannot take into account the strength of each party's case where there is a dispute on the evidence, Laddie J. was unperturbed. He emphasised that relief must be flexible and calculated that Lord Diplock did not intend to prevent consideration of the strength of the cases in most applications for injunctive relief. Accordingly, he argued that where, "the court is able to come to a view as to the strength of the parties' cases on credible evidence then it can do so".[63] Although the interpretation of Laddie J. has received judicial support[64] and, as illustrated above, the *Cyanamid* guidelines have been convincingly criticised, it is probable that *Cyanamid* will continue to be applied. Not least, the approach in *Series 5* seems to ignore the clear requirement that the court concern itself with the balance of convenience and not the parties' prospect of success. As Lord Diplock himself made clear in *NWL Ltd v Woods*, the *Cyanamid* approach, "enjoins the judge on an application for an interim injunction to direct his attention to the balance of convenience as soon as he has satisfied himself that there is a serious issue to be tried".[65]

Qualications to Cyanamid

18.41　As has been discussed, the *American Cyanamid* guidelines are those generally applicable to the grant of an interim injunction. The guidelines are subject to important qualifications i.e. the guidelines will not apply to cases as follows:

- where there is no arguable defence,

- where the grant or refusal of relief will put on end to the action or finally resolve the case,

- as to interim mandatory injunctions.

No arguable defence

18.42　Where a defendant has no arguable defence, there is no basis upon which to consider the *American Cyanamid* guidelines.[66] The reason is logical, because, as James L.J. explained, "Balance of convenience has nothing to do with a case of this kind; it can

---

[62] *Hoffmann La-Roche v Secretary of State for Trade and Industry* [1975] A.C. 295 at 360.
[63] [1996] 1 All E.R. 853 at 865.
[64] For example, see *Barnsley Brewery Co Ltd v RBNB* [1997] F.S.R. 462 per Robert Walker L.J.
[65] [1979] 1 W.L.R. 1294 at 1306.
[66] See, for example, *Official Custodian for Charities v MacKay* [1985] Ch. 168.

only be considered where there is some question that must be decided at the hearing".[67] Accordingly, in cases where the defendant has no arguable defence, an appropriate course is to grant the injunction until trial.

Final resolution of case

Where the grant or refusal of an interim injunction will have the practical effect of **18.43** putting an end to the action, in the sense, for example, that it would give judgment against the defendant without permitting him a right of trial, the *Cyanamid* guidelines will not apply. It is instead necessary to take on board the relative strength of the parties' claims. The approach of the court must be to endeavour to avoid injustice.[68] Lord Diplock, himself, pointed out that the *American Cyanamid* case was not a case where the grant or refusal of an injunction would dispose of the action finally in favour of the successful party. Accordingly, he acknowledged that where:

> "the grant or refusal of the interlocutory injunction will have the effect of putting an end to the action because the harm that will have been already caused to the losing party by its grant or its refusal is complete and of a kind which money cannot constitute any worthwhile recompense, the degree of likelihood that the plaintiff would have succeeded in establishing his right to an injunction if the action had gone to trial, is a factor to be brought into the balance by the judge in weighing the risks that injustice may result from his deciding the application one way rather than the other".[69]

In *Cayne v Global Natural Resources Plc*[70] it was clear that there would be no trial of the action if the claimant obtained an injunction. Here, the applicant sought to restrain a share issue, the effect of which would be to determine the constitution of a board of directors of a company. If the applicants were to succeed, they were likely to take control of the company. The court acknowledged that by that stage it would be inconceivable that they would continue with the present proceedings. For Kerr L.J., therefore, the overriding concern was that, "if an injunction is granted, the effective contest between the parties is likely to have been finally decided summarily in favour of the plaintiffs".[71]

Under markedly different circumstances, the Court of Appeal in *Cambridge Nutrition Ltd v BBC*[72] also viewed the *Cyanamid* guidelines as pertaining to situations where the substantial issues between the parties required to be resolved at trial. The appellate court found that a different set of considerations must be relevant where the crucial issues did not depend on trial, but on the grant of interim relief. The claimants sought an injunction to restrain the BBC from broadcasting a programme until after the publication of a government report on the same issue. If successful, the trial of the

---

[67] *Stocker v Planet Building Society* (1879) 27 W.R. 877 at 878.
[68] See *Cayne v Global Natural Resources* [1984] 1 All E.R. 225.
[69] *NWL Ltd v Woods* [1979] 1 W.L.R. 1294 at 1307.
[70] [1984] 1 All E.R. 225.
[71] [1984] 1 All E.R. 225 at 236.
[72] [1990] 3 All E.R. 523.

action would be unlikely. The claimants would have secured their goal with the grant of interlocutory relief in that the crucial consideration was the postponement of the broadcast. Albeit expressed narrowly, Kerr L.J. felt that the *Cyanamid* guidelines could not extend to, "cases in which the subject matter concerns the right to publish an article, or to transmit a broadcast whose importance may be transitory but whose impact depends on timing, news value and topicality".[73] Such cases do not lend themselves easily to the application of the *Cyanamid* guidelines in that the availability of interim relief will be decisive of the case and make trial of the action unlikely indeed. Instead, the court will assess the merits of the case. On the facts, the existence of a contract was doubtful and could not support the grant of an injunction which would prevent the broadcast by the BBC of a programme on a matter of public interest. No injunction was issued.

Interim mandatory injunctions

18.44   The *Cyanamid* guidelines relate to the grant of prohibitive injunctions on an interim application. Where a mandatory order is sought, the court has jurisdiction to grant it on an interim basis, but it will very rarely do so, "for the Court would not compel a man to do so serious a thing as to undo what he had done except at a hearing".[74] Sensibly, therefore, a high degree of assurance is required that at trial it will appear that the injunction was rightly granted. In *De Falco v Crawley BC*, Bridge L.J. emphasised that the guidelines laid down by Lord Diplock in *Cyanamid* had "no relevance"[75] to the issue of whether a local authority could be ordered to provide accommodation for the homeless claimant.[76] The higher standard required of the applicant was that he show "a strong prima facie case".[77] Indeed in *Leisure Data v Bell*[78] the Court of Appeal has confirmed that the *Cyanamid* guidelines are not applicable to the issue of interim mandatory orders.

It will be recalled that different considerations influence the court where a defendant will be forced into some positive act. It is, indeed, the interim quality of equitable relief that accentuates the pressure on the courts to decline to issue a mandatory order. Megarry J. disclosed the reasons in *Shepherd Homes v Sandham*.[79] First, a mandatory order is larger in scope. The prohibitive injunction focuses on restraining continuance of the act or conduct in the period between the issue of the interim order and the date of the effective hearing. In the words of Megarry J., "it does not attempt to deal with what has happened in the past".[80] By contrast, the mandatory injunction looks at least in part to what has happened in the past because it will require the taking of positive steps to dismantle or undo something already done. Secondly, the danger at an interim stage

---

[73] [1990] 3 All E.R. 523 at 535.
[74] *Gale v Abbot* (1862) 10 W.R. 748 at 750 per Kindersley V.C. See also *Edwin Shirley Productions Ltd v Workspace Management Ltd* [2001] 23 E.G. 158.
[75] [1980] 1 All E.R. 913 at 924.
[76] Under the Housing (Homeless Persons) Act 1977, now repealed.
[77] [1980] 1 All E.R. 913 at 922 per Lord Denning M.R.
[78] [1988] F.S.R. 367 at 371 per Dillon L.J.
[79] [1971] Ch. 340.
[80] [1971] Ch. 340 at 348.

of requiring the defendant to take positive steps is pronounced. Megarry J. drew attention to the, "consequent waste of time, money and materials" if it later transpires that the defendant had been wrongly mandated.[81] Thirdly, Megarry J. described the interim mandatory injunction as a, "once and for all"[82] order, in that once granted, the claimant will receive all that is required. In the destruction of a building, for example, there is no need for the continuance of a mandatory order. Once demolished, the claimant has achieved all that was sought by the action. Accordingly, Megarry J. felt that a case must be, "unusually strong and clear" before the court could exercise its discretion.[83] The *Cyanamid* guidelines are patently inappropriate in this context.

EXCEPTIONS TO CYANAMID

In addition to the general qualifications outlined above, there are a variety of specific **18.45** contexts in which it is inappropriate to import the *Cyanamid* guidelines. A selection of examples will now be considered and explained. These include:

- trade disputes,
- restraining the presentation of a wind up petition,
- Human Rights Act 1998 s.12(3).

Trade disputes

Section 221(2) of the Trade Union and Labour Relations (Consolidation) Act 1992 **18.46** provides an exception in the context of an application for an interim injunction where the defendant claims that he acted in contemplation or furtherance of a trade dispute. Here the court can exercise its discretion and have regard to that party's likelihood of succeeding at trial of the action in establishing a defence under the Act conferring immunity from liability in tort. Accordingly, the *Cyanamid* guidelines have been modified in this particular context.

Restraining the presentation of a winding-up petition

Where a company seeks to restrain a creditor from presenting a winding-up petition, **18.47** the company must show a prima facie case that the petition will fail and be an abuse of process of the court. As Buckley L.J. noted in *Bryanston Finance Ltd v de Vires (No.2)*, the fact that the action is, "an action designed to prevent the commencement of proceedings *in limine* is a special factor. In such a case the court shall not, in my judgment,

[81] [1971] Ch. 340 at 348.
[82] [1971] Ch. 340 at 348.
[83] [1971] Ch. 340 at 349.

interfere with what would otherwise be a legitimate approach to the seat of justice unless the evidence is sufficient to establish prima facie that the plaintiffs will succeed in establishing that the proceedings sought to be restrained would be an abuse of process".[84] Although Buckley L.J. purported to follow *American Cyanamid*, in treating the case as one involving "special factors", both Stephenson L.J. and Sir John Pennycuick regarded the facts as properly outside *Cyanamid's* reach. All three, nonetheless, were minded to refuse the injunction. This exception to *Cyanamid* has recently been endorsed in *Southern Cross Group Plc v Deka Immobilien Investment GMBH*.[85] Here, the applicant sought an injunction restraining the respondent from presenting a winding-up petition. There was no dispute as to the debts owed by the claimant in the form of unpaid rent and service charges. The applicant, however, alleged substantial cross-claims on the basis that the respondent had unreasonably refused its consent to the assignment of the lease. Nicholas Warren Q.C. held that, on the basis of insufficient evidence to support the claim of alleged losses, the court was unable to restrain the respondent. The applicant had failed to present a genuine and serious case to establish a counter claim greater than the debt on which the statutory demands underlying the petition were based.

The Human Rights Act 1998

18.48 The application for interim injunctions now requires to be considered in the context of art.8 (right to respect for private and family life) and art.10 (right to freedom of expression) of the European Convention. More particularly, s.12 of the Human Rights Act 1998 provides a specific test that must be employed by the courts before relief is granted which might affect the exercise of the Convention right to freedom of expression. Under s.12(3), "No relief is to be granted so as to restrain publication before trial unless the court is satisfied that the applicant is likely to be able to establish that publication should not be allowed".[86] Lord Phillips has acknowledged that this is, "a particularly high threshold test",[87] where an applicant seeks interim relief in an action against the media. The *American Cyanamid* threshold of "a serious question to be tried" is, obviously, a more readily surmountable obstacle than the higher test imposed in this context.

Breach of confidence

18.49 In the case of injunctions sought against the media, most of the case law development has occurred in the context of breach of confidence, where the impact of s.12 is most

---

[84] [1976] Ch. 63 at 78.
[85] [2005] BPIR 1010.
[86] Section 12(4) emphasises that, "The court must have particular regard to the importance of the Convention right of freedom of expression and, where the proceedings relate to material which the respondent claims, or which appears to the court to be journalistic, literary or artistic material (or to conduct related to such material), to (a) the extent to which—(i) the material has, or is about to, become available to the public; or (ii) it is, or would be, in the public interest to be published; (b) any relevant privacy code".
[87] *Douglas v Hello!* [2005] EWCA Civ. 595 at [258].

acutely felt. This is because, as Lord Nicholls recognised in *Campbell v MGN Ltd*, "In this country, unlike the United States of America, there is no over-arching, all-embracing, cause of action for 'invasion of privacy' ... But protection of various aspects of privacy is a fast developing area of the law, here and in other jurisdictions".[88] Currently, "the law imposes a 'duty of confidence' whenever a person receives information he knows or ought to know is fairly and reasonably to be regarded as confidential".[89] It is important to note that these circumstances are strikingly different to those that traditionally gave rise to a duty of confidence.[90] Over the last decade, the courts have adopted the values that arts 8 and 10 protect, giving a "new strength and breadth" to the action for breach of confidence.[91] Indeed, as Buxton L.J. acknowledged in *McKennitt v Ash*, "in order to find the rules of the English law of breach of confidence we now have to look in the jurisprudence of Articles 8 and 10".[92] Inevitably, therefore, some aspects of invasion of privacy have come to be protected against, and there is an increasing recognition that, in considering exactly what can be protected as private pursuant to art. 8, regard must be had to the decisions of the European courts. It follows that the capacity of the courts to restrain the, "misuse of private information"[93] in an action for breach of confidence, has seen a host of celebrities in highly publicised cases test the boundaries of the court's jurisdiction as regards articles and photographs pertaining to weddings,[94] extra-marital affairs,[95] drug use[96] and visits to brothels.[97]

The approach of the court is, initially, to discern "a reasonable expectation of privacy".[98] Thereafter, it must weigh up competing Convention rights, with an intense focus on the facts of the individual case. As regards the balancing exercise, no one Convention right takes precedence over another and the court must measure the extent to which the intrusion into the claimant's privacy is justified or proportionate in light of any legitimate public interest in disclosure. **18.50**

As regards the expectation of privacy, the courts are increasingly concerned to protect individuals, whether material is confidential in the context of a pre-existing relationship between the parties,[99] or in cases where no such relationship exists i.e. where "private" information has been purloined for misuse.[1] Here, even where material **18.51**

---

[88] [2004] 2 All E.R. 995 at 1002.
[89] [2004] 2 All E.R. 995 at 1002.
[90] See *Coco v AN Clark (Engineers) Ltd* [1969] R.P.C. 41 at 47 per Megarry J. An overview of relevant developments in the law of confidence is provided by Lord Phillips in *Douglas v Hello!* [2005] EWCA Civ 595 at [54]–[82].
[91] See *A v B* [2002] 2 All E.R. 545 at 549 per Lord Woolf C.J.
[92] [2008] Q.B. 73 at [11].
[93] To adopt the phrasing of Lord Nicholls in *Campbell v MGN Ltd* [2004] 2 All E.R. 995.
[94] *Douglas v Hello!* [2001] Q.B. 967.
[95] See, for example, *A v B* [2002] 2 All E.R. 545 (concerning an unnamed Premiership footballer).
[96] *Campbell v MGN Ltd* [2003] 1 All E.R. 224.
[97] *Theakston v MGN Ltd* [2002] EWHC 137 (QB).
[98] *Campbell v MGN Ltd* [2004] 2 A.C. 457 at 466.
[99] See *McKennitt v Ash* [2008] Q.B. 73 (publication of a book by a former friend of Canadian folk artist revealing personal details about the artist's private life). As Eady J. acknowledged at first instance, "it seems to have been accepted ... that she protected her reputation and her privacy 'with the iron safeguard of a chastity belt'" ([2005] EWHC 3003 (QB) at [6]).
[1] For example, as to medical health, finances or personal or sexual relationships.

is in some sense accessible to the public,[2] the courts have been prepared, in appropriate circumstances,[3] to discern, and to protect, a claimant's legitimate expectation of privacy.[4]

18.52   As to whether there is a compelling public interest in disclosure, (such that greater weight should be attached to freedom of expression), the courts now construe public interest as an increasingly narrow concept. It is no longer sufficient to satisfy the public interest test that public figures must expect higher levels of media intrusion or that such figures are viewed as role models,[5] although such arguments may or may not be relevant on the facts.[6] Disclosure will be justified, however, to expose crime or wrongdoing, to protect the health and safety of the public or to set the record straight where the public has been misled.[7] In such cases, the courts are mindful as to the use to which the defendant puts his freedom of expression to satisfy legitimate public interest. Understandably, therefore, a distinction has been drawn between the revelation of wrongdoing to the general public generally and the broadcast of images and recordings to that effect. These different considerations with images and recordings were summed up in *Douglas v Hello! Ltd (No.3)*,

> "Special considerations attach to photographs in the field of privacy. They are not merely a method of conveying information that is an alternative to verbal description. They enable the person viewing the photograph to act as a spectator, in some circumstances voyeur would be the more appropriate noun, of whatever it is that the photograph depicts. As a means of invading privacy, a photograph is particularly intrusive. This is quite apart from the fact that the camera, and the telephoto lens, can give access to the viewer of the photograph to scenes where

---

[2] In *Mosley v News Group Newspapers* [2008] EWHC 687 (QB), however, an application to restrain the defendant from making available on its website video footage of Mosley (president of the FIA) engaged in sexual activities with five prostitutes was refused. Eady J. explained at [33], "a point *may* be reached where the information sought to be restricted, by an order of the Court, is so widely and generally accessible 'in the public domain that such an injunction would make no practical difference".

[3] As Patten J. acknowledged at first instance in *Murray v Express Newspapers Plc* [2007] EWHC 1908 (Ch) at [59], "there must remain a category of cases involving innocuous, unimportant and unremarkable events, which although private in one sense do not necessarily qualify for protection under Article 8". See also *John v Associated Newspapers Ltd* [2006] EMLR 27 where there was no reasonable expectation of privacy as to a photograph of the claimant, Elton John, standing in the street outside his house.

[4] See *Peck v UK* (2003) 36 E.H.R.R. 41 at [62], where despite the public location of Peck's attempted suicide, such that any passer by may have witnessed it, the broadcast by the local council, (in which Peck's identity was barely shielded), "far exceeded any exposure to a passer-by or to security observation"; *Von Hannover v Germany* (2005) 40 E.H.R.R. 1 at [77] (Princess Caroline of Monaco's campaign over a number of years to restrain the publication of photographs taken of her as she lived her daily life), where there was deemed to be no public interest, "in knowing where the applicant is and how she behaves generally in her private life even if she appears in places that cannot always be described as secluded and despite the fact that she is well known to the public"; *Murray v Express Newspapers Plc* [2008] EMLR 12 (infant son of J.K. Rowling arguably had a reasonable expectation of privacy in relation to the publication of a photograph of him in his buggy with his parents in a public street).

[5] See, for example, *Theakston v MGN Ltd* [2002] EMLR 22 where a report (but not photographs) of a well-known TV presenter's visit to a brothel was justified on the basis that he was a role model to young people.

[6] See *Mosley v News Group Newspapers* [2008] EWHC 1777 (QB) at [12].

[7] See *Campbell v MGN Ltd* [2004] 2 A.C. 457 where the publication of the fact that Naomi Campbell had taken drugs and was receiving treatment for addiction was necessary to set the record straight given her previous statements to the press. Further information, (including photographs), was deemed to be intrusive and should not have been disclosed.

those photographed could reasonably expect that their appearances or actions would not be brought to the notice of the public".[8]

Applying s.12(3)

At an interim stage of proceedings, it is the s.12(3) test that is of primary importance. Not surprisingly, the meaning of "likelihood" in s.12(3) has been extensively litigated. In *Cream Holdings v Banerjee*,[9] Ms Banerjee had been an employee of the Cream group of companies. Cream began a successful nightclub in Liverpool and diversified into areas such as the organisation of music festivals and merchandising. When Banerjee's contract of employment was terminated, she copied company files and made these available to two principal Merseyside newspapers. Her story was one of considerable public interest, that Cream had been involved in serious instances of illegal and improper conduct. On this ground, the House of Lords concluded that the applicants had failed to show that they were more likely than not to succeed at trial in preventing the publication of information. The opportunity was taken explicitly to address the higher threshold that the court must impose in the context of breach of confidence cases. In the words of Lord Nicholls:

18.53

"Section 12(3) makes the likelihood of success at trial an essential element in the court's consideration of whether to make an interim order. But in order to achieve the necessary flexibility the degree of likelihood of success at trial needed to satisfy s.12(3) must depend on the circumstances. There can be no single, rigid standard governing all applications for interim restraint orders, Rather, on its proper construction the effect of s.12(3) is that the court is not to make an interim restraint order unless it is satisfied the applicant's prospect of success at the trial are sufficiently favourable to justify such an order being made in the circumstances of the case. As to what degree of likelihood makes the prospects of success 'sufficiently favourable', the general approach should be that the courts will be exceedingly slow to make interim restraint orders where the applicant has not satisfied the court that he will probably ('more likely than not') succeed at trial. In general, that should be the threshold that an applicant must cross before the court embarks on exercising its discretion, duly taking into account the relevant jurisprudence on Art.10 and any countervailing Convention rights".[10]

Lord Nicholls also warned of difficult cases where this higher standard should not be imposed. By way of clarification, he continued:

"there will be cases where it is necessary for a court to depart from this general approach and a lesser degree of likelihood will suffice as a prerequisite. Circumstances where this may be so include ... where the potential adverse consequences of disclosure are particularly grave, or where a short-lived injunction is needed to

---

[8] [2006] Q.B. 125 at [84]; see also *D v L* [2004] EMLR 1 at [23] per Waller L.J.
[9] [2004] 4 All E.R. 617.
[10] [2004] 4 All E.R. 617 at 625.

enable the court to hear and give proper consideration to an application for interim relief pending the trial or any relevant appeal".[11]

18.54   Lord Nicholls has, therefore, clarified that the word "likely" in s.12(3) cannot have intended to mean "more likely than not" in all situations. He argued that as a test of universal application, this would be a degree of likelihood too high. Some flexibility is essential. He deemed the intention of Parliament to be that "likely" should have an extended meaning that sets as a normal prerequisite to the grant of an injunction before trial a likelihood of success at the trial higher than the commonplace *American Cyanamid* standard of "real prospect" but "permits the court to dispense with this higher standard where particular circumstances make this necessary".[12] This new test has been applied in *E v Channel Four*.[13] Here, the Official Solicitor applied for an interim injunction to prevent the broadcasting of a film and the publication of a newspaper report on the basis that both concerned an adult who, by virtue of her dissociative identity disorder, did not have the mental capacity to consent. If, indeed, E lacked the capacity, the conflict between arts 8 and 10 were directly in point. The court would be required to balance E's rights under art.8 and the public interest in protecting the privacy of a vulnerable individual as against the public and private interest in disseminating information regarding her life. Munby J. applied, without question, the *Cream Holdings Ltd v Banerjee* test. In the light that there was nothing particular to justify departure from the general approach, the Official Solicitor was required to show that success at trial was, "more likely than not". Although Munby J. accepted that success at trial may follow, this was insufficient to convince the court. Accordingly, the injunction was refused.

Freedom of Expression and Libel

18.55   The *Cream Holdings* test was formulated in response to the question of interim relief in cases of alleged breach of confidence and privacy. The applicability of s.12(3) to cases of freedom of expression has been questioned also outside this context. One notable example is that of libel. The court's jurisdiction to issue an interim injunction to restrain a libellous or defamatory publication has always been subject to a very strict test. In *Bonnard v Perryman*[14] the working rule was established that the court would not restrain the publication of an article, even if it were defamatory, when the defendant intends to justify it[15] (unless it is clear that the plea of justification is bound to fail) or to make fair comment on a matter of public interest. As Lord Coleridge C.J. observed, "Until it is clear that an alleged libel is untrue, it is not clear that any right at all has been infringed; and the importance of leaving free speech unfettered is a strong reason

---

[11] [2004] 4 All E.R. 617 at 625.
[12] [2004] 4 All E.R. 617 at 624.
[13] [2005] EWHC 1144 (Fam).
[14] [1891] 2 Ch. 269.
[15] i.e. prove the truth of the statement.

in cases of libel for dealing most cautiously and warily with the granting of interim injunctions".[16] In *Fraser v Evans*,[17] Lord Denning M.R. reflected on the need for the stricter test, "The reason sometimes given is that the defences of justification and fair comment are for the jury, which is the constitutional tribunal, and not for a judge; but a better reason is the importance in the public interest that the truth should out ... There is no wrong done if it is true, or if [the alleged libel] is fair comment on a matter of public interest. The court will not prejudice the issue by granting an injunction in advance of publication".[18] Similarly, in *Herbage v Pressdram Ltd*,[19] Griffiths L.J. restated the law and commented, "These principles have evolved because of the value the court has placed on the freedom of speech and I think also on the freedom of the press, when balancing it against the reputation of a single individual who, if wrong, can be compensated in damages".[20]

On the basis of this established and strict test, it has been understood for some time that the principles laid down in *American Cyanamid* have no application to libel injunctions.[21] More recently, however, the question arose as to whether the *Bonnard v Perryman* rule had been affected by the new test under the Human Rights Act, s.12(3). In *Martha Greene v Associated Newspapers*,[22] the claimant sought interim relief to restrain the publication of a newspaper article alleged to be defamatory and based on forged e-mails. Adopting the *Cream Holdings* test, she argued that she was "more likely than not" to succeed at trial in establishing that the publication should not be allowed. In the Court of Appeal, Brooke L.J. restated the conventional position that there would be no prior restraint on publication unless it was clear that no defence would succeed at trial. The claimant had not met this threshold. Brooke L.J. distinguished *Cream Holdings* as a decision on breach of confidence and not defamation. The potential damage to a reputation could not be compared with the publication of confidential information. Interim relief in the case of the latter is of critical importance to the claimant because, as Lord Nicholls admitted in *Cream Holdings*, "Confidentiality, once breached, is lost for ever".[23] Brooke L.J. looked also to interpret the Act and found nothing therein that could weaken the force of the common law. He claimed, "In a section of an Act of Parliament which is expressly concerned with the protection of freedom of expression and not with undermining it, Parliament cannot be interpreted as having abrogated the rule in *Bonnard v Perryman* by a side wind".[24] Accordingly, as regards libel injunctions the law remains, for the present, untouched by the recent statutory protection afforded to human rights.

[16] [1891] 2 Ch. 269 at 284.
[17] [1969] 1 All E.R. 8 (discharge of an injunction restraining the threatened publication in the *Sunday Times* of a defamatory article).
[18] [1969] 1 All E.R. 8 at 10.
[19] [1984] 2 All E.R. 769 (injunction refused to restrain publication of information relating to the claimant's "spent" convictions under the Rehabilitation of Offenders Act 1974).
[20] [1984] 2 All E.R. 769 at 771.
[21] *J. Trevor & Sons v Solomon* (1977) 248 E.G. 779.
[22] [2005] 1 All E.R. 30.
[23] [2004] 4 All E.R. 617 at 624.
[24] [2005] 1 All E.R. 30 at 48.

PRINCIPLES GOVERNING THE GRANT OF INJUNCTIONS IN SPECIFIC SITUATIONS

18.56   Finally, it remains to discuss two specific injunctions and the principles governing their award, namely the search order (issued to prevent the removal or destruction of evidence) and the freezing injunction (issued to prevent the removal of assets). The search order and the freezing injunction are two particular types of interim injunction, operative in their own special circumstances[25] and governed by a distinct body of case law. Described as the law's "nuclear weapons",[26] detailed guidelines have been developed to circumscribe their use and safeguard the defendant from the obvious risk of oppression.

The search order

18.57   The search order (formerly known as an *Anton Pillar order*)[27] is mandatory in nature and requires the defendant to permit the claimant to enter the defendant's premises for specified purposes.[28] The first reported use of such an order was as recent as 1974,[29] causing Lord Wilberforce to cite the development of this modern day jurisdiction as, "an illustration of the adaptability of equity to new situations".[30] The utility of the order is most evident in cases of breach of copyright, passing off or infringements of patents,[31] where there is a risk that vital documents or files may be destroyed and it is crucial that the claimant be allowed to inspect them. The applicant is required to give an undertaking in damages as a condition of the order that he will compensate the respondent for any damage caused to him by the order and for which the court thinks it necessary for the applicant to pay.

The power to make a search order is now on a statutory footing.[32] Section 7 of the Civil Procedure Act 1997 provides the court with a power for the purpose of securing, in the case of any proposed or existing proceedings in court:

- the preservation of evidence which is or may be relevant, or

- the preservation of property which is or may be the subject matter of the proceedings or as to which any question arises or may arise in the proceedings.

---

[25] Although frequently issued in conjunction.
[26] *Bank Mellat v Nikpour* [1985] F.S.R. 87 at 91 per Lord Donaldson M.R.
[27] Taking its name from *Anton Pillar KG v Manufacturing Processes Ltd* [1976] Ch. 55.
[28] Unlike a search warrant, a search order does not entitle the claimant to enter against the defendant's will, but refusal by the defendant to permit entry and inspection, may leave the defendant in contempt of court with the likelihood of adverse inferences being drawn against him at trial.
[29] See *EMI Ltd v Pandit* [1975] 1 All E.R. 418.
[30] *Rank Film Distributors Ltd v Video Information Centre* [1982] A.C. 380 at 439.
[31] Hence its description by Hoffmann J. in *Lock International Plc v Beswick* [1989] 1 W.L.R. 1268 at 1279 as the "ultimate weapon against fraudulent copyright pirates".
[32] With no attempt to limit the pre-existing jurisdiction.

The order may direct any person to permit any person described in the order, (or secure that any person so described is permitted) to enter premises in England and Wales,[33] and while on the premises to take in accordance with the terms of the order any of the steps specified in the Act. Those steps are:

- to carry out a search for or inspection of anything described in the order, and

- to make or obtain a copy, photograph, sample or other record of anything so described.

The order may also direct the person subject to the order:

- to provide any information or article described in the order, and

- to retain for safe keeping anything described in the order.

In *Anton Pillar KG v Manufacturing Processes Ltd*[34] the claimant believed that the defendant was selling confidential information to its competitors. In order to prove this it required access to documents filed in the defendants' premises. The Court of Appeal made an order requiring the defendant to permit the claimant to enter the premises and inspect the relevant documentation. The order in *Anton Pillar* was made without notice to the defendant. In one sense, this reflects the commonsense requirement that the defendant is not warned in advance. As Templeman L.J. put it in *Rank Film Distributors Ltd v Video Information Centre*, "If the stable door cannot be bolted, the horse must be secured ... If the horse is liable to be spirited away, notice of an intention to secure the horse will defeat the intention".[35] In another, the practice gives rise to the obvious dangers of misuse and oppression. As Hoffmann J. accepted, in *Lock International Plc v Beswick*, "The making of an intrusive order ex parte even against a guilty defendant is contrary to normal principles of justice and can only be done where there is a paramount need to prevent a denial of justice to the plaintiff. The absolute extremity of the court's powers is to permit a search of a defendant's dwelling house, with the humiliation and family distress which that frequently involves".[36]

In *Anton Pillar KG v Manufacturing Processes Ltd*, Ormrod L.J. laid down three conditions for the grant of the order. The claimant must:

18.58

- have an extremely strong prima facie case;

- show actual or potential damage of a very serious nature; and

- have clear evidence that the defendant has incriminating documents or things and a real possibility of their destruction before an application with notice can be made.

Lord Denning M.R. felt it appropriate to add that the inspection must do no real harm to the defendant or his case. In addition, many judges have highlighted that a balancing

---

[33] Premises includes any vehicle: s.7(8).
[34] [1976] Ch. 55.
[35] [1982] A.C. 380 at 418.
[36] [1989] 1 W.L.R. 1268 at 1281.

exercise is required to measure, on the one hand, the claimant's right to his property and to ensure the preservation of evidence, as against, on the other, the invasion of privacy of a defendant where he has no opportunity to put his side of the case.[37] By way of illustration, the court will not grant a search order against a person of good standing who is deemed likely to respond to an order of the court to deliver up. In the words of Hoffmann J., "Not everyone who is misusing confidential information will destroy documents in the face of a court order requiring him to preserve them".[38]

18.59   By the 1980s there was considerable concern that the grant of search orders had become too commonplace. As Scott L.J. described in *Columbia Picture Industries Inc v Robinson*, "the practice of the court has allowed the balance to swing much too far in favour of the plaintiffs and that Anton Pillar orders have been too readily granted and with insufficient safeguards for respondents".[39] In *Lock International v Beswick*,[40] for example, the potential for misuse of the search order was clearly demonstrated. Here, the claimant's solicitors were permitted to search the premises and the homes of three individual defendants. In addition to documents that belonged to the claimant (documents containing specified confidential information), virtually all the defendants drawings, documents records and prototypes were removed. In total, 12 boxes of drawings, five filing cabinet drawers and five prototypes were taken. Hoffmann J. discharged the order. He accepted that it should never have been granted and, with particular regret as to the searches of individuals' private homes, confessed that he could, "only sympathise with the sense of outrage that they must have felt".[41]

Underpinned by the Civil Procedure Rules,[42] more recent practice is to exercise considerable caution in the grant of search orders.[43] For the avoidance of oppression, moreover, certain safeguards help to protect the interests of the defendant. These include:

- the presence of a supervising solicitor (ideally with experience and not a member of the firm of solicitors acting for the claimant);

- execution of the order in office hours;

- where the order pertains to a private house, perhaps occupied by a woman on her own, the solicitor serving the order should be accompanied by a woman;

- unless impracticable, a list of items to be removed should be prepared at the premises and the defendant afforded an opportunity to check the list;

- no items should be taken from the defendant's premises unless covered by the terms of the order;

- the setting aside of the order where the claimant or the claimant's solicitors have acted improperly; and

- the availability of exemplary (i.e. punitive) damages.

---

[37] For example, *Lock International v Beswick* [1989] 1 W.L.R. 1268 per Hoffmann J.
[38] [1989] 1 W.L.R. 1268 at 1281.
[39] [1987] Ch. 38 at 76.
[40] [1989] 1 W.L.R. 1268.
[41] [1989] 1 W.L.R. 1268 at 1283.
[42] See CPR 25, Practice Direction para.7.
[43] See further, the comments of Sir Donald Nicholls V.C. in *Universal Thermosensors Ltd v Hibben* [1992] 1 W.L.R. 840.

The privilege against self-incrimination

In *Rank Film Distributors Ltd v Video Information Centre*,[44] the House of Lords held, reluctantly, that the defendant could invoke the privilege against self-incrimination where to comply with the order (by answering questions or disclosing documents) would give rise to a real and appreciable risk of criminal proceedings against them for conspiracy to defraud. As Lord Wilberforce emphasised, no civil court, "has any power to decide in a manner which would bind a criminal court that evidence of any kind is admissible or inadmissible in that court".[45] In other words, the court could not compel disclosure at the same time as safeguarding the defendant from the consequences of his self-incrimination. This development threatened to make it increasingly difficult to obtain disclosure of information from defendants. Section 72 of the Supreme Court Act 1981 provides, however, that in any High Court proceedings for infringement of intellectual property rights or passing off, a person shall not be excused, by reason that to do so would expose that person[46] to proceedings for a related offence, from answering questions or from complying with any order made in those proceedings. Whilst the section amounts to an important restriction, the privilege against self-incrimination may still be invoked where s.72 does not apply.

18.60

The freezing injunction

Formerly known as the "*Mareva*" injunction,[47] the freezing injunction is interim in nature and, like the search order, comparatively recent in its evolution.[48] The freezing injunction is an order of the court to restrain the defendant from disposing of or removing his assets from the jurisdiction where there is a risk that any judgment will go unsatisfied by reason of that disposal or removal.[49] The jurisdiction of the court is statutory. Section 37(3) of the Supreme Court Act 1981 provides, "The power of the High Court ... to grant an interlocutory injunction restraining a party to any proceedings from removing from the jurisdiction of the High Court, or otherwise dealing with, assets located within that jurisdiction shall be exercisable in cases where that party is, as well as in cases where he is not, domiciled, resident or present within that jurisdiction".[50] As is evident from s.37(1) of the Act, the High Court retains a jurisdiction to grant an injunction when it is "just and convenient" to do so. Indeed, this is an area now governed by the Civil Procedure Rules, as an order may be made, "restraining a

18.61

---

[44] [1982] A.C. 380.
[45] [1982] A.C. 380 at 442.
[46] Or his or her spouse.
[47] Its first reported use was in *Nippon Yusen Kaisha v Karageorgis* [1975] 1 W.L.R. 1093.
[48] Taking its name from *Mareva Compania Naveira SA v International Bulkcarriers SA* [1975] 2 Lloyd's Rep. 509.
[49] The freezing injunction is normally issued pending trial, but it may also be issued post trial where the claimant can show the risk that the defendant will dispose of his assets to avoid execution of the judgment: see, for example, *Babanaft International Co SA v Bassatne* [1990] Ch. 13.
[50] Originally, the freezing injunction was a remedy against a defendant located outside the jurisdiction with assets inside the jurisdiction.

party from removing from the jurisdiction assets located there" or, restraining a party from dealing with any assets "whether located within the jurisdiction or not".[51]

Prior to 1982, the court was unable to grant interlocutory injunctive relief where the substantive proceedings were taking place abroad.[52] This had the effect that a claimant in a foreign court seeking control of a defendant's assets in England was unable to do so on the ground that the English courts did not have jurisdiction over the provision of substantive relief.[53] Nowadays, by virtue of s.25 of the Civil Jurisdiction and Judgments Act 1982,[54] as extended by Civil Jurisdiction and Judgments Act 1982 (Interim Relief) Order 1997,[55] the High Court can grant interim relief in aid of substantive proceedings anywhere else, "of whatever kind and wherever taking place".[56] The claim must be such, nonetheless, that an English court could identify the relief as interim relief in relation to the final order sought abroad.[57]

General guidelines

18.62 Despite the seemingly broad discretion bestowed by s.37, guidelines applicable for obtaining a freezing injunction were previously laid down by Lord Denning M.R. in *Third Chandris Shipping Corpn v Unimarine SA*.[58] Ultimately, of course, the court must ensure that its remedy is not used oppressively against the defendant and that it is just and reasonable in the circumstances of the case to grant the relief sought. The guidelines are as follows:

- the claimant must make a full and frank disclosure of all matters in his knowledge, material for the judge to know;[59]

- the claimant should give the particulars of his claim against the defendant, stating the ground of his claim and the amount thereof, and fairly stating the points made against it by the defendant.[60] The applicant requires a good arguable case;

- the claimant must give some grounds for believing that the defendant has assets here. It is accepted that the claimant will rarely have precise information, but he

---

[51] CPR r.25.1(f). For worldwide freezing orders: see **18.64**.
[52] *The Siskina* [1977] 3 All E.R. 803.
[53] *Mercedes-Benz AG v Leiduck* [1995] 3 All E.R. 929.
[54] Which gave power to the High Court to grant interim relief where substantive proceedings were pending in a Brussels or Lugano Convention state and the subject matter of the proceedings was within the scope of the Brussels or Lugano Conventions.
[55] SI 1997/302; The order extends the effect of s.25 to non-Convention countries and to proceedings outside the scope of the Conventions.
[56] *Crédit Suisse Fides SA v Cuoghi* [1998] Q.B. 818 at 825 per Millett L.J.
[57] *Fourie v Le Roux* [2005] EWCA Civ. 204.
[58] [1979] 2 All E.R. 972.
[59] This involves the applicant in the making of proper inquiries prior to his application: see further, *Brink's-Mat Ltd v Elcombe* [1998] 3 All E.R. 188 per Ralph Gibson L.J.
[60] Most applications are "without notice". As Lord Scott indicated in *Fourie v Le Roux* [2007] 1 W.L.R. 320 at 334, "I find it very difficult to visualise a case where the grant of a freezing order, made without notice, could be said to be properly made in the absence of any formulation of the case for substantive relief that the applicant for the order intended to institute".

is expected to show indications. For example, the existence of a bank account in England will suffice regardless of whether it is in overdraft or not;[61]

- the claimant should give some grounds for believing that there is a risk of the assets being removed before the judgment or award is satisfied. In *Montechi v Shimco*, Lord Bridge spoke of the need for a "real reason to apprehend" that the claimant would be denied a remedy.[62] In *Polly Peck International v Nadir (No.2)*,[63] moreover, Scott L.J. refused an application for a freezing injunction against a bank on the ground that the claimant had no arguable case for liability. Unlike *Cyanamid*, therefore, the court necessarily engages with the question of the strength of the claimant's case; and

- the claimant must give an undertaking in damages. As has been discussed in relation to interim injunctions more generally, the undertaking is required because liability has yet to be determined. The claimant must be prepared to compensate the defendant for the cost and inconvenience incurred should the claimant fail to succeed at trial.

Third parties

A third party who has notice of a freezing injunction against a defendant will be in contempt of court if he knowingly assists in the removal or disposal of assets. Many of the case law illustrations involve banks and bank accounts.[64] As Lord Denning M.R. described in *Z Ltd v A-Z*, "As soon as the bank is given notice of the freezing injunction, it must freeze the defendant's bank account ... It must not allow any drawings to be made on it, neither by cheques drawn before the injunction nor by those drawn after it. The reason is because, if it allowed any such drawings, it would be obstructing the course of justice, as prescribed by the court which granted the injunction, and would be guilty of a contempt of court".[65] Equally, of course, any other asset held by any other person and covered by the terms of the freezing order is subject to the same principle. A third party must not allow the defendant to have access to the asset so as to enable him to dispose of it. Such would be in contempt of court.

In light of the obvious scope for inconvenience to third parties, the claimant is under an obligation to indemnify a third party for any expenses and liabilities incurred as a result of the issue of the injunction. Where a bank is asked to undertake a search to identify the defendant's assets, for example, the claimant must undertake to cover the

18.63

---

[61] *Third Chandris Shipping Corpn v Unimarine SA* [1979] 2 All E.R. 972 at 985 per Lord Denning M.R.
[62] [1979] 1 W.L.R. 1180 at 1183.
[63] [1992] 4 All E.R. 769.
[64] Note that in such cases, no duty of care arises as between the third party Bank and the claimant. The claimant must rely on the court to ensure that injunctions are respected: see *Customs and Excise Commissioners v Barclays Bank Plc* [2007] 1 A.C. 181 at 196, where Lord Bingham claimed that it would be, "unjust and unreasonable that the bank should, on being notified of an order which it had no opportunity to resist, become exposed to a liability which was in this case for a few million pounds only, but might in another case be for very much more".
[65] [1982] Q.B. 558 at 574. Obligations to third parties must be honoured and, accordingly, payments under letters of credit or under bank guarantee are not prevented: see *Intraco Ltd v Notis Shipping Corpn* [1981] 2 Lloyd's Rep. 256. The bank must also honour all credit cards issued to the defendant.

costs. It is vital that assets subject to the order are clearly identified and that third parties are provided with a detailed explanation of what they are permitted to do and restrained from doing. In addition, the court is mindful of the inconvenience caused to third parties by the issue of a freezing injunction. Accordingly, in *Galaxia Maritime SA v Mineralimportexport*,[66] the third party owner of a ship containing the defendant's assets was permitted to sail outside the jurisdiction of the court, his rights ranking in preference to the desire of the claimant to maintain control of those assets.

World-wide freezing orders

18.64 Notwithstanding a location outside the jurisdiction of the court, the court can issue a freezing injunction over the defendant's assets. It will be remembered that the court acts in personam and it has been accepted, therefore, that the injunction may be granted in relation to assets, "whether located within the jurisdiction or not".[67] This "worldwide" injunction is justified only in exceptional circumstances where it can be made effectively, without oppression, and where no conflict exists with the ordinary principles of international law.[68] Such was the case in *BCCI SA (No.9)*[69] where a worldwide freezing order was granted against the defendant employees of BCCI where a major international fraud brought about the collapse of the bank.

18.65   Where a worldwide freezing injunction is deemed appropriate, the court will insist upon an undertaking by the claimant that the claimant will seek permission of the English court before attempting to enforce the order in a foreign jurisdiction. The need for such an undertaking is clearly to protect the defendant from the risk of oppression where the claimant is able to bring proceedings in different jurisdictions. As to the circumstances in which permission should be granted, the Court Of Appeal recently laid down non-exhaustive guidelines for the exercise of judicial discretion in *Dadourian Group International Inc v Simms*.[70] In particular, the guidelines state that:

- the grant of permission should be "just and convenient" and "not oppressive to the parties to the English proceedings or to third parties who may be joined to the foreign proceedings".

- all the relevant circumstances and options need to be considered.

- "the interests of the applicant should be balanced against the interests of the other parties to the proceedings and any new party likely to be joined to the foreign proceedings".

---

[66] [1982] 1 All E.R. 796.
[67] CPR 25.1(1)(f); see also, *Babanaft International Co SA v Bassatne* [1990] Ch. 13, where it was accepted by the Court of Appeal that there is no geographical limitation to the jurisdiction of the court to issue such an injunction.
[68] See *Derby & Co Ltd v Weldon* [1990] Ch. 48.
[69] [1994] 3 All E.R. 764.
[70] [2006] 1 W.L.R. 2499 at 2502–2503.

- "permission should not normally be given in terms that would enable the applicant to obtain relief in the foreign proceedings which is superior to the relief given by the WFO".

- "the evidence in support of the application for permission should contain all the information (so far as it can reasonably be obtained in the time available) necessary to make the judge to reach an informed decision, including evidence as to the applicable law and practice in the foreign court, evidence as to the nature of the proposed proceedings to be commenced and evidence as to the assets believed to be located in the jurisdiction of the foreign court and the names of the parties by whom such assets are held".

- the applicant must show that there is a real prospect that assets are located within the jurisdiction of the foreign court in question.

- there must be evidence of a risk of dissipation of the assets in question.

- normally the application should be made on notice to the respondent, but in cases of urgency, where it is just to do so, the permission may be given without notice to the party against whom relief will be sought in the foreign proceedings but that party should have the earliest practicable opportunity of having the matter reconsidered by the court at a hearing of which he is given notice.

GUIDE TO FURTHER READING

L. Collins, "The Territorial Reach of the *Mareva* Injunction" (1989) 105 L.Q.R. 262.
M. Dockray, H. Laddie, "*Pillar* Problems" (1990) 106 L.Q.R. 601.
S. Gee, "The Undertaking in Damages" [2006] LMCLQ 181.
C. Gray, "Interlocutory Injunctions Since *Cyanamid*" (1981) 40 C.L.J. 307.
G. Phillipson, "Transforming Breach of Confidence? Towards a Common Law Right of Privacy under the Human Rights Act" (2003) 66 M.L.R. 726.
A. Zuckerman, "Interlocutory Injunctions on the Merits" (1991) 107 L.Q.R. 196.

Chapter 19

SPECIFIC PERFORMANCE

An order for specific performance is an order of the court directing a party to a contract **19.01** positively to perform his obligations according to the terms of the order. The remedy operates in personam, i.e. it imposes a personal obligation on the defendant to fulfil his promise. Specific performance developed as part of the jurisdiction of equity to do justice where the common law was inadequate. Traditionally regarded as an "exceptional remedy",[1] it is available only where damages will not adequately compensate the claimant for a breach of contract.

Being equitable in origin, the award of specific performance is a discretionary remedy. Accordingly, a variety of factors can influence the exercise of discretion, such as the conduct of the claimant,[2] any delay in seeking equitable assistance[3] or hardship resulting from the compelled performance of contractual obligations.[4] Nonetheless, as will become evident, the principles upon which specific performance is awarded are established equitable principles.[5] Hence, it has long been possible to say with some certainty that specific performance will be awarded in respect of some types of contract,[6] but not in the case of others.[7] The law is not, however, static for as Millett L.J. observed, "The court is entitled and bound to re-examine its practice to see whether it accords with modern requirements".[8] Notwithstanding the foundation of settled principle, the general trend appears to be to expand the scope of the remedy to order specific performance where it is just and practicable to do so.[9] As will be demonstrated,

---

[1] *Co-Operative Insurance Society Ltd v Argyll Stores (Holdings) Ltd* [1998] A.C. 1 at 11 per Lord Hoffmann.
[2] In accordance with the equitable maxim, "he who comes to equity must come with clean hands".
[3] Under the doctrine of laches.
[4] See **19.32**.
[5] As Lord Chelmsford put it in *Lamare v Dixon* (1873) L.R. 6 H.L. 414, the discretion in the court is, "not an arbitrary or capricious discretion, but one to be governed as far as possible by fixed rules and principles".
[6] For example, contracts relating to the sale of land.
[7] For example, contracts for personal services.
[8] *Co-Operative Insurance Society Ltd v Argyll Stores (Holdings) Ltd* [1996] Ch. 286 at 306.
[9] See *Beswick v Beswick* [1968] A.C. 58 at 102 per Lord Upjohn, "Equity will grant specific performance when damages are inadequate to meet the justice of the case".

recent decisions have brought important incremental developments[10] and modern courts have, on occasion, moulded longstanding principles to meet the needs of contemporary society.[11] The aim of this chapter is to provide a helpful analytical introduction to the key features of the remedy, the principles upon which it is nowadays awarded and the main grounds for its refusal.

Preconditions

19.02 An important precondition is that there can be no specific performance of an agreement unless it is in the form of a legal and binding contract. As equity will not assist a volunteer, it is required that the contracting parties provide consideration.[12] The provision of money or money's worth is, seemingly, adequate consideration,[13] but past consideration will not suffice.[14]

The award of specific performance is not necessarily dependent on a pre-existing breach of contract and can be made in circumstances where there can be no recovery of damages at common law.[15] In *Marks v Lilley*,[16] the claimant commenced an action for specific performance of a contract for the sale of land after the date fixed for completion, but without serving a notice making time of the essence of the contract. Vaisey J. acknowledged that in a strict sense there had been no default and that, subject to the clearing away of the difficulties that were besetting the defendant, the contract would be completed in a reasonable time. Nevertheless, the defendant was under an equitable obligation to make good his promise and the claimant was, therefore, in a position to enforce his rights. Specific performance was awarded.

The effect of an order

19.03 Where an order for specific performance is made the contract remains in existence and is not merged in the judgment of the court.[17] Hence, in the event that the defendant fails, or is unable, to comply with the order, the claimant can seek to dissolve the order and obtain common law damages. In claiming specific performance, however, the claimant essentially surrenders to the court control of how the contract is carried out.[18]

---

[10] For example, in the context of enforcement of leasehold repairing covenants.

[11] See, for example, as to the doctrine of mutuality (see **19.26**).

[12] "The court will never lend its assistance to enforce the specific execution of contracts which are voluntary, or where no consideration emanates from the party seeking performance, even though they may have the legal consideration of a seal": Fry, *Specific Performance*, (6th edn), at p.53.

[13] *Mountford v Scott* [1975] Ch. 258.

[14] *Robertson v St John* (1786) 2 Bro. C.C. 140 (agreement to renew a lease in consideration of previous expenditure).

[15] Conversely, of course, damages may be available where specific performance is refused.

[16] [1959] 1 W.L.R. 749.

[17] Per Greene M.R. in *Austins of East Ham Ltd v Macey* [1941] Ch. 338 at 341.

[18] As Megarry V.C. clarified in *Singh v Nazeer* [1978] 3 All E.R. 817 at 822, "the machinery provisions ... are intended to govern the carrying out of the contract out of court, and are not directed to carrying it out once an order for specific performance has been made ... it is the provisions of the order and not the contract which regulate how the contract is to be carried out".

As such it is necessary that the claimant return to court either to enforce the order or to terminate the contract.[19] The principles governing the entitlements of the parties are authoritatively laid down in *Johnson v Agnew*.[20] Here, the claimant sought specific performance of a contract to sell mortgaged properties to the defendant. The defendant purchaser delayed and the claimant's mortgagee sold the properties rendering performance of the contract impossible. It was held that the claimant was entitled to have an order discharging the specific performance order, termination of the contract and damages at common law for breach of contract.

It is noteworthy also that an order for specific performance is a final order.[21] Unlike the injunction, it is an equitable remedy that is not available on an interim basis.[22]

Enforcement

Enforcement can take a variety of forms. Section 39 of the Supreme Court Act 1981, for example, allows the court to appoint a nominated person other than the defendant to execute a contract or conveyance which the defendant has neglected or refused to execute. Ultimately, however, failure to comply with an order will see the defendant committed to prison for contempt of court. Other options include sequestration of assets pending compliance and the imposition of fines. **19.04**

Damages in addition to or in substitution for specific performance

Principles governing the award of damages have been considered in Ch.18 in the context of injunctions. The same principles operate in the context of specific performance. Damages may be awarded in addition to or in lieu of specific performance,[23] but also in conjunction with other equitable remedies. In *Seven Seas Properties Ltd v Al-Essa*, therefore, an order for specific performance was combined with a *Mareva* injunction restraining the vendor from dealing with the purchase money from a sale.[24] Hoffmann J. regarded it as "excessively formalistic" to require the result to be achieved by two orders rather than one and he was happy that the court had jurisdiction to create a combined order.[25] **19.05**

---

[19] *GKN Distributions Ltd v Tyne Tees Fabrication Ltd* [1985] 2 EGLR 181.
[20] [1980] A.C. 367.
[21] *Co-Operative Insurance Society Ltd v Argyll Stores (Holdings) Ltd* [1998] A.C. 1 at 18 per Lord Hoffmann.
[22] See, however, *Sky Petroleum Ltd v VIP Petroleum Ltd* [1974] 1 W.L.R. 576 where an interim injunction restraining the defendant company from failing to supply the claimant with petrol was tantamount to the specific enforcement of the claimant's contract until the date of the full hearing (see **18.20**).
[23] See **18.11**.
[24] [1989] 1 All E.R. 164.
[25] [1989] 1 All E.R. 164 at 166.

INADEQUACY OF COMMON LAW DAMAGES

19.06   The following section considers the main principle governing the award of the remedy of specific performance, that is, no decree of specific performance will be awarded where the plaintiff can obtain an adequate remedy at law. The laudable aim of the court is to interfere, "only when it can by that means do more perfect and complete justice".[26] Damages will be an inadequate remedy where the obligation is such that successive breaches would necessitate successive actions for damages,[27] or where damages are insufficient to meet the justice of the case[28] or where loss is difficult to quantify.[29] Specific performance will not be awarded where, on the true construction of the contract, the parties have agreed to the payment of a sum of money as an alternative to the performance of an obligation.[30] This is because the court will construe a "formal recognition" by the parties that damages is an adequate remedy for the particular breach.[31] Ultimately, however, the court's discretion to award or to refuse specific performance cannot be fettered by agreement between the parties.[32] The court cannot be bound by the terms of the contract because otherwise, as Stocker L.J. noted, "the function of the court would be reduced to that of a rubber stamp".[33]

The following illustrations provide evidence of the approach of the courts to the issue of adequacy of damages. As is clear, the principle operates in the context of many different types of contract. The types of contract considered here are as follows:

- contracts for the sale or other disposition of interests in land,
- contracts for the sale of personalty,
- contractual licences, and
- contracts to pay money.

Contracts for the sale or other disposition of interests in land

19.07   The remedy of specific performance is almost always granted to compel performance of land contracts. As Sir William Grant said of the Court of Equity, it is "as much a course in this court to decree specific performance, as it is to give damages at law".[34] Land is deemed to be unique and, hence, damages are considered an inadequate remedy to compensate for the failure of a vendor to complete a contract for its sale. In respect

---

[26] *Wilson v Northampton and Banbury Junction Railway Co* (1874) 9 Ch. App. 279 at 284 per Lord Selbourne.
[27] *Beswick v Beswick* [1968] A.C. 58 (payment of an annuity).
[28] For example, where only nominal damages were recoverable by an action at law: *Beswick v Beswick* [1968] A.C. 58.
[29] Older cases state a requirement of impossibility as opposed to a mere difficulty in quantification: see *Hart v Herwig* (1873) 8 Ch. App. 860.
[30] *Legh v Lillie* (1860) 6 H. & N. 165.
[31] See *Warner Bros v Nelson* [1937] 1 K.B. 209 at 220 per Branson J.
[32] Although it remains common practice for the parties to contract that breach of a particular term shall "sound only in damages".
[33] *Quadrant Visual Communications Ltd v Hutchinson Telephone* (UK) Ltd [1993] BCLC 442 at 451.
[34] *Hall v Warren* (1804) 9 Ves. 605 at 608.

of contracts entered into on or after September 27, 1989, however, the Law of Property (Miscellaneous Provisions) Act 1989 requires that a contract for the sale or disposition of any interest in land must be made in writing[35] and signed by or on behalf of each party.[36] The contract must incorporate all express terms in one document, or, where contracts are exchanged, in each document. Failure to comply with the formalities renders the contract ineffective. As a precondition to the award of specific performance of land contracts, therefore, the 1989 Act imports the requirement of a written and signed contract.

Contracts for the sale of personalty

Most items of personal property cannot be said to be unique or of such rarity that a claimant will not be compensated adequately by damages. Traditionally, therefore, specific performance has not be granted to enforce contracts for the sale of most goods and personal property. Such was the case in *Cohen v Roche*[37] where the subject matter of the contract was a set of eight Hepplewhite chairs. McCardie J. declared that the discretion was not to be exercised where the property concerned was an, "ordinary article of commerce and of no special value or interest".[38] Accordingly, he declined to order specific performance and instead awarded damages. The contrasting approach towards contracts for the sale of land and personalty was addressed by Sir John Leach V.C., who explained that, "Courts of Equity decree the specific performance of contracts not upon any distinction between realty and personalty, but because damages at law may not in the particular case, afford a complete remedy".[39] Accordingly, it is not the personal nature of goods that serves to explain the approach of the courts, but simply that in the case of most items of personalty, damages is as satisfactory a remedy as the delivery of the items themselves.

19.08

By contrast, where a chattel can be shown to have a special value or interest, damages has not been deemed to be an adequate remedy. Hence, in *Behnke v Bede Shipping Co*,[40] specific performance was awarded to compel the sale of a steamship. Wright J. noted that the ship was of "peculiar and particularly unique value" to the claimant and that it was required for immediate use.[41] Specific performance was granted, "in order that justice may be done".[42] Similarly, in *Falcke v Gray*, two china jars were considered to be articles of unusual beauty, rarity and distinction such that damages could not

19.09

---

[35] Previously a contract was required only to be evidenced in writing and could be enforced under the doctrine of part performance: Law of Property Act 1925, s.40.
[36] Section 2(5) exempts from the requirement of signed writing a contract to grant a short lease taking effect in possession for a term not exceeding three years, a contract made in the course of a public auction and a contract regulated under the Financial Services Act 2000 other than a regulated mortgage contract.
[37] [1927] 1 K.B. 169.
[38] [1927] 1 K.B. 169 at 181.
[39] *Adderley v Dixon* (1824) 1 Sim. & ST 607 at 610.
[40] [1927] 1 K.B. 649.
[41] [1927] 1 K.B. 649 at 661.
[42] [1927] 1 K.B. 649 at 661.

adequately compensate for their loss.[43] In addition, it has been accepted that heirlooms or articles of particular personal value to the claimant can fall into this category.[44]

Where there is no readily available market, (for example in the case of particular stocks and shares), damages may not be an adequate remedy.[45] Damages will be adequate, however, where the shares are such that, "anyone can go out and buy them".[46] Shares in private limited companies are subject to limitations on transfer and availability to the public. As such, a legitimate claim for specific performance might be made in respect of a contract for the sale of such shares. In *Sky Petroleum Ltd v VIP Petroleum Ltd*,[47] specific performance of a contract for the sale of fuel was ordered on the ground that the contract with the defendant's company was the sole means of keeping the claimant's business afloat. Goulding J. acknowledged the "well established and salutary rule" that there was no specific performance of contracts for the sale of non-specific chattels.[48] Nonetheless, due to the unusual state of the petroleum market, the award of damages was not an adequate remedy in the circumstances.

19.10   Notably, a statutory jurisdiction is provided by the Sale of Goods Act 1979. Section 52 enables the court to decree specific performance of contracts for the sale of "specific or ascertained goods", i.e. goods identified and agreed by the parties when the contract is entered into. Further, the 1979 Act has been amended to provide additional rights to buyers in consumer contract cases.[49] Under s.48E(2) of the 1979 Act,[50] the court has new powers to enforce a seller's obligation to repair or to replace defective goods, i.e. delivered goods which are not in conformity with the contract of sale at the time of delivery.[51] This extension to the availability of specific relief invites a more liberal approach to the exercise of judicial discretion based on the appropriateness of granting the remedy in the circumstances of the particular case.

Contractual licences

19.11   Historically, a court of equity would not protect so called "transient interests". The recent trend in judicial thinking, however, is to disregard the reasoning in earlier authorities and exercise discretion according to the justice of the case. Accordingly the contemporary approach is encapsulated by Roskill L.J. who pitched the duty of the court to be, "to protect, where it is appropriate to do so, any interest, whether it be an estate in land or a licence, by injunction or specific performance as the case may be".[52] As will be shown, adequacy of damages has emerged as the prevailing consideration in the enforcement of such contracts.

The most prominent illustration of equitable intervention is that of *Verrall v Great*

[43] (1859) 4 Drew. 651.
[44] *Thorn v Commissioners of Public Works* (1863) 32 Beav. 490 (stones from the old Westminster Bridge).
[45] *Duncuft v Albrecht* (1841) 12 Sim. 189.
[46] *Re Schwabacher* (1907) 98 L.T. 127 at 128 per Parker J.
[47] [1974] 1 W.L.R. 576.
[48] [1974] 1 W.L.R. 576 at 578.
[49] Sale and Supply of Goods to Consumers Regulations (2002) (SI2002/3045).
[50] See D.Harris, "Specific Performance—a Regular Remedy for Consumers?" [2003] L.Q.R. 541.
[51] Sale of Goods Act 1979 s.48A(2)(a); s.48B.
[52] *Verrall v Great Yarmouth Borough Council* [1981] Q.B. 202 at 220.

Yarmouth Borough Council.[53] Here, the Court of Appeal awarded specific performance of a contractual licence to use a public hall for the purposes of the two-day party conference of the National Front. Specific performance had not hitherto been available because, in the words of Lord Greene M.R., "If a licence is revoked in breach of contract, the remedy is damages and nothing else, the reason being that the licencee has no estate in the land at all".[54] In *Verrall*, a newly constituted council had tried to force a cancellation at last minute. The National Front claimed that it was unable, at such short notice, to locate an alternative venue. The award of damages was not an adequate remedy because even with damages in hand, the claimant was unable to re-organise the planned event. Only performance of the contract would enable the conference to take place.

Contracts to pay money

The adequacy of common law damages also precludes the award of specific perfor-   **19.12**
mance in relation to contracts to pay money.[55] For example, of a contract to make a loan, Lord Herschell stated unequivocally, "I do not think that it is open to any doubt that a person with whom a contract to lend money has been entered into cannot obtain specific performance of that contract".[56] Perhaps surprisingly, however, an agreement to grant an annuity has always been specifically enforceable,[57] with the justification that it is difficult to assess damages with accuracy and, thereby, unjust to leave a claimant to his common law remedy,[58] and because it will prevent recourse to a "series of actions at law to enforce the performance of a continuing obligation".[59] It is certainly questionable whether this reasoning carries force in modern times. For example, such calculations have become commonplace with the growth of life assurance and the ease with which annuities can be bought and sold. This clearly points to the adequacy of damages as the appropriate remedy for the breach of such contracts.

In *Beswick v Beswick*[60] specific performance was awarded in respect of a contract to pay money and in circumstances where, for the House of Lords, justice, seemingly, outweighed settled principles. Peter Beswick entered into an agreement with his nephew that he would transfer his business to him in consideration of his nephew employing Peter as a consultant for the remainder of his life and, thereafter, the payment to Peter's widow of an annuity at the rate of £5 per week for life. Subsequent to Peter Beswick's death, the nephew made only a single payment to the widow. Personally, and in her capacity as administratrix of Beswick's estate, she sued for specific performance.

Arguments for the defendant looked insurmountable. First, the contract was not of a   **19.13**
type for which specific performance was usually granted. Secondly, notwithstanding

---

[53] [1981] Q.B. 202.
[54] *Booker v Palmer* [1942] 2 All E.R. 647 at 677.
[55] A statutory exception can be found in s.195 of the Companies Act 1985 where a contract with a company to take up and pay for any debentures can be enforced by an order for specific performance.
[56] *South African Territories Ltd* [1898] A.C. 309 at 315.
[57] *Keenen v Handley* (1864) 2 De. G. J. & Sim. 283.
[58] See the approach of Leach V.C. in *Adderley v Dixon* (1842) 1 Sim. & St. 607.
[59] *Beswick v Beswick* [1968] A.C. 58 at 78 per Lord Hodson.
[60] [1968] A.C. 58.

that the widow had suffered loss personally, she was not a party to the contract and, accordingly, she had no right of action.[61] Thirdly, in her capacity as administratrix, only nominal damages appeared to be recoverable. The estate had suffered no loss. In such circumstances, it is patently difficult to maintain that nominal damages were inadequate. Lord Upjohn, however, seized on the injustice of the claimant's predicament to hold that, "the court ought to grant a specific performance order all the more because damages are nominal".[62] It was "wholly repugnant to justice and commonsense" that the defendant had received the whole benefit of his bargain, failed to perform his obligations and that the breach would attract only nominal damages.[63] Justice demanded an equitable remedy.

GROUNDS FOR REFUSAL

19.14 Whereas the inadequacy of common law damages is the central principle motivating the award of specific performance, there exist a wide range of grounds for the refusal of the remedy. In some cases the court enjoys a flexible discretion as to whether on the facts of a given case specific performance is the appropriate remedy. In others, the jurisdiction of the court is more tightly constrained. Accordingly, the refusal to award specific performance might be justified on the following bases:

- the need for constant supervision;
- the contract is for personal services;
- the conduct of the claimant;
- want of mutuality;
- impossibility and futility;
- part of a contract;
- illegality and public policy;
- hardship and prejudice to third parties;
- *laches* or delay, and
- mistake, misdescription and misrepresentation.

---

[61] This case pre-dates the Contracts (Rights of Third Parties) Act 1999 under which it is possible for a third party to enforce the contract and obtain substantial damages. It remains unlikely that specific performance will be awarded as equity will not assist a volunteer.

[62] [1968] A.C. 58 at 102.

[63] [1968] A.C. 58 at 89 per Lord Pearce.

Constant supervision of the court

Specific performance has historically been refused where enforcement would require the **19.15** constant supervision of the court. In the nineteenth century case of *Ryan v Mutual Tontine Westminster Chambers Association*,[64] for example, the Court of Appeal was asked to construe a term in a lease which required the constant attendance of a resident porter, or in the event of some temporary absence, a trustworthy assistant. Lord Esher M.R. appeared concerned at the period of time over which the court would be required to compel performance. Declining on the ground of constant superintendence, he explained, "The contract is that those services shall be performed during the whole term of the tenancy; it is therefore a long continuing contract, to be performed from day to day, and under which the circumstances of non-performance might vary from day to day".[65]

Markedly more recently, however, and on very similar facts the rationale underpinning *Ryan* was called into question. *Posner v Scott-Lewis*[66] also concerned the enforcement of a landlord's covenant to employ a resident porter, facts that Mervyn Davies J. was prompted to admit were, "difficult to distinguish" from the *Ryan* case.[67] Here, however, specific performance was granted. Mervyn Davies J. felt that Ryan had to be viewed in the context of its re-evaluation by many later authorities.[68] The modern approach of the courts is to focus on the practicality of enforcing the individual contract before them. In *Tito v Waddell (No.2)*, therefore, Megarry V.C. emphasised that, "The real question is whether there is sufficient definition of what has to be done in order to comply with the order of the court. That definition may be provided by the contract itself, or it may be supplied by the terms of the order, in which case there is the further question whether the court considers that the terms of the contract sufficiently support by implication or otherwise the terms of the proposed order".[69] Accordingly, in *Posner v Scott-Lewis*, Mervyn Davies J. embraced a refinement of general principle. He considered the pertinent questions to be as follows:

"(a) Is there a sufficient definition of what has to be done in order to comply with the order? (b) Will enforcing compliance involve superintendence by the court to an unacceptable degree? (c) What are the respective prejudices and hardships that will be suffered by the parties if the order is made or not made".[70]

On the facts, the work was sufficiently defined and there was no unacceptable level of superintendence.[71] In addition, damages was not an adequate remedy. Although the

---

[64] [1893] 1 Ch. 116.
[65] [1893] 1 Ch. 116 at 123.
[66] [1987] Ch. 25.
[67] [1987] Ch. 25 at 34.
[68] Principally, *Giles & Co Ltd v Morris* [1972] 1 W.L.R. 307 per Megarry J.; *Shiloh Spinners v Harding* [1973] A.C. 691 at 724 per Lord Wilberforce; *Tito v Waddell (No.2)* [1977] Ch. 106 at 321 per Megarry V.C.
[69] [1977] Ch. 106 at 321.
[70] [1987] Ch. 25 at 36.
[71] The porter was to carry out specific domestic functions pertaining to the cleaning of common parts, maintenance of heating services and refuse disposal. Compare *Ryan v Mutual Tontine Westminster Chambers Association* where the porter was subject to such ill-defined obligations as, "to be and act as the servant of the tenants".

landlord had arranged for the functions to be carried out by a non-resident, damages could not adequately compensate for the loss of the feeling of security and opportunities to ask for help that arose form the porter's presence.[72]

Running a business

19.16   The constant supervision principle fell to be reviewed by the House of Lords in *Co-Operative Insurance Society Ltd v Argyll Stores (Holdings) Ltd.*[73] The facts are straightforward. The defendants were granted the lease of the largest unit in a shopping centre. It was envisaged that the unit would be an anchor unit, attracting trade to the smaller businesses in the shopping centre. As any closure of the anchor unit would have a disastrous effect on the other tenants, the defendants were required to covenant to keep their premises open for retail trade during the usual hours of business in the locality. Subsequently, however, the defendants experienced financial loss and sought, in breach of contract, to close down the supermarket. The claimant sought damages and an order for specific performance of the keep-open covenant.

At first instance, the court endorsed the settled approach to award damages. It was a showing of what Leggatt L.J. later described as "unwarrantable reluctance" to award the remedy of specific performance.[74] In the appellate court, he called for the court to intervene and exercise its discretion "afresh unfettered by shibboleths which will otherwise continue to be unthinkingly applied".[75] Leggatt L.J. was patently struck by the "gross commercial cynicism" of Argyll.[76] Roch L.J. too reluctantly faced what he described as the "unedifying spectacle of a large commercial company seeking to rely on its own wanton and quite unreasonable conduct".[77] Forming a majority view in the Court of Appeal,[78] specific performance was awarded on the grounds that damages were inadequate and that the tenant's obligations were defined with sufficient precision. The defendants appealed.

19.17   In the House of Lords, Lord Hoffmann was focused and categorical in denying the availability of the remedy. He drew attention first, to the long settled practice of the court that orders requiring the defendant to run a business would not be made. The practice was not only premised on the adequacy of damages, but also that the order would require the constant supervision of the court (i.e. that it would draw the court into the undesirable position of having to give an indefinite series of rulings to ensure compliance with the order). Secondly, he highlighted deficiencies in the means of forcing compliance. The prospect of imprisonment for contempt of court was a heavy-handed enforcement mechanism wholly ill-suited to adjudicate disputes as to the appropriate running of a business. In Lord Hoffmann's view, it would force the defendant "to make decisions under a sword of Damacles which may descend if the way

---

[72] As Mervyn Davies J. explained above, at 33, "There is to my mind a world of difference between living in a block with a porter in residence and living in a block where there is no porter in residence".
[73] [1998] A.C. 1.
[74] [1996] Ch. 286 at 294.
[75] [1996] Ch. 286 at 294.
[76] [1996] Ch. 286 at 294.
[77] [1996] Ch. 286 at 296.
[78] Millett L.J. gave a dissenting judgment.

the business is run does not conform to the terms of the order.[79] Thirdly, Lord Hoffmann was persuaded that an order for specific performance would allow the claimant to enrich himself at the defendant's expense. The loss suffered by the defendant by running a business at a loss for an indefinite period would be greater than that suffered by the claimant by breach of contract. Accordingly, the landlord would be in a position to extract a high price from the defendant in order to release it from its obligations.[80] Finally, he felt that it was perfectly satisfactory that the defendant rely on legal advice as to the settled practice of the court.[81] In other words the parties entered into the transaction with the knowledge that specific performance was not awarded to enforce performance of such contracts. The obligation was not, therefore, one which the House of Lords was prepared to specifically enforce.

As to the principle of constant supervision generally, Lord Hoffmann emphasised a distinction between orders requiring the defendant to carry out an activity over a more or less extended period of time and orders requiring the defendant to achieve a result. In the former case there was a danger of repeated actions for rulings on compliance with the order, whereas, in the latter case the court would be called upon perhaps once to determine compliance. In addition to the risk of wasteful litigation, a further objection to an order to carry out an activity was the inevitable imprecision in the terms of the order. Lord Hoffmann foresaw a risk of oppression to the defendant in that, "The less precise the order, the fewer signposts to the forensic minefield which he has to traverse".[82]

Whatever the merits of this practical assessment of when concerns as to constant **19.18** supervision can be swept aside, two final observations can be made. First, it is not clear that, even by Lord Hoffmann's own test, the keep-open covenant could not be construed as a covenant to attain a particular result. Is this not a straightforward case where all concerned know exactly what would be required of the defendant? Secondly, the decision of the House of Lords is a noteworthy failure to respond to the justice of the case. Tettenborn describes it as an, "unfortunate failure to liberalise the rules of specific performance and grant an effective remedy to a plaintiff who is clearly deserving and who is liable to be severely short-changed by a mere award of damages".[83] Perhaps on this basis, the approach of the Court of Appeal is to be preferred.

It remains to discuss two further contexts in which the courts have grappled with the principle of constant supervision, namely, that of building contracts and enforcement of leasehold repairing covenants. Notwithstanding the somewhat intransigent stance of the House of Lords in *Argyll*, the courts have been generally responsive in other contexts in which the question of supervision arises.

---

[79] [1998] A.C. 1 at 13. It was not, furthermore, in the interest of public policy to award a remedy which, "yokes the parties together in a continuing hostile relationship" (per Lord Hoffmann at 16).

[80] This finding can be criticised on the basis that the lease could be assigned with the landlord's consent and that the cost to the defendant would be no more than that required to find a new assignee. In any event as Tettenborn argues in [1998] Conv. 23 at 36, "it is hard to see any injustice in this when the defendant can avoid having to pay up by the simple expedient of providing what the plaintiff was justifiably entitled to in the first place".

[81] This was despite the view of Leggatt L.J. in the lower court that there was no evidence of the parties receipt of advice to the effect that the promise could be disregarded upon payment of damages ([1996] Ch. 286 at 294).

[82] [1998] A.C. 1 at 14.

[83] [1998] Conv. 23 at p.38.

Building contracts

19.19 Building agreements appear to fall readily into the class of contract for which, on the ground of constant supervision, the court might decline to award a decree of specific performance. As Kay L.J. explained in *Ryan v Mutual Tontine Westminster Chambers Association*, "Ordinarily the court will not enforce specific performance of works, such as building works, the prosecution of which the court cannot superintend; not only on the ground that damages are generally in such cases an adequate remedy, but also on the ground of the inability of the court to see that the work is carried out".[84] This category has, nonetheless, been the subject of notable exceptions. Of particular historical prominence, a number of cases involving railway companies prompted equity to fashion an exception where land was purchased on terms that certain works would be carried out. In general, these were cases were the award of damages was not an adequate remedy, the works required were sufficiently definite and the companies in question had taken possession of the lands.[85] In addition, judges also appear to have been motivated by the need to respond to the justice of the case. In *Wilson v Furness Railway Company*, for example, Sir W. M. James V.C. commented of the company's refusal to build a road, "It would be monstrous if the company, having got the whole benefit of the agreement, could turn round and say, 'This is the sort of a thing that the court finds a difficulty in doing, and will not do'. Rather than allow such a gross piece of dishonesty, the court would struggle with any amount of difficulties in order to perform the agreement".[86]

As regards building contracts more generally, it is nowadays established that specific performance will be available where the conditions listed by Romer L.J. in *Wolverhampton Corporation v Emmons*[87] are satisfied. *Wolverhampton Corporation v Emmons* involved the sale by the urban sanitary authority in Wolverhampton of a plot of land, part consideration for the sale being the purchaser's covenant to erect a number of houses in line with the Corporation's scheme of improvement for the area. The parties entered into a further written agreement containing the detailed plans for the building scheme. Upon the builder's breach the Corporation commenced an action for specific performance.[88] Although all three judges were content to admit confusion as to the principles on which courts of equity had acted previously, the Court of Appeal was unanimous in its support for the plaintiff. It fell to Romer L.J. to re-iterate the criteria that had, for many years past, allowed a plaintiff to bring himself within the exception generated for building contracts.

19.20 First, the building work must be defined by the contract, to the extent that, "the particulars of the work are so far definitely ascertained that the court can sufficiently see what is the exact nature of the work of which it is asked to order the performance".[89]

---

[84] [1893] 1 Ch. 116 at 128.
[85] See, for example, *Storer v Great Western Railway* (1842) 2 Y. & C. Ch. Cas. 48.
[86] (1869) Law Rep 9 Eq. 28 at 33.
[87] [1901] 1 K.B. 515.
[88] Smith L.J. felt that it would have been "hopeless" to seek specific performance of the covenant contained in the conveyance, but endorsed the view of the lower court that the subsequent agreement was sufficiently specific to justify an order for its specific performance.
[89] [1901] 1 K.B. 515 at 525.

Hence, in any future proceedings, it can be determined accurately what the defendant is required to do.

Secondly, the plaintiff must have, "a substantial interest in having the contract performed".[90] This element serves simply to emphasise that there can be no equitable remedy where damages are adequate. Here, it was of great importance to the sanitary authority that the land, situated in the middle of the town, would not be left vacant and that the houses built upon it would contribute to the rates.

Thirdly, it is a requirement that the defendant has obtained possession of the land on **19.21** which the work is contracted to be done.[91] The crucial consideration here is that it is the defendant alone who can carry out the works. In such circumstances specific performance will be available to the plaintiff and completion of the works compelled by order of the court.

Specific performance of a landlord's covenant

In *Jeune v Queens Cross Properties Ltd*[92] Sir John Pennycuick V.C. successfully crafted **19.22** an analogy with building agreements to allow the court to specifically enforce a lessor's repairing covenant. In that case, the tenants of Westbourne Terrace, London sought specific performance of a covenant requiring the landlord to restore a collapsed balcony to the standard in which it existed before its disrepair. Pennycuick V.C. considered that the work to be completed was sufficiently defined by the contract, that damages were not an adequate remedy and that the defendant's entitlement to possession of the balcony ensured that the plaintiff could not have the work carried out without committing a trespass. Although the *Wolverhampton Corporation v Emmons* conditions were satisfied, an obstacle remained in the form of the decision of Lord Eldon L.C. in *Hill v Barclay* that a landlord cannot obtain against his tenant an order for specific performance of a covenant to repair.[93] Pennycuick V.C. could see no reason in principle why an order should not be made against a landlord to carry out the specific work, although he admitted that, "obviously, it is a jurisdiction which should be carefully exercised".[94]

In the case of dwellings, the jurisdiction to award specific performance of a landlord's repairing covenant is now on a statutory footing. Section 17 of the Landlord and Tenant Act 1985[95] provides:

> "In proceedings in which a tenant of a dwelling alleges a breach on the part of a landlord of a repairing covenant relating to any part of the premises in which the dwelling is comprised, the court may order specific performance of the covenant,

---

[90] [1901] 1 K.B. 515 at 525.
[91] Romer L.J. appears to require the defendant's possession to be obtained by contract. Cf. *Carpenter's Estates Ltd v Davies* [1940] Ch. 160 at 165 where Farwell J. did not consider it a "complete bar" to the granting of specific performance that the defendant "had not obtained by the contract" possession of the land on which the work is to be done.
[92] [1974] Ch. 97.
[93] (1810) 16 Ves. 402 (under the principle of mutuality: see **19.26**).
[94] [1974] Ch. 97 at 101.
[95] Replacing the Housing Act 1974 s.125.

whether or not the breach relates to a part of the premises let to the tenant and notwithstanding any equitable rule restricting the scope of the remedy, whether on the basis of a lack of mutuality or otherwise".

The approach of Pennycuick V.C. in *Jeune v Queens Cross Properties Ltd* has, in any event, been endorsed by subsequent case law[96] and fits with the generally progressive approach of the courts as to the exercise of discretion in this context.

Specific performance of a tenant's covenant

19.23   Where a tenant is in breach of a negative leasehold covenant, it has always been possible for a landlord to seek injunctive relief to restrain the breach. As is evident from the discussion above, the same flexibility has been traditionally lacking where the landlord wishes to compel performance of a tenant's positive covenant to repair.[97] Despite admissions that, in light of *Jeune v Queens Cross Properties Ltd*, the strength of older authority, "may logically be much weakened"[98] it took almost 25 years before doubt was dispelled as to the applicability of specific performance to a tenant's repairing covenant. The decision in *Rainbow Estates Ltd v Tokenhold Ltd*[99] signalled a change in judicial tack that would see specific performance available against a tenant in cases where damages are inadequate but subject to the, "overriding need to avoid injustice and oppression".[1]

The appropriateness of specific performance was plainly evident on the facts. First, the landlord had no adequate alternative remedy. The lease contained no forfeiture clause or proviso for re-entry. Thus, even a breach of repairing covenant did not entitle the landlord to forfeit the lease. Neither did the lease contain a term permitting the landlord to enter for the purpose of carrying out the necessary works and later recovering the costs. Secondly, the property was in a state of serious disrepair and deterioration. Thirdly, the schedule of works was sufficiently certain that the court could see with precision exactly what was required to be done. Quite uncommonly, there was an absence of any dispute regarding the repairs to be carried out. Finally, Epping Forest District Council had served notices pursuant to the Housing Act 1985 and the Environmental Protection Act 1990, non-compliance with which allowed the Council to step in, carry out the repairs and recover its costs. Accordingly, in the view of the court, there was no clearer a case to demonstrate how, "a modern law of remedies requires specific performance of a tenant's repairing covenant to be available in appropriate circumstances".[2]

---

[96] See, for example, *Gordon v Selico Ltd* (1986) 18 H.L.R. 219 per Slade L.J. where specific performance was awarded to compel a landlord to remove dry rot.
[97] *Hill v Barclay* (1810) 16 Ves. 402.
[98] Per Oliver J. in *Regional Properties Ltd v City of London Real Property Co Ltd* [1981] 1 EGLR 33 at 34.
[99] [1999] Ch. 64.
[1] The court must be astute to ensure that the landlord is not, "seeking the decree simply in order to harass the tenant", the mischief at which the Leasehold Property (Repairs) Act 1938 was enacted to prevent: [1999] Ch. 64 at 73 per Lawrence Collins Q.C.
[2] [1999] Ch. 64 at 72.

Contracts for personal services

It is an established equitable rule that equity will not intervene to compel the performance of personal services or the maintenance of a personal relationship between the parties. As Jessel M.R. declared in 1878, the courts, "have never dreamt of enforcing agreements strictly personal in nature whether they are agreements of hiring or service, being the common relation of master and servant, or whether they are agreements for the purpose of pleasure, or for the purpose of scientific pursuits or for the purpose of charity and philanthropy".[3] Accordingly, on this ground, specific performance has been refused to compel performance of contracts of employment,[4] apprenticeship[5] and, recently, as between school and parent.[6] Indeed, s.236 of the Trade Union and Labour Relations (Consolidation) Act 1992 provides that no court can decree specific performance so as to compel an employee to work.[7] A significant underlying motivation in the rule against specific performance is one of public policy. In the memorable language of Fry L.J, "the courts are bound to be jealous lest they should turn contracts of service into contracts of slavery".[8]

19.24

It is also true that the enforcement of contracts for personal services have been rejected as necessitating continuous supervision. In *Giles & Co Ltd v Morris*,[9] however, Megarry J. insisted that the reason was more the futility of equitable intervention:

"The reasons why the court is reluctant to decree specific performance of a contract for personal services (and I would regard it as a strong reluctance rather than a rule) are, I think, more complex and more firmly bottomed on human nature. If a singer contracts to sing, there could no doubt be proceedings for committal if, ordered to sing, the singer remains obstinately dumb. But if instead the singer sang flat, or sharp, or too fast, or too slowly, or too loudly or too quietly, or resorted to a dozen of the manifestations of temperament traditionally associated with some singers, the threat of committal would reveal itself as a most unsatisfactory weapon: for who could say whether the imperfections of performance were natural or self-induced? To make an order with such possibilities of evasion would be vain".[10]

As is apparent, moreover, Megarry J. did not feel that the rule against specific performance in the case of such contracts is an unbending one. In support of his contention, there is authority that in cases where a high degree of confidence exists between the parties the court may be justified in departing from the general rule.[11] Nonetheless,

---

[3] *Rigby v Connol* (1878) 14 Ch. D. 482 at 487.
[4] As Geoffrey Lane L.J. commented in *Chappell v Times Newspapers* [1975] 1 W.L.R. 482 at 506, "The reason is obvious: if one party has no faith in the honesty, integrity or the loyalty of the other, to force him to serve or to employ that other is a plain recipe for disaster".
[5] *Webb v England* (1860) 29 Beav. 54.
[6] *R. v Incorporated Froebel Institute, ex p. L* [1999] E.L.R. 488.
[7] Neither can the same result be achieved by use of the injunction.
[8] *Francesco v Barnum* (1890) 45 Ch. D. 430 at 438.
[9] [1972] 1 W.L.R. 307.
[10] [1972] 1 W.L.R. 307 at 318.
[11] See *Hill v CA Parsons & Co Ltd* [1972] Ch. 305 (interim injunction restraining termination of employment amounting in substance to specific performance).

two significant objections remain. First, damages will be an adequate remedy in almost all cases. Secondly, any order for specific performance must be workable.[12] It is surely open to question whether the court can compel the re-establishment of, for example, the employer/employee relationship against the wishes of either of the parties. As Stamp L.J. convincingly argued in *Hill v CA Parsons & Co Ltd*, the court "will not exercise its discretion where the order will be nugatory, uncertain or as a practical matter impossible to enforce. Nowhere could the consideration be more compelling than where an employee asks for an order on his employer to continue to employ him".[13]

The conduct of the claimant

19.25 The court's concern as to the conduct of the claimant is summed up by two equitable maxims: "he who seeks equity must do equity", and, "he who comes to equity must come with clean hands". In relation to the former, any claimant who wishes to enlist the help of equity must do equity, i.e. fulfil his own obligations of conscience arising out of the disputed agreement. Accordingly, a claimant must show that he has performed his own contractual obligations,[14] or has tendered performance and is willing to perform his future obligations[15] before specific performance will be awarded to him. As to the latter, unconscionable conduct in relation to the contract will also disbar a claimant from the equitable remedy. If the conduct of the plaintiff is "tricky or unfair", the court may refuse the remedy, for "he who comes to equity must come with clean hands".[16]

Want of mutuality

19.26 The doctrine of mutuality has had a prominent influence on equitable intervention. Indeed, want of mutuality has been viewed as a traditional barrier to the award of specific performance. The principle upon which the discretion is exercised is clearly explained in *Price v Strange*.[17] The court, "will not compel a defendant to perform his obligations specifically if it cannot at the same time ensure that any unperformed obligations of the plaintiff will be specifically performed, unless, perhaps, damages would be an adequate remedy to the defendant for any default on the plaintiff's part".[18] The classic illustration of a lack of mutuality appears in *Flight v Bollard*.[19] Here, it was

---

[12] *Robb v Hammersmith and Fulham London Borough Council* [1991] I.C.R. 514.

[13] [1972] 1 W.L.R. 307 at 323.

[14] This requirement does not extend to "non-essential or trivial breaches": see *Dyster v Randall* [1926] Ch. 932 at 942 per Lawrence J. (failure to submit "unexceptionable" plans for the approval of the defendant's architect).

[15] As Lord Radcliffe explained in *Australian Hardwoods Pty Ltd v Railways Commissioner* [1961] 1 W.L.R. 425 at 435, "he must fail unless he can show that he is ready and willing on his part to carry out those obligations, which are in fact part of the consideration for the undertaking of the defendant that the plaintiff seeks to enforce".

[16] *Quadrant Visual Communications Ltd v Hutchinson Telephone* (UK) Ltd [1993] BCLC 442; see C. Harpum, [1992] C.L.J. 263.

[17] [1978] 1 Ch. 337.

[18] [1978] 1 Ch. 337 at 368 per Buckley L.J.

[19] (1828) 4 Russ. 299 at 301.

held that a minor is unable to obtain specific performance for the reason that specific performance cannot be decreed against him. Leach M.R. claimed that, "No case of a bill filed by an infant for the specific performance of a contract made by him has been found in the books".[20] He did not dispute the general principle of equity to interpose, "only where the remedy is mutual".[21] Similarly, it is often said that a person whose contractual obligation amounts to a performance of personal services cannot obtain specific performance for the reason that the remedy cannot be obtained against him.[22]

Historically, much debate has focused upon the time at which the requirement of mutuality must be satisfied, i.e. whether there was a requirement of mutuality at the time at which the contract was entered into,[23] or at all material times later.[24] The issue has now been resolved by the Court of Appeal in *Price v Strange*,[25] wherein a liberal approach was adopted and any need for mutuality at the time of entering into the contract firmly rejected. As Goff L.J. made clear, "want of mutuality raises a question of the court's discretion to be exercised according to everything that has happened up to the decree".[26] In *Price v Strange*, therefore, specific performance of a contract to grant an underlease of a flat was awarded where repairing obligations (not specifically enforceable at the time of the contract) had been performed at the date of the hearing. Although it was the defendant who had, indeed, performed some of the plaintiff's obligations, specific performance was awarded on terms that the plaintiff pay to the defendant appropriate compensation for the actual cost of the works carried out.

Nowadays, the issue of mutuality is emphasised as a discretionary matter for the court. As Lawrence Collins Q.C. emphasised, "it does not follow from the fact that specific performance is not available to one party that it is not available to the other: want of mutuality is a discretionary, and not an absolute, bar to specific performance".[27] The absence of mutuality, after all, does nothing to oust the jurisdiction of the court to award damages in lieu of specific performance. Accordingly, modern courts will award the remedy if it can be done without injustice or unfairness to the defendant.[28] It is, in addition, possible for a claimant to counter the absence of mutuality by agreeing to perform an obligation that cannot be specifically enforced against him[29] or by waiving the benefit of a term in the contract.[30]

The comment of Lawrence Collins Q.C. was made in the context of repairing covenants in leases. It will be recalled that the classic explanation for the failure of the courts to award specific performance of a landlord's repairing covenant was want of

19.27

[20] (1828) 4 Russ. 299 at 301.
[21] (1828) 4 Russ. 299 at 301.
[22] See, for example, *Ogden v Fossick* (1862) 4 De. G.F. & J. 426. Note, however, that "some small element of personal service ... does not destroy the quality of mutuality (otherwise plainly present) want of which may in general terms properly be a ground for refusing a decree of specific performance" (*Beswick v Beswick* [1968] A.C. 58 at 97 per Lord Upjohn).
[23] As famously promoted by Fry, *Specific Performance*, (6th edn) at p.219, above.
[24] See, for example, Spry, *Equitable Remedies* (3rd edn) at p.91.
[25] [1978] 1 Ch. 337.
[26] [1978] 1 Ch. 337 at 354.
[27] *Rainbow Estates v Tokenhold Ltd* [1999] Ch. 64 at 69.
[28] *Price v Strange* [1978] Ch. 337 at 357 per Goff L.J.
[29] See *Scott v Bradley* [1971] Ch. 850 where a purchaser consented to be bound by an omitted term that he pay half of the defendant's legal costs incurred on sale
[30] *Heron Garage Properties v Moss* [1974] 1 W.L.R. 148.

mutuality, that is, that the tenant's covenant could not be specifically enforced.[31] As Lord Eldon L.C. claimed in *Hill v Barclay*, "The difficulty upon this doctrine of a court of equity is, that there is no mutuality in it. The tenant cannot be compelled to repair".[32] The enforcement of leasehold covenants provides a telling illustration of the movement away from the slavish adherence to older authority. It will be recalled that following *Jeune v Queens Cross Properties*, s.17 of the Landlord and Tenant Act 1985 provided a statutory incursion into the principle of mutuality. The section allows the court to order specific performance of a landlord's covenant and despite the existence of equitable rules "based on mutuality or otherwise". Accordingly, the section appears to carve an important exception to the general principle of mutuality.

19.28 In 1999, however, the decision in *Rainbow Estates v Tokenhold Ltd*, (which allowed for the specific performance of a tenant's repairing covenant) had the effect of restoring a semblance of parity to the availability of the remedy to landlords and tenants. It is interesting that the court downplayed the decisiveness of the principle of mutuality in modern judicial thinking, yet emphasised that mutuality is clearly to be preferred. As Lawrence Collins Q.C. admitted, "even if want of mutuality were any longer a decisive factor (which it is not) the availability of the remedy against a tenant would restore mutuality as against the landlord".[33] In view of such recent case law development, it seems difficult to argue, as Megarry did in 1951, that "the doctrine of mutuality still broods heavy over specific performance".[34] In the words of Hayton and Marshall, "The judicial retreat from it must now be almost complete in light of the decision of the High Court in *Rainbow Estates v Tokenhold Ltd*".[35]

Impossibility and futility

19.29 Equity does not act in vain. Where performance is impossible the matter is simply that equity cannot enforce what cannot be done. In *Ferguson v Wilson*, therefore, there could be no specific performance of a contract to allot shares as the shares had been validly allotted to other shareholders before equitable relief was sought.[36] The defence of impossibility can be raised whatever the manner in which the impossibility arose because the remedy cannot be awarded where the defendant simply cannot perform his obligations. Such was the concern in *Jones v Lipman*,[37] where property was transferred to a company controlled by the defendant with the object of defeating the claimant's unprotected contractual interest. Nonetheless, Russell J. held that the defendant's company was a "creature" of the defendant, "a device and a sham, a mask which he holds before his face in an attempt to avoid recognition by the eye of equity".[38] Specific performance was ordered because, by his ownership and control of the company in

---

[31] Other justifications for a refusal included inadequate definition of the works to be carried out and that an award of specific performance would require the constant supervision of the court.
[32] (1810) 16 Ves. 402 at 405.
[33] [1999] Ch. 64 at 73.
[34] R. E. Megarry (1951) 67 L.Q.R. 300.
[35] At p.913.
[36] (1866) L.R. 2 Ch. 77.
[37] [1962] 1 W.L.R. 832.
[38] [1962] 1 W.L.R. 832 at 836.

which the property was vested, the defendant was, indeed, in a position to complete the contract, i.e. performance was possible.

Similarly, where performance is not technically impossible an order for specific performance may be denied on the ground that intervention would be futile. Again, this defence is rooted in the argument that to act would be to act in vain. Accordingly, specific performance has been refused in respect of leases for terms that had already expired[39] and for an agreement to execute a deed constituting a partnership determinable at will.[40]

Part of a contract

The court will decline to award specific performance of a part of a contract if it is not in a position to order performance of the whole. In *Ogden v Fossick*[41] there was an agreement between the parties that the claimant would be granted a lease of a coal wharf and that the defendant would be appointed manager of the wharf. An action for specific performance of the agreement to grant the lease failed because the court could not enforce the employment aspect to the contract, i.e. it could not enforce the whole of the contract. Where, however, an agreement can be construed as a series of separate and distinct contracts, enforcement of one part will cease to depend on whether the court is able to enforce performance of the others.[42]

19.30

Illegality and public policy

Not surprisingly, there can be no specific performance of an illegal contract. As such contracts are void, there is no valid agreement capable of enforcement. Equally, an agreement the enforcement of which will result in an outcome contrary to public policy will not be enforced specifically. An illustration is provided by *Wroth v Tyler*.[43] The defendant Edmund Tyler entered into a contract to sell his bungalow with vacant possession. On the following day, his wife entered a notice in the charges register at the Land Registry, which, under the Matrimonial Homes Act 1967,[44] secured her personal right to occupy the property. When the existence of the charge came to light and the wife refused to vacate it, the husband was unable to deliver the property with vacant possession. The vendor sought specific performance of the contract.

19.31

Two public policy reasons were put forward by Megarry J. to justify a refusal to award specific performance. First, Mr Tyler could only carry out his contractual obligation by embarking on litigation to terminate his wife's right of occupation. Megarry J. warned that the court should be, "reluctant to make an order which requires

---

[39] In *Mundy v Joliffe* (1839) 9 L.J. Ch. 95, the object of the action was to enable a further action to be brought on the covenants contained in the lease.
[40] *Hercy v Birch* (1804) 9 Ves. 357, on the basis that the defendant could simply dissolve the partnership.
[41] (1862) 4 De. G.F. & J. 426.
[42] See *Wilkinson v Clements* (1872) L.R. 8 Ch. App. 96.
[43] [1974] Ch. 30.
[44] Now Family Law Act 1996.

a husband to take legal proceedings against his wife, especially when they are still living together".[45] Secondly, as a consequence of awarding specific performance, the purchaser would take the property subject to the wife's right of occupation. As both the husband and children would be subject to eviction, the inevitable splitting up of the family was against public policy. Accordingly, Megarry J. felt disobliged to award specific performance and he opted for damages as the only feasible alternative. Somewhat unfortunately, however, the award of damages resulted in the husband's bankruptcy and entailed that the property was sold by his trustee in bankruptcy with vacant possession and free from the wife's right of occupation.

Hardship and prejudice to third parties

19.32   It is at the discretion of the court to refuse to award specific performance where unnecessary hardship would result for either of the parties to the contract or, indeed, a third party. In *Warmington v Miller*, for example, the court refused to order specific performance of an agreement to grant an underlease of a ground floor workshop.[46] To do so would leave the defendant landlord in breach of a covenant contained in his head lease and, thereby, cause hardship to his head landlord.

Ordinarily, it is to be expected that the parties to a contract for the sale of land take on the risk that some hardship may result from circumstances arising from entry into that particular contract. Accordingly, refusal to award specific performance of such contracts has traditionally been confined to hardship existing at the date of the contract or hardship arising from the conduct of the plaintiff.[47] In *Patel v Ali*,[48] however, the court resisted performance of a land contract where the hardship was supervening and in no way attributable to the plaintiff. The defendant co-owners entered into a contract for the sale of their house, but the husband's bankruptcy precipitated a long delay for which neither the plaintiffs nor the defendants sought to blame each other. Completion was further hampered by a disastrous change in personal circumstances that befell the defendant. Shortly after the making of the contract, she was diagnosed with bone cancer and, whilst in an advanced state of pregnancy, underwent an operation to amputate her right leg. Thereafter, she came to rely heavily on the support provided by friends and relatives in the neighbourhood. Her reliance became acute in the months that followed as her husband was imprisoned and she continued to speak virtually no English. At the time of the hearing, the defendants had three children and argued that their enforced removal would be unjust.

19.33   Goulding J. accepted that to award specific performance would, "inflict upon her a 'hardship amounting to injustice' ".[49] Of particular significance was the four-year delay, within which the defendant's circumstances had altered in an unforeseeable way, and after which she was being asked to do what had not been contemplated, i.e. complete a sale at that much later time. Accordingly, he felt the proper course was to leave the

[45] [1974] Ch. 30 at 51.
[46] [1973] Q.B. 877.
[47] Fry, *Specific Performance* (6th edn) at p.199.
[48] [1984] Ch. 283.
[49] [1984] Ch. 283 at 288 adopting the phrase employed by James L.J. in *Tamplin v James* [1880] 15 Ch. D. 215 at 221.

plaintiffs to their remedy in damages.[50] Although *Patel v Ali* serves to emphasise the width of judicial discretion, it is important to note that future cases will continue to turn on their own facts. Goulding J. felt that it took such, "extraordinary and persuasive circumstances" to supply an excuse for resisting performance of a contract for the sale of immovable property.[51] Perhaps rarely, therefore, will such compelling evidence be presented to the court.

Laches **and delay**

The general equitable rule is that time is not the essence of a contract[52] and accordingly, **19.34** a claimant may obtain specific performance in circumstances where he has failed to carry out his contractual obligations by the time specified.[53] Nonetheless, a claimant who brings an action after an unreasonable delay may well be unsuccessful. Although there is no statutory period of limitation on the time at which a claim for specific performance may be brought, it is a statement of general principle that, in the absence of special circumstances rendering the position unjust, "relevant equitable rules should accord with comparable legal rules".[54]

Unfortunately, there is no easily applicable definition of an unreasonable delay and little can be gleaned from the copious case law on the doctrine of *laches* to be dug up from previous centuries.[55] As Aldous L.J. put it in *Frawley v Neill*, "The modern approach should not require an inquiry as to whether the circumstances can be fitted within the confines of a preconceived formula derived from earlier cases".[56] In a similar vein, the award of specific performance in *Lazard Bros & Co Ltd v Fairfield Property Co (Mayfair) Ltd*[57] is illustrative of the modern judicial approach. Megarry V.C. argued that if specific performance was to be regarded as a prize to be awarded by equity to the zealous and denied to the indolent then the claimants in the case before him should fail. His view was that whatever the position over a century ago that was the wrong approach today. If it was just that the claimant should obtain his remedy, the court ought not to withhold it merely because he was guilty of delay. This is a long way from the nineteenth century view of Lord Alvanley that, "a party cannot call upon a Court of Equity for a specific performance unless he has shewn himself ready, desirous, prompt

---

[50] There was evidence that sympathetic members of the Muslim community were willing to put up the money to meet the costs of the damages.

[51] [1984] Ch. 283 at 288.

[52] Where the parties agree that time is of the essence of a contract, or the circumstances indicate that completion is of the essence, specific performance will not be awarded if the time limit has not been respected: see *Steedman v Drinkle* [1916] 1 A.C. 275.

[53] The delaying party may, however, be liable to damages for breach of contract: see *Raineri v Miles* [1981] A.C. 1050.

[54] Spry, *Equitable Remedies* (5th edn) at p.419, see further, *P & O Nedlloyd BV v Arab Metals Co* [2007] 1 W.L.R. 2288.

[55] As Laddie J. indicated in *Nelson v Rye* [1996] 1 W.L.R. 1378 at 1396, "some of the factors which must be taken into consideration in deciding whether the defence runs ... include the period of the delay, the extent to which the defendant's position has been prejudiced by the delay and the extent to which that prejudice was caused by the actions of the plaintiff".

[56] [2000] Cp Rep. 20.

[57] (1977) 121 S.J. 793.

and eager".[58] The essence of the contemporary approach, therefore, is to question whether the claimant's actions render it unconscionable for him to assert his rights.[59]

19.35   Delay will not be a bar to specific performance where the claimant has taken possession under the contract and, as equitable owner, seeks to have the legal estate vested in him. In *Williams v Greatrex*,[60] a delay of 10 years was no bar by laches because the purchaser had equitable title to the property by virtue of the contract and he had entered into possession of it.[61] Different considerations apply where it is the transaction creating the proprietary interest that is in dispute.[62] Here the doctrine of *laches* unquestionably applies. It is clear also that the subject matter of the contract is a relevant consideration in determining unreasonableness. Where the subject matter has a "speculative and fluctuating value", for example, delay on the part of the claimant will be prominent in the exercise of judicial discretion.[63]

Further consideration is required of a claimant who commences a timely action for specific performance, but delays in bringing the matter to trial. Generally, delay will not in itself be sufficient to defeat the claim. Neither will detriment to the defendant of itself be sufficient as a ground for the court's refusal of leave to enforce an order. Such was the case in *Easton v Brown*[64] where the plaintiff property developers delayed by eight years an action to enforce an order for specific performance of a contract for the sale of property with vacant possession. Although the defendant argued that such late enforcement was to his detriment, the plaintiffs had acted reasonably throughout and had provided a legitimate explanation for the delay. The delay had been caused by the defendant's former wife and their nine children who remained in occupation of the property. Legal advice suggested litigation to remove them would be unsuccessful. Accordingly, it was not until agreement was reached between the parties that the plaintiffs pressed ahead to enforce their rights. It seems, therefore, that the court will require both an insufficient explanation of the delay by the plaintiff and a detriment to the defendant before it is unjust to enforce the order.

Mistake, misdescription and misrepresentation

19.36   Where a contract cannot be avoided in equity by reason of a mistake or misrepresentation, both can be grounds to defend an action for specific performance.[65] In other words, X may not succeed in his efforts to rescind a contract, but equity will not provide to Y the remedy to compel performance of it. To succeed with the defence of mistake, a defendant is usually required to show, "hardship amounting to injustice".[66]

---

[58] *Milward v Earl of Thanet* (1873) 5 Ves. 720.
[59] *Frawley v Neill* [2000] Cp Rep. 20.
[60] [1956] 3 All E.R. 705.
[61] The possession claimed must be possession under the contract: *Mills v Haywood* (2000) 6 Ch. D. 196.
[62] *Joyce v Joyce* [1979] 1 W.L.R. 1170.
[63] *Mills v Haywood* (1877) 6 Ch. D. 196 at 202 per Cotton L.J.
[64] [1981] 3 All E.R. 278.
[65] As Lindley L.J. put it in *Re Terry and White's Contract* (1886) 32 Ch. D. 14 at 29, "it is well known that a less serious misleading is sufficient to enable a purchaser to resist specific performance than is required to enable him to rescind the contract".
[66] *Tamplin v James* (1880) 15 Ch. D. 215 at 221 per James L.J.

Ignorance as to the legal implications of an agreement[67] or evidence of some fault or mistake solely on the part of the defendant will not generally suffice. In *Tamplin v James*,[68] for example, the defendant purchaser made a unilateral mistake as to the extent of the property being sold; the vendor had accurately described the property by reference to plans. The purchaser, who had first hand knowledge of the property, failed to consult the plans and mistakenly assumed he was buying a portion of land that did not, in fact, belong to the vendor. Specific performance was awarded against the defendant on the basis that his mistake was solely attributable to his own negligence. There was nothing misleading in the particulars. In the words of James L.J., "If a man will not take reasonable care to ascertain what he is buying, he must take the consequences. The defence on the ground of mistake cannot be sustained. It is not enough for a purchaser to swear, 'I thought the farm contained 12 fields which I knew, and I find it does not contain them all' or 'I thought it contained 100 acres and it only contains 80'. It would open the door to fraud if such a defence was to be allowed".[69]

A markedly less rigorous (and frequently criticised[70]) approach was adopted in *Malins v Freeman* where the defendant at auction was mistaken as to the lot put up for sale.[71] Despite the defendant's failure to draw attention to the mistake immediately and that the mistake itself was solely attributable to the defendant, specific performance was refused.[72]

Where the claimant has contributed to, or somehow induced the defendant's mistake, **19.37** the court is legitimately less likely to award specific performance on the ground that it is inequitable to do so. In *Denny v Hancock*,[73] the purchaser's mistake as to the accuracy of the boundary of a property arose due to the misleading layout of the vendor's plans. Mellish L.J. questioned whether the plan and particulars were "naturally calculated to deceive" and concluded: "I cannot but think that they were".[74] Even on a more generous interpretation of the vendor's intentions, (i.e. that the inducement was unintentional) the defendant's mistake was at least attributable to the negligence of the vendor's agents in the production of the plans. The more complicit the claimant in the defendant's mistake, therefore, the less likely the court is to award specific performance. In *Webster v Cecil*,[75] the defendant's error was unilateral, but the purchaser, who must have known of the error, sought to take full advantage. Negotiations as to the sale price of property had been conducted by letter. The vendor mistakenly offered to sell at £1,250. His intention had been to write down a figure of £2,250. The purchaser readily accepted. Immediately, upon realising his mistake, the vendor gave notice of his error. Nonetheless, the purchaser sought to compel the vendor to sell at £1,250. As he had a previous offer of £2200 rejected by the vendor, the purchaser must have realised the mistake. No specific performance was awarded.

---

[67] *Powell v Smith* (1872) L.R. 14 Eq. 85.
[68] (1880) 15 Ch. D. 215.
[69] (1880) 15 Ch. D. 215 at 221.
[70] See, for example, the discussion of Kekewich J. in *Van Praagh v Everidge* [1902] 2 Ch. 266.
[71] (1837) 2 Keen 25.
[72] Lord Langdale admitted that the defendant was, "hurried and inconsiderate" and that when the mistake was made known to him, he was, "not so prompt as he ought to have been in declaring it" ((1837) 2 Keen 25 at 35).
[73] (1870) 6 Ch. App. 1.
[74] (1870) 6 Ch. App. 1 at 14
[75] (1861) 30 Beav. 62.

In the case of a misdescription of subject matter the approach of the courts will depend on the justice of the case. It may be that specific performance will be ordered with an appropriate abatement in the purchase price. In the case of a serious misdescription, the court will refuse to compel performance and, indeed, allow rescission of the contract.

GUIDE TO FURTHER READING

D. Harris, "Specific Performance—A Regular Remedy for Consumers?" (2003) 119 L.Q.R. 541.

A. Tettenborn, "Absolving the Undeserving: Shopping Centres, Specific Performance and the Law of Contract" [1998] Conv. 23.

INDEX